MW01122473

WEINSTEIN'S EVIDENCE MANUAL

A Guide to the United States Rules Based on Weinstein's Evidence

Jack B. Weinstein

Adjunct Professor
Columbia Law School
Judge United States District Court
Eastern District of New York

Margaret A. Berger

Professor and Associate Dean
Brooklyn Law School

1991

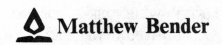 Matthew Bender

Times Mirror
Books

Copyright © 1987, 1988, 1989, 1990, 1991
By MATTHEW BENDER & COMPANY
INCORPORATED

All Rights Reserved
Printed in United States of America
Library of Congress Catalog Card Number: 87-070538
ISBN 0–8205–1419–0

MATTHEW BENDER & CO., INC.
EDITORIAL OFFICES
11 PENN PLAZA, NEW YORK, NY 10001-2006 (212) 967-7707
2101 WEBSTER ST., OAKLAND, CA 94612-3027 (415) 446-7100

PREFACE

This volume comprehensively covers the United States Rules of Evidence. It was designed for judges, lawyers and students who need a concise guide to the practical and theoretical information required in the court, office and classroom.

It is assumed that any user will have access to our multi-volume *Weinstein's Evidence* for purposes of more detailed research and briefwriting. The multi-volume **Treatise** contains comprehensive legislative history, more extensive analysis and citations to federal cases, references to secondary sources, coverage of the evidence law of the states and military that follow the Federal Rules with minor variations, and case citations to the law in those states. Nevertheless, there are enough citations in this single volume to support daily practice and to provide a starting point for more intensive work.

The references to "**Treatise**" throughout this volume are to the multi-volume Treatise.

We have provided the exact language of each of the Rules so that quotations as well as paraphrasing for meaning are readily available to the advocate, judge or student. While the volume is comprehensive, every effort has been made to limit its size so that it can be conveniently carried home or to court and kept for ready reference at the desk.

Now that the Federal Rules have been in effect for more than a decade, some clear lines of interpretation have begun to emerge. We have summarized those areas and indicated places where further clarification is needed.

We have not explicitly covered state rule variations. These details may be found in the multi-volume treatise.

William J. Schneier's assistance in the preparation of this work, while a student at Brooklyn Law School, is gratefully acknowledged.

Jack B. Weinstein

Margaret A. Berger

(Pub.819)

SUMMARY TABLE OF CONTENTS

(Pub.819)

SUMMARY TABLE OF CONTENTS

TABLE OF CONTENTS

vii

TABLE OF CONTENTS

TABLE OF CONTENTS

TABLE OF CONTENTS

TABLE OF CONTENTS

Chapter 8   Authentication and Identification

Chapter 9   Best Evidence Rule

TABLE OF CONTENTS

Chapter 10 Witnesses Generally

Chapter 11 Special Witness Rules

Chapter 13   Expert Witnesses

Chapter 15   Hearsay Exclusions

TABLE OF CONTENTS

TABLE OF CONTENTS xxvi

References to **Treatise** throughout this volume are to
the multi-volume *Weinstein's Evidence* treatise.

CHAPTER 1

Application of Rules and Construction

SYNOPSIS

(Pub.819)

¶ 1.01   All Relevant Evidence Is Admissible With Certain Exceptions—Rule 402[1]

Rule 402, a restatement of Thayer's classic formulation,[2] expresses the only universal rule of evidence:

Rule 402

RELEVANT EVIDENCE GENERALLY ADMISSIBLE; IRRELEVANT EVIDENCE INADMISSIBLE

All relevant evidence is admissible, except as otherwise provided by the Constitution of the United States, by Act of Congress, by these rules, or by other rules prescribed by the Supreme Court pursuant to statutory authority. Evidence which is not relevant is not admissible.

The principal reason for admitting all relevant evidence is that, generally, the probability of ascertaining the truth about a given proposition increases as the amount of the trier's knowledge grows. Truth finding must be a central purpose. Unless we are to assume that the substantive law is perverse or irrelevant to the public welfare, its enforcement is properly the primary aim of litigation. The substantive law can best be enforced if litigation results in accurate determinations of facts made material by the applicable rule of law. The assumption that accurate fact finding is possible is fundamental to our judicial system.

Nevertheless, truth finding is not always the law's overriding aim. Trials in our judicial system are intended to do more than merely determine what happened. Among the goals, in addition to truth finding, which the rules of procedure and evidence seek to satisfy are terminating disputes, economizing resources, inspiring confidences, supporting independent social policies, permitting ease in prediction and application, adding to the efficiency of the

---

[1] See discussion in **Treatise** at ¶¶ 402[01]–[05].

[2] Thayer, A Preliminary Treatise on Evidence at Common Law 530 (1898) ("[T]he rules of evidence should be simplified; and should take on the general character of principles, to guide the sound judgment of the judge, rather than minute rules to bind it. The two leading principles should be brought into conspicuous relief, (1) that nothing is to be received which is not logically probative of some matter requiring to be proved; and (2) that everything which is thus probative should come in, unless a clear ground of policy or law excludes it.").

entire legal system, and tranquilizing disputants. Rule 402 makes no attempt to enumerate the underlying policies that dictate exclusion.

Any set of evidentiary or procedural rules is constantly obliged to strike a balance between these often competing goals. Thus, while Rule 402 acknowledges that relevant evidence is prima facie admissible, it also recognizes that other evidentiary or procedural rules, or Acts of Congress or the Constitution may require the exclusion of evidence that meets the relevancy test of Rule 401.

The constitutional principles, and provisions in statutes and Federal Rules, which exclude otherwise relevant evidence, can be grouped into two classes that have very different objectives. One class—termed "auxiliary rules of probative force" by Wigmore[3] —excludes certain types of evidence, although relevant, because admission would hamper rather than advance the search for truth. The second class of rules limits admissibility in order to implement some extrinsic policy which the law considers more important than ascertaining the truth in a particular law suit.

¶ 1.01[01]   Auxiliary Rules of Probative Force

A law suit involves numerous propositions that cannot be viewed or proved in isolation. A line of proof directed to one proposition may cause confusion or prejudice concerning another. A certain type of proof may be inherently lacking in trustworthiness so that its admission would interfere with ascertaining the truth.

Many of the provisions in the Federal Rules of Evidence are designed to increase the likelihood of accurate determinations. Rule 403 restricts admissibility where the danger of confusion or prejudice is so great that the truth probably would be obscured. See discussion in Chapters 6. The succeeding rules in Article IV of the Rules rest, at least in part, on the same notion. See discussion in Chapter 7, below. Rules governing authentication (Article IX of the Rules, discussed in Chapter 8), best evidence (Article X of the Rules, discussed in Chapter 9), and many of the provisions relating to witnesses (see Chapters 10, 12, and 13) are all grounded in

[3] 8 Wigmore, Evidence ¶ 2175 (McNaughton rev. 1961).

the desire to protect the trier of fact from evidence that may not be worthy of belief. The hearsay rule also finds its main justification in truth finding (see discussion in Chapters 14–17).

This policy is also served by other enactments. Basic to the discovery practice of the Federal Rules of Civil and Criminal Procedure is the underlying assumption that the possibility of ascertaining the truth is enhanced by having witnesses testify orally in open court. Consequently, despite relevancy, depositions of witnesses may not be admitted at trial as substantive evidence unless certain conditions regarding deponents' unavailability are met.[4]

Constitutional doctrine may also further the reliability of evidence. The Supreme Court is viewing reliability as the main concern of the Confrontation Clause, and other constitutional requirements, such as restrictions on the use of eyewitness testimony, also further the trustworthiness objective. See discussion in Chapter 14, *infra.*

¶ 1.01[02]   Rules of Extrinsic Policy

The privilege rules in Article V are the most obvious example of evidentiary rules designed to further some policy other than ascertaining the truth. See Chapter 18, below. Rules 404 through 412 all rest at least in part on the notion that certain evidence may be excluded because of goals other than truth finding. See Chapter 7, below. Even the hearsay rule serves more than a trustworthiness of evidence rationale. Although its main justification lies in truth finding, some of its vitality is due to its psychic value to litigants, who feel that those giving evidence against them should do so publicly and face to face.

The Advisory Committee's notes to Rule 402 list a number of Congressional enactments that restrict the admissibility of evidence through the formulation of a privilege or of a prohibition against disclosure. Procedural rules, such as Rule 37(b)(2)(B) of the Federal Rules of Civil Procedure, that impose sanctions may

---

[4] Rule 32(a) of the Federal Rules of Civil Procedure; Rule 15 of the Federal Rules of Criminal Procedure. Depositions of adverse parties are admissible for any purpose on the same rationale as are other admissions. See Rule 801(d)(2) discussed in Chapter 15, below.

also have the effect of restricting the use of evidence in order to discourage behavior destructive to the judicial process. Constitutional exclusionary rules, though less favored by the Supreme Court than in the past, also operate to exclude relevant evidence in order to further important societal policies such as the deterrence of unlawful police conduct.

¶ 1.02   Purpose and Construction—Rule 102[1]

Rule 102 acknowledges flexibility as the theme of the Federal Rules of Evidence, a theme which is developed in subsequent provisions of the Rules. The rule provides:

Rule 102

PURPOSE AND CONSTRUCTION

These rules shall be construed to secure fairness in administration, elimination of unjustifiable expense and delay, and promotion of growth and development of the law of evidence to the end that the truth may be ascertained and proceedings justly determined.

Flexibility is mandated because the wording of Rule 102 indicates that general, normative goals are preferred over subservience to specific, technical rules. This preference is developed in subsequent provisions of the Rules which eschew mechanical results in favor of judicial discretion. Rule 403 (Chapter 6) and the rules discussed in Chapter 2, which govern the trial court's control over the conduct of the trial, require the judge to take into account the facts of the particular case in ruling on the admissibility of evidence. Such an approach suggests that the trial court's decision will be final except when it clearly amounts to an abuse of discretion.

In addition, to mention only some of the most striking examples, the rules relating to expert testimony, hearsay and privilege have been extensively revised to make them more flexible. Article VII of the Rules eliminates common law restrictions on the use of expert testimony in favor of a "helpfulness" test that recognizes the need for case-by-case analysis. See Chapter 8, *infra*. Even a tradi-

---

[1] See discussion in **Treatise** at ¶¶ 102[01]–[02].

tionally black-letter law like the hearsay rule has been given flexibility by the addition of residual, non-class exceptions. See Chapter 14, *infra,* for a detailed discussion of judicial discretion in the application of the hearsay rule and its exceptions. Congress' action in rejecting the detailed rules on privilege drafted by the Advisory Committee had the effect of dismantling a closed system with absolute rules in favor of a case-by-case approach that evaluates existing privileges and proposed privileges "in the light of reason and experience." See discussion *infra* in Chapter 18.

The flexibility mandated by Rule 102 is inconsistent with the "near miss" theory espoused by a few judges. According to this theory, evidence "which narrowly fails to meet the standards" of a particular hearsay exception cannot be admitted pursuant to the residual hearsay exceptions in Rules 803(24) and 804(b)(5), because the residual exceptions may only "be used in exceptional and unanticipated situations which are not specifically covered by the specific exceptions."[2] Such a narrow, mechanical approach misconstrues the most basic theme of the Federal Rules of Evidence that is expressed in Rule 102—that relevant, reliable evidence should not be kept from the trier of fact unless warranted by some of the other goals stated in the rule. Determinations of technical impeccability are not one of the objectives. Read together, Rule 102 and the residual exceptions indicate that the exclusion of reliable evidence because of a failure to comply with the specific criteria of a class hearsay exception is not consonant with the Federal Rules' disposition to admit rather than to exclude.

The courts obviously need leeway in interpreting the Rules because Rule 102 directs them to competing goals; in the absence of

---

[2] Zenith Radio Corp. v. Matsushita Electric Industrial Co., Ltd., 505 F.Supp. 1190, 1263 (E.D. Pa. 1980). In the course of reversing on a number of evidentiary grounds, the appellate court noted its disapproval of the "near miss" theory, stating that it conflicts with the function of residual exceptions. *In re* Japanese Electronic Products Litigation, 723 F.2d 238, 302–03 (3d Cir. 1983), *rev'd on other grounds,* 106 S.Ct. 1348 (1986). See also Creamer v. General Teamsters Local Union 326, 560 F.Supp. 495, 498 (D. Del. 1983) (agreeing with "near miss" theory); United States v. American Cyanamid Co., 427 F.Supp. 859, 866 (S.D.N.Y. 1977) ("near miss" theory "would negate the requirement of Rule 102"); Lloyd v. American Export Lines, Inc., 580 F.2d 1179 (3d Cir. 1978), *cert. denied,* 439 U.S. 969 (1979) (concurring opinion; testimony that does not satisfy prior testimony exception is admissible pursuant to residual exception).

flexibility, the elimination of unjustifiable expense and delay cannot always be easily reconciled with the ascertainment of the truth. Rule 102 recognizes that judges may be justified in employing procedures that will lead to a cheap and swift, rough and ready approximation of the facts, even though there may be an increased risk of error. Distinctions in practice have to be made between bench and jury trial, between criminal and civil cases, and among various types of cases. A bench-tried federal tort claim involving minor property damage caused by a post office truck does not require the full formalities of a major organized crime prosecution in order to leave the participants with the feeling that due process was fully served.

The emphasis on the ascertainment of truth and justly determined proceedings authorizes judges to determine issues justly even when this requires a modification of the law of evidence and a rejection of precedent. Rule 102 may operate as an escape route from restrictions that have become burdensome because of unforseen contingencies or new developments. Rule 102 encourages courts to utilize rules of evidence to afford parties their substantive rights. The federal practice is, rightly, merits minded.

¶ 1.02[01]   When Does State Law Have To Be Applied?[3]

While Congress specifically provided that state law would govern the effect of civil presumptions,[4] questions of privilege,[5] and the competency of witnesses[6] when state law "supplies the rule of decision," few other rules expressly refer to non-federal law,[7] although there are some implicit references. When, however, a proceeding instituted in a federal court presents claims or defenses

---

[3] See discussion in **Treatise** at ¶ 1101[02].

[4] Rule 302 discussed in Chapter 5.

[5] Rule 501 discussed in Chapter 18.

[6] Rule 601 discussed in Chapter 10.

[7] Rule 903 provides that a writing need not be authenticated by testimony of a subscribing witness unless such testimony "is required by the law of the jurisdiction whose laws govern the validity of the writing." Rule 902(9) refers to the "general commercial law." See Chapter 8. Standard 502, which is discussed in Chapter 18, accords a privilege to reports required by law if the requiring law grants a privilege.

which are governed by substantive state law, as when the action is grounded in diversity jurisdiction or raises pendent claims, the *Erie* doctrine requires a careful analysis of when, whether, and to what extent state law must be used.[8] The state's rule may have to be applied if it is intended to prescribe rights and obligations of the parties not related to fact finding.[9] A court may also be called upon to decide whether a particular matter is covered by a Federal Rule of Evidence, in which case *Hanna v. Plumer*[10] teaches that it need not consider state law because the rule deals with an area that is arguably procedural, or whether the Federal Rule does not apply to the issue in question, in which case state law may have to be applied.[11]

Widespread adoption of the Federal Rules by the states has minimized some of the problems of diverse federal and state rules. To this extent national horizontal uniformity is not inconsistent with state-federal vertical consistency.[12]

---

[8] United States v. Paone, 782 F.2d 386, 393 (2d Cir. 1986) (although predicate acts underlying RICO indictment were New York state law offenses, New York law did not have to be applied; "Congress did not intend to incorporate the various states' procedural and evidentiary rules into the RICO statute.").

[9] See, *e.g.*, Caldarera v. Eastern Airlines, Inc., 705 F.2d 778, 782 (5th Cir. 1983) (state law forbidding use of evidence of remarriage in action for damages for loss of spouse applies in diversity cases); *In re* Air Crash Disaster Near Chicago, Illinois, 701 F.2d 1189, 1091-95 (7th Cir.), *cert. denied,* 464 U.S. 866 (1983) (discusses admissibility of evidence of income tax liability on issue of damages).

[10] 380 U.S. 460 (1965).

[11] This problem arises in connection with Rule 407 discussed in Chapter 8.

[12] See State Adaptations of the Federal Rules of Evidence in **Treatise** at T-1. The states that have adopted a version of the Federal Rules are: Alaska, Arizona, Arkansas, Colorado, Delaware, Florida, Hawaii, Idaho, Iowa, Maine, Michigan, Minnesota, Mississippi, Montana, Nebraska, Nevada, New Hampshire, New Mexico, North Carolina, North Dakota, Ohio, Oklahoma, Oregon, Puerto Rico, South Dakota, Texas, Utah, Vermont, Washington, West Virginia, Wisconsin, Wyoming, Military. See Wroth, "The Federal Rules of Evidence in the States: A Ten-Year Perspective," 30 Vill. L. Rev. 1315 (1985).

¶ 1.03   Applicability of the Federal Rules of Evidence— Rules 101 and 1101[1]

In applying the Federal Rules of Evidence, it must be remembered that they are not "Rules" in the sense of having been adopted through the rule making power provided for by the Rules Enabling Act.[2] Although the Federal Rules originally were intended to become effective as a result of promulgation by the Supreme Court, they ultimately were enacted as a statute.[3] They are, consequently, immune from attack on the ground that they deal with substantive issues beyond the scope of rule-making. The language of the Rules— and particularly those Congress gave great attention to—are sometime accorded great deference because they represent a positive legislative enactment.

Rule 101[4] provides that the Federal Rules of Evidence[5] apply in the courts of the United States and before federal magistrates, except for those situations specifically enumerated in Rule 1101. Subdivisions (a) and (b) of Rule 1101[6] explain in more detail that the Rules

---

[1] See discussion in **Treatise** at ¶¶ 101[01], 1101[01], 1101[03].

[2] 28 U.S.C. § 2071 et seq.

[3] See discussion in Preface of **Treatise** for a summary of the legislative history.

[4] Rule 101:

SCOPE

These rules govern proceedings in the courts of the United States and before United States bankruptcy judges and United States magistrates, to the extent and with the exceptions stated in rule 1101.

[5] Rule 1103:

TITLE

These rules may be known and cited as the Federal Rules of Evidence.

[6] Subdivisions (a) and (b) of Rule 1101 provide:

Rule 1101

APPLICABILITY OF RULES

(a) Courts and magistrates.—These rules apply to the United States district courts, the District Court of Guam, the District Court of the Virgin Islands, the District Court for the Northern Mariana Islands, the United States Courts of Appeals, the United States Claims Court, and to United States bankruptcy judges and United States magistrates, in the actions, cases, and proceedings and to the

apply to civil actions and proceedings, including admiralty and maritime cases, to criminal actions and proceedings, and to cases of non-summary contempt. The Rules also apply in bankruptcy courts, and in territorial courts.[7] Subdivision (c)[8] implements the privilege article of the Rules. It recognizes that confidentiality once destroyed cannot be restored, and that a privilege is effective only if it bars all disclosure at all times.[9]

Except for the privilege rules, however, subdivision (d) of Rule 1101 acknowledges that evidence rules need not be applied in certain specified circumstances:

Rule 1101

APPLICABILITY OF RULE

. . .

(d) Rules inapplicable.—The rules (other than with respect to privileges) do not apply in the following situations:

(1) Preliminary questions of fact.—The determination of questions of fact preliminary to admissibility of evidence when the issue is to be determined by the court under rule 104.

(2) Grand jury.—Proceedings before grand juries.

(3) Miscellaneous proceedings.—Proceedings for extradition or rendition; preliminary examinations in criminal cases; sentencing, or granting or revoking probation; issuance of warrants for arrest, criminal summonses, and search warrants; and proceedings with respect to release on bail or otherwise.

---

extent hereinafter set forth. The terms "judge" and "court" in these rules include United States bankruptcy judges and United States magistrates.

(b) Proceedings generally.—These rules apply generally to civil actions and proceedings, including admiralty and maritime cases, to criminal cases and proceedings, to contempt proceedings except those in which the court may act summarily, and to proceedings and cases under title 11, United States Code.

. . .

[7] See discussion in **Treatise** at ¶ 1101[01].

[8] (c) Rule of privilege. The rule with respect to privileges applies at all stages of all actions, cases, and proceedings.

[9] See, *e.g.,* Appeal of Malfitano, 633 F.2d 276 (3d Cir. 1980).

Although the Federal Rules of Evidence as such do not apply in the situations enumerated in subdivision (d), the rules may in some circumstances offer useful guidance in determining the probative value of evidence.[10]

Subdivision (e) of Rule 1101 is self-explanatory.[11] If an Act of

---

[10] See, *e.g.,* Calhoun v. Bailar, 626 F.2d 145 (9th Cir. 1980), *cert. denied,* 452 U.S. 906 (1981) (court, after extensive discussion, suggests that standards of Rule 803(24) may be helpful in determining whether hearsay declarations have sufficient probative value to constitute substantial evidence in an administrative proceeding); United States v. Samango, 450 F.Supp. 1097 (D. Hawaii 1978), *aff'd,* 607 F.2d 877 (9th Cir. 1979) (while evidentiary rules are inapplicable in grand jury proceedings, they illuminate factors that mitigate prejudice; court considered Rule 403).

[11] (e) Rules applicable in part.—In the following proceedings these rules apply to the extent that matters of evidence are not provided for in the statutes which govern procedure therein or in other rules prescribed by the Supreme Court pursuant to statutory authority: the trial of minor and petty offenses by United States magistrates; review of agency actions when the facts are subject to trial de novo under section 706(2)(F) of title 5, United States Code; review of orders of the Secretary of Agriculture under section 2 of the Act entitled "An Act to authorize association of producers of agricultural products" approved February 18, 1922 (7 U.S.C. 292), and under sections 6 and 7(c) of the Perishable Agricultural Commodities Act, 1930 (7 U.S.C. 499f, 499g(c)); naturalization and revocation of naturalization under sections 310–318 of the Immigration and Nationality Act (8 U.S.C. 1421–1429); prize proceedings in admiralty under sections 7651–7681 of title 10, United States Code; review of orders of the Secretary of the Interior under section 2 of the Act entitled "An Act authorizing associations of producers of aquatic products" approved June 25, 1934 (15 U.S.C. 522); review of orders of petroleum control boards under section 5 of the Act entitled "An Act to regulate interstate and foreign commerce in petroleum and its products by prohibiting the shipment in such commerce of petroleum and its products produced in violation of State law, and for other purposes", approved February 22, 1935 (15 U.S.C. 715d); actions for fines, penalties, or forfeitures under part V of title IV of the Tariff Act of 1930 (19 U.S.C. 1581–1624), or under the Anti-Smuggling Act (19 U.S.C. 1701–1711); criminal libel for condemnation, exclusion of imports, or other proceedings under the Federal Food, Drug, and Cosmetic Act (21 U.S.C. 301–392); disputes between seamen under sections 4079, 4080, and 4081 of the Revised Statutes (22 U.S.C. 256–258); habeas corpus under sections 2241–2254 of title 28, United States Code; motions to vacate, set aside or correct sentence under section 2255 of title 28, United States Code; actions for penalties for refusal to transport destitute seamen under section 4578 of the Revised Statutes (46 U.S.C. 679); actions against the United States under the Act entitled "An Act authorizing suits against the United States in admiralty for damage caused by and salvage service rendered to public vessels belonging to the United States, and for other purposes", approved March 3, 1925 (46 U.S.C. 781–790), as implemented by section 7730 of title 10, United States Code.

Congress, or a rule adopted by the Supreme Court, governing a special type of proceeding, specifically deals with evidentiary matters, the Rules of Evidence apply only to the extent not inconsistent with the statute or rule.[12]

The Federal Rules of Evidence, other than those relating to rules of privilege, may be amended pursuant to 28 U.S.C. § 2076,[13] in conformity with the rule-making process provided, which allows an amendment to take effect unless either House of Congress disapproves of it within one hundred and eighty days after it is reported. Any amendment creating, abolishing, or modifying a privilege must be enacted by Congress.

---

[12] Difficult issues about the applicability of evidence rules may arise as Congress adopts new procedures that cannot easily be classified as civil or criminal. See, *e.g.*, the unanswered questions regarding the Victim and Witness Protection Act of 1982, 18 U.S.C. § 1501 et seq., raised at ¶ 1101[03] of the Treatise.

[13]
Rule 1102

AMENDMENTS

Amendments to the Federal Rules of Evidence may be made as provided in section 2076 of title 28 of the United States Code.

28 U.S.C. § 2076 provides:

The Supreme Court of the United States shall have the power to prescribe amendments to the Federal Rules of Evidence. Such amendments shall not take effect until they have been reported to Congress by the Chief Justice at or after the beginning of a regular session of Congress but not later than the first day of May, and until the expiration of one hundred and eighty days after they have been so reported; but if either House of Congress within that time shall by resolution disapprove any amendment so reported it shall not take effect. The effective date of any amendment so reported may be deferred by either House of Congress to a later date or until approved by Act of Congress. Any rule whether proposed or in force may be amended by Act of Congress. Any provision of law in force at the expiration of such time and in conflict with any such amendment not disapproved shall be of no further force or effect after such amendment has taken effect. Any such amendment creating, abolishing, or modifying a privilege shall have no force or effect unless it shall be approved by act of Congress.

CHAPTER 2*

Control by Trial Court Generally

SYNOPSIS

---

* Chapter revised in 1991 by HELEN B. PARKER, member of the New York bar.

¶ 2.01   Overview of Trial Judge's Control

The trial judge is granted great discretion under the Federal Rules.[1] In this chapter specific reference is made to juducial power to control the mode and order of interrogating witnesses (Rule 611), limited review of error in rulings on evidence (Rule 103), authority to instruct on limited admissibility (Rule 105), application of the fairness concept in related writings (Rule 106), right of the court to call and interrogate witnesses (Rule 614), and the power to sum up and comment by the judge (Standard 107). Other indicia of that discretion are found in Rule 102, on construction of the rules (Chapter 1), Rule 104, on authority to answer preliminary questions as a predicate for admissibility (Chapter 3), Rule 201, on discretionary power to take judicial notice under some circumstances (Chapter 4), Rule 403, on power to weigh probative force against prejudice and other negative factors (Chapter 6), Rule 404, on admissibility of character evidence (Chapter 7), Rules 608 and 609, on discretionary limits on use of character and conviction evidence to impeach (Chapter 12), Rules 702–06, on control of experts (Chapter 13), Rules 803(24) and 804(b)(5), on power to expand use of hearsay (Chapter 14), and in various other places discussed throughout the text.

To prevent abuse of these powers, the trial court must remain cognizant of its limited role. Under our adversary system, primary decisions on tactics and style within very wide limits are assigned to the lawyers. In general, the best run trials have the least ratio of colloquy and interjections by the judge.

Nevertheless, the judge should, whenever a question arises, explain clearly what factors were taken into account in exercising discretion. Rulings in advance should be encouraged so that no surprises take place at trial, leading to pressured and sometimes unwise spur-of-the-moment decisions. The lawyer needs to think through the applicability of the rules before trial in order to request in limine rulings.

Wasteful side bars and continuances should be avoided. Explanations to the jury should be designed to inform on the assumption that the jurors will do a more intelligent job if they

---

[1] *See* **Treatise** at Preface pp. iii–v.

understand what is going on. Given the generally high quality of American jurors, the more information they have, the more likely they are to arrive at a sound and dispassionate estimate of the truth. This assumption underlies the tendency under the Federal Rules to admit rather than to exclude evidence whenever possible.

¶ 2.02 Interrogation and Presentation of Witnesses— Rule 611

¶ 2.02[01] Scope

Rule 611 is one of the rules central to the scheme of the Federal Rules of Evidence. In addition to setting forth basic principles governing the examination of witnesses in subdivisions (b) and (c), subdivision (a) is the source of the trial court's power over the order and mode of the presentation of evidence and the interrogation of witnesses. The rule provides:

Rule 611

MODE AND ORDER OF INTERROGATION AND PRESENTATION

(a) Control by court. The court shall exercise reasonable control over the mode and order of interrogating witnesses and presenting evidence so as to (1) make the interrogation and presentation effective for the ascertainment of the truth, (2) avoid needless consumption of time, and (3) protect witnesses from harassment or undue embarrassment.

(b) Scope of cross-examination. Cross-examination should be limited to the subject matter of the direct examination and matters affecting the credibility of the witness. The court may, in the exercise of discretion, permit inquiry into additional matters as if on direct examination.

(c) Leading questions. Leading questions should not be used on the direct examination of a witness except as may be necessary to develop the witness' testimony. Ordinarily leading questions should be permitted on cross-examination. When a party calls a hostile witness, an adverse party, or a witness identified with an adverse party, interrogation may be by leading questions.

¶ 2.02[02]   Control by Court[1]

Rule 611(a) restates a number of principles which are expressed elsewhere in the rules, particularly in Rules 102 and 403. The Rule reflects the power of the court to control the course of a trial so as to achieve three objectives: the ascertainment of the truth, the avoidance of needless consumption of time, and the protection of witnesses from harassment or undue embarrassment.

In the usual case, the order and mode of the presentation of evidence and interrogation of witnesses are determined by legal conventions and the parties' choice of trial tactics. The court steps in only when it is asked for a ruling, or something out of the ordinary occurs that warrants intervention.[2] If the court is satisfied that the truth is being elicited, it should generally not intrude and insist on a particular mode of questioning or order of proof in defiance of the parties. Even if the court is trying to save time, which is one of the objectives of Rule 611(a), it must bear in mind that counsel are far more familiar with the case, so that a seemingly trivial ruling may impede rather than expedite the search for truth. Once the trial court exercises its power, its decision is virtually immune to attack, and will be overturned only in the rare case where the appellate court finds a clear abuse of discretion that seriously damaged a party's right to a fair trial.[3]

Subdivision (a) authorizes departures from the usual order of proof and innovations in the presentation of evidence. Some of the more frequently occurring examples of a court's power

---

[1] See discussion in **Treatise** at ¶ 611[01].

[2] United States v. Jerde, 841 F.2d 818 (8th Cir. 1988) (judge permitted to interrogate defendant to clarify testimony and elicit necessary facts). *Cf.* United States v. Nivica, 887 F.2d 1110 (1st Cir. 1989), *cert. denied,* 110 S. Ct. 1300 (1990) (not unreasonable for judge to allow self examination of defendant representing himself by asking and answering his own questions while on the witness stand).

[3] *See, e.g.,* United States v. Mickens, 926 F.2d 1323 (2d Cir. 1991) (court's admonitions to counsel and questions to witnesses were proper); Nachtsheim v. Beech Aircraft Corp., 847 F.2d 1261 (7th Cir. 1988) (within trial court's discretion to refuse to allow document to be used for impeachment after witness had been excused and left the courtroom).

are: the reopening of a case after a party has rested;[4] the recalling of a witness;[5] allowing[6] or ordering[7] witnesses to testify out of order; the admission of rebuttal or surrebuttal testimony;[8] permitting witnesses to testify in installments;[9] and

---

[4] The trial court will usually be affirmed whether it reopens or refuses to reopen the case. *See, e.g.,* United States v. Terry, 729 F.2d 1063, 1066–69 (6th Cir. 1984) (within trial court's discretion not to reopen case to present further impeaching evidence against chief prosecution witness, where witness had already been subject to extensive impeachment); Rhyne v. United States, 407 F.2d 657, 661 (7th Cir. 1969) (no abuse of discretion in permitting government to reopen case after defendant had moved for acquittal, where defendant was not surprised, evidence was no more detrimental than it would have been if offered originally, and defendant was given opportunity to meet additional evidence). Once the case is submitted to the jury it is bad practice to allow further evidence except on stipulation in a most unusual situation since the argument and charge has been based on the prior evidence. *But see* United States v. Simtob, 901 F.2d 799 (9th Cir. 1990) (trial court erred in refusing to reopen case before final arguments so that defendant could present evidence to jury of a tape recorded conversation on the issue of defendant's predisposition to commit the crime).

[5] *See, e.g.,* United States v. Anthony, 565 F.2d 533, 536 (8th Cir. 1977), *cert. denied,* 434 U.S. 1079 (1978) (some witnesses called twice because court required government to establish prima facie case of conspiracy prior to admission of co-conspirators' statements; no error where defendants were allowed to cross-examine witnesses on both appearances and no testimony was unnecessarily repeated).

[6] *See, e.g.,* Berroyer v. Hertz, 672 F.2d 334 (3d Cir. 1982) (court permitted defense expert witness to be called during plaintiff's case in chief and then allowed plaintiff to call witness to rebut the defense witness); Lis v. Robert Packer Hosp., 579 F.2d 819 (3d Cir.), *cert. denied,* 439 U.S. 955 (1978) (not error for court to allow defense to qualify plaintiff's witness, a physician, as its witness at the conclusion of cross-examination; court has discretion to accommodate the schedules of expert witnesses even though calling a defense witness during plaintiff's case-in-chief may technically disrupt the normal presentation of the case).

[7] *See, e.g.,* United States v. Leon, 679 F.2d 534 (5th Cir. 1982) (where defense witness had not yet arrived, no error in court directing counsel to put on defendant where defendant had already indicated he would testify and judge was merely trying to keep trial from stalling).

[8] *See, e.g.,* Bhaya v. Westinghouse, 922 F.2d 184 (3d Cir. 1991) (trial court properly limited plaintiffs' questioning on rebuttal where plaintiffs sought to elicit testimony that merely stated in different words what another defense witness had said, and did not tend to refute the defendants' proof); Benedict v. United States, 822 F.2d 1426 (6th Cir. 1987) (abuse of discretion by trial court in excluding criminal defendant's rebuttal evidence even though it

allowing witnesses to testify in a narrative form.[10] This list is in no way exhaustive; the court has the power under Rule 611(a) to experiment with more radical variations on traditional practice, provided that it keeps in mind the goals of the rule and the rights of the parties when it balances the needs of the witness and the judicial system.

Problems relating to the harassment of witnesses usually arise in the context of the permissible scope of cross-examination. The exact point at which the court must step in to prevent abuse is impossible to formulate since it depends on the interaction of the particular factors present. A witness may be intimidated by the manner as well as the questions of the cross-examiner. Likewise, even fighting words may become unobjectionable when said with a smile. Appellate courts are reluctant to disturb a trial judge's decision on cross-examination since the cold record will not adequately reflect the actual situation in the courtroom.

---

belonged in the defendant's case-in-chief); Rodriguez v. Olin Corp., 780 F.2d 491 (5th Cir. 1986) (The court of appeals held that for purposes of proper rebuttal, the evidence introduced in the defense case need not be "brand new." Evidence is considered to be new if, under all the facts and circumstances, the court concludes that the evidence was not fairly and adequately presented to the trier of fact before the defendant's case-in-chief.); United States v. Wilford, 710 F.2d 439 (8th Cir. 1983), *cert. denied,* 464 U.S. 1039 (1984) (refusal to allow surrebuttal testimony); Page v. Barko Hydraulics, 673 F.2d 134 (5th Cir. 1982) (no abuse of discretion in trial court's refusal to allow plaintiff to present important relevant evidence on rebuttal which should have been presented in case-in-chief).

[9] United States v. DeLuna, 763 F.2d 897, 911–12 (8th Cir.), *cert. denied,* 474 U.S. 980 (1985) (no abuse of discretion where defendants were presented ample opportunity to cross-examine witness after each installment).

[10] *See, e.g.,* United States v. Young, 745 F.2d 733, 761 (2d Cir. 1984), *cert. denied,* 470 U.S. 1084 (1985) (qualified expert narrated and offered opinions while a videotape was played for jury); Goings v. United States, 377 F.2d 753, 762–63 (9th Cir. 1967) (discusses pertinent considerations for exercise of trial court's discretion).

¶ 2.02[03]   Cross-examination

[a]   Scope[1]

Rule 611(b), in accord with the majority position in the United States, restricts cross-examination to the subject matter of the direct examination and matters affecting the witness' credibility. Advocates of the rule believe that it "facilitates orderly presentation by each party at trial."[2]

The consequence of the Rule 611(b) formulation is that there will be instances in which a court may prevent questions from being asked on cross-examination as beyond the scope of the direct, as, for example, where an adverse party is called to authenticate a document and then tries to put in a whole defense out of order on cross- examination.[3] While appellate courts confer a good deal of discretion on trial courts to rule upon the appropriate scope,[4] the exercise of discretion must

---

[1] See discussion in **Treatise** at ¶ 611[02]. The **Treatise** discusses in some detail the English, and minority rule, that permits wide-open cross-examination. Rule 611(b) had been drafted as a rule of wide-open cross-examination, but this change was rejected by Congress. See discussion of Congressional Action on Rule 611 in Treatise.

[2] House Comm. on the Judiciary, Rep. No. 650, 93rd Cong., 1st Sess. 12 (1973).

[3] See, e.g., Williams v. Giant Eagle Markets, 883 F.2d 1184 (3d Cir. 1989) (in employment discrimination action, a witness called to authenticate document could not be cross-examined about whether he, a white male, had been treated less severely for acts of insubordination than plaintiff, a black female); United States v. Harris, 761 F.2d 394, 397–98 (7th Cir. 1985) (where fact that investigation of CETA program was discontinued was in issue, not error to limit cross-examination of a witness as to why investigation was discontinued); Lewis v. Rego Co., 757 F.2d 66, 72–73 (3d Cir. 1985) (error to allow expert witness to give his opinion about what had made cylinder burst on cross-examination when he was not asked about the cause on direct examination).

[4] See, e.g., United States v. Vasquez, 858 F.2d 1387 (9th Cir. 1988), cert. denied, 488 U.S. 1034 (1989) (where defendant testified on direct only about events surrounding sale of cocaine to undercover agent, cross-examination about the cocaine, money, photographs and narcotics paraphernalia discovered in his apartment was "reasonably related" to direct testimony); United States v. Beechum, 582 F.2d 898, 905–07 (5th Cir. 1978), cert. denied, 440 U.S. 920 (1979) (where defendant mail carrier, charged with theft of a silver

be consonant with the rule's objective of promoting the orderly presentation of evidence without cutting off inquiry that is germane.[5]

The trial court also has power pursuant to Rule 403 to limit cross-examination that would create prejudice or confusion even though it satisfies the test of Rule 611(b).[6] In a criminal case, the court's right to curtail cross-examination is circumscribed by the defendant's Sixth Amendment right of confrontation,[7] although the Supreme Court has held that an erroneous

---

dollar, testified on direct that he had found silver dollar in mailbox and that he intended to turn it over to supervisor, proper to cross-examine defendant about two credit cards, not made out to him, found in his possession together with dollar when he was arrested).

[5] *See, e.g.,* Lis v. Robert Packer Hosp., 579 F.2d 819, 821–23 (3d Cir.), *cert. denied,* 439 U.S. 955 (1978) (trial judge reversed where he claimed to have "the right to permit inquiry beyond the scope of the direct . . . in every case."); United States v. Wolfson, 573 F.2d 216 (5th Cir. 1978) (where in prosecution of marine surveyor for overstating value of yachts for taxpayers, government called insurance agent who testified that he had received request for the amounts of insurance from the defendant (amounts much lower than reports to taxpayers); reversible error for trial court to have prevented defendant from cross-examining agent about conversation with defendant in which defendant explained that insurance was low because universities in question could not afford more).

[6] *See, e.g.,* United States v. Spivey, 841 F.2d 799 (7th Cir. 1988) (co-defendant's counsel had conducted extensive cross-examination on same issue); Specht v. Jensen, 832 F.2d 516 (10th Cir. 1987) (appropriate to restrict cross-examination that was relevant for one purpose but not another because of danger that jury might misinterpret); United States v. Beltran, 761 F.2d 1 (1st Cir. 1985) (potentially cumulative and harassing); United States v. Sorrentino, 726 F.2d 876, 885 (1st Cir. 1984) (potentially cumulative and harassing); United States v. 10.48 Acres of Land, 621 F.2d 338 (9th Cir. 1980) (appropriate to restrict cross-examination that was relevant for one purpose but not another because of danger that jury might misuse); United States v. Praetorius, 622 F.2d 1054 (2d Cir. 1979), *cert. denied,* 449 U.S. 860 (1980) (co-defendant's counsel had conducted extensive cross-examination on same issue); United States v. Rice, 550 F.2d 1364 (5th Cir.), *cert. denied,* 434 U.S. 965 (1977) (reasonable not to allow inquiry into whereabouts of chief prosecution witness who was in protective custody because he would be endangered).

[7] United States v. Berros, 833 F.2d 455 (3d Cir. 1987) (court did not violate defendant's rights under the confrontation clause when limiting the cross-examination of a witness in order to avoid misleading the jury); United States v. Gregory, 808 F.2d 679 (8th Cir.), *cert. denied,* 483 U.S. 1023 (1987) (right

restriction may constitute harmless error.[8] In a civil case, the restriction of cross-examination rarely rises to constitutional dimensions.

[b] Impact of Privilege Against Self-Incrimination[9]

Rule 611(b) is silent about the extent to which the privilege against self-incrimination limits the permissible scope of cross-examination. The question should be resolved by constitutional principles rather than evidentiary order of proof concerns. The problem arises in civil as well as in criminal cases, and in the case of ordinary witnesses as well as party witnesses, but it is most difficult to solve when the accused takes the stand.

Most cases which have been faced with the problem are not very helpful. Courts generally assume that the scope of the

---

to confrontation not violated where defendant was not completely prohibited from inquiring into bias on the part of the witness). *See also* Kentucky v. Stincer, 482 U.S. 730, 107 S. Ct. 2658, 96 L. Ed. 2d 631 (1987) (defendant's right of confrontation not violated by exclusion from competency hearing where defendant had opportunity of full and effective cross-examination of witnesses at trial); Pennsylvania v. Ritchie, 480 U.S. 39, 107 S. Ct. 989, 94 L. Ed. 2d 40 (1987) (in case where defendant was convicted of rape, involuntary sexual intercourse, incest, and corruption of a minor, defendant's confrontation rights were not violated by the withholding of the state's Children and Youth Services files, since defense counsel was able to extensively cross-examine all trial witnesses). *Cf.* United States v. Springer, 831 F.2d 781 (8th Cir. 1987), *cert. denied,* 485 U.S. 938 (1988) (trial court did not violate defendant's right to confrontation by limiting defendant's cross-examination of informant; judge stated he would allow further questioning about informant's criminal activity if defense counsel could demonstrate some basis for it, since there had already been extensive evidence about informant's background); United States v. Crockett, 813 F.2d 1310 (4th Cir.), *cert. denied,* 484 U.S. 834 (1987) (right to confrontation does not arise merely from status of witness as co-defendant but rather from content of testimony); United States v. Viera, 819 F.2d 498 (5th Cir. 1987), *aff'd,* 839 F.2d 1113 (5th Cir. 1988) (en banc); United States v. Cameron, 814 F.2d 403 (7th Cir. 1987) (no violation of confrontation clause where cross-examination is not allowed but other ample opportunities for impeachment of witnesses' testimony are available to defendant).

[8] Delaware v. Van Arsdall, 475 U.S. 673, 106 S. Ct. 1431, 89 L. Ed. 2d 674 (1986) (trial court erroneously curtailed all cross-examination of prosecution witness relevant to bias; Court remanded for determination of whether error was harmless).

[9] See discussion in **Treatise** at ¶¶ 611[03], [04].

privilege is identical to the scope of cross-examination, permitted by a restricted rule such as Rule 611(b).[10] without examining the differing policies served by the two rules. Consequently, they hold that the defendant must answer questions on cross-examination that are "reasonably related" to the subject of the direct examination and credibility.[11] This reasoning ignores the case of an ordinary witness, since a rule of limited cross-examination affects primarily the order of proof. A defendant, however, is not an ordinary witness; he cannot be recalled by the prosecution. With respect to a defendant's case, a rule of limited cross-examination bars evidence rather than merely postponing it. These cases fail to inquire whether the policy of

---

[10] McEwen v. City of Norman Okla., 926 F.2d 1539 (10th Cir. 1991) (questions concerning use of alias and prior bench warrant on cross-examination were probative of matters directly or inferentially developed during direct examination); United States v. Harper, 802 F.2d 115 (5th Cir. 1986) (when defendant voluntarily testifies he waives his fifth amendment rights and becomes obligated, like any other witness, to answer all relevant questions); Hankins v. Civiletti, 614 F.2d 953 (5th Cir. 1980) (where petitioner testified on direct as to possession, custody and control of records, questions regarding the whereabouts or fate of the records were proper cross-examination within the subject matter of his direct testimony).

[11] McGautha v. California, 402 U.S. 183, 215, 91 S. Ct. 1454, 28 L. Ed. 2d 711 (1971) ("It has long been held that a defendant who takes the stand in his own behalf cannot then claim the privilege against cross-examination on matters reasonably related to the subject matter of his direct examination"; dictum). *See* United States v. Raper, 676 F.2d 841, 846 (D.C. Cir. 1982) ("any question which would have elicited testimony that was reasonably related to the inferences that might reasonably be drawn from his direct testimony would have been permissible."); United States v. Beechum, 582 F.2d 898, 907–09 (5th Cir. 1978) (en banc), *cert. denied*, 440 U.S. 920 (1979) (defendant's denial of unlawful intent on direct waived his privilege against self-incrimination at least to the extent of cross-examination relevant to issues raised by his testimony; he could therefore be cross-examined about evidence of other crimes which was admissible pursuant to Rule 404(b) as negativing innocent intent); United States v. Hearst, 563 F.2d 1331, 1338–44 (9th Cir. 1977), *cert. denied*, 435 U.S. 1000 (1978) (waiver of the privilege and the permissible cross-examination of a defendant are not to be determined by what the defendant actually discussed during direct examination but by whether the government's questions are "reasonably related" to the subjects covered by defendant's testimony; accordingly, where defendant claimed that she had acted under duress during the entire year and a half prior to her arrest, questions about her activities during that year were more than " 'reasonably related' to the subject of her prior testimony").

the privilege (as well as the goal of maximizing information available to the triers) is best served by compelling defendant to respond to any question once he has voluntarily testified, or by allowing him to remain selectively silent even after he has made partial disclosure.

Other restrictions may apply to a defendant who chooses not to testify in his own behalf. For example, if a criminal defendant elects not to take the stand, he cannot claim on appeal that the district court erred in denying his motion in limine to restrict cross-examination.[12]

A party in a civil action who testifies voluntarily in his own behalf is in a position analogous to that of an accused who is testifying by choice in a criminal case.[13] The party waives his privilege at least as to matters relevant to his examination on direct and risks sanctions for the refusal to testify. Moreover, unlike the defendant in a criminal case, even the proper exercise of the privilege by a party warrants a negative inference that unfavorable evidence is being suppressed by the party.

The position of the non-party witness is somewhat different. If subpoenaed he has no right to refuse to testify without being subject to contempt; even if not subpoenaed, he has the good citizen's responsibility to assist the court. Consequently, it is agreed that he does not waive his privilege against self-incrimination by merely taking the stand, and he has a right to claim the privilege if the answers sought may tend to incriminate him. This right is not lost so long as the witness testifies to non-incriminating facts, but testimony as to incriminating facts may constitute a waiver of the privilege. Precisely when waiver occurs is unclear.[14] Some courts will not find a waiver even though incriminating testimony has been given, if the answers sought may lead to further incrimination.[15]

[12] United States v. Nivica, 887 F.2d 1110 (1st Cir. 1989), *cert. denied,* 110 S. Ct. 1300 (1990).

[13] *See* Brown v. United States, 356 U.S. 148, 78 S. Ct. 622, 2 L. Ed. 2d 589 (1958).

[14] *Compare* Rogers v. United States, 340 U.S. 367, 71 S. Ct. 438, 95 L. Ed. 344 (1951) *with* cases cited in note below.

[15] *See, e.g.,* United States v. Seifert, 648 F.2d 557, 561 (9th Cir. 1980); United States v. LaRiche, 549 F.2d 1088, 1096 (6th Cir.), *cert. denied,* 430 U.S. 987 (1977).

If the privilege claim is upheld and the witness does not answer fully on cross-examination, the direct testimony must be stricken if the cross-examiner has been deprived of the ability to test the truth of the witness' direct testimony.[16] Courts have denied motions to strike when they find that the direct testimony related to "collateral" issues,[17] or was merely cumulative,[18] or that the unanswered questions constituted an insignificant portion of the cross-examination.[19]

In criminal cases the government may grant a witness use immunity in order to obtain testimony. The courts have not recognized a defendant's right to demand that his witnesses receive immunity, so long as the government is not using its grant selectively and unfairly.[20] In any case, the trial court may considerably enhance factfinding and fairness by working out an agreement out of the jury's presence that a witness, including a defendant in a criminal trial, will not be asked about certain areas. Considerations of fairness rather than precedent then govern.

¶ 2.02[04]   Leading Questions[1]

Rule 611(c) codifies the traditional mode of dealing with leading questions. It acknowledges that they are generally undesirable on direct examination, that they are usually permissible on cross-examination, and that there are exceptions to both of these statements. Although not explicitly stated, the

---

[16] See discussion in Fountain v. United States, 384 F.2d 624 (5th Cir. 1967).

[17] See, e.g., United States v. Director, Ill. Dept. of Corrections, 871 F.2d 680 (7th Cir. 1989) (exclusion of collateral matters); Air Et Chaleur v. Janeway, 757 F.2d 489 (2d Cir. 1985) (issues concerning a party's credibility are generally collateral); Klein v. Harris, 667 F.2d 274 (2d Cir. 1981).

[18] See, e.g., United States v. Lyons, 703 F.2d 815, 818–19 (5th Cir. 1983).

[19] See, e.g., Toolate* v. Borg, 828 F.2d 571 (9th Cir. 1987); United States v. Seifert, 648 F.2d 557 (9th Cir. 1980).

[20] See, e.g., United States v. Turkish, 623 F.2d 769, 772–73 (2d Cir. 1980), cert. denied, 449 U.S. 1077 (1981) (reviewing arguments). Most commentary is to the contrary. See, e.g., Notes, 91 Harv. L. Rev. 1266 (1978), 30 Stat. L. Rev. 1211 (1978).

[1] See discussion in **Treatise** at ¶ 611[05].

rule implies what has in fact long been the case—that the matter falls within the area of trial court discretion.[2] Reversals on the basis of non-compliance with Rule 611(c) are exceedingly rare,[3] probably occurring most frequently in criminal cases where a prosecutor, in the guise of asking leading questions, brings prohibited material to the attention of the jury.[4]

Rule 611(c) does not define a leading question, which is, however, well recognized in case law as a question which "so suggests to the witness the specific tenor of the reply desired by counsel that such a reply is likely to be given irrespective of an actual memory."[5] The tenor of the desired reply can be suggested in any number of ways, as, for example, by the form of the question, by emphasis on certain words, by the tone of the questioner or his nonverbal conduct, or by the inclusion of facts still in controversy. Because of these myriad ways in which a suggestion can be conveyed, only the judge actually presiding at the trial is in a position to assess fully the impact of the question on the witness and the effect of any impropriety on the conduct of the litigation. The trial judge is also the one

---

[2] Alpha Display Paging Inc. v. Motorola Co. & Elec., 867 F.2d 1168 (8th Cir. 1989) (court has discretion to allow leading questions to be used by defendant on cross-examination of defendant's employee who had been called by plaintiff as witness identified with adverse party); United States v. Demarrias, 876 F.2d 674 (8th Cir. 1989) (court did not abuse discretion in allowing victim who was reluctant to answer to be questioned by reading her the contents of her prior statement and then having her acknowledge that she had written the statement); Ellis v. City of Chicago, 667 F.2d 606 (7th Cir. 1981) (trial court's decision in this area will not be reversed absent a clear showing of prejudice).

[3] See, e.g., Miller v. Fairchild Indus. 885 F.2d 498 (9th Cir. 1989), cert. denied, 110 S. Ct. 1524 (1990) (although it was not clear that defense counsel's leading questions were necessary within the meaning of Rule 611(c), they would be allowed because the testimony they produced "did not substantially expand or alter earlier testimony elicited through proper, non-leading questions");

[4] See, e.g., United States v. Meeker, 558 F.2d 387 (7th Cir. 1977) (leading questions implied prior misconduct in violation of Rule 404(b) and suggested that defendant had engaged in conduct for which he was on trial); United States v. Shoupe, 548 F.2d 636 (6th Cir. 1977) (prosecutor incorporated unsworn remarks allegedly made by witness into leading questions in the guise of refreshing recollection).

[5] United States v. Durham, 319 F.2d 590, 592 (4th Cir. 1963).

to decide whether the questioner may rephrase a question after an objection has been sustained on the ground of leading.

Rule 611(c) acknowledges that leading questions may be necessary to develop the testimony. Among the situations in which the court is most likely to permit leading are the following: a witness who has less than a normal adult capacity,[6] a witness whose memory is exhausted,[7] and when the testimony relates to undisputed matters[8] or is at the periphery of the case.

If the witness is hostile to the examiner there is no reason to prohibit leading questions since there is no danger of false suggestions. Accordingly, Rule 611(c) provides that interrogation may be by leading questions when a party calls a hostile witness, an adverse party, or a witness identified with an adverse party. In the case of a hostile witness, the examiner will have to demonstrate the requisite degree of hostility, bias or reluctance to the satisfaction of the court.[9] Adverse parties are

---

[6] United States v. Grey Bear, 883 F.2d 1382 (8th Cir. 1989), *cert. denied,* 110 S. Ct. 846, (1990) (prosecution in a murder case was properly allowed to use leading questions in its direct examination of one "unusually softspoken and frightened witness"; the leading questions were used "infrequently and judiciously in order to develop testimony. . . "). *See* United States v. Demarrias, 876 F.2d 674 (8th Cir. 1989) (in sexual child abuse case, the district court properly used its discretion in allowing a leading question to be asked of victim on direct examination, since the young victim had exhibited a reluctance to testify).

[7] *See, e.g.,* Roberson v. United States, 249 F.2d 737, 742 (5th Cir. 1957), *cert. denied,* 356 U.S. 919 (1958) (leading questions to refresh the recollection of a witness).

[8] *See, e.g.,* United States v. Schepp, 746 F.2d 406 (8th Cir. 1984), *cert. denied,* 469 U.S. 1215 (1985) (leading questions on preliminary and collateral matters to expedite the trial); McClard v. United States, 386 F.2d 495, 501 (8th Cir. 1967), *cert. denied,* 393 U.S. 886 (1968) (leading questions on preliminary and collateral matters to expedite the trial).

[9] *See, e.g.,* United States v. Diaz, 662 F.2d 713 (11th Cir. 1981) (refusal to declare witness hostile was entirely proper where despite grant of immunity, hostility was directed against government rather than defendant); Riverside Ins. Co. of America v. Smith, 628 F.2d 1002 (7th Cir. 1980) (no error in trial court's refusal to treat as hostile witnesses owner of car, and her daughter, who had lent car to accident victim, but were not parties to action); United States v. Librach, 520 F.2d 550 (8th Cir. 1975), *cert. denied,* 429 U.S. 939 (1976) (proper to use leading questions where witness "evasive").

automatically subject to leading questions, as is the witness identified with an adverse party, once the examiner has made a sufficient showing to place the witness in this category.[10]

The second sentence of subdivision (c) restates the traditional view that leading questions can usually be asked on cross-examination as a matter of right, but that the right is not absolute. Where the witness is biased in favor of the cross-examiner, the same danger of leading questions arises as on direct and the court may, in its discretion, prohibit their use.[11] The Advisory Committee noted two circumstances in which the prohibition may be applied: (1) where a party is "cross-examined by his counsel after having been called by his opponent" and (2) where an "insured defendant proves to be friendly to the plaintiff."

¶ 2.03 Rulings on Evidence—Rule 103

¶ 2.03[01] Scope[1]

Rule 103 makes two major points: (1) that the initiative for raising and preserving error in the admission or exclusion of evidence lies with the party and not with the court, and (2) that in applying Rule 103 a court's objective is to avoid reversals on purely technical grounds while remaining ready to rectify errors which affect substantial rights of the parties. Although subdivisions (b) and (c) specify in some detail how objections to rulings are to be made, Rule 103 is silent as to the factors a court must consider in determining whether substantial rights have been affected. This indicates that the court must proceed on a case-by-case basis rather than apply a mechanical rule. The

---

[10] *See, e.g.,* United States v. Hicks, 748 F.2d 854, 859 (4th Cir. 1984) (not abuse of discretion to allow prosecution to ask two leading questions of defendant's girlfriend who was called as a government witness as she was a person identified with an adverse party).

[11] *See, e.g.,* Ardoin v. J. Ray McDermott & Co., 684 F.2d 335 (5th Cir. 1982) (court recognizes that trial court has power to require party cross-examining a friendly witness to employ non-leading questions but refuses to adopt per se rule that an employer cross-examining his own employees must use non-leading questions).

[1] See discussion in **Treatise** at ¶ 103[01].

rule governs civil and criminal[2] cases, as well as jury and non-jury cases. It applies when an appellate court reviews a decision of an inferior court, or when a trial court rules on a motion for a new trial. The rule provides:

Rule 103

RULINGS ON EVIDENCE

(a) Effect of erroneous ruling. Error may not be predicated upon a ruling which admits or excludes evidence unless a substantial right of the party is affected, and

(1) Objection. In case the ruling is one admitting evidence a timely objection or motion to strike appears of record, stating the specific ground of objection, if the specific ground was not apparent from the context; or

(2) Offer of proof. In case the ruling is one excluding evidence, the substance of the evidence was made known to the court by offer or was apparent from the context within which questions were asked.

(b) Record of offer and ruling. The court may add any other or further statement which shows the character of the evidence, the form in which it was offered, the objection made, and the ruling thereon. It may direct the making of an offer in question and answer form.

(c) Hearing of jury. In jury cases, proceedings shall be conducted, to the extent practicable, so as to prevent inadmissible evidence from being suggested to the jury by any means, such as making statements or offers of proof or asking questions in the hearing of the jury.

(d) Plain error. Nothing in this rule precludes taking notice of plain errors affecting substantial rights although they were not brought to the attention of the court.

The rule does not prescribe the precise form which objections should take. The following objectives need to be considered in deciding whether a particular objection was properly made: (1) it should give the opponent a sufficient idea of what is objectionable so that the error may be corrected, if that is possible;

---

[2] In criminal cases, because of constitutional guarantees, errors in the admission or exclusion of evidence may at times, though rarely, be raised by collateral attack. *See, e.g.,* Kimmelman v. Morrison, 477 U.S. 365, 106 S. Ct. 2574, 91 L. Ed. 2d 305 (1986).

(2) it should bring the objection to the trial court's attention so that it can rule on the matter intelligently and quickly; and (3) it should be construed in a way which will reduce the necessity for reversals and new trials—i.e., the trial court's determination should be upheld wherever decently possible by approving or disapproving the form of the objection to support the ruling below.

Although plain error is the only class of error mentioned by name in Rule 103, the rule deals with three categories of error well recognized in statutory law and judiciary opinion. "Harmless error" is error raised at trial but found not to affect substantial rights. "Prejudicial" or "reversible" error is error raised at trial which is found to affect substantial rights. "Plain error" is error not raised at trial, but nevertheless considered by a reviewing court, which is found to affect substantial rights. The distinction between harmless and reversible error thus turns on whether substantial rights are affected, and the distinction between harmless and plain error on whether the particular error in the case at hand excuses the party's failure to bring it properly to the trial court's attention.

¶ 2.03[02] Objections to the Admission of Evidence[1]

Subdivision (a)(1) of Rule 103 provides that error cannot be predicated on a ruling admitting evidence unless "a timely objection or motion to strike appears of record stating the specific ground of objection." Calling error to the attention of the trial court gives it an opportunity for correction which may obviate the need for further proceedings. In addition, continued questioning in response to an objection may clarify a situation which may be otherwise unclear to the reviewing court.

[a] Waiver

"A rule of evidence not invoked, is waived."[2] Thus, the decision whether or not to object should not be taken lightly.

---

[1] See discussion in **Treatise** at ¶ 103[02].

[2] Wigmore, Evidence § 18 (1985).

Although subdivision (d) of Rule 103 relieves a party of the consequences of a failure to object in the case of "plain error," appellate courts often discern underlying strategical patterns and are extremely reluctant to consider errors in the admission of evidence when they suspect that the failure to object is attributable to legitimate trial tactics.[3] An attorney can also waive the right to assert on appeal an error in the admission of evidence by deliberately eliciting[4] or relying on inadmissible

---

[3] *See, e.g.,* United States v. Parikh, 858 F.2d 688 (11th Cir. 1988) (documents that were admittedly written by defendant were correctly admitted into evidence because defendant failed to object at trial to lack of in camera hearing concerning the documents); United States v. Hall, 845 F.2d 1281 (5th Cir.), *cert. denied,* 488 U.S. 860, (1988) (defense counsel opened door on cross-examination to hearsay information elicited on re-direct examination as part of trial strategy to deal with expected testimony by surprise government witness; since counsel failed to move to strike or to have the court instruct the jury to disregard the hearsay testimony, the trial court's failure to sua sponte instruct the jury did not amount to plain error); Ward v. United States, 838 F.2d 182 (6th Cir. 1988) (admission of medical records that were read into the record at trial was proper because plaintiffs failed to object until appeal and failed to show "that a substantial right was violated" as required by Rule 103); Johnson v. Ashby, 808 F.2d 676 (8th Cir. 1987) (in medical malpractice action plaintiff waived right to challenge trial court's time limits on the presentation of evidence; plaintiff failed to make a timely objection to those limits and an offer of proof concerning the evidence he was unable to introduce); Lazzara v. Howard A. Esser, Inc., 802 F.2d 260 (7th Cir. 1986) (plaintiff argued on appeal that uncertified copy of first page only of judgment arising from automobile accident was inadmissible under Rule 902; failure to raise specific objection at trial did not reserve argument for appeal); United States v. Dysart, 705 F.2d 1247, 1252-55 (10th Cir.), *cert. denied,* 464 U.S. 934 (1983) (no plain error in admission of testimony derived from court-ordered psychiatric examination; court found that defense counsel "was obviously alerted to the statute" which makes such testimony inadmissible; defense cross-examined doctor about examination; cross-examination together with failure to object "demonstrate that a trial decision was made to . . . attack the Government's sole witness on competency . . . rather than to make the objections and confine his testimony").

[4] *See, e.g.,* United States v. Vachon, 869 F.2d 653 (1st Cir. 1989) (where defendant's expert witness had offered testimony on defendant's mental state, the trial court was within its discretion in allowing rebuttal evidence on the part of the government; defendant waived any right he had to object to the testimony of the government's expert witness by eliciting inadmissible testimony from his own witness); Burgess v. Premier Corp., 727 F.2d 826, 834 (9th Cir. 1984) (defendant waived objection to expert testimony on redirect concerning how and by whom securities fraud was perpetrated by raising the subject during cross-examination).

evidence.[5] Waiver has been applied even where the error involves a defendant's constitutional rights.[6]

[b] Timing

An objection must be timely.[7] Some objections may have to be raised even before trial. For example, motions for the suppression of evidence obtained through an illegal search or seizure,[8] or through a tainted out-of-court identification,[9] and objections relating to depositions must ordinarily be raised prior to trial or be deemed waived.[10] In criminal cases, there should be a pretrial hearing at which the trial court can determine whether any motions to suppress will be made.

Raising the evidentiary issue before trial will not necessarily relieve counsel from having to repeat the objection when the evidence to which the objection was made is offered at trial.[11]

_____

[5] *See, e.g.,* United States v. Silvers, 374 F.2d 828, 832 (7th Cir.), *cert. denied,* 389 U.S. 888 (1967) (defense counsel objected to testimony on prior convictions but relied on defendant's long prison experiences in presenting insanity defense; "a defendant's reference to or use of an erroneously admitted line of evidence cures or waives the error.").

[6] *See, e.g.,* Shaw v. United States, 403 F.2d 528, 530 (8th Cir. 1968) ("[B]arring* plain error, we will not notice errors raised for the first time in the appellate court, including errors involving a defendant's constitutional right."); United States v. White, 377 F.2d 908 (4th Cir.), *cert. denied,* 389 U.S. 884 (1967).

[7] United States v. Rivera-Santiago, 872 F.2d 1073 (1st Cir. 1989), *cert. denied,* 110 S. Ct. 105 (1989) (where defendant failed to object to a witness's statement when given, a motion to strike the statement at the close of the evidence did not meet the requirement of a "timely" objection under Rule 103(a)(1)). *See* United States v. Solomonson, 908 F.2d 358 (8th Cir. 1990) (motion to strike a government agent's testimony at the end of redirect not sufficient to preserve the objection for appeal; grounds for objection were apparent at the time of the agent's statement).

[8] *See* Rule 12(b) and (f) of the Federal Rules of Criminal Procedure.

[9] *See* Wade v. United States, 388 U.S. 218, 87 S. Ct. 1926, 18 L. Ed. 2d 1149 (1967).

[10] *See* Rule 32(b) of the Federal Rules of Civil Procedure.

[11] *Compare* Collins v. Wayne Corp., 621 F.2d 777 (5th Cir. 1980) (plaintiffs' in limine motion to exclude evidence with respect to the negligence of third parties had been granted, and to exclude cross-examination of experts as to their fees had been denied; court held that plaintiffs had waived their

The circuits are divided as to whether an objection at trial is necessary if the same issue was raised in an unsuccessful pretrial motion in limine. Some circuits require that "[o]bjection must be made in the trial court unless a good reason exists not to do so."[12] However, other circuits have held that no formal trial objection is necessary if the pretrial motion adequately resolves the issue with no suggestion that the trial court would reconsider the matter at trial.[13] Because of the danger that a pretrial objection will not be preserved for appeal, the wiser course is to renew any objection at trial.[14] The opportunity for additional reflection, particularly in light of details elicited in court, may cause a change in the court's view of the evidence.

objection when evidence on these subjects was admitted at trial without objection) *with* Sherrod v. Berry, 827 F.2d 195 (7th Cir. 1987) (when defendant objected to admission of certain evidence at a motion in limine, it was unnecessary to renew objections when evidence was admitted at trial).

[12] United States v. Griffin, 818 F.2d 97, 102–105 (1st Cir.), *cert. denied*, 484 U.S. 844 (1987) (no appellate review of in limine motion unless defendant raises issues in actual context of trial); Rojas v. Richardson, 703 F.2d 186, 189–90 & n.3, *opinion set aside for other reasons on rehearing*, 713 F.2d 116 (5th Cir. 1983) (plaintiff waived his objection by not raising it again at trial because he had no good reason not to do so); *see also* Northwestern Flyers, Inc. v. Olson Bros. Mfg. Co., 679 F.2d 1264, 1275 n.27 (8th Cir. 1982). *Cf.* United States v. DeGeratto, 876 F.2d 576 (7th Cir. 1989) (defendant's objection to admission of bad acts evidence viewed as a continuing objection to use of bad acts evidence in closing argument).

[13] Palmerin v. City of Riverside, 794 F.2d 1409, 1412–1413 (9th Cir. 1986) (in civil rights action arising out of plaintiff's arrest, court rejected an invariable requirement that objection that is the subject of an unsuccessful motion *in limine* be renewed at trial; "[an opposite rule] will serve as a trap for unwary counsel and bar an appeal of a meritorious issue on essentially technical grounds"; reviews cases); *see also* Thronson v. Meisels, 800 F.2d 136 (7th Cir. 1986); Adams v. Fuqua, 806 F.2d 770 (8th Cir. 1986); American Home Assurance Co. v. Sunshine Supermarket, Inc., 753 F.2d 321, 324–35 (3d. Cir. 1985).

[14] *See* United States v. Vest, 842 F.2d 1319 (1st. Cir.), *cert. denied*, 488 U.S. 965 (1988) (defendant's failure to object when prosecution witness testified at trial was fatal to a review of the issue on appeal; although the testimony was covered in defendant's pretrial motion in limine, this would not preserve the issue for appeal since the trial court stated that it would not rule on admissibility until the witness was presented by the government); United States v. Roenigk, 810 F.2d 809 (8th Cir. 1987) (defendant properly preserved the issue of admissibility by motion in limine and by making a timely objection at trial).

The requirement of a timely objection means that counsel cannot gamble on letting inadmissible evidence in as long as it is favorable. For instance, if a witness makes statements that violate the hearsay rule, counsel cannot sit back while helpful testimony is given, and then object on the basis of hearsay once the witness gives damaging testimony.[15] Nor can counsel remain silent when an error is committed at trial in the hope that this will be the basis for a new trial if they lose.[16]

Speed and alertness of counsel are essential. Once the answer to an improper question has been given the court is likely to rule that the objection came too late.[17]

[c] Form

Subdivision (a)(1) of Rule 103 requires that the objection or motion to strike state "the specific ground of objection." Some leeway is afforded because courts recognize that the requirement of a timely objection may not give counsel sufficient time to fully analyze the error in the split second they are rising to their feet. Courts generally understand this and will give counsel some assistance that will lead to rephrasing the objection with the requisite specificity.

"I object," or the phrase "incompetent, irrelevant and immaterial" will not usually satisfy the specificity requirement unless the ground for exclusion is obvious to the court and

---

[15] *See, e.g.,* United States Aviation Underwriters, Inc. v. Olympia Wings, Inc. 896 F.2d 949 (5th Cir. 1990); Willco Kuwait Trading v. de Savary, 843 F.2d 618 (1st Cir. 1988).

[16] *See* Collins v. Wayne Corp., 621 F.2d 777, 785–86 (5th Cir. 1980) (court refused to allow appellant to predicate error on the trial court's admission of evidence in violation of its in limine ruling: "Had plaintiffs' counsel promptly objected to the violations . . . the trial court could have either avoided the violations or given an instruction to cure any harm . . . The courts cannot adopt a rule that would permit counsel to sit silently when an error is committed at trial with the hope that they will get a new trial because of that error if they lose.").

[17] *But see* United States v. Serrano, 870 F.2d 1 (1st Cir. 1989) (where counsel was late in objecting to admission of hearsay but eventually did object and government failed to raise tardiness in its appellate brief, court decided "to disregard defense counsel's otherwise very serious default in objecting"; citing **Treatise**).

opposing counsel,[18] or is intended to claim that the evidence proffered does not meet the test of relevancy specified in Rule 401. All other objections to the admission of evidence must, according to Rule 103(a), be stated specifically. If a general objection is overruled when a specific objection should have been made, the party objecting to the evidence is precluded from asserting the proper objection on appeal.[19] A specific objection made on the wrong grounds and overruled precludes a party from raising a specific objection on other, tenable grounds on appeal.[20] An improper specific objection does not, however, preclude a motion at trial to strike the answer on a different ground since counsel did not gamble on a favorable answer, and the policy of the rule—encouraging the elimination of error in the trial court—is not thwarted by permitting a motion to strike while the witness is still testifying. If the trial

---

[18] *See, e.g.,* United States v. Cummiskey, 728 F.2d 200, 205 (3d Cir.), *cert. denied,* 471 U.S. 1005 (1985) (court rejected prosecutor's contention that defense counsel's general objection to questioning was not sufficiently specific to satisfy Rule 103(a)(1) where objection was sustained immediately and specific ground for objection was apparent from context).

[19] United States v. Mann, 884 F.2d 532 (10th Cir. 1989) (objections on the ground of lack of relevancy and failure to authenticate did not raise issue of prejudice); United States v. Carroll, 871 F.2d 689 (7th Cir. 1989) (objection on relevancy and prejudice grounds did not preserve objection to evidence on Rule 404(b) grounds). *See* United States v. Mejia, 909 F.2d 242 (7th Cir. 1990) (defendant's general objections to the admission of certain evidence were insufficient under Rule 103(a)(1) to preserve them for appeal); Bryant v. Consolidated Rail Corp., 672 F.2d 217, 220 & n.4 (1st Cir. 1982) (plaintiff's objection to admission of evidence of other injuries and medical absences from work on relevancy grounds was not sufficient to alert court to theory asserted on appeal that admission was precluded by Rule 404(a)).

[20] *See, e.g.,* United States v. Holland, 880 F.2d 1091 (9th Cir. 1989) (objection on the ground of hearsay to admissibility of tape recording did not preserve an objection to failure to redact the tape); United states v. Piva, 870 F.2d 753 (1st Cir. 1989) (defendant's objection to prior consistent statement as hearsay failed to apprise judge that evidence was inadmissible; objection was made after declarant had acquired a motive to fabricate); United States v. Mennuti, 679 F.2d 1032, 1036 (2d Cir. 1982) (defendant barred from asserting on appeal that testimony should have been excluded under Rule 608 where objection below was based solely on Rule 403); Falcon v. General Telephone Co. of Southwest, 626 F.2d 369 (5th Cir.), vacated and remanded on other grounds, 450 U.S. 1036 (1981) (plaintiff which objected at trial on grounds of hearsay and relevancy could not assert new ground, though valid, at trial).

court errs in overruling a specific objection and admits the proffered evidence, the appellate court may permit the proponent of the evidence to advance a theory of admissibility that was never argued at trial, and on which the trial court never ruled.[21]

In all cases, objecting counsel should be prepared to explain to the court—if the court wishes such an explanation or does not itself obviously see the point—precisely how the admission of the evidence in question would transgress a rule of evidence. The explanation should be brief and to the point. Often it is enough to merely cite a Rule of Evidence number.

¶ 2.03[03]   Objections to the Exclusion of Evidence[1]

Rule 103 is silent about the consequences of a trial court's exclusion evidence on the basis of an incorrect specific objection. A flexible test utilizing the plain and harmless error rules in the circumstances of the case is suggested. If other defects exist that would have made the evidence inadmissible, the trial court should not be reversed for giving a wrong reason in support of a correct ruling unless the consequence is that the proponent of the evidence was prevented from modifying his proffer and presenting admissible evidence of substantial value.

Subdivision (a)(2) of Rule 103 provides that error may not be predicated on a ruling excluding evidence unless the judge was informed of the substance of the evidence by an offer of proof, or could ascertain the substance from the context of the questions asked. As the Fifth Circuit has bluntly put it, "this circuit will not even consider the propriety of the decision to exclude the evidence at issue, if no offer of proof was made at

---

[21] United States v. Williams, 837 F.2d 1009 (11th Cir.), *cert. denied,* 488 U.S. 965 (1988) (where evidence was erroneously admitted pursuant to business records exception, court held that proponent could rely on an admissions theory on appeal; the court reasoned that the evidentiary grounds relied on at trial and on appeal serve the same purpose, *i.e.,* to permit the introduction of evidence proving the truth of the matter asserted; court distinguished this and a situation based "on a theory wholly unrelated to the ground advanced at trial"; citing **Treatise**).

[1] See discussion in **Treatise** at ¶ 103[03].

trial."[2] A "formal proffer" need not always be made.[3] What is required is for the proponent of the excluded evidence to make known the substance of the proposed testimony in sufficient detail so that the trial court can determine whether the evidence would be available for any purpose, and so that the appellate court can assess the impact of the ruling to determine whether the exclusion of the evidence constituted reversible error.[4]

In making an offer of proof, counsel must be careful to specify every way in which the evidence satisfies an evidentiary rule,[5]

---

[2] United States v. Winkle, 587 F.2d 705, 710 (5th Cir.), *cert. denied,* 444 U.S. 827 (1979); United States v. Winograd, 656 F.2d 279, 284 (7th Cir. 1981), *cert. denied,* 455 U.S. 989 (1982) ("It is well-established . . . that the appellant cannot raise theories or issues for the first time on appeal which were not presented to the trial court . . ."). *Accord* United States v. Leisure, 844 F.2d 1347 (8th Cir.) *cert. denied,* 488 U.S. 932 (1988) (the court was within its discretion in limiting the scope of cross-examination by prohibiting defendant's attorney from cross-examining government witnesses who were former clients; the attorney had made no offer of proof as required by Rule 103(a)(2)); Rabb v. Orkin Exterminating Co., 677 F. Supp. 424 (D.S.C. 1987) (plaintiffs sued exterminator alleging misapplication of termicide; at trial, plaintiffs' evidence of their alleged "increased risk of disease" was properly excluded pursuant to Rule 103, in the absence of an offer of proof).

[3] *See, e.g.,* Collins v. Wayne Corp, 621 F.2d 777 (5th Cir. 1980) (no need for offer of proof where district court was fully aware of what plaintiffs sought to show by excluded deposition, and the district court in allowing record to be supplemented with deposition noted that it had reviewed parts thereof through pretrial motions and briefs); Charter v. Chleborad, 551 F.2d 246 (8th Cir.), *cert. denied,* 434 U.S. 856 (1977) (no formal offer of proof necessary where clear from transcript that court was aware of general nature of evidence to be offered).

[4] *See, e.g.,* Parliament Insurance Co. v. Hanson, 676 F.2d 1069, 1074 (5th Cir. 1982) (purpose of rule "is to alert the court and opposing counsel to the thrust of the excluded evidence . . . and to provide an appellate court with a record allowing it to determine whether the exclusion was erroneous or not;" trial court did not err in refusing to allow proffer of witness' testimony and notes where substance of proposed evidence and purpose thereof had been made known).

[5] *See, e.g.,* Reese v. Mercury Marine Div. of Brunswick Corp., 793 F.2d 1416 (5th Cir. 1986) (it is the proponent's duty to clearly articulate every ground for which the evidence is admissible); United States v. Pugliese, 712 F.2d 1574, 1580–81 (2d Cir. 1983) (co-defendant who did not raise issue of admissibility of certain evidence pursuant to Rule 804(b)(3) during trial colloquy between other party and trial court concerning admissibility of evidence under Rule 804(b)(5) is precluded from raising issue on appeal); Huff v. White Motor Corp., 609 F.2d 286 (7th Cir. 1979) (party must notify trial court of specific rule of evidence on which he relies).

and to articulate the purpose for which the evidence is being offered.[6] A purpose not identified at the trial level will not provide a basis for reversal on appeal.[7] Many problems are obviated if the trial court informs the parties on what ground it is sustaining a general objection, or on which of several urged specific grounds it is sustaining a specific objection; if the judge does not do so, the burden is on the proponent to request such a ruling. In addition, if the district court has been unclear in explaining the ground for its decision to admit or exclude evidence, the appellate court can sometimes avoid a reversal and the resulting new trial by remanding to the district court for a hearing on the admissibility or excludability of the evidence.[8]

An offer of proof need not be made where it would be futile and would only result in an unseemly argument with the court—as where the trial judge prevents a formal offer.[9]

[6] *See, e.g.,* Strong v. Mercantile Trust Co., 816 F.2d 429 (8th Cir. 1987), *cert. denied,* 484 U.S. 1030 (1988) (in employment discrimination action plaintiff offered to prove at trial that defendant's representatives at an EEOC meeting were the same individuals who later fired her; on appeal, plaintiff contended she would have testified that one of defendant's representatives was "visibly outraged" by her allegations; court held that since the plaintiff's offer of proof did not mention the visible reaction to the charges, the offer of proof was insufficient; citing **Treatise**); Reese v. Mercury Marine Div. of Brunswick Corp., 793 F.2d 1416 (5th Cir. 1986) (in wrongful death action appellate court refused to grant new trial for error in excluding evidence that had been offered at trial solely on issue of causation, but which plaintiff later argued as relevant on theory of failure to warn). *See also,* Fox v. Dannenberg, 906 F.2d 1253 (11th Cir. 1990) ("putting a proffered witness on the stand is not the only way to adequately make an offer of proof; it is also sufficient for counsel to 'state with specificity what he . . . anticipates will be the witness' testimony . . . ").

[7] United States v. McDonald, 837 F.2d 1287 (5th Cir. 1988) (failure at trial to specify Rule 804(b)(5) as basis for admissibility results in waiver). See discussion in Robbins v. Whelan, 653 F.2d 47 (1st Cir. 1981).

[8] *See, e.g.,*United States v. Judge, 846 F.2d 274 (5th Cir. 1988) (evidence of DEA procedures for taking inventory of contents of seized automobile); United States v. Downing, 753 F.2d 1224 (3d Cir. 1985) (concerning admissibility of testimony of expert); United States v. Sebetich, 776 F.2d 412 (3d Cir. 1985), *cert. denied,* 484 U.S. 1017 (1988) (reliability of expert testimony concerning the reliability of eyewitness identification).

[9] *See, e.g.,* Gray v. Lucas, 677 F.2d 1086, 1100 (5th Cir.), *cert. denied,* 461 U.S. 910 (1983) (court criticized lower court for refusing to allow offer of

Prompt filing of a written proffer may be helpful should the judge be non-cooperative.

Sometimes a proffer is not practical because the attorney is not aware of what the witness will say, as when a question on cross-examination is held improper, or when an adverse witness is being examined on direct. Although appellate judges will, in principle, excuse the lack of an offer where the question suggests a favorable answer,[10] they may not always be in agreement as to whether this has occurred.[11] Accordingly, careful counsel should protect the record by requesting the witness to make a statement to the trial judge outside the hearing of the jury as to what he actually would have answered.

There are instances where an offer of proof in connection with an unfriendly witness not adverse to tailoring his testimony may tip the attorney's hand. This is particularly true on cross-examination. In such circumstances, the attorney should make the proffer outside the presence of the jury and the witness, preferably when a recess is not imminent so that the witness will not hear of the offer.

¶ 2.03[04]   Procedures[1]

The purpose of subdivision (b) of Rule 103 is to ensure that an objection to the admission or exclusion of evidence will be preserved in a form enabling the appellate court to have a clear idea of what occurred at the trial level. Although the subdivision is couched in terms of what the judge may do, it is the

---

proof, but finds that substance of proposed evidence is apparent from context of questions and that appellate court can review evidentiary ruling).

[10] *See, e.g.,* Harris v. Smith, 372 F.2d 806 (8th Cir. 1967) (in medical malpractice case, plaintiff's father, a doctor, was barred from testifying because of court's erroneous belief that he needed to be expert in particular specialty; appellate court excused lack of offer of proof because question was proper on its face and indicated answer favorable to appellant).

[11] *See, e.g.,* Beech Aircraft v. Rainey, 488 U.S. 153, 109 S. Ct. 439, 102 L. Ed. 2d 445 (1988) (majority opinion stated that nature of defendant's testimony was abundantly apparent from the questions posed by counsel; dissent thought that the proposed testimony was being offered on an entirely different theory than that advanced by the majority, and stated that Rule 103(a)(2) requires a specific offer of proof; citing **Treatise**).

[1] See discussion in **Treatise** at ¶¶ 103[04]–[05].

responsibility of counsel to request action by the court if it does not appear disposed to take the initiative. Rule 103 does not insist on a particular form of offer of proof although subdivision (b) indicates that a question and answer form may be used.[2] The object of any method should be to resolve doubts as to what testimony the witness should, in fact, have given.

Subdivision (c) is self-explanatory. It states that in jury cases, whenever practicable, proceedings shall be conducted in such a way as to prevent inadmissible evidence from being suggested to the jury.[3] Too much emphasis can be placed upon sidebar discussions outside the jury's presence. Much depends upon the nature of the case, the kind of jurors, and the kind of counsel trying the case. Constant interruption of an examination for rulings on points of evidence wastes a great deal of time, breaks up the force of an examination designed to reach a climax, and makes the jury fidgety. It is often sound to rule right in the presence of the jurors, explaining to them why the ruling is being made so that they feel a more responsible part of the administration of justice.

¶ 2.03[05]   Harmless Error[1]

Subdivision (a) of Rule 103 provides that an error brought to the trial court's attention may be the basis for a reversal on appeal only if the error affected "a substantial right of a party." Error that does not affect substantial rights is commonly termed "harmless error."

---

[2] *See* United States v. Barta, 888 F.2d 1220 (8th Cir. 1989) (witness was present in the courtroom at the time of the exclusionary ruling, so an offer of proof by question and answer could have been made).

[3] United States v. Wood, 851 F.2d 185 (8th Cir. 1988) (pretrial determination of admissibility of evidence need not be made to prevent jury from hearing inadmissible or prejudicial statements; court decided to use the procedures set forth in *United States v. Bell,* because *Bell* "was designed to deal with problems that are addressed by [Rules 103(c) and 104(c)]"); United States v. Griffin, 818 F.2d 97, *cert. denied,* 484 U.S. 844 (1987) (court properly excluded evidence on motion in limine and noted that controversial evidence need not be revealed to the jury prior to ruling; use of side bar conference is encouraged).

[1] See discussion in **Treatise** at ¶ 103[06].

In making its determination, the appellate court must view the alleged error in the context of the particular circumstances of the case. Initially the type of case must be considered. The harmless error rule may require a different judgment from the reviewing court in a criminal case than in a civil one, and the appellate court can be expected to scrutinize the record more harshly in a death penalty case than in one involving a short term of imprisonment.[2] Harmless error may be found more frequently in the bench trial, where the trial court will be assumed to have ignored inadmissible evidence in arriving at its findings, than in a jury trial.[3] The cost and duration of a retrial undoubtedly enter into the appellate court's determination.[4]

In both civil and criminal cases, the particular way in which the questionable evidence was utilized at trial must be considered.[5] The courts frequently hold error harmless when the

---

2 *See, e.g.,* Kotteakkos v. United States, 328 U.S. 750, 762, 66 S. Ct. 1239, 90 L. Ed. 1557 (1946) ("Necessarily the character of the proceeding, what is at stake upon its outcome, and the relation of the error asserted to casting the balance for decision on the case as a whole, are material factors in judgment. The statute in terms makes no distinction between civil and criminal cases. But this does not mean that the same criteria shall always be applied regardless of this difference.").

3 *See, e.g.,* United States v. Menk, 406 F.2d 124, 127 (9th Cir. 1968), *cert. denied,* 395 U.S. 496 (1969) ("a trained, experienced Federal District Court judge, as distinguished from a jury, must be presumed to have exercised the proper discretion in distinguishing between the improper and the proper evidence introduced at trial, and to have based his decision only on the latter, in the absence of a clear showing to the contrary by appellant.").

4 *See, e.g.,* Litton Systems, Inc. v. American Tel. & Tel. Co., 700 F.2d 785, 819 (2d Cir. 1983), *cert. denied,* 464 U.S. 1073 (1984) (court noted that trial began after four and a half years of pretrial proceedings and lasted five months).

5 *See* Greer v. Miller, 483 U.S. 765, 107 S. Ct. 3102, 97 L. Ed. 2d 618 (1987) (although the prosecutor's question regarding the defendant's post-arrest silence constituted an attempt to violate the rule in *Doyle v. Ohio,* the Supreme Court held that there was no denial of due process in the context of this trial; the judge immediately sustained defense counsel's objection, no further discussion was had, and two curative instructions were given); United States v. Vaccaro, 816 F.2d 443 (9th Cir.), *cert. denied,* 484 U.S. 914 (1987) (admission by co-conspirator was proper where testimony was elicited by defense on cross-examination to impeach).

evidence in issue was merely "cumulative" of other properly admitted evidence.[6] On the other hand, a court is more likely to find reversible error when the evidence in question— erroneously admitted or excluded below—was the only or primary evidence in support of or in opposition to a claim or defense.[7]

Some courts hold error harmless when the other evidence supporting the verdict is strong or "overwhelming," without making an independent determination regarding the impact of the error on the judgment of the jury or judge.[8] On the other

---

[6] Kostelecky v. NL Acme Tool/NL Indus., 837 F.2d 828 (8th Cir. 1988) (trial court abused its discretion in admitting report of witness to accident which concluded that accident was caused by the "injured's own conduct"; where causation is in dispute, an opinion as to causation would serve only to indicate to the jury what result to reach); United States v. Austin, 823 F.2d 257 (8th Cir.), *cert. denied,* 484 U.S. 1044 (1987) (improper admission of hearsay evidence not a ground for mistrial; court instructed the jury to disregard the testimony since other evidence on these matters was properly before the jury); United States v. Wright-Barker, 784 F.2d 161 (3d Cir. 1986) (error in a report prepared as part of business duty was harmless where it was merely cumulative of testimony given at trial and subject to cross-examination); Burns v. Clusen, 798 F.2d 931 (7th Cir. 1986) (court's ruling that rape victim was unavailable as a witness was harmless error; victim's testimony from preliminary hearing was cumulative and there was other overwhelming physical evidence of defendant's guilt); Dixon v. International Harvester Co., 754 F.2d 573, 582 (5th Cir. 1985) (since erroneously admitted regulations were almost identical to properly admitted regulations, admission was merely cumulative).

[7] *See, e.g.,* United States v. Sarmiento-Perez, 633 F.2d 1092, 1104 (5th Cir. 1981), *cert. denied,* 459 U.S. 834 (1982) (admission of confession of non-testifying co-conspirator, which was "the only direct evidence identifying the defendant as the source of the illicit drugs, and as a full-fledged participant in the criminal enterprise" was prejudicial error); Huff v. White Motor Corp., 609 F.2d 286 (7th Cir. 1979) (wrongful death action based on theory that defective design of fuel system caused fire; exclusion of statement by deceased that there was fire in cab of truck prior to accident held prejudicial where statement was only direct evidence on whether fire occurred before or after crash).

[8] *See, e.g.,* United States v. Nabors, 707 F.2d 1294 (11th Cir.), *cert. denied,* 465 U.S. 1021 (1984) (even if erroneously admitted evidence called attention to defendant's failure to testify, admission harmless in light of the other evidence of defendant's guilt); United States v. Iron Shell, 633 F.2d 77, 92 (8th Cir. 1980), *cert. denied,* 450 U.S. 1001 (1981) (no prejudicial error from admission of knife found on defendant when arrested for assault with intent to rape, where "the evidence of defendant's guilt was strong").

hand, other courts insist that the test is not simply whether the non-tainted evidence was independently sufficient to support the verdict, but whether "the error had a substantial influence on the jury's judgment."[9] These tests may not, of course, be inconsistent; it often appears from the courts' discussions that the court concluded that the error had no substantial impact on the jury's judgment precisely because the erroneously excluded or admitted evidence was cumulative or the other evidence supporting the outcome was "overwhelming."[10]

Other factors that may be crucial in a particular case are: the number of errors in relation to the length of the trial,[11] the closeness of the factual disputes,[12] the centrality of the issue to which the evidence is directed,[13] the prejudicial impact of the evidence,[14] the judge's instructions with regard to the

[9] *See, e.g.,* Kowalski v. Gagne, 914 F.2d 299 (1st Cir. 1990) (no error or miscarriage of justice resulted from erroneous admission of tainted evidence; substantial untainted evidence existed on the same issue to support the jury's verdict); United States v. Pisari, 636 F.2d 855 (1st Cir. 1981) (despite government's strong case, testimony regarding prior inconsistent statement of defendant was prejudicial).

[10] *See, e.g.,* Burger v. Kemp, 483 U.S. 776, 107 S. Ct. 3114, 97 L. Ed. 2d 638 (1987) (trial court's charge in a murder case, that a person of sound mind and discretion is presumed to intend the natural and probable consequences of his acts, was harmless beyond a reasonable doubt in light of overwhelming evidence of defendant's guilt); United States v. Wolf, 839 F.2d 1387 (10th Cir.), *cert. denied,* 488 U.S. 923 (1988) (error in admission of hearsay evidence was harmless where evidence of defendant's guilt was overwhelming); United States v. Winfelder, 790 F.2d 576 (7th Cir. 1986) (harmless error to allow opinion evidence of defendant's mental state which constituted an element of the crimes charged; other evidence of defendant's guilt was overwhelming); United States v. Mouzin, 785 F.2d 682 (9th Cir.), *cert. denied,* 479 U.S. 985 (1986) (admission of computer printout without proper foundation was harmless error in light of overwhelming evidence).

[11] *See, e.g.,* Rabon v. Automatic Fasteners, Inc., 672 F.2d 1231, 1239 (5th Cir. 1982) ("a mere shred of the totality of the evidence").

[12] *See, e.g.,* Jordan v. Medley, 711 F.2d 211 (D.C. Cir. 1983) (reversible error where improperly admitted testimony went directly to central issue of case and evidence on that issue was closely balanced).

[13] *See, e.g.,* Contractor Utility Sales Co. v. Certain-Teed Prods., 638 F.2d 1061, 1085 (7th Cir. 1981) (prejudicial error where excluded evidence was critical).

[14] *See, e.g.,* United States v. Escobar, 674 F.2d 469, 474–76 & n. 12 (5th Cir. 1982) (in narcotics prosecution, erroneous admission of information

evidence,[15] the degree to which the evidence corroborates other evidence,[16] and counsels' reliance on the tainted evidence in their arguments.[17] Constitutional error is discussed in a separate section below.

The Supreme Court has not clearly articulated the standard of probability to be used in evaluating errors of a non-constitutional nature. Three possible tests have been suggested for finding harmless error: "(a) that it is more probable than not that the error did not affect the judgment, (b) that it is highly probable that the error did not contribute to the judgment, or (c) that it is almost certain that the error did not taint the judgment."[18] Several circuits have opted for a "more-probable-than-not" standard for non-constitutional error in criminal cases.[19] In fact, this may be the standard that is often applied throughout the other circuits as well. It is hard to discern from the cases whether the articulation of a particular

from police computer stating that defendant was a "suspected narcotics smuggler" was reversible error). See discussion of Rule 403 in Chapter 6 *infra*.

[15] *See, e.g.,* United States v. Holman, 680 F.2d 1340, 1351–52 (11th Cir. 1982) (no error where judge immediately gave instruction to disregard testimony); United States v. Smith, 635 F.2d 411 (5th Cir. 1981) (harmless error where court instructed jury to disregard testimony and polled jury).

[16] Harris v. Wainwright, 760 F.2d 1148, 1153 (11th Cir. 1985) (error in admission not harmless where crux of state's case was uncorroborated identification testimony); United States v. Sampol, 636 F.2d 621, 639–40 (D.C. Cir. 1980) (prejudicial error where insufficient limiting instructions were given and evidence "furnished strong corroboration for the testimony of . . . the principal witness of the government.").

[17] *See, e.g.,* United States v. Ruffin, 575 F.2d 346, 360 (2d Cir. 1978) (substance of erroneously admitted testimony "must have been in the forefront of the jurors' minds when they retired to deliberate," because of "the extent to which the prosecutor dwelt [on it] both in his opening summation and his rebuttal."); Mueller v. Hubbard Milling Co., 573 F.2d 1029, 1037 (8th Cir.), *cert. denied,* 439 U.S. 865 (1978) ("plaintiff's counsel pointedly emphasized the pivotal nature of the parol testimony during closing argument.").

[18] Government of Virgin Islands v. Toto, 529 F.2d 278, 284 (3d Cir. 1976) (the three options were put forth by Justice Traynor of California in The Riddle of Harmless Error (1970)).

[19] *See* United States v. Echavarria-Olarte, 904 F.2d 1391 (9th Cir. 1990); United States v. Neuroth, 809 F.2d 339 (6th Cir.), *cert. denied,* 482 U.S. 916 (1987); United States v. Lewis, 671 F.2d 1025 (7th Cir. 1982).

test really matters. The appellate court will affirm, regardless of whether a high probability, more-probable-than-not, or reasonable possibility test is applied, when, after assessing the factors discussed above, it does not have a serious doubt about either the fairness of the trial or the outcome of the case.[20]

¶ 2.03[06]   Plain Error[1]

Although Rule 103 requires that both reversible error and plain error affect substantial rights, the rule does not distinguish between the former, which suffices as a ground for reversal only when the error was called to the attention of the trial judge, and the latter, which subdivision (d) acknowledges may be recognized by the appellate court even though it was not raised below. The courts have been equally taciturn; about the most that can be said is that there is some point at which a reviewing court will not tolerate the error below even though it was not adequately raised and preserved by counsel.

The plain error rule operates to mitigate the harsh results that flow from counsels' failures and omissions, or mistaken trial strategy. It is not a concept that can safely be relied upon by the bar, since the cases clearly indicate that appellate courts are extremely reluctant to find plain error except in the most egregious cases, a result which is hardly surprising given the size of federal dockets.[2]

---

[20] *See* Kotteakos v. United States, 328 U.S. 750, 765, 66 S. Ct. 1239, 90 L. Ed. 1557 (1946) ("But if one cannot say, with fair assurance, after pondering all that happened without stripping the erroneous action from the whole, that the judgment was not substantially swayed by the error, it is impossible to conclude that substantial rights were not affected. The inquiry cannot be merely whether there was enough to support the result, apart from the phase affected by the error. It is rather, even so, whether the error itself had substantial influence. If so, or if one is left in grave doubt, the conviction cannot stand.").

[1] See discussion in **Treatise** at ¶ 103[07].

[2] *See* United States v. Bernard, 877 F.2d 1463 (10th Cir. 1989) (trial court did not err in admitting testimony of defense counsel concerning his relationship with client; client himself had breached attorney client confidentiality by disclosure to another witness; in addition, defendant failed to establish that a substantial right was affected by the testimony); United States v. Snyder, 872 F.2d 1351 (7th Cir. 1989) (although the trial court erred in

A few generalizations can be made. Although the plain error rule is sometimes applied in civil cases, an appellate court undoubtedly subjects the record in a serious criminal case to a more searching scrutiny. Children, pro se litigants, and others who need the assistance of a court are more likely to have the plain error rule invoked in their behalf.[3] Beyond this point the court proceeds by examining the facts of the particular case, the gravity of the offense, the probable effects of the error, and the other factors noted in the discussion of the harmless error rule.[4] An appellate court may, at times, be willing to notice counsel's failure to raise an issue at trial where a decisive issue of substantive law has been ignored below, particularly if it is one counsel may have overlooked because it is subtle or new.[5]

¶ 2.03[07] Constitutional Error[1]

It has been clear since the Supreme Court's 1967 decision in *Chapman v. California*[2] that not all constitutional errors

admitting grand jury testimony pursuant to Rule 804(b)(5), testimony of defendant provided sufficient corroboration to satisfy the Confrontation Clause; harmless error).

[3] *See, e.g.,* Rojas v. Richardson, 703 F.2d 186, 190–92 (5th Cir. 1983) (defense counsel's description of plaintiff in closing remarks as "illegal alien," which was totally unsupported by evidence, was "obvious and blatant appeal . . . to racial and ethnic prejudice" and constituted plain error); Government of the Canal Zone v. P (Pinto), 590 F.2d 1344, 1353 (5th Cir. 1979) ("We are especially sensitive in criminal cases . . . in which the defendants were represented by a series of court-appointed attorneys;" violation of hearsay rule constituted plain error).

[4] *See, e.g.,* Pinkham v. Maine Cent. R.R., 874 F.2d 875 (1st Cir. 1989) (although plaintiff should not have been questioned about prior drug use, it was not plain error; jury knew plaintiff had passed drug test administered by defendant after accident, thereby decreasing likelihood of improper inference that drugs caused the accident; in addition, there was other substantial evidence from which jury could deduce responsibility for plaintiff's injuries).

[5] *See, e.g.,* United States v. Moore, 571 F.2d 76, 88–89 (2d Cir. 1978) (court reversed conviction hinging on presumption court found to be unconstitutional although counsel below had not challenged constitutionality or objected to trial judge's charge).

[1] See discussion in **Treatise** at ¶ 103[08].

[2] 386 U.S. 18, 87 S. Ct. 824, 17 L. Ed. 2d 705 (1967).

require an automatic reversal of the verdict below. In the years since *Chapman,* the Court has gradually expanded the category of errors that may be considered harmless, and has changed the contours of the harmless constitutional error test.

The Court has held that a rule of per se reversal is justified only for those errors that "necessarily render a trial fundamentally unfair."[3] A criminal trial is fundamentally unfair when it "cannot reliably serve its function as a vehicle for determination of guilt or innocence."[4] Those errors that interfere with fundamental fairness are, however, "the exception and not the rule. . . . [I]f the defendant had counsel and was tried by an impartial adjudicator, there is a strong presumption that any other errors that may have occurred are subject to harmless error analysis."[5] Pursuant to this approach, the Supreme Court has found that a wide variety of constitutional errors may be harmless.[6]

---

[3] Rose v. Clark, 106 S. Ct. 3101, 3106 (1986). The Court gave the following examples: Payne v. Arkansas, 356 U.S. 560, 78 S. Ct. 844, 2 L. Ed. 2d 975 (1958) (introduction of coerced confession); Gideon v. Wainwright, 372 U.S. 335, 83 S. Ct. 792, 9 L. Ed. 2d 799 (1963) (complete denial of counsel); Tumey v. Ohio, 273 U.S. 510, 47 S. Ct. 437, 71 L. Ed. 2d 749 (1927) (adjudication by biased judge); United States v. Martin Linen Supply Co., 430 U.S. 564, 97 S. Ct. 1349, 51 L. Ed. 2d 642 (1977) (judge directing verdict of guilty in jury case).

[4] Rose v. Clark, 478 U.S. 579.

[5] *Id.* at 579–80. Justice Stevens, concurring, objected "that the Court's dictum about a sweeping presumption in favor of harmless error review is not only unnecessary, but also unsound." *Id.* at 589.

[6] *See, e.g.,* Rose v. Clark, 478 U.S. 570, 106 S. Ct. 3101, 92 L. Ed. 2d 460 (1986) (jury instructions that violated the principles of Sandstrom v. Montana, 442 U.S. 510 (1979)); Delaware v. Van Arsdall, 106 S. Ct. 1431, 89 L. Ed. 2d 674 (1986) (prohibiting all cross-examination into prosecution witness' bias in violation of Confrontation Clause); Rushen v. Spain, 464 U.S. 114, 99 S. Ct. 2450, 61 L. Ed. 2d 39 (1983) (per curiam) (denial of right to be present at trial); United States v. Hasting, 461 U.S. 499, 103 S. Ct. 1974, 76 L. Ed. 2d 96 (1983) (improper comment on defendant's silence at trial); Moore v. Illinois, 434 U.S. 220, 98 S. Ct. 458, 54 L. Ed. 2d 424 (1977) (admission of identification obtained in violation of right to counsel); Milton v. Wainwright, 407 U.S. 371, 92 S. Ct. 2174, 33 L. Ed. 2d 1 (1972) (admission of confession obtained in violation of right to counsel); Schneble v. Florida, 405 U.S. 427, 92 S. Ct. 1056, 31 L. Ed. 2d 340 (1972) (*Bruton* error); Chambers v. Maroney, 399 U.S. 42, 90 S. Ct. 1975, 26 L. Ed. 2d 419 (1970) (admission of evidence obtained in violation of the Fourth Amendment);

In *Chapman,* the Supreme Court had stated that "before a federal constitutional error can be held harmless, the court must be able to declare a belief that it was harmless beyond a reasonable doubt."[7] It appeared to require the courts to focus on the possible impact on the minds of the jurors of the specific, erroneously admitted (or excluded) evidence, without considering the non-tainted evidence. Subsequent Supreme Court cases, however, suggest that when the non-tainted evidence of guilt is "overwhelming," no further inquiry into the effect of the error need be made.[8]

By stressing that a correct determination in the court below is the central concern of the harmless error rule, the Court has abandoned the deterrence of prosecutors from engaging in conduct violative of constitutional standards as a rationale justifying a higher standard for constitutional error. As long as the reviewing court is persuaded that "the record developed at trial establishes guilt beyond a reasonable doubt,"[9] it is commanded to affirm the judgment regardless of constitutional errors or other errors below. For example, in *Delaware v. Van Arsdall,*[10] the Supreme Court held that "the constitutionally improper denial of a defendant's opportunity to impeach a witness for bias" could constitute harmless error.[11] The opinion of Justice Rehnquist for the Court explained the task of the appellate court as follows:

> The correct inquiry is whether, assuming that the damaging potential of the cross-examination were fully realized, a reviewing court might nonetheless say that the error was harmless beyond a reasonable doubt. Whether such an error is harmless in a particular case depends upon a host of factors, all readily accessible to reviewing courts. These factors include the importance of the witness'

Harrington v. California, 395 U.S. 250, 89 S. Ct. 1726, 23 L. Ed. 2d 284 (1969) (admission of non-testifying co-defendant's statement in violation of *Bruton*).

[7] 386 U.S. at 24.

[8] *See, e.g.,* Milton v. Wainwright, 407 U.S. 371, 377, 92 S. Ct. 2174, 33 L. Ed. 2d 1 (1972) ("we do not close our eyes to the reality of overwhelming evidence of guilt fairly established . . . ").

[9] Rose v. Clark, 478 U.S. 570, 583.

[10] 478 U.S. 673 (1986).

[11] *Id.* at 684.

testimony in the prosecution's case, whether the testimony was cumulative, the presence or absence of evidence corroborating or contradicting the testimony of the witness on material points, the extent of cross-examination otherwise permitted, and, of course, the overall strength of the prosecution's case.[12]

This approach suggests that some members of the Supreme Court are prepared to rule that there is no higher standard for constitutional error than for any other kind of error, unless the error is of that rare variety that renders a trial fundamentally unfair. Most judges will, however, continue to be more sensitive to errors constituting a violation of the Constitution because of their greater interest in deterring similar errors in the future.

¶ 2.04   Limited Admissibility—Rule 105

¶ 2.04[01]   Scope and Theory[1]

The concept of admissibility for limited purposes is fundamental to the Anglo-American law of Evidence. Together with Rule 403 permitting the exclusion of relevant evidence on the ground of prejudice, confusion and waste of time, and Standard 107 permitting comment by the judge. Rule 105 gives the trial court substantial control over both the admissibility of evidence and the limitations on its use. Evidence may be limited as to the persons against whom it may be used, or may be limited as to the purposes for which it may be employed. When a proper objection is made to the general admission of evidence, pursuant to Rule 103, it becomes the task of the proponent to suggest an evidentiary hypothesis that will convince the court to admit the evidence for limited purposes. If the court agrees to restrict the scope of the evidence, Rule 105 provides that it shall, upon request, inform the jurors[2] through limiting

---

[12] *Id.* at 684.

[1] See discussion in **Treatise** at ¶¶ 105[01]–[02].

[2] While the rule speaks only of instructions to the jury, the trial court should, on request, rule even in a bench trial on how it intends to limit the use of the evidence. Lawyers are entitled to know how the court is restricting the evidence so that they can decide how to try the case. The ambiguous phrase, "I'll take it for what it's worth," gives little guidance. It may mislead a lawyer into failing to make an adequate record.

instructions that they may only use the evidence for specified purposes. Since there is often little point in instructing the jury not to consider the evidence for unauthorized purposes, limiting instructions are not required in a jury trial unless they are sought. In this respect Rule 105 serves much the same purpose as Rule 103(a)—which requires a specific objection if an error is to be preserved for appeal. The rule provides:

Rule 105

LIMITED ADMISSIBILITY

When evidence which is admissible as to one party or for one purpose but not admissible as to another party or for another purpose is admitted, the court, upon request, shall restrict the evidence to the proper scope and instruct the jury accordingly.

Rule 105 accords with modern evidentiary theory that as a general rule, evidence should be received if it is admissible for any purpose, notwithstanding the fact that it may be inadmissible for another. The rule represents a compromise between two competing interests—the desire to admit all relevant evidence and the recognition that a jury composed of untrained triers of fact may not, in the absence of some control by the judge over the evidence presented, accurately assess its probative value or confine its use to its proper legal scope.

Limiting instructions have become more important since the distinct tendency of the Federal Rules of Evidence is to admit rather than to exclude.[3] It is assumed that the more information available to the trier of fact, the greater will be its knowledge of the events in question and the more likely will it be that resolution of the factual disputes will approximate the truth.

The opposing party must be specific in stating the grounds for limiting the evidence.[4] The absence of a precise request will not prevent an appellate court from holding that the failure of the trial judge to give limiting instructions despite the lack of a request or the insufficiency of a general objection was plain error where a substantial right was adversely affected.[5]

---

[3] *See* discussion in Chapter 1 *supra* and Chapter 6 *infra*.

[4] *See* Rule 103(a).

[5] *See* discussion of Rule 103(d), *above*.

The jury may be instructed either as the evidence is admitted or as part of the general charge.[6] There are sound reasons for encouraging the practice of giving limiting instructions as the evidence is received. The impact of evidence in a case tends to be cumulative, each segment building on the evidence that preceded it. The jury will probably get a clearer picture of the interrelation between the evidence and the factual issues to which it is relevant if the limitations of the evidence are spelled out as it is presented. It is unrealistic to expect jurors to selectively suppress their impressions of the facts until the end of the trial, after all the evidence has been received. Repetition of the instructions at that time, if accompanied by a summary of the evidence, may help to clear up doubts and refresh the jury's memory.

¶ 2.04[02]   Applying Rule 105[1]

[a]   Civil Cases

Since the thrust of the Federal Rules is to admit relevant evidence, the usual consequence in a civil case is that a court will admit evidence that is not generally admissible but that clearly passes the Rule 401 hurdle as to a particular purpose. The Federal Rules' preference for admitting evidence even though it may lead jurors to draw prohibited inferences can be seen in Rules 407–409, and 411, which are specialized applications of the doctrine of limited admissibility. Even though these rules are grounded on a variety of social policies that dictate that certain inferences are prohibited, the Rules recognize that there are acceptable purposes for which the evidence may be used.[2]

---

[6] *See* United States v. Garcia, 848 F.2d 1324 (2d Cir. 1988), *rev'd on other grounds sub nom.* Gomez v. United States, 490 U.S. 858, 109 S. Ct. 2237, 104 L. Ed. 2d 923 (1989) (it was not error for the trial court to refuse to give a contemporaneous limiting instruction that physical evidence was not admissible against all defendants; trial court gave instruction as part of its general charge; citing **Treatise**).

[1] See discussion in **Treatise** at ¶¶ 105[03]–[05].

[2] *See* discussion in Chapter 7 *infra.*

The extensive pretrial discovery procedures available under the Federal Rules of Civil Procedure will usually reveal potential sources of prejudice that would result from the admission of evidence competent against one party but not another. The court has the power to sever joint trials pursuant to Rule 20(b) of the Federal Rules of Civil Procedure to avoid embarrassment, delay, undue expense or prejudice to any party, but will only rarely do so in a civil case. For example, where an insurance company is a proper party, the risk that the jury will be prejudiced by the knowledge of the insurance company's involvement in the case is generally thought to be insufficient to warrant the granting of separate trials.

In some instances, the split trial device may be useful in avoiding prejudice where evidence may be misused on an issue. For example, evidence that would be relevant on a damage issue—such as the decedent's alcoholism in determining his earning ability and the support his family would have received—may be so prejudicial on the liability issue that the two issues should be bifurcated pursuant to Rule 42 of the Federal Rules of Civil Procedure.

Parties will usually be aware of the possibility of prejudice and they should bring it to the court's attention before the trial so that adequate measures can be taken. Counsel has the opportunity to advise the court of the problem either at the Rule 16 pretrial conference, or by a motion to sever or to try different issues separately.

Primarily, however, Rule 105 contemplates that prejudice will be averted through the device of the limiting instruction.[3] The instruction must be responsive to the needs of the case.

---

[3] *See, e.g.,* Mauldin v. Upjohn Co., 697 F.2d 644, 648 (5th Cir.), *cert. denied,* 464 U.S. 848 (1983) (probative value of "adverse reactions" reports, admitted to show drug company's knowledge of problems associated with subject drugs, not outweighed by possibility of unfair prejudice and jury confusion although reports detailed many complications other than those in issue, where trial judge instructed jury to consider reports solely on issue of notice); *In re* Beverly Hills Fire Litig., 695 F.2d 207 (6th Cir. 1982), *cert. denied,* 461 U.S. 929 (1983) (court stated that at retrial, certain documents could, at trial court's discretion, be offered against some but not all defendants with appropriate limiting instructions, instead of bifurcating causation from liability issues).

At times, telling the jurors that they may use the evidence for certain purposes will not suffice; jurors will also have to be instructed about the inferences they are prohibited from drawing. At other times, because the danger of prejudice is less, a court will be justified in using a simpler and less detailed instruction.[4]

[b]   Criminal Cases

Although Rule 105 does not distinguish between civil and criminal cases, the danger of prejudice is far greater in a criminal case when the evidence in question is being offered by the prosecution. Evidence admissible for one purpose may clearly prejudice the defendant if the jurors use it in an unauthorized manner. Evidence of other crimes or wrongs committed by the defendant offers particularly difficult problems. Although the evidence may not be admitted to show that the defendant had a greater propensity to commit the crime, it may be used to show such matters as intent, motive and similarity of plan, or to impeach the credibility of defendant's character witness or to rebut an entrapment defense. The efficacy of limiting instructions in restricting the consideration of other crimes by the jury to the purposes for which it was admitted is questionable in many cases. Application of the Rule 403 balancing test may disclose that cautionary instructions will not adequately protect the defendant from prejudice and that the other crimes evidence will have to be excluded. See discussion in Chapter 7 *infra*.

If the court determines that the evidence is admissible, defense counsel may request a limiting instruction pursuant to

---

[4] *See, e.g.,* Sprynczynatyk v. General Motors Corp., 771 F.2d 1112 (8th Cir. 1985), *cert. denied,* 475 U.S. 1046 (1986) (in products liability action, court admitted videotape of driver's hypnosis session without giving the instruction defendant had requested in the presence of the jurors, warning them against using the tapes to prove the truth of the facts asserted; court did state that tapes could be used for explanatory purposes; appellate court held that by failing to warn of prohibited use, court failed to restrict scope of the evidence; by rejecting defendant's request jury was improperly led to think proffered instruction was wrong; in this case, trial court's action was not harmless).

Rule 105. It is fully within the court's power to instruct the jury, sua sponte, without request from counsel. This power, however, should be exercised with caution because counsel may have concluded that a limiting instruction will actually call the juror's attention to the prohibited inference.[5] If counsel fails to request an instruction, the appellate courts will seldom find error even if a substantial right of the defendant has been adversely affected.[6]

For the most part, situations where evidence is admissible against one party, but not another, arise in joint trials of criminal defendants. The evidence involved may be so important and the possibility of prejudice so great that neither exclusion nor a limiting instruction will provide adequate protection. In such cases a severance pursuant to Rule 14 of the Federal Rules of Criminal Procedure constitutes the only practical alternative even though repetitive trials are burdensome.

The joint trial is most often employed in a criminal case where it is designed to reconcile the right of a defendant to be tried solely on evidence indicative of his personal guilt or innocence with the interests of the state in reducing expense, delay and harassment of witnesses by holding multiple trials where two or more defendants have been accused of sharing responsibility for the crime.

It is, of course, one of the basic tenets of our jurisprudence that each person accused of a crime must be judged solely on

---

[5] *See* United States v. Lewis, 693 F.2d 189, 197 (D.C. Cir. 1982) (noting that reversible error occurs when court fails to give cautionary instruction after admission of highly prejudicial evidence, even in absence of request, but court must give counsel opportunity to waive instruction; no error arises from lack of instruction when evidence is not highly prejudicial).

[6] *See, e.g.,* United States v. Prati, 861 F.2d 82 (5th Cir. 1988) (court's failure to provide instruction limiting jury's consideration of evidence of extraneous acts and offenses was not plain error; failure was not so prejudicial as to affect the substantial rights of the accused); United States v. Garcia, 530 F.2d 650, 653, 656 (5th Cir. 1976) (court declined to find plain error where defendant had not requested limiting instruction on use of impeachment testimony but noted that, under other circumstances where impeaching testimony was extremely dangerous and prejudice high, failure to give instruction would amount to plain error).

the basis of evidence indicating personal culpability for the act charged. In the situation, however, where several persons are accused of having acted together with a common purpose, the law recognizes that there is also a measure of responsibility shared equally by all the participants and evidence offered to establish that collective guilt may be admissible against all of the defendants. In a conspiracy trial, for example, extrajudicial statements, normally admissible only against the declarant, may be admissible against all the co-conspirators if the statement was made during and in furtherance of the conspiracy. See discussion in Chapter 14 *infra.*

Often not all the evidence presented in a joint trial will be admissible against all of the defendants. For example, extrajudicial statements made outside the framework of the joint venture, evidence used to impeach the credibility of one of the defendants who takes the witness stand, evidence of one defendant's participation in other similar crimes, or evidence seized in violation of one defendant's Fourth Amendment rights will be admissible against less than all of those on trial.

The dangers presented by admitting evidence for limited purposes vary with the type of evidence offered. Consequently, the Rules, as well as current practice, recognize that the measures required to ensure that the evidence is not misused by the jury must be shaped to fit the needs of the particular offer of evidence.

The admission of hearsay evidence which is usable against only one of the defendants also has a constitutional dimension. In 1968, in *Bruton v. United States,*[7] the Supreme Court held that a limiting instruction did not sufficiently protect the defendant from the prejudice that resulted when a confession by his co-defendant implicating the defendant was admitted. The Court found that there was too great a risk "that the jury, despite instructions to the contrary, looked to the incriminating extrajudicial statements in determining petitioner's guilt . . . ."[8] In the immediate aftermath of *Bruton,* many courts reacted by routinely granting severances in cases where the

---

[7] 391 U.S. 123, 88 S. Ct. 1620, 20 L. Ed. 2d 476 (1968).

[8] *Id.* at 126.

government intended to introduce admissions of a co-defendant inculpating a defendant.

The impact of *Bruton* has, however, been blunted by a number of developments. In the first place, the Supreme Court has held that not every violation of *Bruton* constitutes reversible error.[9] With the expansion of the harmless error doctrine discussed above, more cases can be expected to fall into this category. Second, the Supreme Court has held that the confession of a nontestifying co-defendant may be admitted into evidence where the confession was effectively redacted to omit all references to the defendant and defendant's existence, and the jury was instructed not to use the confession against the defendant.[10] Finally, although the Supreme Court held in 1987 that *Bruton* still applies even when the defendant's own confession, which corroborates that of his co-defendant, is introduced against him,[11] the Court also acknowledged that there are instances in which a nontestifying co-defendant's statement may be directly admissible against the defendant.[12]

The co-conspirators exception and the declaration against penal interest will often operate to authorize evidentiary use against a defendant of a statement made by a co-defendant. In the case of the co-conspirators exception, the Supreme Court has held that a statement that satisfies Federal Rule 801(d)(2)(E) automatically satisfies the Confrontation Clause. See discussion in Chapters 14 and 15. Prosecutors may have somewhat more difficulty in establishing that a declaration against penal interest

---

[9] Schneble v. Florida, 405 U.S. 427, 92 S. Ct. 1056, 31 L. Ed. 2d 340 (1972).

[10] Richardson v. Marsh, 481 U.S. 200, 107 S. Ct. 1702, 95 L. Ed. 2d 176 (1987) (no violation of *Bruton* that confession became incriminating when linked to defendant through defendant's own testimony). *See* United States v. Vasquez, 874 F.2d 1515 (11th Cir. 1989), *cert. denied,* 110 S. Ct. 845 (1990) (admission of non-testifying defendant's confession satisfied *Bruton* where it was redacted to eliminate all reference to the other defendant's name; although the redaction did not eliminate reference to the defendant's existence, the jury was not compelled to conclude that the defendant was the individual referred to in the confession).

[11] Cruz v. New York, 481 U.S. 186, 107 S. Ct. 1714, 95 L. Ed. 2d 162 (1987) (Court rejected view that *Bruton* does not apply to interlocking confessions; consequently the co-defendant's confession must be excluded or separate trials must be held.).

[12] *Id.* at 193, 107 S. Ct. at 1719, 95 L. Ed. 2d at 172.

can pass constitutional muster. But even when the declaration was made in custody by an accomplice, a situation characterized by the Supreme Court as "presumptively unreliable," the Court has conceded "that the presumption may be rebutted" if sufficient "indicia of reliability" are present.[13] A confession by a co-defendant inculpating the defendant that was not made in a custodial setting is obviously more likely to be directly admissible against the defendant. See Chapter 17. Regardless of how the co-defendant's statement satisfies the hearsay rule, *Bruton* will not be implicated because the *Bruton* rule applies only when the co-defendant's statements are inadmissible because of evidentiary constraints.

¶ 2.05   Remainder of Related Writings or Recorded Statements—Rule 106[1]

Rule 106 gives the opponent against whom part of a writing or recorded statement is offered the right to request that the proponent of the evidence be required to put in other parts of the statement necessary to tell a complete story. The trial court must then decide whether to honor the request and thus restrain the proponent from exercising a lawyer's full adversarial power to carve up the evidence in order to present the case in the most favorable light. The Advisory Committee note points out that the rule is designed to avoid two dangers: "The first is the misleading impression created by taking a statement out of context, and the second is the inadequacy of repair work when delayed to a point later in trial." The rule provides:

---

[13] Lee v. Illinois, 476 U.S. 530, 106 S. Ct. 2056, 2063, 90 L. Ed. 2d 514, 527 (1986) (Dissenters found sufficient "indicia of reliability" to admit co-defendant's confession. The Court acknowledged that the interlocking nature of the defendant's and co-defendant's statements might enhance reliability so as to make the confession directly admissible against the defendant.). *Id.* at 544, 106 S. Ct. at 2064–65, 90 L. Ed. 2d at 529. *See also* Cruz v. New York, 481 U.S. 186, 190, 107 S. Ct. 1714, 1718–19, 95 L. Ed. 2d 162, 171 (1987).

[1] See discussion in **Treatise** at ¶¶ 106[01]–[04].

Rule 106

REMAINDER OF OR RELATED WRITINGS OR RECORDED STATEMENTS

When a writing or recorded statement or part thereof is introduced by a party, an adverse party may require the introduction at that time of any other part or any other writing or recorded statement which ought in fairness to be considered contemporaneously with it.

Rule 106 was drafted so as not to directly involve a question of admissibility, but to regulate a detail of the order of proof. In practice it is often a powerful device for an opponent to introduce otherwise excludable evidence.[2] For example, reliance by a defendant on snippets of information from 3500 materials may be the basis for putting the whole report of an agent before the jury. On the other hand, the need to place a portion of evidence in context may require even the otherwise admissible portion to be excluded under Rule 403. Rule 611(a) should be interpreted to give the court the power to require the introduction of the balance of oral statements, which are not covered by Rule 106. Depositions in civil cases are governed by Rule 32(a)(4) of the Federal Rules of Civil Procedure.[3]

Rule 106 wisely avoids any attempt to set a hard and fast rule. The trial court has been granted power to determine whether "fairness" requires the proponent to introduce all of the writing or other form of recording that relates to the fact sought to be proved. Insistence on procedural protocol should never prevent the orderly and coherent presentation of relevant and competent evidence. Thus, the trial judge must weigh in

---

[2] United States v. Gravely, 840 F.2d 1156 (4th Cir. 1988) (defendant proffered portions of grand jury testimony pursuant to the former testimony exception; government could then introduce other portions, pursuant to Rule 106, even though they might not have been admissible standing alone); United States v. Sutton, 801 F.2d 1346, 1368 (D.C. Cir. 1986) ("Rule 106 can adequately fulfill its function only by permitting the admission of some otherwise inadmissible evidence . . . .").

[3] Rule 32(a)(4) provides: "If only part of a deposition is offered in evidence by a party, an adverse party may require the offeror to introduce any other part which ought in fairness to be considered with the part introduced, and any party may introduce any other parts."

each case the adequacy of the repair work necessary to rectify the misleading impression possibly created by incompleteness against the waste of time and attention and the unfairness involved in blunting the proponent's presentation of the case when everything is required to be read at one time.

Rule 106 does not require the automatic introduction of an entire document if the proponent offers only a part, and the opponent demands more.[4] At times, honoring the request would lead to unfairness where the additional material is neither explanatory of, nor relevant to, the passages already admitted.[5] At other times, however, Rule 106 will require even more than having the proponent offer the balance of a particular document or recording. There may be instances where a misleading impression can be created by introducing a whole writing or recording without accompanying documents or without the related correspondence.[6] Admission of the

---

[4] United States v. Pendas-Martinez, 845 F.2d 938, 943–45 (11th Cir. 1988) (although defense counsel in cross-examining case agent made some general use of case agent's written report, counsel did not read from the report to suggest that testimony was inconsistent with report or to attack agent's credibility; government did not point out any portion of report used by defense "for which the remainder was relevant and necessary to harmonize the introduced portions.").

[5] United States v. Alvardo, 882 F.2d 645 (2d Cir. 1989), *cert. denied,* 110 S. Ct. 1114 (1990) (court found that admitting defendant's statements in redacted form, omitting name of co-defendant, did not distort the meaning of the statements nor did it exclude exculpatory information; ruling protected co-defendant's right to confrontation and served judicial economy by allowing joint trial); United States v. Costner, 684 F.2d 370, 373 (6th Cir. 1982) (reversible error to have admitted all of report made by defense witness which he used to refresh his recollection of conversation with prosecution witness; since defense witness had been called to impeach prosecution witness, his testimony was limited by scope of prosecution witness' testimony; report contained matters that did not bear on prosecution witness' credibility but related to prior bad acts by defendant; "Rule 106 is intended to eliminate the misleading impression created by taking a statement out of context. The rule covers an order of proof problem; it is not designed to make something admissible that should be excluded.").

[6] United States v. Boylan, 898 F.2d 230 (1st Cir. 1990), *cert. denied,* 111 S. Ct. 139 (1990) (no misleading impression was created by presenting personnel orders without the remainder of the files); Brewer v. Jeep Corp., 724 F.2d 653, 657 (8th Cir. 1983) (trial court did not abuse discretion in refusing to admit into evidence a film unless companion report was also

surrounding documents is desirable if it may assist the jury to understand the full significance of the document offered by the proponent. If for some reason, such as privilege, evidence necessary to correct a misleading impression cannot be admitted, the misleading evidence may also have to be excluded.[7]

In *Beech Aircraft Corp. v. Rainey,*[8] the Supreme Court found that the district court had abused its discretion when it refused to allow the plaintiff, called as an adverse witness by the defense, "to present a more complete picture"[9] of a letter he had written, two statements of which had been used by the defense in questioning him.[10] The Court declined to place its holding squarely on Rule 106 grounds, although it stated that "[c]learly the concerns underlying Rule 106 are relevant here."[11] Rather the Court relied on the general rules of relevancy:

. . .when one party had made use of a portion of a document, such that misunderstanding or distortion can be averted only through presentation of another portion, the material required for completeness is *ipso facto* relevant and therefore admissible under Rules 401 and 402.[12]

In the case of a single document, attached documents or related documents, it is convenient to mark them in evidence at one time with a single exhibit number or a series of numbers, whether or not they are all actually read or shown to the jury

offered into evidence); *In re* Saco Local Development Corp., 30 B.R. 862 (Bankr. Ct. D. Me. 1983) (court excluded financial statements because the notes, which were an integral part of the statements, were missing).

[7] United States v. LeFevour, 798 F.2d 977, 981 (7th Cir. 1986) (dictum).

[8] 488 U.S. 153, 109 S. Ct. 439, 102 L. Ed. 2d 445 (1988).

[9] *Id.* at 169, 109 S. Ct. at 450, 102 L. Ed. 2d at 463.

[10] Plaintiff was suing for the death of his wife, a Navy flight instructor, in the crash of a Navy training plane. The only disputed issue was whether the crash was due to pilot error or malfunctioning equipment. Plaintiff, also a Navy flight instructor, had written to the investigator setting forth his own theory of what had happened. The defense questioned him about two statements that were consistent with pilot error without allowing him to explain that his letter, read in its entirety, was fully consistent with equipment failure.

[11] *Id.* at 17, 109 S. Ct. at 451, 102 L. Ed. 2d at 465.

[12] *Id.* at 172, 109 S. Ct. at 451, 102 L. Ed. 2d at 465 (citing **Treatise** at ¶ 106[02], p. 106–20 (1986)].

at the time of introduction. Reference to the documents both at the time of introduction and subsequently is then much simpler and they are easier to find. A good deal of useless colloquy can also be avoided about which portions have or have not yet been introduced. All these decisions should be made before trial by counsel, wherever possible without the court's intervention.

¶ 2.06   Calling and Interrogation of Witnesses by Court— Rule 614[1]

Rule 614 is in accord with usual practice and the common law tradition in recognizing the trial court's right to call and question witnesses. The source of this right springs from the nature of the judicial function: "A judge is more than a moderator; he is charged to see that the law is properly administered, and it is a duty which he cannot discharge by remaining inert."[2] It is a right that is not unlimited; excessive intervention by the court interferes with the jury's right to decide facts, is at odds with the adversary system, and deprives parties of their right to an impartial arbiter. The rule provides:

Rule 614

CALLING AND INTERROGATION OF WITNESSES BY COURT

(a) Calling by court. The court may, on its own motion or at the suggestion of a party, call witnesses, and all parties are entitled to cross-examine witnesses thus called.

(b) Interrogation by court. The court may interrogate witnesses, whether called by itself or by a party.

(c) Objections. Objections to the calling of witnesses by the court or to interrogation by it may be made at the time or at the next available opportunity when the jury is not present.

By providing that the trial court "may" call witnesses, Rule 614(a) recognizes that calling witnesses is a matter of judicial

---

[1] See discussion in **Treatise** at ¶¶ 614[01]–[04].

[2] United States v. Marzano, 149 F.2d 923, 925 (2d Cir. 1945) (Learned Hand, J.).

discretion rather than duty, and that the failure to call a witness on its own, or at the suggestion of a party, is not a ground for reversal.[3] Ordinarily, the court's exercise of its right will not lead to a reversal either, unless the appellate court concludes that the trial court's action interfered with the fairness of the trial.[4] Rule 614(a) provides that all parties are entitled to cross-examine a witness called by the court.

Although Rule 614(b) acknowledges the court's power to interrogate all witnesses,[5] it is often suggested that this right be exercised sparingly. The court must at all times retain its role of impartial arbiter. Although it has a duty to assist the jurors in eliciting the truth, it also has an obligation to ensure that they reach their own conclusions. In a criminal case, in particular, the right to a fair trial may be jeopardized by over-zealous questioning by the trial court.[6] In an extreme case, the

---

[3] *See, e.g.,* United States v. Lester, 248 F.2d 329, 331 (2d Cir. 1957); Steinberg v. United States, 162 F.2d 120, 124 (5th Cir. 1947). *Cf.* Cunningham v. Housing Authority of the City of Opelousas, 764 F.2d 1097 (5th Cir. 1985) (district court did not abuse its discretion in ordering parties to take a deposition after the court had taken the case under submission; equivalent of court calling its own witness under Rule 614(a)).

[4] *See, e.g.,* United States v. Karnes, 531 F.2d 214 (4th Cir. 1976) (error for court to have called prosecution witnesses essential to government's case whom prosecutor refused to call); United States v. Marzano, 149 F.2d 923, 926 (2d Cir. 1945) (in narcotics prosecution, court called witnesses awaiting sentencing by him after they pleaded guilty under a separate indictment; calling, coupled with questions by the judge which clearly suggested that he would increase their sentences if they persisted in their denials, held to amount to abuse of discretion).

[5] *See* Hanson v. Waller, 888 F.2d 806, 812–813 (11th Cir. 1989) (the authority of the judge to question witnesses is well established).

[6] *See, e.g.,* United States v. Gill, 909 F.2d 274 (7th Cir. 1990) (critical inquiry is whether, by its conduct in questioning witnesses, the court has conveyed to the jury its bias or belief regarding defendant's guilt); United States v. Victoria, 837 F.2d 50 (2d Cir. 1988) (it was clear error for a trial judge to ask questions bearing on the credibility of a defendant-witness prior to the completion of direct examination; the interrogation here served to convey to the jury the judge's opinion that the witness was not worthy of belief and the credibility of the defendant-witness was a key issue); United States v. Mazzilli, 848 F.2d 384 (2d Cir. 1988) (where credibility is crucial to a defense, the jury's impression that court disbelieves defendant's testimony affects his right to a fair trial). *But see* United States v. Mickens, 926 F.2d 1323 (2d Cir. 1991) (district court's admonitions to counsel and

appellate court will reverse if it finds that the judge acted as an advocate, or invaded the province of the jury.[7] Reversals are, however, rare. It is the impact the questioning had on the rights of the litigants, and not the sheer volume of the court's questions that is decisive.[8]

Unless counsel are particularly obtuse it should be enough for the court to suggest a line to counsel.[9] Particularly where expert testimony or technical terminology is involved, the court may suggest to counsel that the witness be asked to clarify or define so that the lay jurors can follow.

As when it applies Rule 103, or Standard 107, the appellate court will consider the trial judge's actions in the context of the case. Factors a reviewing court may consider are: the extent to which the witnesses' testimony needed clarification; whether the witnesses were unusually hesitant and in need of assurance; the trial court's use of leading questions; the degree to which the court interfered with cross-examination, and whether the court's interruptions favored one side exclusively; whether the court instructed the jury to arrive at its own conclusions; whether the parties were adequately represented; the objections made to the court's questioning; and the complexity of the facts and the trial judge's familiarity with them.[10]

questions to witnesses did not deprive defendants of fair trial); United States v. Beaty, 722 F.2d 1090, 1095–96 (3d Cir. 1983) (trial judge's questioning of key alibi witnesses was in effect an attack on witnesses' credibility since questioning was unrelated to offenses charged and alibi defense offered); United States v. Welliver, 601 F.2d 203 (5th Cir. 1979) (reversible error for judge to have repeatedly usurped questioning of witnesses from counsel who were competently conducting examination).

[7] Rocha v. Great Am. Ins. Co, 850 F.2d 1095 (6th Cir. 1988) (trial judge's questioning of plaintiff's expert's testimony deprived plaintiff of impartial trial).

[8] *See, e.g.,* Moore v. United States, 598 F.2d 439, 442–43 (5th Cir. 1979) (judge asked almost the same number of questions as defense counsel and prosecutor combined; appellate court stated that "[w]hile such statistical comparisons are not without significance . . . the court's questioning here was unbiased, patient and temperate, never argumentative or accusatory.").

[9] *See* Holland v. Commissioner, 853 F.2d 675 (6th Cir. 1987) (trial judge's suggestion that the government procure a handwriting expert was "somewhat unusual," but was in substantial compliance with Rule 614).

[10] *See* cases cited in **Treatise** at ¶ 614[03].

Subdivision (c) of Rule 614 is designed to accommodate the aims of Rule 605 (automatic objection when judge called as witness) and Rule 103 (parties have responsibility for making timely objection). It seeks to protect the attorney against the possible embarrassment attendant upon making objections in the presence of the jury, but insists on counsel's responsibility to object at a time when corrective measures can still be taken. Since counsel need not object until the next opportunity when the jury is absent, counsel do not forfeit their rights by failing to object when the judge asks the first question. Rather, they have some opportunity[11] to assess the judge's attitude towards the particular witness before deciding whether an objection is required to protect their client's rights.

¶ 2.07 Summing Up and Comment by Judge—Standard 107[1]

Standard 107 authorizes the trial court to summarize and comment on the evidence, provided it informs the jurors that they have the ultimate responsibility for resolving issues of fact. The text is consistent with long standing federal practice; it was not enacted by Congress, however, because of opposition by attorneys trained in states where the trial judge does not have these powers.[2] In striking the provision, Congress did not intend to affect federal practice. Consequently, the proposed rule should be viewed as a standard to be consulted as a useful restatement of existing law. The standard provides:

---

[11] If a witness' testimony extends over a number of days, the objector may not be able to wait until the witness is finished testifying before making an objection. *See* United States v. Billups, 692 F.2d 320 (4th Cir. 1982), *cert. denied,* 464 U.S. 820 (1983) (defense waived objection where it did not object to judge's interrogation of defendant until after testimony concluded; appellate court states that defendant could have objected at end of first day of testimony or at the beginning of the proceedings on the next day when the jury was absent; court also concluded that trial court had not deprived defendant of fair trial).

[1] See discussion in **Treatise** at ¶¶ 107[01]–[07].

[2] *See* Congressional Action on Standard 107 in Treatise.

Standard 107

SUMMING UP AND COMMENT BY JUDGE

After the close of the evidence and arguments of counsel, the judge may fairly and impartially sum up the evidence and comment to the jury upon the weight of the evidence and the credibility of the witnesses, if he also instructs the jury that they are to determine for themselves the weight of the evidence and the credit to be given to the witnesses and that they are not bound by the judge's summation or comment.

¶ 2.07[01]   Summing Up

Standard 107 authorizes the judge to summarize the evidence in the case for the benefit of the jury after the close of arguments by counsel. By retaining this traditional power, the federal courts preserve one of the most effective tools the judge has at his disposal to assist the jury in arriving at a just verdict.[3] A statement by the court of its recollection of the evidence immediately following the summations of counsel can do much to place counsel's unavoidably partisan restatements in proper perspective.

The distinction between the court's power to summarize and its right to comment on the evidence should not be over-emphasized; some courts, in fact, use the terms interchangeably. To the extent that a summary given by the court falls short of a recitation of the entire transcript, the very process of choosing which testimony to review and which to leave out is in itself a comment on the evidence and the court must, under

---

[3] Nudd v. Burrows, 91 U.S. 426, 23 L. Ed. 286, 289 (1875) ("[I]t is the right and duty of the court to aid them [the jury], by recalling the testimony to their recollection; by collating its details; by suggesting grounds of preference where there is contradiction; by directing their attention to the most important facts, . . . by resolving the evidence, however complicated, into its simplest elements, and by showing the bearing of its several parts and their combined effect, stripped of every consideration which might otherwise mislead or confuse them. How this duty shall be performed depends in every case upon the discretion of the judge. There is none more important resting upon those who preside at jury trials. Constituted as juries are, it is frequently impossible for them to discharge their function wisely and well without this aid. In such cases, chance, mistake, or caprice, may determine the result.").

Standard 107, remind the jurors that if their recollection of the evidence is different from that of the court, then they should reach a verdict based upon the evidence as they remember it.

Although the court has broad discretion on when and how[4] to summarize, it is improper for the court to assume the existence of facts at issue by characterizing the evidence "as facts rather than as testimony"[5] to be considered by the jury in deciding the facts. In a criminal case where the facts are not in dispute, the court may not assume that the defendant committed the acts charged with the requisite criminal intent by failing to charge the jury that it must find intent.[6] Nor is it proper without the accused's consent for the court to characterize as "uncontroverted" or "undisputed" any fact which the prosecution must establish as true in order for the defendant to be found guilty.

When summarizing the case for the jury, the court must be careful to review only the evidence actually presented to the jury. Thus, it is error, without the consent of the parties, to inform the jury of facts brought to the court's attention during hearings or colloquies conducted outside the jury's presence, or upon a hypothetical or conjectural state of facts not established by the evidence.

The court's summary of the evidence must be accurate. Although misstatements of facts of a minor nature will rarely be the source of reversible error, serious distortions of the evidence or the theories proffered to explain it can constitute the basis for a reversal if the party was deprived of having the evidence impartially considered by the jury.

If a party requests the court to charge on a particular theory, the theory should be put before the jury, along with a statement of the evidence that supports it, as long as the theory is supported by evidence sufficient to go to the jury, even though the evidence is weak or improbable. It is not for the court to decide whether the evidence is worthy of belief; that is a

---

[4] See discussion of different ways in which the court can summarize the evidence in **Treatise** at ¶ 107[02].

[5] Hardy v. United States, 335 F.2d 288, 290 (D.C. Cir.), *rev'd on other grounds,* 375 U.S. 277 (1964).

[6] See discussion of presumptions in criminal cases in Chapter 5 *infra.*

question only the jury can resolve. It is reversible error "to submit the evidence and theory of one party prominently and fully . . . and not call attention to the main points of the opposite party's case."[7]

Regardless of the instructions offered by the parties, the court has an independent duty to charge the jury correctly on the law. Although numerous cases state that a court is relieved of its obligation to charge on a particular theory when a party does not appropriately request it, a reversal on the basis of plain error may occur, if the reviewing court believes that substantial rights were ignored. As in the case of erroneous rulings on evidence governed by Rule 103, the appellate court's determination will hinge on the particular facts presented. It will consider factors such as the party's failure to object, the type of case—criminal or civil, complicated or simple—the length of the trial, the nature of the trial judge's summary and instructions, and the context in which they were given, in determining whether the trial court properly exercised its Standard 107 discretion in reviewing the evidence.

In the vast majority of cases there are no inflexible rules dictating the requisite method of summation. It is preferable for the court to keep an open mind as to which method should be used in a particular case or in a portion of the case. When appropriate, the court should not hesitate to adopt the form of evidentiary review best suited to meet the exigencies of the case before it. Some elements of the charge may require a detailed marshaling of the facts implicated by the charge, and for other portions a brief summary will suffice.

The jury should get the impression that the court is presenting its own—rather than a party's—summary and charge. Nevertheless, the jury will sometimes be made aware of the source of an instruction or partial summary because it hears the court adopt the suggestion of counsel. Even when the objection is made at side bar after the main charge and the court turns to the jury and makes a further statement, it will

---

[7] Pullman v. Hall, 46 F.2d 399, 404 (4th Cir. 1931); Bentley v. Stromberg-Carlson Corp., 638 F.2d 9 (2d Cir. 1981) (reversible error for trial judge to stress defendant's contentions at great length by "an almost verbatim reading of [its] trial brief," and to make no reference to plaintiff's evidence).

be apparent that the addition favors a particular side and was made at the request of the side it favors. For this reason, among others, it is preferable to go over a full draft of the charge before it is delivered. The judge should photocopy the entire proposed charge, mark it as an exhibit, and use it as a basis for discussion. After agreement, the amended charge should be recopied and distributed so that side bars can be avoided. In reading the charge, the court will depart slightly from non-critical language to keep up the jurors' and its own interest. Communication to the jurors even more than pandering to the appellate court is desirable.

Many errors can be avoided if counsel submit their requests for instructions and confer with the court well in advance of summation when there is still time to clear up misunderstandings and to ensure that the instructions will reflect accurately the theories asserted by both sides. If a conference is impractical or disagreement persists, counsel must protect their clients by objecting at the time the instructions are delivered so that the court has a final opportunity to correct its remarks, and the objectors are assured of a record on which to appeal.

¶ 2.07[02] Comments on the Evidence

The power to comment on the evidence, as authorized by Standard 107, is broad. Generally no error results, if the court confines its remarks to the evidence in the case, specifically instructs the jury that the opinions expressed are those of the court and are not binding, and informs the jurors that they have the ultimate responsibility for resolving issues of fact.[8] Whether

---

[8] *See, e.g.,* United States v. Sanchez-Lopez, 879 F.2d 541 (9th Cir. 1989) (trial judge's comments to defendants' witness during cross-examination permissible; court instructed jury that its comments were merely expressions of opinion of the facts and the jury was free to disregard them); United States v. Nelson, 570 F.2d 258, 262 (8th Cir. 1978) (no error where trial court repeatedly told jurors that its comments were not evidence but recollections which may have been mistaken, and that jury should rely on its own recollections). *Cf.* United States v. Gill, 909 F.2d 274 (7th Cir. 1990) (trial judge's questioning of government witnesses did not improperly convey to the jury a bias regarding defendant's guilt; questions were not aimed at defendant and the jury was instructed that no personal opinion should be inferred from the court's questions).

or not to comment on the evidence under the circumstances of a particular case lies almost entirely within the discretion of the trial court.[9] A failure to comment on the evidence, as opposed to reviewing the evidence and stating the applicable law, does not constitute error. Although the court has the option of indicating its own opinions on the evidence, it rarely does so explicitly.

In practice, the primary significance of the court's power to comment is that it enables an appellate court to uphold a jury verdict when the trial court did not intend to express an opinion on the evidence but where the record shows that the jurors could have inferred that it did from the wording of the charge or other remarks. If the trial court is so carried away in its remarks as to lose its sense of propriety and impartiality, the reviewing court may find that the parties have been deprived of their right to a fair and impartial trial.[10]

There is almost never any justification for informing the jurors which witnesses the trial court thinks are telling the truth. Advising the jury about the factors to consider in evaluating a witness' credibility may be considerably more helpful. Jurors

---

[9] There are some limitations on the judge's power to comment imposed by rule, case law and statute. *See, e.g.,* discussion of Standard 513 (prohibiting comment on assertion of a testimonial privilege) in Chapter 18 *infra;* Griffin v. California, 380 U.S. 609, 85 S. Ct. 1229, 14 L. Ed. 2d 106 (1965) (comments on defendant's invocation of privilege against self-incrimination violated Fifth amendment); 18 U.S.C. § 4241(f) ("A finding by the court that the defendant is mentally competent to stand trial shall not prejudice the defendant in raising the issue of his insanity as a defense to the offense charged, and shall not be admissible as evidence in a trial for the offense charged.").

[10] *See, e.g.,* United States v. Hickman, 592 F.2d 931, 936 (6th Cir. 1979) (when one combines the limitation on cross-examination, the anti-defendant tone of the judge's interruptions, the wholesale taking over of cross-examination of defense witnesses by the trial judge, one is left with the strong impression that these two defendants did not receive the fair and impartial trial which the Sixth Amendment to the Constitution guarantees them); United States v. Yates, 553 F.2d 518 (6th Cir. 1977) (court's comment that defendant had clearly admitted participation in robbery adversely affected substantial right of defendant to have defense fairly heard and guilt determined by jury). See discussion in **Treatise** at ¶ 107[07] of standards of review employed by the appellate courts in determining whether the trial judge's comments amounted to reversible error.

are, for instance, generally unaware of all the factors that should be taken into consideration in evaluating the testimony of an accomplice or an informer; and a court may wish to caution the jury to treat such evidence with suspicion and caution.[11] In the case of witnesses who have no clearly defined biases, the better practice is simply to advise the jury with respect to the general factors used in evaluating the credibility of any witness and the freedom to reject part or all of a witness' testimony.[12]

The occasions where the exercise of the prerogative of federal judges to express views on the ultimate issues of a trial—guilt and liability—would be appropriate are extremely rare. In civil cases, the power is superfluous. The court should direct a verdict if its opinion is based upon the conclusion that no other finding could be made by a reasonable juror. In a criminal case, the court must direct a verdict of acquittal if it believes that the evidence produced by the government, with all the inferences viewed in its favor, would not support a verdict of guilty beyond a reasonable doubt. If the court thinks that a verdict of acquittal is not indicated, the court is of most help to the jury when it confines its remarks to the considerations that the jury should take into account in order to reach a just verdict.

The power of a trial judge to comment on the weight and sufficiency of the evidence is one of the tools for exercising

---

[11] *See, e.g.,* United States v. Dove, 916 F.2d 41 (2d Cir. 1990) (failure to give balanced instructions is reversible error); United States v. Gleason, 616 F.2d 2, 15 (2d Cir. 1979), *cert. denied,* 444 U.S. 1082 (1980) (court has duty to give balanced instructions; where it points out that certain witnesses' testimony is suspect, such as that of accomplices or co-conspirators, those who have made plea bargains or are awaiting sentence, those granted immunity, and defendants, "it must also direct the jury's attention to the fact that it may well find these witnesses to be truthful, in whole or in part.").

[12] *See, e.g.,* United States v. Anton, 597 F.2d 371 (3d Cir. 1979) (trial court's statement that he regarded defendant as "devoid of credibility" deprived defendant of right to have credibility determined by jury; reversible error when combined with favorable comments on testimony of 13 Roman Catholic priests who testified for prosecution); United States v. Allsup, 566 F.2d 68, 72–73 (9th Cir. 1977) (trial court intervened in cross-examination of identification witness, who had erroneously identified picture of defendant, and brought out that she had been scared; appellate court found that trial judge destroyed effect of cross-examination, rehabilitated witness, and committed prejudice because of implication that defendant had frightened witness).

substantial control over the admission and presentation of evidence. Together with Rule 105 (authorizing limiting instructions), Rule 403 (permitting the exclusion of relevant but unduly prejudicial evidence), Rule 611 (allowing the court to regulate the mode and order of the presentation of the evidence) and Rule 614 (allowing a judge both to call and to question witnesses), it allows the trial court to structure the reception of evidence in a manner which effectively promotes the search for truth while avoiding needless waste of time and unfairness to either party.

In addition to the obvious advantages afforded by allowing the court to give the jury the benefit of its experience by explaining and analyzing the evidence, the power to comment on the probative value of the proof offered by the parties, coupled with the option of giving the jury an instruction limiting the application of the evidence to its proper scope, has an inevitably liberalizing impact upon the standards governing the admissibility of evidence. If the trial court had no power to control the effect of an offer of evidence once it was admitted, the tendency would be to admit less.

There are, however, few occasions where the court should reveal its own conclusions on the weight of the evidence. When the court does comment, it should be careful to explain the reasoning behind its conclusions so that the jury will be given a clear basis in the evidence upon which it can accept or reject the court's opinion. In such instances, the adequacy of the court's reminder to the jury that the remarks are not binding also becomes important.

Comments by the court can do much to clear up ambiguities in the testimony, and to indicate to the jury which inferences may rationally be drawn from the evidence before it. The court's comments should be guided by the same general principles of relevancy and prejudice that govern the introduction of evidence-in-chief. The court is expected to be more circumspect, less emotional, and more rational in its analysis than attorneys for the parties. Comments which are of an ad hominem nature are not within the scope of the power to comment on the weight and sufficiency of the evidence.

The federal trial court is not required to refrain from remarking on the evidence until after counsel have finished their closing arguments. It is fully consistent with the rationale underlying Standard 107, for the trial court to clarify the purpose for which evidence is being offered, to explain the evidentiary law underlying the court's ruling, or to offer any other advice concerning the evidence being presented which will enable the jury to better understand its significance. In fact, this will generally be the better practice during a protracted trial, since the jury may have a difficult time relating instructions which they receive at the end of the trial to evidence which they heard earlier in the course of the trial.

CHAPTER 3

Power of Court in Relation to Jury

SYNOPSIS

3–1

¶ 3.01   Preliminary Questions in General—Rule 104

¶ 3.01[01]   Scope[1]

The admissibility of proffered evidence frequently depends upon resolution of a multitude of difficult preliminary questions of fact. Rule 104 partially resolves the dilemma by stating in subdivision (b) that the jury determines preliminary questions upon which the relevance of evidence depends but that the court, pursuant to subdivision (a), makes other determinations such as the "qualification of a person to be a witness, the existence of a privilege, or the admissibility of evidence." The allocation of functions between judge and jury rests on the notion that only a judge can appropriately apply technical, evidentiary rules grounded in policy concerns. Lay persons are ill-equipped to engage in the necessary legal reasoning or to evaluate certain kinds of evidence, and will be less likely to disregard evidence that should not have been admitted once it comes to their attention.

Subdivision (e) provides that the admissibility of evidence relevant to weight or credibility—issues that clearly must be resolved by the fact-finder—is unaffected by Rule 104. The last sentence of subdivision (a) and subdivisions (c) and (d) of Rule 104 govern some of the procedures at preliminary hearings.

The rule provides:

Rule 104

PRELIMINARY QUESTIONS

(a) Questions of admissibility generally. Preliminary questions concerning the qualification of a person to be a witness, the existence of a privilege, or the admissibility of evidence shall be determined by the court, subject to the provisions of subdivision (b). In making its determination it is not bound by the rules of evidence except those with respect to privileges.

(b) Relevancy conditioned on fact. When the relevancy of evidence depends upon the fulfillment of a condition of fact, the court shall admit it upon, or subject to, the introduction of evidence sufficient to support a finding of the fulfillment of the condition.

---

[1] See discussion in **Treatise** at ¶¶ 104[01]–[02].

(c) Hearing of jury. Hearings on the admissibility of confessions shall in all cases be conducted out of the hearing of the jury. Hearings on other preliminary matters shall be so conducted when the interests of justice require, or when an accused is a witness and so requests.

(d) Testimony by accused. The accused does not, by testifying upon a preliminary matter, become subject to cross-examination as to other issues in the case.

(e) Weight and credibility. This rule does not limit the right of a party to introduce before the jury evidence relevant to weight or credibility.

¶ 3.01[02]   Questions of Fact Allocated to the Court[1]

Instead of setting forth a formula for allocating functions between judge and jury, Rule 104(a) specifies two instances of preliminary fact-finding that must be left to the court—the qualifications of a witness and the existence of a privilege—and then lists a third, the admissibility of evidence, which is, however, subject to the provisions of subdivision (b). The combination of subdivisions (a) and (b) results in the court having to determine those preliminary questions of fact that hinge on the application of technical or exclusionary evidentiary rules. Rule 104(a) is silent about the applicable standard of proof. The Supreme Court has held in *Bourjaily v. United States*[2] that the courts must use a preponderance of the evidence standard in determining pursuant to Rule 104(a) whether the conditions for admitting a co-conspirator's statement have been satisfied. See discussion in Chapter 15, *infra*. Without explicitly so stating, courts may use a prima facie standard in admitting other evidence pursuant to Rule 104(a) as consistent with the preference for admitting relevant evidence expressed in the Federal Rules of Evidence.

[a]   Qualification of Witness

The trial court's responsibility under Rule 104(a) to determine preliminary questions concerning the qualification of witnesses is largely vitiated by Rule 601 which makes all witnesses competent except where state law supplies the rule of decision and declares a

---

[1] See discussion in **Treatise** at ¶¶ 104[03]–[07].

[2] — U.S. —, 107 S.Ct. 2775, 97 L.Ed.2d 144 (1987).

witness incompetent. The rules in Article VI of the Federal Rules rely on the jury's capacity to evaluate the relative credibility of witnesses. They discard insanity, infancy, interest in the proceedings, and religious belief as absolute grounds of incompetence and retain only the requirement that the witness have personal knowledge of the matter to which the testimony relates. See Rule 602, discussed in Chapter 10, *infra.* Only if no reasonable person could give any credence to the witness, so that the probative weight of his testimony is at or close to zero, can the testimony be excluded. An example is where the witness could not physically see what he describes, making his testimony excludable on hearsay or opinion grounds.

The court does, however, retain its power to decide preliminary questions with regard to the qualification of expert witnesses under Rule 702. The danger that a jury will accept "expert" conclusions and opinions as fact without exercising normal scrutiny makes it imperative that this sort of evidence be admitted after preliminary consideration by the judge of the witness' qualifications and the basis for the opinion. See discussion of Rules 702 and 703 in Chapter 13, *infra.*

[b] Privileges

Numerous preliminary factual questions may have to be decided in ruling on the validity of a claim of privilege. For instance, a claim of attorney-client privilege may require resolution of such issues as whether the requisite relationship existed between the lawyer and the client, the communication in question was intended to be confidential, a waiver occurred, or an exception applied. All of these preliminary questions should be decided by the trial court pursuant to Rule 104(a). Any other rule that allows the privileged material to be divulged to the jury before the court finally decides on the existence of the privilege undermines the policies that led to the creation of the privilege in question. Irreparable damage to the confidential relationship may be sustained at the moment of disclosure regardless of whether the evidence is ultimately used by the trier of fact in reaching its verdict.

[c]   Hearsay

Rules 801, 803 and 804 require resolution of many preliminary issues of fact before it can be determined whether or not a proffered statement is excluded by the hearsay rule.

Although Rule 104 is silent about the proper allocation of responsibility for this fact-finding as between court and jury, the decisions pursuant to the Federal Rules clearly indicate that it is the court pursuant to subdivision (a), rather than the jury pursuant to subdivision (b), that is making these determinations.

Allocating responsiblity for preliminary questions about the applicability of the hearsay rule to the court makes sense in terms of the principle underlying Rule 104(a)—that jurors should not have the responsibility of applying evidentiary rules of a technical and exclusionary nature with a great potential for prejudice. Jurors will not appreciate the relevant policy concerns underlying these rules, will not assess the value of the evidence accurately, and will be unable to disregard the improperly admitted evidence in reaching their conclusions.

The courts' treatment of the allocation issue can be seen most clearly with respect to co-conspirators' statements governed by Rule 801(d)(2)(E). As is discussed more fully in connection with that rule in Chapter 15, *infra,* the Supreme Court has held[3] that the court, rather than the jury, must find that the requirements that allow co-conspirators' statements to be admitted have been satisfied. To ask the jurors to consider highly prejudicial statements of co-conspirators only if they first find the existence of the conspiracy and defendant's participation in it, is to present them with too tricky a task. In cases where the conspiracy is charged, it creates the absurdity of asking the jury to in effect decide the issue of guilt before it may consider evidence which is probative of guilt. Although the court will be deciding a preliminary fact that coincides with an ultimate fact in the case, the parties are not deprived of a jury trial on the issue, since the judge and jury need not agree on the resolution. Giving these preliminary questions to the jury would violate the spirit of Rule 104, which calls for preliminary determinations by the judge in all cases involving a high potential for prejudice.

---

[3] Bourjaily v. United States , — U.S. —, 107 S.Ct. 2775, 97 L.Ed.2d 144 (1987).

[d] Coerced Confessions, Illegal Searches, and Improper Trial Procedures

On an evidentiary level, the exclusionary rules pose the same issues as the hearsay rule discussed above—the inability of the jury to comprehend the governing policies, to assess the reliability of the evidence, or to avoid being prejudiced by evidence that should have been excluded. Rule 104(a) would, therefore, govern the admissibility of this type of evidence. In addition, constitutional requirements demand the same result.

¶ 3.01[03] Questions of Fact Allocated to the Jury[1]

Rule 104(b) creates a significant category of preliminary questions that are finally decided by the jury. Where evidence is offered which is relevant only if some preliminary fact is first established, the judge is directed to admit the evidence subject to a jury determination of the conditioning fact. The judge must determine that a reasonable jury could make the requisite factual determination based on the evidence before it.[2]

The rationale behind giving such questions to the jury is that since no protective evidentiary policy is at stake the jury is just as capable as the judge in making a determination. The only real discriminations required of the jurors in this process are evaluations of probative force such as they customarily make. Consequently, following the judge's instructions to disregard the primary evidence if they find against the preliminary fact does not entail the intellectual control required when told to ignore matters which should have been excluded under the rules discussed in connection with subdivision (a). In effect Rule 104(b) is an illustration of the order of proof rule, Rule 611(a).

---

[1] See discussion in **Treatise** at ¶ 104[09].

[2] Tate v. Robbins & Myers, Inc., 790 F.2d 10, 12 & n.1 (1st Cir. 1986) (in products liability action against hoist manufacturer for failure of duty to warn, there was insufficient evidence to support a finding that defendant knew injured party had purchased the hoist, thereby making a 1980 Manual irrelevant to plaintiff's duty to warn theory; citing **Treatise**).

Rule 104(b) must be read in conjunction with Rules 901(a) and 1008 which are discussed below.

¶ 3.01[04] Procedural Aspects of Preliminary Fact Determinations[1]

[a] Applicability of Evidentiary Rules

The last sentence of Rule 104(a) states that when a court is determining a preliminary question of fact pursuant to Rule 104(a) it need not apply any of the evidentiary rules except those with respect to privileges. The trial judge's experience and legal training can be relied upon to properly evaluate the evidence and to put out of mind that which should be excluded. Thus, the judge will generally be fully cognizant of the inherent weakness of evidence by affidavit or hearsay and will take such weakness into account when evaluating its weight on the preliminary question.[2] Furthermore, the opportunity to disregard the evidentiary rules expedites the proceedings. Privilege rules are treated differently because any substantial breach of confidentiality threatens serious damage to the relationship protected by the privilege.

[b] Presence of Jury at Preliminary Hearings

Except for two specified instances, Rule 104(c) vests broad discretion in the trial court to decide whether preliminary hearings should be conducted outside the presence of the jury. Granting this flexibili-

---

[1] See discussion in **Treatise** at ¶¶ 104[02], [10]–[12]. ¶ 104[12] discusses some issues that occur at preliminary hearings in criminal cases.

[2] Despite the last sentence of Rule 104(a), courts are often uncomfortable in considering the very statement seeking admission when deciding whether such statement satisfies the hearsay rule. In Bourjaily v. United States, — U.S. —, —, 107 S.Ct. 2775, 2780, 97 L.Ed.2d 144, 154 (1987), the Supreme Court held that Rule 104(a) "mean[s] what is says" so that a trial court may rely on the very hearsay statements seeking admission in determining whether the statement satisfies the hearsay rule. Because of their reluctance to allow "bootstrapping," a majority of the circuits had insisted that the trial judge may only rely on evidence independent of the coconspirator's statement seeking admission when determining whether Rule 801(d)(2)(E) requirements have been satisfied. See discussion in Chapter 15, *infra.*

ty is in accord with the fundamental concern of this rule for the protection of the parties. The primary consideration of the court in deciding whether to remove the jury is the potential for prejudice inherent in the evidence that the parties will produce on the preliminary question. A court will, therefore, frequently exercise its prerogative to exclude the jury when, for instance, it

(*Text continued on page 3–9*)

has to rule on the admissibility of highly incriminating evidence proffered under an exception to the hearsay rule.

In deciding to exercise its discretion under this subdivision, the court must, however, always be cognizant of the possible adverse effect on the jury's attitude toward the court and the parties if it is repeatedly excluded from what are apparently important decisions. The goal of this rule is protection of the interests of the parties and the possibility of an alienated jury must be weighed heavily against the potential harm involved in letting them hear the evidence on the preliminary question. In many instances the trial will move more swiftly and the intelligent jury will be less likely to fall into error if there are not constant interruptions for side-bar and other discussions outside the presence of the jury.

The court has no discretion when it is ruling on the admissibility of confessions or admissions of a defendant. The jury may not be present if there is a preliminary hearing on such a matter. As a matter of sound practice, "in the interests of justice," hearings on the admissibility of illegally obtained evidence or the admissibility of eyewitness identification should also be conducted outside the presence of the jury because of the high likelihood of prejudice. Even if the evidence turns out to be admissible the jury may get the impression that the defendant falsely accused the law enforcement authorities of illegal activities to keep the jurors from learning the truth.

Rule 104(c) also requires the court to exclude the jury from a hearing on a preliminary matter when the accused is a witness, and so requests. Without this option, the defendant might not be in a position to testify freely on preliminary matters, and would be unable to take advantage of the protections afforded by Rule 104(d).

[c] Testimony of Accused at Preliminary Hearing

Under Rule 104(d), if the accused testifies upon a preliminary matter, he does not subject himself to cross-examination as to other issues in the case. The government may cross-examine only on issues relevant to suppression of the evidence and credibility. The accused does not, therefore, completely waive his right to claim the privilege against self-incrimination when he takes the stand on the preliminary question.[3]

¶ 3.02 Preliminary Questions of Authentication and Identification—Rule 901(a)[1]

Rule 901(a) treats preliminary questions of authenticity of writings and of identification as specialized applications of Rule 104(b). The rule states:

Rule 901

REQUIREMENT OF AUTHENTICATION OR IDENTIFICATION

(a) General provision. The requirement of authentication or identification as a condition precedent to admissibility is satisfied by evidence sufficient to support a finding that the matter in question is what its proponent claims.

The condition of fact which must be fulfilled by every offer of real proof is whether the evidence is what its proponent claims it to be. The standard of admissibility is identical to that required under Rule 104(b) relating to matters of conditional relevance generally —would a finding of fulfillment of the condition be supported by the evidence?[2] Since the court must decide whether a reasonable juror might find for the proponent, the court should base its decision on the same evidence the jury will have before it—admissible evidence only. Once a prima facie showing of authenticity or identity is made, the evidence must be admitted.

The trier may ultimately disbelieve the proponent's proof and entirely disregard or substantially discount the persuasive impact of the real proof. The opposing party may introduce evidence disputing genuineness and argue the point to the jury. Rule 901(a) recognizes that because the question for the jury is one of credibility and probative force, the jury is as competent as the court in deciding if the proffered evidence is what it purports to be.

---

[3] United States v. Gomez-Diaz, 712 F.2d 949 (5th Cir. 1983) (defendant could not limit his testimony at suppression hearing to answering a single question bearing on consent; Rule 104(d) permits full cross-examination on the "preliminary matter").

[1] See discussion in **Treatise** at ¶¶ 901(a)[01]–[02].

[2] See Chapter 8, *infra,* for discussion of different methods of authentication.

¶ 3.03 Preliminary Questions Concerning the Contents of Writings, Recordings and Photographs—Rule 1008[1]

Rule 1008 is a specialized application of the approach to preliminary questions adopted in Rule 104. It recognizes that those preliminary issues that involve only questions of probative force are for the jury, while issues that turn on the satisfaction of technical legal standards such as the best evidence rule, adopted to ensure adequate protection against unreliable evidence, are for the court. The rule provides:

Rule 1008

FUNCTIONS OF COURT AND JURY

When the admissibility of other evidence of contents of writings, recordings, or photographs under these rules depends upon the fulfillment of a condition of fact, the question whether the condition has been fulfilled is ordinarily for the court to determine in accordance with the provisions of rule 104. However, when an issue is raised (a) whether the asserted writing ever existed, or (b) whether another writing, recording, or photograph produced at the trial is the original, or (c) whether other evidence of contents correctly reflects the contents, the issue is for the trier of fact to determine as in the case of other issues of fact.

The theory of Rule 1008 becomes easier to grasp when this rule is considered with Rules 104(b), 401, 402, 602 and 901(a). All are consistent in providing that even when the jury is deciding an issue, the court must first determine if a reasonable juror could be persuaded. In this respect the court has a limited fact-finding function with respect to all evidence.

When, however, the court is actually deciding whether a fact exists necessary to satisfy a condition of the best evidence rule, before allowing evidence to be admitted—as in deciding if an adequate search for a "lost" document was made—it is actually deciding the fact and must be persuaded. Even in such circumstances, if it admits the evidence and finds that the document was lost, the same issue may be posed to the jury as one of credibility, probative force and spoliation. It is apparent, therefore, that the

---

[1] See discussion in **Treatise** at ¶¶ 1008[01]–[05].

judge and jury functions are often closely intertwined whether the judge or the jury is to make a determination under Rule 1008.

Where the jury must make a factual determination, the court must decide if enough evidence has been introduced "to support a finding." See Rule 104(b). In making this determination the court does not decide credibility but leaves the matter to the jury so that a prima facie case suffices.

Where the court makes the preliminary factual determination in deciding if the best evidence rule is satisfied, it decides credibility and probative force so that a prima facie case may not suffice. In this latter circumstance the court must be satisfied that it is more probable than not that the fact exists. The burden of more probable than not with respect to preliminary matters is generally applicable in both civil and criminal cases. As a practical matter, the court, much like a jury, will act on the rule that "where the missing original writings in dispute are the very foundation of the claim, . . . more strictness in proof is required than where the writings are only involved collaterally."[2]

¶ 3.03[01]   Questions for the Court

Administration of exclusionary rules established to vindicate some public policy—here encouragement of the use of original writings at trial—is appropriately lodged in the trial court. Accordingly, it is the court that decides whether the conditions of fact that allow secondary evidence to be introduced have been fulfilled according to the requirements of Rule 1002. Giving the jury the burden of deciding whether certain documents should be admitted because it has been established that a search has been "diligent" or an original destroyed in "bad faith" (Rule 1004(1)) would confuse and distract. The trial court also decides all hearsay, privilege, or constitutional challenges to the receipt of writings.

¶ 3.03[02]   Questions for the Jury

The second sentence of Rule 1008 allocates the burden of re-

---

[2] Sylvania Electric Products, Inc. v. Flanagan, 352 F.2d 1005, 1008 (1st Cir. 1965).

solving preliminary questions of conditional relevance of writings to the trier of fact. Such objections to admissibility of other evidence are based neither on technical exclusionary rules arising from the best evidence rule nor on the general incompetence of the evidence, but rather upon the lack of probative force of the secondary evidence—an issue for the jury. The three instances enumerated are not all-inclusive; they are the issues that will most frequently arise that must receive the treatment specified in Rule 1008 and Rule 104(b).

CHAPTER 4*

Judicial Notice

SYNOPSIS

---

* Chapter revised in 1991 by PHILIP S. GUTIERREZ, an associate with the firm of Cotkin, Collins & Franscell, Santa Ana, California.

¶ 4.01   Judicial Notice: Scope of Rule 201[1]

Rule 201—the only one of the Rules of Evidence to deal with judicial notice—was deliberately drafted to cover only a small fraction of material usually subsumed under the concept of "judicial notice."[2] The rule provides:

Rule 201

JUDICIAL NOTICE OF ADJUDICATIVE FACTS

(a) Scope of rule. This rule governs only judicial notice of adjudicative facts.

(b) Kinds of facts. A judicially noticed fact must be one not subject to reasonable dispute in that it is either (1) generally known within the territorial jurisdiction of the trial court or (2) capable of accurate and ready determination by resort to sources whose accuracy cannot reasonably be questioned.

(c) When discretionary. A court may take judicial notice, whether requested or not.

(d) When mandatory. A court shall take judicial notice if requested by a party and supplied with the necessary information.

(e) Opportunity to be heard. A party is entitled upon timely request to an opportunity to be heard as to the propriety of taking judicial notice and the tenor of the matter noticed. In the absence of prior notification, the request may be made after judicial notice has been taken.

(f) Time of taking notice. Judicial notice may be taken at any stage of the proceeding.

(g) Instructing jury. In a civil action or proceeding, the court shall instruct the jury to accept as conclusive any fact judicially noticed. In a criminal case, the court shall instruct the jury that it may, but is not required to, accept as conclusive any fact judicially noticed.

The Advisory Committee sought to limit the rule to that aspect of judicial notice intrinsic to the law of evidence by using the word "adjudicative" in the title of the rule. The Committee

---

[1] *See* **Treatise** at ¶¶ 201[01]–[02].

[2] United States v. Gould, 536 F.2d 216, 219–20 (8th Cir. 1976) (the reach of Rule 201 extends only to adjudicative facts, not legislative facts; the court described legislative facts as "established truths, facts or pronouncements that do not change from case to case but apply universally, while adjudicative facts are those developed in a particular case"; citing **Treatise**).

used the term in the sense proposed by Professor Kenneth Culp Davis, the originator of the terminology. Professor Davis wrote:

adjudicative facts are those to which the law is applied in the process of adjudication. They are the facts that normally go to a jury in a jury case. They relate to the parties, their activities, their properties, their business.[3]

In the body of the rule, subdivision (a) states that "[t]his rule governs only judicial notice of adjudicative facts." Facts from which the nonexistence of facts in issue can be inferred should also be subject to Rule 201. The test is really one of relevancy: might a reasonable trier find that the fact being judicially noted tends to make the existence of any material fact more or less probable?

Excluded as inappropriate subjects for formalized treatment in the Rules of Evidence are: the general knowledge and reasoning ability a judge employs in fulfilling each task; the materials a judge uses in finding, interpreting or reviewing the substantive law; the extra-record information a judge utilizes in formulating evidential hypotheses by which the admissibility and sufficiency of evidence are determined; and the non-evidence data a judge consults when ascertaining "political facts," or in carrying out a number of functions specifically excepted in Rule 1101.[4]

¶ 4.02 Facts Subject to Notice[1]

Rule 201 imposes no artificial limits on the range of facts which may be judicially noticed. The broad scope of possible notice varies with the facts and issues in each case and the evolving state of knowledge.

The obvious cost of establishing adjudicative facts in an adversary proceeding—in terms of time, energy and money— justifies dispensing with formal proof when a matter is not really disputable. Since there is no real issue of fact, the right to trial by jury is not infringed; nor is the Sixth Amendment

---

[3] Davis, "Judicial Notice," 55 Colum. L. Rev. 945, 952 (1955).

[4] For an analysis of the doctrine of judicial notice in its larger sense *see* **Treatise** at ¶¶ 200[01]–[10].

[1] *See* **Treatise** at ¶ 201[03].

right to confront witnesses abridged.[2] When facts do not possess this requisite degree of certainty, our traditional procedure has been to require proof within the framework of the adversary system. Confrontation and cross-examination are central to ascertaining the truth in our system of litigation. The narrowness of Rule 201 does not apply to stipulations; they should be encouraged to avoid wasting time with issues the parties really do not dispute.

Because the Advisory Committee omitted "propositions of generalized knowledge" as one of the types of fact subject to judicial notice, treatises—such as medical treatises—or statements in treatises cannot be admitted to prove the truth of the matter stated except as provided in Rule 803(18),[3] unless the fact satisfies one of the two tests specified in Rule 201. A generally known or verifiable fact will not be excluded because it appears in a treatise, but specialized opinion requires proof by an expert.

Rule 201 contains two different tests for determining whether a proposition of fact has attained a high enough degree of certainty so that it would be consonant with fair procedure to dispense with proof. The first, traditional test, is whether the fact is "generally known" within the community.[4] The second,

---

[2] United States v. Mentz, 840 F.2d 315, 321–23 (6th Cir. 1988) (for criminal defendants, however, the court must tread very carefully in considering requests for judicial notice, particularly as to facts constituting elements of the government's burden of proof; moreover, the cautionary instruction of Rule 201(g) must be given in all criminal cases where the court proposes to take judicial notice).

[3] See ¶ 16.08 infra, for a discussion of how learned treatises can be admitted into evidence in conjunction with the testimony of an expert witness.

[4] See Carey v. Populaton Servs. Int'l, 431 U.S. 678, 697 (1977) (in suit challenging state law restricting access of contraceptives to minors, Court took judicial notice that "with or without access to contraceptives, the incidence of sexual activity among minors is high, and the consequences of such activity are frequently devastating"); Nationalist Movement v. City of Cumming, 913 F.2d 885, 893 (11th Cir. 1990) (court took judicial notice "that plaintiff's rallies and marches are often loud and attract boisterous and sometimes violent counter-demonstrators," and that "the potential for noise and violence is great"); In re Olson, 884 F.2d 1415, 1424 n.14 (D.C. Cir. 1989) (court took judicial notice of reasonableness of $260.00 per hour billing rate of attorney whose legal abilities were "generally well known within this circuit").

more modern test, is whether the fact is verifiable by reference
to authoritative sources "so that the fact is not subject to
reasonable dispute."[5] When neither test is satisfied, judicial
notice of adjudicative facts will not be taken. Facts which are
known to the judge, but are not generally known or verifiable,
do not satisfy the Rule.[6]

In practice, the extent to which a court will be willing to take
judicial notice will depend on the type of case, and the practicalities of every-day trials. Lawyers and judges accept differences between civil and criminal trials, between bench and jury
trials, between hearings and trials where standards of probative
force are high and there is time for a full trial, and hearings
on such matters as preliminary injunctions when short cuts are
desirable to accommodate the system's need for speed. Much
more formality is required in jury trials—particularly in criminal trials—than in bench trials. In the latter case, adjournments, continuances and conferences can be used to allow the
court to instruct itself from outside sources, and rules such as
those limiting access to treatises have little applicability. What
is vital, however, even in a bench trial, is that the parties be
made aware of what the judge is using and that they be given
time to submit other information to meet what they consider
to be unreliable data.[7] In point of fact most courts are not

[5] Massachusetts v. Westcott, 431 U.S. 322 (1977) (Coast Guard records);
Knox v. Butler, 884 F.2d 849, 852, n.7 (5th Cir. 1989), *cert. denied,* 110 S.
Ct. 1828 (1990) (census records); Sinaloa Lake Owners Ass'n v. City of Simi
Valley, 882 F.2d 1398, 1403, n.2 (9th Cir. 1989), *cert. denied,* 110 S. Ct. 1317
(1990) (data on the median length of trial for complaint-to-trial).

[6] United States v. Lewis, 833 F.2d 1380, 1386 (9th Cir. 1987) (district court
judge erred in concluding that, based upon his personal knowledge of the
effects of an anesthetic upon him, the criminal defendant in this case was
not able to make a voluntary and knowing statement when she was awakened
from general anesthetic).

[7] Oneida Indian Nation of New York v. State, 691 F.2d 1070, 1086 (2nd
Cir. 1982), *cert. denied,* 110 S. Ct. 200 (1989) ("when facts or opinions found
in historical materials or secondary sources are disputed, it is error to accept
the data (however authentic) as evidence"; moreover, it was error for the trial
judge not to afford an opposing party the opportunity to present information
which might challenge the fact or the propriety of noticing it); Reed v.
Rhodes, 607 F.2d 714, 735 (6th Cir. 1979), *cert. denied sub nom.* Cleveland
Bd. of Educ. v. Reed, 445 U.S. 935 (1980) (in school desegregation action,
where trial judge used maps which may have been subject to judicial notice,

inclined to go outside the record. Where the importance of the case and their disquietude with the lawyer's presentation induces them to look at standard works, they should not be discouraged from doing so by a too narrow view of the power granted under Rule 201.

Judges should not confuse lack of information with indisputability. Unless convinced that the matter satisfies the tests of subdivision (b), the judge should seek the parties' assistance in deciding whether the matter is indisputable. If still unconvinced, the court should require proof by expert and other testimony in the usual manner, even though it considers the existence of the fact to be more probable than not.[8]

A proper analysis of the case before trial increases the likelihood that the parties will focus on the issues which will be raised in the appellate courts. A full contested record will often be more useful than the suppositions of the appellate judges. But in many cases it is simply not possible to cover all the possible factual issues which the appellate court will deem decisive. The appellate courts, of course, may remand so the facts can be developed by experts, statistical data and other means, where the trial attorneys could not reasonably predict that the issues would develop as they did on appeal. Or they may, by setting the case down for reargument or for further briefs, permit the parties to indicate why the court's assumptions are questionable.

Adequate development of the facts at the trial level in a jury case protects the party's right to have questions of fact resolved by the jury. In the non-jury case, the parties will have the benefit of cross-examination and the right to submit contrary evidence; moreover, there will be a record subject to appellate review.

---

but without saying so or complying with Rule 201, appellate court eliminated from its consideration any findings made relying on the extrajudicial information).

   [8] Oneida Indian Nation of New York v. State, 691 F.2d 1070 (2nd Cir. 1982), *cert. denied,* 110 S. Ct. 200 (1989) (discussed at n.7 *supra*).

¶ 4.03 Judicial Notice: Discretionary and Mandatory[1]

Subdivisions (c) and (d) provide that a court must take judicial notice only when a party so requests and furnishes it with the necessary information. It may, however, in its discretion take notice regardless of request.

The grant of discretionary authority does not mean, as it does in other situations, that the trial judge's determination is virtually insulated from appellate review. An appellate court is often in as good a position as the trial court to ascertain the degree of probability of a judicially noticeable fact. There is no need for the appellate court to defer to the trial judge's feel for the case. Accordingly, subdivision (b) must be read in conjunction with subdivision (f) authorizing judicial notice "at any stage of the proceedings." If the trial judge failed to notice a fact which the appellate court feels was a proper subject for judicial notice, the appellate court may notice the fact despite the grant of discretionary authority. This does not mean that "judicial notice . . . should be used as a device to correct on appeal an almost complete failure to present adequate evidence to the trial court."[2]

Appellate courts have adequate power in the reverse situation where they disagree with the trial judge's recognition of a fact. The reviewing court may reverse if it finds that the fact was neither "generally known" nor "verifiable."

There are no limitations on methods of providing the court with information enabling it to decide whether it will take judicial notice. Nor are formal requirements specified for the request to notice. If not made on the record at trial it is best to provide it in writing so that a copy can be served apprising adverse parties, thereby enabling them to make arrangements to be heard pursuant to subdivision (e).

---

[1] *See* **Treatise** at ¶ 201[04].

[2] United States v. Campbell, 351 F.2d 336, 341 (2d Cir. 1965), *cert. denied*, 383 U.S. 907 (1966) (court refused to take notice of Canadian law urged as applicable for first time on appeal).

¶ **4.04   Judicial Notice: Opportunity to Be Heard**[1]

Subdivision (e) provides that upon timely request a party will be given the opportunity to be heard on the propriety of taking judicial notice and the tenor of the matter to be noticed. If the party was not notified before notice was taken, the party must be given an opportunity to object afterwards. No formal requirements are specified for the hearing which would, of course, be conducted outside the hearing of the jury, and would generally resemble a hearing on preliminary questions of admissibility pursuant to Rule 104.

Where taking notice is requested pursuant to subdivision (d), all parties are aware that judicial notice is a possibility and can prepare to request a hearing. Where the judge takes judicial notice without request, there is an obligation on the court to notify the parties where it would not be clear to them that judicial notice was being taken.

There are undoubtedly situations where a failure to notify would conflict with constitutional guarantees of a fair trial. While in a civil case, notice of a completely indisputable fact without affording the adverse parties an opportunity to be heard would not violate the right to trial by jury, procedural fairness includes the right to notification and an opportunity to be heard. To date, the question of notification in civil cases has been raised primarily in the context of administrative law. There is no reason to set the standards for bench trials any lower than those for administrative hearings.[2]

Where the fact in question is debatable, judicial notice without notification may deprive the adversely affected party of the right to trial by jury as well, since the party will miss an opportunity to request a hearing at which rebutting information may be introduced, and subdivision (g) commands the judge to instruct a civil jury to accept as conclusive any facts judicially noticed.

---

[1] *See* **Treatise** at ¶ 201[05].

[2] Ohio Bell Tel. Co. v. Public Util. Comm'n, 301 U.S. 292 (1937) (In striking down determinations by the commission the Supreme Court declared: "[w]hen price lists or trade journals or even government reports are put in evidence upon a trial, the party against whom they are offered may see the evidence or hear it and parry its effect." *Id.* at 302.).

In a criminal case, subdivision (g) acknowledges that the scope of judicial notice is circumscribed by the constitutional protections afforded an accused.

¶ 4.05 Judicial Notice at Any Stage of the Proceedings[1]

Subdivision (f) provides that a court may take judicial notice at any stage of the proceeding. A judge may therefore dispense with formal proof of adjudicative facts at any time during the course of a litigation, however, the court must abide by the requirements of Rule 201 when doing so.

The failure or refusal of a court to take judicial notice at one stage of the proceedings does not preclude notice at a later stage. Although subdivision (f) does not so specifically state, judicial notice is permissible on appeal even if it had not been urged below, despite the usual rule limiting appeals to points raised at trial.[2]

An appellate court contemplating original judicial notice should notify the parties of its intent to take judicial notice so that the propriety of taking notice and the tenor of the matter to be noticed can be argued. The point obviously may be decisive of the appeal or the court would not be considering it. Even where the fact appears indisputable it may be fairer to allow the adversely affected party to challenge its relevancy or raise the possibility of remanding for further proof. If oral argument has already been completed, the court should at least afford the parties an opportunity to submit supplemental briefs.

---

[1] *See* **Treatise** at ¶ 201[06].

[2] In criminal cases, however, the authorization in subdivision (f) for taking judicial notice at the appellate level may, at times, come into conflict with the policy expressed in subdivision (g) that gives the jury in a criminal trial the right to disregard a judicially noted fact. *See, e.g.,* United States v. Jones, 580 F.2d 219 (6th Cir. 1978) (in a prosecution for intercepting a telephone conversation, the government failed to prove that the telephone company which had furnished the tapped phone was a common carrier as required by applicable statute, and the trial court did not instruct the jury that it could choose to take judicial notice of the character of the telephone company; appellate court held that a judgment of acquittal, after jury's verdict of guilty, had to be affirmed); this case seems extreme.

¶ 4.06   Judicial Notice: Effect of Taking in Civil Cases [1]

When subdivisions (e) and (g) of Rule 201 are read together, the following pattern of consequences of taking judicial notice emerges in civil cases.

¶ 4.06[01]   Non-Jury Cases

If the court took judicial notice without having previously notified the parties that it would do so, procedural fairness requires, and subdivision (e) provides, that the parties have an opportunity to object to the taking of notice.[2] In a bench trial, granting a hearing after notice was taken would do no harm because the objections and the evidence would be heard by the same trier. The trial court should include all facts that it has judicially noticed in its findings of fact. See Rule 52 of the Federal Rules of Civil Procedure.

¶ 4.06[02]   Jury Cases

If the judge declared the fact indisputable after a hearing pursuant to subdivision (e), permitting the jury to hear further proof would defeat the principal reason for taking judicial notice. As the Reporter of the New Jersey Supreme Court Committee on Evidence stated:

> In light of the thoroughness with which a judge should consider the taking of judicial matter in the first place, it would be a waste of time to receive evidence on the matter again; moreover, to submit an indisputable fact . . . to a jury would permit the possibility of irrational results which the judicial notice rules are designed to prevent.[1]

---

[1] *See* **Treatise** at ¶ 201[07].

[2] *Cf.* Siderius v. M.V. Amilla, 880 F.2d 662, 666–67 (2d Cir. 1989) (court distinguished between those situations "when a court takes judicial notice of facts extraneous to a record, and when it takes notice of facts that are integrally related to the record"; here, the parties to this maritime suit had incorporated the "Interclub Agreement" by reference in their Charter Party; this agreement was therefore not extraneous to the record but a part of it; a post-trial hearing on whether the agreement should be noticed was not required).

[1] Report of the New Jersey Supreme Court Committee on Evidence 37–38 (1963).

Furthermore, allowing the jury to hear evidence would destroy some of the flexibility inherent in judicial notice procedure. A jury may hear only admissible evidence, while one of the principal advantages of judicial notice is that the rules of evidence do not apply and the parties may introduce any pertinent material. It would be impossible for the jury to weigh the probative force of the evidence admitted against that considered by the judge and not admitted. Finally, the Advisory Committee felt that importing the consequences of presumptions into the law of judicial notice would affect "the substantive law to an extent and in ways largely unforeseeable." Consequently, subdivision (g) provides that the jury may not pass upon a fact once it is judicially noticed but must accept it as true for the basis of its deliberations in civil cases.

Where no hearing was held because the court did not indicate that it was planning notice, the aggrieved party's remedy is to ask for a hearing if the case is still pending, or petition for a rehearing. The party would argue that information could have been presented indicating that the fact was not a proper subject for judicial notice. This offer of proof must be made to the judge, outside the presence of the jury. See Rule 103(c). Even after a hearing has taken place on the issue, if a party is able to produce new information throwing doubt on the judge's determination, the matter of taking judicial notice should be reopened. Since the hearings and proffers take place outside the jury's presence they can be worked into odd moments of the trial day without any loss of time.

¶ 4.07 Judicial Notice: Instructions to Jury in Criminal Case [1]

Subdivision (g) provides that a judge must instruct a jury in a criminal case that it may, but need not, accept as conclusive any adjudicative fact in a case.[2] In a criminal case, therefore,

---

[1] *See* **Treatise** at ¶ 201[08].

[2] United States v. Deckard, 816 F.2d 426, 428 (8th Cir. 1987) (in prosecution for interception of telephone communications, the trial judge properly took judicial notice that interstate communications are transported over Southwestern Bell telephone lines, including telephone lines to victim's residence, where judge instructed jury, as required by Rule 201, that it could, but was not required to, accept as conclusory any fact judicially noticed).

the court's function of judicially noting facts against the defendant should be no greater than general power to comment on the evidence. See discussion in Chapter 2 *supra.*

This approach to judicial notice is analogous to the operation of presumptions in criminal cases, which leaves juries free not to find the presumed fact even though the basic fact is established beyond a reasonable doubt. The unique treatment afforded criminal cases is probably compelled by constitutional guarantees expressed in the axiom "that a verdict cannot be directed against the accused . . . with the corollary that the judge has no authority to direct the jury to find against the accused as to any element of the crime."[3]

The Advisory Committee did not intend Rule 201 to apply to the utilization of general knowledge and reasoning abilities which are part of every normal person's mental equipment. In its Notes to an earlier draft of subdivision (g) (which was ultimately enacted), the Committee stated that "[w]hile matters falling within the common fund of information supposed to be possessed by jurors need not be proved, these are not, properly speaking, adjudicative facts but an aspect of legal reasoning."[4] The Committee cites *State v. Dunn*[5] for this statement, a case in which the trial judge was held to have properly instructed that a club 22 inches long, 2½ inches wide and ¾ inch thick used to beat the victim was a "deadly weapon and that the

---

[3] Advisory Committee's Notes to subdivisions (b) and (c) of Rule 301. *See* United States v. Southard, 700 F.2d 1, 26 (1st Cir. 1983) (court held that although court could take judicial notice of the minimum driving time between New Haven and Rhode Island, the defendant's actual knowledge could not be determined solely from this judicially-noticed fact: "When the knowledge to be proved is an element of the crime it cannot be assumed, even though such assumption is reasonable. It is the personal knowledge of the defendant that must be proved.").

[4] *Cf.* United States v. Gould, 536 F.2d 216 (8th Cir. 1976) (court did not err in instructing jury that if it found confiscated substances to be cocaine hydrochloride then the applicable law classified the substance as a Schedule II Controlled Substance; this was legislative rather than adjudicative fact and consequently Rule 201(g) is inapplicable); Smith v. United States, 431 U.S. 291, 307 (1977) (in obscenity cases in addition to jurors' knowledge of community standards, state statute was part of evidence of that standard).

[5] 221 Mo. 530, 120 S.W. 1179 (1909).

defendant therefore must be assumed to have known the consequences of such use."[6]

It would not seem unreasonably burdensome for the judge to notify the parties of the impending instruction so that a hearing could be requested if they wished to debate the point. If the judge fails to notify the parties, a verdict against defendant would probably not be reversed if the appellate court found that the noticed fact was indisputable, provided that the judge made it clear to the jurors that they need not agree with his opinion but were free to draw their own conclusion.[7] However, where the judge does not inform the jurors that they are free to ignore the judicially noted fact, the principles of harmless error discussed under Rule 103 should govern, the trial court's failure being treated as error.[8]

---

[6] *Id.* 120 S.W. at 1182. That part of the *Dunn* instruction which directs the jury to presume the defendant's intent to kill is in conflict with *Sandstrom v. Montana,* 442 U.S. 510 (1979), in which the Supreme Court held unconstitutional an instruction that "the law presumes a person intends the ordinary consequences of his voluntary acts." The Court held that the instruction may have been interpreted as shifting the burden of persuasion, and therefore would have violated the Fourteenth Amendment's requirement that the state prove every element of a criminal offense beyond a reasonable doubt. *See* Chapter 5 *infra.* and, for a discussion of the constitutional issues involved in presumptions in criminal cases, *see* **Treatise** at ¶¶ 303[02]–[06].

[7] *See* United States v. Mentz, 840 F.2d 315, 322 (6th Cir. 1988) (reversible error for court in bank robbery prosecution to have instructed jury that banks in question were FDIC insured, thereby directing a verdict on an essential element of the charge; instruction erroneous according to Rule 201(g); concurring opinion would have dissented as to this point on the basis of harmless error); United States v. Jones, 580 F.2d 219, 224 (6th Cir. 1978) (the government's failure to prove the essential fact—that the tapped telephone in question was furnished by a "common carrier"—could not be cured by taking judicial notice at the appellate level; in a criminal trial, if the fact is one appropriate for judicial notice it must be submitted to the jury with instructions that the jury may disregard the fact if it so chooses; "Congress intended to preserve the jury's traditional prerogative to ignore even uncontroverted facts in reaching a verdict"; citing **Treatise**).

[8] United States v. Berrojo, 628 F.2d 368 (5th Cir. 1980) (in prosecution for possession with intent to distribute Schedule II controlled substance, where government witness identified substance as cocaine hydrochloride but government offered no proof that substance was listed on Schedule II, trial court after motion for judgment of acquittal took judicial notice that cocaine is a derivative of coca leaves and denied the motion; court without objection

charged jury that cocaine is a controlled substance; appellate court held that failure to give Rule 201(g) charge did not amount to plain error); United States v. Piggie, 622 F.2d 496 (10th Cir. 1980) (failure of court to instruct jury that it had taken judicial notice that Leavenworth Penitentiary was an area of special wartime and territorial jurisdiction of United States and that jury did not have to treat fact as conclusive did not constitute prejudice to defendant).

CHAPTER 5

Presumptions

SYNOPSIS

(Pub.819)

¶ 5.01   Overview of Presumptions

As indicated below, Congress decided to give presumptions the least weight possible. In civil cases they generally will merely shift the burden of coming forward. In criminal cases they left case law where it was, with negligible effect in federal criminal cases where the burden of proof beyond a reasonable doubt on all material elements of the crime lies with the government.

Presumptions, despite their theoretically minimal impact, still enthrall the bench and bar. In the face of codification they still create difficulties in application. Their very ambiguity makes them attractive to legislatures since they provide room for compromise with each lawmaking side gaining a sense that the rule will favor its view of which way the substantive law should lean.

For the judge and lawyer, a fundamental rule is: "never mention the word presumption to a jury." The rules of presumption are for the court: they tell the judge which side has, and has met, the burden of coming forward and which side has the burden of persuasion. All the jury has to know—if the matter gets to it—is who has the burden of persuasion. If the judge wishes to alert the jury to a legislative finding on weight of evidence, it should do so in terms of allowable inferences rather than of presumptions.

As indicated below, presumptions have no evidentiary weight. They represent purely procedural rules.

Rules 301 and 302 are the only rules on presumptions that emerged from Congress. In civil cases, Congress recognized that Rule 301 does not apply when state law governs the rule of decision in the case (see Rule 302), or Congress has created a different kind of presumption.

Proposed Rule 303, which had been promulgated by the Supreme Court, was omitted. This scheme means that at this time there is no Federal Rule of Evidence governing presumptions in criminal cases. The discussion below discusses the present status in the federal courts of presumptions in criminal cases, and the extent to which proposed Rule 303 can be relied upon as a Standard.

¶ 5.02   Presumptions in General in Civil Cases—Rule 301

¶ 5.02[01]   Definition and Procedure[1]

Rule 301 adopts one uniform rule for all presumptions in civil actions and proceedings, except those governed by state law (see Rule 302), or those as to which Congress provides otherwise.[2] The rule provides:

Rule 301

PRESUMPTIONS IN GENERAL IN CIVIL ACTIONS AND PROCEEDINGS

In all civil actions and proceedings not otherwise provided for by Act of Congress or by these rules, a presumption imposes on the party against whom it is directed the burden of going forward with the evidence, to rebut or meet the presumption, but does not shift to such party the burden of proof in the sense of the risk of nonpersuasion, which remains throughout the trial upon the party on whom it was originally cast.

The term "presumption" is used to describe a procedural rule which requires the existence of fact B (presumed fact) to be assumed when fact A (basic fact) is established unless and until a certain specified condition is fulfilled. An inference is not a presumption. In the case of an inference, the existence of B may be deduced from A by the ordinary rules of reasoning and logic; in the case of a presumption, the existence of B must initially be assumed because of a rule of procedural law.

A so-called irrebuttable presumption does not satisfy the definition of a presumption because fact B must be assumed conclusively rather than conditionally. Fact B becomes a euphemism for fact A if B is irrebuttable. An irrebuttable presumption is a rule of substantive law when B is a material proposition.

---

[1] See **Treatise** at ¶ 300[01] for discussion of different varieties of presumptions, and see ¶¶ 300[02], [03] for discussions of reasons for the creation of presumptions and policies underlying choice of a particular definition of a presumption.

[2] For a discussion of some of the Congressional statutes which establish presumptions, see **Treatise** at ¶ 301[03].

A presumption has the procedural consequence of shifting a burden of proof.[2a] From Thayer on, commentators have recognized that there are two aspects to the burden of proof—the burden of coming forward with proof and the burden of persuasion—and it is on the question of whether a presumption operates to shift only one of these burdens or both that the theorists divide into two main camps.

A presumption governed by Rule 301 operates only to shift the burden of producing evidence; it has no effect on the assignment of the burden of persuasion.[3] In other words, once the basic fact giving rise to the presumption has been established, the presumed fact must be assumed to exist until the burden of producing sufficient evidence to establish the negative of the presumed fact has been satisfied by the opponent of the presumption. Consequently, assuming no controversy about the basic fact, if the opponent produces no evidence, the party in whose favor the presumption operates is entitled to a directed verdict in a civil case.

Rule 301 does not specify how much contrary evidence must be introduced by the opponent for the presumption to be rebutted. The appropriate burden on the opponent is to produce enough evidence so that a reasonable juror could be convinced that the contrary of the presumed fact is true. An argument could be made that the burden of coming forward should vary, giving some flexibility to the rule. Two reasons militate against such a flexible standard, however

---

[2a] *Cf.* Basic Incorporated v. Levinson, — U.S. —, —, 108 S.Ct. 978, 990–91, 99 L.Ed.2d 194, 217 (1988) (in a class action alleging that defendant had made false and misleading statements in violation of Rule 10b-5, district court relied on a presumption of reliance by members of the plaintiff class on defendant's public statements to conclude that action was maintainable as a class action because common questions or fact or law predominated over particular questions pertaining to individual plaintiffs; the Court found that "[t]he presumption of reliance employed in this case is consistent with, and by facilitating Rule 10b-5 litigation, supports, the congressional policy embodied in the 1934 Act." Citing Rule 301, the Court explained: "Arising out of considerations of fairness, public policy, and probability, as well as judicial economy, presumptions are also useful devices for allocating the burdens of proof between parties.")

[3] As drafted by the Advisory Committee, presumptions would have had the effect of shifting the burden of persuasion to the opponent on the issue governed by the presumption. This view was rejected by Congress for reasons that are discussed in the **Treatise.** See Congressional Action on Rule 301. Paragraph 301[01] in the **Treatise** discusses the constitutionality of presumptions that operate to shift the burden of persuasion.

desirable it might be as a policy. First, the legislative history of the rule demonstrates that everyone concerned with drafting Rule 301, including Congress, favored a rule of uniformity and simplicity and rejected a rule that would vary depending upon the reasons underlying the creation of the particular presumption. Second, if the proponent's burden of persuasion to establish the basic facts is higher than a preponderance, the opponent's should be lower since he is concerned with establishing the contrary of the presumed fact—*i.e.,* a reciprocal. Reducing the burden of coming forward to rebut to less than enough for a reasonable jury to be persuaded of the contrary of the presumed factor attenuates the presumption's effect too greatly. Increasing it gives the presumption more weight than the drafters intended.

The word presumption should not be mentioned to the jury.[4] The court may discuss with the jury the normal inferential value of the basic fact in assisting it to decide whether it is persuaded by the proponent of the existence of the presumed fact. This does not mean that a reversal is warranted because a court slips and uses the word presumption rather than inference. It is unlikely that it will be understood by the jury in its technical sense rather than as a synonym for inference.

For example, the court should handle as follows a case in which a presumption of negligence arises from proof that a bailed article was delivered in good condition but returned in damaged condition:

(1) When insufficient evidence has been introduced to permit a reasonable juror to find no negligence by the bailor, the judge should instruct the jury: "If you find from the evidence that it is more probable than not that the bailed article was delivered in good condition, then you must find that the bailee was negligent. The burden of proof is on the bailor."

(2) When the presumption has been rebutted by evidence sufficient to support an inference by the bailee of non-negligence, the judge should instruct: "If from all the evidence you find that it is more probable that the bailee was negligent, you will find that the bailee was negligent; otherwise you will find that the bailee was not negligent. The burden of proof is on the bailor."

---

[4] Support for this statement can be derived from the legislative history of Rule 301. The House of Representatives had proposed that presumptions be treated as evidence to be considered by the jury. This proposal was rejected.

(3) Nothing prevents the judge from informing the jury that it can infer that something delivered in good condition will generally remain so in the absence of some intervening cause, or commenting at greater length on the fact that the bailee is in a better position to explain what happened than the bailor. It is probably best, however, to leave such arguments to counsel.

(*Text continued on page 5–7*)

¶ 5.02[02] Application of Rule 301[1]

Despite the fact that Rule 301 dictates one uniform rule having the incidents discussed above unless "otherwise provided for" by Congress, cases decided since the adoption of the rule indicate that there is still a considerable lack of uniformity. First, the cases reveal that the courts are not always in agreement as to whether or not Congress exercised its prerogative to adopt a different type of presumption when creating a statutory presumption;[2] such statutory presumptions may not only shift burdens of persuasion but change the weight of the burden.[3] Second, some cases dealing with presumptions do not base their holding on Rule 301. Even when the results are consistent with the rule, it is impossible to tell whether the court is aware that Rule 301 controls.[4] Finally, although Rule 301 purports to apply "in all civil actions and proceedings," a number of courts have improperly bypassed Rule 301, finding that it applies to "procedural" presumptions but not to "substantive" ones.[5]

---

[1] See **Treatise** at ¶ 301[04] for discussion of conflicting presumptions.

[2] *Compare* Presbyterian-St. Luke's Medical Center v. NLRB, 653 F.2d 450, 453 (10th Cir. 1981) (Rule 301 applicable to presumption adopted under National Labor Relations Act that a single facility bargaining unit was appropriate) *with* Big Y Foods, Inc. v. NLRB, 651 F.2d 40, 45 (1st Cir. 1981) (Rule 301 not applicable to presumption that meat department bargaining unit was appropriate in multi-department retail food store, because presumption is "substantive," rather than procedural).

[3] See, *e.g.*, United States v. Banco Cafetero Panama, 797 F.2d 1154, 1160 (2d Cir. 1986) (in forfeiture of narcotics proceeds, government need only show more than a suspicion that property was drug related, not prima facie proof; under Congressional scheme, claimant must show proceeds of bank account not traceable to drug transactions).

[4] See, *e.g.*, Texas Dep't of Community Affairs v. Burdine, 450 U.S. 248, 254, 101 S.Ct. 1089, 67 L.Ed.2d 207 (1981) (establishment of prima facie case of unlawful discrimination pursuant to Title VII creates a presumption that shifts burden of production to defendant; Court noted in footnote 8 that the function of the presumption was a traditional one, citing Rule 301).

[5] See, *e.g.*, James v. River Parishes Co., Inc., 686 F.2d 1129 (5th Cir. 1982) (holding that custodian of drifting vessel bears risk of non-persuasion that vessel was not cast adrift through negligence and that this is matter of substantive law to which Rule 301 does not apply; dissent argued that Rule 301 applies to all civil proceedings and that prior decisions were over-turned by enactment of Rule 301); Bunge Corp. v. M/V Furness Bridge, 558 F.2d 790 (5th Cir. 1977).

A careful practitioner must therefore check all cases construing the presumption in question regardless of whether the presumption is statutory or judicially created. Of course, counsel also needs to be aware of the operation of rule 301 so that appropriate request or objections can be made to the court.[6]

¶ 5.03 Presumptions Governed by State Law—Rule 302

Rule 302 recognizes that the rationale of the *Erie* decision[1] requires the effect of some presumptions in civil actions to be governed by state law.[2] Presumptions in which the presumed fact is a material proposition involve substantive law. The wording of the rule is designed to restrict the applicability of state law to the area actually encompassed by the *Erie* decision. The rule provides:

Rule 302

APPLICABILITY OF STATE LAW IN CIVIL ACTIONS AND PROCEEDINGS

In civil actions and proceedings, the effect of a presumption respecting a fact which is an element of a claim or defense as to which State law supplies the rule of decision is determined in accordance with State law.

----

[6] See, *e.g.*, Sharp v. Coopers & Lybrand, 649 F.2d 175, 186, 189 n.2 (3d Cir. 1981), *cert. denied*, 455 U.S. 938 (1982) (court upheld presumption that cast burden of production and persuasion on defendant; on appeal, defendants argued that trial court had erred in creating presumption, but did not argue that if presumption was proper, shifting burden of persuasion to defendants was improper under Rule 301; appellate court noted requirement of Rule 301, but refused to consider issue since defendant had not objected to instruction).

[1] Erie v. Tompkins, 304 U.S. 64, 58 S.Ct. 817, 82 L.Ed. 1188 (1938).

[2] The Supreme Court in a number of cases has held that rules governing burdens of proof are substantive for *Erie* purposes. See, *e.g.*, Dick v. New York Life Ins. Co., 359 U.S. 437, 446, 79 S.Ct. 921, 3 L.Ed.2d 935 (1959) ("Under the Erie rule presumptions (and their effects) and burden of proof are 'substantive' "); Palmer v. Hoffman, 318 U.S 109, 63 S.Ct. 477, 87 L.Ed. 645 (1943) (federal courts in diversity cases must apply state law on burden of proof as to contributory negligence); Cities Service Oil Co. v. Dunlap, 308 U.S. 208, 60 S.Ct. 201, 84 L.Ed. 196 (1939). A rule allocating the burden of proof has an effect equivalent to a presumption that shifts the burden of proof. See **Treatise** at ¶ 300[01].

¶ 5.03[01]   State Law Supplies Rule of Decision[1]

Rule 302 applies only when "state law supplies the rule of decision." This phrase was deliberately chosen as more accurately descriptive of the requirements of *Erie* than the commonly used term "diversity cases." *Erie* does not apply to a federal claim or issue even if jurisdiction is based on diversity, but does govern a non-federal claim or issue even in non-diversity cases.[2]

When state law provides the rule of decision on the effect of a presumption where the presumed fact is an element of a claim or defense, a federal court pursuant to Rule 302 must determine what the state court would have done and act accordingly. This may be exceedingly difficult.[3] Although theoretically adhering to one particular view of presumptions, the state court may actually be applying a number of different theories and requiring a different measure of proof depending on the particular type of presumption involved.[4] Since identical situations rarely recur, the court may have difficulty in ascertaining which presumption is to apply to the particular facts at hand, or what the state court would have done in a case of first impression, or what to do with conflicting presumptions. The problem is compounded when the parties are relying on causes of action based upon both federal and state substantive law. To avoid confusing the jury, and as a matter of practical judicial administration, some discretion should be used to ignore state presumptions that are not clearly substantive.

¶ 5.03[02]   Element of Claim or Defense[1]

Some presumptions do not express a state's substantive policy;

---

[1] See **Treatise** at ¶ 302[02].

[2] See, *e.g.*, Maternally Yours, Inc. v. Your Maternity Shop, Inc., 234 F.2d 538 (2d Cir. 1956).

[3] See, *e.g.*, Melville v. American Home Assurance Co., 443 F.Supp. 1064 (E.D. Pa. 1977), *rev'd*, 584 F.2d 1306 (3d Cir. 1978) (whether to apply New York, Delaware or Pennsylvania presumption against suicide in case with multi-state contacts).

[4] See, *e.g.*, the type of problem that may arise in applying presumptions in the Uniform Commercial Code discussed in **Treatise** at ¶ 302[03].

[1] See **Treatise** at ¶ 302[01].

they are referred to as tactical. An instance is establishing the receipt of a mailed letter. Such presumptions are designed to operate tactically as rules of convenience, regardless of whether they favor plaintiff or defendant, and regardless of the nature of the case in which they are invoked. *Erie* does not require state law to be applied in such situations because the presumption operates as a minor rule of procedure, rather than as a rule of substantive law. Rule 302 embodies the substantive-procedure dichotomy by limiting the applicability of state law to situations where the presumption operates upon "a fact which is an element of a claim or defense"—that is to say, where the presumed fact is a material fact.

There may, nevertheless, be instances where the distinction between rules of substantive policy and procedural convenience remains blurred, even after a court has analyzed the reasons giving rise to the presumption. In case of doubt, the policy embodied in Rule 302 suggests the application of federal rather than state law, since the drafters of the rule deliberately chose to interpret the *Erie* doctrine as narrowly as possible.

¶ 5.04　　Presumptions in Criminal Cases—Standard 303

¶ 5.04[01]　　In General[1]

In criminal cases, theories must yield to constitutional considerations when a presumption is directed against an accused.[2] Although in a civil case, a presumption operates as a rule of procedure that requires a "presumed" fact to be found once the "basic" fact is established, in a criminal case, Standard 303 circumscribes a presumption to a much more limited effect: once the "basic" fact is established, an inference may, rather than must, be drawn that the "presumed" fact also exists. The procedural device created in Standard 303 does not meet the usual criteria of a presumption. Even if the defendant offers no evidence contrary to the presumed

---

[1] See **Treatise** at ¶ 303[01].

[2] Presumptions against the government should be governed by Rule 301 practice since the constitutional limitations which underlie the adoption of Standard 303 apply only in the case of an accused.

fact, the court may refuse to submit the case to the jury, or if it does, the jury may refuse to convict.

Standard 303 is designed to instruct federal judges in the use of federal statutes in federal criminal cases. They should follow the standard. In construing state statutes applied by state judges more tolerance in accepting conduct not appropriate for federal judges is allowed.

Standard 303 provides:

SUPREME COURT STANDARD 303—PRESUMPTIONS IN CRIMINAL CASES

(a) Scope. Except as otherwise provided by Act of Congress, in criminal cases, presumptions against an accused, recognized at common law or created by statute, including statutory provisions that certain facts are prima facie evidence of other facts or of guilt, are governed by this rule.

(b) Submission to Jury. The judge is not authorized to direct the jury to find a presumed fact against the accused. When the presumed fact establishes guilt or is an element of the offense or negatives a defense, the judge may submit the question of guilt or of the existence of the presumed fact to the jury, if, but only if, a reasonable juror on the evidence as a whole, including the evidence of the basic facts, could find the guilt or the presumed fact beyond a reasonable doubt. When the presumed fact has a lesser effect, its existence may be submitted to the jury if the basic facts are supported by substantial evidence, or are otherwise established, unless the evidence as a whole negatives the existence of the presumed fact.

(c) Instructing the Jury. Whenever the existence of a presumed fact against the accused is submitted to the jury, the judge shall give an instruction that the law declares that the jury may regard the basic facts as sufficient evidence of the presumed fact but does not require it to do so. In addition, if the presumed fact establishes guilt or is an element of the offense or negatives a defense, the judge shall instruct the jury that its existence must, on all the evidence, be proved beyond a reasonable doubt.

The existence of a presumption may still affect the outcome of a criminal case in two ways: (1) in a borderline case a trial court may be influenced by the legislative judgment of Congress to submit a basic fact to a jury which it would not have submitted as merely circumstantial evidence of the presumed fact. The appellate court may, of course, reverse on the ground that the jury could not have found the presumed fact from the basic fact beyond a reasonable doubt (a requirement discussed below), but it too may defer to the Congressional finding. (2) Insofar as the trial court refers to the presumption (using the word inference) in instructing the jury, the jury may be influenced by hearing that the court (expressing Congressional will) considers proof of the basic fact sufficient evidence to convict of the charged crime. Though both of these effects are difficult to evaluate since their impact is subjective and psychological, the existence of a statutory presumption probably does enhance the value of a basic fact for the prosecution beyond its purely inferential significance.

The constitutional limitations on the impact of presumptions in criminal cases have been spelled out by the Supreme Court in a number of cases,[3] some of which were decided after Standard 303 was drafted by the Advisory Committee.[4] The Court has exercised control over the operation of presumptions in criminal cases by means of the "rational connection" test, restrictions on shifting the burden of proof to an accused, and requirements for instructing the jury. These mechanisms are discussed below.

The Supreme Court's decisions reveal the sensitivity of the drafters of Standard 303 to those issues which have emerged as constitutionally significant. With one possible caveat discussed below—the burden required for proof of the basic fact—Standard 303 satisfies constitutional requirements, and should be followed by the lower federal courts until advised to the contrary by Congress or the Supreme Court.

¶ 5.04[02]   Scope of Standard 303; Tactical Presumptions[1]

Standard 303 accords identical treatment to statutory and non-statutory presumptions, and recognizes a variety of statutory patterns as establishing presumptions. A typical provision, which the Advisory Committee had in mind as within the compass of the Standard, is one that provides that proof of a specific fact (such as possession or presence) is sufficient to authorize conviction.

---

[3] Pre-1975 Supreme Court cases are discussed in the **Treatise** at ¶¶ 303[02]–[04].

[4] Post-1975 Supreme Court cases are discussed in the **Treatise** at ¶ 303[05].

[1] See **Treatise** at ¶¶ 303[01], [02].

Equally the concern of Standard 303 were provisions that add the qualification "unless the defendant explains the possession [or presence] to the satisfaction of the jury," and provisions that make possession evidence of a particular element of a crime. The Standard is expressly applicable when a statute provides "that certain facts are prima facie evidence of other facts or of guilt."

Subdivisions (b) and (c) accord different treatment to those presumptions upon which the prosecution relies as establishing guilt or negating a defense, and those presumptions that are merely tactical in nature. Non-tactical presumptions may not be submitted to the jury unless a reasonable jury could find the presumed fact (through normal inferential analysis) from the basic fact beyond a reasonable doubt (subdivision b), and the jury must be so instructed (subdivision c). See discussion below.

Standard 303 is silent as to any requisite connection between the basic fact and the presumed proposition of fact when the presumption is merely tactical in nature (as, for example, a presumption that a letter mailed by one codefendant was received by another to show knowledge of an event). The court still must be satisfied that there is "substantial" evidence of the basic proposition of facts, or that they "are otherwise established," and that the evidence as a whole does not "negative[] the existence of the presumed fact." Furthermore, even in the case of a tactical presumption, the court must instruct the jury that it may, but need not, regard the basic facts as sufficient evidence of the presumed fact.

¶ 5.04[03]   The Rational Connection Test[1]

[a]   The Supreme Court's Position

In a series of decisions predating the promulgation of Standard 303, the Supreme Court had held that there must be a "rational connection" between the basic fact and the presumed fact in order for a presumption to pass constitutional muster.[2] Rational connec-

---

[1] See **Treatise** at ¶¶ 303[02], [05].

[2] See, *e.g,* Barnes v. United States, 412 U.S. 837, 93 S.Ct. 2359, 37 L.Ed.2d 380 (1973); Turner v. United States, 396 U.S. 398, 90 S.Ct. 642, 24 L.Ed.2d 610 (1970); Leary v. United States, 395 U.S. 6, 89 S.Ct. 1532, 23 L.Ed.2d 57 (1969);

tion, according to the Court, meant that there had to be a connection between the basic fact and the presumed fact "in common experience."[3] It was not, however, clear from the Court's opinions whether the presumed proposition of fact must be inferable from the basic propositon of fact beyond a reasonable doubt, or whether the constitutional standard is met if the basic fact is more likely than not to support an inference of the truth of the presumed proposition.

In 1979, the Supreme Court returned to this issue in *County Court of Ulster County v. Allen,*[4] and muddied the waters. It avoided addressing the problem by treating the presumption as an inference which was not subject to the rules of presumptions. Inference type presumptions were called "permissible presumptions" and what standard 303 refers to as presumptions were called "mandatory presumptions."

Allen was a case which challenged the constitutionality of a New York statute providing that, with certain exceptions, the presence of a firearm in an automobile is presumptive evidence of its illegal possession by all the occupants of the vehicle. The evidence against defendants was strong and supported a verdict with or without the statutory presumption on normal inferential grounds. Four persons, three adult males and a sixteen year-old girl, had been convicted of possession of two loaded firearms. The guns, protruding from the handbag of the girl, were said to be in plain view when a police officer stopped the car in which the four were

---

United States v. Romano, 382 U.S. 136, 86 S.Ct. 279, 15 L.Ed.2d 210 (1965); United States v. Gainey, 380 U.S. 63, 85 S.Ct 754, 13 L.Ed. 2d 658 (1965); Tot v. United States, 319 U.S. 463, 63 S.Ct. 1241, 87 L.Ed. 1519 (1943).

[3] Tot v. United States, 319 U.S. 463, 468, 63 S.Ct. 1241, 87 L.Ed. 1722 (1943). See, *e.g.,* United States v. Romano, 382 U.S. 136, 141, 144, 86 S.Ct. 279, 15 L.Ed.2d 210 (1965) (Court struck down statute which provided that presence at an illegal still is sufficient to authorize conviction for possession of still; Court had previously in United States v. Gainey, 380 U.S. 63, 85 S.Ct 754, 13 L.Ed.2d 658 (1965), approved statute which provided that same basic fact of presence was sufficient to authorize conviction for carrying on the business of distilling without giving bond; Court explained that "anyone present at the site is very probably connected with the illegal enterprise . . . [b]ut presence tells us nothing about what the defendant's specific function was . . . [and] its connection with possession is too tenuous to permit a reasonable inference of guilt . . . ").

[4] 442 U.S. 140, 99 S.Ct. 2213, 60 L.Ed.2d 777 (1979).

riding for speeding. Counsel for all four defendants objected to the introduction of the handguns into evidence on the ground that the state had not adequately demonstrated a connection between the defendants and the guns. The state trial court overruled the objection and the defendants were convicted. The case reached the Supreme Court after a writ of habeas corpus had been granted on the ground that the statute was unconstitutional.

In upholding the constitutionality of the statute, a plurality of the Court distinguished between "permissive" and "mandatory" presumptions, and held that only mandatory presumptions have to meet a reasonable doubt standard. The opinion for the Court set forth the following definitions:

> [T]he entirely permissive inference or presumption . . . allows—but does not require—the trier of fact to infer the elemental fact from proof by the prosecutor of the basic one and . . . places no burden of any kind on the defendant. . . . A mandatory presumption . . . tells the trier that he or they must find the elemental fact upon proof of the basic fact, at least until the defendant has come forward with some evidence to rebut the presumed connection between the two facts.[5]

The plurality in *Allen* also stated that the classification of a presumption as permissive or mandatory depends upon the instructions the court gives to the jury. After looking at these instructions, the plurality concluded that the New York statutory presumption at issue in *Allen* "gave rise to a permissible inference available only in certain circumstances, rather than a mandatory conclusion of possession . . . ."[6] When the prosecution utilizes a mandatory presumption, it may not rest its case entirely on the presumption "unless the fact proved is sufficient to support the inference of guilt beyond a reasonable doubt."[7] When, however, as in *Allen,* the prosecution relies on a permissive presumption—i.e., inference—the presumed fact need only be more likely than not to

---

[5] 442 U.S. at 157. This analysis of the effect of a "mandatory presumption" seems incorrect insofar as federal prosecutions are involved, since the court is never authorized to direct the jury to find for the prosecution on a material proposition. Perhaps the court was thinking of a form of affirmative defense or treatment by some states of insanity. It is also incorrect since the rules of presumption are designed to control judges, not juries.

[6] *Id.* at 161.

[7] *Id.* at 167.

flow from the basic fact, "[a]s long as it is clear that the presumption is not the sole and sufficient basis for a finding of guilt."[8] The beyond a reasonable doubt standard is apparently applicable when the prosecution relies solely on a presumption.

To determine whether the permissive presumption in question satisfies the more likely than not standard, the court must look to the evidence presented in the case before it, rather than to the general experience of the community or the validity of the legislative findings.[9] A review of the evidence persuaded the Court that in this case the presumption (or, under our analysis, inference) of possession was "entirely rational."[10]

[b] The 303 Standard

Standard 303 more than satisfies the rational connection test because it employs a beyond the reasonable doubt standard for all presumptions, other than those that are merely tactical, instead of the lesser more likely than not standard authorized by *Allen* for permissive presumptions.

¶ 5.04[04] Instructing the Jury[1]

[a] The Supreme Court's Position

The Supreme Court's opinion in the *Allen* case, discussed above, has made the judge's instructions to the jury a crucial component of the constitutionality of presumptions. The Court perceived a significant distinction between what the Court termed mandatory and permissive presumptions, and rested the determination of which category a presumption falls into almost entirely on the formulation of the jury instructions.[2]

---

[8] *Id.*

[9] *Id.* at 162–63. As applied to the Allen case, the Court noted such factors as the age of the girl, the size of the handbag and guns, the driver's easy access to the guns, and the presence of older men who were not hitchhikers or other casual passengers.

[10] *Id.* at 163.

[1] See **Treatise** at ¶¶ 303[04], [06].

[2] The Court stated: "In deciding what type of inference or presumption is in-

In cases decided subsequently to *Allen,* the Court has continued to stress the importance of instructions to the jury. In *Sandstrom v. Montana,*[3] the Court insisted on "careful attention to the words actually spoken to the jury,"[4] and in *Francis v. Franklin,*[5] the Court found the crucial question to be "what a reasonable juror could have understood the charge as meaning."[6] It is not, however, entirely clear from looking at the instructions that were given in the cases decided by the Supreme Court precisely which words need to be used by the charging judge to ensure that the jury understands that it need not find the presumed fact.[7] What seems clear is that a federal judge (and a well advised state judge) should not use the word "presumption" in charging the jury. It should also instruct the jury that the burden is on the prosecution to prove each element of the crime by proof beyond a reasonable doubt.[8]

volved in a case, the jury instructions will generally be controlling, although their interpretation may require recourse to the statute involved." County Court of Ulster County v. Allen, 442 U.S. 140, 157 n.16, 99 S.Ct. 2213, 60 L.Ed.2d 777 (1979).

[3] 442 U.S. 510, 99 S.Ct. 2450, 61 L.Ed.2d 39 (1979).

[4] 442 U.S. at 514.

[5] 471 U.S. 307, 105 S.Ct. 1965, 85 L.Ed.2d 344 (1985).

[6] 105 S.Ct at 1972.

[7] Some of the instructions in the *Allen* case itself could have been understood to mean that the jury must find possession unless the defendant comes forward with some rebuttal evidence—the definition of a mandatory rather than a permissive presumption. See, *e.g.,* County Court of Ulster County v. Allen, 442 U.S. 140, 161, n.20 ("In other words, those presumptions or this latter presumption upon proof of the presence of the machine gun and the hand weapons, you may infer and draw a conclusion that such prohibited weapon was possessed by each of the defendants who occupied the automobile at the time when such instruments were found. The presumption or presumptions is effective only so long as there is no substantial evidence contradicting the conclusion flowing from the presumption, and the presumption is said to disappear when such contradictory evidence is adduced."). Although the Court has indicated that the jury charge has to be taken as a whole in determining what a reasonable juror would have understood, there has been considerable disagreement among the Justices in determining the impact of any particular jury charge. See, *e.g.,* Francis v. Franklin, 471 U.S. 307, 105 S.Ct. 1965, 85 L.Ed.2d 344 (1985) (5–4 decision).

[8] The Court had indicated in a footnote in United States v. Gainey, 380 U.S. 63, 70–71, n.7, 85 S.Ct. 754, 13 L.Ed.2d 658 (1965), that "the better practice would be to instruct the jurors that they may draw the inference unless the evidence in the case provides a satisfactory explanation for the defendant's presence at the

[b]   The 303 Standard

Subdivision (c) of Standard 303 clearly requires a federal judge to instruct the jury that it may decline to regard the basic facts as sufficient evidence of the presumed fact. The judge is also required to instruct the jury that, except in the case of a purely tactical presumption, it must make its own finding that the presumed fact exists beyond a reasonable doubt. These instructions will satisfy the constitutional concerns expressed in *Allen* in all cases where the particular facts compel the conclusion that the prosecution was not relying solely on the presumption. This will usually be the case since the presumed fact is very likely to have some probability relationship to the basic facts; that is often why the presumption was created in the first place.

If, however, after looking at all of the facts, it appears that the prosecution relied solely upon the permissive presumption, according to *Allen,* the basic facts have to give rise to the presumed fact beyond a reasonable doubt. In such a situation Standard 303 may perhaps not afford sufficient constitutional protection because it does not require an instruction to the jury directing it to find the basic facts beyond a reasonable doubt. Such an instruction should be given in federal prosecutions.[9]

¶ 5.04[05]   Shifting Burdens of Proof[1]

[a]   The Supreme Court's Position

Considerable uncertainty existed prior to the promulgation of Standard 303 as to whether a presumption in a criminal case could constitutionally fulfill its usual civil case function of shifting either

---

still, omitting any explicit reference to the statute itself in the charge." In County Court of Ulster County v. Allen, 442 U.S. 140, 99 S.Ct. 2213, 60 L.Ed.2d 777 (1979), the trial court had informed the jurors that a presumption exists in the New York Penal Law.

[9] Hawaii and Oregon, which adopted rules governing criminal presumptions after the Supreme Court's decisions in *Allen* and *Sandstrom,* require the basic facts to be proved beyond a reasonable doubt. See Hawaii Evidence Rule 306; Oregon Evidence Rule 309.

[1] See **Treatise** at ¶¶ 303[03], [04].

the burden of production or the burden of persuasion to the party against whom the presumption operates when the party is the accused. Traditionally, the law had recognized that not every element which might conceivably affect the outcome of a case rests initially with the prosecution. Affirmative defenses existed which required the defendant, rather than the prosecution, to produce evidence on particular issues, or even to persuade the jury with respect to them. A presumption has identical procedural consequences, although not until the basic fact is established. Nevertheless, language in the Supreme Court's 1965 opinion in *United States v. Gainey*[2] suggested that presumptions shifting the burden of disproof to the accused might be unconstitutional. The Court was silent as to the theoretical analogy between presumptions and affirmative defenses.

Cases decided by the Supreme Court since the promulgation of Standard 303 have not clarified the relationship between presumptions and affirmative defenses. In a series of cases dealing with a state's allocation of a burden of persuasion to the defendant via an affirmative defense, the Court declined to hold that affirmative defenses may never be shifted to a defendant. Instead, the Court adopted a formalistic test that disposed of the cases before it, but established no standard by which to test the constitutionality of affirmative defenses.

In *Mullaney v. Wilbur*,[3] the Court had reversed a Maine murder conviction. The jury had been instructed that were it to find the homicide both intentional and unlawful, then malice aforethought, essential to a finding of murder as opposed to manslaughter, was to be conclusively implied unless the accused proved by a fair preponderance of the evidence that he acted in the heat of passion. Noting that Maine imposed very different penalties for murder and manslaughter, the Court explained that it could not "dra[w] this distinction, while refusing to require the prosecution to establish beyond a reasonable doubt the fact upon which it turns."[4] Two years later, in *Patterson v. New York*,[5] the

---

[2] 380 U.S. 63, 68, 85 S.Ct. 754, 13 L.Ed.2d 658 (1965) (existence of basic fact does not require court to submit case to jury, or jury to convict).

[3] 421 U.S. 684, 95 S.Ct. 188, 44 L.Ed.2d 508 (1975).

[4] 421 U.S. at 698. The Court explained that "Maine denigrates the interests

Court upheld a New York statute which defined second degree murder as an intentional killing, and allowed the defendant to reduce the homicide to the less culpable crime of manslaughter if he proved by a preponderance of the evidence that he had acted under "extreme emotional disturbance." The majority explained that unlike the Maine statute, the New York provision does not require the prosecution to prove malice aforethought: New York's affirmative defense "does not serve to negative any acts of the crime which the State is to prove in order to convict for murder. It constitutes a separate issue on which the defendant is required to carry the burden of persuasion."[6] The *Patterson* opinion ruled out interpreting *Mullaney* to mean that the prosecution has the burden of proving every fact that bears on culpability.

At this time, therefore, it appears that a state generally will be able to require a defendant to prove some factor bearing on guilt, provided the definition of the crime does not require the prosecution to prove the nonexistence of that factor. To be sure, the *Patterson* majority conceded that there is some constitutional limit beyond which a legislature may not go in shifting affirmative defenses to a defendant, regardless of how it goes about defining crimes. But it failed to indicate how those limits may be found. Allocating the affirmative defense of insanity to the defendant has been upheld as constitutional.[7] The Court has also held in *Martin v. Ohio*[8] that the burden of proving self-defense may be placed on a defendant in a homicide case pursuant to a statute that, according to

---

found critical in Winship." In *In re* Winship, 397 U.S. 358, 364, 90 S.Ct. 1068, 25 L.Ed.2d 368 (1970), the Court had stated that "the Due Process Clause protects the accused against conviction upon proof beyond a reasonable doubt of every fact necessary to constitute the crime with which he is charged."

[5] 432 U.S. 197, 97 S.Ct. 2319, 53 L.Ed.2d 281 (1977).

[6] 432 U.S. at 207.

[7] In Riviera v. Delaware, 429 U.S. 877, 97 S.Ct. 226, 50 L.Ed.2d 160 (1976), the Supreme Court dismissed, for want of a substantial federal question, an appeal challenging the placement of the burden of insanity on defendant. An earlier decision of the Court had upheld an Oregon statute requiring defendant to prove insanity beyond a reasonable doubt. Leland v. Oregon, 343 U.S. 790, 72 S.Ct. 1002, 96 L.Ed. 1302 (1953).

[8] 107 S.Ct. 1098 (1987).

the state's courts does not require the prosecution to prove unlawfulness.[9]

Although the *Mullaney-Patterson* line of cases allow the burden of proof to be placed on the defendant under the circumstances indicated above, the Supreme Court's decisions on presumptions would bar allocating a functionally identical burden to the defendant by means of a presumption. Suppose, for instance, that a statute defines first-degree robbery as a robbery committed with what *appears* to be a firearm, and permits defendant to prove as an affirmative defense by a preponderance of the evidence that the firearm was not loaded, thereby reducing the crime to second-degree robbery. The constitutionality of such a statute was upheld by the Second Circuit in *Farrell v. Czartnetzky,*[10] as not violating *Mullaney* or *Patterson.*

Suppose, however, that the legislature had instead chosen to define first-degree robbery as a robbery committed with a loaded weapon, and had further provided that when what appears to be a firearm is displayed in the course of committing a robbery, it will be presumed to be loaded unless the contrary is shown. Such a statute would suffer from a double infirmity. It would be invalidated under the burden of proof line of cases because it shifts to the defendant the proof of a factor—the gun was not loaded—the non-existence of which the prosecution is required to prove as an element of the crime.[11] It might also be invalidated under the Court's presumption line of cases, because for a mandatory presumption to be constitutional, the presumed fact—the gun was loaded—must flow from the basic fact—the gun was displayed during a robbery—beyond a reasonable doubt.[12] Whether any such inference could be drawn beyond a reasonable doubt is questionable considering the number of robberies committed with

---

[9] *Id.* at 1103 (5-4 opinion; majority and dissent disagreed on whether elements of aggravated murder and self-defense overlap, and on the degree of deference to be given to a state's judgment).

[10] 566 F.2d 381 (2d Cir. 1977), *cert. denied,* 434 U.S. 1077 (1978).

[11] See Sandstrom v. Montana, 442 U.S. 510, 99 S.Ct. 2450, 61 L.Ed.2d 39 (1979) (presumption unconstitutional that relieves prosecution from proving intent). But *cf.* Rose v. Clark, 106 S.Ct. 3101, 92 L.Ed.2d 460 (1986) (a *Sandstrom* error may be harmless).

[12] See discussion of *Allen* case, *supra.*

what turn out to be water pistols, cap guns and starter pistols, as well as authentic, but unloaded, guns. Of course, in the affirmative defense case, the legislature has chosen to penalize using a firearm that *appears* to be loaded, whereas in the presumption case, first-degree robbery has been defined as using a gun that *is* loaded. Functionally, however, the result in both cases would be the same. The jury would find the defendant guilty of first-degree robbery if it believed that he committed the robbery, unless he came forward with a satisfactory explanation about the gun not being loaded.

Constitutional distinctions should not be based on technicalities in draftsmanship that do not affect the merits. Yet *Patterson* has the advantage of requiring the legislature to directly confront the political and policy problems of what the definition of the crime and defenses should be. There is a difference between "appears to be loaded" and "is loaded." Guns of the latter type can kill, while guns of the former type merely intimidate.

[b] The 303 Standard

The Supreme Court's burden of proof cases have no bearing on criminal presumptions governed by a rule such as that set forth in Standard 303, because the Standard does not shift either the burden of production or persuasion to the defendant. Presumptions will not be able to play a greater role in criminal cases until the decisions on presumptions are harmonized with the decisions on burdens of proof.

CHAPTER 6

Relevancy Generally

SYNOPSIS

(Pub.819)

¶ 6.01   Definition of Relevant Evidence—Rule 401

¶ 6.01[01]   Nature of Concept[1]

The concept of relevancy is basic to the law of evidence; it is the cornerstone on which any rational system of evidence rests. Without regard to any other rules or considerations, an item of evidence cannot be admitted unless it meets the test of relevancy. Rule 401 is, therefore, the foundation on which the Federal Rules of Evidence rest. The rule provides:

Rule 401

DEFINITION OF "RELEVANT EVIDENCE"

"Relevant evidence" means evidence having any tendency to make the existence of any fact that is of consequence to the determination of the action more probable or less probable than it would be without the evidence.

The nature of the concept of relevancy is such as to elude exact definition. "Relevancy," as the Advisory Committee notes, "is not an inherent characteristic of any item of evidence but exists only as a relationship between an item of evidence and a matter properly provable in the case." According to Rule 401, relevancy is a relationship between a proffered item of evidence and a "fact that is of consequence to the determination of the action". Although some situations discussed below recur with sufficient frequency to permit formulation of particular rules of relationship, most cases do not fall into any set pattern and must be considered on an ad hoc basis. Rule 401 was designed as a general guide for handling such cases. Rules 404 through 412 provide more particular guidance as to relevancy with respect to recurrent fact patterns which also entail considerations of substantive policy. See Chapter 7, *infra*.

In some situations, the relevancy of an item of evidence depends upon the existence of a particular preliminary fact. This category of relevancy raises questions of the judge-jury relationship and is discussed as an aspect of Rule 104(a) in Chapter 3, *infra*.

---

[1] See **Treatise** at ¶ 401[01]–[02]

¶ 6.01[02]　　Consequential or Material Fact[1]

The Rules themselves are not consistent in their use of terminology. This is particularly true of what we refer to in this volume as a material proposition of fact, following Professor Jerome Michael's approach.[2] This is the ultimate proposition of fact being proved that is required by the rule of substantive law to make out a prima facie case. In Rule 401 it is referred to as a "fact that is of consequence to the determination of the action" and in Rule 405(b) as "an essential element of a charge, claim, or defense." In the **Treatise** it is referred to from time to time as a "material" or "consequential" or "material, consequential" fact and sometimes as the "ultimate fact in issue." Whether or not a proposition of fact is material—*i.e.,* of consequence—is determined not by the rules of evidence but by substantive law. In a diversity case, this means that the federal court will have to look to applicable state law because of the *Erie* rule.[3] Every legal controversy is governed by a rule of substantive law which may be represented in syllogistic terms. The major premise embodies the rule of substantive law controlling the litigation, the minor premise represents the case specific examples of these general terms, and the conclusion is that the pleader is entitled to a legal remedy to be embodied in a judgment of the court.

Although an understanding of the concept that what is consequential or material controls what is provable in a case is crucial for analytical purposes, the idea is implied in the definition of relevancy. It need not, therefore, be made the basis of a separate ob-

----

[1] See **Treatise** at ¶ 401[03].

[2] For the most systematic discussion, see Michael and Adler, The Nature of Judicial Proof (1931); Michael and Adler, The Trial of An Issue of Fact (1934) (reprinted in 34 Colum. L. Rev. 1224, 1252 (1934)); Michael, "The Basic Rules of Pleading," 5 Record of the Assoc. of the Bar of the City of New York 175 (1950).

[3] See, *e.g.,* Greiner v. Volkswagenwerk Aktiengesellschaft, 540 F.2d 85 (3d Cir. 1976) (whether evidence that automobile driver had been drinking was admissible pursuant to Pennsylvania law). See also Conway v. Chemical Leaman Tank Lines, Inc., 540 F.2d 837, 838 (5th Cir. 1976) (error to exclude evidence that widow had remarried in wrongful death action where fact of remarriage would be admissible by statute in state court; statute constitutes "one of those rare evidentiary rules which is so bound up with state substantive law that federal courts sitting in Texas should accord it the same treatment as state courts in order to give full effect to Texas' substantive policy"). See also **Treatise** at ¶ 110l[02].

jection where evidence fails to relate to a consequential fact. This is so because the definition of relevancy posits that one term of the relationship is, as Rule 401 indicates, a "fact of consequence to the determination of the action." If an item of evidence tends to prove a fact not of consequence to the determination of the action, it is, therefore, according to the terminology of the Federal Rules, irrelevant.[4]

¶ 6.01[03]   Credibility; Evidential Hypothesis[1]

Evidence that does not relate to any proposition of substantive law that must be proved may be admitted in order to evaluate the credibility of witnesses.[2] It has been suggested that, at least when there is other evidence to that effect, a jury may draw a negative inference from disbelief of the witness.[3] The test here is not

---

[4] See, *e.g.,* United States v. Hall, 653 F.2d 1002, 1005–6 (5th Cir. 1981) (in prosecution for narcotics conspiracy and possession with intent to distribute, where defendant's counsel stressed lack of physical evidence, testimony of drug enforcement agent who had no connection with the case regarding the general problems the government has in obtaining physical evidence "had no tendency whatsoever to make the existence of any fact of consequence to the government's case in chief either more or less probable than it would have been without his testimony;" cites 401 and **Treatise**); United States v. Hyman, 741 F.2d 906, 913–14 (7th Cir. 1984) (in affirming defendant's conviction for conspiracy, possession and sale of stolen goods, court of appeals found no error in exclusion of evidence proffered by defendant regarding market prices for different types of steel; excluded evidence dealt with prices for types other than galvanized, which was the type stolen, and thus failed to meet the threshold requirement of relevance).

[1] See **Treatise** at ¶ 401[05], [09].

[2] See, *e.g.,* Berkey Photo, Inc. v. Eastman Kodak Co., 603 F.2d 263, 305–08 (2d Cir. 1979), *cert. denied,* 444 U.S. 1093 (1980) (destruction or concealment of documents unfavorable to defendant's case by attorney and expert for defendant; extensive analysis of relevancy).

[3] See Dyer v. MacDougall, 201 F.2d 265, 268–69 (2d Cir. 1952) (Judge Learned Hand). See also Doe v. New York City Department of Social Services, 649 F.2d 134, 149 (2d Cir. 1981) (in action against agency which placed plaintiff in foster home for damages she suffered as a result of child abuse, including forced sexual relations with foster father, trial judge elicited information that plaintiff had recently borne an out-of-wedlock child; court found that while such evidence presumably is relevant to damages showing that plaintiff's capacity to perform and enjoy sex was not greatly harmed, "such a conception of relevancy [is] highly attenuated and of dubious validity;" furthermore there should have been caution-

whether the proffered evidence tends directly to prove or disprove any consequential fact, but whether it will aid the court or jury in evaluating the probative value of other evidence offered to affect the probability of the existence of a consequential fact.[4]

Evidence may also be admissible to assist the juror in evaluating the validity of an evidential hypothesis used in drawing an inference (through deductive reasoning) from evidence introduced in the trial to a consequential fact.[5] Such information is normally supplied by the trier's own general knowledge of life; it results from inductive reasoning. An evidential hypothesis may also be supplied by experts and may require evidence directed to its proof or disproof. See discussion of Rules 702 and 703 in Chapter 13, *infra.* Where the hypothesis can be demonstrated beyond dispute it may be a matter for judicial notice. See discussion of Rule 201 in Chapter 4, *supra.*

¶ 6.01[04]　Altering the Probabilities[1]

Whether the relevancy relationship exists also depends, in the words of Rule 401, on whether the proffered evidence has "any

---

ary instruction that her sexual conduct should not be taken as bearing on credibility).

[4] United States v. Iaconetti, 406 F.Supp 554, 557 (E.D.N.Y.), *aff'd,* 540 F.2d 574 (2d Cir. 1976), *cert. denied,* 429 U.S. 1041 (1977) (evidence that witness reported alleged bribe to business partner is relevant as reinforcing witness' credibility); United States v. Robinson, 530 F.2d 1076, 1079 (D.C. Cir. 1976). See also United States v. Giese, 597 F.2d 1170 (9th Cir. 1979), *cert. denied,* 444 U.S. 979 (1979) (strong disagreement among members of court as to whether evidence of the contents of books owned by defendant was relevant to credibility).

[5] See, *e.g.,* Saladino v. Winkler, 609 F.2d 1211, 1214 (7th Cir. 1979) (in civil rights action brought by motorist who was shot by policeman when he emerged from his car with a shotgun, defense was entitled to prove that plaintiff was legally intoxicated at time of incident; "evidence tends to make more probable that the plaintiff acted as the defendant contended he did or that plaintiff otherwise conducted himself in such a manner as to place the defendant reasonably in fear of his life"); Mathiesen v. Panama Canal Co., 551 F.2d 954 (5th Cir. 1977) (suit by owner of vessel involved in a collision, while being piloted by employee of defendant, for expenses incurred in settlement of a lawsuit in Holland; testimony of foreign attorneys as to likely results of Dutch litigation was relevant in determining whether settlement was reasonable).

[1] See **Treatise** at ¶¶ 401[06]–[07].

tendency to make the existence" of the fact to be proved "more probable or less probable than it would be without the evidence." Any proffered item that would appear to alter the probabilities of a consequential fact is relevant,[2] although it may be excluded because of other factors.

Any standard requiring more than an apparent altering of the probabilities has been rejected by the Committee as "unworkable and unrealistic." As the Committee notes, quoting Professor McCormick, "a brick is not a wall," and "it is not to be supposed that every witness can make a home run."[3] Unlike Rule 401's standard of logical relevancy, a standard of legal relevancy would require evidence to have more than minimum probative value in order to be admitted. Such a test confuses relevancy with the sufficiency of a party's proof enabling him to get to the jury on an issue.[4] Evidence tending to make a consequential fact "less probable" is as relevant as evidence tending to make it "more probable."[5] Either increases our knowledge and enhances the likelihood of ascertaining the truth about the fact at issue.

---

[2] United States v. Beechum, 582 F.2d 898, 913 (5th Cir. 1978), *cert. denied,* 440 U.S. 920 (1979).

[3] Falknor, "Extrinsic Policies Affecting Admissibility," 10 Rutgers L. Rev. 574, 576 (1956) (quoting Professor McBaine).

[4] United States v. Kreimer, 609 F.2d 126, 131 (5th Cir. 1980) (in prosecution for mail fraud, evidence concerning the amount realized on certain collateral had some logical tendency to support the argument that collateral was overvalued, and it was therefore relevant and admissible but it was too weak of itself to establish that the defendants did not require the collateral that they had stated each loan would require); United States v. Schipani, 289 F.Supp. 43, 56 (E.D.N.Y. 1968) (The court's function in determining relevancy is "only to decide whether a reasonable man might have his assessment of the probabilities of a material proposition changed by the piece of evidence sought to be admitted. If it may affect that evaluation it is relevant and, subject to certain other rules, admissible. . . . Even, therefore, if a juror decides that the probability is only 40% that the document referred to above is authentic, it may help him determine whether the material proposition is more probably true than not.").

[5] See, *e.g.,* Dente v. Riddell, Inc., 664 F.2d 1 (1st Cir. 1981) (in personal injury action in which plaintiff claimed permanent brain damage resulting from use of defective football helmet, which caused fatigue and depression resulting in, among other things, a diminished social life, evidence of plaintiff's sexual activity, gambling and drinking, which could have been interpreted to make plaintiff's claims less probable, was relevant); United States v. Morgan, 581 F.2d 933 (D.C.

It should be borne in mind that not every additional piece of evidence will permit the trier to approach more closely to the truth. For, if all the additional evidence is on one side and the other side is not placed before him, he will receive an unbalanced view of the matter which may result in a less accurate decision on the facts. The adversary system is intended to guard against this result. Moreover, the additional evidence may be "cumulative," that is, it may be repetitive of a line already established and the small increment of probability it adds may not warrant the time spent on introducing it. Rule 403 provides that such evidence may be excluded.

In short, the test of relevancy is whether a reasonable person might believe the probability of the truth of the consequential fact to be different if he or she knew of the proffered evidence.[6] The "probabilities are determined [in the usual case] in a most subjective and unscientific way . . . according to the trier's limited experience."[7] Precise attempts to fix probabilities in quantitative form are usually impossible because of the absence of adequate experimental data. Rule 401, by furnishing no standards for the determination of relevancy, implicitly recognizes that questions of relevancy cannot be resolved by mechanical resort to legal formulae. The court in making its determination must be allowed flexibility in drawing on its own experience to evaluate the probabilities on which relevancy turns.

Cir. 1978) (in prosecution for possession of drug with intent to distribute, where government introduced evidence of drugs found in basement, error to exclude evidence that another person was selling drugs from the house; since there was no evidence of actual sales by defendant, jury might not have drawn inference about defendant's intent to distribute had evidence suggested that a third person was the distributor).

[6] United States v. Brashier, 548 F.2d 1315, 1325 (9th Cir. 1976), *cert. denied,* 429 U.S. 1111 (1977) (quoting **Treatise**).

[7] Hart & McNaughton, "Evidence and Inference in the Law." Hayden Colloquium on Scientific Concept and Method 54 (Lerner ed. 1958). See United States v. Williams, 545 F.2d 47, 50 (8th Cir. 1976) ("The relevance of a given piece of circumstantial evidence must be determined by the trial judge in view of his or her experience, judgment and knowledge of human motivation and conduct"; citing Rule 401).

[a] Statistical Evidence

Some commentators believe that jurors should be made aware of the range of probabilities that exists with regard to an item of proof and should be instructed on how their assessment of the applicable probability would affect their conclusions. In some areas involving life expectancy, diseases, blood types and the like, judicial notice and expert witnesses can provide a numerical basis for evaluating probability, but even in such cases care must be taken in instructing the jury on the significance of such information.[8] Statistical information for which a proper foundation is laid is admissible if it makes the existence of a consequential fact more or less probable.[9] See discussion of judicial notice in Chapter 4, *supra,* and Chapter 13, *infra,* on expert witnesses.

¶ 6.01[05] How Relevancy is Determined[1]

Rule 401 is silent about the factors the court must consider in determining whether the requisite standard of probability is met.

---

[8] See United States v. Massey, 594 F.2d 676, 681 (8th Cir. 1979) (identification of hair samples; "prosecutor confused[d] the probability of concurrence of the identifying marks with the probability of mistaken identification of the bank robber") (quoting McCormick on Evidence, § 204 at 487 (E. Cleary ed. 1972)); Marx & Co., Inc. v. Diners Club, Inc., 550 F.2d 505, 511 (2d Cir.), *cert. denied,* 434 U.S. 861 (1977) (in action alleging securities fraud and breach of obligation to register stock, statistic that median time in which registration statements become effective was 70 days after filing was relevant but "should not have been given to the jury as if it were akin to a statute of limitations without regard to the particular facts").

[9] See, *e.g.,* United States v. Hickey, 596 F.2d 1082, 1089 (1st Cir.), *cert. denied,* 444 U.S. 853 (1979) (analysis of hair samples taken from ski mask and sweater found in getaway car after bank robbery and defendant's hair "while not affirmatively implicating [the defendant], 'enhanced the probability of guilt,' and was therefore probative"); Oi Lan Lee v. District Director of Immigration and Naturalization Service, 573 F.2d 592, 595 (9th Cir. 1978) (blood test which showed extreme improbability, though not impossibility, that petitioner was mother of child for whom preference status was sought properly admitted); Contemporary Mission, Inc. v. Famous Music Corporation, 557 F.2d 918, 927–28 (2d Cir. 1977) (in action for breach of contract by record company, statistics showing probabilities that plaintiff's record would have reached top ends of popularity charts should have been admitted; relevant on issue of damages).

[1] See **Treatise** at ¶ 401[01],[08].

Consequently, the appellate court's power of review is relatively limited. The court will accord the trial judge "a limited right to be wrong,"[2] and within these limits will not reverse the determination, even if it disagrees with the ruling.[3] The test the appellate court is forced to apply, since it was not present at the trial, will normally require it to assume the maximum probative force a reasonable jury might assess and the minimum prejudice to be reasonably expected.[4] Two major factors account for this limited review: first, recognition by the appellate court that the cold record cannot fully convey the trial's atmosphere and that the trial judge —attuned to nuances and intangibles to which the reviewing court is deaf—is in a better position to take cognizance of factors crucial to a just result; and second, recognition by the appellate court that it may be so difficult to determine whether a contrary ruling would have led to an appreciably better overall result that in the interests of economy, finality and judicial morale, the trial judge's determination had best be left undisturbed.

The task of the trial court in ruling on questions of relevancy is more complex because of the superior vantage point from which it assesses probative force and prejudice and because of its ability to minimize prejudice by limiting rulings, by instruction and by other techniques. It should not assume maximum prejudice and minimum probative force since it can actually observe and evaluate both with a fair degree of assurance, and it has such effective power to minimize prejudice.[5] Nor need it assume maximum probative force and minimum prejudice (although it will be aware

---

[2] Rosenberg, "Judicial Discretion," 38 The Ohio Bar 819, 823 (1965).

[3] United States v. Aulet, 618 F.2d 182, 191 (2d Cir. 1980) ("this Court is reluctant to overturn evidentiary rulings in the absence of an abuse of the district court's broad discretion in these matters."); United States v. Ashley, 555 F.2d 462, 465 (5th Cir. 1977), cert. denied, 434 U.S. 869 (1978) ("district court has wide discretion in determining relevance and materiality and its ruling will not be disturbed except for an abuse of discretion").

[4] F&S Offshore, Inc. v. K.O. Steel Castings, Inc., 662 F.2d 1104, 1107–08 (5th Cir. 1981) ("In reviewing the district court decision, an appellate court should assume the maximum probative force and the minimum prejudice to be reasonably expected"); United States v. Robinson, 560 F.2d 507 (2d Cir. 1977), cert. denied, 435 U.S. 905 (1978) (en banc) (court noted it could not review demeanor of witnesses nor assess emotional reaction of jury).

[5] See **Treatise** at ¶ 401[09] for illustrative examples.

that this is the boundary that will lead to reversal if it steps beyond it, absent an appellate finding of harmless error).

Despite the fact that the trial court's rulings are in large measure insulated from full appellate review, it is not justified in being silent on how it arrived at its decision. Whenever there is a close question it should identify and articulate the circumstances, factors, and hypotheses crucial to its ruling so that the appellate court can discern whether or not an arbitrary exercise of power adversely affected rights of the party. Discretion does not mean immunity from accountability. The court which fails to analyze and justify its decision risks being charged with arbitrariness by the bar, as well as by a reviewing court. More importantly it may deny itself the effective assistance of counsel in reaching a result necessary for a fair trial. Detailed analysis is also a prerequisite for applying Rule 403 because the court must balance the probative value of the evidence against the dangers specified in that rule to see whether or not the evidence should be admitted. See discussion of Rule 403, below.

Where relevancy is not immediately apparent, the judge and counsel should clearly identify the terms of the relevancy relationship in the particular case. That is, they should describe the item of evidence being proffered, the consequential fact to which it is directed, and the hypothesis required to infer the consequential fact from the evidence. Without this analysis it is impossible to decide how the evidence may alter the probability of the existence of the consequential fact, especially because evidence irrelevant to one proposition may be relevant to another.

If it cannot be demonstrated that an item of evidence may affect the trier's evaluation of the probability of a consequential fact, it should be excluded. Of course, information on credibility, or on the probability of an evidential hypothesis—*e.g.*, suicide is a sign of a guilty mind—will help a trier evaluate a line of proof. So will some charts, diagrams and the like used by the experts.

Except in a case where the evidence sought to be introduced is relevant on its face, the court may without error sustain an objection to its introduction if the attorney fails to explain its significance. See Chapter 2, *supra.* But it is wrong for the court not to assist the attorney, if the court is more capable of suggesting possible relevancy relationships. The court fulfills its role by helping the attorneys present their case, not by acting as a cold and impartial computer which rejects proffered proof because the attorney does not utter the right words.

¶ 6.01[06]   Recurring Problems[1]

Some types of categories of facts appear on a recurring basis in the case law to prove the same or similar issues. The Federal Rules of Evidence single out a number of areas for specific evidentiary treatment in Rules 404–412. See Chapter 7, *infra*. Other instances of recurring problems of relevancy are discussed below, as well as a few categories which are of interest because they indicate the interrelationship between relevancy disputes and the development of the substantive law.

[a]   Similar Incidents or Accidents

Evidence of prior or subsequent similar accidents is frequently offered by plaintiffs in personal injury actions as relevant to a variety of issues, such as, for instance, to show the defendant's notice,[2] magnitude of the danger involved, the defendant's ability to correct a known defect, the lack of safety for intended uses, strength of a product, the standard of care, and causation.[3]

Courts frequently state without qualification that the relevancy of such accidents depends on "whether the conditions operating to produce the prior failures were substantially similar to the occurrence in question"[4] and whether there was a close proximity in time of the accidents to each other. The requisite similarity and proximity will vary depending on what the other accident is designed to prove. If dangerousness is the issue, a high degree of similarity will be essential. On the other hand, if the accident is of-

---

[1] See **Treatise** at ¶ 401[09].

[2] Koloda v. General Motors Parts Division, General Motors Corp., 716 F.2d 373, 375 (6th Cir. 1983); Stoler v. Penn Central Transportation Co., 583 F.2d 896 (6th Cir. 1978).

[3] Payne v. A.O. Smith Corp., 99 F.R.D. 534, 537–39 (S.D. Ohio 1983); **Rhodes** v. Michelin Tire Corporation, 542 F.Supp. 60, 62 (E.D. Ky. 1982).

[4] Jones & Laughlin Steel Corp. v. Matherne, 348 F.2d 394, 400 (5th Cir. 1965).

fered to prove notice, a lack of exact similarity of conditions will not cause exclusion provided the accident was of a kind which should have served to warn the defendant. Of course, a greater degree of similarity and proximity will usually enhance the probative value of the evidence.

[b]   Possession of Weapons or Other Paraphernalia Used in Committing Crimes

Evidence, such as that offered by ballistics experts, which links the defendant to the weapon actually used in committing a crime, is obviously relevant.[5] So is evidence that the defendant possessed weapons or other paraphernalia that may have been used in committing a crime.[6] In some cases, the courts have held that evidence of the possession of weapons or paraphernalia not used in the crime charged may also be relevant, because it shows the opportunity to commit the crime or an awareness that the crime involves highly dangerous activity and may require the use of weapons.[7]

---

[5] See, *e.g.,* United States v. Peltier, 585 F.2d 314, 325 (8th Cir. 1978), *cert. denied,* 440 U.S. 945 (1979) (government introduced firearms used by defendants in shoot-out).

[6] See, *e.g.,* United States v. Bear Killer, 534 F.2d 1253 (8th Cir.), *cert. denied,* 429 U.S. 846 (1976) (testimony that defendant owned weapon of particular caliber was relevant when government established that fatal shot had been caused by same caliber; cites Rules 401 and 104(b)); United States v. Eatherton, 519 F.2d 603, 611–12 (1st Cir.), *cert. denied,* 423 U.S. 987 (1975) (briefcase containing three ski masks and loaded gun properly admitted; "[t]he point of which the jury could properly take notice is not that innocent people do not carry the particular combination of items, but rather that the bundle of implements is distinctive enough to support the Government's argument that appellant was one of the individuals making use of very similar instruments several days earlier"); United States v. Robinson, 560 F.2d 507 (2d Cir. 1977), *cert. denied,* 435 U.S. 905 (1978) (en banc) (same caliber weapon in defendant's possession as was used in earlier bank robbery).

[7] See, *e.g.,* United States v. Arnott, 704 F.2d 322, 326 (6th Cir.), *cert. denied,* 464 U.S. 948 (1983) (in prosecution for drug offenses, including distribution of cocaine, weapons seized from co-conspirator's residence where contraband stored relevant as "tools of the trade" of trafficking in narcotics; court cites Rule 401); United States v. Marino, 658 F.2d 1120, 1123 (6th Cir. 1981) (involved conspiracy to import cocaine; guns found in defendants' possession at time of arrest relevant to prove intent to engage in conspiracy, because "dealers in narcot-

Such evidence should be excluded where the crime charged is not of such a nature as to suggest a clear possibility of the need for dangerous weapons because the evidence then has low probative value coupled with a high potential for prejudice. See also discussion of Rule 403, below.

[c]   Consciousness of Guilt

Under the rubric of consciousness of guilt, evidence is often offered of a party's behavior which, through a series of inferences, is deemed relevant to show that he committed the charged crime or act. Courts admit on a consciousness of guilt theory evidence of such behavior as flight,[8] attempted suicide,[9] furtive conduct,[10] false exculpatory statements,[11] threats directed at witnesses,[12]

---

ics are well known to be dangerous criminals usually carrying weapons") (quoting United States v. Korman, 614 F.2d 541, 566 (6th Cir.), *cert. denied,* 446 U.S. 952 (1980)).

[8] United States v. Borders, 693 F.2d 1318, 1324–28 (11th Cir. 1982), *cert. denied,* 461 U.S. 905 (1983) (evidence that co-conspirator immediately left hotel without paying bill and flew home upon hearing that FBI had arrested defendant and wanted to question him admissible as evidence of consciousness of guilt; court reviews cases); United States v. Howze, 668 F.2d 322, 324 (7th Cir. 1982); United States v. Peltier, 585 F.2d 314 (8th Cir. 1978); *cert. denied,* 440 U.S. 945 (1979) (elaborate discussion of probative value of flight).

[9] *Cf.* Tug Raven v. Trexler, 419 F.2d 536 (4th Cir. 1969), *cert. denied,* 398 U.S. 38 (1970) (suicide as destroying credibility of witness).

[10] See, *e.g.* United States v. Rice, 652 F.2d 521 (5th Cir. 1981) (use of false names); United States v. Carrillo, 565 F.2d 1323 (5th Cir.), *cert. denied,* 435 U.S. 955 (1978) ("nervousness" as evidence of guilt); United States v. Lind, 542 F.2d 598 (2d Cir. 1976), *cert. denied,* 430 U.S. 947 (1977) (defendant's attempt to change his appearance before surrendering).

[11] See, *e.g.,* United States v. Green, 680 F.2d 520, 523–24 (7th Cir.), *cert. denied,* 459 U.S. 1072 (1982) (defendant's inconsistent exculpatory statements); United States v. Ingram, 600 F.2d 260 (10th Cir. 1979) (statement by defendant that he had left Fort Carlson four hours after robbery took place was clearly intended to be exculpatory and thereby rendered admissible government's evidence that he had in fact left Fort Carlson six days before robbery).

[12] See, *e.g.,* United States v. Gonsalves, 668 F.2d 73, 75 (1st Cir.), *cert. denied,* 456 U.S. 909 (1982) ("threats made by a defendant respecting a specific hostile witness may imply that the party making the threat has something specific to hide").

spoliation of evidence, the failure to produce witnesses who could exculpate the defendant[13] or the refusal of a person suspected of driving while intoxicated to submit to a blood-alcohol test.[14]

The probative value of this type of evidence may become seriously attenuated in a particular case where it is not clear that the defendant's behavior was prompted by a consciousness of guilt,[15] or where another reason exists, other than the charged crime, which would adequately explain his behavior.[16] The same objection could be raised to the admission of many other items of circumstantial evidence which nevertheless satisfy the minimal relevancy test of Rule 401. See discussion of Rule 403, below.

[d]   Evidence of Indebtedness or a Sudden Acquisition of Large Amounts of Cash

In prosecutions for crimes whose purpose is pecuniary gain, evidence of sudden acquisition of large amounts of cash has frequently been held highly relevant.[17] Similarly, evidence of substantial indebtedness is relevant to prove the motive for committing such crimes.[18] At times, of course, evidence that a defendant

---

[13] See, *e.g.*, Stanojev v. Ebasco Services, Inc., 643 F.2d 914, 924, n.7 (2d Cir. 1981) (in age discrimination case, if plaintiff had established prima facie case, jury could have drawn adverse inference from defendant's failure to produce certain personnel records); Berkey Photo, Inc. v. Eastman Kodak Co., 603 F.2d 263, 305–08 (2d Cir. 1979), *cert. denied,* 444 U.S. 1093 (1980) (destruction or concealment of documents unfavorable to defendant's case by attorney and expert for defendant; extensive analysis of relevancy).

[14] South Dakota v. Neville, 459 U.S. 553 (1983) ("similar to other circumstantial evidence of consciousness of guilt").

[15] Miller v. United States, 320 F.2d 767, 771 (D.C. Cir. 1963) (extensive discussion by Bazelon, J. about assumptions underlying evidence of flight); United States v. Beahin, 664 F.2d 414 (4th Cir. 1981).

[16] See, *e.g.,* United States v. Myers, 550 F.2d 1036, 1048–51 (5th Cir. 1977), *cert. denied,* 439 U.S. 847 (1978) (error to have given instruction on flight where flight was inconclusively established and defendant may have fled because he felt guilty about unrelated crime which he had committed).

[17] United States v. Ariza-Ibarra, 605 F.2d 1216, 1225 (1st Cir. 1979), *cert. denied,* 454 U.S. 895 (1981) (cash in excess of $55,000,000); United States v. Barnes, 604 F.2d 121, 146 (2d Cir. 1979), *cert. denied,* 446 U.S. 907 (1980).

[18] See, *e.g.,* United States v. Hernandez, 588 F.2d 312 (6th Cir. 1978).

was owed money may be relevant as exculpatory evidence. [19]

[e] Future Earnings, Inflation and Future Taxes

It is well settled that estimates of future earnings are relevant to the issue of damages in wrongful death and personal injury actions. [20] More controversial is the issue of whether evidence of future inflation [21] may be admitted as part of the proof of future earnings and future tax liability. [22]

[f] Governmental, Professional and Industry Codes and Standards; Custom and Practice

Governmental, professional and industry codes, regulations and standards are often admitted in federal criminal cases as relevant to proving knowledge, intent or lawful duty, [23] and in federal tort actions as relevant evidence of the appropriate standard of care. [24]

---

[19] United States v. Carriger, 592 F.2d 312 (6th Cir. 1979) (in net worth income tax evasion prosecution, error to have excluded evidence of notes evidencing indebtedness by defendant's brother since they tended to make more probable defendant's claim that some of his expenditures came from a nontaxable source—the repayment of a pre-existing debt).

[20] See, *e.g.*, Chesapeake & Ohio R. Co. v. Kelly, 241 U.S. 485, 36 S.Ct. 630, 60 L.Ed. 1117 (1916).

[21] See, *e.g.*, Norfolk and Western Railway Co. v. Liepelt, 444 U.S. 490, 100 S.Ct. 755, 62 L.Ed.2d 689 (1980); Culver v. Slater Boat Co., 688 F.2d 280, 299 (5th Cir. 1982), *cert. denied sub nom.* Heinrich Schmidt Reederei v. Byrd, 467 U.S. 1252 (1984) (28 page opinion reviews arguments for and against consideration of inflation); Doca v. Marina Mercante Nicaraguense, S.A., 634 F.2d 30 (2d Cir. 1980), *cert. denied*, 451 U.S. 971 (1981). See note 22, *infra*.

[22] Norfolk and Western Railway Co. v. Liepelt, 444 U.S. 490 (1980) (where impact of future taxes would be minimal, evidence might be excludible on Rule 403 grounds). This kind of issue is commonly handled at trial by an expert on economics.

[23] See, *e.g.*, United States v. Head, 641 F.2d 174 (4th Cir. 1981) (in prosecution for bribery of IRS agent, IRS manual on employee conduct was relevant to show the lawful duty of agent); United States v. Ford, 632 F.2d 1354 (9th Cir. 1980), *cert. denied*, 450 U.S. 934 (1981) (AFL-CIO Codes of Ethics relevant to issue of criminal intent).

[24] See, *e.g.*, Brown v. Cedar Rapids Iowa City R. Co., 650 F.2d 159, 163 (8th

[g] Comparable Sales to Show Value of Real Property

The issue of the value of real property arises most often in federal court in condemnation cases, although it may also arise in other contexts, such as misuse of property.[25] The courts have held that the market value of real property may be proven with evidence of sales (or comparable transactions) of similarly situated property. To be relevant, such evidence must be of reasonably recent sales and of property substantially comparable to the property in issue.

[h] Profile Evidence

One issue currently before the courts in a number of contexts is the relevancy of testimony by an expert that a person involved in a lawsuit is a member of a class with certain characteristics. This kind of testimony has been offered with regard to victims,[26] criminal defendants,[27] and witnesses.[28]

Cir. 1981) (Safety Codes promulgated by governmental authority); *In re* Air Crash Disaster, 635 F.2d 67 (2d Cir. 1980) (noncompliance with Federal Air Regulations).

[25] See, *e.g.*, United States v. 179.26 Acres of Land in Douglas County, Kansas, 644 F.2d 367, 371 (10th Cir. 1981); United States v. 429.59 Acres of Land, 612 F.2d 459, 462 (9th Cir. 1980) (condemnation proceeding).

[26] See, *e.g.*, United States v. Bowers, 660 F.2d 527, 529 (5th Cir. 1981) (battered child syndrome).

[27] See, *e.g.*, United States v. Burgess, 691 F.2d 1146 (4th Cir. 1982) (post-traumatic stress disorder); United States v. Torniero, 735 F.2d 725 (2d Cir. 1984) (compulsive gambling disorder); Ibn-Tamas v. United States, 407 A.2d 626 (D.C. App. 1979) (battered wife syndrome).

[28] See, *e.g.*, United States v. Downing, 753 F.2d 1224 (3d Cir. 1985) (accuracy of eyewitness testimony).

¶ 6.02 Exclusion on Grounds of Prejudice, Confusion, or Waste of Time—Rule 403

¶ 6.02[01] Facts to be Considered in Excluding Relevant Evidence in General[1]

Rule 403 is the major rule that explicitly recognizes the large discretionary role of the judge in controlling the introduction of evidence. Being in terms unlimited, it applies to all forms of evidence: direct and circumstantial, testimonial, hearsay, documentary, real proof, and demonstration. The one instance in which Rule 403 arguably does not accord discretion to a court is in ruling on the admissibility of a conviction of a prosecution witness and on the admissibility of defense convictions pursuant to Rule 609(a)(2). See discussion in Chapter 12, *infra*. The balancing approach of Rule 403 should be utilized in deciding on the admissibility of other types of evidence offered for impeachment.

The rule provides:

Rule 403

EXCLUSION OF RELEVANT EVIDENCE ON GROUNDS OF PREJUDICE, CONFUSION, OR WASTE OF TIME

Although relevant, evidence may be excluded if its probative value is substantially outweighed by the danger of unfair prejudice, confusion of the issues, or misleading the jury, or by considerations of undue delay, waste of time, or needless presentation of cumulative evidence.

Rule 403 recognizes that passing the minimum relevancy test of Rule 401 does not guarantee admissibility—the question remains whether the value of the evidence in contributing to a rational solution is outweighed by attendant costs. The court must consider whether the search for truth will be helped or hindered by the interjection of distracting, confusing or emotionally charged evidence.

In making this determination, the court must assess the probative value of the proffered item as well as the harmful conse-

---

[1] See **Treatise** at ¶¶ 403[01]–[02].

quences specified in Rule 403 that might flow from its admission. The countervailing factors to admissibility specified in the Rule—prejudice, confusion of issues, danger of misleading the jury, and considerations of delay, waste of time or needless presentation of cumulative evidence—predate enactment of the Rule.

Surprise is not specified as a separate ground for exclusion, and a continuance will often be more appropriate than a refusal to admit. When, however, counsel is taken unawares, Rule 403 requires the court to assess whether a continuance can adequately protect against unfair prejudice or confusion. If the proffered evidence is insignificant, the delay ensuing from a continuance may justify exclusion. In this sense, surprise may still prove a factor in determining admissibility. Where the court in a pretrial order requires listing of witnesses and exchange of data expert's reports before trial, preclusion is proper on grounds independent of Rule 403.

The court has sufficient flexibility pursuant to Rule 403 to admit part of a line of proof while excluding the more prejudicial details. A conditional ruling which admits some proof provided other evidence is excluded is also justified. If there is doubt about the existence of unfair prejudice, confusion of issues, misleading, undue delay, or waste of time, it is generally better practice to admit the evidence taking necessary precautions by way of contemporaneous instructions to the jury followed by additional admonitions in the charge. In limine motions to exclude evidence on the basis of Rule 403 objections are being increasingly utilized by the courts.[2] An *in limine* motion will not necessarily relieve counsel from raising the issue at trial in order to preserve the matter for appeal.[3] See discus-

---

[2] See, *e.g.,* Zenith Radio Corp. v. Matsushita Electric Industrial Co., Ltd., 505 F.Supp. 1125, 1141 (E.D. Pa. 1980) (review of cases in which pretrial rulings have been made under Rule 403).

[3] See United States v. Griffin, 818 F.2d 97, 102–105 (1st Cir.), *cert. denied,* 108 S.Ct. 137 (1987) (prosecution witness had refused to cooperate for over a year; government attributed his reticence to threat by co-defendant; when witness was called, counsel for defendant objected at sidebar to any reference to prior threats, citing Rule 403; court ruled that if witness was cross-examined about his reticence, government could question witness on redirect as to threats, but that government was foreclosed from bringing up threats on direct; no *voir dire* was held and witness never acknowledged that he had in fact been threatened; when trial resumed, defense never cross-examined witness about his reluctance to testify, and prosecution never brought out threat; defendant objected to the judge's ruling on appeal; court held

sion of limiting instructions and motions in limine in Chapter 2, *supra.*

Unlike some of the subsequent rules in Article IV, Rule 403 purports to set no absolute standard but rather is designed as a guide for handling situations for which no specific rules have been formulated. Consequently, as the cases decided since the enactment of the Federal Rules consistently acknowledge, the trial court has considerable discretion in applying Rule 403.[4] The appellate court will not reverse simply because it would have weighed highly subjective factors differently. Reversals are likely to occur only when the trial court did not engage in the balancing process mandated by the Rule or when it is impossible to determine from the record whether it did. Counsel cannot, therefore, safely hold back arguments on Rule 403 grounds for appeal. They must be prepared at the trial level to identify with precision both the probative value of the evidence and any factors inimical to admissibility since the chances of a successful appeal on the point are remote.

¶ 6.02[02]   Exclusion of Relevant Evidence: Prejudice[1]

In the absence of redeeming probative value, exclusion of evidence because of its capacity for prejudice has long been the practice. "Of course," as the Fifth Circuit has remarked on a number of occasions, " 'unfair prejudice' as used in Rule 403 is not to be equated with testi-

---

that because counsel never cross-examined witness about why he procrastinated, "the actual issue which the appellant seeks to have us decide never arose. . . . Although the court telegraphed what its ruling was likely to be if defense counsel opened the door, the latter never knocked. And we will not venture to pass upon issues such as this in a vacuum. . . . [I]t is too great a handicap to bind a trial judge to a ruling on a subtle evidentiary question, requiring the most delicate balancing, outside a precise factual context." Court relies on Luce v. United States, 469 U.S. 38 (1984) (see ¶ 12.04[03][e]).

[4] See, *e.g.,* United States v. Long, 574 F.2d 761, 767 (3d Cir.), *cert. denied,* 439 U.S. 985 (1978) ("If judicial self-restraint is ever desirable, it is when a Rule 403 analysis of a trial court is reviewed by an appellate tribunal."). See also United States v. Robinson, 560 F.2d 507 (2d Cir. 1977), *cert. denied,* 435 U.S. 905 (1978) (en banc court reversed panel which had reversed trial judge for abusing his discretion under Rule 403; strong support of trial court discretion).

[1] See **Treatise** at ¶ 403[03].

mony simply adverse to the opposing party. Virtually all evidence is prejudicial or it is not material. The prejudice must be 'unfair.' "[2]

The Committee's Notes explain that "unfair prejudice" means an "undue tendency to suggest decision on an improper basis, commonly, though not necessarily, an emotional one." Evidence that appeals to the jury's sympathies,[3] arouses its sense of horror,[4] provokes its instinct to punish,[5] or triggers other mainsprings of human action[6] may cause a jury to base its decision on something other than the

---

[2] Dollar v. Long Mfg., N.C. Inc., 561 F.2d 613, 618 (5th Cir. 1977), *cert. denied*, 435 U.S. 996 (1978).

[3] See, *e.g.*, Iris Betancourt v. J.C. Penney Co., Inc., 554 F.2d 1206, 1207 (1st Cir. 1977) (evidence that plaintiff did not go to hospital the night of the alleged accident because her alcoholic ex-husband showed up and caused a commotion until he was finally removed by the police, "has obvious potential to engender sympathy for the plaintiff and her family so as to cause an inflated verdict"); Grimes v. Employers Mutual Liability Insurance Co. of Wisconsin, 73 F.R.D. 607 (D. Alaska 1977) (while film of plaintiff's daily activities was relevant to showing impact plaintiff's injury had on his life, scenes with his daughter and quadriplegic brother served little purpose except to create sympathy for plaintiff).

[4] See, *e.g.*, United States v. Qamar, 671 F.2d 732 (2d Cir. 1982) (analysis of the admissibility of death threat evidence against Rule 403 challenge); United States v. Anderson, 584 F.2d 849 (6th Cir. 1978) (in trial for conspiracy to transport marijuana, expert testimony about effects of drug was irrelevant and highly prejudicial).

[5] United States v. Sostarich, 684 F.2d 606 (8th Cir. 1982) (error to admit testimony that witness who identified defendant from bank surveillance photograph knew defendant in prison; while testimony of witness was relevant to issue of defendant's identity, fact that defendant had been in prison was of no probative value and highly prejudicial).

[6] See, *e.g.*, United States v. Millen, 594 F.2d 1085 (6th Cir.), *cert. denied*, 444 U.S. 829 (1979) (in prosecution for first-degree murder and distribution of controlled substance, prosecutor's question which intentionally elicited highly prejudicial reply that defendant physicians, victim and witness were engaged in homosexual relationship required reversal of involuntary manslaughter conviction; appellate court noted the government's complete failure to spell out a theory as to how this relationship, if it existed, was probative of the crimes charged); Harless v. Boyule-Midway Division, American Home Products, 594 F.2d 1051 (5th Cir. 1979) (in wrongful death action against manufacturer of household product which had been intentionally inhaled by fourteen year-old-boy, evidence of deceased's having smoked marijuana should have been excluded as highly prejudicial; defendant had argued that evidence was relevant to assist jury in placing a value on the loss plaintiff had sustained as a result of her son's death).

established propositions in the case.[7] The appellate court may conclude that "unfair prejudice" occurred because an insufficient effort was made below to avoid the dangers of prejudice,[8] or because the theory on which the evidence was offered was designed to elicit a response from the jurors not justified by the evidence. Rules 407 through 410 are to some degree based on the assumption that certain evidence is inherently prejudicial and must be excluded.

Particular difficulties arise where the proffered evidence connects a party with a highly charged public issue, such as communism, organized crime, or narcotics. Despite undoubted resulting prejudice, the probative value of the proffered evidence may compel its admission.[9] In other instances, the probative value may be so low as to warrant exclusion when prejudicial factors are present.

Judges may differ in their assessment of probative value because, like jurors, they may disagree with respect to the evidential hypothesis and, consequently, its significance to the case. The usual approach on the question of admissibility on appeal, as noted above, is to view both probative force and prejudice most favorably towards the proponent, that is to say, to give the evidence its maximum reasonable probative force and its minimum reasonable prejudicial value. The

---

[7] United States v. Figueroa, 618 F.2d 934, 943 (2d Cir. 1980) ("All evidence introduced against a defendant, if material to an issue in the case, tends to prove guilt, but is not necessarily prejudicial in any sense that matters to the rules of evidence. . . . Evidence is prejudicial only when it tends to have some adverse effect upon a defendant beyond tending to prove the fact or issue that justified its admission into evidence. . . . The prejudicial effect may be created by the tendency of the evidence to prove some adverse fact not properly in issue or unfairly to excite emotions against the defendant. . . . When material evidence has an additional prejudicial effect, Rule 403 requires the trial court to make a conscientious assessment of whether the probative value of the evidence on a disputed issue in the case is substantially outweighed by the prejudicial tendency of the evidence to have some other adverse effect upon the defendant.").

[8] United States v. McManaman, 606 F.2d 919, 926 (10th Cir. 1979) ("the explosive portions were not excised, as can be done to avoid such dangers of prejudice.").

[9] United States v. Sickles, 524 F.Supp. 506 (E.D. Pa. 1981), aff'd, 688 F.2d 827 (3d Cir. 1982) (in prosecution for violation of federal firearms laws, court did not err in admitting some evidence of defendant's connection with Ku Klux Klan; evidence was relevant to conspiracy charge and to defense of entrapment, and mention of Klan was unavoidable; but court excluded Klan-related material whose probative value was slight and potential for prejudice high, including a Klan robe and racist portions of rules and regulations).

trial court will lean towards this approach since the thrust of the Federal Rules favor admissibility. Admission may be proper in some instances even though the party against whom it is offered would have been willing to stipulate to the proposition for which it is offered, for the stipulation may not provide the jury with a basis for evaluating probative force.[10] Nevertheless, the court should generally be decidedly receptive to stipulations that will avoid some prejudicial aspects of evidence. The saving in time and in risk of prejudice may be substantial.

¶ 6.02[03]   Exclusion of Relevant Evidence: Confusion of Issues, Misleading Jury[1]

Rule 403 recognizes that evidence may be excluded if it might confuse the issues or mislead the jury. As with prejudice, each case of possible confusion, or misleading the jury, turns on the facts in the particular case. It is impossible to state that any particular factors will dictate exclusion. Courts are reluctant to admit evidence which is seemingly plausible, persuasive, conclusive and significant if detailed rebuttal evidence or complicated judicial instructions would be required to demonstrate that the evidence actually has little probative value.[2]

---

[10] See, *e.g.*, United Sates v. Sampol, 636 F.2d 621 (D.C. Cir. 1980) (no error in allowing government to introduce evidence about explosion which killed victim of assassination even though defendants offered to stipulate that deaths had been caused by bomb since stipulation would have diluted value of proof). *Cf.* United States v. Allen, 798 F.2d 985, 1001–02 (7th Cir. 1986) (in prosecution for transportation of explosives by a convicted felon, where prior felony conviction was an element of the charged crime, trial court did not abuse its discretion by not accepting defendant's offer to stipulate to a prior felony conviction; stipulation might be even more prejudicial because jury might infer that felony was recent although conviction was 36 years old; "no suitable stipulation was offered and it is clearly conceptually difficult, if not impossible, to construct a nonprejudicial one").

[1] See **Treatise** at ¶ 403[04].

[2] See, *e.g.*, United States v. Kail, 804 F.2d 441, 446 (8th Cir. 1986) (in mail fraud prosecution of coin dealer, 1977 finding by administrative law judge that there were no industry-wide standards for the grading and valuation of coins would have confused jurors; testimony indicated that standards have been developed since then, that defendant was not aware of administrative finding until his trial, and jury would have been forced to decide legal issue and been distracted from issue of defendant's intent to defraud); Benna v. Reeder Flying Service, Inc., 578 F.2d 269 (9th Cir.

Courts also hesitate to admit evidence that has an aura of scientific infallibility,[3] particularly where the jury may use the evidence for purposes other than that for which it is introduced. Courts are careful to scrutinize evidence of statistical probabilities. Statistics can easily become, in the words of one court, "an item of prejudicial overweight."[4] They may suggest to the jury that the probability that the ultimate fact to be proved is true can be equated with the statistical probability offered in evidence.[5] When, however, there is an adequate foundation for the statistical probabilities, and they are properly used and explained, their probative value will usually outweigh their tendency to confuse and mislead, thereby warranting their admission into evidence.[6] The confusion the courts fear with respect to scientif-

---

1978) (in suit brought for injuries suffered in air crash against airplane owner and engine seller, trial court properly admitted only the one page of a report on the engine's overhaul prepared by the seller where that page dealt with the only engine parts as to which there was a controversy; plaintiffs wanted to introduce other pages because they were sloppily prepared so that jury would infer that overhaul was negligently performed; trial court properly concluded that jury might be misled into thinking that the condition of other parts was at issue).

[3] See, *e.g., In re* Air Crash Disaster at John F. Kennedy International Airport on June 24, 1975, 635 F.2d 67, 73 (2d Cir. 1980) (trial judge clearly did not abuse discretion in refusing to admit chart that compared the established glide slope path used by a landing airplane with the actual path of the airplane that crashed; appellate court explained: "The thickness of the lines on the chart, and the fact that the times of conversation marked on the chart did not match the stipulated conversation times could have misled the jury.").

[4] Marx & Co., Inc. v. Diners' Club, Inc. 550 F.2d 505, 511 (2d Cir.), *cert. denied,* 434 U.S. 861 (1977) (securities' fraud case; court held that statistic regarding the median time in which registration statements filed with the Securities and Exchange Commission become effective was misused as "if it were akin to a statute of limitations"; the jury based its damage award on apparent conclusion that registration statement actually became effective on date established by statistical probability).

[5] United States v. Massey, 594 F.2d 676 (8th Cir. 1979) (reversal where prosecutor on closing argument suggested that statistical odds showed a better than 99.44 percent chance of defendant's guilt).

[6] See, *e.g.,* United States v. Gwaltney, 790 F.2d 1378, 1383 (9th Cir. 1986), *cert. denied,* 107 S.Ct. 1337 (1987) (statistical evidence that defendant was part of only 12 percent of male population whose semen contained certain blood type and particular enzyme, and that he was in five percent of that 12 percent having antisperm antibodies was properly admitted; no attempt by prosecution to suggest that percentages could be used to predict odds of defendant's guilt); United States v. Hickey, 596 F.2d 1082, 1089 (1st Cir.), *cert. denied,* 444 U.S. 853 (1979) (no error in admission of hair samples taken from a ski mask and sweater found in the getaway car; court

ic and statistical evidence might often be avoided were time allowed for explanatory testimony.

In many cases involving confusion or misleading, the courts exclude evidence because an inordinate amount of time would be consumed in clarifying the situation.[7]

¶ 6.02[04]   Special Problems Related to Real Proof[1]

Real proof, otherwise known as real evidence, demonstrative evidence or autoptic proference, refers to evidence which is directly cognizable by the senses of the trier of fact. Photographs, tape recordings, guns, and clothing are some of the categories of real proof most commonly encountered. Real proof may have such a powerful and unwarranted impact upon the trier that special care must be taken in considering its admissibility in connection with Rule 403.

Before an object can be admitted, it must be authenticated or identified as being that which its proponent claims it to be. See discussion of Rule 901 in Chapter 8, *infra*. This requirement is an aspect of relevancy, since the object obviously is not relevant if it has no connection with that which is being proved. The process of identification is twofold: the object must be related to an issue in the case, and the condition of the object must be shown to be substantially the same as when the event in question took place, since if significant physical changes have occurred, the object, in the form it would be shown to the trier, may no longer be relevant. Courts sometimes view the latter requirement, not as an aspect of relevancy, but as an instance of refusing to admit relevant evidence because of the danger that the jury might be confused by the change in condition.[2] The problem is particularly acute in the case of posed photographs, or experi-

---

found where "jury was made well aware of the limitations of this evidence" and "the link between the sweater and mask and the robbery was strong, and the similarity of hairs, while not affirmatively implicating [the defendant], 'enhanced the probability of guilt' and was therefore probative").

[7] See **Treatise** at ¶ 403[04].

[1] See **Treatise** at ¶ 403[05].

[2] **King v. Ford Motor Co.**, 597 F.2d 436 (5th Cir. 1979) (trial court did not abuse its discretion in excluding photographs of motor vehicle chassis which showed chassis at different state of completion than chassis involved in accident).

ments, because the trier may fail to keep in mind hearsay and opinion elements which went into the artificially created event.

The usual objection raised to the admissibility of real proof is, however, not confusion, but the danger of unfair prejudice. The impact produced by the object itself is often so much greater than that produced by testimony about the object that it is feared that jurors will overestimate its probative value. There is a general mental tendency, when a corporal object is produced as proving something, to assume, on sight of the object, all else that is implied in the case about it. The sight of it seems to prove all the rest. In addition, there is the further danger that if the object exhibited has gruesome or repulsive characteristics, the jury may be so emotionally aroused as to fail to assess the probative value of the other evidence in the case accurately.

This objection to the overpowering effect of real proof is often raised when a person seeks to display his injuries to the jury. Simple black and white pictures are usually the most neutral way to get this information to the jury. Color pictures or slides may be useful as may movies or TV pictures, but staged "Day in the Life" films are usually too prejudicial and often contain elements of hidden hearsay and opinion evidence.[2a]

Evidence may not, however, be excluded merely because it is unpleasant. "[A] court cannot arrange for lively music to keep the jury cheerful while the state's case in a murder trial is being presented, and grewsome [sic] evidence cannot be suppressed merely because it may strongly tend to agitate the jury's feelings."[3] The possibility of prejudice is in itself insignificant; it is the danger of prejudice substantially outweighing the probative value of the proffered evidence that is determinative. Otherwise, the more gruesome the crime or the greater the injuries, the more difficult it would become for the prosecutor or plaintiff to prove its case.

[2a] But see Bannister v. Town of Noble, 812 F.2d 1265, 1270 (10th Cir. 1987) (review of dangers; court concludes that no abuse of discretion in admitting "Day in the Life" film).

[3] State v. Moore, 80 Kan. 232, 236 (1909) (bloodstained jacket of deceased admitted into evidence). See United States v. Bowers, 660 F.2d 527, 529–30 (5th Cir. 1981) (in prosecution for child abuse admission of color photograph of child's lacerated heart not error; although "the photograph had the potential to inflame the jury," it was necessary to prove that defendant used cruel and excessive force on child).

Objections are frequently raised to the admission of photographs—particularly color photographs—because disturbing objects or events may be represented which could not otherwise be visually viewed by the jury. With proper instruction, the danger of jurors overvaluing such proof is slight. Jurors, exposed as they are to television, the movies, and picture magazines, are fairly sophisticated. If a fair audio or visual presentation would assist the jury, the court should not discourage its use.

Where probative value outweighs the danger of undue prejudice, the federal courts have admitted photographs and moving pictures of such unsavory objects and events as murder victims,[4] rape victims,[5] accident victims,[6] assault victims,[7] and the actual commission of a crime.[8] Demonstrations have also been permitted.[9] As in other

---

[4] See, *e.g.,* Giblin v. United States, 523 F.2d 42 (8th Cir. 1975), *cert. denied,* 424 U.S. 971 (1976) (photograph of victim's skeleton as it was exhumed showed position of body and corroborated testimony that victim had climbed into his grave and waited to be executed; probative value outweighed prejudice).

[5] Papp v. Jago, 656 F.2d 221 (6th Cir.), *cert. denied,* 454 U.S. 1035 (1981) (defendant's right to fair trial was not prejudiced by admission of colored autopsy slides of rape victim's intimate parts of anatomy; although such photographs are highly prejudicial, they were directly probative on essential element of penetration on rape charge); United States v. Shoemaker, 542 F.2d 561 (10th Cir.), *cert. denied,* 429 U.S. 1004 (1976) (color photographs of partially nude victim murdered in rape attempt; photographs had probative value in establishing the attempted rape and in substantiating government testimony as to cause of death).

[6] Jenkins v. Associated Transports, Inc., 330 F.2d 706, 711 (6th Cir. 1964) (colored photographs); Luther v. Maple, 250 F.2d 916, 921 (8th Cir. 1958) (motion picture showing treatment of injuries).

[7] United States v. Authemant, 607 F.2d 1129 (5th Cir. 1979) (photographs of victim in prosecution of police officer for willful deprivation of civil rights); United States v. Bailey, 537 F.2d 845, 846 (5th Cir. 1976), *cert. denied sub nom.* Harstrom v. United States, 429 U.S. 1051 (1977) (Polaroid photographs properly admitted; while they "may be stark, they are not so gruesome or sensational as to be unduly prejudicial").

[8] See, *e.g.,* United States v. Weiss, 718 F.2d 413, 431 (D.C. Cir. 1983), *cert. denied,* 465 U.S. 1027 (1984) (videotape of Congressman accepting bribe money).

[9] See Schleunes v. American Casualty Co. of Reading, Pa., 528 F.2d 634 (5th Cir. 1976) (trial court should have permitted court-supervised demonstration of whether gun could be discharged accidentally in action on life insurance policy in which insurer claimed the insured had committed suicide; cites other cases in which courts allowed highly relevant demonstrations); Curry v. American Enka, Inc., 452

instances where the admissibility of evidence is challenged on Rule 403 grounds, counsel and the trial court must carefully analyze and evaluate the probative value of the proffered evidence and balance it against the factors specified in Rule 403.

¶ 6.02[05]   Exclusion of Evidence: Waste of Time[1]

Rule 403 provides that relevant evidence may be excluded if its probative value is substantially outweighed by considerations of undue delay, waste of time, or needless presentation of cumulative evidence.

Exclusion is generally harmless where the evidence excluded merely repeats what has already been admitted.[2] In the case of cumulative evidence, the trial court clearly must have wide discretion to exclude if it is to conduct a trial efficiently.[3] Certainly, Rule 403 does not mean that a court may exclude evidence that will prolong a trial regardless of its probative value. The exclusion of crucial evidence may amount to an abuse of discretion.

F.Supp. 178 (E.D. Tenn. 1977) (discusses whether jurors should be permitted to touch injured plaintiff's hands).

[1] See **Treatise** at ¶ 403[06].

[2] Contemporary Missions, Inc. v. Bonded Mailings, Inc., 671 F.2d 81 (2d Cir. 1982) (evidence of independent litigation against plaintiff which was cumulative and potentially extensive was properly excluded in contract action, where evidence was not necessary to any issue; dissent argued that evidence was relevant to determine proper measure of damages); United States v. Hearst, 563 F.2d 1331, 1348–49 (9th Cir. 1977), *cert. denied,* 435 U.S. 1000 (1978) (not abuse of discretion to exclude one hour and 45-minute long tape recording of interview of defendant by psychiatrist where psychiatrist had testified fully about interview and government had invited witnesses to read "particular" parts of transcript of tape; district court has discretion to exclude material as cumulative).

[3] See, *e.g.,* MCI Communications v. American Tel. & Tel. Co., 708 F.2d 1081 (7th Cir.), *cert. denied,* 464 U.S. 891 (1983) (time limits ordered by trial judge restricting presentation of each party's case-in-chief were not prejudicial where litigation was protracted, limits were flexible, not absolute, and had effect of excluding cumulative testimony).

CHAPTER 7

Special Rules of Relevancy

SYNOPSIS

(Rel.2–9/89 Pub.819)

¶ 7.01 Character and Criminal Conduct To Prove an Event—Rule 404

¶ 7.01[01] Rationale and Scope[1]

Rule 404 is the basic rule governing the admissibility of character evidence to prove that an event did or did not take place as one of the parties contends. It applies to both civil and criminal cases, although it is obviously of far greater significance in criminal cases. Rule 404 is applicable whether or not the person whose character is being disputed is a witness. The Rule reads as follows:

Rule 404

CHARACTER EVIDENCE NOT ADMISSIBLE TO PROVE CONDUCT; EXCEPTIONS; OTHER CRIMES

(a) Character evidence generally. Evidence of a person's character or trait of character is not admissible for the purpose of proving action in conformity therewith on a particular occasion, except:

(1) Character of accused. Evidence of a pertinent trait of character offered by an accused, or by the prosecutor to rebut the same;

(2) Character of victim. Evidence of a pertinent trait of character of the victim of the crime offered by an accused, or by the prosecution to rebut the same, or evidence of a character trait of peacefulness of the victim offered by the prosecution in a homicide case to rebut evidence that the victim was the first aggressor;

(3) Character witness. Evidence of the character of a witness, as provided in rules 607, 608, and 609.

(b) Other crimes, wrongs, or acts. Evidence of other crimes, wrongs, or acts is not admissible to prove the character of a person in order to show action in conformity therewith. It may, however, be admissible for other purposes, such as proof of motive, opportunity, intent, preparation, plan, knowledge, identity, or absence of mistake or accident. *Amended '91 (11.1.91)*

Methods of proof are governed by Rule 405. For distinction between character and habit *see* discussion of Rule 406, *infra* this chapter at ¶ 7.03. For the use of character as bearing on credibility see the discussion of Rule 608 in Chapter 12.

---

[1] *See* **Treatise** at ¶ 404[01].

Character and habit (Rule 406) are not synonymous. The former faces in the direction of Freud, the latter towards Pavlov. "Character" is not defined. Like habit, it is not descriptive of any qualitative or quantitative characteristics recognizable by a scientist, but it is a helpful concept, useful in administering trials, since people who have been careful, honest or peaceable—or the opposite—in the past tend to meet new situations in a way consistent with these observed "traits" or "dispositions."

Rule 404 provides that character evidence is not admissible for the purpose of proving that a person acted in conformity with it except in the case of a victim, or in some instances an accused, or where the evidence is being used for purposes of impeachment. *See* Rules 607, 608 and 609. Character evidence, offered to prove character when it is a material proposition rather than to prove an act, does not fall within the prohibition of the rule and consequently is admissible. *See* ¶ 7.01[02], Character in Issue, *infra.* Character evidence offered to prove an act is similarly admissible if it can be utilized without resort to the inference that a person of certain character is more likely than persons generally to have committed the act in question.

Character evidence used circumstantially has traditionally been excluded for two basic reasons: 1) lack of probative value, and 2) the likelihood of prejudice or confusion resulting from its admission. The rule rests on the theory that the risk that the jury will convict for crimes other than those charged, or because defendant deserves punishment for his prior bad acts, outweighs the probative value of the inference, "he's done it before, he's done or will do it again."

The solution adopted in Rules 404, 405, 608 and 609 is not strictly logical. Shaped by evidentiary concerns and constitutional pressures, the resulting maze of interconnecting rules concerning character is difficult to negotiate. Central to the Anglo-American system of criminal law is the concept that the accused must be protected against inculpation through proof of his past misdeeds. Closely analogous is the familiar rule that a person is innocent until proven guilty of the particular act charged. One form of protection is constitutional—the privilege against compelled self-incrimination. A second—which may not be constitutionally guaranteed[2] but which is accepted by all American jurisdictions—is the exclusionary rule embodied in Rule 404; it renders inadmissible, as part of the prosecution's evidence in chief, character evidence offered solely to show the accused's propensity to commit the crime with which he is charged.

Despite the exclusionary rule, evidence of the accused's character is admissible in a variety of situations. A basic exception to Rule 404, expressed in subparagraph (a)(1), permits the accused to introduce evidence of his good character. If he does so, additional character evidence may be adduced from the prosecution's rebuttal witnesses, as well as on cross-examination of the accused's witnesses. The exceptions in (a)(2) allow limited proof of the victim's character by defendant and prosecutor. The exception embodied in subparagraph (a)(3) of Rule 404 makes character evidence admissible to impeach the credibility of a witness, a category to which the accused is consigned if he takes the stand. Subdivision (b) of Rule 404 provides that character evidence is admissible if it is relevant to prove something other than that the accused acted in conformity with his character.

If the accused raises the defense of entrapment, arguing that he would not have committed the crime but for the solicitation of the police, his character and prior conduct become relevant in determining whether he was predisposed to commit the offense; if he was, the fact that he was apprehended through government solicitation will not excuse him.[3] The inquiry into character allowed by the courts has included evidence of general character[4] and of prior criminal convictions. Testimony is also allowed relating to prior or subsequent criminal activity for which the accused was not convicted.[5]

Concerned observers have noted that the conjunction of these

---

[2] For discussion of constitutional attacks on propensity rule and a general discussion of propensity in American law *see* **Treatise** at ¶ 404[04].

[3] *See, e.g.,* Sorrells v. United States, 287 U.S. 435, 53 S. Ct. 210, 77 L. Ed. 413 (1932) (leading case); United States v. Russell, 411 U.S. 423, 93 S. Ct. 1637, 36 L. Ed. 2d 366 (1973) (reaffirming *Sorrells*).

[4] United States v. Newman, 849 F.2d 156, 163–66 (5th Cir. 1988) (discussion of admissibility of expert psychiatric testimony seeking to show that defendant was peculiarly susceptible to inducement).

[5] *See* discussion in **Treatise** at ¶ 404[04].

rules and exceptions may cause the defendant with a criminal past to be deprived of both constitutional and common law protection. Although he has an absolute right not to testify, and no adverse inference may be drawn from his failure to take the stand,[6] studies indicate (what every lawyer assumes) that "jurors notice and tend to infer guilt from silence."[7] If he takes the stand, he becomes a witness who may be impeached by evidence of his prior crimes. Although the defendant is entitled to a limiting instruction that the jury may consider these crimes only as affecting credibility, it seems clear that juries consider such evidence as evidence of guilt. Nor can the defendant gain protection by not taking the stand himself but by calling witnesses to vouch for his good character. The witnesses may be cross-examined as to specific offenses committed by the defendant on the theory that the validity of their assertions about defendant's good character should be tested by whether they had heard of his previous misdeeds. Here again the issue is credibility of the witness, not guilt of the defendant, but a limiting instruction is of dubious efficacy. Regardless of whether or not the defendant takes the stand, evidence relating to prior offenses may become admissible if he pleads entrapment, or the court finds the evidence relevant for some purpose other than merely showing a propensity to commit the crime charged. The defendant may even discover to his dismay that by his defense he has inadvertently "opened the door" to evidence of his character being admitted on the government's case in rebuttal.[8]

The Federal Rules—although retaining all the rules and exceptions discussed above—have sought to make defendant's theoretical protection more effective. Character witnesses for the defendant are

---

[6] Griffin v. California, 380 U.S. 609, 85 S. Ct. 1229, 14 L. Ed. 2d 106 (1965).

[7] Note, "To Take the Stand or Not to Take the Stand: The Dilemma of the Defendant With a Criminal Record," 4 Colum. J. of L. & Soc. Prob. 215, 221 (1968).

[8] *See, e.g.,* United States v. Giese, 597 F.2d 1170 (9th Cir. 1979) and cases discussed in **Treatise** at ¶ 404[04]. United States v. Holladay, 566 F.2d 1018 (5th Cir. 1978) (after witness for prosecution was cross-examined vigorously about prior inconsistent testimony favorable to the accused, it was not error for witness to state on redirect that he had testified differently in the past because of fear of defendant, evidence was admissible because issue had been injected by the defense); United States v. Corey, 566 F.2d 429 (2d Cir. 1977) (where defendant asked witness called by prosecution about his opinion of defendant's character prior to discovery of fraud, defendant "opened the door" to prosecutor asking witness on cross-examination about his opinion of defendant's character after fraud was discovered).

no longer confined to testifying in vague generalities about defendant's reputation in the community but may express their own opinions. More important, the factors of unfair prejudice, confusion of issues or misleading the jury have been given explicit recognition. If the probative value of the proffered character evidence is outweighed by these dangers, the judge, pursuant to Rule 403, must exclude the evidence regardless of whether it is being offered to rebut an entrapment defense or, pursuant to Rule 404(b), to prove a relevant proposition such as motive. If the evidence is being offered to impeach the accused as a witness or to impeach any other witness, Rule 609 requires the court to balance the prejudicial effect to the defendant except in the case of felonies involving dishonesty or false statement. Whether Rule 403 applies in this latter situation is not yet completely clear. *See* discussion at ¶ 12.04, *infra.*

Consequently, a defendant may take the stand or introduce evidence of good character with some confidence that he will be protected against unfavorable character evidence whose probative value is substantially outweighed by the countervailing factors of Rule 403. Before taking the stand the defendant should request a conference outside the presence of the jury to determine how the court expects to rule on the character issues in the case.[9]

Read literally, Rules 404 and 405 prohibit a defendant from proving specific good acts as a basis for inferring that he acted in accordance with his character and, accordingly, did not commit the charged act. Although there is an exception in Rule 404(a)(2) for character offered by an accused, it authorizes proof by reputation and opinion, not proof by specific acts.

While this prohibition of good acts may at times make sense on relevance grounds—besides opening up collateral issues, the proof may be of dubious worth as even the greatest villain may pass up some opportunities for reprehensible conduct—exclusion does not comport with the policy of protecting the accused which is the paramount concern of the propensity rule. In an appropriate case, testimony about defendant's good acts should be admitted. For instance, once the prosecution is permitted to show other crimes as part of a common plan or scheme, evidence that defendant did not commit bad acts during the time this scheme was allegedly flourishing would

---

[9] *See* **Treatise** at ¶ 404[19].

be highly relevant.[10] But even in the absence of other crimes evidence offered by the prosecution, evidence of defendant's good acts may be relevant to show that it was highly unlikely that he acted in the way described by a prosecution witness when he had, in fact, rejected such criminal proposals under strikingly similar circumstances.[11] In general, evidentiary rules which restrict a defendant's right to present exculpatory material are suspect.[12]

A related problem is whether defendant should be permitted to show a third person's character for the inference that this person acted in conformity with his character and committed the crime with which defendant is charged. This use of character evidence does not fall within any of the exceptions listed in Rule 404(a), since only evidence of the defendant's own character or that of a victim is, at times, permitted. Nevertheless, there may be instances when such evidence is highly relevant and necessary for a fair determination.

¶ 7.01[02]   Character in Issue[1]

Possession of a particular trait of character may be a material proposition of fact which under the substantive law determines the rights and liabilities of the parties. In such a case character evidence is being offered not to prove that a person "acted in conformity therewith on a particular occasion" but rather is being offered because the character traits themselves are of significance as an element of a crime, claim or defense.

As illustrative of character in issue, the Advisory Committee referred to the chastity of a victim under a statute specifying chastity as an element of the crime of seduction. Character evidence may be

---

[10] *See, e.g.,* United States v. Garvin, 565 F.2d 519 (8th Cir. 1977) (insurance fraud; where government had been allowed to introduce defendant's applications for other insurance policies in order to prove common plan or scheme, error to exclude proof of defendant's truthful responses on these and contemporaneous insurance application forms).

[11] *But see* United States v. O'Connor, 580 F.2d 38, 43 (2d Cir. 1978) (testimony of defendant's non-receipt of bribes from other meat packers excluded as "attempt to demonstrate . . . [defendant's] good character by proof of specific good acts").

[12] Chambers v. Mississippi, 410 U.S. 284, 93 S. Ct. 1038, 35 L. Ed. 2d 297 (1973).

[1] *See* **Treatise** at ¶ 404[02].

admissible in an action for negligently entrusting a vehicle to an incompetent driver,[2] and has also been admitted in wrongful death actions as relevant to the issues of damages and loss to the beneficiary.[3]

Character evidence is customarily received in Hobbs Act prosecutions,[4] and in connection with prosecutions pursuant to the Extortionate Credit Transaction Act.[5] Since the government must prove that property was extorted from the victim by threats, the defendant's reputation for violence—when known to the victim—is relevant in ascertaining the victim's fear and its reasonableness. The accused's character and criminal conduct may also be essential factors for the court to consider in determining whether a defendant is "dangerous" under the dangerous special offender statute.[6] The use of character evidence when the accused raises an entrapment defense is discussed in ¶ 7.01[01], *supra.*

Prosecutions under the Racketeer Influenced and Corrupt Organizations (RICO) Act provisions have enhanced the opportunity of prosecutors to circumvent Rules 404 and 405 through proof of a pattern of conduct incorporating many criminal predicate acts.[7] Such proof could often not be used directly in proving character where only individual crimes were charged. The individual counts might have been severed as providing too great a threat that the jury might infer predisposition, bad character or impermissible proof of pattern or practice, but, under RICO, severance would be contrary to the

---

[2] *In re* Air Crash in Bali, Indonesia on April 22, 1974, 684 F.2d 1301, 1315 (9th Cir. 1981) (aircraft pilot's training records were admissible under Rule 404 to show that employer had notice of pilot's alleged incompetence and should not have allowed him to fly). For discussion of admissibility of character in negligence cases *see* **Treatise** at ¶ 404[20].

[3] *See* discussion in **Treatise** at ¶ 404[02].

[4] United States v. Billingsley, 474 F.2d 63, 66 (6th Cir. 1973) ("[T]he reputation of the defendant is admissible not to show that he was a bad man and likely to commit a crime, but to indicate that the threats of the defendant were not idle.").

[5] *See, e.g.,* United States v. Dennis, 625 F.2d 782, 800 (8th Cir. 1980) (reputation evidence may be used to show the state of mind of both the defendant and the victim).

[6] *See* United States v. Schell, 692 F.2d 672 (10th Cir. 1982) (construing 18 U.S.C. § 3575).

[7] *See* 18 U.S.C. § 1961 (5) defining a "pattern of racketeering activity," and 18 U.S.C. § 1962 (e) making participation in such a pattern illegal.

substantive theory of the case, which requires proof of repeated individual acts of racketeering.[8]

There are other instances not connected with guilt-determination where propensity is considered. Sentencing is an obvious example.[9] Under the Bail Reform Act of 1984,[10] other crimes may be considered in deciding whether the defendant should be detained prior to trial to protect the community.

When character is in issue, proof may be made by specific acts; otherwise only opinion or reputation may be used. Specific acts create more powerful proof as a general rule, with greater possibilities of prejudice.[11]

¶ 7.01[03]   Character in Civil Cases[1]

Rule 404 adopts the orthodox position of rejecting evidence of character in civil actions offered as a basis for inferring an act. This exclusion does not prohibit the introduction of character evidence in a civil case where character is in issue or the evidence is being offered to reflect upon the credibility of a witness, or as proving something other than that defendant acted in conformity with his character.[2]

It is not reasonable, particularly in view of the Advisory Committee notes, to read Rule 404(a)(1) and (2) as permitting evidence of character in a civil case if the conduct involved would be a crime.

---

[8] *See* G. Robert Blakey, *Material on RICO: Criminal Overview* 18, 19 (1979) (statute was designed by drafters to permit the jury to receive evidence about other crimes which would have been excluded under traditional evidence rules).

[9] United States v. Pirovolos, 844 F.2d 415, 420 (7th Cir.), *cert. denied,* 109 S. Ct. 147 (1988) (court concluded that under statute governing offense of possession of firearm by convicted felon, defendant's prior convictions were relevant only to sentence-enhancement and error, but harmless, to have admitted them as stating separate offenses).

[10] 18 U.S.C. § 3141 *et seq.*

[11] *See* discussion of Rule 405 in ¶ 7.02, *infra.*

[1] For a discussion of character in civil cases generally *see* **Treatise** at ¶ 404[19].

[2] For discussion of use of character evidence in negligence cases *see* **Treatise** at ¶ 404[20].

This is so because the terms "accused" and "prosecutor" are used.[3] Nevertheless, the courts in interpreting Rule 404(a) do not always seem to be aware that the rule bars the use of character evidence in civil cases, perhaps because the Rule does not state so explicitly, or perhaps because of a reluctance to apply a blanket rule of exclusion instead of balancing probative worth against possible prejudice.[4] This is a sensible result, though not in accord with classic practice or the plain implication of the Rule's language.

Despite Rule 404's rejection of circumstantial use of character evidence in civil cases, some evidence of this nature may be admissible in diversity cases because of the thrust of the *Erie* rule. Some states have a no-eyewitness rule which permits evidence concerning the carefulness and prudence of the deceased to be introduced in a wrongful death action where there is no eyewitness to the fatal accident. A minority of jurisdictions admit character evidence in other situations—such as assault and battery cases, or defamation cases, or where a crime is involved. These rules might arguably be considered as expressing state substantive policy which a federal judge should follow despite the exclusion mandated by Rule 404. *Erie* should not apply in the absence of a clear indication by the state that a substantive result was intended under the state's rule.

---

[3] For explanation and criticism of Rule 404's blanket rejection of circumstantial character evidence in civil cases *see* **Treatise** at ¶ 404[03].

[4] *See, e.g.,* Harbin v. Interlake Steamship Co., 570 F.2d 99, 106 (6th Cir.), *cert. denied,* 437 U.S. 905 (1978) (court suggested that plaintiff could have offered evidence as to his good character); Gray v. Sherrill, 542 F.2d 953 (5th Cir. 1976) (civil rights action against police for arresting plaintiff for no apparent reason; court stated that since plaintiff had put his character in issue by testifying that he was calm and temperate, no error in permitting testimony by witness concerning plaintiff's character trait of having emotional outbursts and being argumentative; no mention of Federal Rules). *See also* Crumpton v. Confederation Life Ins. Co., 672 F.2d 1248, 1253–54 & n.7 (5th Cir. 1982) ("when evidence would be admissible under Rule 404(a) in a criminal case, we think it should also be admissible in a civil suit where the focus is on essentially criminal aspects, and the evidence is relevant, probative, and not unduly prejudicial;" alternative holding).

¶ 7.01[04]   Character of Accused; Offered by Accused and in Rebuttal[1]

Rule 404 restates the common law rule which bars the prosecution from the circumstantial use of bad character in the first instance, but allows the accused to introduce evidence of good character.[2] The inconsistency is not based upon a difference in probative force, but rather upon an underlying policy somewhat akin to that involved in the privilege against self-incrimination which seeks to protect a defendant from "uncontrollable and undue prejudice, and possible unjust condemnation."[3] The accused has an absolute right to introduce character evidence, although the trial court, in its discretion, may limit the scope of the proof, as by limiting the number of witnesses;[4] or by controlling the order of proof.[5] Often this option is vital to the defendant. In a case of mistaken identity, where the defendant has no alibi but his own, good character evidence may be the only thing that can save him from mistaken witnesses.

Although many courts speak of the defendant as putting his character "in issue" when he introduces good character evidence, the terminology is misleading; the issue is not whether defendant is "good" but whether he committed a given act, and the evidence is being used

---

[1] *See* **Treatise** at ¶ 404[05].

[2] The classic statement of the common law rule codified by Rule 404(a)(1) is contained in Justice Jackson's opinion in Michelson v. United States, 335 U.S. 469, 69 S. Ct. 213 (1948). *See* **Treatise** at ¶ 404[05].

[3] United States v. Hewitt, 634 F.2d 277 (5th Cir. 1981) (reversible error to have excluded all proffered evidence).

[4] United States v. MacDonald, 688 F.2d 224, 227–28 (4th Cir. 1982), *cert. denied,* 459 U.S. 1103 (1983) (in prosecution for murder of defendant's wife and children, trial court did not abuse discretion in excluding psychiatrist's testimony regarding defendant's non-violent character where evidence would have been cumulative and would have engendered "battle of experts" which would have been more confusing than helpful).

[5] United States v. Southers, 583 F.2d 1302, 1309 (5th Cir. 1978) (trial judge did not err in refusing to allow defendant to introduce character evidence though cross-examination of prosecution's witnesses during government's case-in-chief given potential confusion in the government's subsequent cross-examination of its own witnesses; defendant was free to call witnesses on his direct case and his failure to do so cannot be blamed on trial court's efforts "to maintain an orderly and coherent presentation of the evidence").

circumstantially to show that a person of such character is unlikely to have committed such an act.

The prosecution may come forward with evidence rebutting good character only when the accused has called character witnesses to testify to his character.[6] A defense witness who has knowledge of the defendant's character but who has not been called as a character witness cannot be converted into a character witness at the election of the prosecution before defendant has opened up the issue by proof of good character.[7] However, the defense may convert a prosecution witness into a character witness if it elicits testimony about the defendant's reputation on cross-examination of the witness.[8] Taking the stand does not expose defendant's character to attack,[9] except indirectly insofar as certain evidence of bad character may be used to attack defendant's credibility as a witness, or unless defendant opens the door to cross-examination about prior acts.[10]

---

[6] *See, e.g.,* United States v. McLister, 608 F.2d 785, 790 (9th Cir. 1979) (defense opening statement and testimony by defendant about his legitimate life style did not place his character in issue; government could not introduce evidence of narcotics conviction); United States v. Masino, 275 F.2d 129, 133 (2d Cir. 1960) (testimony as to service with the armed forces and introduction of honorable discharge did not put character in issue).

[7] United States v. Gilliland, 586 F.2d 1384 (9th Cir. 1978) (reversible error for court to have allowed defendant's purported eyewitness, his stepson, to be cross-examined about defendant's prior convictions where witness had not been called as a character witness).

[8] United States v. Grady, 665 F.2d 831 (8th Cir. 1981) (where prosecution witness testified to defendant's good reputation for truth and honesty on cross-examination, proper for government to ask him about the arrests of the defendant reflecting on his truth and veracity).

[9] United States v. Gillespie, 852 F.2d 475, 479–80 (9th Cir. 1988) (defendant's testimony did not put his character in issue; reversible error for clinical psychologist to testify for prosecution about the profile of a child molester); United States v. Reed, 700 F.2d 638, 645 (11th Cir. 1983) (in prosecution for theft, after character witnesses had testified for defense, prosecution could not introduce evidence during cross-examination of defendant that defendant smoked marijuana since government had not sought to use evidence to impeach character witnesses).

[10] *See, e.g.,* United States v. Burkett, 821 F.2d 1306, 1310 (8th Cir. 1987) (where defendant claimed that he had helped police solve other burglaries, and answered in the negative when asked on cross-examination whether he had been involved in other burglaries, court found no error in introduction of evidence about defendant's involvement in other burglaries); United States v. Draiman, 784 F.2d 248, 254 (7th

The appropriate methods of proving and rebutting good character as evidence-in-chief are covered by Rule 405. Methods of attacking and rehabilitating the character of a witness for credibility purposes are covered in Rules 608 and 609. The majority of the circuits[11] favor an instruction advising the jury that character evidence is to be considered in connection with all the other evidence in the case. In the Tenth Circuit, the circumstances of a particular case, but not every case, may require the giving of the "standing alone" instruction.[12] The position of the District of Columbia Circuit is unclear.[13]

Cir. 1986) (where cross-examination left chief prosecution witness in bad personal light, trial court permitted prosecution to introduce prior crimes evidence court had previously excluded in order to explain that witness had contacted FBI about defendant's other crimes).

[11] *First Circuit:* United States v. Winter, 663 F.2d 1120, 1146–49 (1st Cir. 1981), *cert. denied,* 460 U.S. 1011 (1983) ("standing alone" instruction need not be given; reviews cases in other circuits). *Second Circuit:* United States v. Lowenthal, 224 F.2d 248, 249 (2d Cir. 1955). *Third Circuit:* United States v. Klass, 166 F.2d 373, 378–80 (3d Cir. 1948). *Fourth Circuit:* Mannix v. United States, 140 F.2d 250, 253–54 (4th Cir. 1944). *Fifth Circuit:* United States v. Callahan, 588 F.2d 1078, 1085 (5th Cir. 1979) ("character evidence is to be treated together with all other evidence and not segregated merely to tip the scales"). *Sixth Circuit:* Poliafico v. United States, 237 F.2d 97, 114 (6th Cir. 1956), *cert. denied,* 352 U.S. 1025 (1957). *Seventh Circuit:* United States v. Burke, 781 F.2d 1234 (7th Cir. 1985) (extensive discussion). *Eighth Circuit:* Black v. United States, 309 F.2d 331, 343–44 (8th Cir. 1962), *cert. denied,* 372 U.S. 934 (1963). *Ninth Circuit:* Carbo v. United States, 314 F.2d 718, 746 (9th Cir. 1963); Smith v. United States, 305 F.2d 197, 205–07 (9th Cir.), *cert. denied,* 371 U.S. 890 (1962). *Eleventh Circuit:* United States v. Borders, 693 F.2d 1318, 1328–30 (11th Cir. 1982), *cert. denied,* 461 U.S. 905 (1983) (error to convey impression that character evidence to be considered only if evidence is close; but no error in instant case where jury instructed to consider evidence of character "along with all the other evidence").

[12] United States v. McMurray, 656 F.2d 540 (10th Cir. 1980), *rev'd on other grounds,* 680 F.2d 695 (1981) ("standing alone" instruction unnecessary where defendant did not rely solely on good character defense).

[13] *Compare* United States v. Lewis, 482 F.2d 632 (D.C. Cir. 1973) (good character may of itself generate reasonable doubt as to guilt and accused is entitled to have jury so instructed) *with* Marzani v. United States, 168 F.2d 133, 138–39 (D.C. Cir.), *aff'd per curiam,* 335 U.S. 895, *aff'd per curiam on rehearing,* 336 U.S. 922 (1948) ("evidence of good character, taken in conjunction with all the other evidence before you, might be sufficient to create in your minds a reasonable doubt"; court found no error in omission of requested clause; "where, without it, you may have been convinced of his guilt").

Certainly it is not reversible error in any circuit to give the standing alone charge. It seems far fetched to assume that a federal jury will take this instruction as an invitation to ignore all the other evidence. If this is considered to be a danger the jury can be told explicitly that the character evidence should be considered with the other evidence in the case but that in and of it itself [or standing alone] it may be sufficient basis for a reasonable doubt.

¶ 7.01[05]   Character of Victim[1]

Paragraph (2) of subdivision (a) of Rule 404 represents an exception to the prohibition against introducing evidence of character for the purpose of proving that a person acted in a specified way. It permits both the accused and prosecutor to introduce evidence of the character of a victim under specified circumstances.

Rule 404 no longer applies to rape victims. A special rule, Rule 412, enacted in 1978, makes the character of a rape victim generally inadmissible, except under specified circumstances.[2] In a homicide case, the accused may introduce evidence of the victim's reputation for violence or aggression in support of a claim of self-defense.[3] If it is proved that the accused knew of deceased's reputation, this evidence does not transgress the policy expressed in Rule 404 of excluding evidence of character as proof of conduct; it is being offered not to prove the deceased's acts but to establish the accused's apprehension and the reasonableness of his defensive measures.[4] Even if the accused was unaware of deceased's reputation, evidence of this reputation may be introduced pursuant to Rule 404(a)(2).

The prosecutor in a homicide case may offer evidence of a victim's

---

[1] *See* **Treatise** at ¶ 404[06].

[2] *See* **Treatise** at ¶¶ 412[01]–[02] and ¶ 7.09 *infra*.

[3] United States v. Greschner, 647 F.2d 740 (7th Cir. 1981) (in prosecution of inmate for stabbing of another inmate involving a claim of self-defense, error to have excluded evidence that victim had formerly stabbed another inmate).

[4] Gov't of Virgin Islands v. Carino, 631 F.2d 226 (3d Cir. 1980) (Rules do not change prior precedents admitting evidence of victim's acts of violence in order to show defendant's fear).

character for peacefulness in order to rebut evidence that the victim was the aggressor.[5]

¶ 7.01[06] Other Crimes; Permissible Scope[1]

The fact that a defendant committed another crime may be relevant to a wide variety of material propositions depending on the kind of circumstantial steps with which it is used. Only one series of evidential hypotheses is forbidden in criminal cases by Rule 404: a person who commits a crime probably has a defect of character; a person with such a defect of character is more likely than people generally to have committed the act in question. Rule 404(b), which allows evidence of other crimes, wrongs or acts for purposes other than to show that a person acted in conformity with his character, is not an exception to Rule 404(a) since Rule 404(a) does not apply when criminal propensity is not used circumstantially as the basis for inferring an act. In this sense, Rule 404(b) is redundant; it appears as a rule, although the result would have been the same in its absence, to alert the reader to this avenue of admitting evidence of other criminal acts and to detail the most usual instances in which admissibility may be achieved.

Although all American jurisdictions agree that no evidence may be introduced which seeks solely to prove that the accused has a criminal disposition, the question of when evidence of a particular criminal act may be admitted is perplexing. Rule 404(b) is relied upon more frequently in the reported cases than any other Federal Rule of Evidence with the exception of Rule 403, which obviously is a rule of far more general application. Furthermore, even a cursory sampling of judicial opinions reveals that the cases are frequently impossible to reconcile.[2]

---

[5] For discussion of why Congress added this provision to Rule 404 *see* **Treatise** at ¶ 404[06].

Note that the use of character evidence to impeachment witnesses is discussed in detail in commentary to Rule 608 and 609, Chapter 12, *infra.*

[1] *See* **Treatise** at ¶ 404[08].

[2] The judges in the same case may not see eye-to-eye either. *See, e.g.,* United States v. Rubio-Estrada, 857 F.2d 845 (1st Cir. 1988) (extensive discussion by majority and dissent of whether defendant's prior conviction for possessing cocaine with in-

It has not been possible to verbalize a formula which can be applied with any precision because the factors in each case are so varied and unique, and the counterthrusting pressures—constitutional and otherwise—so great. Some aid to fairness is afforded by analyzing each proffer of other crime proof to determine what evidential hypotheses the jury is expected to use, and weighing the probative force of the line of proof against the need of the prosecutor and the risks specified in Rule 403. The more reason there is in the decision to admit or exclude, the more apt it is to be fair. Both bench and bar benefit at a trial if critical questions of admissibility are exposed and reasons clearly stated.[3] As with any determination pursuant to Rule 401, counsel must be prepared to 1) identify the consequential fact to which the proffered evidence of other crimes, wrongs or acts is directed, 2) prove the other crimes, wrongs or acts and 3) articulate precisely the evidential hypothesis by which the consequential fact may be inferred from the proffered evidence.[4] Evidence which passes

tent to distribute, and for aiding and abetting similar possession by others should have been admitted in prosecution for possession of cocaine with intent to distribute; police found cocaine in defendant's house, concealed in closet, and found electronic scales, a ledger which an expert testified contained accounts of transactions that appeared to be drug sales, substantial amounts of cash, and a white powder, never identified, although an expert testified that various white powders are used to cut cocaine; defendant claimed lack of knowledge and intent, and counsel suggested that defendant used scales to weigh gold; majority found that relevance of prior conviction was "fairly obvious" because it made it more likely that one so convicted would know use of scales and ledger books and white powder and how to use these items and to think that cocaine distribution was going on in his house when he noticed items; cites **Treatise**; dissent argues that relevance of these items lies in defendant's possession of them and his prior conviction does not make it more likely that he was using them to deal cocaine except through a propensity inference).

[3] United States v. Rubio-Estrada, 857 F.2d 845, 854 (1st Cir. 1988) ("The importance of making these logical chains explicit for the jury *during trial,* and not when the case is on appeal, is that it provides a minimal safeguard against the jury's improper use of the evidence"; cites **Treatise**; dissenting opinion; majority excused failure to spell out inference in detail on the ground that relevancy of other crimes evidence to knowledge and intent "seemed fairly obvious to the district court"; *id.* at 847; *see also* n.2 *supra*).

[4] United States v. Rivera, 837 F.2d 906, 912–13 (10th Cir. 1988) (court condemned "laundry list" approach whereby government recited purposes listed in Rule 404(b) without identifying which of the Rule 404(b) elements were in dispute and "without affirmatively demonstrating the nexus of the other acts evidence to the resolution of the disputed issue"; error compounded by court's having told jury that it could

muster up to this point must, in addition, satisfy the balancing test imposed by Rule 403 which requires the probative value of the other crimes evidence to outweigh the harmful consequences that might flow from its admission.

The problem is most acute when defendant—by refusing to take the stand and failing to call character witnesses—has closed the other channels through which evidence of other crimes may enter. The Supreme Court's holding in *Griffin v. California*[5] that no comment may be made on defendant's failure to take the stand was intended to further insulate the defendant from inferences that might suggest a criminal past. As a consequence, the prosecutor has more incentive than ever for seeking to introduce evidence of other crimes. For, while disagreement is rife as to the proper scope of an exclusionary rule, everyone agrees that evidence of other crimes is most convincing.

Rule 404(b) does not authorize automatic admission. The Rule lists some of the instances in which other crimes evidence may be admissible, but these categories are neither exhaustive nor conclusive.[6] The terminology "crimes, wrongs, or acts" indicates that conduct that is neither criminal nor unlawful is included if it is relevant to something other than propensity. The proffered item may tend directly to prove or disprove a consequential fact, such as intent or knowledge, or it may tend to establish a proposition, such as motive, which through a series of inferences may tend to establish the probability of a material proposition of fact such as intent.

---

use other crimes evidence as direct evidence of the crime of continuing criminal enterprise).

[5] 380 U.S. 609, 85 S. Ct. 1229, 14 L. Ed. 2d 106 (1965).

[6] For example, if proof of another crime is being offered to satisfy a jurisdictional fact, it is not being used for a propensity inference and is, therefore, admissible. Sanabria v. United States, 437 U.S. 54, 98 S. Ct. 2170, 57 L. Ed. 2d 43 (1978). United States v. Scarfo, 850 F.2d 1015, 1018–21 (3d Cir.), *cert. denied,* 109 S. Ct. 263 (1988) (evidence that prosecution witnesses on order of defendant murdered other members of organization who broke rules was relevant to witnesses' credibility as it bore on their motives for cooperating with government). *See also* **Treatise** at ¶ 404[17].

¶ 7.01[07] Other Crimes; When Is There a Controverted Issue?[1]

Rule 404(b) lists only some of the material propositions of fact which typically may be at issue in a given case. Evidence directed to a category other than propensity is not, however admissible unless this issue is actually being controverted. This is simply a specialized application of the usual rule that evidence must be probative of a proposition of fact that is material, that is to say relevant. *See* discussion of Rule 401, Chapter 6, *supra.* Although this is an elementary principle of the law of evidence, it has proven difficult to apply in a number of contexts involving other crimes evidence.

[a] Stipulations

If the defendant is willing to stipulate as to a particular issue—for example, that if the charged criminal act is proven, the defendant will not contest intent—is there still a controverted proposition of fact to which other crimes evidence may be adduced? The courts generally say no,[2] but a close reading of the cases indicates that trial courts are reluctant to cut off evidence that would have probative value,[3] and careful analysis is essential to identify the material proposition of fact and the evidentiary hypothesis for which the evidence is being offered.[4] Too tight and rigid a view by appellate courts in such cases leads to trials so aseptic as to be out of touch with reality.

---

[1] *See* **Treatise** at ¶ 404[09].

[2] *See, e.g.,* United States v. DeVaughn, 611 F.2d 42 (2d Cir. 1979) (where concession removed identity as issue, reversible error to introduce evidence of subsequent possession of heroin as relevant to identity); United States v. Mohel, 604 F.2d 748 (2d Cir. 1979); United States v. Webb, 625 F.2d 709 (5th Cir. 1980) (dictum).

[3] *See, e.g.,* United States v. Perry, 643 F.2d 38, 51 (2d Cir.), *cert. denied,* 454 U. S. 835 (1981) (in prosecution for conspiring to distribute heroin where defendants had distributed substances which were themselves legal and uncontrolled but which were used as cutting agents for heroin, not error to introduce evidence of defendant's prior large scale heroin dealings where his defense was that he was simply a little mannite dealer; defendant had stipulated that he had sold mannite on three occasions with knowledge of its ultimate use).

[4] United States v. Bass, 794 F.2d 1305, 1312 (8th Cir.), *cert. denied,* 107 S. Ct. 233 (1986) ("a proper Rule 403 balancing analysis will incorporate some assessment of

[b] Timing

Must the court defer admission of the other crimes evidence until the defense is concluded, since the court will only then be in a position to determine which issues are controverted? Certainly, when it is apparent from the opening statement,[5] or previous proceedings,[6] that a certain consequential fact will be in issue, the appellate courts have refused to find error in the admission of other crimes evidence as part of the government's direct case. But suppose the defendant has done nothing other than to interpose a plea of not guilty. In such a situation may the prosecution offer other crimes evidence in its case-in-chief? The circuits have not used a uniform approach in dealing with this problem.

The Second Circuit differentiates among the issues as to which the other crimes evidence is being offered. When the prosecution seeks to use the similar acts to prove design or identity, the Second Circuit

---

the need for the allegedly prejudicial information in light of a valid stipulation"; cites **Treatise**).

[5] *See* United States v. Price, 617 F.2d 455 (7th Cir.1979)(in Hobbs Act prosecution, defendant suggested in opening statement that jury could find that payments constituted "gifts" or "contributions"); United States v. Olsen, 589 F.2d 351 (8th Cir. 1978), *cert. denied,* 440 U.S. 917 (1979) (although admission of evidence of other crimes should perhaps have been deferred until after defendant had testified to his purported lack of knowledge, no abuse of discretion since defendant's opening statement raised lack of knowledge as his defense, and because of other circumstances of case). *Cf.* United States v. Beechum, 582 F.2d 898, 914 (5th Cir. 1978) (en banc), *cert. denied,* 440 U.S. 920 (1979) (court reserved decision on whether intent may be proved on direct case where clear before trial that accused would contest intent, and any objection to order of proof waived when he took stand and professed lack of criminal intent).

[6] United States v. Brunson, 549 F.2d 348, 361 n.20 (5th Cir.), *cert. denied,* 434 U.S. 842 (1977) (appellate court suggests that it would be preferable for government to wait until conclusion of defense case before offering other crimes evidence, rather than introducing it at the end of its case-in-chief because the trial court would then be "in a better position to determine whether the element which the other crimes evidence is offered to prove has become a material issue in the case and how substantial the need for the evidence is"; however, no error in instant case where defense of lack of intent was "foreshadowed" by evidence and defendant did not object on this ground to introduction of other crimes evidence); United States v. McMahon, 592 F.2d 871 (5th Cir.), *cert. denied,* 442 U.S. 921 (1979) (obvious that intent would be issue because of grand jury testimony; furthermore waiver of objection to order of proof when defendant took stand).

permits the other crimes evidence to be introduced in the government's case-in-chief.[7] When, however, the evidence is relevant to intent, it may not be introduced until the conclusion of the defense case, since the need for the evidence may be obviated by the possibility of inferring intent from proof of the act itself.[8] Deferral to rebuttal, however, does not solve the problem when the defendant fails to introduce any evidence. In such a case, the Second Circuit permits the government to reopen if, upon reconsideration and rebalancing under Rule 403, the court concludes that the evidence is relevant to intent.[9] The Second Circuit also holds that intent is not a controverted issue where defendant claims he did not do the charged act at all, rather than claiming he did it innocently or mistakenly.[10]

This Second Circuit approach is useful in preventing the prosecutor from circumventing the other crime rule when it is not necessary for its case to do so, but it sometimes leads to awkwardness in presenting the prosecution's case[11] and is inconsistent with the trial courts' broad discretion to fix the order of proof under Rule 611. Other circuits, accordingly, properly reject the Second Circuit's rigid approach and hold that at least in those cases where the government must prove specific intent as an element of the crime charged, evidence of other crimes may be introduced without timing limits to establish that intent.[12] A reading of the cases indicates that in some

---

[7] United States v. Reed, 639 F.2d 896 (2d Cir. 1981); United States v. Danzey, 594 F.2d 905 (2d Cir.), *cert. denied,* 441 U.S. 951 (1979).

[8] United States v. Danzey, 594 F.2d 905 (2d Cir.), *cert. denied,* 441 U.S. 951 (1979).

[9] United States v. Figueroa, 618 F.2d 934 (2d Cir. 1980).

[10] United States v. Manafzadeh, 592 F.2d 81 (2d Cir. 1979).

[11] The problems that may ensue are graphically illustrated by United States v. Ortiz, 857 F.2d 900 (2d Cir. 1988) (*see* discussion at ¶ 7.01[11], n.4 *infra*).

[12] *See, e.g.,* United States v. Hamilton, 684 F.2d 380 (6th Cir.), *cert. denied,* 459 U.S. 976 (1982) (intent to defraud is statutory element of crime which government must prove in prosecution for passing altered bills); United States v. Weidman, 572 F.2d 1199 (7th Cir.), *cert. denied,* 439 U.S. 821 (1978) (specific intent is required element of mail fraud); United States v. Adcock, 558 F.2d 397 (8th Cir.), *cert. denied,* 434 U.S. 921 (1977) (extortion). *See also* United States v. Norton, 846 F.2d 521, 524 (8th Cir. 1988) ("While Norton asserts that his intent was not an issue in question because his only defense was that he was coerced to take part in the transactions, the government is not limited in its proof of its case by a defendant's representations of what his case will be after the government rests.").

instances the courts admit other crimes evidence, offered to prove intent, on the government's direct case even when the government is not required to prove specific intent.[13] Such unnecessary use constitutes an abuse of the rules and should not be permitted.

[c] Conspiracy

Some courts appear to give the prosecution an especially broad leeway in the use of other crimes evidence when a conspiracy has been charged. Acts in furtherance of the conspiracy which occur during the time the conspiracy is operative are not other crimes at all; they are part of the conspiracy itself. But other crimes, wrongs or acts, extraneous to the conspiracy, are sometimes admitted as relevant to the existence of a conspiracy with virtually no analysis by the court of why defendant's participation in conspiracies amounts to anything more than proof of his propensity to engage in crime.[14]

---

[13] *See, e.g.,* United States v. Harrod, 856 F.2d 996, 1000 (7th Cir. 1988) (specific intent is an essential element of bank theft and bank fraud, and defendant cannot remove intent as an element of government's proof by merely claiming that he did not participate in charged crime); United States v. Webb, 625 F.2d 709 (5th Cir. 1980) (defendant was charged with firing at a helicopter; appellate court found that evidence that someone on defendant's property shot at helicopter several days after charged incident was relevant since defendant might have claimed that the shooting was accidental; defendant actually raised an alibi defense).

[14] *See, e.g., Second Circuit:* United States v. Bermudez, 526 F.2d 89, 95–96 (2d Cir. 1975), *cert. denied,* 425 U.S. 970 (1976) (narcotics-related equipment seized six weeks after conspiracy had terminated); United States v. Tramunti, 513 F.2d 1087, 1116 (2d Cir.), *cert. denied,* 423 U.S. 832, 96 (1975) (narcotics seized after termination of conspiracy); United States v. Mallah, 503 F.2d 971, 981 (2d Cir. 1974), *cert. denied,* 420 U.S. 995 (1975) (post-conspiracy possession of thermometers (apparently used in testing heroin) as evidence of intent to participate in prior narcotics conspiracy). *Fifth Circuit:* United States v. Renteria, 625 F.2d 1279, 1281 (5th Cir. 1980) (in prosecution charging conspiracy to import and distribute cocaine and marijuana, evidence of possession of a commercially saleable amount of cocaine properly admitted; "It is sufficient if the extrinsic offense is similar to the substantive offense at the core of the conspiracy."); United States v. Bobo, 586 F.2d 355, 372 (5th Cir. 1978) (where statement indicating defendant had been involved in other crime was being used to prove the existence of a conspiracy, the evidence was relevant to an issue other than defendant's character and was therefore admissible pursuant to Rule 404(b) unless the trial judge should have exercised his discretion to exclude pursuant to Rule 403; not error to admit because "incremental probity of the evidence was substantial"). *Ninth Circuit:* United States v. Uriarte, 575 F.2d 215, 218

Conspiracy cases present special dangers and care must be exercised not to load matters too heavily against defendants by other crime and co-conspirator hearsay. This is not to say that other crimes evidence, such as that used to prove plan or design, motive or intent, may not be relevant to something other than propensity in conspiracy prosecutions.

¶ 7.01[08]   Other Crimes; Proof of Other Crime[1]

[a]   Assessing Probative Value

Once the material proposition of fact is identified, the probative force of the other crime evidence must be assessed. One serious and nagging doubt that must be considered by the trial judge is whether the prior crime caused the police to focus on the particular defendant because of his known proclivity so that they then failed to investigate fully other possibilities. This danger is particularly acute when deviate sex acts, counterfeiting, narcotics, or other criminal specialties are involved.

Another obvious problem is that of proving the other crime.[2] To the extent that there is a serious question about whether the accused committed another crime, the probative force of the entire line of

---

(9th Cir. 1978) (not error in prosecution for conspiracy to import marijuana for witness to testify that he had initially worked for defendant in smuggling aliens: "Evidence relevant to the existence and aims of the conspiracy is admissible."). *Tenth Circuit: See, e.g.,* United States v. Bridwell, 583 F.2d 1135, 1140 (10th Cir. 1978) (appellate court found that evidence of drug transaction subsequent to charged drug conspiracy was properly admitted although it "approaches the outer limits of permissible use of rule 404(b) evidence"). *Eleventh Circuit:* United States v. Kopituk, 690 F.2d 1289, 1334–35 (11th Cir. 1982), *cert. denied,* 461 U.S. 928 (1983) (plea of "not guilty" in conspiracy case sufficiently raises issue of intent to justify admission of extrinsic offense evidence; rule based on difficulty of proving intent in conspiracy cases, particularly where defendant is "passive" member of conspiracy).

[1] *See* **Treatise** at ¶ 404[10].

[2] An authenticated copy of a prior conviction would be admissible pursuant to Rule 803(22) if the requirements of Rule 404 are met.

proof is seriously attenuated.[3]

There is no requirement that the other criminal activity have culminated in a criminal conviction,[4] or even that it has resulted in a criminal charge.[5] All that is required is proof that the defendant was connected to the other offense. In making this determination, the Supreme Court has held that the trial court need not make a preliminary finding that the government has proved the other act by a preponderance of the evidence before the court may submit the evidence to the jury.[6] Rather, because similar act evidence is governed by Rule 104(b) and not Rule 104(a), the trial court:

> simply examines all the evidence in the case and decides whether the jury could reasonably find the conditional fact . . . by a preponderance of the evidence . . . . Often the trial court may decide to allow the proponent to introduce evidence concerning a similar act and at a later point in the trial assess whether sufficient evidence has been offered to permit the jury to make the requisite finding. If the proponent has failed to meet this

---

[3] United States v. Peterson, 808 F.2d 969, 974 (2d Cir. 1987) (in prosecution for knowingly possessing a stolen check from the United States mail, reversible error to admit another check which, according to the government's handwriting expert defendant had endorsed, where government failed to show that check had been stolen, or that defendant had received proceeds of check, or that endorsement was unauthorized); United States v. Brown, 608 F.2d 551 (5th Cir. 1979) (in prosecution for causing injury to defendant's child, reversible error to have admitted evidence that two weeks previously child had suffered severe multiple bruises where government failed to show that injuries were the result of any offense, or that the defendant committed the offense); United States v. DeVaughn, 601 F.2d 42 (2d Cir. 1979) (in prosecution for distribution of heroin, where defendant allegedly exchanged heroin for quinine supplied by DEA agent, evidence that three days later defendant was found in possession of heroin cut with quinine did not corroborate evidence of heroin-quinine exchange in absence of any evidence that quinine found in heroin was the same or sufficiently identical to quinine supplied by agent; reversible error to have admitted other-crime evidence).

[4] United States v. Nolan, 551 F.2d 266 (10th Cir.), cert. denied, 434 U.S. 904 (1977) (court rejected contention that other crime could not be used because it had resulted in a British conviction which would not meet federal constitutional standards; Rule 404 unlike Rule 609 does not require proof of a conviction).

[5] United States v. Fowler, 735 F.2d 823 (5th Cir. 1984) (Rule 404 refers to evidence that reflects adversely on defendant's character regardless of whether there has been a conviction or indictment).

[6] United States v. Huddleston, — U.S. —, 108 S. Ct. 1496, 99 L. Ed. 2d 771 (1988).

minimal standard of proof, the trial court must instruct the jury to disregard the evidence.[7]

Although the Court acknowledged that other crimes evidence may be unduly prejudicial, the Court explained that the usual rules for admissibility provide adequate safeguards:

> We think, however, that the protection against such unfair prejudice emanates not from a requirement of a preliminary finding by the trial court, but rather from four other sources: first, from the requirement of Rule 404(b) that the evidence be offered for a proper purpose; second, from the relevancy requirement of Rule 402—as enforced through Rule 104(b); third, from the assessment the trial court must make under Rule 403 to determine whether the probative value of the similar acts evidence is substantially outweighed by its potential for unfair prejudice, . . . and fourth, from Federal Rule of Evidence 105, which provides that the trial court shall, upon request, instruct the jury that the similar acts evidence is to be considered only for the proper purpose for which it was admitted.[8]

[b]   Convictions Resulting in Acquittals or Dismissals

In *Dowling v. United States,*[9] the Supreme Court resolved a conflict as to whether evidence might be introduced of another crime of which defendant had been acquitted. The Court concluded "that neither the Double Jeopardy nor the Due Process clause barred the use of this testimony."[10] The court explained

---

[7] *Id.* at —, 108 S. Ct. at 1501, 99 L. Ed. 2d at 782–83; United States v. Fortenberry, 860 F.2d 628 (5th Cir. 1988) (in prosecution of defendant for allegedly placing small explosive device on his ex-father-in-law's automobile, trial court admitted evidence of numerous unusual incidents that occurred after defendant's ex-wife regained custody of their children; *inter alia,* crossbow arrows were shot at wife's attorney's house and defendant's ex-father-in-law, pipe bombs exploded in restaurants owned by ex-father-in-law, and wife's attorney's cars were destroyed by incendiary devices similar to those used on ex-father-in-law's car and restaurant; conviction reversed on the ground that the other crimes occupied more of the jury's time than the charged offenses and were of a magnitude greater than the charged offenses, and that the government failed to present direct proof that defendant committed these other acts).

[8] United States v. Huddleston, —U.S.—, 108 S. Ct. 1502, 99 L. Ed. 2d 783–84.

[9] — U.S. —, 110 S. Ct. 668, — L. Ed. 2d — (1990).

[10] *Id.* at —, 110 S. Ct. at 670, — L. Ed. 2d at —.

that the government does not have to prove beyond a reasonable doubt that defendant committed the other crime in order to use other crimes evidence. Furthermore, evidence relating to an acquittal is not inherently unreliable so as to raise due process concerns. Defendant must look to the evidentiary rules for protection against this type of evidence. Evidence of acquittals will be subject to a Rule 403 balancing test and may be excluded if the probative value is outweighed by undue prejudice.

[c] Other Crime Versus Same Crime

Rule 404(b) presupposes the existence of other crimes, wrongs or acts. Sometimes, however, it is very difficult to draw a line between the crime charged and other wrongful circumstances with which it is inextricably intertwined.[10a] It may be quite impossible to prove the

(Text continued on page 7–29)

10a United States v. Ball, 868 F.2d 984 (8th Cir. 1989) (in prosecution for assaulting federal officer with a chain, defendant claimed that officer tripped over the chain as defendant was connecting it between his friends' disabled vehicle and a pick-up truck; court held that threatening statements to police officer made by defendant after he was arrested were highly probative of defendant's state of mind at time of alleged assault; court did not consider that statements might have been reaction to arrest).

case without revealing other crimes.[11] If an understanding of the event in question, or if a description of the immediate circumstances reveals crimes other than those charged, exclusion will lead to a highly artificial situation at the trial making understandable testimony unlikely. In spite of all precautions some suggestion of the related crime is bound to creep in.

The underlying rationale of Rule 404—to protect the defendant from undue prejudice—should be kept in mind. Consequently, only as much of related crimes as is necessary to make comprehensible the evidence relating to the charged crime should be admitted. Naturally, judges differ in their assessment of where the line should be drawn.[12]

¶ 7.01[09]   Other Crimes Evidence; the Evidential Hypothesis[1]

In order for evidence to be admitted pursuant to Rule 404(b), the proponent of the evidence must be able to convince the court of the soundness of the evidential hypothesis which makes the other crime relevant to prove an issue in controversy other than propensity.[2] Evidence of a subsequent crime may be admissible provided the eviden-

---

[11] United States v. Tate, 821 F.2d 1328, 1331–32 (8th Cir. 1987) (federal weapons violations; evidence that defendant had shot two state troopers with weapons "was admitted as an integral part of the overall criminal transaction").

[12] *See, e.g.,* majority and dissenting opinions in United States v. Day, 591 F.2d 861 (D.C. Cir. 1978) and other cases discussed in **Treatise** at ¶ 404[10].

[1] *See* **Treatise** at ¶ 404[11].

[2] United States v. Lynn, 856 F.2d 430, 436 (1st Cir. 1988) (in prosecution for participation in international smuggling operation, proof of defendant's prior sale of marijuana to undercover agent six years previously was of questionable probative value; inference to be drawn seems to be that the defendant had the propensity and therefore more probably the intent to commit the crime and this seems very close to inference Rule was designed to avoid; cites **Treatise**); United States v. Lau, 828 F.2d 871, 874–75 (1st Cir. 1987), *cert. denied,* 108 S. Ct. 1729 (1988) (evidence that defendant had participated in a prior drug smuggling scheme was admissible to prove identity of defendants and to refute innocent or naive explanations of defendants' behavior; court stated that it "need not decide whether either of these two sets of inferences, standing alone, would justify the admission of the prior bad act evidence .... Together ... they have sufficient probative value to bring the probity-versus-prejudice balance within the scope of the district court's lawful powers.").

tial hypothesis with which it is utilized demonstrates relevancy to the controverted issue.[3] Although the proffer of the evidence of other crimes—whether subsequent to or prior to the offense charged—may have a surface plausibility, counsel must be prepared with a detailed analysis of how the evidence alters the probabilities.[4]

The discussion below focuses on the hypotheses most commonly used to make other crimes evidence admissible pursuant to Rule 404(b).

[a]   Intent[5]

As noted there is some disagreement among the courts as to when intent is a material proposition in a case. The circuits do not take a completely uniform approach in ascertaining when intent is a controverted issue to which proof can be directed. Some defenses, however, such as intoxication,[6] non-consent,[7] duress,[8] or entrapment[9]

---

[3] *But see* United States v. Echeverri, 854 F.2d 638, 645 (3d Cir. 1988) (presence of cocaine in defendant's apartment eighteen months after the termination of the alleged conspiracy and four years after last overt act as to which there was direct evidence was not probative of knowledge or intent of conspirators during relevant period; cites **Treatise**).

[4] United States v. Mothershed, 859 F.2d 585, 588–92 (8th Cir. 1988) (reversible error for trial court to have admitted prior conviction that reviewing court found was not relevant to any element of charged crimes; court disapproved of government having simply read "laundry list" of issues for which other crimes can be admitted under Rule 404(b) because it left reviewing court with burden of reconstructing all the issues from the trial and determining whether prior conviction was relevant).

[5] *See* **Treatise** at ¶ 404[12].

[6] United States v. Smith, 552 F.2d 257 (8th Cir. 1977) (evidence of other narcotics activity relevant to intent which had been placed in issue by intoxication defense); United States v. Kirk, 528 F.2d 1057 (5th Cir. 1976) (prior conviction for threatening president relevant at trial for similar violation where defendant raised intoxication defense).

[7] United States v. Holman, 680 F.2d 1340 (11th Cir. 1982) (in drug distribution conspiracy where one defendant argued that he had only allowed son to use boat because of threats on son's life, not error to introduce evidence of past smuggling activities).

[8] United States v. Hearst, 563 F.2d 1331 (9th Cir. 1977), *cert. denied,* 415 U.S. 1000 (1978).

clearly allow evidence relevant to intent to be introduced. Showing that intent is material is only the first step; the profferer must also persuade the court that the other crimes evidence is relevant, *i.e.,* that it alters the probability of defendant's having had the requisite state of mind termed intent.[10]

The courts have articulated a number of evidential hypotheses which allow other crimes evidence to be utilized as a basis for inferring intent, rather than propensity, the inference prohibited by Rule 404. Since criminal intent is a state of mind inconsistent with inadvertence or accident, evidence of another crime which tends to undermine defendant's innocent explanation for his act will be admitted.[11] Furthermore, repetition of an act affords an "opportunity for

---

[9] *See, e.g.,* United States v. Henciar, 568 F.2d 489 (6th Cir. 1977). Other courts treat entrapment pursuant to Rule 404(a) as an instance of character in issue.

[10] United States v. Payne, 805 F.2d 1062 (D.C. Cir. 1986) (guns recovered from defendant's apartment admitted to show intent to distribute marijuana; discusses cases).

[11] *See, e.g.,* United States v. Dworken, 855 F.2d 12, 27 (1st Cir. 1988) (in narcotics prosecution, evidence of defendant's substantial involvement in drug smuggling in three prior years was properly admitted as defendant's intent is "much more readily comprehended when viewed in full circumstantial context. Dworken's claim that his entreaties and inquiries were but casual explorations of a drug deal that he did not seriously intend to make is belied by the evidence of the prior endeavors"; cites **Treatise**); United States v. Bennett, 848 F.2d 1134, 1136–38 (11th Cir. 1988) (where defendants claimed that they were just fishing when police observed them approaching unoccupied boat containing over 750 kilograms of cocaine, trial court did not err in admitting evidence that one of the defendants (the father of the other) had engaged in narcotics smuggling on other occasions); Young v. Rabideau, 821 F.2d 373, 382 (7th Cir. 1987), *cert. denied,* 108 S. Ct. 263 (1987) (civil rights action for excessive force by correctional officers; court affirmed the admission of general questions concerning plaintiff's prior assaults on correctional officers as probative of intent and absence of mistake or accident, issues that the plaintiff raised by alleging that his acts of poking his finger in a guard's face and grabbing a chain from a guard's hand were reflexive or accidental); United States v. Calandrella, 605 F.2d 236 (6th Cir. 1979) (evidence of uncharged business transaction in which witness claimed he was duped relevant to show defendant's business sophistication in transactions involving his companies, and contradicted defendant's contention that he was merely consultant for business); United States v. McPartlin, 595 F.2d 1321, 1343–45 (7th Cir. 1979) (in prosecution for bribing foreign officials, where defendant claimed that he made the payments only to satisfy extortionate demands, evidence of other instances in which defendant had been willing to make such payments without incentive of extortion properly admitted). *See* other cases cited in **Treatise** at ¶ 404[12].

reflection and for foresight of the consequences,"[12] so that even if defendant did not possess criminal intent initially, it may be inferred that defendant in a number of incidents, must have arrived at a mental state inconsistent with innocence by the time of the charged act.[13] There is substantial overlap between intent and knowledge, which are often lumped together by the courts because in many instances both are disputed and must be proved by the prosecution.

Although courts often stress the similarity of the charged and uncharged acts,[14] the degree of similarity required will depend on the

---

[12] People v. Gerks, 243 N.Y. 166, 171, 153 N.E. 36, 38 (1926) (Cardozo, J.).

[13] United States v. Gordon, 780 F.2d 1165, 1173–74 (5th Cir. 1986) (in prosecution for defrauding an insurance company by having his tractor-trailer "stolen," the district court properly admitted evidence that, one month earlier, defendant had asked co-conspirators to burn his house so he could receive insurance proceeds; "defendant's prior attempt to defraud an insurance company meets the relevancy requirement because intent to defraud an insurance company was an issue."); United States v. Stump, 735 F.2d 273, 275 (7th Cir. 1984) (in prosecution for illegally prescribing controlled substances, evidence of disproportionately large number of prescriptions written by defendant was properly admitted because it showed that defendant was engaged in a pattern of continuing unlawful conduct outside the scope of a legitimate medical practice); United States v. Sciortino, 601 F.2d 680 (2d Cir. 1979) (in prosecution stemming from defendant's acts in forging endorsements upon and cashing two fire insurance checks, where defendant claimed he was under an honest belief that he owned property involved, or in the alternative, was mistaken about his authority to cash checks, evidence that defendant also forged endorsement upon and cashed third fire insurance check was properly admitted); United States v. Fairchild, 526 F.2d 185, 189 (7th Cir. 1975), cert. denied, 425 U.S. 942 (1976) (evidence of possession of counterfeit bills tended to prove that passing of single bill was "not a mere accident or mistake," relying on Federal Rules of Evidence). See also O'Neil v. Krzeminski, 839 F.2d 9, 11, 14 (2d Cir. 1988) (in prosecution against police officers for using excessive force against plaintiff after he was arrested, majority finds that prior judgment against defendant for using excessive force was admissible, not to prove base line intent, which was undisputed, but to prove intent to inflict needless injury; dissent found evidence irrelevant since defendant did not claim accident or negligence and, in addition, evidence was excludable under Rule 403 as substantially more prejudicial than probative).

[14] See, e.g., United States v. Griffin, 579 F.2d 1104 (8th Cir. 1978) (in prosecution for fraud in connection with loans made by federally organized credit institution, evidence of other similar transactions also involving land deals and same persons was properly admitted); United States v. Wilkerson, 548 F.2d 970 (D.C. Cir. 1976) (prosecution for kidnapping federal officer during course of attempted escape from prison; evidence of prior escape attempts admitted).

evidential hypothesis that is being employed.[15] This requirement affords considerable leeway to the trial judge, both in making the initial determination under Rule 404(b) that the evidence is relevant to a consequential fact other than propensity, and subsequently in assessing probative value in order to apply the balancing test of Rule 403.[16]

[b] Knowledge[17]

Knowledge is properly in issue when defendant's claim is that he was unaware that a criminal act was being perpetrated.[18] Here the evidentiary hypothesis is similar to the one used with intent, discussed above: the unlikelihood that repeated instances of behavior, even if originally innocent, would not have resulted in defendant's having acquired the requisite state of knowledge by the time of the charged crime.[19] Knowledge may also be in issue when it is an ele-

---

[15] *See, e.g.,* United States v. Flores Perez, 849 F.2d 1 (1st Cir. 1988) (reversible error to have admitted evidence of pending charges in Puerto Rico for possessing an unlicensed weapon and receiving a stolen gun as showing defendant's intent with regard to aiding and abetting in the knowing receipt of guns with obliterated serial numbers); United States v. Beechum, 582 F.2d 895 (5th Cir. 1978) (en banc) *cert. denied,* 440 U.S. 920 (1979) (court noted that if physical elements match, evidence may have higher probative value but that evidence satisfies relevancy test if it alters probabilities).

[16] *See* Treatise at ¶ 404[12] for discussion of narcotics cases in which courts appear to allow considerable discretion in admitting other crimes evidence as relevant to intent, and for extensive citations by circuits of other cases in which other crimes evidence was admitted pursuant to an intent hypothesis.

[17] *See* Treatise at ¶ 404[13].

[18] *See* United States v. Rubio-Estrada, 857 F.2d 845 (1st Cir. 1988) (*see* discussion at ¶ 7.01[06], ns.2 and 3 *supra*); Commodity Futures Trading Commission v. Co Petro Marketing Groups, Inc., 680 F.2d 573, 584 (9th Cir. 1982) (consent judgments and conviction of defendant arising out of illegal sales of commodity options relevant to show defendant's familiarity with commodities laws and to rebut his contention that corporate defendant's actions "were, at worst, innocent, technical violations"); Doe v. New York City Dep't of Social Services, 649 F.2d 134, 147 (2d Cir. 1981), *cert. denied,* 464 U.S. 864 (1983) (in suit by foster child against placement agency for failing to supervise placement properly so that she was, inter alia, subjected to rape by foster father, court erred in excluding evidence of foster sister's abuse since it was relevant to agency's notice and knowledge of risk of harm to plaintiff).

[19] *See, e.g.,* United States v. Fleming, 739 F.2d 945, 949 (4th Cir. 1984) (defendant was convicted of second-degree murder arising out of an accident in which he lost

ment which the prosecution has to prove because of the statutory definition of the crime. Such crimes include the knowing possession of stolen property,[20] or the knowing possession of an unregistered firearm,[21] or the importation of obscene matter.[22]

---

control of his car while traveling at a high rate of speed; defendant's driving record which showed previous convictions for driving while intoxicated was admissible under Rule 404(b) to establish that he had grounds to be aware of the risk his driving while intoxicated presented to others); United States v. Moccia, 681 F.2d 61, 63 (1st Cir. 1982) (in prosecution for possession of marijuana and diethylpropion, where defendant contended that he did not know that there was marijuana and diethylpropion under dog food in freezer room and in barn under chicken coop, prior conviction of defendant for possession of marijuana was relevant to issue of knowledge; because past possessor is more likely to spot marijuana, or less likely to throw it away, or more likely to associate with those who use and keep and talk freely about lost marijuana all of which conclusions support knowledge); United States v. Chiarella, 588 F.2d 1358, 1372 n.21 (2d Cir. 1978), *rev'd on other grounds,* 445 U.S. 222 (1980) (in prosecution for using confidential information obtained through job in financial printing house to anticipate impending tender offers, where defendant denied that he was subject to Rule 10b-5, court held that evidence of repeated similar acts was properly admitted because "the fact that he engaged in five separate transactions over a period of fifteen months would permit the jury to infer that his mind was focused on the nature of his acts").

[20] United States v. DeFillipo, 590 F.2d 1228, 1240 (2d Cir.), *cert. denied,* 442 U.S. 920 (1979) (in prosecution for receiving stolen goods where defendants claimed that they were simply hired hands who loaded and unloaded the goods without knowing they were stolen, evidence of possession of a large quantity of goods stolen three months prior to charged acts was highly probative of knowledge and intent; "this case involves a classic use of similar act evidence"); United States v. Dooley, 587 F.2d 201 (5th Cir.), *cert. denied,* 440 U.S. 949 (1979) (other stolen cars on defendant's used car lot).

[21] United States v. Johnson, 562 F.2d 515 (8th Cir. 1977) (prosecution for knowing possession of an unregistered firearm; evidence concerning defendant's offer to sell machine guns and hand grenades was properly admitted even though specific intent is not an element of the charged offense, knowing possession is, and testimony about offer to sell firearms was probative of defendant's knowledge regarding shotgun with the possession of which he was charged). For cases involving other statutory crimes in which knowledge is an element *see* **Treatise** ¶ 404[13].

[22] United States v. Garot, 801 F.2d 1241, 1246–1247 (10th Cir. 1986) (where obscene matter was found in defendant's bedroom, which is not illegal, it "was vital evidence on the essential element of defendant's knowledge that the package he received through the mail contained obscene materials.").

[c] Motive[23]

When other crimes evidence is admitted as proof of motive, two evidentiary steps are involved: 1) the evidence is admitted to show that defendant has a reason for having the requisite state of mind to do the act charged, and 2) from this mental state it is inferred that he did commit the act. Evidence of another crime has been admitted to show the likelihood of defendant having committed the charged crime because he needed money,[24] sex,[25] or goods to sell,[26] was filled with hostility,[27] sought to conceal a previous crime,[28] to

---

[23] *See* **Treatise** at ¶ 404[19].

[24] *See, e.g.,* United States v. Feldman, 788 F.2d 544, 557 (9th Cir. 1986), *cert. denied,* 107 S. Ct. 955 (1987) (in prosecution for bank robbery, evidence that defendant's joint bank account with his father was overdrawn by $8,000 and that defendant forged his father's signature on bad checks, was admissible to suggest a motive for a crime involving financial gain); United States v. Seastrunk, 580 F.2d 800 (5th Cir. 1978), *cert. denied,* 439 U.S. 1080 (1979) (bank robbery; testimony that when defendant was told to leave by motel manager on day of robbery because he had exceeded credit limit on credit card which defendant was using under an alias, defendant had told him not to worry because he would get money from the bank); United States v. Jackson, 576 F.2d 46 (5th Cir. 1978) (in prosecution for illegally dispensing controlled substances, evidence of 5,000 prescriptions for methaqualone that did not relate to any charged counts properly admitted to show that after doctor had lost surgical privileges at two hospitals he had gone into business of selling street drugs in order to maintain his income).

[25] United States v. Free, 574 F.2d 1221 (5th Cir. 1978) (in prosecution for murdering fellow inmate who refused to engage in homosexual relations with defendant, evidence of letters defendant received from homosexual lover in other prison and testimony from prisoners about defendant coercing homosexual relations was properly admitted as relevant to intent and motive); United States v. Weems, 398 F.2d 274, 275 (4th Cir. 1968), *cert. denied,* 393 U.S. 1009 (1969) (kidnapping; evidence of rape permitted to show motive to prove that victim held "for ransom or reward or otherwise" as statute provides).

[26] Theobald v. United States, 371 F.2d 769, 770 (9th Cir. 1967) (conspiracy to import marijuana; testimony relating to purchase of marijuana from defendant admitted: "This evidence was offered to show motive—that appellant had reason to import a substantial quantity of marijuana because he was engaged in the sale of marijuana").

[27] United States v. Buchanan, 787 F.2d 477, 481 (10th Cir. 1986) (prior threats against owner of trailer home that was firebombed); United States v. Hernandez, 780 F.2d 113, 117–18 (D.C. Cir. 1986) (in prosecution for unlawful possession of a machine gun and silencer, evidence that one defendant was engaged in a fight several hours before his arrest was properly admitted to show motive to possess firearm;

escape after its commission,[29] or to silence a potential witness.[30]

---

reversible error to have admitted against other defendant without limiting instruction when there was insufficient evidence to prove that he was a participant in the fight); United States v. Franklin, 704 F.2d 1183, 1187–88 (10th Cir.), *cert. denied,* 464 U.S. 845 (1983) (in prosecution for murder of two black men on night on which victims had each been jogging with white women, evidence that defendant had previously followed and assaulted an interracial couple and had stated that he thought interaction between races was wrong admissible to show motive); United States v. Goehring, 585 F.2d 371 (8th Cir. 1978) (in prosecution for mailing threatening letter to police officer, proof was properly admitted that defendant had started making threatening calls to officer after officer had issued three speeding citations to defendant).

[28] *See, e.g.,* United States v. Haldeman, 559 F.2d 31, 88–91 (D.C. Cir. 1976) (in Watergate cover-up trial, evidence of break-in at offices of Daniel Ellsberg's psychiatrist was properly admitted; "concealing responsibility for the Ellsberg break-in was part of the motivation for the payment of money to those involved in Watergate," was indicative of a motive to conceal the identities of higher-ups involved in Watergate and cast light on Hunt's threats to reveal what he had done if he were not paid); United States v. Dansker, 537 F.2d 40 (3d Cir. 1976), *cert. denied,* 429 U.S. 1038 (1977) (defendant convicted of bribery to obtain zoning variances; testimony that defendants had previously diverted large sums of corporate money to their own use under pretext of obtaining property for project was relevant since it indicated why a large project which would justify these expenditures was essential even though barred by existing zoning ordinances).

[29] *See, e.g.,* Hernandez v. Cepeda, 860 F.2d 260, 265 (7th Cir. 1988) (evidence of charges on which plaintiff was being arrested at the time of the alleged civil rights violation was admissible to demonstrate his motive to resist which was relevant because it would tend to make more probable the defendants' testimony that plaintiff did in fact resist thereby justifying the use of some additional force); United States v. Smith, 605 F.2d 839 (5th Cir. 1979) (in prosecution of wholesale car dealer for receiving cars from suppliers, taking possession of them, signing bank drafts in exchange, and then pocketing proceeds and instructing bank to dishonor drafts, trial court properly admitted evidence that defendant had pleaded guilty to another offense and knew that he was about to start serving sentences, as part of his plan was to seek refuge from creditors in jail; evidence showed both defendant's motive and plan); Bowden v. McKenna, 600 F.2d 282 (1st Cir.), *cert. denied,* 444 U.S. 899 (1979) (in civil rights action brought by wife and children of man shot by two experienced policemen allegedly for failing to get out of car, evidence that victim had been identified in armed robbery committed that day should not have been excluded as it would have shown that victim had a motive to resist officers).

[30] United States v. Bufalino, 683 F.2d 639 (2d Cir. 1982), *cert. denied,* 459 U.S. 1104 (1983) (tape of extortion attempt admitted in prosecution stemming from attempt to kill person to whom threat was made); United States v. Benton, 637 F.2d 1052 (5th Cir. 1981) (evidence of Florida homicides introduced to show that defendant had reason for killing victim who might implicate him).

[d] Identity[31]

Courts admit other crimes evidence in the name of identity either 1) when the evidence proves indirectly that defendant is the person who committed the particular act with which he is charged, or 2) when the evidence relates directly to identity. In the first type of case identity is being proved indirectly through proof of motive, design or plan. Some courts, instead of applying the identity label, classify these situations as instances of the signature or modus operandi exception.[32] In the second type of case, the evidence relates directly to identity, as when it consists of a photograph or testimony relating to it,[33] a handwriting[34] or voice[35] specimen, an object associating the

---

[31] *See* **Treatise** at ¶ 404[15].

[32] United States v. Lau, 828 F.2d 871, 874 (1st Cir. 1987), *cert. denied* 108 S. Ct. 1729 (1988) (evidence that defendant had participated in a prior drug smuggling scheme under parallel circumstances was admissible to establish that defendants and not others present were owners of cocaine found aboard their helicopter, and to establish common scheme); United States v. DiGeronimo, 598 F.2d 746 (2d Cir.), *cert. denied,* 444 U.S. 886 (1979) (hijacking properly admitted where hijacking was one of the real issues and prior hijacking also occurred at Kennedy Airport, was committed in a similar fashion and stolen merchandise was sold in the same bar); United States v. Bohr, 581 F.2d 1294, 1298 (8th Cir.), *cert. denied,* 439 U.S. 958 (1978) (prosecution for wire fraud; evidence of "scheme very similar to the one charged" perpetrated by defendant properly admitted as relevant to identity; no further details about scheme in opinion). *Compare* United States v. Gubelman, 571 F.2d 1252, 1255 & n.12 (2d Cir.), *cert. denied,* 436 U.S. 948 (1978) (where defendant raised issue by cross-examining prosecution witnesses as to their ability to identify defendant as one of the corrupt meat inspectors allegedly taking bribes, evidence of two uncharged bribes was properly admitted since it made it much more unlikely that main prosecution witnesses had picked out wrong persons; majority stated that it did "not agree with our dissenting brother that only unique signature crimes are admissible under the rubric of identity;") *with* United States v. O'Connor, 580 F.2d 38, 42 (2d Cir. 1978) (in one of series of cases like *Gubelman* court reversed where other crime evidence was sought to be used on identity theory since "not part of a unique scheme . . . there is nothing unique about receiving bribes in cash each week without conversation or spectators.").

[33] *See* **Treatise** at ¶ 404[15] for discussion about admissibility of mug shots.

[34] *See, e.g.,* Abernathy v. United States, 402 F.2d 582 (8th Cir. 1968) (check forgery; primary issue was identity of forger; witness who testified that defendant forged check in his presence was suspect because of his criminal associations; police officer allowed to testify that he had on previous unrelated occasion taken handwriting specimen from individual who signed defendant's name, that this procedure was routinely followed in the case of all arrests, and that he could not identify the defen-

defendant with the crime,[36] or the testimony of a witness called for identification purposes.[37] Evidence may also be admissible to show that defendant at times used another identity.[38]

---

dant as the person who gave the handwriting exemplar; handwriting expert testified that it was highly probable that person who signed exemplar also forged check; appellate court held that "case falls squarely within the identity exception" and affirmed despite reference to previous unrelated arrest). In *Abernathy,* defense counsel might have offered to freely provide non-prejudicial exemplars to avoid use of this prejudicial specimen.

[35] United States v. Tibbetts, 565 F.2d 867 (4th Cir. 1977) (prior recorded threat, identified as being made by defendant, introduced in trial for making false bomb threat).

[36] *See, e.g.,* United States v. Evans, 848 F.2d 1352, 1360–61 (5th Cir. 1988) (in prosecution for purchasing firearms and ammunition using a driver's license issued in a false name, court did not err in admitting pistol, ammunition, gun case, wigs, glasses and false identification documents found in defendant's possession and in her apartment; all of the items were relevant to the question of who purchased the weapons and ammunition charged); United States v. Two Eagle, 633 F.2d 93 (8th Cir. 1980) (where material issue existed as to identity of assailant who attacked the victim and fled in the victim's car, evidence regarding defendant's relationship to the car was clearly relevant to a determination of defendant's identity); United States v. Miller, 589 F.2d 1117, 1136 (1st Cir.), *cert. denied,* 440 U.S. 958 (1979) (in prosecution for smuggling hashish and marijuana with intent to distribute, evidence that defendant had bought another boat shortly before his arrest was relevant where receipt for boat bearing defendant's name was found on island where smuggling operation was taking place, thus linking defendant to smuggling).

[37] *See, e.g.,* McClendon v. United States, 587 F.2d 384 (8th Cir. 1978), *cert. denied,* 440 U.S. 983 (1979) (evidence of other conversations between defendant and government witnesses concerning sales of drugs before and after offense charged were properly admitted where defendant claimed alibi and hence identification of defendant by the witnesses was in issue; evidence of repeated meetings is probative in that it indicates a greater likelihood of accurate identification); United States *ex rel.* Barksdale v. Sielaff, 585 F.2d 288 (7th Cir. 1978), *cert. denied,* 441 U.S. 962 (1979) (after defense witnesses testified that defendant had a long Afro and a moustache at the time of the crime in contradiction of complaining witness' description, rebuttal witness for government could properly testify that defendant had short hair and no mustache even though jury could have inferred that another crime took place when she was with defendant; court noted that defendant was primarily responsible for bringing out references to other crimes).

[38] United States v. Phillips, 664 F.2d 971, 1028–29 (5th Cir. 1981), *cert. denied,* 457 U.S. 1136 (1982) (evidence showing that defendant had driver's license in another name was relevant because phone calls were made to individual with phone listed under that name by other members of the conspiracy).

If there is no issue as to defendant's identity because defendant admits committing the act, then the other crimes evidence should not be admissible on this theory.[39] A defendant in order to prove mistaken identity may show that other crimes similar in detail have been committed at or about the same time by some person other than himself.[40]

[e] Plan or Design[41]

Courts use the plan or design label to admit proof of other crimes in a variety of somewhat overlapping situations:

(1) Same or common or connected or inseparable plan or scheme or transaction, or res gestae. Evidence that reveals defendant's connection with a bad act other than the one with which he is charged is often admitted as background to place the charged act in context, or because it is impossible to prove the charged act without revealing the other act.[42]

(2) Continuing plan, scheme or conspiracy. The object of such evidence is to prove the existence of a definite project of which the charged crime is a part.[43] The cases reveal a continuum ranging from situations close to the common design,[44] to cases where the bounda-

---

[39] United States v. DeVaughn, 601 F.2d 42 (2d Cir. 1979) (in prosecution for possession with intent to distribute and distribution of heroin, where government claimed that defendant had received quinine in exchange for heroin, error to have introduced evidence of defendant's subsequent possession of heroin as relevant to identity since defendant had offered to concede that he had received quinine).

[40] *See, e.g.,* United States v. O'Connor, 580 F.2d 38, 41 (2d Cir. 1978).

[41] *See* **Treatise** at ¶ 404[16].

[42] *See* cases at **Treatise** ¶ 404[16].

[43] United States v. Vest, 842 F.2d 1319, 1324–28 (1st Cir.), *cert. denied,* 109 S. Ct. 489 (1988) (in prosecution of police officer for making false statements before grand jury in which he denied receiving pay-offs from Waters, trial court properly admitted testimony that another witness, a close business associate of Waters, also had made pay-offs to defendant; government's theory was that Waters and various members of the Boston police, including defendant, were members of an ongoing conspiracy to provide protection for illegal sales of marijuana at Waters' variety stores).

[44] *See* United States v. Lewis, 693 F.2d 189, 194 (D.C. Cir. 1982) (in prosecution for passing 20 false money orders, no error in admitting evidence that appellant passed other false money orders where such evidence "covered the same time period

ries of the scheme are astonishingly wider.[45]

As with other applications of Rule 404(b), each case in which admission is sought on a plan or design rationale turns on its own peculiar facts.[46] Individual judges may well differ in their evaluation of the validity and value of the evidential hypothesis on which the profferor of the evidence is relying. Since the court will admit proof of acts performed during the period of the plan's existence, the court's evaluation of the scope of the scheme obviously determines admissibility, but begs the question of how scope is to be ascertained. No rule is more than suggestive. In light of the policy of the rule to protect the defendant against unnecessary prejudice while permitting the government to rely on highly relevant necessary evidence, any balancing requires narrowing the scope of the provable scheme so it is no broader than is clearly required to give the trier an understanding of the evidence necessary to prove the crime charged.

(3) Unique plan or scheme or pattern. There are many instances when details of the crime show an individuality that, if repeated, are highly probative of the conclusion that they were committed by the same person. The issue here is whether defendant committed the act at all, not as in intent cases, whether defendant committed the act

---

as the transactions charged in the indictment, showed appellant's possession of the tools necessary to commit the crimes charged, and tended to show a 'design or plan' to commit crimes of this sort"); United States v. Krezdorn, 639 F.2d 1327 (5th Cir. 1981), *cert. denied,* 465 U.S. 1066 (1984) (where immigration inspector was charged with falsely making and forging signature of other inspector on border-crossing cards, evidence of payments to person other than defendant was relevant where there was independent evidence to show concerted action between defendant and payee).

[45] *See* United States v. Rohrer, 708 F.2d 429 (9th Cir. 1983) (a scale and baggies seized from a defendant's home fifteen months and two and a half years after the last acts forming the bases of counts against that defendant properly admitted; evidence was not too remote in time to be admissible; indicative of a continuing conspiracy and probative of plan); United States v. Carson, 702 F.2d 351, 368–69 (2d Cir.), *cert. denied,* 462 U.S. 1108 (1983) (two vials containing traces of heroin and cocaine taken from defendant at time of arrest admissible as tools of drug trade even if "they relate[d] to transactions outside the scope of the conspiracy"; also, other evidence that defendant engaged in narcotics-related activities unrelated to crime charged similarly admissible because " '[n]arcotics is a business . . . and evidence that the defendants were in the business at a closely related time is relevant, and is not a mere showing of bad character.' ").

[46] *See* cases discussed at **Treatise** ¶ 404[16].

with the requisite state of mind. While not rising to the same certainty of chisel marks or rifling marks, they are no different as identifying marks than the fact that the defendant limped or had a scar over his eye. If, for example, the same or a similar false name is used, the check is almost the same amount, the same kind of purchase is made in the same kind of store and the approach is the same, there is good reason to suspect identity. Criminals are not generally highly intelligent and creative artists. They tend easily to fall into detailed patterns serving as "prints" of their crimes. Proof of the commission of the same type of crime is not sufficient on this theory unless the particular modus operandi is analyzed.[47] A defendant cannot be identified as the perpetrator of the charged act simply because he has at other times committed the same commonplace variety of criminal act except by reference to the forbidden inference of propensity. The question for the court is whether the characteristics relied upon are sufficiently idiosyncratic to permit an inference of pattern for purposes of proof.[48]

Other categories of other crimes are almost limitless.[49] Rule 404 does not prevent reliance on other reasonable inferential hypotheses. Since the design of the rule is to protect the defendant against the inference of bad man therefore bad charged act, these unclassified cases present what are essentially Rule 403 balancing problems.

¶ 7.01[10] Other Crimes Evidence; Balancing[1]

Even if the court finds that the proffered evidence of other crimes has probative value in proving something other than defendant's propensity to commit the charged crime, admission of the evidence does

---

[47] United States v. Lail, 846 F.2d 1299 (11th Cir. 1988) (in bank robbery prosecution, reversible error to have admitted evidence of uncharged bank robberies where dissimilarities between uncharged and charged robberies were more striking than similarities).

[48] *See* United States v. Beasley, 809 F.2d 1273, 1278 (7th Cir. 1987) ("Unless something more than a pattern and temporal proximity is required, the fundamental rule is gone. This is why 'pattern' is not listed in Rule 404(b) as an exception. Patterns of acts may *show* identity, intent, plan, absence of mistake, or one of the other listed grounds, but a pattern is not itself a reason to admit the evidence"; cites **Treatise**).

[49] *See* **Treatise** at ¶ 404[17].

[1] *See* **Treatise** at ¶ 404[18].

not follow as a matter of course.[2] Rule 404(b) provides only that the evidence may be admissible.

If the Rule 404(b) test is met—*i.e.,* the evidence is relevant—the court must turn to an assessment of the evidence's probative worth so that it can be weighed against the preclusive factors specified in Rule 403.[3] In determining the probative value of the proffered evidence, the courts consider such factors as the similarity between the charged and uncharged acts,[4] the reliability of the evidence being proffered, the remoteness of the other crime,[5] and the need for the evidence. Need in this sense means more than the customary principle that evidence may not be introduced on issues that are not controverted. The inclusion of need as a factor to be considered stems from the courts' recognition that the incremental value of other crimes evidence depends on how much other evidence there is.[6] If the government has a strong case, the other crimes evidence will add

---

[2] Hernandez v. Cepeda, 860 F.2d 260, 265 (7th Cir. 1988) ("In the future, . . . we encourage district courts to explicitly acknowledge the balancing process when admitting evidence under Rule 404(b).").

[3] United States v. Zabaneh, 837 F.2d 1249, 1262–66 (5th Cir. 1988) (extensive discussion of court's obligation to identify and weigh the potentially prejudicial effect of other crimes evidence; uncertainty in record led to remand).

[4] United States v. Wiley, 846 F.2d 150, 155–56 (2d Cir. 1988) (error to have admitted Iowa court order stating that defendant and one Wiley had engaged in making false, deceptive, fraudulent and misleading statements; although evidence was probative of defendant having lied when he told witness that Wiley was honest, evidence should have been excluded as too prejudicial because Iowa order related to precisely the kind of charges for which defendant was on trial so that jury likely to use evidence as relevant to defendant's propensity rather than knowledge).

[5] United States v. Harrod, 856 F.2d 996, 1102 (7th Cir. 1988) (whether prior act is close enough in time to be relevant depends on theory of admissibility; where acts were so similar to charged acts that they showed a pre-existing scheme as well as knowledge and intent, acts occurring in 1981 and 1984 were not too remote).

[6] Morgan v. Foretich, 846 F.2d 941, 945–46 (4th Cir. 1988) (in civil suit by plaintiff on behalf of her minor daughter against father of child and his parents for damages arising out of defendants' alleged sexual abuse of child, error for trial court to have excluded evidence that child's half-sister had also been sexually abused; court found need for other act evidence "compelling" in this type of case because "there are seldom any eyewitnesses"; evidence was relevant to counter defenses of self-infliction, fabrication or abuse by mother).

little.[7]

Ascertaining the incremental probative value of the proof fixes but one side of the scale; prejudice must also be weighed. In a joint trial, the court must consider not only the prejudice to the defendant whose other crimes are being revealed but spill-over prejudice to co-defendants.[8] All evidence of other crimes is prejudicial, but some—such as evidence of prior sexual offenses[9] or previous connections with organized crime—is probably more prejudicial than other. The result in each case is, of course, dependent on the particular facts the court is assessing.[10] *See*, in general, discussion of Rule 403, above.

As the foregoing discussion should indicate, details of other cases, though suggestive of possible techniques of advocacy, are not very helpful as precedents, since the same combination of identical factors is unlikely to recur. Generalizations have an initial appearance of solidity but crumble on close examination. In the final analysis, admissibility will depend on the individual judge's evaluation of the

---

[7] *See, e.g.,* United States v. Vest, 842 F.2d 1319, 1327 (1st Cir.), *cert. denied,* 109 S. Ct. 489 (1988) (there was a strong need for other crimes evidence that corroborated testimony of witness in a case that centered to a large degree on the credibility of that witness; "[n]ecessity can be an important element of Rule 403 balancing," citing **Treatise**); United States v. Beechum, 582 F.2d 898 (5th Cir. 1978) (en banc), *cert. denied,* 440 U.S. 920 (1979). Other cases are discussed in **Treatise** at ¶ 404[18].

[8] United States v. Dworken, 855 F.2d 12, 28–29 (1st Cir. 1988) (no error where trial court emphasized that each defendant was to be accorded distinct, individualized treatment, and jury's verdict discriminated among defendants and charges).

[9] Cohn v. Papke, 655 F.2d 191, 194 (9th Cir. 1981) (civil rights action against police officers who had arrested plaintiff on charge that he had solicited one officer to engage in homosexual act; reversible error for trial court to have allowed evidence of plaintiff's past homosexual and bisexual experiences and sexual fantasizing; Rule 404 does not permit inference that because plaintiff was a homosexual he would have solicited a homosexual act; but even assuming arguendo that evidence was admissible under Rule 404, it should have been excluded under Rule 403: "There was a clear potential that the jury may have been unfairly influenced by whatever biases and stereotypes they might hold . . . .").

[10] United States v. Lynn, 856 F.2d 430, 436–37 (1st Cir. 1988) (government added to the prejudice caused by the admission of other crimes evidence for which there was minimal need by placing agent on the stand, eliciting his lack of memory, and then reading his investigatory reports of the prior crime; defendant was presented with the Hobson's choice of ignoring the information in the reports or attempting to cross-examine a witness about details admittedly forgotten, thereby stressing the prior conviction in front of the jury).

justification for the rule as an appropriate device to protect accused persons.

Appellate courts recognize that "The trial judge must have wide discretion to determine whether the probative value of the evidence is outweighed by its prejudicial character."[11] Thus the parties must be prepared to convince the trial judge at the time the evidence is offered. Since both sides will probably be aware of the possibility that the issue will arise, it should be adequately briefed before the judge must rule. More important than lists of cases in such a brief is the detailed analysis of the facts to show why the proof of other crimes is needed, why its use may be prejudicial and how some compromise or limitation may protect both parties. Holding arguments back for the appeal is dangerous and unsound. The appellate court may well take into account the situation as it was presented to the trial judge, rather than the more fine spun analysis presented on appeal.[12] Furthermore, the harmless error rule will apply.

The legislative history of Rule 404 suggests that the policy of protecting the accused should be embraced in good faith by prosecutor and judge. Accordingly, the onus of showing that prejudice is overbalanced by need and good faith should rest on the government. This consideration calls for prosecutorial restraint.[13]

---

[11] United States v. Montalvo, 271 F.2d 921, 927 (2d Cir. 1959), *cert. denied,* 361 U.S. 961 (1960). *See* also United States v. Derring, 592 F.2d 1003, 1007 (8th Cir. 1979) (in prosecution for interstate transportation of stolen vehicles, majority held that trial judge had not abused his discretion in admitting statements defendant had made about murdering the owner of the stolen car: "We do not reweigh the value of the material against its potential for harm to the defendant, but determine only whether the district judge abused his discretion in admitting it"; dissent held evidence should have been excluded pursuant to Rule 403).

[12] United States v. Zelinka, 862 F.2d 92, 98–99 (6th Cir. 1988) (court reversed where evidence was admitted that defendant possessed cocaine and plastic bags seventeen months after the conspiracy charged to distribute cocaine had ended; government had failed to articulate any theory of admissibility).

[13] *See, e.g.,* United States v. Harvey, 845 F.2d 760, 763 (8th Cir. 1988) (in reversing conviction in tax conspiracy prosecution, court noted that prosecutors' zeal had outrun their discretion; trial court had erroneously admitted testimony about unrelated drug activities and related monetary gains in the '60's and '70's and had not given any limiting instruction); United States v. Biswell, 700 F.2d 1310, 1317 & n.5 (10th Cir. 1983) (burden on government to show relevancy of evidence to proper issues); United States v. Williams, 596 F.2d 44 (2d Cir. 1979) (court expressed concern

¶ 7.01[11]   Procedural Aspects[1]

Rule 404 is silent on when and how the admissibility of other crimes, wrongs or acts is to be determined. Obviously, it is to defense counsels' advantage to ascertain if the prosecution intends to offer such evidence against their clients, and to limit such proof as narrowly as possible. The earlier in the litigation process that counsel can make these determinations, the more effectively they can plan a defense.

Rule 404 does not require the government to give notice of an intention to use other crimes evidence at trial. Nevertheless, individual prosecutors should in fairness inform the defense of other crimes evidence they plan to introduce, and many judges require disclosure in conjunction with the pretrial conference,[2] or at the time of argument of a motion to sever or to obtain a bill of particulars.[3]

A desirable way of raising the other crimes issue is by a motion in limine which asks the court before trial to determine how it will rule on the character issues in the case. Whenever possible, the court should indicate before trial how it expects to exercise its discretion so that counsel can realistically plan an effective defense. If the ruling is adverse the issue should be raised again at trial; failure to do so may constitute a waiver.[4] If the court defers a decision until trial,

---

"over the government's readiness to jeopardize a conviction by use of other crimes evidence when the question of admissibility, as here, is a close one.").

[1] *See* **Treatise** at ¶ 404[19].

[2] *See, e.g.,* United States v. Foskey, 636 F.2d 517 (D.C. Cir. 1980) (court suggested that in the future government should exercise its discretion to give defendant notice before trial of its intention to introduce other crimes evidence, and provide defendant with analysis of evidence if defendant moves to suppress).

[3] For a discussion of the interrelationship between other crimes evidence and motions to sever offenses joined pursuant to Rule 8(a)(1) of the Federal Rules of Criminal Procedure *see* **Treatise** at ¶ 404[19].

[4] *Cf.* Luce v. United States, 105 S. Ct. 460 (1984) (to obtain review of claim of improper impeachment with prior convictions, defendant may not rest on adverse in limine ruling but must take stand). United States v. Ortiz, 857 F.2d 900 (2d Cir. 1988) (In a prosecution for possession of heroin with intent to distribute, the defendant made an in limine motion to exclude defendant's prior conviction for selling a controlled substance. The defense theory was that defendant had never possessed any heroin, and had not made a sale to a narcotics agent; accordingly the trial court ruled that the conviction could not be used as there was no issue of intent. The de-

or defendant does not seek a ruling until such time, any conference at which the admissibility of other crimes evidence is discussed should be conducted outside the presence of the jury. A judicial determination before defendant takes the stand affords the accused the most protection consonant with his constitutional right to testify.

Once the question of admissibility has been raised, the profferor of the evidence has the burden of convincing the court that it is relevant other than on the theory of propensity and that Rule 403 does not require exclusion. A court's failure to make explicit findings on how it balanced probative value versus prejudice will not mandate reversal of the conviction when it is apparent to the appellate court that the trial judge considered the appropriate factors in reaching a determination.[5] Counsel should provide a record on this point by briefs and transcribed oral argument.

The court may decide to admit only some of the proffered evidence and may limit inquiry into some of the more prejudicial details.[6] A limiting instruction which explains for what purposes the evidence

---

fense, however, subsequently wished to argue that defendant's act of throwing away six envelopes of heroin when she was about to be arrested, as testified to by arresting officer, was as consistent with personal use as intent to distribute. The trial court, without engaging in Rule 403 analysis, ruled that the prior conviction would become admissible if counsel made this argument. Counsel did not make the argument and defendant contended on appeal that the restriction on closing argument deprived defendant of a fair trial. The court unanimously affirmed the conviction; the majority, however, by analogy to *Luce* held that the defense had waived the point by failing to make the personal use argument. The dissent found that the trial court acted within its discretion when it refused to allow defense counsel to take unfair advantage of defendant's earlier concession to take intent out of case, but strongly rejected the majority's waiver theory, stating that "unlike in *Luce,* the courts would not have to indulge in unreasonable speculation in undertaking the type of Rule 403 balancing demanded here by the appellant." *Id.* at 907).

[5] United States v. Rawle, 845 F.2d 1244, 1247 (4th Cir. 1988) (on-the-record determination by the trial court is not required and failure of court to identify purpose for which evidence was offered does not constitute reversible error even though explicit ruling may be preferable).

[6] United States v. Dworken, 855 F.2d 12, 28 (1st Cir. 1988) (in narcotics prosecution, although appellate court conceded that with hindsight it was perhaps true that trial judge could have excluded more other crimes evidence as not necessary to prove intent, no error where trial court was "not at all indiscriminate" in its rulings and excluded much of the proffered evidence, limited method and timing of proof, and gave limiting instructions).

may be used may have a substantial impact in reducing prejudice.[7] While a failure to give such an instruction, if required, may be a factor leading the appellate court to find reversible error, a failure to give an instruction is not generally held to constitute plain error.[8]

¶ 7.01[12] Character Used for Other Purposes: Negligence[1]

Negligence cases often present the question of to what extent evidence of other accidents may be introduced. Under some circumstances such evidence may be relevant. An extensive body of literature exists which tends to prove that some persons are more accident prone than others. However, under Rule 404, which applies to civil cases, and in most jurisdictions such evidence may not be introduced to prove that a given plaintiff or defendant was more likely to have been at fault in the accident case being tried. The evidence may be admissible pursuant to subdivision (b) of Rule 404 if its purpose is to prove something other than a person's negligent act, as for example, to dispute injuries, or to provide the motive for instituting suit. Where the action is against the employer, parent or owner who allowed the driver to operate the car, evidence of other accidents is admissible if the plaintiff claims that the owner was negligent in entrusting the car to the driver, since the driver's character for driving is then in issue.

Evidence of other accidents in the same place or involving the same machinery or instrumentality is generally admissible, not because it shows that defendant has a general tendency to be negligent, but because it tends to prove either 1) the existence of a dangerous or defective condition where this is in issue or 2) that defendant knew or should have known of the dangerous or defective condition.

In order to be admissible, the evidence must also meet the test of

---

[7] United States v. Hernandez, 780 F.2d 113, 119 (D.C. Cir. 1986) (reversible error not to have instructed jury to be especially cautious about using other crimes against one of the defendants).

[8] United States v. Cooper, 577 F.2d 1079 (6th Cir. 1978) (but would have been better part of discretion for court to have given instruction sua sponte). For cases dealing with the use of limiting instructions in conjunction with Rule 404 *see* **Treatise** at ¶ 404[19].

[1] *See* **Treatise** at ¶ 404[20].

Rule 403. If the evidence of other accidents raises a disproportionate risk of prejudice, confusion or undue consumption of time, it will be excluded. The lawyer should be prepared to present his arguments against admissibility before the trial judge; the cases indicate that trial rulings are rarely reversed.

¶ 7.02 Methods of Proving Character—Rule 405

¶ 7.02[01] In General[1]

Rule 405 provides for three different ways of proving character: (1) by testimony as to reputation, (2) by testimony in the form of opinion or (3) by evidence of specific instances of conduct. Which method may be used depends on the status of character in the case.

The rule reads as follows:

Rule 405

METHODS OF PROVING CHARACTER

(a) Reputation or opinion. In all cases in which evidence of character or a trait of character of a person is admissible, proof may be made by testimony as to reputation or by testimony in the form of an opinion. On cross-examination, inquiry is allowable into relevant specific instances of conduct.

(b) Specific instances of conduct. In cases in which character or a trait of character of a person is an essential element of a charge, claim, or defense, proof may also be made of specific instances of that person's conduct.

When character is a material, consequential fact as defined in ¶ 7.01, *supra*—referred to in Rule 405(b) as an "essential element"—which must be proved, permitting the introduction of all relevant evidence is most likely to yield the truth about a crucial issue. Consequently, evidence of specific instances is allowed, in addition to proof by reputation or opinion.

Rule 405 does not, however, allow evidence of specific instances

---

[1] *See* **Treatise** at ¶ 405[01].

of conduct to be admitted to prove character in those instances in which Rule 404(a) authorizes the circumstantial use of character as a basis for inferring that the person in question acted in conformity with his character. Consequently, an accused, seeking to prove his good character pursuant to Rule 404(a)(1), may only offer reputation or opinion evidence, and the same limitation applies to proof of the character of a victim pursuant to Rule 404(a)(2). Rules 608 and 609, rather than Rule 405, govern the proof of character when used for impeachment. *See* ¶ 12.03, *infra.*

Rule 405 prohibits evidence of specific instances in these circumstances for practical reasons. This type of evidence is so convincing that it may cause a jury to give it too much weight as well as put the defendant to the difficult task of preparing to refute numerous charges covering the entire period of his life. Moreover, it is likely to lead to claims of surprise and confusion. Disputes about whether the conduct took place, and what the surrounding mitigating circumstances were, may take a great deal of time.

Rule 405 departs from customary practice[2] in allowing proof of opinion of the witness himself as well as reputation both in cases where character is a material proposition of fact and where it is being used circumstantially as a basis for inferring that a given act was committed.

The limits on methods of proof in Rule 405 do not apply where the evidence is being introduced not to prove that a person acted in conformity with his character, but to prove something else, such as motive or intent under Rule 404(b). In such a case, even though character is proved incidentally, any method of proof including extrinsic proof of other crimes, wrongs or acts is acceptable.

¶ 7.02[02]   Methods of Proving Character; Reputation[1]

When a defendant elects to call character witnesses to testify to his good reputation, the testimony must relate to his reputation in the community in which he resides, though particularly in urban

---

[2] For a discussion of the historical antecedents of Rule 405 and its legislative history *see* **Treatise** at ¶ 405[01].

[1] *See* **Treatise** at ¶ 405[02].

communities where a next-door neighbor may be a stranger, the defendant's reputation in non-residential business or professional groups with which he associates is acceptable. The witness must be able to demonstrate that he is familiar with the defendant's reputation, and competent to speak for the relevant community.[2] The testimony must relate to a time contemporaneous with the acts charged[3] and to character traits relevant to the offense in question.[4] It is admitted despite the hearsay rule, which would ordinarily bar the admission of uncross-examined opinions expressed outside the courtroom, primarily because reputation evidence is a convenient way of obtaining the views of a large number of people. Even in big cities, television has not completely displaced gossip, and reputation does exist as a major factor in people's lives.

Once the defendant has opened the door to consideration of his

---

[2] United States v. Perry, 643 F.2d 38, 52 (2d Cir.), *cert. denied,* 454 U.S. 835 (1981) (excluded private investigator's proffered testimony about conversations he had with persons in defendant's community since character witness must be able to demonstrate his own familiarity with defendant's reputation).

[3] United States v. Lewis, 482 F.2d 632, 641 (D.C. Cir. 1973) ("Since proof of a reputation at a given time may tend to indicate what the reputation at a later time is, his character witnesses might have been allowed to testify as to a reputation existent during a period prior to and not remote from the offense date. On the other hand, since the community's view of the accused's character could well be affected by the gossip which frequently follows on the heels of a criminal charge, his reputation in the community after the charge became publicized might not be a trustworthy index to his actual character. For this reason, the courts have generally held that a reputation subsequent to publication of the charge on trial is not admissible in evidence") (footnotes omitted).

[4] United States v. Angelini, 678 F.2d 380 (1st Cir. 1982) (in narcotics prosecution, reversible error to have excluded evidence of defendant's "lawabidingness"; federal rule was intended to restate the common law and there is no indication of a general common law rule against the admissibility of such evidence as compared to evidence of good character generally which is excluded because it does not qualify as relating to a specific trait; however, evidence of truthfulness was properly excluded as not pertinent to trait charged); United States v. Hewitt, 634 F.2d 277 (5th Cir. 1981) (drafters of Federal Rules of Evidence did not intend to preclude proof of such a general trait as lawfulness; only restriction is that character trait must be relevant); United States v. Jackson, 588 F.2d 1046, 1055 (5th Cir. 1979) (in prosecution for conspiracy to distribute and possess heroin, trial judge did not err in excluding character evidence as to defendant's truth and veracity).

character by calling character witnesses under Rule 404(a)(l),[5] the prosecution may both cross-examine the defendant's witnesses and call its own witnesses in rebuttal. Rebuttal witnesses may testify only to reputation and to opinion. Testimony pertaining to specific acts by the defendant is not allowed. When cross-examining the defendant's character witnesses, however, the prosecution may ask them whether they have heard about or know about specific acts of misconduct committed by the defendant incompatible with the good character traits they testified to on direct.[6] Since the cross-examination is designed to test the witnesses' knowledge and standards, inquiries into defendant's prior arrests and rumors are permitted.[7] Exposing his character witnesses to a searching cross-examination is the price the defendant pays for being allowed to open up the subject of character which otherwise had been closed for his benefit.

There are some restrictions on the cross-examination. The prosecution must have a good faith basis for asking about the specific acts allegedly committed by the defendant.[8] Some courts prohibit the prosecutor from asking character witnesses whether their favorable opinions of the defendant's reputation would change if they assumed the charges were true.[9] Rule 405 is subject to Rule 403 so that the

---

[5] United States v. Gilliland, 586 F.2d 1384, 1389 (10th Cir. 1978) (if defendant does not utilize witnesses as a character witness, "government may not turn him into a character witness by asking him what kind of man defendant was, and then use those questions to bootstrap into the case evidence of defendant's prior convictions which it was prohibited from using in its case-in-chief.").

[6] *See* **Treatise** at ¶ 405[02] for extensive discussion of the leading case of Michelson v. United States, 335 U.S. 469, 69 S. Ct. 213, 93 L. Ed. 2d 168 (1948), and subsequent cases. *See also* United States v. Alvarez, 860 F.2d 801, 826–27 (7th Cir. 1988) (no error in allowing character witnesses to be cross-examined about events that occurred approximately ten years before witnesses knew defendant; since witnesses were testifying as to reputation it was possible they may have heard or have known something about defendant's past even though the events had occurred in Miami and witnesses were testifying in Chicago).

[7] *See* cases cited in **Treatise** at ¶ 405[02].

[8] *See, e.g.,* United States v. Reese, 568 F.2d 1246, 1249 (6th Cir. 1977) (suggesting that trial judge should hold voir dire examination to determine whether there were rumors about defendant buying stolen goods before allowing cross-examination).

[9] *See, e.g.,* United States v. Curtis, 644 F.2d 263 (3d Cir. 1981), *cert. denied,* 459 U.S. 1018 (1982) (reputation witness cannot be asked about opinion); United States v.

trial court, in its discretion, may limit cross-examination when prejudice substantially outweighs probative value.[10] When requested, the
court should give an instruction advising the jury of the limited purpose for which the evidence of misconduct is admitted.[11]

¶ 7.02[03]   Method of Proving Character; Opinion[1]

When character is being used circumstantially, Rule 405 permits
proof by opinion evidence.[2] This broadening of the common law rule
was intended to encourage testimony illuminating the defendant's
unique characteristics in place of empty formulae equally applicable
to all. Jurors may possibly be less overwhelmed by inquiries as to
the defendant's misdeeds elicited on cross-examination of the character witness if the testimony on direct is more personal.[3]

Opinion evidence may be offered either through lay or expert witnesses. The lay category usually consists of persons enjoying close,
personal relationships with the defendant. The trial court will have
to exercise firm control over the proceedings to insure that the witness does not relate the particular incidents on which the opinion
of defendant is based—for proof of character by specific acts is still
prohibited. And as with all testimony probative value must be
weighed against the countervailing factors to admissibility specified
in Rule 403.

Expert testimony by a psychiatrist or psychologist that the defendant does not fit the character profile of the perpetrator of the
charged acts is more questionable. Although Rule 405 poses no obstacles to the admission of testimony by experts as to the defendant's

---

Candelaria—Gonzales, 547 F.2d 291 (5th Cir. 1977) (questions destroyed presumption of innocence).

[10] *See* discussion in **Treatise** at ¶ 405[02].

[11] *See* instruction proposed by Federal Judicial Center reprinted in **Treatise** at
¶ 405[02].

[1] *See* **Treatise** at ¶ 405[03].

[2] For discussion of change from the common law rule limiting proof to reputation
only *see* Congressional Action on Rule 405, **Treatise** at 405–2.

[3] United States v. Manos, 848 F.2d 1427, 1431 (7th Cir. 1988) (both opinion and
reputation witnesses are subject to cross-examination regarding specific instances
of conduct).

character, the defendant wishing to present such evidence faces numerous hurdles. In the first place, the evidence must meet the general relevancy test of Rule 401. Courts may be more likely to admit evidence that the defendant is sexually normal and is unlikely to have committed a crime of homosexual perversion or that abusive behavior is not compatible with defendant's background than that the defendant is well-adjusted and could not have passed a bad check. The court's decision will depend on judicial evaluation of the dependability of psychiatric and other expert opinion as to the trait in question;[4] expert evidence and writings should be made available to the court to permit an informed ruling on this point. The liberality of the expert evidence rules tends to encourage this type of testimony.

The expert seeking to express an opinion about the defendant's character has to be appropriately qualified pursuant to Rules 702 and 703, and the proffered testimony must meet the test of Rule 403. Opponents of psychiatric testimony have expressed concern that if the prosecution offers rebutting evidence, the resulting battle of the experts will bewilder the jury. Rebuttal testimony that causes the jury to infer that the defendant has committed similar deviant acts in the past (although testimony as to specified acts is not permitted), may seriously prejudice the defendant. An even greater risk of prejudice arises on cross-examination of the defendant's witnesses. If the witness is asked whether he was aware of particular misdeeds of the defendant so that the jury may consider his familiarity with the defendant in evaluating weight and credibility, the resulting prejudice may require the judge to exclude the evidence pursuant to Rule 403.[5] Once this expert testimony is admitted, however, there is an almost certain need for some specificity under Rule 703, which allows the expert to state the basis of the opinion; this should be permitted.

---

[4] United States v. MacDonald, 688 F.2d 224 (4th Cir. 1982), *cert. denied,* 459 U.S. 1103 (1983) (in murder prosecution of defendant for killing his wife and children, court rejected testimony of defense psychiatrist that defendant did not possess the personality type to commit charged acts; testimony would lead to battle of experts); United States v. Staggs, 553 F.2d 1073, 1075 (7th Cir. 1977) (assault; error to exclude psychologist's testimony that defendant would be more likely to hurt himself than others).

[5] *See* **Treatise** at ¶ 405[03] for discussion of constitutional implications arising from expert character testimony.

¶ 7.02[04]   Methods of Proving Character; Specific Acts[1]

The limitations of Rule 405 do not apply when evidence of misconduct is offered not as circumstantial evidence of other misconduct but as evidence of some other fact in issue. *See* Rules 404(a) and 405(b). Accordingly, proof of specific acts committed by either the accused or his victim or by a party in a civil action may be introduced to evidence intent, knowledge, plan or some fact other than character pursuant to Rule 404(b).

As noted above, character witnesses for the defendant may be asked on cross-examination whether they had heard of specific acts committed by the defendant, because the inquiry is not directed toward proving the conduct of the defendant but toward evaluating the credibility of the witness.

Evidence of specific acts is permissible to prove character pursuant to Rule 405(b) in cases in which the character of a person is an essential element of a charge, claim or defense.[2]

---

[1] *See* **Treatise** at ¶ 405[04].

[2] *See, e.g.,* Pagano v. Hadley, 100 F.R.D. 758, 760 (D. Del. 1984) (in defamation action by priest against law enforcement officers, alleging damage to plaintiff's reputation as a result of false and malicious accusations of criminal activity, court ordered diocese to produce certain documents relating to plaintiff's performance as a priest; in order for defendants to be able to defend against claim, they were entitled to discovery of evidence which would be admissible on issue of plaintiff's reputation, or which might lead to discovery of evidence which would be so admissible; citing Rule 405); Crawford v. Yellow Cab. Co., 572 F. Supp. 1205, 1209–10 (N.D. Ill. 1983) (in action for wrongful entrustment of cab, brought by passenger injured in collision, court held that evidence of driver's employment record was admissible as specific instance of conduct, since character was an essential element of charge); *In re* Irvin, 31 B.R. 251 (D. Colo. 1983) (evidence of prior conduct of debtor was admissible to show that debtor's tortious actions, which resulted in personal injury judgment for petitioner, were willful and malicious so that debt should not be discharged). *See* **Treatise** at ¶ 405[04] for discussion of admissibility of character evidence in prosecutions pursuant to the Extortionate Credit Transaction Act.

¶ 7.03   Habit and Routine Practice to Prove an Event—Rule 406.

¶ 7.03[01]   Rationale and Scope[1]

Rule 406 allows the use of "habit" and "routine practice," but nowhere defines these terms.[2] The rule reads as follows:

Rule 406

HABIT; ROUTINE PRACTICE

Evidence of the habit of a person or of the routine practice of an organization, whether corroborated or not and regardless of the presence of eye-witnesses, is relevant to prove that the conduct of the person or organization on a particular occasion was in conformity with the habit or routine practice.

The reason there is no definition of these terms is that they do not have any precise psychological or organizational content descriptive of real world experience. Nevertheless, they are helpful as broad suggestive categories giving the judge great latitude in administering trials. Rule 406 is a subcategory of Rule 403 in requiring a balancing of limited probative force against the costs of time for proof and possible prejudice.

As indicated in the discussion of Rule 404 under character and criminal conduct,[3] the law recognizes that people often act differently than their generalized or specific past conduct would lead the observer to expect even though past conduct, and background are helpful guides to future conduct. The more specific the conduct and the more consistent the pattern, the more likely in general that it will be repeated by the individual in comparable circumstances. Thus habit has some probative force. In cases of institutional conduct—routine practice—there is greater organizational pressure for unifor-

---

[1] *See* **Treatise** at ¶ 406[01].

[2] *See* **Treatise** at ¶ 406[01], ns. 1–3 for a discussion of antecedents and legislative history.

[3] *See* **Treatise** at ¶ 404[01] for additional discussion of the difference between habit and character.

mity if all parties in the organization and outsiders are to react predictably in carrying on the enterprise.

In the continuum of 1) character, 2) habit, and 3) routine practice, the courts are least likely to be impressed with the first as proof that an act was done in conformity with the character trait in question and most likely to accept the third; in the case of the second the courts will want to consider how narrow the practice was, that is to say how automatic and non-thinking, and how difficult the proof—*e.g.,* whether one witness as opposed to many is required. The categories, in short, are defined and applied in terms of the needs of trial administration, as well as in terms of lay and psychological experience.

Rule 406 adopts the well-established practice of admitting evidence of habit or routine practice as relevant to prove that an act was done in conformity with the pattern. The reason for accepting evidence of habit when evidence of character is excluded has generally been explained on grounds of greater probative value.

While Rule 406 does not define habit, the Reviser's Notes indicate they relied upon McCormick's oft-quoted paragraph contrasting habit with character:

> Character and habit are close akin. Character is a generalized description of one's disposition, or of one's disposition in respect to a general trait, such as honesty, temperance, or peacefulness. "Habit" in modern usage, both lay and psychological, is more specific. It describes one's regular response to a repeated specific situation. If we speak of character for care, we think of the person's tendency to act prudently in all the varying situations of life, in business, family life, in handling automobiles and in walking across the street . . . The doing of the habitual acts may become semiautomatic.[4]

Disagreements arise mainly in resolving the question of how frequent, consistent[5] and voluntary[6] behavior must be in order to rise

---

[4] McCormick, Evidence § 195 at 462–63 (1954) (footnote omitted).

[5] *See, e.g.,* Keltner v. Ford Motor Co., 748 F.2d 1269, 1266, 1268–69 (8th Cir. 1984) n a negligence case in which there was evidence of intoxication at the time of the :cident and plaintiff "characterized his pattern of drinking as a 'habit,' " testimony at plaintiff regularly drank a six-pack of beer four nights a week admissible as ibit evidence); Reyes v. Missouri Pacific Railroad Co., 589 F.2d 791 (5th Cir. 179) (introduction of plaintiff's four prior convictions for public intoxication span-

to the status of habit. Adequacy of sampling and uniformity of response are key factors.[7] Precise standards cannot be formulated since admissibility, as in other instances of relevancy, depends on the judge's evaluation of the particular facts of the case. Consequently, appellate courts will accord great deference to the trial court's judgment[8] and the trial court will depend upon counsel's persuasiveness in argument and briefing.

As is noted below, the decision as to whether a particular pattern of conduct rises to the level of a habit will often depend upon the type of actor—individual or organization—and the type of action—criminal[9] or civil. Particular types of fact patterns which repeatedly

---

ning a three and one half period was of "insufficient regularity to rise to the level of 'habit' evidence").

[6] *Compare* United States v. Sampol, 636 F.2d 621, 657 n.21 (D.C. Cir. 1980) (relying on McCormick's statement that it is the "semi-automatic" character of behavior which makes habit evidence trustworthy, to exclude testimony that witness made a "habit" of assassinating Chilean exiles) and United States v. Holman, 680 F.2d 1340, 1351 (11th Cir. 1982) ("purported use of coercive tactics vis-a-vis drug transactions in isolated instances [could not be transformed] into a stimulus-response habit") *with* Keltner v. Ford Motor Co., 748 F.2d 1265, 1268–69 (8th Cir. 1984) (concluding that Advisory Committee's statement that evidence of intemperate behavior " 'is generally excluded when offered as proof of drunkenness in accident cases' because of 'failure to achieve the status of habit,' . . . is at odds with the probability theory of habit seemingly adopted elsewhere in the Notes to Rule 406").

[7] Perrin v. Anderson, 784 F.2d 1040, 1046 (10th Cir. 1986) (in civil rights action arising out of the fatal shooting of decedent when being questioned by police officers, the court found that sufficient evidence had been presented to district court to enable it to find that decedent "invariably reacted with extreme violence to any contact with a uniformed police officer"; court acknowledged that it "seems rather extraordinary" that there can be such a habit); Wilson v. Volkswagen of America, Inc. 561 F.2d 494, 512 (4th Cir. 1977), *cert. denied,* 434 U.S. 1020 (1978) ("no finding is supportable under Rule 406 . . . which fails to examine critically the 'ratio of reactions to situations' ").

[8] Loughan v. Firestone Tire & Rubber Co., 749 F.2d 1519, 1524 (11th Cir. 1985).

[9] For example in United States v. Angelilli, 660 F.2d 23 (2d Cir. 1981), *cert. denied,* 455 U.S. 910 (1982), the Second Circuit held that the evidence of the practice of a group cannot be used for the further inference that membership in the group proved that the defendant himself had committed the crime. This is contrary to the practice in civil cases where evidence of a routinized practice of a business or organization is admitted for the inference that a member acted in conformity with that practice on a particular occasion.

arise pursuant to Rule 406 are also emphasized.[10]

¶ 7.03[02]   Habit and Routine Practice in Business and Organizations[1]

Courts are inclined to leniency in admitting evidence of business custom.[2] There is no confusion with character, and the business nature of the behavior in question is a greater guarantee of regularity than in the case of purely personal, voluntary acts. As a practical matter large organizations cannot exist unless much of their work is routinized. If it were not for such routine much of the predicate for business entries would be lost. So many events involving changing staff occur that reliance on routine to prove that events occurred in a certain way is essential.

An objection to the reception of evidence of private business custom should be made on the basis of sufficiency of the proof, not admissibility, except where low probative value accompanied by the danger of resulting prejudice, confusion or waste of time mandates

---

[10] Numerous courts have considered the question of when repeated alcohol consumption rises to the level of habit. Other courts have considered when the practice of obtaining informed consent becomes habitual. *See* Habit and Routine in Negligence Cases *infra*.

[1] *See* **Treatise** at ¶ 406[03].

[2] Commonwealth v. Porter, 659 F.2d 306 (3d Cir. 1981, *cert. denied,* 458 U.S. 1121 (1982) (evidence of pattern of civil rights violations occurring more than two years prior to filing of suit and subsequent thereto relevant to show routine practices of defendant); Wetherill v. University of Chicago, 570 F. Supp. 1124, 1127–29 (N.D. Ill. 1983) (evidence that organizers of study had promulgated "protocol" for study which required doctors to make full disclosure to patients and obtain their consent sufficient to imply a routine practice); United States v. General Foods Corp., 446 F. Supp. 740, 752 (N.D.N.Y.), *aff'd mem.,* 591 F.2d 1332 (2d Cir. 1978) (to rebut allegations of a violation of Federal Food, Drug and Cosmetic Act, defendant may introduce evidence of routine customs, or business habits, involving established cleanup, sanitation and maintenance procedures); United States v. Floulis, 487 F. Supp. 1350, 1355 (W.D. Pa. 1978) (testimony about INS procedure established that INS official notified defendant-alien that he was entitled to counsel). *See also* Williams v. Alexander, 562 F.2d 1081, 1086 n.7 (8th Cir. 1977) (proof of racially discriminatory practice prior to period for which relief is available is relevant "since it creates the inference that the discrimination continued, particularly when there has been little change in the decision making process").

exclusion pursuant to Rule 403.[3] The broad definition of a business in Rule 803(b)(6) applies in defining custom of a business.

Courts have been divided as to the quantum of proof necessary for a proper foundation for the inference that the custom was followed. Generally, if a jury might be persuaded that the custom was followed evidence of it ought to be admitted. The usual and fixed course of dealings between two parties has sometimes been characterized as a habit by the courts. If the relationship is of a commercial or other routine nature it should be characterized as routine practice rather than habit to ease admission.

Recently there has been a trend toward admitting evidence of business transactions between one of the parties and a third party as tending to prove that the same bargain or proposal was made in the litigated situation.[4] It should be noted, however, that there are strong arguments in favor of the rejection of proof concerning third party contracts where similarities are weak and comparisons strained,[5] but there is no excuse for absolute exclusion of evidence that outlines a clear course of dealing or routine way of doing business. Subsidiary evidence of parallelism must be strong and convincing when dealing

---

[3] *See, e.g.,* Utility Control Corp. v. Prince William Construction Co., 558 F.2d 716 (4th Cir. 1977) (alternatively holding that habit evidence should have been excluded pursuant to Rule 403).

[4] *See, e.g.,* Amoco Production Co. v. United States, 619 F.2d 1383 (10th Cir. 1980) (in dispute about contents of original deed, evidence of routine practice to reserve one-half mineral interest in all property transferred during relevant period admitted); United States v. Callahan, 551 F.2d 733, 736 (6th Cir. 1977) (in prosecution of union agent for extortion, company's practice of paying off other union representatives in similar circumstances should have been admitted since "such evidence may well have established a routine practice . . . of paying off local unions for the sake of expediency and not out of fear"). *Cf.* United States v. Riley, 550 F.2d 333 (5th Cir. 1977) (in determining whether defendant-banker intended to injure and defraud bank, evidence of eighty instances where bank had issued check without contemporaneous payment should have been admitted). *But see* United States v. Lambert, 580 F.2d 740, 747 (5th Cir. 1978) (trial court did not abuse discretion pursuant to Rule 403 to exclude evidence of third party transactions).

[5] Simplex, Inc. v. Diversified Energy Systems, Inc., 847 F.2d 1290, 1293–94 (7th Cir. 1988) (not error to exclude evidence of plaintiff's late and inadequate performance of other contracts; behavior does not approach "level of specificity necessary to be considered semi-automatic conduct" and, in addition, defendant failed to allege adequately the frequency of the alleged conduct).

with third party situations, and the court will be less likely to admit than when dealing with transactions between the same parties.[6]

¶ 7.03[03]   Habit and Routine Practice in Negligence Cases[1]

Evidence of habit or custom is offered in a variety of situations in negligence cases and may involve the habits of an individual or the routine practice of an organization.[2] For example, a defendant may wish to introduce such evidence to prove that plaintiff was contributorily negligent because he was intoxicated,[3] that a claimed dangerous condition could not have existed,[4] or could not have been

---

[6] *See* Seven Provinces Ins. Co. Ltd. v. Commerce & Industry Ins. Co., 65 F.R.D. 674, 689 (W.D. Mo. 1975) (evidence of payments by other reinsurer offered by plaintiff to establish custom and usage with respect to duration of provisional binders rejected because it would have led to litigation of collateral issues).

[1] *See* **Treatise** at ¶ 406[02].

[2] The Advisory Committee's endorsement of McCormick's distinction between habit and character indicates that evidence of prudence or carefulness, or, conversely, recklessness or carelessness, should not be admitted unless these traits manifest themselves in some specific response to a regularly repeated situation. The result as to admissibility may, therefore, under Rule 406, be somewhat more stringent than in jurisdictions adhering to rules where courts tend not to be as strict in their definition of habit. If, however, the admission of what theoretically is character rather than habit evidence is due to a state's substantive policy favoring recovery by plaintiffs in wrongful death actions where no witnesses are present, but plaintiff has the burden of proving freedom from contributory negligence, the thrust of the Erie decision argues for admission despite Rule 406. *See* **Treatise** at ¶ 1101[02].

[3] *See* Loughan v. Firestone Tire & Rubber Co., 749 F.2d 1519, 1523 (11th Cir. 1985) (upholding district court's conclusion that evidence adduced from three sources: the plaintiff, his former employer, and his supervisor, demonstrates a drinking habit); Keltner v. Ford Motor Co., 748 F.2d 1265, 1266, 1268–69 (8th Cir. 1984) (in a negligence case in which there was evidence of intoxication at the time of the accident and plaintiff "characterized his pattern of drinking as a 'habit,' " testimony that plaintiff regularly drank a six-pack of beer four nights a week admissible as habit evidence); Reyes v. Missouri Pacific Railroad Co., 589 F.2d 791 (5th Cir. 1979) (introduction of plaintiff's four prior convictions for public intoxication spanning a three and one half years period was of "insufficient regularity to rise to the level of 'habit' evidence").

[4] *See, e.g.,* Hambrice v. F.W. Woolworth Co., 290 F.2d 557 (5th Cir. 1961) (defendant's employee permitted to testify as to his "habit" of sweeping the floor every morning).

known[5] or that there was informed consent.[6] Plaintiff may wish to introduce such evidence to prove that defendant had a duty to warn him of impending danger,[7] or that he had a right to rely on defendant's previous warnings,[8] and that, consequently, he was not guilty of contributory negligence. Or plaintiff may resort to custom in order to identify the defendant as the wrongdoer.[9]

Evidence of habit or custom is frequently introduced in negligence cases in order to establish a standard of conduct or care. This usage is not governed by Rule 406 since the evidence is not being intro-

---

[5] *See, e.g.,* Eaton v. Bass, 214 F.2d 896, 899 (6th Cir. 1954) (testimony as to the custom of the company to check every unit before it was sent on road was sufficient to take the question of negligence to jury even though defendant's witness "had no records or personal knowledge about the check which was given the particular truck involved in the accident.").

[6] Salis v. United States, 522 F. Supp. 989, 995 n.4 (M.D. Va. 1981) (treating physician who could not remember why he selected particular course of conduct could testify about his normal practice); *In re* Swine Flu Immunization Products Liability Litigation, 533 F. Supp 567, 573–74 (D. Colo. 1980) (evidence of Health Center's routine practice of obtaining signed consent forms prior to administering swine flu vaccine admitted); Mayer v. United States, 464 F. Supp. 317 (D. Col. 1979), *aff'd,* 638 F.2d 155 (10th Cir. 1980) (evidence that dentist had routine of advising patients of potential risk of molar extraction admitted).

[7] *See, e.g.,* Stratton v. Southern Ry., 190 F.2d 917, 918–19 (4th Cir. 1951) (because defendant railroad would have had duty to warn people crossing between cars if it had notice of the practice, plaintiff should have been allowed to introduce evidence of the practice).

[8] *See, e.g.,* Kozman v. Trans World Airlines, 236 F.2d 527, 531–32 (2d Cir.), *cert. denied,* 352 U.S. 953 (1956) (action against airline by window cleaner who was injured when TWA revved up plane engines without warning so that air blast and sound waves knocked down plaintiff and ladder on which he was working; "error" to exclude evidence of a custom or habit on the part of TWA's employees to warn the window washers at the hangar of the proposed operation).

[9] *See, e.g.,* Mahoney v. N.Y. Central RR., 234 F.2d 923 (2d Cir. 1956) (railroad employee injured by piece of wire protruding from gondola car; claim against Universal Pipe based on its alleged negligence in unloading car without removing the wire; car had been picked up from Universal a few hours prior to accident; plaintiff should have been allowed to show that there was a general custom of securing the type of shipment Universal had just unloaded by means of wires attached to sides of gondola). *See also* Howard v. Capital Transit Co., 97 F.Supp. 578 (D.D.C. 1951), *aff'd,* 196 F.2d 593 (D.C. Cir. 1952) (action against bus company for wrongful death; evidence of decedent's habit of using defendant's buses to return home from work admitted on issue of whether decedent was passenger on bus).

duced to prove that a person acted in conformity with the habit. Admissibility would be pursuant to the general relevancy Rules 401 to 403.

¶ 7.03[04] Methods of Proof[1]

Rule 406 provides for the admission of habit evidence despite the existence of eyewitnesses to the event.[2] The rule specifically provides that evidence of routine practices may be admitted "whether corroborated or not." The effect of this language is that evidence of one witness or admitted document evidencing the custom will suffice. Proof of custom may, therefore, be utilized even when the person who engaged in the routine practices is unavailable to testify. Even if the person is available, another witness may testify to the custom, though probative force will usually be enhanced by having the person testify as to his or her custom. Thus, a proponent need not offer the testimony of the actual clerk who mailed an item in order to establish that it was in fact mailed.[3] Similarly in a denaturalization case[4] where the government sought to divest the defendant of his citizenship on the ground that he had concealed his criminal record, a former INS employee was permitted to testify that the checkmarks and initials on the defendant's application indicated that the actual examiners asked the defendant questions relating to arrests and received the same answers that the defendant had given in writing.

---

[1] *See* **Treatise** at ¶¶ 406[02]–[04].

[2] For a discussion of Rule 406's rejection of the eyewitness rule, *see* **Treatise** at ¶ 406[02].

[3] *See, e.g.,* Envirex, Inc. v. Ecological Recovery Associates, Inc., 454 F.Supp. 1329 (M.D. Pa. 1978), *aff'd mem.,* 601 F.2d 574 (3d Cir. 1979) (in dispute over whether complete contract was sent to defendant, officer of plaintiff-corporation permitted to testify that as part of its routine business practice plaintiff would have sent a complete proposal). *See also* United States v. Leathers, 135 F.2d 507, 510 (2d Cir. 1943) (practice of sending bank letters and checks by mail).

[4] United States v. Oddo, 314 F.2d 115 (2d Cir.), *cert. denied,* 375 U.S. 833 (1963). *See also* United States v. Quezda, 754 F.2d 1190, 1195–96 (5th Cir. 1985) (in addition to admitting physical evidence that defendant had been served with a warrant of deportation, INS agent permitted to testify about "normal procedures followed in executing a warrant . . . [,even though] he had never personally observed the execution of a warrant").

¶ 7.04 Subsequent Repairs—Rule 407.

¶ 7.04[01] Scope and Theory[1]

Rule 407 codifies the almost uniform practice of American courts of excluding evidence of subsequent remedial measures as proof of an admission of fault. The rule states:

Rule 407

SUBSEQUENT REMEDIAL MEASURES

When, after an event, measures are taken which, if taken previously, would have made the event less likely to occur, evidence of the subsequent measures is not admissible to prove negligence or culpable conduct in connection with the event. This rule does not require the exclusion of evidence of subsequent measures when offered for another purpose, such as proving ownership, control, or feasibility of precautionary measures, if controverted, or impeachment.

The use of the phrase "remedial measures" is designed to bring within the scope of the rule any post-accident[2] change, repair or precaution. Rule 407 is broad enough to cover such diverse situations as the discharge of the employee responsible for the accident,[3] the change in company operating procedures or rules,[4] or the removal of a hazardous condition from the premises where the accident took

---

[1] *See* **Treatise** at ¶ 407[01]–[02], [06]–[07].

[2] Rozier v. Ford Motor Co., 573 F.2d 1332 (5th Cir. 1978) (in suit for wrongful death due to negligent design of fuel tank, document relating to alternative locations for tanks prepared prior to date of accident admissible).

[3] *Cf.* Elliot v. Webb, 98 F.R.D. 293 (D. Idaho 1983) (records and transcripts of disciplinary and reinstatement hearings fall within the Rule because they appeared to be essentially remedial in nature).

[4] Ford v. Schmidt, 577 F.2d 408 (7th Cir. 1978) (new regulation issued by prison excluded); Noble v. McClatchy Newspapers, 533 F.2d 1081 (9th Cir. 1976), *cert. denied,* 433 U.S. 908 (1977) (deletion of provisions in contracts); Vander Missen v. Kellogg-Citzens Nat'l Bank of Green Bay, 481 F. Supp. 742 (E.D. Wis. 1979) (in action alleging violation of Equal Credit Opportunity Act, steps taken to prevent future acts of sex discrimination after alleged violation inadmissible).

place.[5] But the rule should not be applied to exclude evidence contained in post-event tests or reports.[6] Whether the rule applies to products liability causes of action is discussed below.

The subsequent repair rule may not apply where a change has been made in the product after delivery of the defective model but prior to the event sued on since there may have been a duty to warn those using the product.[7] This issue should be controlled by the substantive law with respect to duty to warn ultimate users of dangers after sale. The subsequent repair rule should not apply where the product was manufactured prior to the change, but the product was delivered subsequent to the change in the product. There should be some duty to control the product before it gets to the ultimate consumer—but this too seems more a matter of substantive than of evidentiary law.[8]

Because the controlling ground for excluding evidence has been the promotion of the policy of encouraging people to take safety precautions, remedial measures carried out by persons not party to the suit are not covered.[9] Since the person taking the remedial measures

---

[5] Hall v. American Steamship Company, 688 F.2d 1062 (6th Cir. 1982) (change in policy of hosing down deck in rough weather inadmissible).

[6] Rocky Mountain Helicopters, Inc. v. Bell Helicopters, Textron, A Division of Textron, Inc., 805 F.2d 907, 918–19 (10th Cir. 1986) (error, but harmless, for attorney to argue that by conducting the test defendant admitted that it had been negligent in failing to conduct the test sooner; remarks had effect of characterizing test as a remedial measure).

[7] See Chase v. General Motors Corp., 856 F.2d 17, 21–22 (4th Cir. 1988) (court holds that design change made after purchase of car but before accident is admissible because the "event" spoken of in Rule 407 is the date of the accident).

[8] Kaczmarek v. Allied Chemical Corp., 836 F.2d 1055, 1060 (7th Cir. 1987) (evidence that defendant decided to change coupling on hose before plaintiff's accident was admissible, but no error in trial court's refusing to admit evidence that the decision was carried out after the accident); Ramos v. Liberty Mutual Insurance Co., 615 F.2d 334, 341 (5th Cir. 1980), cert. denied, 449 U.S. 1112 (1981) (trial court erred in excluding evidence of changes made in a mast delivered approximately ten days after the collapse, since testimony indicated that the new mast was produced before the accident). But cf. Foster v. Ford Motor Co., 621 F.2d 715 (5th Cir. 1980) (refusal to admit model redesigned after manufacture of vehicle in question, but before accident).

[9] Farner v. Paccar, Inc., 562 F.2d 518, 525 n.20 (8th Cir. 1977) ("rule against the admission of subsequent remedial measures in negligence cases may not apply in any event since the corrective measures were not carried out by the defendant").

is not prejudiced by having the evidence admitted as an admission of fault, the admissibility of the evidence should be governed by the general relevancy requirements of Rules 401–403 rather than Rule 407.[10] Determining the scope of Rule 407 is particularly important because the cases which raise issues of subsequent remedial measures generally fall under the court's diversity jurisdiction. When a federal court holds that Rule 407 governs the admissibility of the evidence in question, *Hanna v. Plumer*[11] suggests that state law may not need to be considered if Rule 407 is viewed as a special rule of relevancy that is arguably procedural. But if the court concludes that Rule 407 does not apply, an *Erie* inquiry must be made. The court must determine whether the general relevancy approach of Rule 401 and 403 should be used or whether reference must be made to pertinent state law. Ordinarily the *Erie* issue does not emerge in cases tried solely on a negligence theory because virtually all states have a rule almost identical to Rule 407.[12] The question does arise in the products liability area which is discussed *infra*.

Finally, it should be recognized that the standard of admissibility established by Rule 407 for evidence of subsequent remedial measures is not the same as that for pretrial discovery. Some courts have failed to make the distinction and denied discovery on the grounds of relevancy.[13] The better view is to permit discovery,[14] not only be-

---

[10] Middleton v. Harris Press and Shear, Inc., 796 F.2d 747, 752 (5th Cir. 1986) (in products liability action, even though evidence of a subsequent repair was not barred by Rule 407 because the repairs were made by someone other than the defendant, Rule 403 barred the evidence "[because] of its tendency 'to confuse the jury by diverting its attention from whether the product was defective at the relevant time . . . to what was done later' "). *Cf.* Russel v. Page Aircraft Maintenance, Inc., 455 F.2d 190 (5th Cir. 1972) (plaintiff injured in nighttime accident at army base by vehicle operated by defendant, contractor for U.S. Army; defendant alleged vehicle was being operated without lights in compliance with Army instructions; not error to exclude subsequent Army regulations authorizing lights where defendant never claimed that it could not have improved on safety, but maintained that Army had sole rule-making authority, and possibility of prejudice to defendant on issue of negligence "is quite great").

[11] 380 U.S. 460, 85 S. Ct. 1136, 14 L. Ed. 2d 8 (1965).

[12] *But see* Rule 407 of the Maine Rules of Evidence, allowing proof of subsequent repairs to prove negligence.

[13] Elliot v. Webb, 98 F.R.D. 293 (D. Idaho 1983) (dicta).

[14] Rozier v. Ford Motor Co., 573 F.2d 1332, 1345 (5th Cir. 1978) (reversing verdict

cause Rule 407 is a rule of public policy as well as relevancy, but also because subsequent remedial measures might be admissible to prove an issue other than negligence.

Two separate distinct grounds have long been recognized as justifying exclusion of evidence of subsequent remedial measures to prove negligence. Such evidence is often irrelevant. While it is reasonable to interpret such conduct as an acknowledgement that the prior condition was capable of causing harm, the inference that subsequent remedial measures indicate a consciousness of prior lack of due care can vary considerably in probative force. A further ground for exclusion is the policy of encouraging people to take safety precautions.

Nevertheless, Rule 407 has only a marginal justification. Its underlying assumption is that a person will not take remedial measures because his corrective actions might be used in evidence at a future trial. Such an assumption seems absurd. Not every defendant will be aware of the possibility that subsequent remedial measures might constitute an admission. Of those who would know of the rule, any responsible insured defendant will not be likely to refrain deliberately from taking action to prevent the recurrence of subsequent serious injuries. In any subsequent case, evidence of the earlier accident would be admissible to show that defendant knew of a dangerous condition. Even if defendants are as cold-blooded as the rule suggests, their awareness of the many exceptions to the general exclusionary rule would make it risky to refrain from making the needed repairs. A prompt and adequate admonition following an improper reference to a subsequent remedial measure should ordinarily suffice. The trial court is in the best position to say whether a mistrial is required because the jury has been prejudiced.

¶ 7.04[02]   Products Liability[1]

An unresolved issue is whether Rule 407 bars evidence of post-accident remedial measures in a strict liability case. The notes of the Advisory Committee and the legislative history are silent on this

---

for defendant who failed to turn over document that defendant argued would have been excluded at trial because of Rule 407 because document "might have been catalyst for an entirely different approach to the case").

[1] *See* **Treatise** at ¶ 407[03].

point. In *Ault v. International Harvester Co.,*[2] the California court held that a statute virtually identical to Rule 407 did not bar evidence of subsequent remedial change in a strict liability action. Since the products liability action seeks to prove a defect in the product rather than culpable conduct, the court found the subsequent repair rule inapplicable. Furthermore, the court found that the policy underlying the rule of encouraging the adoption of safety measures would not be served in a strict liability case by excluding evidence of subsequent repairs, because:

> it is manifestly unrealistic to suggest that such a producer will forgo making improvements in its product, and risk innumerable additional lawsuits and the attendant adverse effect upon its public image, simply because evidence of adoption of such improvement may be admitted in an action founded on strict liability for recovery on an injury that preceded the improvement.[3]

A number of federal courts have endorsed the *Ault* approach.[4] On the other hand, other courts stress the questionable relevancy of evidence of subsequent repairs. In addition, fears have been expressed that jurors are likely to view products liability cases as entailing culpable conduct, thus forcing the defendant to prove due care (not an element of proof in this type of action). Because of questionable relevance and possible prejudice, a number of federal courts have applied Rule 407 to bar evidence of subsequent repairs or warnings[5] in products liability actions.[6] In addition, Rule 407 has been applied to strict

---

[2] 13 Cal. 3d 113, 528 P.2d 1148 (1975).

[3] *Id.* at 120, 117, 528 P.2d at 1152.

[4] Roth v. Black & Decker, 737 F.2d 779, 782 (8th Cir. 1984); Herndon v. Seven Bar Flying Service, Inc., 716 F.2d 1322 (10th Cir. 1983); Robbins v. Farmers Union Terminal Ass'n, 552 F.2d 788, 793 (8th Cir. 1977); Farner v. Paccar, Inc., 562 F.2d 518, 528 (8th Cir. 1977).

[5] Petree v. Victor Fluid Power, Inc., 831 F.2d 1191, 1197–98 (3d Cir. 1987) (in products liability action predicated on failure to warn, Rule 407 requires exclusion of evidence of warning subsequent to the date of sale but prior to the accident; fact that warning was affixed to newly manufactured products before injury "is equally as consistent with knowledge gained through experience as with an inference that such misuse was forseeable when older products were sold").

[6] Gauthier v. AMF, Inc., 788 F.2d 634 (9th Cir. 1986) (Rule 407 applies to strict liability case alleging defective design); Flaminio v. Honda Motor Co., 733 F.2d 463, 468–72 (7th Cir. 1984) (rejected plaintiff's contention that Rule 407 did not apply to strict liability cases); Alexander v. Conveyors & Dumpers, Inc., 731 F.2d

liability claims involving prescription drugs where the defendant's liability is based on its alleged failure to warn adequately of possible adverse reactions and side-effects.[7]

The most desirable approach is to treat products liability cases as governed by Rule 403 rather than Rule 407, thereby giving the judge discretion to admit the evidence of subsequent repairs when relevance exceeds prejudice to the defendant.[8] Some courts have been sensitive to the state law issue that lurks in the background of these diversity cases—should Rule 407 or the state's provision on subsequent remedial measures be applied? If the federal court views Rule

---

1221, 1229 (5th Cir. 1984) (reaffirming Fifth Circuit's prior decision holding Rule 407 applicable to strict liability actions); Hall v. American Steamship Company, 688 F.2d 1062, 1066 (6th Cir. 1982) (in action alleging unseaworthy condition, a species of strict liability, court found that operating ship with an unseaworthy condition is a form of "culpable conduct," and that "the reasons for excluding the evidence [of a change in policy] as proof of negligence or culpable conduct . . . apply here"); Cann v. Ford Motor Co., 658 F.2d 54, 60 (2d Cir. 1981), cert. denied, 456 U.S. 960 (1982); Werner v. Upjohn Co., 628 F.2d 848, 856–58 (4th Cir. 1980), cert. denied, 449 U.S. 1080 (1981) (holding that rule does not speak of strict liability cases but that policy of encouraging repairs applies equally in strict liability and negligence cases); Wolf v. Procter & Gamble Co., 555 F.Supp. 613, 623–24 (D.N.J. 1982) (evidence that the defendant removed tampon product from market after plaintiff contracted disease inadmissible to prove strict liability; court finds that to allow evidence of causation "would certainly thwart the policy behind the rule").

[7] Werner v. Upjohn Co., 628 F.2d 848, 858 (4th Cir. 1980); cert. denied, 449 U.S. 1080 (1981) (Rule 407 should apply in failure to warn cases involving an unavoidably dangerous drug because the standard for liability under strict liability and negligence is essentially the same). The Werner court's reasoning was adopted by the Eighth Circuit in DeLuryea v. Winthrop Laboratories, 697 F.2d 222, 227–29 (8th Cir. 1983).

[8] Grenada Steel Industries, Inc. v. Alabama Oxygen Company, 695 F.2d 883, 885–87 (5th Cir. 1983) (evidence of post-accident change in design of valve used to seal cylinder containing gas excluded because of low probative value and danger of confusion); Foster v. Ford Motor Co., 621 F.2d 715 (5th Cir. 1980) (trial court's refusal to admit model was not error where defendant had conceded that design change was technologically feasible because physical evidence at best would have been cumulative or, at worst, unfair, misleading or confusing); Knight v. Otis Elevator Co., 596 F.2d 84, 91 (3d Cir. 1979) (evidence of placing guards around elevator buttons subsequent to accident properly excluded); Smyth v. Upjohn Co., 529 F.2d 803 (2d Cir. 1975) (diversity case relying on New York law "or indeed, on that of most jurisdictions" for making an exception to the subsequent repair doctrine in cases involving a mass-produced product; court held that the probative value of subsequent repair evidence is outweighed by prejudice to the defendant).

407 as a specialized rule of relevancy that governs product liability cases, it is free under *Hanna v. Plumer* to disregard state law.[9] On the other hand, if the court concludes that Rule 407 does not apply in the strict liability context, the question remains whether the court may resort to the general principles of Rules 401 and 403, or whether it must decide the issue by reference to state law. The result should turn on whether the state excludes such evidence 1) because of low probative value or 2) because, as a matter of policy, it holds that such evidence should be excluded in order to encourage voluntary repairs by manufacturers. In the first instance, the court is free to forge its own rules; in the second instance, the court should implement the state rule. Ultimately, it may well be that the issue of admissibility will be resolved by substantive legislative developments, such as Congressional action, rather than judicial interpretations of an evidentiary rule.

¶ 7.04[03]   Recall Letters

The arguments for admitting recall letters sent by automobile manufacturers to car owners notifying them of possible defects are identical to those urged for admitting evidence of subsequent repairs in product liability actions: 1) that the issue in controversy is defect

---

[9] *See, e.g.,* Flaminio v. Honda Motor Co., 733 F.2d 463, 470–73 (7th Cir. 1984) (holding that Rule 407 applies in diversity case because Congress intended the Federal Rules to apply in such cases and that while Rule 407 has substantive consequences, it is sufficiently procedural so as not to violate the federal courts' constitutional obligation to decide diversity cases in accordance with state substantive law); Rioux v. Daniel Int'l. Corp., 582 F. Supp. 620 (D. Me. 1984) (in dicta court stated that under Hanna v. Plumer, 380 U.S. 460, 85 S. Ct. 1136, 14 L. Ed. 2d 8 (1965), Rule 407 could rationally be considered procedural and therefore should be applied instead of state rule in diversity actions). *But see* Moe v. Avions Marcel Dassault-Breguet Aviation, 727 F.2d 917, 932 (10th Cir.), *cert. denied,* 105 S. Ct. 176 (1984) (court disregarded *Hanna v. Plumer* and concluded that Rule 407 was designed to promote state policy in substantive law area, and determination as to whether subsequent remedial measures should be excluded from evidence is a matter of state policy). *See also* Oberst v. International Harvester Co., 640 F.2d 863 (7th Cir. 1980) (majority rejected argument that Rule 407 does not apply to strict liability actions on ground that this argument is contrary to Illinois law; dissent found the question of whether state law had to be applied was difficult but not necessary for decision since it concluded that neither state law nor Rule 407 would bar subsequent repair evidence in strict liability).

rather than conduct, making Rule 407 inapplicable, and 2) that the policy underlying the rule is not implicated since the adoption of safety measures will not be discouraged. Both of these arguments are stronger in the recall letter context. When the plaintiff seeks recovery because of the very defect which is the subject of the letter, the probative value of the evidence in proving defect is usually far greater than when evidence of subsequent repairs is offered to show that the product must have been defective. Furthermore, since car manufacturers are required by federal law to send out recall notices, it would be unreasonable "to assume that the manufacturers will risk wholesale violation of the National Traffic and Motor Vehicle Safety Act and liability for subsequent injuries caused by defects known by them to exist in order to avoid the possible use of recall evidence as an admission against them".[1] Most courts, presented with the recall letter issue, have ruled in favor of admissibility.[2] This would normally be the result under a Rule 403 analysis.

¶ 7.04[04]   Exceptions[1]

Rule 407 precludes the use of evidence of subsequent remedial measures only when offered to prove negligence or culpable conduct. The second sentence of the rule explicitly recognizes that such evidence may be admissible to prove material facts in issue other than

---

[1] Farner v. Paccar, Inc., 562 F.2d 518, 527 (8th Cir. 1977).

[2] Rozier v. Ford Motor Co., 573 F.2d 1332, 1343 (5th Cir. 1978) (document prepared by defendant in anticipation of a revised safety standard to be required by National Highway Traffic Safety Administration did not meet exclusion rationale of Rule 407). *But see* Chase v. General Motors Corp., 856 F.2d 17, 20–22 (4th Cir. 1988) (evidence of actual recall of plaintiffs' vehicle after date of accident must be excluded as a subsequent remedial measure in a products liability case which the circuit holds is barred by Rule 407); Vockie v. General Motors Corp., Chevrolet Division, 66 F.R.D. 57, 61 (E.D. Pa.), *aff'd mem.,* 523 F.2d 1052 (3d Cir. 1975) (automobile manufacturer's recall letter excluded in trial charging manufacturer with negligent design: "If such statements are admissible on a wholesale basis, manufacturers will be reluctant to come forth and make a full unqualified disclosure of any potential safety hazards which they discover." Court also noted that "[s]uch evidence has minimal probative value to the existence of a defect in a particular vehicle.").

[1] *See* **Treatise** at ¶¶ 407[04]–[05].

negligence or culpable conduct.[2]

[a]   Control or Ownership

Evidence of subsequent remedial measures is admissible to prove control or ownership of the place or object causing the injury. In addition, a photograph, taken the day after an accident, may be admitted where it serves to acquaint the jury with the scene, and no more neutral pictures are available, even though it indicates that repairs were made.[3] This situation provides a typical Rule 403 problem requiring the exercise of discretion and an instruction to the jury.

[b]   Feasibility

Rule 407 explicitly permits evidence of subsequent remedial measures to be used to show the feasibility of precautionary measures when the issue is controverted.[4] This exception is troublesome because the feasibility of a precaution may bear on whether it was negligent not have taken the precaution; thus negligence and feasibility

---

[2] Rimkus v. Northwest Colorado Ski Corp., 706 F.2d 1060 (10th Cir. 1983) (evidence of defendant's subsequent remedial measures admissible to rebut contributory negligence defense and to refute testimony); Wetherill v. University of Chicago, 565 F. Supp. 1553 (N.D. Ill. 1983) (subsequent released publications containing warnings admissible to prove causation).

[3] See, e.g., Jaeger v. Henningson, Durham & Richardson, Inc., 714 F.2d 773, 776 (8th Cir. 1983) (district court did not err in admitting photographs that were offered to show what the original specifications required).

[4] See Reese v. Mercury Marine Division of Brunswick Corp., 793 F.2d 1416 (5th Cir. 1986) (manufacturer's subsequent warnings were admissible to rebut defendant's claim that only the retailer could properly instruct the ultimate consumer); MCI Communications v. American Tel. & Tel. Co., 708 F.2d 1081 (7th Cir.), cert. denied, 464 U.S. 891 (1983) (testimony concerning technical arrangements between the parties set forth in a prior agreement admissible since the evidence was relevant to demonstrate technical feasibility, inter alia); Chute v. United States, 449 F. Supp. 172, 177 (D. Mass. 1978) (evidence that coast guard was planning to blow up wreck was admissible to show that there were other feasible ways of protecting boating public); Doyle v. United States, 441 F. Supp. 701 (D.S.C. 1977) (subsequent warnings as to danger of cable admitted to show feasibility of precautionary measures where feasibility was contested).

are often not distinct issues.[5] There is no difficulty when the defendant opens up the issue by claiming either that all possible care was being exercised at the time of the accident or that further precautionary measures were not practicable or feasible.[6] By raising the issue of feasibility, the defendant in effect has waived the protection of Rule 407, for it would be unfair not to allow the plaintiff to meet the issue by showing the defendant's conflicting conduct—the subsequent remedial measures.[7] When the defendant has not raised the issue, however, the trial court should consider whether the offer of

---

[5] *See, e.g.,* Rimkus v. Northwest Colorado Ski Corp., 706 F.2d 1060 (10th Cir. 1983) (no abuse of discretion to admit evidence of defendant's subsequent remedial measures where jury was instructed that evidence was admissible as to feasibility and not to be considered as bearing on defendant's negligence); Lindsay v. Ortho Pharmaceutical Corp., 481 F. Supp. 314 (E.D.N.Y. 1979) (in action alleging manufacturer of oral contraceptives failed to adequately warn plaintiff of risk, letter from defendant to Bureau of Drugs stating its intent to put a warning label on future packages admissible as bearing on defendant's knowledge of inadequacy of past warnings).

[6] Anderson v. Malloy, 700 F.2d 1208, 1213 (8th Cir. 1983) (defendants controverted feasibility when they testified that peepholes and chains would not be useful but would provide false sense of security, because "[w]hether something is feasible relates not only to actual possibility of operation, and its cost and convenience, but also to its ultimate utility and success in its intended performance"); Grenada Steel Industries, Inc. v. Alabama Oxygen Company, Inc., 695 F.2d 883, 888–89 (5th Cir. 1983) (feasibility must be explicitly contested to trigger exception to Rule 407; court rejects plaintiff's contention "that, in design defect cases, feasibility is 'inherently' an issue and an integral element of its proof"); Bauman v. Volkswagenwerk Aktiengesellshaft, 621 F.2d 230 (6th Cir. 1980) (error to admit evidence of subsequent changes in door latch where feasibility not in issue); Wetherill v. University of Chicago, 565 F. Supp. 1553 (N.D. Ill. 1983) (manufacturer's publication, which mentioned that several researchers opposed drug's prenatal use, did not deny feasibility of placing warning language in product literature).

[7] Patrick v. South Central Bell Tel. Co., 641 F.2d 1192, 1196 (6th Cir. 1981) (where witness testified that wire had been at proper height prior to storm not error to admit evidence that cables had been placed considerably higher after accident); Davis v. Fox River Tractor Co., 518 F.2d 481 (10th Cir. 1975) (proper to admit evidence that plaintiff's employer had welded a grid on to machine to make it safer before completing job on which plaintiff was injured where defendant had testified that a grid would render machine ineffective). *But cf.* Wheeler v. John Deere Co., 862 F.2d 1404, 1410–11 (10th Cir. 1988) (where defendant conceded feasibility by stipulation, the stipulation was the only evidence the jury should have heard relating to design changes and reversible error to admit photograph showing changes).

evidence is not designed merely to permit the jury improperly to infer negligence and whether the standards of Rule 403 are met.[8]

[c] Proof of Conditions

Another situation permitting a justifiable use of evidence of repairs involves a defendant's attempt to use proof of conditions at the time of the trial to prove the non-existence of a dangerous condition. It is obvious that plaintiff should, in rebuttal, be able to show that conditions have changed in material respects since the accident's occurrence.[9] If the jury has been apprised of the conditions of the place or object at the time of the trial, then the plaintiff may need to show post-accident changes. But even in such clear situations, counsel can eliminate much of the potential prejudice by introducing the evidence in such a way as to emphasize the original conditions and not the subsequent remedial measures.

[d] Proof of Duty

The Advisory Committee's Note includes among the other purposes for which exclusion is not called for "existence of duty." The difference between "duty" and "negligence" is at best unclear, and attempts to distinguish the elements for purposes of evidentiary rulings in a jury trial seem futile in most cases. As in the case of the

---

[8] *See, e.g.,* Probus v. K-Mart, Inc., 794 F.2d 1207, 1210 (7th Cir. 1986) (in products liability action against seller and manufacturer of a ladder, defendants' testimony that material used was appropriate did not open door to proof that defendants subsequently used different material; defendants did not claim that material was either best material available or that use of another material would not have been feasible); Robbins v. Farmers Union Grain Terminal Ass'n., 552 F.2d 788, 792 and n.8 (8th Cir. 1977) (plaintiff's request that defendant admit feasibility forced them "to openly admit the fact of feasibility to the jury or to allow the plaintiffs to prove the same. This offered the defendant little choice and it remains questionable that the issue can thus be 'controverted' within the intent of Rule 407."). *Cf.* Gardner v. Chevron U.S.A., Inc., 675 F.2d 658 (5th Cir. 1982) (trial court properly balanced concerns of Rules 407 and 403).

[9] Kenny v. Southeastern Pennsylvania Transportation Authority, 581 F.2d 351 (3d Cir. 1978) (because it countered defendant's inference that light was adequate, evidence that several light bulbs were replaced soon after rape attack and new fluorescent fixture was installed was properly admitted).

attempt to separate "feasibility" from "negligence," the result is often an arbitrary decision made without regard to the underlying reasons for Rule 407. Before admitting evidence to show existence of duty, the trial judge should be satisfied that the need for such evidence is substantial, that the issue is actually in dispute, and that the plaintiff's need outweighs the danger of misuse of the evidence by the jury.

[e] Impeachment

The second sentence of Rule 407 explicitly recognizes that evidence of subsequent remedial measures may be used for impeachment.[10] The enactment of Rule 407, with its explicit recognition of the "exception" for impeachment, should not affect the traditional reluctance of the courts to permit cross-examination that reflects on the witness only by means of a prohibited inference of negligence from the subsequent remedial measures.[11]

In applying the exceptions, particularly in the case of feasibility and impeachment, care should be taken that a mechanical reliance on the permissible uses specified in Rule 407 does not subvert the policy goals the rule is designed to promote. Prejudice and waste of time remain for consideration under Rule 403.

---

[10] Bickerstaff v. South Central Bell Telephone Co., 676 F.2d 163 (5th Cir. 1982) (trial court committed error, but harmless, in not allowing consultant for defendant and defense engineering expert to be impeached); Dollar v. Long Mfg., N.C., Inc., 561 F.2d 613, 618 (5th Cir. 1977), *cert. denied,* 435 U.S. 996 (1978) (reversible error for trial judge not to have permitted plaintiffs to impeach defendant's design engineer in products liability case by asking him about letter he had sent to dealers warning them of "death dealing propensities of [product] when used in the fashion employed in [instant case]").

[11] *See, e.g.,* Bickerstaff v. South Central Bell Telephone Co., 676 F.2d 163, 169 n.6 (5th Cir. 1982) (discussion of danger that impeachment exception can swallow up rule); Avery v. Rann Sons Co., 91 F.2d 248, 250 (D.C. Cir. 1937).

¶ 7.05   Compromise Offers—Rule 408

¶ 7.05[01]   Definition, Rationale and Scope[1]

Rule 408 codifies and extends the federal courts' longstanding practice of excluding evidence of proposed or accepted compromises when it is offered to prove the validity or invalidity of a claim or amount of damage. The Rule states:

Rule 408

COMPROMISE AND OFFERS TO COMPROMISE

Evidence of (1) furnishing or offering or promising to furnish, or (2) accepting or offering or promising to accept, a valuable consideration in compromising or attempting to compromise a claim which was disputed as to either validity or amount, is not admissible to prove liability for or invalidity of the claim or its amount. Evidence of conduct or statements made in compromise negotiations is likewise not admissible. This rule does not require the exclusion of any evidence otherwise discoverable merely because it is presented in the course of compromise negotiations. This rule also does not require exclusion when the evidence is offered for another purpose, such as proving bias or prejudice of a witness, negativing a contention of undue delay, or proving an effort to obstruct a criminal investigation or prosecution.

The Rule extends the exclusionary treatment to cover "evidence of conduct and statements made in compromise negotiations." Rule 408 reflects the judgment that free and frank settlement negotiations should be fostered.[2] Evidence of an offer to compromise is also excluded because it is of such low probative value. A settlement offer may be motivated by a desire to "buy peace" rather than by an acknowledgement of the merits of a claim.

The Rule applies to a number of different situations: 1) offers to compromise disputes; 2) completed compromises; and 3) conduct occurring and statements made during settlement negotiations.

---

[1] *See* **Treatise** at ¶¶ 408[01]–[04].

[2] *See* Reichenbach v. Smith, 528 F.2d 1072, 1074 (5th Cir. 1976); Bottaro v. Hatton Assocs., 96 F.R.D. 158, 160 (E.D.N.Y. 1982); Young v. Verson Allsteel Press Co., 539 F. Supp. 193, 196 (E.D. Pa. 1982).

[a] Offers to Compromise Disputes

Evidence of offers to compromise is excluded only if there is a dispute about either the validity or the amount of the claim. The Advisory Committee Note also states that "the effort . . . to induce a creditor to settle an admittedly due amount for a lesser sum" would not further the underlying policy of the rule and is therefore not protected. Yet a careful distinction must be made between a frank disclosure during the course of negotiations—such as "All right, I was negligent. Let's talk about damages" (inadmissible)—and the less frequent situation where both the validity of the claim and the amount of damages are admitted—"Of course, I owe you the money, but unless you're willing to settle for less, you'll have to sue me for it" (admissible). Likewise, an admission of liability made during negotiations concerning the time of payment and involving neither the validity nor amount of the claim is not within the rule's exclusionary protection.[3] When interpreting Rule 408 to determine whether a statement was an offer to compromise, the court should construe the term "valuable consideration" broadly. For example, an apology or some private or public acknowledgement of a new policy is often the basis for bringing parties together, particularly when there is a continuing relationship. In the context of this rule, such a statement is a valuable consideration.[4]

---

[3] *See* United States v. Peed, 714 F.2d 7, 9–10 (4th Cir. 1983) (statement was not made in an effort to settle a civil claim because there was no civil suit pending when statement was made); Deere & Co. v. International Harvester Co., 710 F.2d 1551 (Fed. Cir. 1983) (evidence of patentee's offer to license patent to infringer admissible because offer was made at a time when no claim was in dispute); Mendelovitz v. Adolph Coors Co., 693 F.2d 570, 580 (5th Cir. 1982) (letter admissible because it was not part of settlement negotiation and did not offer to compromise or settle any claim in instant action); United States v. 320.0 Acres of Land, More or Less in County of Monroe, State of Fla., 605 F.2d 762, 822–25 (5th Cir. 1979) (in condemnation proceeding, statements of just compensation which had been provided to landowners by Department of Interior were not excludible as offers of compromise since at the time the statements were provided there was no disputed claim); United States v. Meadows, 598 F.2d 984 (5th Cir. 1979) (remark by defendant that he knew checks were issued by mistake was in no sense offer to compromise claim).

[4] *See, e.g., In re* B.D. Int'l Discount Corp., 701 F.2d 1071, 1074 n.5 (2d Cir.), *cert. denied,* 464 U.S. 830 (1983) (evidence of bankrupt's acknowledgment of debt not inadmissible under Rule 408 where bankrupt was not disputing liability but was negotiating to get more time to pay); Perzinski v. Chevron Chemical Co., 503 F.2d 654, 658 (7th Cir. 1974) (statements made by defendant's salesman that the compa-

It is clear that Rule 408 includes offers both by the person against whom the claim is asserted and by the person asserting the claim. If the person makes an offer of compromise to a person other than the potential litigant, the offer should be protected.

[b] Completed Compromises

Rule 408 extends the exclusionary treatment not only to offers of compromise, but also to completed compromises when offered against a compromiser.[5] A party cannot introduce evidence of an adversary's completed compromises with third persons if the agreement arose out of the transaction being litigated.[6]

[c] Conduct Occurring During Settlement Discussions

Rule 408 also explicitly excludes evidence of all conduct occurring

---

ny was prepared to stand in back of its product were not offers of compromise and settlement).

[5] *See* Belton v. Fibreboard Corp., 724 F.2d 500, 504–05 (5th Cir. 1984) (court's instructions directing jury to consider amount of settlement in determining damage award violated Rule 408 and constituted reversible error).

[6] *See* Quad Graphics v. Fass, 724 F.2d 1230, 1234–35 (7th Cir. 1983) (evidence of settlement agreement between plaintiff and third person inadmissible to show invalidity of plaintiff's claim); McHann v. Firestone Tire & Rubber Co., 713 F.2d 161, 166 (5th Cir. 1983) (evidence that service station paid money to owner as part of covenant not to sue inadmissible in tire owner's action against manufacturer for injuries arising from tire explosion during mounting); American Ins. Co. v. North Am. Co., 697 F.2d 79, 82 (2d Cir. 1982) (evidence about defendant's discussions with third party insurance company regarding commutation inadmissible); United States v. Contra Costa County Water Dist., 678 F.2d 90 (9th Cir. 1982) (evidence of settlement between United States and landowner was inadmissible to decrease liability for landowner's actions). *But see* Kennon v. Slipstreamer, Inc., 794 F.2d 1067, 1069–70 (5th Cir. 1986) (products liability action; not error for trial judge to disclose that plaintiff had settled with other defendants; admissible to avoid jury confusion due to the sudden absence of the co-defendants; but disclosing the amount of the settlement ($10) was a prejudicial error because it suggested that the settling co-defendants were not liable and the remaining defendant was; dissent argued that Rule 408 does not apply to trial judge's comments and that a Rule 403 analysis would not require exclusion of the amount of the settlement).

and statements made during settlement negotiations.[7] The rule eliminates the common law requirement that admissions of fact are not protected unless stated hypothetically "for the sake of discussion only" or "without prejudice." Deciding whether or not there were compromise negotiations is a question for the court pursuant to Rule 104(a) and not for the jury. When making this determination, the trial judge should bear in mind that the principal purpose of the expanded exclusionary rule is to insure freedom of communication with respect to compromise negotiations. Since the rule interferes with the admissibility of relevant evidence, some courts have, in spite of the rule's policy, limited its exclusionary effect by holding that the statement in question was not an explicit offer of compromise or was not made within the context of express negotiations.[8]

Rule 408 is not, as its last sentence points out, intended to cover efforts to "buy off" the prosecution or a prosecuting witness. But a distinction must be made between such illicit offers and legitimate "plea bargaining" protected under Rule 410. If a transaction gives rise to both civil and criminal remedies, it is unclear whether a good faith offer to compromise the civil claim will be protected in both proceedings.[9]

---

[7] Ramada Dev. Co. v. Rauch, 644 F.2d 1097, 1106 (5th Cir. 1981) (trial court did not err in excluding architect's report that functioned as a basis for settlement negotiations); Saf-Gard Prods., Inc. v. Service Parts, Inc., 491 F. Supp. 996 (D. Ariz. 1980) (licensing agreements entered into in compromise of infringement claims could not be admitted as measure of patent owner's damages); *In re* Golden Plan of Cal., Inc. 39 B.R. 551 (Bkrtcy. E.D. Cal. 1984) (in proceeding to set aside foreclosure sale of land, evidence inadmissible that trustee's attorney wrote defendants' attorney during the course of settlement negotiations that the trustee no longer asserted an interest in the property).

[8] *See* Mendelovitz v. Adolph Coors Co., 693 F.2d 570, 580 (5th Cir. 1982) (letter admissible because litigation was in progress; letter not part of settlement negotiation and did not offer to compromise or settle any claim in instant action); Big O Tire Dealers v. Goodyear Tire & Rubber Co., 561 F.2d 1365, 1373 (10th Cir. 1977), *cert. denied,* 434 U.S. 1052 (1978) (district court's ruling that discussions between plaintiff and defendant were business communications and not offers to compromise was sustainable because "discussions had not crystallized to the point of threatened litigation").

[9] *See, e.g.,* United States v. Gonzales, 748 F.2d 74, 78 (2d Cir. 1984) (statements made in the course of settlement negotiations are admissible to establish that one committed a crime because they are not offered to prove the validity or amount of a claim and their exclusion would not encourage the settlement of claims). The

The rules should not be construed so as to render inadmissible otherwise discoverable evidence solely because it was presented during the settlement negotiations. The policy of allowing open and free negotiations between parties by excluding conduct or statements made during the course of these discussions is not intended to conflict with the liberal rules of discovery embodied in the Federal Rules of Civil Procedure.[10]

Rule 408 should be applied even though a state has an evidentiary rule which may embody a substantive policy favoring the disclosure of all relevant evidence, since the promotion of compromises is essential to the integrity of the federal court system.[11]

[d] Use of Offers and Agreements of Compromise for Other Purposes[12]

The last sentence of Rule 408 contains two limitations on the general exclusionary treatment for evidence of offers or agreements of compromise. First, such evidence may be used to prove a material

---

matter may become particularly important in a RICO or mail fraud case. A compromise of the civil claim should not be used in the criminal case. As to the converse problems, *cf.* Rule 803(22).

[10] Center for Auto Safety v. Department of Justice, 576 F. Supp. 739, 749 & n.23 (D.D.C. 1983) (documents were not protected by "settlement negotiation" privilege because Rule 408 limits admissibility of evidence of settlement negotiations at trial, but does not affect its disclosure for other purposes); Mfg. Systems, Inc. of Milwaukee v. Computer Tech., 99 F.R.D. 335, 336 (E.D. Wis. 1983) (fact that information might be inadmissible at trial under Rule 408 was not necessarily a bar to discovery; there need only be reasonable likelihood that information sought would lead to discovery of admissible evidence). *But cf.* Bottaro v. Hatton Assocs., 96 F.R.D. 158, 160 (E.D.N.Y. 1982) (discovery into terms of settlement agreement between plaintiff and one codefendant inadmissible in absence of "particularized showing of a likelihood that admissible evidence will be generated"); Ramada Dev. Co. v. Rauch, 644 F.2d 1097, 1107 (5th Cir. 1981) (documents that would not have existed but for negotiations are not discoverable because in this circumstance the negotiations are not being used as a device to thwart discovery).

[11] *Cf.* Morris v. LTV Corp., 725 F.2d 1024, 1030–31 (5th Cir. 1984) (although controlling Mexican law provided that offers to compromise are binding admissions of liability, trial court did not err in concluding that evidentiary questions are procedural in nature and governed by law of forum).

[12] *See* **Treatise** at ¶ 408[05].

fact other than validity or invalidity of the claim or its amount.[13] Accordingly, evidence of offers or agreements of compromise has been admitted to prevent abuse of the general exclusionary rule and its policy of promoting compromises.[14] The existence of negotiations for compromise is admitted to demonstrate the existence of other parties that may have been responsible for the plaintiff's injury,[15] or to demonstrate the extent of a party's liability,[16] or to establish that a party was not successful for purposes of awarding attorney's fees,[17] or to show that the real party in interest had already settled with the defendant all claims outstanding from the transaction.[18] It would also be permissible to show that a party had relevant knowledge,[19] ·or that a party acted in bad faith,[20] or to rebut a claim that the behav-

---

[13] *Cf.* Rule 68 of the Federal Rules of Civil Procedure which makes certain offers of judgment, which are otherwise inadmissible, admissible in proceeding to determine costs.

[14] *In re* General Motors Corp. Engine Interchange Litigation, 594 F.2d 1106 (7th Cir. 1979) (in class action where fairness of settlement was being appealed, conduct of the negotiations was relevant and evidence was not barred by Rule 408).

[15] Belton v. Fibreboard Corp., 724 F.2d 500, 504–05 (5th Cir. 1984) (in products liability action, evidence of settlements between plaintiff and fifteen other named defendants admitted to prove plaintiffs had been exposed to products of other defendants).

[16] Catullo v. Metzner, 834 F.2d 1075, 1079 (1st Cir. 1987) (testimony to prove terms of agreement admissible to enforce agreement; citing **Treatise**); Thomas v. Resort Health Related Facility, 539 F. Supp. 630, 638 (E.D.N.Y. 1982) (employer's offer to reinstate plaintiff admissible to show that pay loss during period after offer was made was not attributable to discrimination).

[17] B & B Investment Club v. Kleinert's Inc., 472 F. Supp. 787 (E.D. Pa. 1979).

[18] Central Soya Co., Inc. v. Epstein Fisheries, Inc., 676 F.2d 939 (7th Cir. 1982) (in action by seller on guaranty, testimony about settlement of contract dispute between seller and buyer was admissible because it was highly relevant to determining amount of debt which had been guaranteed).

[19] Breuer Elec. Mfg. Co. v. Toronado Systems of Am., Inc., 687 F.2d 182, 185 (7th Cir. 1982) (settlement evidence properly presented on motion to set aside entry of default judgment to rebut defendants' assertions that they were not aware of issues in suit prior to filing of action); United States v. Gilbert, 668 F.2d 94 (2d Cir. 1981), *cert. denied,* 456 U.S. 946 (1982) (earlier civil consent decree signed by defendant was properly admitted to prove defendant's knowledge of SEC reporting requirements).

[20] Urico v. Parnell Oil Co., 708 F.2d 852 (1st Cir. 1983) (testimony which detailed settlement negotiations between parties was not inadmissible where it was offered

ior in question was a mistake or accident.[21] In addition, where the settlement negotiations and terms explain and are a part of another dispute, they must often be admitted if the trier is to understand the case.[22] In *Cassino v. Reichhold Chemicals, Inc.,*[23] an age discrimination suit, the court drew a distinction between cases in which an employee relinquishes the right to a judicial determination in return for a valuable consideration after the employee has claimed to be the victim of illegal discrimination (settlement protection under Rule 408), and those cases where an employment situation is terminated and the employer offers a severance pay package in exchange for a release of all potential claims. In the latter situation, the "policy behind Rule 408 does not come into play. Rule 408 should not be used to bar relevant evidence concerning the circumstances of the termination itself simply because one party calls its communication with

---

to show defendant unreasonably prevented plaintiffs from mitigating their damages in an effort to reach an advantageous settlement); Iberian Tankers Co. v. Gates Constr. Corp., 388 F. Supp. 1190 (S.D.N.Y. 1975) (settlement negotiations admissible to determine whether defendant was liable for prejudgment interest).

[21] Bradbury v. Phillips Petroleum Co., 815 F.2d 1356, 1363 (10th Cir. 1987) (suit for trespass, outrageous conduct and assault arising from defendant's hiring of drilling company which erroneously drilled on one plaintiff's land and whose employees assaulted other plaintiff; jury awarded substantial exemplary damages; trial court properly admitted evidence of seven similar incidents in which defendant compensated the landowners since they "bore on the central question of whether the driller engaged in reckless behavior or whether it was a mistake or accident"; in response to defendant's argument that evidence of other incidents might have led jury to conclude that defendant deserved to be punished for its treatment of other landowners, court acknowledged that risk of prejudice was high, but found no abuse of discretion because district court had carefully considered the issue which was briefed and decided *in limine* before trial).

[22] United States v. Wilford, 710 F.2d 439 (8th Cir. 1983), *cert. denied,* 464 U.S. 1039 (1984) (not error to admit evidence of settlement agreement between the union and the N.L.R.B. that union would cease its disputed activities and refund fees paid by non-union drivers where the settlement was offered to show the circumstances surrounding the refunds); MCI Communications v. American Tel. & Tel. Co., 708 F.2d 1081 (7th Cir.), *cert. denied,* 464 U.S. 891 (1983) (the trial court did not err in admitting testimony set forth in a prior agreement since the evidence explained another dispute, assisted the factfinder in understanding the case, demonstrated technical feasibility, and proper limiting instructions were given at the time the evidence was introduced).

[23] 817 F.2d 1338 (9th Cir. 1987).

the other party a 'settlement offer.' "[24]

The second general exception to Rule 408's exclusionary force is proof of bias or prejudice of a witness. Need for the evidence is most common when the witness had compromised his claims against a litigant in the suit being tried.[25] Rule 408 has determined, in effect, that the need to evaluate a witness's credibility normally outweighs the policy of encouraging compromises.[26] Yet the trial judge should guard against needless inquiry and concern over credibility factors, which could well result in unnecessarily undercutting the basic exclusionary rule.[27] The danger that the evidence will be used substantively as an admission is especially great when the witness sought to be impeached, by showing the compromise with a third party, is one of the litigants in the suit being tried.

Despite the exceptions to Rule 408, care should be taken that an indiscriminate and mechanistic application does not result in undermining the rule's public policy objective. The almost unavoidable impact of disclosure about compromises is that the jury will consider the evidence as a concession of liability. The problem is similar to that of proof of other crimes, subsequent remedial measures, and liability insurance. The trial judge should weigh the need for such evidence against the potentiality of discouraging future settlement negotiations and apply Rule 403[28] to exclude when the balance so

[24] *Id.* at 1343.

[25] *See* County of Hennepin v. AFG Industries, Inc., 726 F.2d 149, 152–53 (8th Cir. 1984) (evidence of settlement between plaintiff and cross-defendant's insurer was held properly admitted against plaintiff to impeach testimony of plaintiff's witnesses).

[26] John McShain, Inc. v. Cessna Aircraft Co., 563 F.2d 632, 635 (3d Cir. 1977) (court properly admitted evidence that a sister corporation of witness' employer had been released from liability by plaintiff in exchange for witness testifying for plaintiff).

[27] *Cf.* Hardware Mut. Ins. Co. v. Lukken, 372 F.2d 8, 14–15 (10th Cir. 1967) (not abuse of discretion to deny cross-examination when witness' testimony was not damaging).

[28] Ramada Dev. Co. v. Rauch, 644 F.2d 1097, 1107 (5th Cir. 1981) (trial court had not abused discretion in excluding report since exception "was not intended to completely undercut the policy behind the rule," and "notice could be effectively provided by means less in conflict with the policy behind Rule 408"); John McShain, Inc. v. Cessna Aircraft Co., 563 F.2d 632, 635 (3d Cir. 1977) ("A sensitive analysis of the need for the evidence as proof on a contested factual issue, of the prejudice which

dictates. Even if such evidence is admitted pursuant to an exception, an opponent can still argue to the jury that the admission has little probative force because of the accompanying circumstances.

¶ 7.05[02]   Curing Error[1]

Rule 408's exclusionary treatment is broad. It covers all conduct occurring and statements made during compromise negotiations. It is therefore unlikely that every erroneous admission of evidence will be prejudicial. Automatic declarations of mistrial are not required. Rather, the trial judge should determine whether, after an adequate instruction, such a fixed impression of a concession of liability has been made on the minds of the jury as to probably influence its verdict.[2]

¶ 7.06   Payment of Medical and Other Expenses—Rule 409[1]

Rule 409 excludes evidence of furnishing or offering or promising to pay medical, hospital or similar expenses occasioned by an injury. The rule provides:

---

may eventuate from admission, and of the public policies involved is in order before passing on such an objection.")

[1] *See* **Treatise** at ¶ 408[06].

[2] *Compare* Almonte v. National Union Fire Ins. Co., 705 F.2d 566 (1st Cir. 1983) (judgment for plaintiff reversed because trial court failed to give instruction to counteract prejudice created by receipt of evidence which would otherwise have been excluded because, inter alia, it partially concerned settlement negotiations) and Hawthorne v. Eckerson Co., 77 F.2d 844, 847 (2d Cir. 1935) (in case in which verdict was similar to amount of compromise with another accident victim, court concluded that evidence of compromise was improperly admitted to show agency) *with* Meyer v. Capital Transit Co., 32 A.2d 392, 393–94 (D.C. Mun. App. 1943) (inference from counsel's argument that client always settled with reasonable claimants to show unreasonableness of suit; careful instruction removed any prejudice).

[1] *See* **Treatise** at ¶¶ 409[01]–[03].

Rule 409

PAYMENT OF MEDICAL AND SIMILAR EXPENSES

Evidence of furnishing or offering or promising to pay medical, hospital, or similar expenses occasioned by an injury is not admissible to prove liability for the injury.

The ground for exclusion relied upon by the drafters is the social policy of encouraging assistance to the injured party by removing the risk that such action will be used in a subsequent trial as an admission. Rule 409 excludes all such offers or payments to prove liability, even if the only motivation was the desire to mitigate the damages for which the aider might be subsequently held legally liable.

Where the state rule is different, the court may consider the *Erie* problem. Since it is unlikely that the state rule on this matter is of great significance, uniformity needs will almost always result in application of the federal rule even where state substantive law is applied. Exclusion is required by the terms of Rule 409 only when the evidence is offered to prove liability. Where the evidence is offered to prove another material proposition,[2] such as control or the status of the alleged tort-feasor,[3] the court may consider the underlying policy and exclude pursuant to Rule 403 if there is little probative force in the line of proof.

A troublesome question arises when an express admission of liability is coupled with an offer of assistance. Although Rule 409 excludes all such offers or tenders of assistance, the express admissions are generally admissible. If the admission can be disclosed without mentioning the furnishing, offering or promise to pay medical expenses,

---

[2] Employers Mut. Cas. Co. v. Mosqueda, 317 F.2d 609, 613 (5th Cir. 1963) (insurance company's payment of attorney fees for negligent driver admissible on issue whether driver had permission to drive insured's truck); Hartford Accident & Indem. Co. v. Sanford, 344 F. Supp. 969 (W.D. Okla. 1973) (insurance company payment of medical expenses admissible on issue of estoppel in action by company against insured).

[3] Savoie v. Otto Candies, Inc., 692 F.2d 363, 370 & n.7 (5th Cir. 1982) (in Jones Act action, evidence that employer made "maintenance payments" to plaintiff admissible to show plaintiff's status as seaman).

then it should be admitted.[4] Non-severable admissions—such as "Don't worry about it; since it's my fault, I'll pay your bills"—should generally be excluded, unless the circumstances are so compelling as to prevail over the rule's general social policy.

¶ 7.07 Plea Bargaining—Rule 410

¶ 7.07[01] Rationale and Scope[1]

Rule 410 excludes evidence of withdrawn guilty pleas, nolo contendere pleas, and statements made in the course of federal or state plea proceedings. In addition, statements made in the course of plea discussions with the prosecutor are excluded. The evidence excluded by the rule may not be admitted against the defendant who made the plea or statement either for substantive or impeachment use in any civil or criminal proceeding.

The rule provides:

Rule 410

INADMISSIBILITY OF PLEAS, PLEA DISCUSSIONS, AND RELATED STATEMENTS

Except as otherwise provided in this rule, evidence of the following is not, in any civil or criminal proceeding, admissible against the defendant who made the plea or was a participant in the plea discussions:

(1) a plea of guilty which was later withdrawn;

(2) a plea of nolo contendere;

(3) any statement made in the course of any proceedings under Rule 11 of the Federal Rules of Criminal Procedure or comparable state procedure regarding either of the foregoing pleas; or

(4) any statement made in the course of plea discussions with an attorney for the prosecuting authority which do not result in a plea of guilty or which result in a plea of guilty later withdrawn.

---

[4] Sims v. Sowle, 238 Or. 329, 395 P.2d 133 (1964) (statements defendant made when he returned to apologize two days after paying plaintiff's medical expenses admissible).

[1] *See* **Treatise** at ¶¶ 401[01], ¶ 410[05].

However, such a statement is admissible (i) in any proceeding wherein another statement made in the course of the same plea or plea discussions has been introduced and the statement ought in fairness be considered contemporaneously with it, or (ii) in a criminal proceeding for perjury or false statement if the statement was made by the defendant under oath, on the record and in the presence of counsel.

The rule does not exclude evidence of witnesses' withdrawn pleas or plea bargaining statements. Such evidence may be admitted to impeach the witness. Nor does the rule cover the admissibility of pleas of guilty or of nolo contendere against an alleged co-offender.[2] Even though a plea or statement is excluded by the rule, evidence of the underlying acts is admissible pursuant to other rules, such as Rule 404(b).[3] The rule is identical to Rule 11(e)(6) of the Federal Rules of Criminal Procedure.

Although the justification for excluding each category of evidence varies, a common policy thread runs throughout: the promotion of plea bargaining and the avoidance of undue prejudice to the defendant. Rule 410 creates, in effect, a privilege of the defendant.

A defendant may proffer evidence of offers to plead or pleas that might be excluded were a prosecutor to offer them. Generally, the court should give a defendant considerable leeway in introducing such evidence. There are two clear exceptions to this rule of leniency in applying Rule 410. First, the defendant should not be permitted to prove a withdrawn plea or an offer to plead in order to show that a government attorney had doubts about his guilt.[4] The prosecutor's view of the defendant's guilt or innocence is irrelevant. Second, where there are joint trials, the introduction of such evidence by one defendant may prejudice a co-defendant.

---

[2] The admissibility of such evidence is discussed in the **Treatise** at ¶ 410[07]. For a discussion of the use of criminal pleas, which have not been withdrawn, in other causes of action, see **Treatise** at ¶ 410[06].

[3] United States v. Wyatt, 762 F.2d 908, 909 (11th Cir. 1985) ("admissibility of underlying facts unaffected by nolo plea").

[4] See United States v. Verdoorn, 528 F.2d 103, 107 (8th Cir. 1976) (trial court excluded evidence of plea bargaining which according to defendants would "disclose the lengths to which the government went in attempting to obtain vital testimony"; court relied on Fed. R. Crim. P. 11(e)(6)); United States v. Collins, 305 F. Supp. 629 (M.D. Pa. 1975).

¶ 7.07[02]   Evidence of Pleas Excluded[1]

Rule 410 excludes evidence of withdrawn pleas, rejected pleas, and pleas of nolo contendere. Evidence of any withdrawn plea is excluded in any proceeding regardless of knowledge and willingness of the pleader.[2] Exclusion is required because permitting use of the withdrawn plea would make the trial meaningless. It is unlikely that the jury would use the plea merely as evidence of conduct inconsistent with the defendant's claim of innocence.[3] Withdrawn pleas are also excluded because flexibility, in making and withdrawing them without prejudice, is necessary to encourage negotiations between defense and prosecution counsel. A constitutional basis for exclusion has been suggested by a few courts.[4]

Evidence of rejected pleas is also inadmissible against the defendant. Exclusion effectuates the policy of promoting "plea bargaining" by protecting defendants against the use of unaccepted offers at subsequent trials.

As in the case of withdrawn pleas, the impact on the jury of the seeming admission of guilt cannot normally be overcome by an admonition. A defendant might well be forced to take the stand to explain the offer or to leave the evidence unrebutted, thereby creating a constitutional issue.

If information about a withdrawn or a rejected plea is disclosed, a mistrial may have to be declared. Certainly, if the prosecution or court deliberately reveals the existence of such pleas, the prejudice would seem to be incurable. The defendant, in view of the clarity of Rule 410, is in effect deliberately being tried by means declared to be unfair.

---

[1] *See* **Treatise** at ¶¶ 410[03]–[04].

[2] United States v. Lawson, 683 F.2d 688 (2d Cir. 1982) (statement may not be used for impeachment).

[3] Bruton v. United States, 391 U.S. 123, 135, 88 S. Ct. 1620, 20 L. Ed. 2d 476 (1968) ("[T]here are some contexts in which the risk that the jury will not, or cannot, follow instructions is so great, and the consequences of failure so vital to the defendant, that the practical and human limitations of the jury system cannot be ignored.").

[4] *See, e.g.,* Wood v. United States, 128 F.2d 265 (D.C. Cir. 1942) (admission of the withdrawn plea would be a form of self-incrimination since the court had compelled a plea).

Counsel and the trial court can, without much effort, avoid the disclosure of the withdrawn or rejected plea or the plea of nolo contendere. Unlike matters of widespread knowledge—such as the existence of liability insurance—the probability of an inadvertent or unintentional disclosure by an unsuspecting witness of pleas barred by Rule 410 is not significant. Nevertheless, automatic retrials should not be granted if in fact it is perfectly clear that disclosure was inadvertent and reference to the plea did not affect the verdicts.

¶ 7.07[03]   Statement Made in Connection with Plea Bargaining[1]

Rule 410 expressly makes inadmissible statements made in the course of any proceedings under 1) Rule 11 of the Federal Rules of Criminal Procedure,[2] 2) state plea proceedings, and 3) plea discussions with an attorney for the prosecuting authority. Such statements are excluded to ensure that plea discussions are immunized sufficiently to promote the practice of plea bargaining.

A number of grey areas remain for treatment on a case by case basis. It is not always clear whether the statements were made in the course of plea bargaining, a pre-requisite if the rule is to apply.[3] A clear record obviously best enables the court to characterize accurately the nature of the discussions between the defendant and the

---

[1] See **Treatise** at ¶¶ 410[04], [08].

[2] Rule 11 of the Federal Rules of Criminal Procedure governs procedures for pleas in the federal courts and establishes requirements designed to enhance the visibility and fairness of plea discussions.

[3] See, e.g., United States v. Leon Guerrero, 847 F.2d 1363, 1367–68 (9th Cir. 1988) (FBI investigatory interview held before defendant had been arrested or charged was not transformed into plea negotiation because United States Attorney made brief appearance and made vague promise that cooperation would be taken into consideration); United States v. Serna, 799 F.2d 842, 848–49 (2d Cir. 1986), cert. denied, 107 S. Ct. 1887 (1987) (defendant's preliminary discussion with DEA agent to determine the defendant's sincerity in cooperating with the Assistant United States Attorney was part of the overall plea bargaining process since the AUSA arranged the discussion with the DEA agent); United States v. Gazzara, 587 F.Supp. 311 (S.D.N.Y. 1984) (statements made by defendant to Secret Service agents in the presence of his attorney were not protected by Rule 410 where attorney never asked to speak with an Assistant United States Attorney about formal plea bargaining negotiations).

prosecution. The careful United States Attorney will make it clear on a recording of the conversation and a form signed by the defendant that the statements were not made in connection with any plea negotiations or because of any promise of a plea or leniency.[4] In addition, the prosecutor should urge the defendant to obtain an attorney before speaking. If defense counsel is present and plea bargaining is taking place, counsel should make a written record as soon as possible, by exchange of letters or by stipulation, that any statements made by his client are in the course of plea negotiations pursuant to Rule 11(e)(6) and Rule 410.

Some statements may be protected from disclosure even though they were not made to a prosecuting attorney. The government should not be permitted to by-pass Rule 410 by authorizing law enforcement officials to conduct plea negotiations.[5] Furthermore, there may be instances where law enforcement officials misrepresent their authority and induce a defendant to make inculpatory statements while he is under the mistaken impression that he is engaging in plea bargaining. Such cases are governed not by Rule 410 but by the body of law dealing with the voluntariness of statements made while in police custody[6] and inhibitions against trickery by the police.

Once there has been an indictment or information filed, there is a strong inference that admissions were made in the course of plea negotiations. Prior to this event, a contrary inference would be reasonable and sound. Admissions in open court prior to trial at arraignment or pretrials will almost always be protected by Rules 11(e)(6) and Rule 410.

¶ 7.07[04]   Attacks on Credibility

The evidence excluded by Rule 410 may not be used in impeaching the defendant. Such use would usually compel defendant to remain

---

[4] United States v. Cunningham, 723 F.2d 217, 227–28 (2d Cir. 1983), *cert. denied,* 466 U.S. 951 (1984) (stipulation made by defendant at outset of interview that anything said could later be used against him made it clear that the interview was not a plea bargaining session).

[5] *See* discussion in Rachlin v. United States, 723 F.2d 1373, 1376 (8th Cir. 1983).

[6] *See* discussions in Rachlin v. United States, 723 F.2d 1373, 1377–78 (8th Cir. 1983); United States v. Gazzara, 587 F. Supp. 311 (S.D.N.Y 1984).

off the witness stand. The remedy for brazen lying is prosecution for interfering with governmental activities or perjury.[1]

¶ 7.07[05]   Exceptions[1]

Statements made by a defendant in connection with a plea or an offer to plead may be used in a criminal proceeding for perjury or false statement if the statements were made by the defendant under oath,[2] on the record, and in the presence of counsel.[3] They should be usable in a prosecution for obstruction of justice where government agents are deliberately lied to by the defendant.

If a defendant introduces statements made during plea discussions, then other relevant statements made in the same plea discussions are admissible under the rule of completeness.[4] Caution by de-

---

[1] United States v. Udeagu, 110 F.R.D. 172 (E.D.N.Y. 1986).

[1] *See* **Treatise** at ¶ 410[02].

[2] *Cf.* United States v. Abrahams, 604 F.2d 386 (5th Cir. 1979) (statement made before magistrate could not be used against defendant in perjury proceeding where defendant was never placed under oath).

[3] Rule 17.1 of the Federal Rules of Criminal Procedure provides: "No admission made by the defendant or his attorney at the conference shall be used against the defendant unless the admissions are reduced to writing and signed by the defendant and his attorney." *Cf.* Cupac, Inc. v. Mid-West Ins. Agency, 100 F.R.D. 440, 442 (S.D. Ohio 1983) (although plea discussions might be inadmissible at trial under Rule 410, defendant was not entitled to protective order precluding their discovery since they appeared reasonably calculated to lead to discovery of admissible evidence); United States v. Hinton, 703 F.2d 672, 679 (2d Cir.), *cert. denied,* 462 U.S. 1121 (1983) (government may use statements made during plea negotiations to change theory of case and reindict); United States v. Tesack, 538 F.2d 1068 (4th Cir.), *cert. denied,* 429 U.S. 1025 (1976) (not error to allow withdrawn guilty plea to be used to impeach codefendant after he took stand and categorically denied any connection whatever with charged offenses). Tesack seems clearly inconsistent with Rule 410 and is explicable only on the harmless error principle. The proper remedy for bold faced lies of this kind is a perjury prosecution. *See* United States v. Udeagu, 110 F.R.D. 172 (E.D.N.Y. 1986).

[4] United States v. Doran, 564 F.2d 1176 (5th Cir. 1977), *cert. denied,* 435 U.S. 928 (1978) (where defendant testified on direct that he had refused plea offer because he was innocent, on cross-examination prosecution was permitted to ask him about a counter-offer he had made to the government; appellate court found that doctrine of "invited error" applied; defendant was permitted to explain his plea offer and trial judge gave cautionary instruction).

fense counsel is called for. In addition, plea statements made pursuant to an agreement with the prosecutor may be admitted if the defendant withdraws or violates the agreement.[5]

The plea and surrounding circumstances can be used in deciding the sentence in the case in which it is entered. It should also be usable in other criminal cases in deciding whether a nolo contendere plea should be accepted. A judge or administrative agency should be entitled to use the plea in determining a penalty either in a civil or criminal action.[6]

Courts still have to determine whether statements induced in ways that avoid the operation of Rule 410 should be immunized. For example, a court may have to determine whether statements made to a United States Attorney by a suspect after he is given Miranda warnings and advised that he is a target of an investigation are protected by Rule 410, when the United States Attorney stated, "If you cooperate fully and tell us who else is involved, I will tell the court about your cooperation and forget about the gun count; otherwise you'll face 25 years." The rule of admissibility prevails unless there

---

[5] In United States v. Stirling, 571 F.2d 708, 731–32, 736–37 (2d Cir. 1978), the Second Circuit held that plea statements that the defendant made before the grand jury may be used against him because he withdrew from a written agreement with the prosecutor to plead guilty and testify for the government. The court concluded that the defendant's failure to live up to the agreement "justly exposed him to prosecutorial use of his Grand Jury Testimony." The District of Columbia Circuit endorsed this approach in United States v. Davis, 617 F.2d 677 (D.C. Cir. 1979). Unlike Stirling, the plea agreement expressly provided for the use of defendant's testimony in case of breach. The District of Columbia Circuit, while conceding the difference, found that the two cases were nevertheless indistinguishable because excluding grand jury testimony simply because the defendant later "wants out" of the plea agreement would not serve the purpose of the rule. *See also* United States v. Perry, 643 F.2d 38, 52 (2d Cir.), *cert. denied,* 454 U.S. 835 (1981) (statements made by defendant after violating his plea agreement properly admitted); United States v. Arroyo-Angulo, 580 F.2d 1137, 1149 (2d Cir. 1978) (court noted as alternative ground for not extending Rule 410 to statements in question that "[i]n view of Arroyo's blatant breach of the cooperation arrangement with the Government, to prohibit the introduction of his admissions would make a mockery of the investigation processes employed to secure evidence of serious crimes.").

[6] United States v. Schipani, 315 F. Supp. 253 (E.D.N.Y.), *aff'd,* 435 F.2d 26 (2d Cir. 1970), *cert. denied,* 401 U.S. 983 (1971) (use of illegally obtained evidence for sentence).

is a special reason to exclude, such as a *Miranda* violation or unacceptable trickery.

¶ 7.08   Liability Insurance—Rule 411

¶ 7.08[01]   Rationale and Scope[1]

Rule 411 specifically excludes evidence not only of the existence but also of the nonexistence of insurance against liability upon the issue of defendant's negligence or other wrongful conduct. The Rule provides:

Rule 411

LIABILITY INSURANCE

Evidence that a person was or was not insured against liability is not admissible upon the issue whether the person acted negligently or otherwise wrongfully. This rule does not require the exclusion of evidence of insurance against liability when offered for another purpose, such as proof of agency, ownership, or control, or bias or prejudice of a witness.

Such evidence is excluded in the first instance because it is irrelevant. In the average automobile case the evidential hypothesis would be: "an insured person is more apt to be careless or reckless or to do an intentional harm than an uninsured person, because someone else will pay for any damages caused by his activity." The probative force of this line of proof is almost nil; no normal person operates a car more carelessly because he is insured. On the contrary, in a state where insurance is not required, carrying insurance shows a thoughtfulness warranting application of the hypothesis: "an insured person is more responsible than an uninsured person, and more responsible people are more apt to drive cars carefully." Even if the hypothesis of carefulness had any substantial probative force, it is likely that this line of proof would prove prejudicial because a juror might think, "After all, some rich insurance company will pay, so we might as well decide for this plaintiff without respect to the law and facts." Taking into account the low probative force and the pos-

---

[1] *See* **Treatise** at ¶¶ 411[01]–[03].

sibility of prejudice, evidence of insurance in an automobile liability case would probably be excluded under Rules 401 and 403, even without Rule 411.

Seen wholly from the standpoint of relevancy, the whole issue seems somewhat artificial, particularly in those states where automobile insurance is required, because jurors probably assume that most defendants are either insured or judgment proof. The same assumption is probably made with respect to other types of liability insurance.

Rule 411, in addition to excluding evidence of low probative force, also seeks to implement a general public policy favoring insurance. Both insurers and insured are, in effect, encouraged to enter into contracts of insurance with the implied promise that they will not, as a result of their forethought, have what they believe to be the somewhat harmful inference of carelessness used against them.

Although the rule might be literally interpreted as not covering evidence of the existence or non-existence of the *plaintiff's* liability insurance, such a position would be without merit. Evidence of insurance would be relevant and prejudicial as indicative of fault on the part of the plaintiff. Such evidence would further be prejudicial because it suggests that the plaintiff either may be seeking a double recovery or that the real party in interest is the subrogated insurer.

Rule 411, however, is not applicable to direct actions against the insurer. In such cases, it is not possible to keep the jury unaware of the insurance. It is, of course, appropriate for the court to attempt to minimize the possibilities of prejudice by appropriate instructions.[2]

---

[2] While there is discretion to deny impleader under Rule 14 of the Federal Rules of Civil Procedure or to grant separate trials under Rule 42(b) because of prejudice if the jury learns that the defendant is insured, Rule 411 ordinarily does not inhibit courts from exercising their discretion to resolve an entire dispute in one litigation whenever possible. *See, e.g.,* Schevling v. Johnson, 122 F. Supp. 87 (D. Conn. 1953) (impleader permitted), *aff'd on opinion below,* 213 F.2d 959 (2d Cir. 1954); Baker v. Moons, 51 F.R.D. 507, 510 (W.D. Ky. 1971) (impleader permitted); Crockett v. Baysen, 26 F.R.D. 148 (D.C. Minn. 1960) (motion for separate trials denied). *But see* Arnold v. Eastern Air Lines, Inc., 712 F.2d 899 (4th Cir. 1983), *cert. denied,* 464 U.S. 1040 (1984) (consolidation reversible error where it resulted in counsel's revelation to the jury of existence of insurance coverage and compensatory damages

¶ 7.08[02]   Exceptions[1]

Evidence of defendant's insurance against liability is relevant and therefore admissible if its existence tends to prove some material issue and it does not require use of the forbidden hypothesis that "an insured person tends to be more careless (or more careful) than one who is uninsured." Rule 411 sets forth the most common situations in which such evidence has generally been deemed admissible. These explicit exceptions are not all inclusive but are only illustrative.[2]

[a]   Control, Agency or the Like

Evidence concerning insurance against liability is admissible in vicarious liability cases when the issue of agency is contested. If the principal carries liability insurance covering the person alleged to be a agent or employee, this fact is strong evidence of the relationship. Evidence of insurance is also admissible to prove that defendant had control over certain property, or that defendant was the owner of

awarded were extremely disproportionate to average recovery of similarly situated plaintiffs).

Even if an insured co-defendant voluntarily discloses the presence of insurance, the uninsured co-defendant will generally not be permitted to show lack of insurance despite the possibility that the jury will assume all the defendants have insurance. City of Villa Rica v. Couch, 281 F.2d 284, 291-92 (5th Cir. 1960); Jenkins v. Nicholson, 162 F. Supp. 167, 170 (E.D. Pa. 1958). On request, appropriate instructions should be given.

[1] *See* **Treatise** at ¶¶ 411[03]–[04].

[2] B. H. Morton v. Zidell Explorations, Inc., 695 F.2d 347 (9th Cir. 1982), *cert. denied,* 460 U.S. 1039 (1983) (evidence that plaintiff secured liability insurance, effective day after contract signed, admitted to show that plaintiffs knew that agreement was binding); Varlack v. SWC Caribbean, Inc., 550 F.2d 171 (3d Cir. 1977) (in support of argument that amendment adding party should relate back, evidence that proposed defendant provided insurance carrier with information and that carrier was real party in interest admitted); Posttape Assocs. v. Eastman Kodak Co., 537 F.2d 751, 758 (3d Cir. 1976) (evidence of indemnification insurance admitted to show party knew it was the custom of trade to limit damages to replacement costs); Maggord Truck Line, Inc. v. Deaton, Inc., 573 F. Supp 1388, 1392 (N.D. Ga. 1983) (carrier's insurance coverage admitted because it tended to prove the existence of a special agreement shifting liability from broker to carrier).

the instrumentality causing the accident.[3]

If the evidence of insurance is admitted, the insured should be given a full opportunity to introduce evidence showing why, in the special circumstances of the case, insurance does not indicate control, agency or the like.

Evidence of the nonexistence of liability insurance would normally be less probative of the negative of issues such as control or agency than insurance is probative of the issue. Evidence of noninsurance should, therefore, not normally be admissible, since the possible prejudice outweighs any probative force. Where insurance by the person claimed to be in control is an invariable practice, lack of insurance may be evidence of his belief that he was not in control. *See* ¶ 7.03 *supra*.

[b] Credibility

Evidence disclosing the existence of defendant's liability insurance is admissible for purposes of impeachment.[4] Thus, should an attempt be made to impeach a witness by use of a written statement, plaintiff should be permitted to show that the person procuring the statement was an employee or a representative of a defendant's insurance company if that fact bears on trustworthiness.[5] Yet this rule is not without its limits; if the court has good reason to believe that the insurance question has almost no bearing on credibility but that it will be used prejudicially, it should exercise its power to exclude.[6] For

---

[3] Hunziker v. Scheidemantle, 543 F.2d 489, 495 n.10 (3d Cir. 1976) (trial court should consider, outside hearing of the jury, whether insurance contract was evidence of agency relationship in order to determine whether exclusion would be more prejudicial to the plaintiff than its admission would be to the defendant).

[4] *See, e.g.* Charter v. Chleborad, 551 F.2d 246 (8th Cir.), *cert. denied,* 434 U.S. 856 (1977) (reversible error for court to restrict impeachment of defendant's witness who was employed by insurance carrier representing defendant).

[5] Complete Auto Transit, Inc. v. Wayne Broyles Eng'r Corp., 351 F.2d 478, 481–82 (5th Cir. 1965); Zanetti Bus Lines, Inc. v. Hurd, 320 F.2d 123, 129 (10th Cir. 1963); Mideastern Contracting Corp. v. O'Toole, 55 F.2d 909, 912 (2d Cir. 1932).

[6] Brown v. Walter, 62 F.2d 798, 799 (2d Cir. 1933) (L. Hand, J.); Meek v. Miller, 38 F. Supp. 10, 12 (M.D. Pa. 1941); Coble v. Phillips Petroleum Co., 30 F. Supp. 39, 40 (N.D. Tex. 1939).

example, where the witness admits both the authenticity and correctness of the written statement, it has properly been held that it is proper to refuse isclosure.[7] If the evidence of insurance is disclosed, courts should, if requested, specifically charge the jury that this information can be used only on the issue of credibility and not in determining defendant's liability or in fixing the measure of damages.

¶ 7.08[03]   Application[1]

The standard of admissibility established by Rule 411 for evidence of liability insurance is not the same as that for pre-trial discovery. Discovery is permitted whenever the existence of insurance would tend to prove a material proposition of fact in the case. In addition, Rule 26(b)(2) of the Federal Rules of Civil Procedure permits widespread discovery of insurance.

Nor is Rule 411 intended to cover the troublesome question of the propriety of questioning prospective jurors as to possible interest in connection with any insurance carrier, since the issue does not involve a rule of evidence. But the extensive practice of permitting such examinations on voir dire undermines the rule's efficacy by reminding prospective jurors of the probable existence of insurance.

Federal courts have sought to "strike a balance between the probability of danger to plaintiffs that someone sympathetic to insurance companies may remain on the jury and the danger to defendant that the jury may award damages without fault if aware that there is insurance coverage to pay the verdict."[2] The general practice is that the panel may be questioned with respect to any interest or connection with any insurance company interested in the litigation, although the company is not a party.[3] If, however, the defendant does

---

[7] Brown v. Edwards, 258 F. Supp. 696, 699 (E.D. Pa. 1966) (applying Pennsylvania law).

[1] *See* **Treatise** at ¶¶ 411[05], [07]–[11].

[2] Langley v. Turner's Express, Inc., 375 F.2d 296, 297 (4th Cir. 1967) (examination not permitted, relying in part on state law).

[3] While some courts require plaintiffs to exhibit good faith in making the inquiry, Hinkle v. Hampton, 388 F.2d 141, 144 (10th Cir. 1968); Socony Mobil Oil Co. v. Taylor, 388 F.2d 586, 589 (5th Cir. 1967); Langley v. Turner's Express Inc., 375 F.2d 296, 297 (4th Cir. 1967), the Third Circuit in Kiernan v. Van Schaik, 347 F.2d

not possess insurance against liability, some courts refuse to permit questioning.[4] Others have suggested that questioning will be permitted, but the defendant will have the right to show absence of insurance coverage in order to counteract prejudice.[5] When the judge conducts the voir dire—the usual federal practice—a routine low key question on the subject buried among many other queries reduces the significance of the issue and its possible prejudice to the vanishing point.

The insurance rule sometimes does present difficult tactical and ethical problems for the practitioner. If a statement contains both an objectionable reference to insurance and admissible evidence and redaction may lead to misinterpretation, the whole statement will be admitted despite the resulting prejudice. *See* discussion in Chapter 2, *supra,* of Rule 106 and the rule of completeness. The general principle of Rule 403 provides the court with ample discretion to weigh prejudice against probative force.[6] Counsel for an insured party must be wary of unnecessary participation by insurance investigators in presenting the case, since opposing counsel may expose the insurance carrier's role by means of cross-examination. Thus, counsel must sometimes choose between using a written statement of a party in impeaching his credibility and allowing the testimony to go uncontradicted. Using the statement for the purpose of refreshing memory without actually introducing it can sometimes suffice to bring the witness around without disclosing the presence of the insurer. A not uncommon situation is a non-responsive or inadvertent reference to insurance by a witness in response to a proper question. Such refer-

---

775 (3d Cir. 1965), held that plaintiffs in accident cases may make reasonable inquiries as a matter of right.

[4] Socony Mobil Oil Co. v. Taylor, 388 F.2d 586, 588–89 (5th Cir. 1967) (relying in part on Texas law); Hinkle v. Hampton, 388 F.2d 141, 143–44 (10th Cir. 1968).

[5] Eppinger & Russell Co. v. Sheely, 24 F.2d 153, 155 (5th Cir. 1928) (dictum); Socony Mobile Oil Co. v. Taylor, 388 F.2d 586, 588 (5th Cir. 1967).

[6] An admission of a party bearing on the issue of negligence or damages is normally highly probative so that the statement is admissible even if it contains a nonseverable reference to his insurance. Garee v. McDonell, 116 F.2d 79, 80 (7th Cir. 1940), *cert. denied,* 313 U.S. 561 (1941). But if the witness' testimony is clear without revealing the existence of insurance, or if the reference to insurance can be easily deleted from documentary evidence, disclosure is unnecessary and should be avoided. Jamison v. A. M. Byers Co., 330 F.2d 657, 661 (3d Cir. 1964) (failure to delete insurance provisions of a contract caused new trial).

ences will be stricken on request. They will not call for a mistrial in the absence of any indication of bad faith on the part of the witness or of the examining counsel.[7]

In the absence of unusual circumstances,[8] the prejudicial effect of an improper disclosure of insurance can be sufficiently reduced to avoid a mistrial by striking and admonishing the jury to disregard the information.[9] A related problem—the jurors' discovery of the existence of insurance from sources outside the courtroom—also should be handled by admonition rather than a new trial. In the event of improper disclosure, counsel should note the objection and request the attorney to desist at a sidebar conference. By making the objection outside the presence of the jury, counsel avoids waiving the right to object to subsequent remarks about a client's insurance, avoids making the remark more prominent in the jury's mind, and preserves the record.

¶ 7.09   Rape Victim's Past Behavior—Rule 412[1]

Rule 412 makes inadmissible, except in specified instances, the sexual behavior of the victim of a rape or attempted rape.[2] Unlike

---

[7] *Compare* Cotter v. McKinney, 309 F.2d 447, 450–51 (7th Cir. 1962) (relying on strict Illinois rule to grant mistrial) and F.W. Woolworth Co. v. Davis, 41 F.2d 342, 345–46 (10th Cir. 1930) (court expressed disapproval of volunteered testimony suggesting presence of defendant's insurance, but reversed on other grounds) *with* Marks v. Mobil Oil Corp., 562 F. Supp. 759 (E.D. Pa. 1983), *aff'd,* 727 F.2d 1100 (3rd Cir. 1984) (inadvertent mention by witness of contact with an insurance company agent in a context which did not affect the substantive rights of the parties was insufficient to support a mistrial).

[8] Cotter v. McKinney, 309 F.2d 447, 450 (7th Cir. 1962) (improper argument by counsel; relying on strong Illinois policy); Transit Cas. Co. v. Transamerica Ins. Co., 387 F.2d 1011, 1013–14 (8th Cir. 1967) (jury verdict indicated influence by improper references to reinsurance); Indamer Corp. v. Crandon, 217 F.2d 391, 394–95 (5th Cir. 1954) (in light of disproportionate damage award, new trial on damages ordered because of inadequate admonition).

[9] Crusan v. Ackmann, 342 F.2d 611, 613 (7th Cir. 1965).

[1] *See* **Treatise** ¶ 412[01].

[2] *Cf.* Government of Virgin Islands v. Scuito, 623 F.2d 869 (3rd Cir. 1980) (holding that trial judge did not abuse discretion in holding that spirit of Rule 412 required him to deny motion by defendant seeking psychiatric examination of rape complainant).

Rule 404, which only makes evidence of one's character inadmissible if offered to prove that one acted in conformity therewith, Rule 412 excludes evidence of sexual behavior regardless of the evidentiary hypothesis that is proffered.[3] The Rule provides:

Rule 412

SEX OFFENSE CASES; RELEVANCE OF VICTIM'S PAST BEHAVIOR

(a) Notwithstanding any other provision of law, in a criminal case in which a person is accused of an offense under chapter 109A of title 18, United States Code, reputation or opinion evidence of the past sexual behavior of an alleged victim of such offense is not admissible.

(b) Notwithstanding any other provision of law, in a criminal case in which a person is accused of an offense under chapter 109A of title 18, United States Code, evidence of a victim's past sexual behavior other than reputation or opinion evidence is also not admissible, unless such evidence other than reputation or opinion evidence is—

(1) admitted in accordance with subdivisions (c)(1) and (c)(2) and is constitutionally required to be admitted; or

(2) admitted in accordance with subdivision (c) and is evidence of—

(A) past sexual behavior with persons other than the accused, offered by the accused upon the issue of whether the accused was or was not, with respect to the alleged victim, the source of semen or injury; or

(B) past sexual behavior with the accused and is offered by the accused upon the issue of whether the alleged victim consented to the sexual behavior with respect to which such offense is alleged.

---

[3] United States v. Azure, 845 F.2d 1503, 1506 (8th Cir. 1988) (in child sex abuse prosecution, proffered testimony by witness who claimed to have had sexual relations with victim was properly excluded; defense claimed that evidence should have been admitted for impeachment purposes since victim had denied any contact with witness, and to demonstrate her capability to fabricate); United States v. Cardinal, 782 F.2d 34 (6th Cir.), *cert. denied,* 106 S. Ct. 2282 (1986) (evidence that complainant had previously charged the defendant and her stepfather with sexual assault, but later withdrew the charge, was properly excluded even though this proof was offered for the purpose of impeaching the complainant's character for truthfulness); Not all courts recognize this distinction. *See* Doe v. United States, 666 F.2d 43 (4th Cir. 1981) (reputation evidence admissible when offered solely to show defendant's state of mind).

(c)(1) If the person accused of committing an offense under chapter 109A of title 18, United States Code intends to offer under subdivision (b) evidence of specific instances of the alleged victim's past sexual behavior, the accused shall make a written motion to offer such evidence not later than fifteen days before the date on which the trial in which such evidence is to be offered is scheduled to begin, except that the court may allow the motion to be made at a later date, including during trial, if the court determines either that the evidence is newly discovered and could not have been obtained earlier throught the exercise of due diligence or that the issue to which such evidence relates has newly arisen in the case. Any motion made under this paragraph shall be served on all other parties and on the alleged victim.

(2) The motion described in paragraph (1) shall be accompanied by a written offer of proof. If the court determines that the offer of proof contains evidence described in subdivision (b), the court shall order a hearing in chambers to determine if such evidence is admissible. At such hearing the parties may call witnesses, including the alleged victim, and offer relevant evidence. Notwithstanding subdivision (b) of rule 104, if the relevancy of the evidence which the accused seeks to offer in the trial depends upon the fulfillment of a condition of fact, the court, at the hearing in chambers or at a subsequent hearing in chambers scheduled for such purpose, shall accept evidence on the issue of whether such condition of fact is fulfilled and shall determine such issue.

(3) If the court determines on the basis of the hearing described in paragraph (2) that the evidence which the accused seeks to offer is relevant and that the probative value of such evidence outweighs the danger of unfair prejudice, such evidence shall be admissible in the trial to the extent an order made by the court specifies evidence which may be offered and areas with respect to which the alleged victim may be examined or cross-examined.

(d) For purposes of this rule, the term "past sexual behavior" means sexual behavior other than the sexual behavior with respect to which an offense under chapter 109A of title 18, United States Code is alleged.

As the legislative history indicates, the rationale is to prevent the victim, rather than the defendant, from being put on trial. The low incidence of reports of rape is in part believed to stem from the victim's reluctance to be cross-examined about her sexual past as was permitted under the common law approach. Effective November 18, 1988, the Rule was made applicable to sex offenses as defined in chapter 109A of title 18, United States Code.[4]

---

[4] *See Anti-Drug Abuse Act of 1988, P.L. No. 100-690.*

Rule 412 recognizes that evidence of the victim's unchastity is ordinarily of no probative value on the issue of whether a rape occurred. Congress acknowledged, however, that under some circumstances a victim's sexual behavior may be relevant. Three situations are specified in Rule 412(b) which authorize the defendant to proffer evidence of the victim's sexual behavior: 1) if the Constitution would so require;[5] 2) if the defendant is trying to show that someone else was the source of the semen or injury to the victim;[6] and 3) if defendant is claiming consent and wishes to show that the victim had previously engaged in sexual behavior with the accused. While some of the Congressional discussion suggests that the bill protects only female victims, the bill itself is stated generally to protect male victims of rape where such a crime has been charged.

Rule 412(c) requires the defendant to make a written motion in advance of trial of an intention to offer evidence pursuant to the exceptions in subdivision (b), accompanied by a written order of proof. If the defendant could not with due diligence have made the motion prior to trial, a motion during trial may be entertained by the court.[7]

The court upon receipt of the motion must determine whether the offer of proof indicates the existence of one of the three circumstances specified in subdivision (b). If the court so finds, an evidenti-

---

[5] United States v. Bartlett, 856 F.2d 1071, 1088–89 (8th Cir. 1988) (court did not err in excluding alleged prior false accusation of rape made by victim against a third party which was offered only to attack general credibility of witness).

[6] United States v. Shaw, 824 F.2d 601, 602–08 (8th Cir. 1987), *cert. denied,* 108 S. Ct. 1033 (1988) (defendant, charged with carnal knowledge of his eleven year old stepdaughter, proffered testimony by seven witnesses that they had had sexual intercourse with girl; government had offered proof that condition of girl's hymen was consistent with her having engaged in sexual conduct; court held that evidence of prior sexual acts was properly excluded as condition of hymen did not constitute an injury; despite conceded authority to the contrary, court refused to broaden the injury exception to authorize the introduction of past sexual behavior evidence to prove the source of any physical consequence of rape; court relied on legislative history of Rule 412; defendant had not raised constitutional right to present evidence pursuant to Rule 412(b)(1) and court found waiver).

[7] United States v. Nez, 661 F.2d 1203 (10th Cir. 1981) (not error for trial court to have excluded evidence of complainant's past sexual behavior where defendant never indicated purpose for which evidence was being offered, and only on appeal characterized the evidence as relevant to complainant's motive in bringing the charge).

ary hearing will be held in chambers.[8] Even if the proffered evidence is found to be relevant to the issues specified in subdivision (b), subdivision (c)(3) provides that exclusion is still warranted under a Rule 403 test if its probative value does not outweigh the danger of unfair prejudice.[9]

Difficult problems of relevancy may arise when evidence of prior behavior is offered pursuant to Rule 412(b)(1) because "it is constitutionally required." The questions usually arise in the context of a consent defense where defendant wishes to claim that the victim's reputation warranted his belief in her consent. Does the defendant have a constitutional right to present this defense despite the victim's interest in privacy? The rule suggests the answer most judges would give—the defendant's right to a fair trial must be given precedence over the alleged victim's right to privacy.[10]

---

[8] The Fourth Circuit has held that a pre-trial ruling that is adverse to the victim may be directly appealed. Doe v. United States, 666 F.2d 43 (4th Cir. 1981).

[9] United States v. One Feather, 702 F.2d 736, 739 (8th Cir. 1983) (trial court did not err in refusing, on Rule 403 grounds, to allow defense counsel to inquire into rape victim's marriage and divorce where defense sought to indirectly present evidence of victim's past sexual behavior by bringing fact that victim had illegitimate child to jury's attention).

[10] Doe v. United States, 666 F.2d 43, 47 (4th Cir. 1981) (court held that reputation and opinion evidence of past sexual behavior of witness had to be excluded as irrelevant but reserved decision on whether admission of such evidence might in extraordinary situation be justified to preserve defendant's constitutional rights).

CHAPTER 8*

Authentication and Identification

SYNOPSIS

* Chapter revised in 1991 by WALTER BARTHOLD, of counsel to Ferber Greilsheimer Chan & Essner, New York, New York.

¶ 8.01   Requirement of Authentication or Identification—Rule 901

¶ 8.01[01]   Scheme of Rule 901[1]

Rule 901(a)—the basic rule governing authentication—makes two major points: 1) it recognizes that all evidence, not solely writings, must be shown to be genuine, and 2) it provides that evidence challenged on the grounds of authenticity must be admitted once a prima facie showing of genuineness is made to the trial court. This second aspect of Rule 901(a), which implicates the relationship between judge and jury, is discussed in Chapter 3 *supra*.

Rule 901(a) provides:

Rule 901

REQUIREMENT OF AUTHENTICATION OR IDENTIFICATION

(a) General provision. The requirement of authentication or identification as a condition precedent to admissibility is satisfied by evidence sufficient to support a finding that the matter in question is what its proponent claims.

In order to be relevant—that is to have the necessary relationship with a material issue in a case—a piece of evidence must be shown to be what it purports to be.[2] For instance, the profferor may have to show that the letter in question was sent by the defendant, that the handwriting in issue is the plaintiff's, or that this gun being displayed in the courtroom is the gun used in the robbery. Preliminary questions such as these raise

---

[1] *See* **Treatise** at ¶¶ 901(a)[01]–[02].

[2] *See* United States v. Harrington, 923 F.2d 1371 (9th Cir. 1991) (in prosecution for armed bank robbery, contents of bag seized from defendant upon his arrest was admissible, where the arresting officer testified that at the time of trial the bag contained all the items seized at the time of arrest; the prosecution is not required to produce at trial the custodian of the evidence or every person who had possession of the evidence, but merely sufficient proof that the evidence is in substantially the same condition as when it was seized).

conditions of fact upon which the relevancy of the proffered evidence depends.

This rule of genuineness is, of course, subject to common sense. If, for example, a forged bill is offered to show that the defendant passed counterfeit currency, the proof will be that it is not genuine. It is authenticated, however, by showing that it is "genuinely" the bill passed by defendant.

Rule 901(b) lists some of the more common techniques for showing that these conditions of fact have been satisfied. It provides:

(b) Illustrations. By way of illustration only, and not by way of limitation, the following are examples of authentication or identification conforming with the requirements of this rule:

(1) Testimony of witness with knowledge. Testimony that a matter is what it is claimed to be.

(2) Nonexpert opinion on handwriting. Nonexpert opinion as to the genuinesss of handwriting, based upon familiarity not acquired for purposes of the litigation.

(3) Comparison by trier or expert witness. Comparison by the trier of fact or by expert witnesses with specimens which have been authenticated.

(4) Distinctive characteristics and the like. Appearance, contents, substance, internal patterns, or other distinctive characteristics, taken in conjunction with circumstances.

(5) Voice identification. Identification of a voice, whether heard firsthand or through mechanical or electronic transmission or recording, by opinion based upon hearing the voice at any time under circumstances connecting it with the alleged speaker.

(6) Telephone conversations. Telephone conversations, by evidence that a call was made to the number assigned at the time by the telephone company to a particular person or business, if (A) in the case of a person, circumstances, including self-identification, show the person answering to be the one called, or (B) in the case of a business, the call was made to a place of business and the conversation related to business reasonably transacted over the telephone.

(7) Public records or reports. Evidence that a writing authorized by law to be recorded or filed and in fact recorded or filed in a public office, or a purported public record, report, statement, or data compilation, in any form, is from the public office where items of this nature are kept.

(8) Ancient documents or data compilations. Evidence that a document or data compilation, in any form, (A) is in such condition as to create no suspicion concerning its authenticity, (B) was in a place where it, if authentic, would likely be, and (C) has been in existence 20 years or more at the time it is offered.

(9) Process or system. Evidence describing a process or system used to produce a result and showing that the process or system produces an accurate result.

(10) Methods provided by statute or rule. Any method of authentication or identification provided by Act of Congress or by other rules prescribed by the Supreme Court pursuant to statutory authority.

Not mentioned in Rule 901(b) is one of the most frequently used methods of showing the genuineness of an item of evidence, that is, through a chain of custody whereby the profferor accounts for each instance in which the object changed hands and for its custody between changes in possession.[3] This omission shows that the examples in Rule 901(b) are illustrative only. Any other technique will suffice if it supports a finding that the evidence being proffered is what its proponent claims.[4]

Considerable trial time can be spent authenticating physical evidence. This time can be saved and the need for authenticating witnesses obviated when parties deal with the problem prior

---

[3] *See* United States v. Casto, 889 F.2d 562, 568–69 (5th Cir. 1989, *cert. denied,* 110 S. Ct. 1164 (1990) (break in the chain of custody affects only the weight and not the admissibility of the evidence); United States v. Ladd, 885 F.2d 954, 956–57 (1st Cir. 1989) (discusses chain of custody for samples tested in state laboratory and private laboratory and concludes that although some links in state laboratory chain were rusty, none was missing; because of discrepancy in numbering of sample that private laboratory received from state laboratory, test result from private laboratory should not have been admitted, but error harmless); United States v. Cardenas, 864 F.2d 1528 (10th Cir. 1989), *cert. denied,* 109 S. Ct. 3197 (1989) (when prosecution relies on chain of custody, chain need not be perfect, and prosecution need not produce at trial all persons who had custody of the evidence).

[4] *See, e.g.,* United States v. Rembert, 863 F.2d 1023 (D.C. Cir. 1988) (discussion of the admissibility of photographs taken by automatic teller machine surveillance camera; the court admitted photographs although authenticating witness had no personal knowledge of the events; "the contents of photographic evidence . . . need not be merely illustrative, but can be admitted as evidence independent of the testimony of any witness as to the evidence depicted").

to trial. In civil cases this can be achieved through interrogatories, depositions and requests for admissions. Stipulations as to authenticity or waivers of authentication should also be utilized. Also helpful, particularly in large, complex litigation, are agreements to limit the number of exhibits.

The parties should mark their documents with labels obtained from the clerk, and make a list and a set for each other and the court before trial. Important documents should be copied in sufficient numbers so that, where permissible, each juror can have a copy. In complex cases, a looseleaf notebook for each juror will facilitate the trial.

Where no agreement on authenticity can be reached before trial, rulings on the admissibility of documents should be made prior to trial; documents unconditionally admitted may then be used at trial without further rulings, while those conditionally admitted may be reoffered. Documents held inadmissible prior to trial should not be reoffered unless circumstances change. It would be well, however, for counsel to have a clear ruling on the record that no further proffer is required to avoid the argument on appeal that the motion in limine was not sufficient under Rule 103. In criminal cases, the parties, by agreement and with the consent of the court, can use depositions for authentication.

Rule 901(b) is subject to Rules 902 and 903. Rule 902, which is discussed below, relieves the profferor from initially having to produce extrinsic evidence to prove the authenticity of documents in certain instances where the likelihood of forgery or mistaken attribution is extremely rare. The rule sets up presumptions of authenticity. None of the presumptions is irrebuttable and ultimately the trier of fact must determine authenticity under Rule 902 as well as Rule 901(a).

Rule 903[4] adds an additional requirement to establishing authenticity in instances involving documents which under state law require the testimony of an attesting witness. The Rule provides:

---

[4] *See* **Treatise** at ¶¶ 903[01]–[03].

Rule 903

SUBSCRIBING WITNESS' TESTIMONY UNNECESSARY

The testimony of a subscribing witness is not necessary to authenticate a writing unless required by the laws of the jurisdiction whose laws govern the validity of the writing.

Only where the validity of the document is in issue need the state's law on execution be followed. Thus, for example, if the issue is whether a will is valid and state law requires proof by subscribing witnesses, then the state's law should be followed. But if the will is to be admitted to prove a statement made in it as an admission, or to show contents for other purposes, or to show delivery, then the attesting witness is not required and authenticity can be demonstrated under Rules 901 and 902 rather than under the state statute.

¶ 8.01[02]   Testimony of Witness With Knowledge[1]

A competent lay or expert witness with knowledge of relevant facts can testify that a matter is what it is claimed to be.[2] A person who participates in or witnesses a transaction, occurrence or other event can also testify.[3] In addition, witnesses who have circumstantial knowledge about events which occur outside their presence can testify if their testimony is based on

---

[1] *See* **Treatise** at ¶ 901(b)(1)[01].

[2] United States v. Hawkins, 905 F.2d 1489, 1494 (11th Cir. 1990) (letter was authenticated by testimony of defendant that corporation had received it, and that he was familiar with it); United States v. Cowley, 720 F.2d 1037, 1044 (9th Cir. 1983) *cert. denied sub nom.* Clair v. United States, 465 U.S. 1029 (1984) (at trial for perjury before grand jury, introduction of witness' testimony about postmark, rather than introduction of postmark itself, did not require extrinsic evidence of authenticity); United States v. Helberg, 565 F.2d 993, 997 (8th Cir. 1977) (ledger recording drug transactions was properly authenticated by testimony of three drug customers listed in ledger and by policeman who was present throughout search during which ledger was seized).

[3] *In re* Clifford, 566 F.2d 1023, 1025 (5th Cir. 1978) (security deed lacking notarial seal, making it unrecordable under Georgia law, could be authenticated in bankruptcy proceeding by testimony of notary public).

their own observations and perceptions.[4] Testimony about the custom or practice of a firm as well as the habit of an individual (see Rule 406) is often helpful in proving authenticity circumstantially.

Relevant testimony concerning knowledge obtained by any of the five senses is ordinarily admissible. Absolute precision and certainty are not essential.[5]

¶ 8.01[03]   Nonexpert Opinion on Handwriting[1]

A witness who is not an expert may identify a signature or handwriting if he is sufficiently familiar with the calligraphy so that his testimony will aid the jury. Knowledge of a person's writing can be acquired by any means so long as it is not obtained especially for the trial. Nonexperts typically acquire their knowledge in two ways.

First, anyone who has seen a person write is competent to identify that person's handwriting. Once the court has concluded that the witness is competent to testify (see Rule 602), the extent of the opportunity a witness has had to become familiar with a person's handwriting by having observed him write goes to the weight and not the admissibility of his testimony.[2]

---

[4] United States v. Jimenez Lopez, 873 F.2d 769, 773 (5th Cir. 1989) (photostatic copy of document purporting to be record of proceeding in magistrate's court in California was authenticated by testimony of agent of Immigration and Naturalization Service in Texas who explained that he received copy from INS agent in California; court noted that no hearsay objection had been made and refused to consider hearsay objection on appeal); United States v. McNair, 439 F. Supp. 103 (E.D. Pa. 1977), aff'd, 571 F.2d 573 (3d Cir.), cert. denied, 435 U.S. 976 (1978) (bank tellers could authenticate surveillance photographs even though they did not perceive all of the items in the photographs at the moment the pictures were taken).

[5] See Rule 701.

[1] See **Treatise** at ¶ 901(b)(2)[01].

[2] See United States v. Mauchlin, 670 F.2d 746 (7th Cir. 1982) (prison official could testify that documents in prison file were written by defendant, since he has observed defendant write on approximately six occasions); United States v. Standing Soldier, 538 F.2d 196 (8th Cir.), cert. denied, 429 U.S. 1025 (1976) (police officer could testify that signature on note requesting interview was same as that on statement which defendant signed).

The second way a witness can become familiar with another's handwriting is through observation of documents which the person in question has written. For example, a bank employee who has seen the signature of a bank customer may have sufficient familiarity with the witness' handwriting to identify the customer's signature. No minimum number of specimens or observations is required to render a witness competent to testify, but there must be some proof, circumstantial or otherwise, that the writings which the witness observed were genuine.[3] A course of business transactions between the witness and another may be sufficient to authenticate writings which the witness received from the other person.

A nonexpert's testimony can be outweighed or overturned by his own lack of credibility, by the contradictory testimony of an expert, by the jury's own comparison (Rule 901(b)(3)), or by inconsistency with other evidence. Such credibility issues affect probative force, not admissibility.

A nonexpert witness can be cross-examined in order to aid the jury in deciding how much weight to give his testimony. The nonexpert can be questioned as to the extent of his familiarity with the handwriting in question or his skill in identifying the signature or handwriting, but he should not be asked questions of an abstract or scientific nature dealing with handwriting identification. His ability to identify the questioned handwriting or signature can be tested by his being asked to identify a genuine specimen among false copies. Another method of testing the merit of a witness' handwriting identification is to ask the witness whether or not he would rely on the signatures he identified in an ordinary business transaction.

¶ 8.01[04]   Comparison With Authenticated Specimens[1]

Rule 901(b)(3) allows triers of fact and expert witnesses to authenticate physical evidence by comparing it with

---

[3] See United States v. Binzel, 907 F.2d 746, 749–750 (7th Cir. 1990) (familiarity of witness with handwriting must be sufficient to have raised an issue of fact precluding summary judgment).

[1] See **Treatise** at ¶¶ 901(b)(3)[01]–[05].

authenticated specimens.[2] Authenticity is established if it is concluded that the compared items share characteristics that make it likely that they had the same source. Thus a bullet can be identified through the weapon from which it was fired by comparing that bullet with a bullet known to have been fired from that weapon. In addition, authentication by comparison can be used to identify writing, typewriting, tire tread marks, jimmy marks on door jambs, shoe prints, hair, blood and the like. The specimen used for comparison must be authenticated. This initial authentication is necessary because if the source of the exemplar is in doubt, even the most precise comparison will not resolve doubt about the source of the exhibit in question. A specimen can be authenticated by using any of Rule 901's methods or by satisfying one of the conditions specified in Rule 902.

Any item may serve as a standard for comparison if the trial court finds it sufficiently trustworthy to permit a reasonable comparison. While the rule in terms does not require a higher standard of proof for authentication of the exemplar, judges will normally demand that there be a stipulation or clear proof on the point. The jury will have to consider the exemplar's authenticity to determine that of the specimen in question so that questionable exemplars tend to add to, rather than clear up doubts. Care must therefore be taken that the specimen is not prejudicial. It should not be utilized to present information that would be kept out under Rule 403.[3]

Comparisons may be made by the triers of fact unless specialized knowledge is required for the task. If such knowledge is

---

[2] *See, e.g.,* Fagiola v. National Gypsum Co. AC&S., Inc., 906 F.2d 53, 58 (2d Cir. 1990) (comparison of quantity of documents with authenticated documents previously received in evidence justified receipt in evidence of the former); Zenith Radio Corporation v. Matsushita Electric Industrial Co., Ltd., 505 F. Supp. 1190, 1226 (E.D. Pa. 1980), *rev'd on other grounds,* 723 F.2d 238 (3d Cir. 1983), *rev'd on other grounds,* 475 U.S. 574 (1986) (authentication of one document which is member of a group of documents sharing similar characteristics may serve as basis for authenticating others in group).

[3] *See, e.g.,* United States v. Turquitt, 557 F.2d 464, 470 (5th Cir. 1977) (error to have admitted lease which defendant apparently signed with false name as a handwriting exemplar where "other known and less prejudicial specimens would have achieved the same result").

(Matthew Bender & Co., Inc.)   (Rel.4–8/91 Pub.819)

required, experts should make the comparison and submit their conclusions to the triers of fact for evaluation. Expert testimony is also admissible even if the trier of fact is making the primary comparison. The testimony of an expert is admitted because it might aid the jury in reaching its decision as to the identity of an item. The expert's opinion need not be followed blindly. In its instructions, the court should remind the jurors that the question whether or not an item is genuine is for them to decide. A jury should normally be allowed to take the specimen into the jury room to compare it with the item to be identified. Since counsel and witnesses are permitted to argue about authenticity and the court can instruct the jury on what is a reasonable comparison, the danger of prejudice arising from a comparison in the jury room is reduced.

[a]   Handwriting[4]

The trier of fact may use as a specimen any authenticated writing at the court's disposal, including documents in the case file. The court has discretion to exclude exemplars specially prepared for the specific purpose of showing dissimilarity of handwriting.[5] The trier of fact is competent to make the comparison. A handwriting expert's testimony is admissible, since his special knowledge or skill permits him to aid the trier of fact in the identification of a writing. Experts will normally wish to demonstrate to the trier of fact which aspects of handwriting they considered in making their comparison. The court should permit them to use blown-up copies, or to distribute copies of a specimen to the jury. Experts may be

---

[4] *See* **Treatise** at ¶ 901(b)(3)[03].

[5] *Compare* United States v. Lam Muk Chiu, 522 F.2d 330, 331 (2d Cir. 1975) (court rejected samples of defendant's handwriting intended to show that his handwriting was not the same as in letters to informant relied upon by government) *with* United States v. Pastore, 537 F.2d 675, 677–78 (2d Cir. 1976) (court properly admitted exemplars prepared by witnesses to show that they had not endorsed checks as argued by the defense; appellate court distinguished *Lam Muk Chiu* on the ground that there were sufficient indicia of reliability in *Pastore*; witnesses had less of a motive to falsify than the defendant, and there was cross-examination about preparation of exemplars; appellate court suggested it might be better practice to have exemplars prepared under court supervision).

cross-examined and their skill in handwriting identification may be tested. One type of test is to give the expert several signatures, some genuine and some not, and to ask him to identify the genuine signatures. Any reasonable test of skill should be admissible so long as the court thinks it will aid the jury in deciding what weight to give to the expert's testimony. Some courtroom tests are unfair because they deny the use of photographic and other equipment used in an expert's laboratory. An acknowledged expert's refusal to conduct tests without the necessary equipment should be respected as professionally justified.

[b]   Typewriting[6]

Typewriting can be identified by comparison with a typewritten specimen which has been authenticated. Where the identifying characteristics of the typewritings are obvious to a person of ordinary knowledge, the trier of fact can conduct the comparison without the aid of an expert. A typewriter expert may be called upon to make the comparison. A person making a typewriting comparison may consider the physical characteristics of the typewriting as well as the spelling, the grammatical errors, the word patterns, and the operational peculiarities of the typist. Linguistic analysis may require an expert different from the one who depends upon purely mechanical features.

[c]   Ballistics[7]

Authentication by comparison may be used to identify the gun from which a bullet was fired. The use of an expert witness in ballistics comparisons is justified by the ordinary person's lack of skill in comparing weapons and spent bullets.

Normal procedure is for the experts to show the jury enlarged photographs of the bullets which were compared. The photographs themselves must, of course, be authenticated before they are admitted.

---

[6] *See* **Treatise** at ¶ 901(b)(3)[04].

[7] *See* **Treatise** at ¶ 901(b)(3)[05].

¶ 8.01[05]   Distinctive Characteristics[1]

Rule 901(b)(4) provides that a proponent can authenticate an item by demonstrating that it has distinctive characteristics that identify its source. This method is typically used to identify the author of a communication.[2] A writing's content, physical characteristics, internal patterns, or its relationship to other writings or transactions may be alone or in combination distinctive enough to identify its source.[3]

[a]   Contents

Written communications may contain references to activities of the writer which only the author and a few others would be likely to know. When these references are sufficiently specific to the author, the writing may be authenticated solely on the basis of content.[4] As the number of persons who knew the

---

[1] *See* **Treatise** at ¶¶ 901(b)(4)[01]–[05].

[2] *See, e.g.,* United States v. Hoag, 823 F.2d 1123, 1126–27 (7th Cir. 1987) (letters bearing letterhead of defendant's real estate company were properly utilized, where they referred to unique real estate transactions that occurred on or about the date of the letter, where HUD official and other HUD employees testified as to the manner in which the letters were handled, and where letters were signed by defendant; citing Rule 901(b)(4)). *Cf.* United States v. Stearns, 550 F.2d 1167, 1171 (9th Cir. 1977) (details in photographs authenticated the time and place where the pictures were taken).

[3] United States v. Blackwood, 878 F.2d 1200, 1201–02 (9th Cir. 1989) (defendant was charged with submitting false income tax returns in others' names; returns were authenticated by expert testimony linking defendant to handwriting on the forms in conjunction with fact that defendant's name and address were listed as place to send refunds, citing **Treatise**); United States v. Helmel, 769 F.2d 1306 (8th Cir. 1985) (in illicit gambling operation case, a ledger, recording expenses of the defendants' gambling operation, was properly authenticated; contents of document revealed that its author had to be someone intimately acquainted with gambling operation; ledger was found in home of one defendant, along with gambling paraphernalia, and had fingerprints of two co-defendants on it).

[4] United States v. One 56-Foot Yacht Named Tahuna, 702 F.2d 1276, 1284–85 (9th Cir. 1983) (diary properly admitted where contents, including name used as alias by alleged owner, address, some personal belongings of alleged owner and specific entries, demonstrated that it was what government claimed it to be); United States v. Gordon, 634 F.2d 639 (1st Cir. 1980) (in prosecution for mail fraud, questioned documents were properly authenti-

details increases, the number of persons who may have written the document increases. Thus, evidence of unique content alone may not suffice to identify the source.[5] However, even if other persons knew the details of the writing, it can be shown that under the circumstances it is unlikely that they wrote the letter.

Proof of these circumstances and the contents of the writing can then sufficiently authenticate the document.[6] Often this method is combined with other methods.[7]

[b] Physical Attributes[8]

A letter's physical appearance, postmark, return address, contents, and letterhead may alone or in combination sufficiently authenticate the writing.[9] Writings can be authenticated by the identification of a signature affixed by a rubber stamp. There should usually be some testimony that it was the purported writer's custom to use a rubber stamp, and the writing should in some other way be connected to the purported writer.

cated where they were part of an interlocking pattern followed with respect to each of a score of alleged victims of a single scheme).

[5] *See* Zenith Radio Corp. v. Matsushita Elec. Indus. Co., 505 F. Supp. 1190, 1225 (E.D. Pa. 1980), *rev'd on other grounds,* 723 F.2d 238 (3d Cir. 1983), *rev'd on other grounds,* 475 U.S. 574 (1986) (court holds that if information contained in documents is shown to be known to limited number of persons, this factor will be considered in determining whether sufficient evidence to authenticate exists).

[6] *See* United States v. Luschen, 614 F.2d 1164, 1174 (8th Cir.), *cert. denied,* 446 U.S. 939 (1980) (context and external circumstances).

[7] *See, e.g.,* United States v. Whitworth, 856 F.2d 1268, 1283 (9th Cir. 1988), *cert. denied,* 489 U.S. 1084 (1989) (anonymous letters sent to FBI revealing spy conspiracy were authenticated as having been written by defendant by showing that description of conspiracy coincided with known facts, as well as other evidence such as postmarks coinciding with defendant's location on the days when mailed, and newspapers found in defendant's home that corresponded to the editions in which the FBI had been advised to reply).

[8] *See* **Treatise** at ¶ 901(b)(4)[02].

[9] California Ass'n of Bioanalysts v. Rank, 577 F. Supp. 1342, 1355 n.23 (C.D. Cal. 1983) (reports held admissible under Rule 901(b)(4), since they were on agency letterhead and signed by officials of that agency, and content of reports made it unlikely that they were prepared by entity other than agency).

A letter whose signature is stamped can also be authenticated by showing that it was sent in response to a communication already authenticated.

When the postmark corresponds to the return address contained in the letter itself, there is sufficient indication that the letter originated from the address indicated. Thus, a letter written on a company's letterhead, postmarked at the post office nearest the company is location and purporting to bear the signature of a company employee should be admitted.[10]

A letterhead alone may authenticate a letter. If the letterhead would not normally be available to anyone but the sender, corresponds to letterheads in general use, and the typing and form of the letter corresponds to usual practice in the purported sender's office, there is good reason to accept the letter as authentic.

[c]   Internal Patterns; Psycholinguistics[11]

Writings can be authenticated by evidence that the internal word or thought patterns are particularly characteristic of the purported writer.[12] Experts versed in psycholinguistics—the

---

[10] See United States v. Bagaric, 706 F.2d 42, 67 (2d Cir.), cert. denied, 464 U.S. 917 (1983) (letter linking a defendant in an extortion scheme to another co-defendant was admissible where postmark and contents demonstrated its authenticity). See also United States v. Sinclair, 433 F. Supp. 1180, 1196 (D. Del.), aff'd, 556 F.2d 1171 (3d Cir. 1977). But see United States v. Weinstein, 762 F.2d 1522, 1534–35 (11th Cir. 1985) (receipt in evidence of incriminating letter, addressed to one defendant, and envelope, addressed to another defendant, "as one exhibit, stapled together, with no testimony or other evidence linking the two documents" held reversible error).

[11] See **Treatise** at ¶ 901(b)(4)[03].

[12] See United States v. Clifford, 704 F.2d 86, 90–91 (3d Cir. 1983) (lower court erred in excluding correspondence allegedly written by defendant offered for comparison with threatening letter; fact that expert testimony on similarities between letter and other correspondence was inadmissible did not mean that jury could not compare writings itself); United States v. Larson, 596 F.2d 759, 765 n.10 (8th Cir. 1979) (jury considered misspelling of "approach" as "approuch" in kidnapper's ransom note and in defendant's letter to parole board); United States v. Pheaster, 544 F.2d 353, 371–72 (9th Cir. 1976), cert. denied, 429 U.S. 1099 (1977) (jury considered similar misspellings in kidnapper's notes and in defendant's exemplars).

study of the relationship between messages and characteristics of the persons sending messages—may testify.[13]

Likewise, evidence of a letter's internal patterns can be used to contest authenticity. A standard argument of attorneys is that this witness, whom the jury observed speaking on the witness stand, could not possibly have used the language and style attributed to him in a writing. Experts in linguistics can add to or detract from the force of such arguments by demonstrating consistency or inconsistency in language and grammar. By attributing certain styles to persons of particular social or educational backgrounds, they may have an important impact on the authentication of documents. Usually such evidence will be used not to determine admissibility but to evaluate probative force.

[d]   Relationship to Other Writings or Transactions[14]

The circumstances preceding,[15] surrounding,[16] and following the transmission of a writing may sufficiently authenticate the writing. For example, where the purported author of a writing carries on a continuing correspondence and transacts business with a particular person in such a way that the business transacted corresponds to the information transmitted by the writings, the circumstances of the correspondence and business tend to authenticate the writing.[17] In addition writings may

---

[13] *But see* United States v. Hearst, 412 F. Supp. 893 (N.D. Cal. 1976), *aff'd,* 563 F.2d 1331 (9th Cir. 1977), *cert. denied,* 435 U.S. 1000 (1978) (court rejected testimony of psycholinguist).

[14] *See* **Treatise** at ¶ 901(b)(4)[04].

[15] United States v. Bruner, 657 F.2d 1278, 1284 (D.C. Cir. 1981) (authentication through testimony by DEA agent that prescriptions were obtained from physician by subpoena and testimony by state pharmacist that seized prescriptions matched numbers of state-issued prescription blanks issued to physicians); United States v. Natale, 526 F.2d 1160, 1172 (2d Cir. 1975), *cert. denied,* 425 U.S. 950 (1976).

[16] *In re* Japanese Elect. Prod. Litig., 723 F.2d 238, 286–87 (3d Cir. 1983), *rev'd on other grounds,* 475 U.S. 574 (1986) (totality of circumstances, especially fact that documents were obtained from defendants during course of litigation, were sufficient to support a finding that documents were what profferor claimed them to be).

[17] For a number of pre-Federal Rule cases illustrating how external circumstances can authenticate a writing *see* **Treatise** at ¶ 901(b)(4)[04].

correspond to a series of events and be so related to these events that the combination can demonstrate authenticity.[18]

[e]   Reply Letter Technique[19]

Correspondence can be authenticated by testimony or other proof that it was sent in reply to a duly authenticated writing.[20] A reply letter needs no further authentication because it would be unlikely for anyone other than the purported writer to know and respond to the contents of an earlier letter addressed to him.

A letter or telegram received in due course and purporting to respond to a communication previously sent is admissible because of the general assumption that messages are ordinarily delivered to the addressee rather than someone else, and that, consequently, it would be unlikely for someone else to know of, and respond to, the message.

¶ 8.01[06]   Voice Identification[1]

Rule 901(b)(5) provides for the identification of any voice by any person who can connect the voice with the alleged

---

[18] *See* United States v. Eisenberg, 807 F.2d 1446, 1452–53 (8th Cir. 1986) (letter authenticated by proof that it was found among defendant's possessions, and contained references to defendant's car and to a trip, which matched known facts); United States v. DeGudino, 722 F.2d 1351, 1355 (7th Cir. 1984) (during trial for conspiracy to transport illegal aliens, lists of illegal aliens' names were properly authenticated since they were seized from the headquarters of the operation, and since the testimony outlining techniques of the operation indicated that they were written by someone involved in conspiracy); United States v. Gutierrez, 576 F.2d 269, 276 (5th Cir.), *cert. denied,* 439 U.S. 954 (1978) (where evidence showed that heroin came from Culiacan, Mexico, court did not err in admitting cashier's check which was purchased by someone with defendant's name who though not positively identified had characteristics of defendant).

[19] *See* **Treatise** at ¶ 901(b)(4)[05].

[20] United States v. Weinstein, 762 F.2d 1522, 1533 (11th Cir. 1985).

[1] *See* **Treatise** at ¶¶ 901(b)(5)[01]–[03].

speaker by "hearing" the voice.[2] Voice identification is a prerequisite for playing recordings to the trier of fact.[3]

The Rule has been interpreted by the courts to allow a voice to be identified by direct hearing, by indirect hearing, and by voiceprints, although some courts question the reliability of the voiceprint technique. See discussion below.

---

[2] *See, e.g.,* United States v. Carrasco, 887 F.2d 794, 803–04 (7th Cir. 1989).

[3] However, it should be noted that the recording procedure must be authenticated as well. What constitutes a proper foundation is a matter of dispute. The Third Circuit, United States v. Starks, 515 F.2d 112, 121, n.11 (3d Cir. 1975) and Eighth Circuit, United States v. McMillan, 508 F.2d 101 (8th Cir. 1974), *cert. denied,* 421 U.S. 916 (1975); United States v. Jankowski, 713 F.2d 394, 398 (8th Cir. 1983), *cert. denied,* 464 U.S. 1051 (1984), have adopted the rigid formula enunciated in United States v. McKeever, 169 F. Supp. 426 (S.D.N.Y. 1958), *rev'd on other grounds,* 271 F.2d 669 (2d Cir. 1959). The *McKeever* court held that to establish a proper foundation for the admission of recordings a proponent must show: 1) that the recording device was capable of taping the conversation now offered; 2) that the operator of the device was competent to operate it; 3) that the recording was authentic and correct; 4) that changes, additions, or deletions have not been made in the recording; 5) that the recording has been preserved in a manner that is shown to the court; 6) that the speakers are identified; and 7) that conversation elicited was made voluntarily and in good faith without any kind of inducement. The Eighth Circuit has held, however, that the *McMillan* requirements should be applied less stringently when the recording was made by the defendant rather than by the government or at the government's request. United States v. O'Connell, 841 F.2d 1408, 1420 (8th Cir. 1988), *cert. denied,* 488 U.S. 1011 (1989). *See also* United States v. Kandiel, 865 F.2d 967 (8th Cir. 1989) (mechanical requirements of *McMillan* do not apply when recording is found in defendant's possession). The District of Columbia Circuit, United States v. Sandoval, 709 F.2d 1553 (D.C. Cir. 1983), the Second Circuit, United States v. Fuentes, 563 F.2d 527, 532 (2d Cir.), *cert. denied,* 434 U.S. 959 (1977); the Ninth Circuit, United States v. Mouton, 617 F.2d 1379, 1384 (9th Cir.), *cert. denied,* 449 U.S. 860 (1980), and Tenth Circuit, United States v. Smith, 692 F.2d 693, 698 (10th Cir. 1982) have properly declined to impose a rigid formula for the proper authentication of tape recordings, deferring instead to the broad discretion of the trial judge in the admission of evidence and requiring only that the judge "be satisfied that the recording is accurate, authentic, and generally trustworthy." United States v. King, 587 F.2d 956, 961 (9th Cir. 1978).

[a]   Voice Heard Directly

A witness may identify a person solely on the basis of voice recognition.[4] As a preliminary matter, the court should decide whether or not the witness alleges a sufficient familiarity with the voice so that a jury could find that the witness was in fact able to make the identification.[5] A voice identification is sufficient to go to the jury so long as the witness has some familiarity with the voice he seeks to identify.[6] This familiarity can be acquired either before or after hearing the voice to be identified and need only establish a prima facie case of identity.[7] The witness need not be able to point out any particular

---

[4] United States v. Taylor, 905 F.2d 239, 240 (8th Cir. 1990) (testimony of conversation held admissible where witness could not see defendant but recognized him by his voice); United States v. Scully, 546 F.2d 255, 270 (9th Cir. 1976), *vacated and remanded on other grounds sub nom.,* United States v. Cabral, 430 U.S. 902, *cert. denied,* 430 U.S. 970 (1977). *Cf.* Burtis v. Dalsheim, 536 F. Supp. 805, 807–08 (S.D.N.Y. 1982) (voice identification valid; witness could not give visual description of assailant).

[5] United States v. Hyatt, 565 F.2d 229, 232 (2d Cir. 1977) (not error to exclude testimony about telephone call proposed witness had received where she was not acquainted with alleged caller; citing Rule 901).

[6] *See* United States v. Vega, 860 F.2d 779, 782, 788 (7th Cir. 1988) (identification by police officer who had had two-hour conversation with defendant two years previously in English; voice on tape that officer identified was speaking Spanish, which officer did not speak); United States v. Hughes, 658 F.2d 317 (5th Cir. 1981), *cert. denied,* 455 U.S. 922 (1982) (past conversations); United States v. Cuesta, 597 F.2d 903, 915 (5th Cir.), *cert. denied,* 444 U.S. 964 (1979) ("Rule 901(b)(5) merely requires that the witness have some familiarity with the voice which he identifies."); United States v. Thomas, 586 F.2d 123 (9th Cir. 1978) (prosecution established that agent-witness had conversed with defendant on phone on three separate occasions); United States v. Vitale, 549 F.2d 71 (8th Cir.), *cert. denied,* 431 U.S. 907 (1977) (testimony of witness that he had spoken twice to defendant and recognized his voice on telephone was sufficient foundation); Burtis v. Dalsheim, 536 F. Supp. 805, 807–08 (S.D.N.Y. 1982) (voice identification of defendant by rape victim who could hardly see assailant, given within one hour of rape, valid).

[7] United States v. Alvarez, 860 F.2d 801 (7th Cir. 1988), *cert. denied,* 490 U.S. 1051 (1989) (court also found that identification procedures used were not impermissibly suggestive); United States v. Bice-Bey, 701 F.2d 1086, 1090 (4th Cir.), *cert. denied,* 464 U.S. 837 (1983) (no error in permitting FBI agents to identify voice recorded from telephone conversation as that of defendant, where agents met defendant after conversation occurred); United

characteristics of the voice or show a particular intimacy with the speaker so long as he shows some basis for being able to associate the voice heard with the person he designates as the speaker.[8] The witness has been allowed to testify even though his familiarity with the voice to be identified was acquired at least in part though illegal wiretaps.[9] The uncertainty of a voice identification should not bar admission of the testimony as long as the witness claims to have recognized the voice and states some fact permitting a jury to find that he in fact did so.[10]

The jury can give a voice identification as much or as little weight as it sees fit within the bounds of reasonableness and in light of all the testimony. The opportunity a witness has had to become familiar with the speaker's voice, its peculiarities, the time between hearing and identification, the acuteness of the witness' hearing and the witness' state of awareness and proximity to the speaker at the time the voice was heard may all be considered in weighing a voice identification.[11] The fact

States v. Smith, 692 F.2d 693, 698 (10th Cir. 1982) (identification of defendant's voice on tape based on later meeting with defendant permissible); United States v. Watson, 594 F.2d 1330 (10th Cir.), *cert. denied,* 444 U.S. 840 (1979) (witness could authenticate defendant's voice on telephone intercept even though he did not speak with defendant until after the date of the intercept).

[8] People v. Sullivan, 290 Mich. 414, 287 N.W. 567, 569 (1939) (defendant in police-station identification spoke in a "low undertone" as had perpetrator of hold-up).

[9] United States v. DiMuro, 540 F.2d 503, 514 (1st Cir. 1976), *cert. denied,* 429 U.S. 1038 (1977).

[10] *See, e.g.,* United States v. Kirk, 534 F.2d 1262, 1277 (8th Cir. 1976), *cert. denied,* 433 U.S. 907 (1977) (testimony of agents who had heard voices; comparison of voice exemplars with tapes and proof of connecting telephone numbers, addresses and names or nicknames mentioned on the tapes constituted sufficient cumulative evidence to permit identification issue to be submitted to jury); United States v. Biggins, 551 F.2d 64, 67 (5th Cir. 1977) ("correspondence between the agents' accounts of the conversation and the version evidenced by the sound recording [was] sufficiently close to lessen the importance of explicit testimony that the recording itself was accurate.").

[11] Burtis v. Dalsheim, 536 F. Supp. 805, 807–08 (S.D.N.Y. 1982) (court finds that indicia of reliability of voice identification by rape victim included short time interval between crime and identification—less than one hour—high level of certainty demonstrated by victim, and close attention which victim was probably paying to assailant's statements when he threatened to kill her).

that "to date, no single technique of voice identification is completely reliable" may be pointed out to the jury.[12]

A transcript of a tape recording may be admitted in evidence in lieu of the recording itself if the recording has been lost or destroyed through no fault of the party offering the transcript. This presents a best evidence problem. See Chapter 9 *infra*.

Where the recording is available and the transcript of the recording is shown to be accurate, the court should normally permit the jury to use copies of the transcript at the time the recording is played for the purpose of identifying the speakers and following the recording more easily, provided the person making the transcript had been told who each of the speakers is by a person able to identify them. The transcripts are marked for identification only. If, during deliberations, the jury asks for the transcripts, they should not be sent to the jury room unless all parties stipulate on the record to do this.[13] Normal practice is to have the jurors come back into court to hear the recordings while they look at the transcripts, just as they did at trial.

If the recordings are in a foreign language, listening to them is usually a waste of time and the parties should stipulate to have the jury read the transcript in court.[14] Unless the parties stipulate otherwise, the court should make clear, however, that it is the recording, not the transcript that is in evidence.

[b]   Voice Heard Indirectly

A voice heard over a transmitting device can be identified in the same way and with almost the same degree of certainty

---

[12] Tosi, "Voice Identification," *Scientific and Expert Evidence* 971, 973 (E. Imwinkelried ed. 1981).

[13] *But see* United States v. Ulerio, 859 F.2d 1144 (2d Cir. 1988) (transcripts contained notations purporting to identify the speakers; no error where jury well aware that defendants were contesting the accuracy of the identification and judge charged jury to scrutinize identification testimony with care).

[14] See United States v. Briscoe, 896 F.2d 1476 (7th Cir.), *cert. denied sub. nom* Usman v. United States, 111 S. Ct. 173 (1990) (the trial court had received in evidence both the foreign-language tapes and the transcripts, the court of appeals reviewing at length the requirements for authentication).

as the voice of the speaker heard directly.[15] Identification can be based upon familiarity acquired either before or after the disputed conversation and need only be so reliable as to make out a prima facie case of identification.[16] Where a participant in a telephone conversation cannot identify the other speaker, listeners-in can authenticate the fact that a conversation took place and can identify the other speaker so that all persons who heard the other speaker can testify.

A witness who offers to testify to a conversation over an electronic device should first testify that the device was capable of accurately reproducing the sound and then identify the speaker heard over the device. Police and other law enforcement agents have been allowed to testify to conversations overheard by various eavesdropping and transmitting devices. Counsel are entitled to develop the witness' experience in using any listening device and its efficacy in reproducing sound without distortion.

[c] Voiceprints

Rule 901(b)(5) does not preclude expert witness voice identification by the voiceprint technique. Some of the circuits have explicitly approved the use of voicegram testimony.[17] Other

---

[15] *See* United States v. Degaglia, 913 F.2d 372, 375–376 (7th Cir. 1990) (extended review of requirements for authentication of voice recorded on tape); *See* Fabacher v. United States, 84 F.2d 602, 603 (5th Cir. 1936); United States v. Verlin, 466 F. Supp. 155 (N.D. Tex. 1979).

[16] United States v. Smith, 692 F.2d 693, 698 (10th Cir. 1982) (identification of defendant's voice on tape based on later meeting with defendant permissible); United States v. Albergo, 539 F.2d 860 (2d Cir.), *cert. denied,* 429 U.S. 1000 (1976) (officer who had listened to over 500 taped conversations although he had never met defendant could identify his voice; reliability of identification is for jury); United States v. Armedo-Sarmiento, 545 F.2d 785, 792 (2d Cir. 1976), *cert. denied,* 430 U.S. 917 (1977) (witness permitted to compare unidentified voice on disputed tapes with voice samples on other tapes, admittedly those of defendant; "voice identification may be adequate although the witness and the speaker have never personally met.").

[17] **Second Circuit:** United States v. Williams, 583 F.2d 1194 (2d Cir. 1978), *cert. denied,* 439 U.S. 1117 (1979); **Fourth Circuit:** United States v. Baller, 519 F.2d 463 (4th Cir.), *cert. denied,* 423 U.S. 1019 (1975) (conviction of telephone bomb threats; tapes of voice exemplars and threats submitted to

circuits question the reliability of this technique.[18]

¶ 8.01[07]   Telephone Calls[1]

A participant, bystander, eavesdropper,[2] or wiretapper[3] can testify about a telephone conversation if the requisites of 901(b)(6) are satisfied. The Rule provides a liberal standard for the authentication of telephone calls and treats personal calls and business calls differently.

---

voicegram expert who was permitted to testify); **Sixth Circuit:** United States v. Franks, 511 F.2d 25, 33 (6th Cir.), *cert. denied*, 422 U.S. 1042 (1975) ("trend favors the admissibility of voiceprints," compiles cases in note 10 of opinion).

[18] United States v. Addison, 498 F.2d 741 (D.C. Cir. 1974) (but admission constituted harmless error). *See also* United States v. McDaniel, 538 F.2d 408, 413 (D.C. Cir. 1976) (court found itself bound by its prior opinion in *Addison* so that voicegram evidence is still inadmissible in District of Columbia Circuit; however court noted that "[t]he reliability of spectrographic voice identification and its general acceptability within the scientific community may have changed so dramatically in the past two years that we may explain that earlier opinion as a reflection of the then primitive state of spectrographic voice identification"; court found admission of voiceprint evidence to be harmless error). *See also* United States v. Baynes, 687 F.2d 659, 671–72 (3d Cir. 1982) (court declined to decide whether spectrograms are admissible in criminal trials, but concluded that the "district court erred in attaching controlling weight to the spectrogram prepared in this case"). *See also* Report, *On the Theory and Practice of Voice Identification* (Nat'l Research Council 1979). For a discussion of the admissibility of novel scientific evidence, see generally **Treatise** at ¶ 702[03].

[1] *See* **Treatise** at ¶¶ 901(b)(6)[01]–[02].

[2] *See, e.g.,* United States v. Scully, 546 F.2d 255, 270 (9th Cir. 1976), *vacated and remanded on other grounds sub nom.* United States v. Cabral, 430 U.S. 902 (1977), *cert. denied*, 430 U.S. 900 (1970) (authentication by circumstantial evidence).

[3] United States v. Rengifo, 789 F.2d 975 (1st Cir. 1986) (testimony of individual who supervised wiretap); United States v. McMillan, 508 F.2d 101, 104–105 (8th Cir. 1974), *cert. denied*, 421 U.S. 916 (1975) (voice identification of a defendant by wiretapper who overheard informant's side of conversation).

[a] Personal Calls

Personal calls are authenticated by a reasonable showing that the telephone call actually took place. Testimony or other evidence (such as telephone company records) that the witness placed or received a call and identification of the person or persons spoken to is required.

There is no fixed identification requirement for all calls.[4] If the witness will be testifying about a call that he placed, testimony that the person answering identified himself and engaged in a conversation reasonable for the person purporting to answer is sufficient.[5] There is, of course, always the risk of receiving a wrong number and of having a prankster mislead the caller, but the chance of this happening is so remote that it should not prevent admission of the conversation. Because the opportunity for fraud is greater, self-identification of the person calling without more is insufficient to admit the testimony of a caller.[6] However, circumstances surrounding a self-identification may tend to justify the inference that the calling speaker is the person he purports to be.[7] The identification

---

[4] United States v. Allessi, 638 F.2d 466, 480 (2d Cir. 1980) (illustrations in Rule 901(b)(6) are illustrations not limitations on methods of identification; Rule satisfied where witness had called number listed in name of defendant's wife, and identified defendant at trial and testified to arranging meeting for purchases of tickets which plan was thereafter carried out by mail).

[5] See United States v. Hines, 717 F.2d 1481, 1491 (4th Cir. 1983), cert. denied sub nom. Jackson v. United States, 467 U.S. 1214 (1984) and cert. denied sub nom. Peed v. United States, 467 U.S. 1219 (1984) (in cocaine conspiracy prosecution, evidence that recipient of phone call identified himself as "Ronnie," defendant's first name, that phone was registered in the name of defendant's parents, and that defendant was at the house when a government investigator visited house was held sufficient to identify call recipient as defendant); O'Neal v. Morgan, 637 F.2d 846, 850 (2d Cir. 1980), cert. denied, 451 U.S. 972 (1981).

[6] United States v. Pool, 660 F.2d 547, 560 (5th Cir. 1981) (identification not sufficient where witness had never met caller and no voice comparisons were made).

[7] See United States v. Sawyer, 607 F.2d 1190, 1193 (7th Cir. 1979), cert. denied, 445 U.S. 943 (1980) (Rule 901(b)(6) satisfied where personal nature of information sought by agent in telephone conversation with defendant made it "highly unlikely that anyone else would have answered for [defendant]" and number listed in agent's report was defendant's business number).

requirement is also satisfied if the witness is able to identify the voice of the speaker.[8] Events prior or subsequent to a telephone conversation or the subject of the conversation may identify the person with whom the witness spoke. No further identification of the caller is required if the call was made in reply to a previous conversation.

[b]   Business Calls

Telephone calls to a business can be authenticated by testimony that the place of business was called and that someone at the place answered and purported to act for the business establishment. Identification of the person answering is not necessary when the issue is the identity of the place of business called and not the individual purporting to represent that business. It is assumed that the person answering has the authority to act for the business. Identification of the answering party is not required because a listed business telephone number is assumed to be an invitation to the public to transact business with the company by calling that number.[9] Business persons should know that the public will act on this assumption. They cannot prevent the admission of testimony concerning a call placed to their business office by claiming that the person answering was not authorized to do so. Telephone calls to a public utility or municipal office can similarly be authenticated by testimony that the number listed in a directory or obtained from some other reliable source was dialed and that someone answered purporting to represent the office called.

---

[8] *See, e.g.,* United States v. Leon, 679 F.2d 534 (5th Cir. 1982) (tapes of telephone call between witness and person she did not know properly admitted where caller gave description of himself, arranged meeting with witness, told witness he had picture of her, and subsequently witness met man who fit description at arranged for meeting place at which he showed her picture).

[9] *See, e.g.,* United States v. Portsmouth Paving Corp., 694 F.2d 312, 322 (4th Cir. 1982) (witness' testimony that he called defendant's business office supports "inference that the one who answered the telephone was [defendant's] agent. One would usually and properly assume upon the dialing of a business office phone number that the person who answers is employed by and has the authority to speak for the business.").

Rule 901(b)(6) states that the conversation must relate to "business reasonably transacted over the telephone" for the business telephone call assumptions to operate. The person answering need not reveal any special knowledge peculiar to the business called. He need only speak with apparent understanding of the matter put to him.

The requirements for authenticating calls from a business are more rigorous than the requirements for authenticating calls to a business. The person offering the testimony should be able to identify the business office from which he was called by some evidence other than the mere self-identification of the caller. Testimony that the caller spoke with knowledge of a matter peculiar to the office from which he purported to call should be enough to authenticate the call.

¶ 8.01[08]   Public Records[1]

Public records[2] kept by a public office authorized by law to keep such records are admissible under Rule 901(b)(7) upon a showing that such records are what they purport to be. The proponent of the evidence need only show that the office from which the records were taken is the legal custodian of the records. Legal custodianship can be shown by a certificate of authenticity from a public office,[3] by the testimony of a public official whose duty it is to keep such records,[4] or by the

---

[1] *See* **Treatise** at ¶ 901(b)(7)[01].

[2] A public record can be a writing, data compilation or other form of recorded material authorized by law to be kept in a public office. This includes acts of legislatures, judicial records, reports of administrative offices, and video tapes or other nonprinted matter kept by a public office, United States v. Wilson, 535 F.2d 521 (9th Cir.), *cert. denied,* 429 U.S. 850 (1976) (map prepared and maintained by Navy Department), as well as any writing or data compilation authorized by law to be recorded or filed in a public office. In addition, the reliance of public offices on computers justifies the admission of data compilations prepared or stored in public offices.

[3] Bury v. Marietta Dodge, 692 F.2d 1335, 1338 (11th Cir. 1982) (certified affidavit from senior attorney at Federal Reserve Board that copies of letters were true and correct copies of letters sent by Federal Reserve Board).

[4] *See* United States v. Central Gulf Lines, Inc., 747 F.2d 315, 319–20 (5th Cir. 1984) (court held that short-landing certificates and cargo surveys prepared in compliance with government regulations were public records and

testimony of a witness with knowledge that the evidence is in fact from a public office authorized to keep such a record.[5] The court may also take judicial notice of the genuineness of a purportedly public record if there is no reason to suspect that the material is not what it purports to be.

Public records need not be in any particular form to be deemed authentic, and minor irregularities in appearance should not preclude admission if the record is apparently authentic. If the material has a suspicious appearance, however, or if the material appears to have been altered in any way, the court can refuse to admit such material unless the suspicious circumstances are adequately explained.

The confidence placed in official records is based on the assumption that a person in an official capacity can reasonably be relied upon to perform his task with objectivity and with the minimum efficiency requisite for authentication. Falsification of public documents would be not only an irregularity but also a breach of duty and, usually, a violation of criminal law. Courts have therefore assumed that public officers properly perform their duties and that records kept in a public office are ordinarily what they purport to be.

¶ 8.01[09]   Ancient Documents and Data Compilations[1]

Rule 901(b)(8) liberalizes the common law ancient document rule. It provides that a document maybe admitted when certain requirements pertaining to age, nonsuspicious condition and appropriate custody are satisfied.

[a]   Age

A document must exist twenty years before it can be admitted under 901(b)(8).[2] The age of a document or data

---

were properly authenticated through the uncontroverted testimony of the custodian of the documents).

[5] United States v. Binzel, 907 F.2d 746, 749 (7th Cir. 1990).

[1] *See* **Treatise** at ¶ 901(b)(8)[01].

[2] United States v. Koziy, 728 F.2d 1314, 1320 (11th Cir. 1984), *cert. denied,* 469 U.S. 835 (1984).

compilation can be shown by the testimony of a witness with knowledge, by expert testimony, by the physical appearance of the proffered evidence, or even by the contents of the material itself together with surrounding circumstances. See Rule 803(16). These elements of proof are not exclusive, however, and any facts supporting the inference that the document or data compilation has been in existence for twenty years or more should satisfy the age requirement for admission under the Rule.

The age of a document or data compilation is to be determined from the date of first existence until it is offered in evidence, but the figure of twenty years should not be regarded as an absolute. The admission of evidence is in all cases within the discretion of the trial judge, and it has been held that a document not quite satisfying the requirement for admission as an ancient document may nevertheless be admitted where it appears to be authentic.[3] This exception to the age requirement should be applied liberally under the Federal Rules, since the shift in emphasis for the justification of the ancient document rule has been from the unavailability of attesting witnesses to the presumption of authenticity after a longstanding existence in proper custody.

[b]　Nonsuspicious Condition

For a document or data compilation to be admitted under Rule 901(b)(8) it must be free of suspicion concerning its authenticity. Thus, a document can be excluded from evidence either because of its suspicious appearance or because of some question as to its origin or safekeeping.[4]

---

[3] Lee Pong Tai v. Acheson, 104 F. Supp. 503, 506 (E.D. Pa. 1952) (26 years when requisite age for ancient document was 30).

[4] Stewart Oil Co. v. Sohio Petroleum Co., 202 F. Supp. 952–58 (E.D. Ill. 1962), *aff'd,* 315 F.2d 759 (7th Cir. 1962), *cert. denied,* 375 U.S. 828 (1963) ("document contained a great number of variances between it and other document of similar nature"; "in the opinion of the court it smacks of fraud").

[c]   Appropriate Custody

For a document or data compilation to be admitted under Rule 901(b)(8) it must be shown to have been in a place where, if authentic, it would likely be.[5] Nevertheless, the rule does not require that the whereabouts of the material be accounted for at all times for the last twenty years. The fact that possession of the document or data compilation may have changed hands several times does not render the material inadmissible or untrustworthy as long as all custodians or places of custody accounted for are consistent with the nature of the material.[6] What is proper custody of the material offered depends primarily upon the nature of the material itself.

¶ 8.01[10]   Process or System[1]

Rule 901(b)(9) provides that the accuracy of a system or process must be established before the data produced by that system or process can be admitted. The rule covers the data produced by recording devices[2] and computers as well as the results generated by samples, polls and other scientific surveys. The accuracy of the type of system may be either judicially

---

[5] *See* Dartez v. Fibreboard Corp., 765 F.2d 456 (5th Cir. 1985) (documents more than twenty years old inadmissible because plaintiff failed to introduce evidence to establish that papers were found in expected places).

[6] McGuire v. Blount, 199 U.S 142, 145, 26 S. Ct. 1, 2–3, 50 L. Ed. 125 (1905) ("While the testimony tends to show that these documents were subjected to various changes of possession during the transition of the government of Florida from Spain to the United States and upon the evacuation of Pensacola during the Civil War, there is nothing to establish that they were ever out of the hands of a proper custodian."); United States v. Kairys, 782 F.2d 1374, 1379 (7th Cir.), *cert. denied*, 476 U.S. 1153 (1986) (district court properly admitted a "Personalbogen," a German SS identity card, in a proceeding to revoke defendant's citizenship because, *inter alia*, the card was found in the Soviet archives in a repository for German SS documents).

[1] *See* **Treatise** at ¶¶ 901(b)(9)[01]–[03].

[2] United States v. Taylor, 530 F.2d 639 (5th Cir. 1976), *cert. denied*, 429 U.S. 845 (1976) (film was properly authenticated by testimony as to manner in which bank camera operated, a showing that film was removed immediately after robbery, and proof of chain of possession).

noticed if it is generally known or its accuracy may be established through the use of experts.

Any relevant computer output can be admitted into evidence if the person offering the evidence shows that the system which produced the data was reliable. The court can judicially notice that a computer performs operations that would otherwise be done by people who might possibly use more rudimentary mechanical or electronic aids. The court can also recognize that human participation in computer operations is a potential source of inaccuracies. Since there is a chance that the computer output is inaccurate, the person offering computer printouts in evidence should, in addition to explaining the programming methods used, give a description of the controls used to detect both human and machine errors.[3] This precaution is not required as a foundation for admissibility but as a tactical precaution to forestall any doubt in the trier's mind. The person who provides the foundation for the admission of electronically produced data need not be the person who actually operated the computer. It is enough if the witness is familiar with the operation of the equipment used. The witness should describe the computer's operations with enough detail to support a finding that the result is accurate and reliable.

Before the results of samples, polls, and other forms of scientific surveys are admitted, the offeror should show that the sample was selected or the poll was conducted in a scientifically acceptable manner and that the conclusions are statistically acceptable.[4] Wherever possible, all parties should participate in devising the mode of procedure and the court should approve the method before trial.

After admission of the evidence, the method or process by which the sampling was conducted should be described with sufficient particularity so that the trier of fact can determine how much weight should be given to the evidence. Data produced by a process or system such as computers or surveys must

---

[3] United States v. Sanders, 749 F.2d 195 (5th Cir. 1984) (after information was transferred to magnetic tapes, check for accuracy by two employees before transmission of tapes).

[4] Keith v. Volpe, 858 F.2d 467, 480–481 (9th Cir. 1988), *cert. denied sub nom.* City of Hawthorne v. Wright, 110 S. Ct. 61 (1989); Brunswick Corp. v. Spinit Reel Co., 832 F.2d 513, 522 (10th Cir. 1987) (citing **Treatise**).

be made known to opponents and courts well in advance of trial so that the accuracy of the system and its results can be checked, by experts if necessary. Sufficient information must be made available to opposing counsel so that he or she can intelligently question the accuracy of the results by cross-examination and rebuttal. Experts must have access to the data, work sheets, and results well in advance of trial so that they can advise counsel properly.

¶ 8.01[11]   Authentication Pursuant to Statute or Rule 901(b)(10)[1]

Rule 901(b)(10) provides that any method of authentication or identification provided for by an Act of Congress or by the Rules of Civil or Criminal Procedure satisfies the authentication requirement of Rule 901.[2] The fact that a particular situation is expressly covered by language in Rule 901(b)(1)–(9), by any rules of procedure, or by a specific statute, does not make the method of authentication exclusive. Any other method which would be applicable may be used.

¶ 8.02   Self-Authenication—Rule 902

¶ 8.02[01]   Scope and Theory[1]

Rule 902 makes self-authenticating certain classes of writings where various considerations make it unreasonable to require further authentication.

The Rule provides:

Rule 902

SELF-AUTHENTICATION

Extrinsic evidence of authenticity as a condition precedent to admissibility is not required with respect to the following:

---

[1] *See* **Treatise** at ¶ 901(b)(10)[01].

[2] A list of statutory authentication provisions can be found in **Treatise** at ¶ 901(b)(10)[01].

[1] *See* **Treatise** at ¶ 902[01].

(1) Domestic public documents under seal. A document bearing a seal purporting to be that of the United States, or of any State, district, Commonwealth, territory, or insular possession thereof, or the Panama Canal Zone, or the Trust Territory of the Pacific Islands, or of a political subdivision, department, officer, or agency thereof, and a signature purporting to be an attestation or execution.

(2) Domestic public documents not under seal. A document purporting to bear the signature in the official capacity of an officer or employee of any entity included in paragraph (1) hereof, having no seal, if a public officer having a seal and having official duties in the district or political subdivision of the officer or employee certifies under seal that the signer has the official capacity and that the signature is genuine.

(3) Foreign public documents. A document purporting to be executed or attested in an official capacity by a person authorized by the laws of a foreign country to make the execution or attestation, and accompanied by a final certification as to the genuineness of the signature and official position (A) of the executing or attesting person, or (B) of any foreign official whose certificate of genuineness of signature and official position relates to the execution or attestation or is in a chain of certificates of genuineness of signature and official position relating to the execution or attestation. A final certification may be made by a secretary of an embassy or legation, consul general, consul, vice consul, or consular agent of the United States, or a diplomatic or consular official of the foreign country assigned or accredited to the United States. If reasonable opportunity has been given to all parties to investigate the authenticity and accuracy of official documents, the court may, for good cause shown, order that they be treated as presumptively authentic without final certification or permit them to be evidenced by an attested summary with or without final certification.

(4) Certified copies of public records. A copy of an official record or report or entry therein, or of a document authorized by law to be recorded or filed and actually recorded or filed in a public office, including data compilations in any form, certified as correct by the custodian or other person authorized to make the certification, by certificate complying with paragraph (1), (2), or (3) of this rule or complying with any Act of Congress or rule prescribed by the Supreme Court pursuant to statutory authority.

(5) Official publications. Books, pamphlets, or other publications purporting to be issued by public authority.

(6) Newspapers and periodicals. Printed materials purporting to be newspapers or periodicals.

(7) Trade inscriptions and the like. Inscriptions, signs, tags, or labels purporting to have been affixed in the course of business and indicating ownership, control, or origin.

(8) Acknowledged documents. Documents accompanied by a certificate of acknowledgment executed in the manner provided by law by a notary public or other officer authorized by law to take acknowledgments.

(9) Commercial paper and related documents. Commercial paper, signatures thereon, and documents relating thereto to the extent provided by general commercial law.

(10) Presumptions under Acts of Congress. Any signature, document, or other matter declared by Act of Congress to be presumptively or prima facie genuine or authentic.

These classes of documents are made self-authenticating because the slight obstacle to fraud presented by authentication requirements is outweighed by the time and expense of proving authenticity. In addition, in some cases, the facts that would provide further evidence of authenticity are within the knowledge of the opponent of the evidence, making it even more unfair to require the proponent to present this evidence.

The trial judge should, therefore, not use discretion to exclude documents coming within Rule 902's classifications. The opponents of the evidence are in no way precluded from contesting authenticity, and evidence may be presented to the jury to be considered in deciding how much weight to give the document. They are only precluded from disputing admissibility on the ground of authentication.[2]

---

[2] *See* United States v. Giacalone, 408 F. Supp. 251, 253 (E.D. Mich. 1975) (defendant moved to dismiss indictment on ground that special United States Attorney had no authority to conduct grand jury proceedings; certified copy of oath of office established authority where defendant "neither contradicted nor challenged the authenticity of this document"), *rev'd on other grounds,* 541 F.2d 508 (6th Cir. 1976).

¶ 8.02[02] Domestic Public Documents Under Seal— Rule 902(1)[1]

Rule 902(1) provides that domestic public documents under seal are self-authenticating. The rule's application to public documents and the requirement of a political entity, subdivision, department, officer or agency precludes the use of private signets. The rule places no cut-off point on the scale of public authority below which the court will refuse to recognize the genuineness of the seal of an official without further authentication, whether the seal be that of an executing officer on the original documents, or the seal of a custodian on a certificate authenticating copies of public documents.[2]

¶ 8.02[03] Domestic Public Documents Not Under Seal— Rule 902(2)[1]

A document signed by an official without a seal is self-authenticating if the seal of another official is affixed.[2] The

---

[1] *See* **Treatise** at ¶ 902(1)[01].

[2] United States v. Mackenzie, 601 F.2d 221 (5th Cir. 1979), *cert. denied,* 444 U.S. 1018 (1980) (order of Texas Board of Medical Examiners cancelling license to practice medicine); United States v. Moore, 555 F.2d 658 (8th Cir. 1977) (certificate of United States Postal Service); United States v. Trotter, 538 F.2d 217 (8th Cir.), *cert. denied,* 429 U.S. 943 (1976) (copy of motor vehicle registration).

[1] *See* **Treatise** at ¶ 902(2)[01].

[2] United States v. Wilson, 732 F.2d 404, 413 (5th Cir.), *cert. denied,* 469 U.S. 1099 (1984) (affidavit of Executive Director of the CIA self-authenticating because it was executed by the third highest official in the CIA whose duties include overall management, and it was attested to by the General Counsel of the CIA who is the custodian of the seal of the CIA); Hunt v. Liberty Lobby, 720 F.2d 631, 651 (11th Cir. 1983), *further proceedings sub nom.* Hunt v. Marchetti, 824 F.2d 916 (11th Cir. 1987). (affidavits of CIA officials, with certificates bearing the CIA official seal and a certificate of the CIA's general counsel certifying that each affiant occupied the position stated in his affidavit were self-authenticating).

Rule 901(a) permits courts to assume genuineness of a signature alone, without the necessity of further authentication. There is also no reason why a state statute adopting blanket presumptions of genuineness for official signatures as well as for official seals should not be followed.

authenticating official must have "official duties" in the district or public subdivision of the officer whose signature is certified.[3] Rule 902(2) applies only to officials "having no seal" but the officer using his seal to authenticate another officer's signature will by inference also be certifying that there is no seal in the other's possession which he himself could have used. The certifying official will by inference also be certifying that the executing officer signed in his official capacity.[4] See Rule 902(1).

Without a seal, a public record is not self-authenticating.[5]

¶ 8.02[04] Foreign Public Documents Rule—Rule 902(3)[1]

Originals as well as copies of foreign public documents are presumed authentic if attested to by authorized foreign or American officials.[2] The authenticating official can certify to

---

[3] This requirement means only that there be some minimum connection between him and the other officer so as to enable him to have enough knowledge of the other officer to say that the signature is genuine. There need be no preliminary showing of this fact since the seal raises the inference that the officer has the capacity to certify that officer's signature. See Rule 901(a).

[4] See United States v. Combs, 762 F.2d 1343, 1348 (9th Cir. 1985) citing United States v. Beason, 690 F.2d 439, 444 (5th Cir. 1982), cert. denied, 459 U.S. 1177 (1983) (certification of custodial authority is not required).

[5] Nolin v. Douglas County, 903 F.2d 1546, 1552 (11th Cir. 1990).

[1] See **Treatise** at ¶ 902(3)[01].

[2] See, e.g., United States v. Herrera-Britto, 739 F.2d 551 (11th Cir. 1984) (certified document, signed and attested to by officials of Honduras, which stated that no registration for a vessel was found in a search of vessel registration records, self-authenticating); United States v. Koziy, 728 F.2d 1314, 1322 (11th Cir.), cert. denied, 469 U.S. 835 (1984) (documents used by Ukrainian Police bearing defendant's signature were self-authenticated under Rule 902(3) since a Russian official authorized to authenticate such documents attested to the documents at issue here; district court did not abuse discretion in admitting documents); United States v. Montemayor, 712 F.2d 104 (5th Cir. 1983) (Mexican official records of birth were admissible where they were properly authenticated by certification of American consular officials); United States v. Regner, 677 F.2d 754 (9th Cir.), cert. denied, 459 U.S. 911 (1982) (court admitted certified records of state-run Hungarian taxicab company).

The formulation for the authentication of foreign public documents is adapted from Rule 44(a) of the Federal Rules of Civil Procedure.

(1) the genuineness of the signature of the executing official; or (2) the genuineness of the signature of the last officer in a chain of authenticating certificates.[3]

Rule 902(2) explicitly gives the trial judge discretion to forego final certification or to admit instead attested summaries with or without final certification. This final provision is a narrow exception to the hearsay and best evidence rules.

Where the parties have had an opportunity to check on the authenticity of the document, exclusion for lack of a final certificate is seldom justified.[4] Certainly it should be too late to raise the issue for the first time on appeal.[5]

Documents originating with a foreign government may be admissible by a route other than Rule 902 when, for example, they are offered other than as official records.[6]

---

[3] United States v. Howard-Arias, 679 F.2d 363, 366 (4th Cir.), *cert. denied,* 459 U.S. 874 (1982) (statement by affiant that he is official designated by Colombian law to certify that vessel on which marijuana was seized was not of Colombian registry was not required where official's signature was attested to as genuine by series of Colombian officials and certified by American consul).

[4] *See, e.g.,* United States v. Leal, 509 F.2d 122 (9th Cir. 1975) (court admitted foreign immigration record without final certificate where foreign immigration officer refused to appear at United States embassy but instead followed his country's authentication procedures; court noted that defendant was not prevented from investigating the authenticity and accuracy of the records); Black Sea & Baltic General v. S.S. Hellenic Destiny, 575 F. Supp. 685, 691–92 (S.D.N.Y. 1983) (magistrate correct in concluding that Saudi customs certificates were admissible as presumptively authentic, even absent a final certification; defendant did not produce any evidence casting doubt upon their authenticity, and there was independent deposition testimony supporting authenticity).

[5] United States v. Rodriguez Serrate, 534 F.2d 7 (1st Cir. 1976) (counsel given extra day to examine documents and raised no objection directed to the absence of good cause); United States v. Padeco-Lovio, 463 F.2d 232 (9th Cir. 1972) (defense counsel was aware of copy government intended to use without a final certificate and made no objection).

[6] Henein v. Saudi Arabian Parsons Ltd., 818 F.2d 1508, 1512 (9th Cir. 1987), *cert. denied,* 484 U.S. 1009 (1988).

¶ 8.02[05]   Treaty May Make Compliance With Rule 902(3) Unnecessary[1]

Compliance with Rule 902(3) is no longer necessary in many instances because of the Convention Abolishing the Requirement of Legalization for Foreign Public Documents.[2] Under the Convention, each country designates those public officials, by their titles, who may affix a form of certification known as the "apostille." The certificate simply states that the document was signed by an individual in his official capacity and that the seal or stamp is genuine. Public documents from countries which are parties to the Convention[3] are recognized in the courts here so long as the apostille is affixed.

Four categories of documents are deemed to be public documents: first, documents emanating from a judicial or other tribunal, including documents from a public prosecutor, clerk of court, or process server; second, administrative documents; third, notarial acts; and fourth, private documents that bear official certifications, such as a certificate of registration or an official authentication of a signature.

The treaty specifically excludes two categories of documents: (a) documents executed by diplomatic or consular officers, and (b) administrative documents dealing directly with commercial or customs operations.

---

[1] *See* **Treatise** at ¶ 902(03)[02].

[2] The relevant portions of the text of the Convention and a form of an Apostille can be found in **Treatise** at ¶ 902(03)[02].

[3] A list of countries which have signed or ratified the convention appears in 20 International Legal Materials, 1516–17 (1981). They are: Austria, Belgium, Finland, France, Federal Republic of Germany, Greece, Ireland, Italy, Japan, Lichtenstein, Luxembourg, Netherlands, Norway, Portugal, Spain, Sweden, Turkey, United Kingdom, United States, Yugoslavia.

¶ 8.02[06] Certified Copies of Public Records—Rule 902(4)[1]

Rule 902(4) provides that certified copies of public records are self-authenticating.[2] The Rule is to be used in conjunction with Rules 902(1), (2) or (3). Copies are certified by a certificate complying with those subdivisions to which reference should be made for the manner in which certificates must be executed.

Rule 902(4) requires no additional certification to the fact of custody or to the custodian's authority.[3] The purported custodian's signature under a statement that he has custody of the original and that the copy is correct, whether or not accompanied by a seal, suffices to assure the accuracy of the copy as a substitute for the original. The authenticity of the original is guaranteed by a certificate complying with Rule 902, paragraphs 1, 2 or 3.

The rule is silent as to what the custodian's certificate should contain. Any reasonable statement implying custody and correctness should suffice. For records kept within the boundaries of the United States, Rule 902 requires that the copy be a literal copy and not a summary. If a literal copy is not obtainable, Rules 1004, 1005 and 1006 permit use of summaries. Rule 1005, for example has an escape clause for copies which "cannot be obtained by the exercise of reasonable diligence." Copies of foreign official documents are explicitly permitted to be in summary form. See discussion of Foreign Public Documents, Rule 902(3) *supra*.

---

[1] *See* **Treatise** at ¶ 902(4)[01].

[2] *See, e.g.,* United States v. Torres, 733 F.2d 449, 455 n.5 (7th Cir.), *cert. denied,* 469 U.S. 864 (1984) (certificate of enrollment prepared by Menominee enrollment clerk and certified by her at trial to be an accurate representation of the information contained in the original tribal roll was admissible under Rule 902(4) as a certified copy of an original public record).

[3] United States v. Beason, 690 F.2d 439, 444 (5th Cir. 1982), *cert. denied,* 459 U.S. 1177 (1983) (certificate by custodian of National Firearms Registration and Transfer Record that no registration in defendant's name existed sufficed without requiring certificate from Secretary of Treasury that custodian had been given custody).

Rule 902(4) also provides that any form of certification may be used for copies of public records which comply with an Act of Congress or rule adopted by the Supreme Court.[4]

¶ 8.02[07]   Official Publications—Rule 902(5)[1]

Publications that purport to be printed by public authority are admissible without further proof of authenticity. In point of fact, any reputable private printer's version should be accepted since typically it is such versions upon which the bench and bar rely. *Cf.* Rules 803(17), 902(6). Almost never is there an error of critical importance in these conveniently obtainable volumes. Although most frequently applied to statutes, the same rule also applies to officially printed volumes of court decisions and miscellaneous public documents.[2]

Rule 902(5) is silent on what level of government must authorize the publication. The levels of government included here should be construed to be as broad as those outlined in Rule 902(1). Judicial notice provides ample authority for recognizing such publications.

¶ 8.02[08]   Newspapers and Periodicals—Rule 902(6)[1]

Rule 902(6) eases, with respect to newspapers and periodicals, the common law requirements of authentication for non-official publications. In the case of newspapers and periodicals there is good reason not to require any more evidence of authenticity than that in the purported publication itself. The realities of newspaper publishing make forgery highly unlikely. This is as true of publications of general circulation as it is of specialized journals with a limited readership. For example, the pink sheets showing over the counter prices are relied upon by a small group but the chance of forgery is remote.

---

[4] These provisions are listed and discussed in **Treatise** at ¶ 902(4)[01].

[1] *See* **Treatise** at ¶ 902(5)[01].

[2] California Association of Bioanalysts v. Rank, 577 F. Supp. 1342, 1355 n.23 (C.D. Cal. 1983) (report of USDHHS, which bore facsimile of official seal of that agency on its cover page, was self-authenticating under Rule 902(5)).

[1] *See* **Treatise** at ¶ 902(6)[01].

The problem of authentication of these publications arises most often in libel actions. Since the opponent in a libel case is in a particularly good position to prove the forgery by producing a genuine copy of the publication, and facts that would prove or disprove genuineness are within his knowledge, it is not unreasonable to shift the burden to him to prove any forgeries.

¶ 8.02[09]   Trade Inscriptions and the Like—Rule 902(7)[1]

Trade inscriptions affixed "in the course of business" are admissible without further proof of authentication. The over-whelming reliability of trade and brand names support Rule 902(07). The rationale for the rule is further based on the fact that many of the cases will involve trademarks and brand names registered under federal or state laws which no one else would have the right to use. A number of federal maritime cases have held labels indicating foreign origin are prima facie evidence that the goods so labeled are in fact of foreign origin.[2] This provision can be used to authenticate machinery, cans of food or clothing to which labels have been attached.

¶ 8.02[10]   Acknowledged Documents—Rule 902(8)[1]

Rule 902(8) extends prima facie authenticity to all documents accompanied by a certificate of acknowledgment under the seal of a notary public or other authorized officer. The basis for this extension is the theory that if the notary is permitted to authenticate documents of title, which are documents of great legal effect, there is no reason for not allowing other writings to be proved in the same way.

Rule 902(8) states that the seal on the certificate of acknowledgment may, in addition to the seal of the notary, be that of

---

[1] *See* **Treatise** at ¶ 902(7)[01].

[2] 19 U.S.C. § 1615(2) ("Marks, labels, brands, or stamps, indicative of foreign origin, upon or accompanying mechandise [sic] or containers or merchandise, shall be prima facie evidence of the foreign origin of such merchandise.").

[1] *See* **Treatise** at ¶ 902(8)[01].

some "other officer authorized by law to take acknowledgments." The rule itself does not authorize any particular officer to take an acknowledgment. It speaks only to those already authorized to do so. Thus, whether a particular officer will be able to take an acknowledgment under 902(8) will depend on whether he is authorized to take an acknowledgment under state or federal law. In the absence of contrary evidence, there is no reason for not presuming that the officer whose seal is affixed to the certificate of acknowledgment is authorized by law. This presumption is based on the theory that evidence to the contrary would be easily obtainable by the party opposing admission of the document.

¶ 8.02[11]   Effect of Uniform Commercial Code—Rule 902(9)[1]

Documents covered by Sections 3-307, 3-510, 8-105(2) and 1-202 of the Uniform Commercial Code are treated as self-authenticating under paragraph 9 of Rule 902.[2] Other documents offered in connection with a suit governed by the Commercial Code's substantive provisions may or may not be self-authenticating depending upon whether they fall within Rule 901 or 902.

¶ 8.02[12]   Presumption Under Acts of Congress—Rule 902(10)[1]

Paragraph (10) indicates that any mode of self-authentication provided for in an Act of Congress[2] may continue to be employed concomitantly with the procedures specified in Rule 902. The applicable acts often deal with best evidence aspects

---

[1] See **Treatise** at ¶¶ 902(09)[01]–[02].

[2] See United States v. Hawkins, 905 F.2d 1489, 1493 (11th Cir. 1990) (returned checks held self-authenticating); In re Richter & Phillips Jewelers & Dist., Inc., 31 B.R. 512 (S.D. Ohio 1983) (original check was admissible without extrinsic evidence of authenticity); United States v. Carriger, 592 F.2d 312, 316–17 (6th Cir. 1979) (mere production of promissory note is prima facie evidence of its validity).

[1] See **Treatise** at ¶ 902(10)[01].

[2] The relevant statutes are discussed in the **Treatise** at ¶ 902(10)[01].

as well, allowing the prima facie authentic copies to be used instead of the original documents. See discussion of Rule 1002, Chapter 9 *infra*. In addition, they often operate as exceptions to the hearsay rule.

CHAPTER 9*

Best Evidence Rule

SYNOPSIS

---

* Chapter revised in 1991 by RANDALL K. ANDERSON, member of the New York and District of Columbia Bars.

¶ 9.01　Requirement of Original—Rules 1001 and 1002

¶ 9.01[01]　Overview of Best Evidence Rule [1]

Rule 1002 adopts and somewhat expands in scope the so-called "best evidence" rule. There is no general rule that proof of a fact will be excluded unless its proponent furnishes the best evidence.[2] Rule 1002 only requires production of an "original" if a proponent is seeking to prove the content of a "writing," "recording," or "photograph." These terms are defined in Rules 1001(1), (2) and (3) which are discussed below.

The requirement of the rule is expressly dispensed with if other rules in Article X of the Federal Rules or Acts of Congress so provide.[3] These exceptions have proven to be sufficiently comprehensive to allow the admission of many writings, recordings, and photographs that were not originals.[4]

Rule 1002 states:

Rule 1002

REQUIREMENT OF ORIGINAL

To prove the content of a writing, recording, or photograph, the original writing, recording, or photograph is required, except as otherwise provided in these rules or by Act of Congress.

The function of the best evidence rule is to ensure that the trier of fact is presented with the most accurate evidence practicable in those situations where informed legal judgment has concluded that precision is essential. There are many built in exceptions to the rule because the need for the rule is often obviated by the existence of modern techniques of reproduction and broad discovery rules that make it unlikely that a party would produce a fraudulent copy.

---

[1] See **Treatise** at ¶¶ 1002[01]–[02] & [04].

[2] Significantly, neither the article in which it appears nor the rule or its caption refer to "best evidence." This omission was deliberate on the part of the Advisory Committee which hoped thereby to hasten "the demise of a term regarded as misleadingly broad in its scope."

[3] The relevant statutes are discussed in the **Treatise** at ¶ 1002[04].

[4] See ¶¶ 9.02–9.05 infra.

By giving accurate counterparts the status of duplicates (Rule 1001(4)) which can ordinarily be admitted to the same extent as originals (Rule 1003), the Federal Rules of Evidence recognize that a narrow concept of an original is usually not required as a protective device when modern technology is involved, but that respect for the goal of preciseness is still necessary when dealing with documents, photographs and recordings.

Rule 1005 acknowledges that public writings by their very nature call for specialized treatment. Rule 1006 allows a departure from the general rule in the case of voluminous material which cannot conveniently be produced in court. Rule 1007 dispenses with application of the rule if the adverse party made an admission of the contents in writing or in the course of testifying. Rule 1002 itself acknowledges that the requirement of the original may be dispensed with in other situations provided for in statutes or other federal rules. Rule 1004(1) to (3) codifies situations in which the original cannot be produced but its production is nevertheless excused. Rule 1004(4) excuses production without inquiring whether the original is available when the "writing, recording or photograph is not closely related to a controlling issue." Overtechnical application of the rule is also avoided by the federal courts' insistence on applying waiver if an objection on the basis of the rule had not been properly raised at trial, and on finding that errors in admission were harmless unless a substantial possibility existed that the contents of the improperly admitted document were inaccurate and might therefore have affected the result.

When there is any doubt about whether the rule is applicable, secondary evidence should be admitted, leaving it to the jury to determine probative force discounted by the failure to produce an original. Reversals for admission will be rare to the vanishing point since almost never is there real prejudice that the opponent cannot overcome. Wrongful exclusion can, however, have more serious consequences and reversals for this kind of error are to be expected.

¶ 9.01[02]   Application[5]

Rule 1002 is in accord with the traditional view in providing that an original is required when the object is "to prove the content of a writing, recording or photograph." When the content is involved is not always easy to discern.

The best evidence rule has been interpreted as not applying when a witness refreshes his memory with a document,[6] when an expert resorts to material as a basis for his opinion,[7] or when a witness testifies that examined books or records do not contain a particular entry.[8] Some transactions, such as wills, contracts and deeds, as a matter of substantive law take the form of a writing and any attempt to prove their happening necessarily involves the content of the writing and brings the best evidence rule into play. But if an event does not take the form of a writing,[9] recording,[10] or photograph and is only

---

[5] *See* **Treatise** at ¶ 1002[03].

[6] While it makes no difference whether refreshment was with a copy or original, the opponent may be entitled to see the document actually used by the witness. Where there is a claim that the document may have been shown in copy form to mislead the witness, the court should insist on production of the original for comparison purposes.

[7] *See, e.g.,* United States v. Ratliff, 623 F.2d 1293, 1296–97 (8th Cir.), *cert. denied,* 449 U.S. 876 (1980). See discussion under Rule 703.

[8] *See, e.g.,* United States v. Madera, 574 F.2d 1320, 1323 n.3 (5th Cir. 1978) (original document need not be produced when witness testifies that it does not contain a reference to a designated matter, but court notes that although the document is not the best evidence in the evidentiary sense it may actually be better evidence because jury can check for itself).

[9] *See* R & R Associates, Inc. v. Visual Scene, Inc., 726 F.2d 36, 38 (1st Cir. 1984) (in contract action, trial court properly permitted witness to testify even though written contract existed, where witness was in no way attempting to prove the contents of the writing but rather was attempting to prove cost to plaintiff to procure goods).

[10] *See, e.g.,* United States v. Fagan, 821 F.2d 1002, 1008 n.1 (5th Cir. 1987), *cert. denied,* 484 U.S. 1005 (1988) (prosecution sought to prove content of conversation, not tape recording; "best evidence" rule does not preclude proving conversation by testimony of witness even though tape recording of conversation existed); United States v. Rose, 590 F.2d 232, 237 (7th Cir. 1978), *cert. denied,* 442 U.S. 929 (1979) (where government sought to prove contents of conversation, not contents of tape recording, best evidence rule is inapplicable); United States v. Gonzales-Benitez, 537 F.2d 1051, 1053 (9th Cir.), *cert. denied,* 429 U.S. 923 (1976) (where conversations

incidentally memorialized, the rule does not apply and the witness may testify to the underlying event.

Accordingly, where the issue is what was said at a former time the best evidence rule does not apply, so that any witness who heard may testify to the words even though they were transcribed or recorded.

The best evidence rule is triggered even if an event is only incidentally memorialized, if a proponent chooses to prove the event by the content of the recordings. It can be difficult to distinguish between when a writing is being used to prove content and when it is being used to prove something else which does not fall within the ambit of the best evidence rule.[11] Such problems should be settled at a pretrial conference. If opponents raise any questions about a recording, the original should be made available to them, so that they can test it or explain it away. Apart from best evidence rules, fairness requires that opponents see the key materials that will be used against them.

¶ 9.01[03] Writings, Recordings, and Photographs Defined—Rule 1001(1)–(2)[12]

Paragraph (1) of Rule 1001 contains the definitions of "writings" and "recordings," while "photographs" are covered in paragraph (2).

Rule 1001(1) states:

---

with informers were tape-recorded, court did not err in allowing participant to conversation to testify; "if the ultimate inquiry had been to discover what sounds were embodied on the tapes in question, the tapes themselves would have been the "best evidence'" but here the issue was not the content of the tapes but the content of the conversation).

[11] *Cf.* Time Share Vacation Club v. Atlantic Resorts, Ltd., 735 F.2d 61, 64, 65 (2d Cir. 1984) (plaintiff corporation appealed dismissal of its breach of contract action for lack of in personam jurisdiction; since plaintiff had burden of proving defendant's minimum contacts with the forum for the purpose of establishing jurisdiction and was relying solely on contract with defendant towards that end, plaintiff had burden of producing a copy of the entire contract or proffering an explanation for its absence; citing Rules 1002, 1003, 1004).

[12] *See* **Treatise** at ¶ 1001(1) & ¶¶ 1001(2)[01]–[04].

(Matthew Bender & Co., Inc.)

Rule 1001

DEFINITIONS

For purposes of this article the following definitions are applicable:

(1) Writings and recordings. "Writings" and "recordings" consist of letters, words, or numbers, or their equivalent, set down by handwriting, typewriting, printing, photostating, photographing, magnetic impulse, mechanical or electronic recording, or other form of data compilation.

The rule as adopted is broad enough to encompass any future development that uses symbols as the equivalent of words. Symbols that do not have a verbal connotation have generally not been considered subject to the rule. It does seem desirable to extend the rule to drawings whose exact form and content are critical.[13]

The extent to which the requirement of an original should be applied to chattels which have something written or marked on them is not free from doubt. Clearly, uninscribed chattels are not subject to the rule; there is no general rule of best evidence requiring the production of objects. However, numerous objects bear some kind of number or inscription. Money, badges, flags, and tombstones certainly fall within this category. Should one require production of the original inscribed chattel in court? While few courts have considered the question, most modern courts would probably agree that no hard and fast rule applies. Rather most courts would probably apply a balancing test in which the ease of producing the chattel and the need for producing are considered. A photograph of the inscribed object which cannot be conveniently brought into court should suffice.

Rule 1001(2) recognizes that there are instances when photographs of non-writing or non-documentary materials should be subject to the application of the best evidence rule because the contents of the photograph—*i.e.,* the photograph itself—will be sought to be proved. The rule states:

For purposes of this article the following definitions are applicable:

---

[13] Seiler v. Lucasfilm, Ltd., 808 F.2d 1316, 1318–19 (9th Cir. 1986), *cert. denied,* 484 U.S. 826 (1987) (drawings).

. . .

(2) Photographs. "Photographs" include still photographs, X-ray films, video tapes, and motion pictures.

The best evidence rule will usually apply in cases where the photographs or motion pictures are utilized in cases involving such matters as infringement of copyright, defamation and libel, pornography and the invasion of privacy. In such cases the rationale of the best evidence rule warrants specifically including photographs within the rule even though it is unlikely that, in the absence of the requirement, a witness will attempt to testify about what he saw in a film or photograph without actually producing the disputed item itself.

While in many instances photographs are used to illustrate and explain what a witness testifies about from his independent observation, there are situations where a photograph or motion picture will have independent probative value. It will be the best evidence of things which the witness has not described or mentioned. Because the photograph continues to speak for itself and may have details not testified to by a witness, it is important to examine it carefully before it is introduced. If it is to be used for a limited purpose only this fact should be made known to the jury at the time of introduction.

The ability of a photograph to speak for itself is of growing importance since automatic camera equipment is now used for such purposes as check cashing and in taking pictures of bank robbers. In such instances the photographs have been described as " 'mute', 'silent,' or 'dumb' independent photographic witnesses." Evidence of the way the camera was arranged and worked is sufficient to identify the picture even if it was taken as a result of a trip wire or photoelectric cell having snapped the shutter with no one present to observe the event other than the person pictured. Similarly, infra-red or light sensitive film or telescope lenses may reveal matters that cannot be described by an observer.

The best evidence rule will not bar photographs of nondocumentary objects on the theory that the subject of the picture would be the best evidence. Such items of real evidence are not included in the definitions of Rule 1001 so that the best evidence rule does not apply to them. Their characteristics can be shown by testimony or photographs or both. As a matter of trial tactics to maximize probative force it is often desirable to show the object by views, or by bringing it to court or by the use of models and diagrams, but this is a matter of choice, not compulsion.

Under normal circumstances the negative of a photograph and any print made from it are treated interchangeably as originals. See Rule 1001(3) *infra.* A negative film may show more gradations of tone than any ordinary paper print. Hence some delicate tonal differences readily observable on the negative may not be detectable on a paper print when the print is viewed by ordinary reflected light as is ordinarily the case. For all practical purposes a print is usually good enough from the tonal gradation standpoint and, of course, jurors ordinarily can understand positives better than negatives. There may be rare instances, however, especially in the scientific fields as for example, fingerprints, firearms identification, and documents photography, when a print cannot be made that will show essential details. In these instances if the reversal of light and shade does not matter, the negative should be produced.

Properly verified enlargements enhance the value of an exhibit because many details which are not readily discernible in a small print are made obvious by enlargement. So long as cutting and rearranging do not distort or mislead, use of enlargements of specific areas should be permitted.

The best evidence rule needs to be applied with flexibility to X-rays. Since it is the contents of the X-ray that are in dispute, i.e., what the X-ray purports to represent, and no one can directly see the internal structure the X-ray portrays, the best evidence rule is obviously theoretically applicable. But an X-ray photograph alone is often relatively meaningless to the layperson without secondary evidence in the form of expert testimony to interpret and clarify the nebulous image. More modern equipment showing internal arrangements by sound, radar, or electromagnetic processes should be treated in the same liberal way as X-rays.

Usually, for tactical reasons as well as because the Rules require it, the X-ray should be in court. At times when evidence other than X-rays is presented for the purpose of aiding the court in understanding the contents of the X-ray and no prejudice is shown, the X-ray itself will not be required.

Since Rule 705 allows an expert to give his opinion without first disclosing the data upon which he relies, where the opposing party has had an opportunity to examine the X-rays outside of court, such as through the discovery process, the court should allow the expert to testify without requiring production of the X-rays, unless prejudice can be shown.

Although an X-ray means little to an average jury of laymen, when it is produced in court the opposing party is entitled to see and examine it for cross-examination purposes. Discovery will normally have made the X-ray available to both parties and their expert witnesses who are able to interpret and explain the X-ray. The best evidence rule is not inflexible as applied to X-rays or equivalent material.

¶ 9.01[04]   Original Defined (Rule 1001(3))[14]

An "original" in the technical sense used in this rule may be quite different from an "original" in lay terms. The "original" is the document whose contents are to be proved. Its jural significance makes it the original whether or not it was written before or after another, was copied from another, or was itself used to copy from.[15]

Rule 1001(3) defines an original as:

(3) Original. An "original" of a writing or recording is the writing or recording itself or any counterpart intended to have the same effect by a person executing or issuing it. An "original" of a photograph includes the negative or any print therefrom. If data are stored in a computer or similar device, any printout or other output readable by sight, shown to reflect the data accurately, is an "original".

---

[14] See **Treatise** at ¶ 1001(3)[01].

[15] See, e.g., United States v. Taylor, 648 F.2d 565, 568 n.3 (9th Cir.), cert. denied, 454 U.S. 866 (1981) (court noted without deciding, that where letter was telecopied from San Diego to Houston, either telecopied letter or photocopy thereof may have been the document on which Texas bank relied, making it the legally operative original).

The question of what is an original is essentially one of relevancy. If we ask, "what is the document being offered to prove?" the identity of the original often becomes apparent. If it is the terms of a contract, then the signed agreement is the contract containing its terms. If we are trying to show delivery of goods, the original is the signed receipt. If we are trying to show shipment of goods, the original may be the shipping clerk's tally sheet. If we are trying to show an offer, the original may be the signed letter received. If we are trying to show authority to make the offer, the original may be a carbon copy of the agent's letter in the principal's file.

Often the intent of the parties in creating the document controls, particularly in contract actions. When the party or parties to a writing intend that a specific duplicate or copy shall serve as the original, either instead of the chronological original or as an additional original, their intentions govern. Thus, where the writing constituting a bilateral transaction is executed by the parties in several counterparts, each of these parts is "the" writing because each counterpart was intended to be legally effective, hence of equal standing and an original. Any question of preferring one over the other in evidence is thus foreclosed. Similarly, mere simultaneous production of two counterparts does not make each an "equivalent" original if only one of them is recognized by the parties through their acts and intentions as an original.

Where several counterparts are created but only one is signed, it is the original. Where a document is executed in duplicate but each party signs a different counterpart, then to show his agreement the document signed by him is the original. The signature gives the document jural significance.

Depending upon the issue, a document may be both a copy and an original in the same case. To show an offer, the original signed copy of a letter is the original. To show that someone knew of the offer, a carbon copy in his file would be the original. The carbon would, however, be a copy when seeking to show what was received by the offeree, and the signed letter a copy to show what was in the file.

Mere referral by the parties to a document as a "copy" is not decisive; they may have been using the term in its lay sense.

Common usage will often label original telegraphs, autographs and writings as "copies" even in situations where there is no copy. Substantive law indicates which of several documents will be relevant and therefore the original.

At times practical need controls what can be denominated an original. For example, the first permanent business records rather than the preliminary and temporary slips, tags and invoices are originals. They must however, have been made in the regular course of business and must be fairly contemporaneous with the items entered. Many persons may be required to produce such an entry and the rationale of practicality and accuracy is identical to that supporting Rule 803(6). This position is recognized by state and federal business entry statutes which allow the first permanent entries to be recognized as originals.

A related situation controlled by practicalities rather than theory is where a counterpart other than the chronological original is accepted as a best evidence original because it is the first comprehensible document. Examples of this are prints made from a negative. While the negative is the chronological original, all but the best trained photographers cannot accurately visualize the scene photographed. Therefore any print made from the negative is recognized as an original for it is the first to be produced in a medium readily understood by the average person. This is also true of computer printouts because the underlying permanent sources of information—the magnetic tapes and punched cards—cannot be readily understood. The printout represents the first readable counterpart of this information and therefore is the original.

¶ 9.01[05]   Original Recordings [16]

The original of a recording is the recording itself. Unlike documentary evidence where the term original is defined by the circumstances of the case, Rule 1001(4) provides that the original recording is always the original while a rerecording is a duplicate. The only exception to this position is where a specific rerecording is at issue, then it is the original to be

---

[16] *See* **Treatise** at ¶ 1001(3)[02].

(Matthew Bender & Co., Inc.)

produced for the court. This distinction is treated with great flexibility by the courts since all parties concur in the need for enhancement, redaction and the like in presenting recordings in court.

¶ 9.02   Accurate Duplicates Admissible—Rule 1003

¶ 9.02[01]   Scope and Definition[1]

Rule 1003 sets out guidelines for admitting a duplicate as if it were an original. The rule states:

Rule 1003

ADMISSIBILITY OF DUPLICATES

A duplicate is admissible to the same extent as an original unless (1) a genuine question is raised as to the authenticity of the original or (2) in the circumstances it would be unfair to admit the duplicate in lieu of the original.

The rule recognizes that because of the accuracy of modern techniques of reproduction, duplicates and originals should, for evidentiary purposes, normally be treated interchangeably. An original will be insisted upon only when a substantial question is raised as to the authenticity of either the original or the duplicate, or when it is unfair under the circumstances to admit the duplicate in place of the original.

¶ 9.02[02]   Duplicate Defined—Rule 1001(4)[2]

Rule 1001(4) defines the term duplicate. It states:

(4) Duplicate. A "duplicate" is a counterpart produced by the same impression as the original, or from the same matrix, or by means of photography, including enlargements and miniatures, or by mechanical or electronic re-recording, or by chemical reproduction, or by other equivalent techniques which accurately reproduces the original.

---

[1] *See* **Treatise** at ¶ 1003[01].

[2] *See* **Treatise** at ¶¶ 1001(4)[01]–[02].

The definition requires only that the reproduction measure up to a standard of accuracy, "designed to insure an accurate reproduction of the original." It is designed to save the time and expense previously wasted in producing the original when an equally reliable counterpart was at hand. The rule still properly excludes from the definition of duplicate manually produced copies which are subject to human error in the process of reproduction. A duplicate of an original writing, recording, photograph, or computer printout is admissible regardless of the status of the original when the requirements of Rule 1001(4) and 1003 are satisfied.[3]

[a] Writings[4]

The definition of duplicate includes carbon, microfilmed,[5] and Xerographic copies of writings as well as copies produced by other reliable techniques for reproducing originals, such as holography and electronic image storage. Reproduction of the original in color or exact size is ordinarily not called for and enlargements of microfilm should be considered as equal to the microfilm itself. All that is usually required where no objection is offered by the opposing party is that testimony be offered that the copy is an accurate reproduction of its counterpart.

To admit carbon copies, the parties need not have signed the carbon or have shown a specific intention to treat it as part of the writing itself. Simultaneous production by the same impression as the original is all that is required.[6] Exact duplicates of

---

[3] United States v. Gerhart, 538 F.2d 807, 810 n.4 (8th Cir. 1976) (photo-copy could have been admitted as a "duplicate" under Rule 1003 instead of secondary evidence under Rule 1004 where the original was lost).

[4] See **Treatise** at ¶¶ 1001(4)[03]–[05].

[5] United States v. Carroll, 860 F.2d 500, 507–08 (1st Cir. 1988) (where originals of checks were either lost or destroyed, but not by proponent, microfilm prints of checks were admissible).

[6] See CTS Corp. v. Piher International Corp., 527 F.2d 95, 104 n.29 (7th Cir. 1975), *cert. denied,* 424 U.S. 978 (1976) ("Although there is no direct testimony describing the document as a 'carbon copy', in the absence of any evidence to the contrary, we draw this inference from the copy of the document which was offered for examination in light of the testimony of the witnesses").

books, printed notices and the like should be considered originals under Rule 1001(3). They are to be distinguished from
printed copies of contracts where only the signed copies are
originals. Changes on printed form leases, for example, are
common. But some contracts of adhesion, such as bills of
lading, are not commonly changed and any printed form should
prove general terms as an original. The printed and unsigned
copies, if they are shown to be identical to the executed copies,
would be duplicates under Rule 1001(4).

[b] Recordings[7]

Re-recordings should be accepted as duplicates where shown
to have been made by a technique designed to ensure an
accurate reproduction of the original.[8] In order to insure an
accurate re-recording of the recorded conversation it sometimes becomes necessary to edit tapes in order to delete irrelevant material and to suppress noise. Where such editing or
noise suppressing is done by experts or under the court's
supervision, the re-recordings will be admitted into evidence,[9]

---

[7] *See* **Treatise** at ¶ 1001(4)[06].

[8] United States v. Carrasco, 887 F.2d 794, 802–03 (7th Cir. 1989) (accuracy
of duplicate tape may be established through recollection of eyewitness to
the event recorded); United States v. Balzano, 687 F.2d 6, 7–8 (1st Cir. 1982)
(accuracy of tape established by testimony concerning method used for
replication).

[9] United States v. DiMatteo, 716 F.2d 1361, 1368 (11th Cir. 1983), *vacated
and remanded on other grounds,* 469 U.S. 1101 (1985) (where informant had
tape-recorded his conversations with a conspirator and then forwarded tapes
to DEA which in turn made copies of tapes, court held there was no error
in admission of tapes; government properly established that introduced tapes
were duplicates of originals by introduction of informant's testimony that
duplicates were "exact recordings of conversations that were on the original
tapes"). *Cf.* United States v. Scully, 546 F.2d 255, 270 (9th Cir. 1976), *vacated
and remanded on other grounds sub nom.,* United States v. Cabral, 430 U.S.
902 (1977) (no error in permitting government to introduce single master
tape of all conversations which eliminated need to switch tape reels constantly; court noted that originals were also introduced, that master had
quality equal to original, and that defendants had opportunity to inspect
original); United States v. Conway, 507 F.2d 1047, 1052 (5th Cir. 1975) (in
pre-Rule case duplicate recording containing only six out of eleven conversations admissible where there was "no evidence, indeed no intimation, that

but where parties other than the court selectively edit the tapes, the condensed version will sometimes be disallowed because of the risk of fraud or misleading.

Typewritten transcripts of recordings are often introduced for purposes of aiding the jury in understanding and following the recorded conversations. Sometimes they are placed in evidence in conjunction with, or in place of, recordings. Where this is done a proper foundation must be laid by testimony that the transcript was compared with the original recording and found to be a true copy.[10] The transcript is not, however, a duplicate original because it was not made by mechanical or electronic means assuring identity, but rather was copied by a person. Moreover, since the recording will reflect tones, inflections and pauses, it should be produced to be played if the opponent or the court wishes. If a jury wishes to see the transcript during deliberations, unless all parties consent, the recording must be played for them in court while they examine the transcript.

As a matter of sound practice, the original recording should be kept even after it is copied electronically or transcribed into written form. Even if the copy is admitted—as it generally should be—there will be some doubt in the trier's mind as to its completeness. An astute opponent can properly argue on the ground of spoliation that it should not be weighed against his client. Wire tapping and bugging statutes must be complied with in their details as to sealing of originals within specified periods and the like. This is a substantive rather than an evidentiary requirement.

[c] Computer Printouts[11]

While Rule 1001(3) defines printouts as originals, such computer records should be considered duplicates if they are

---

this erasure was intentional, and the authenticity of the tapes remain[ed] unquestionable." Only those conversations supplied to defense counsel prior to trial were admitted).

[10] United States v. Slade, 627 F.2d 293, 302–03 (D.C. Cir.), *cert. denied,* 449 U.S. 1034 (1980) (discussion of appropriate procedures for use of transcripts not introduced into evidence).

[11] *See* **Treatise** at ¶ 1001[04](07).

offered in evidence in place of underlying documents such as purchase orders, sales slips, invoices and notes. Thus a record of a single sale by a department store would come under 1001(4) but an analysis of all sales for a period would be an original creation of the computer and would thus be classified under 1001(3). In practice it makes little difference whether a printout is characterized as coming within 1001(3) or 1001(4).

There is a technical problem in admitting computer records as duplicates because some of the copying of the source data into cards or other inputs is accomplished not, in the words of Rule 1001(4), by "electronic re-recording," but by people. This problem is overcome by use of Rule 803(6).

¶ 9.02[03]　Grounds for Excluding Duplicates[12]

When the opposing party concedes the duplicate's accuracy or does not object pursuant to Rule 1003, or fails to raise a genuine issue of authenticity,[13] the duplicate must be admitted unless the court has strong reason to believe that the parties are conspiring to commit a fraud on the court. Even when accuracy is not conceded, the court should require persuasive reasons for rejecting duplicates which should be routinely

---

[12] *See* **Treatise** at ¶ 1003[01].

[13] United States v. Chang An-Lo, 851 F.2d 547, 557 (2d Cir.) *cert. denied,* 488 U.S. 966 (1988) (copies of telephone logs from hotel in Rio de Janiero were properly admitted because defendant raised no genuine issue of authenticity); United States v. Hausmann, 711 F.2d 615, 618 (5th Cir. 1983) *per curiam* (court affirmed conviction for making false statements to a United States agency holding that duplicates of falsified receipts were admissible since defendant did not raise a genuine issue as to their authenticity or show any unfairness resulting from their admission and the agency director testified that original receipts are normally copied and returned to the owner); United States v. Wilson, 690 F.2d 1267, 1276 n.2 (9th Cir. 1982), *cert. denied,* 464 U.S. 867 (1983) (photocopy of two false pieces of identification admissible as duplicate of originals; no objection at trial); United States v. Barnes, 443 F. Supp. 137, 139 n.2 (S.D.N.Y. 1977) (no reason not to admit state court hearing records where no issue had been raised as to their authenticity). *Cf.* Fidelity Philadelphia Trust Co. v. Pioche Mines Consol., Inc., 587 F.2d 27, 29 (9th Cir. 1978) (fact that records were lost is no excuse for lack of prosecution since Rules 1003 and 1004 allow copies to be used and copies were available).

accepted as a convenience to the court and the parties.[14] A specific objection indicating why the original is needed should be required.[15]

Rule 1003 expressly provides two grounds for objection. It states that a duplicate can be excluded if the authenticity of the original is in doubt or if the admission of the duplicate would be unfair.

[a] Question as to Authenticity of Original [16]

Duplicates can be excluded if there is a genuine question about the authenticity of the original. There are situations in which problems of authenticity will arise with respect to the original or the duplicate, despite the fact that Rule 1001(4) *supra,* requires that a duplicate be produced by a technique designed to insure an accurate reproduction of the original. One common situation is where an original and a duplicate are prepared but subsequently one is corrected or altered while such changes are omitted from the other counterpart, possibly out of forgetfulness or carelessness. The duplicate must have been made after the original took on its final form: extensive conforming by hand makes it the equivalent of a hand drawn

---

[14] United States v. Georgalis, 631 F.2d 1199, 1205 (5th Cir. 1980) (that government had exclusive possession of duplicates for five years raises no issue).

[15] United States v. Benedict, 647 F.2d 928, 932–33 (9th Cir.), *cert. denied,* 454 U.S. 1087 (1981) (duplicate of false passport properly admitted since there was testimony that original had been lost in the State Department; since there was no credible showing of prejudice to defendant, unnecessary to decide whether loss of passport constituted negligence attributable to prosecution); CTS Corp. v. Piher Int'l Corp., 527 F.2d 95, 104 (7th Cir. 1975), *cert. denied,* 424 U.S. 978 (1976) (error for trial judge to have excluded carbon copy of purchase order where there was no basis in record for questioning its authenticity; on remand party against whom offered retains right to question authenticity); Diplomat Homes, Inc. v. Commercial Standard Ins. Co., 394 F. Supp. 558, 565–66 (W.D. Mo. 1975) (unexecuted machine copy of duplicate original properly admitted pursuant to Rule 1003 where there is no real question of lack of authenticity or unfairness); United States v. Rodriguez, 524 F.2d 485, 487–89 (5th Cir. 1975), *cert. denied,* 424 U.S. 972 (1976) (Xerox copy of vehicle certificate of title; citing Rule 1003).

[16] *See* **Treatise** at ¶ 1003[02].

copy. Where there is a dispute about whether the parties authorized changes in a document and when it was changed, both the claimed unaltered version and the corrected counterpart should be admitted.[17]

Questions as to the authenticity of the original also arise where the circumstances surrounding the execution of the writing present a substantial possibility of fraud and where the party offering the duplicate has intentionally destroyed the original. In the latter case, courts look to see what intention the party had in destroying the original. Where it is done by accident, mistake or in the regular course of business or for any nonfraudulent purpose, the duplicate is admissible.[18] Where fraud is raised as an issue the court may exclude the duplicate or any secondary evidence.

Under Rule 1003 the mere supposition that the original may have been altered should not prevent introduction of the duplicate without some indication that the original was altered. There must be a "genuine" dispute about the authenticity of the original.[19]

---

[17] Amoco Production Co. v. United States, 619 F.2d 1383, 1391 (10th Cir. 1980) (in action to quiet title where there was dispute as to whether recorded deed accurately reflected original deed, trial court did not err in holding that what purported to be a conformed copy of the original deed could not be used to prove the contents of the original deed because the critical part of the conformed copy (the mineral reservation clause) was not completely reproduced).

[18] *See, e.g.,* United States v. Balzano, 687 F.2d 6, 7–8 (1st Cir. 1982) *per curiam* (duplicate tape admitted where original was by necessity erased in process of transferring it to second cassette and appellant submitted no evidence suggesting lack of good faith).

[19] United States v. DiMatteo, 716 F.2d 1361, 1368 (11th Cir. 1983) (defendant never met his burden under Rule 1003 of raising genuine question as to authenticity, and even if he had, informant's testimony would have been a sufficient response).

[b] Circumstances of Unfairness[20]

Exclusion of the duplicate is also justified if it would be unfair to admit the duplicate in lieu of the original.[21] When deciding whether to exclude duplicates on unfairness grounds, the court should bear in mind the purpose of the rule. Rule 1003 was designed to make evidence easier to admit by taking advantage of modern accurate means of reproduction.[22]

Unfairness will sometimes arise even when accuracy of the contents of the writing would readily be conceded as where something of substantial value may be gained by inspecting the original. The duplicate may, for example, fail to represent the entire writing and the undisclosed portion of the writing might either qualify the duplicated portion (see Rule 1006) or disclose additional relevant information or there may be doubt about whether the original was executed. Or the original may be a pasted together version which gives an entirely different impression than a smooth Xerox copy; interlineations in different color inks or pencils may be more readily seen in the original.[23]

---

[20] *See* **Treatise** at ¶¶ 1003[01]&[03].

[21] *See* Fox v. Peck Iron and Metal Co., 25 B.R. 674, 679–80 (Bkrtcy. S.D. Cal. 1982) (in nonjury trial, court refused to admit alleged copy after finding testimony from uncooperative witness regarding original unreliable and admission of duplicate unfair "where the original could be of much value" in resolving issues).

[22] United States v. Enstam, 622 F.2d 857, 866 (5th Cir. 1980), *cert. denied,* 450 U.S. 912, *cert. denied,* 451 U.S. 907 (1981) (Xerox copy of corporate letterhead properly admitted as duplicate where it was properly identified as copy of original; court termed as "spurious" questions defendants raised as to authenticity: that there was no explanation for disappearance of original and that copy did not show original's colorings).

[23] Greater Kansas City Laborers Pen. Fund v. Thummel, 738 F.2d 926, 928 (8th Cir. 1984) (court of of appeals upheld the trial court's decision admitting carbon copy of the contract as an original, even though at the signature line of the carbon someone had written defendant's name over the very dim carbon signature, stating that the fact that the signature was obscured would go to the weight not the admissibility of the document); Federal Deposit Ins. Corp. v. Rodenberg, 571 F. Supp. 455, 457–58 (D. Md. 1983) (in suit by assignee of promissory notes against personal guarantor of the notes, court held photocopies of relevant documents to be admissible despite the fact that minor portions were deleted in photocopying; relevant terms of promissory note and guaranty were clear and subject to only one reasonable interpretation).

Determining authenticity of the signature may require production of the original where the signature on the original writing or type or ink color may have to be analyzed. The duplicate itself may be so mutilated, interlined, erased, unintelligible or illegible that fairness requires the original. In short, the category of unfairness encompasses any set of circumstances which enables the opposing party to show that there is a substantial likelihood of prejudice if the duplicate is admitted rather than requiring the original to be produced.

¶ 9.03   When Is an Original Not Required—Rule 1004

¶ 9.03[01]   Scope[1]

Rule 1004 is primarily a restatement of the common law rule excusing production of the original in four specified circumstances. Production of the original is excused in these instances because the best evidence rule is one of preference, not absolute exclusion, that gives way when efficiency and the need for relevant evidence become paramount. The rule states:

Rule 1004

ADMISSIBILITY OF OTHER EVIDENCE OF CONTENTS

The original is not required, and other evidence of the contents of a writing, recording or photograph is admissible if—

(1) Originals lost or destroyed. All originals are lost or have been destroyed, unless the proponent lost or destroyed them in bad faith; or

(2) Original not obtainable. No originals can be obtained by any available judicial process or procedure; or

(3) Original in possession of opponent. At a time when an original was under the control of the party against whom offered, that party was put on notice, by the pleadings or otherwise, that the contents would be a subject of proof at the hearing, and that party does not produce the original at the hearing; or

(4) Collateral matters. The writing, recording, or photograph is not closely related to a controlling issue.

---

[1] *See* **Treatise** at ¶ 1004[01].

If production is excused because one of the four conditions enumerated in Rule 1004 is satisfied, secondary evidence of the contents is admissible. Rule 1004 recognizes no degrees of secondary evidence. In other words, once the conditions of Rule 1004 are met, the party seeking to prove the contents of a writing, photograph or recording may do so by any kind of secondary evidence ranging from photographs and handwritten copies to oral testimony of a witness whose credibility is suspect. Of course, the opponent may attack the sufficiency of the secondary evidence including the credibility of the witness. This attack, however, goes not to admissibility but to the weight of the evidence and is a matter for the trier of fact to resolve.

While a rule establishing a hierarchy of secondary evidence may appear a natural complement of a "best evidence" rule, such a requirement was rejected because it is difficult to apply, and tactical factors ensure that the parties produce the best available evidence. Parties are naturally motivated to produce the best available evidence for fear of inferences the triers of fact might draw from their failure to do so; under the Federal Rules the trial judge has significant latitude to comment on the evidence (Standard 107)[2] and to amplify the questioning of witnesses (Rule 614), and discovery and pretrial procedures enable the opponent to discover what type of secondary evidence the proponent has in his possession. In the case of public records where the utmost accuracy is required and the originals cannot be produced without disruptive effects on public business, Rule 1005 sets forth special requirements for secondary evidence. See ¶ 9.04 *infra*.

¶ 9.03[02]   Original Lost or Destroyed—Rule 1004(1)[3]

Rule 1004(1) follows long recognized state and federal practice by providing that the non-fraudulent loss or destruction

---

[2] Quercia v. United States, 289 U.S. 466 (1933) ("The privilege of the judge to comment on the facts has its inherent limitations. . . . In commenting upon testimony he may not assume the role of a witness. He may analyze and dissect the evidence, but he may not either distort it or add to it. . . . [a]n expression of opinion upon the evidence 'should be so given as not to mislead, and especially that it should not be one sided.' ").

[3] *See* **Treatise** at ¶¶ 1004(1)[01]–[05].

of an "original" creates a basis for the admission of secondary evidence.[4] By limiting the exclusion of secondary evidence to cases involving bad faith, the rule rejects the notion that any intentional destruction by the proponent bars the admissibility of secondary evidence.[5] The Rule excludes secondary evidence when the loss of the original can be attributed to the proponent's bad faith. There is then too great a risk that any secondary evidence that the proponent might offer would be false or misleading. A proponent offering secondary evidence to prove the content of a lost or destroyed original has the burden of proving absence of bad faith. To satisfy this burden, the proponent must account for the loss or destruction of the absent document. Direct evidence of the destruction of the original will usually not be available except in those cases in which the proponent was responsible. A diligent search is required if the destruction of the document is in doubt.

While some courts have attempted to lay down strict rules as to what constitutes a diligent search, the better reasoned decisions have recognized that the sufficiency depends upon the circumstances. Loss of a deed may require turning the house upside down while loss of an easily replaced doctor's bill requires only turning a desk drawer over. The courts consider

---

[4] United States v. Shoels, 685 F.2d 379, 384 (10th Cir. 1982), *cert. denied,* 462 U.S. 1134 (1983) (prosecution could introduce photographs of checks taken by FBI when original checks were stolen and no bad faith shown); United States v. Cambindo Valencia, 609 F.2d 603, 633 (2d Cir. 1979), *cert. denied,* 446 U.S. 940 (1980). Diplomat Homes, Inc. v. Commercial Standard Ins. Co., 394 F. Supp. 558, 566 (W.D. Mo. 1975).

[5] Estate of Gryder v. CIR, 705 F.2d 336, 338 (8th Cir.), *cert. denied,* 464 U.S. 1008 (1983) (because originals were destroyed by Internal Revenue Service "negligently but not in bad faith," contents could be proved by secondary evidence); United States v. Balzano, 687 F.2d 6, 8 (1st Cir. 1982) (duplicate of tape admissible where tape was knowingly erased by government in order to transfer tape to cassette capable of audio replay and appellant made no allegation of bad faith nor was there any evidence thereof and government made extensive showing of mechanics of original recording and transcription); United States v. Conry, 631 F.2d 599, 600 (9th Cir. 1980) (where government's suit to collect taxes would be barred by statute of limitations unless government could establish that taxpayers had executed waiver extending limitation period, and waiver had been destroyed pursuant to standard IRS procedures, proof of the contents of waiver through circumstantial evidence was appropriate pursuant to Rule 1004).

the following factors: (1) any circumstances suggesting fraud on the proponent's part; (2) the importance of the document and; (3) the age of the instrument. In addition, courts should consider the character of the document in question. It may be such that an inference of loss or destruction is so highly likely that a search will be excused or the degree of diligence required greatly minimized.[6] Good faith destruction may also be assumed when the proponent can demonstrate that the original was destroyed pursuant to a routine business practice.

In addition to accounting for the absence of the original, the proponent must authenticate the absent document. Before proof of contents can be admitted, the court should be satisfied that a reasonable juror could find the existence and due execution of the original in the same manner as if the original were produced. See discussion of authentication requirements in Chapter 8 *supra*.

¶ 9.03[03]   Original Not Obtainable—Rule 1004(2)[7]

Rule 1004(2) is in accord with prevailing practice in excusing production of the original if it cannot "be obtained by an available judicial process or procedure."[8] The rationale is obvious: if the original cannot be obtained by either party or court it is as inaccessible as though it had been lost or destroyed. The need for relevant evidence takes precedence over the dangers of inaccuracy and fraud—issues left to the trier in assessing probative force—and allows the admission of secondary evidence.

While the rule is written in absolute terms, the courts are afforded a good deal of discretion to use common sense. *See, e.g.,* Rule 102. For example, it would be ludicrous to force a litigant to expend thousands of dollars to obtain a document

---

[6] United States v. Carroll, 860 F.2d 500, 507–08 (1st Cir. 1988) (where originals of checks were either lost or destroyed but not by proponent, microfilm prints of checks were admissible).

[7] *See* **Treatise** at ¶ 1004(2)[01].

[8] United States v. Benedict, 647 F.2d 928, 933 (9th Cir.), *cert. denied,* 454 U.S. 1087 (1981) (testimony by DEA agents as to business records in Thailand).

from abroad when $10,000 or so is at stake. The phrase "to the extent practicable and reasonable" should be read into the rule. In most instances the court can exercise its good offices at the pretrial conference to avoid making the litigation prohibitively expensive. This is a particularly important matter when a defendant in a criminal case finds it difficult to obtain an original.

The main difficulty with this exception to the best evidence requirement is determining the extent of the showing that must be made to demonstrate that resort to judicial process is ineffective. If the original is in the possession of the party against whom it is offered, the proponent need only show notice pursuant to Rule 1004(3) *infra,* rather than resort to process. If the original is within the possession of a third party within the jurisdiction of the court, service of a subpoena duces tecum would itself constitute a sufficient showing.[9] If the original is possessed by a person who is in the United States but outside of the court's jurisdiction, proof of service of an order to produce the original at a deposition should suffice to fulfill the condition of Rule 1004(2).

Where the person who has possession of the document is outside the United States, the proponent must convince the court that no available practicable judicial process or procedure will bring forth the original. Procedures do exist for the production of documents in foreign countries. Does this mean that parties must invoke these procedures to prove compliance with Rule 1004(2) even if they know that such efforts will be fruitless because the particular country in which the item is sought will not cooperate? Certainly, if the fact of non-cooperation is so well known that a court would take judicial notice thereof, no further showing should be required. Otherwise, the court might wish to insist upon a letter from the State Department or possibly a representation of counsel that efforts to secure

---

[9] United States v. Taylor, 648 F.2d 565, 570 (9th Cir.), *cert. denied,* 454 U.S. 866 (1981) (trial court did not err in admitting photocopy of crucial letter where government represented that subpoenas requesting the original letter had been served on the parties and the original was not produced, and defendant's counsel failed to object to admission of copy).

cooperation with the judicial machinery of the United States are unavailing in the country involved.[10]

In criminal cases, because of the narrow scope of discovery, much less of a showing will ordinarily have to be made to convince the court that material outside the subpoena jurisdiction of the court cannot be obtained.

Privileged material is not subject to discovery,[11] and will not be produced subject to subpoena. A claim of privilege is sufficient to excuse production of the original.

¶ 9.03[04] Original in Possession of Opponent—Rule 1004(3)[12]

Production of an original is excused if a party in possession of the item fails to produce it upon demand. The sufficiency of the proof of possession is a preliminary question for the judge to be determined pursuant to Rule 1008. Notice implies a mere request without compulsive force. If the proponent actually requires the original, his remedy is resort to discovery procedures or a subpoena duces tecum. The purpose of Rule 1004(3) is to excuse production of the original not to compel it.

Rule 1004(3), apart from stating that notice may be given by the pleadings, is silent as to other methods of notification. Notice by the pleadings is given by implication, where it is clear from the pleadings the contents of a document are essential to proof of the case.

Rule 1004(3) does not provide for any exceptions under which notice is unnecessary before secondary evidence of the original in the opponent's control may be used. Thus, although there have been some traditional exceptions dispensing with the need for notice when the opponent has fraudulently

---

[10] *But cf.* United States v. Ratliff, 623 F.2d 1293, 1296–97 (8th Cir.), *cert. denied,* 449 U.S. 876 (1980) (trial court assumed it had no subpoena power over documents in Germany; in absence of demonstration, appellate court did not find court's finding to be clearly erroneous).

[11] Rule 26(b)(1) of the Federal Rules of Civil Procedure.

[12] *See* **Treatise** at ¶ 1004(3)[01].

suppressed the original or the original is itself a notice, the proper course under Rule 1004(3) is to notify the opponent in any case.

Notification is also required by Rule 1004(3) when the original sought is in the hands of the accused in a criminal prosecution. Ordinarily notice should be given before trial, and specific notice may be excused if defendant is put on notice by the indictment that the contents of a particular document will be a subject of proof. Certainly, notice may not be given in the presence of the jury as this would amount to a derogation of the accused's privilege against self-incrimination. The requirement of Rule 1004(3) is merely intended to give defendant the opportunity to produce the original before secondary evidence can be used.

¶ 9.03[05] Collateral Matters—Rule 1004(4)[13]

Rule 1004(4) recognizes the exception commonly found in American jurisdictions for so-called collateral matters. This provision—which eliminates the need for an original when the document is only tangentially related to the material issues in the case—promotes efficiency and gives the trial judge discretion to apply the best evidence rule flexibly rather than over-technically. Although the term "collateral" is elusive and vague and few cases discuss the exception, Rule 1004(4) is useful as another vehicle for the exercise of common sense since it recognizes that the cost of producing an original may greatly outweigh the importance of the document and the financial capacity of the litigant.

¶ 9.04 Public Records Exceptions—Rule 1005[1]

Rule 1005 creates a limited exception to the best evidence rule. The Rule states:

---

[13] *See* **Treatise** at ¶ 1004(4)[01].

[1] *See* **Treatise** at ¶¶ 1005[01]–[06].

Rule 1005

PUBLIC RECORDS

The contents of an official record, or of a document authorized to be recorded or filed and actually recorded or filed, including data compilations in any form, if otherwise admissible, may be proved by copy, certified as correct in accordance with rule 902 or testified to be correct by a witness who has compared it with the original. If a copy which complies with the foregoing cannot be obtained by the exercise of reasonable diligence, then other evidence of the contents may be given.

Rule 1005 is concerned with copies of two kinds of public[2] records: (1) official records—normally records produced by a government employee—and (2) documents authorized to be recorded or filed—normally those produced by private persons. The Rule departs from Article X's rejection of the concept of degrees of secondary evidence and establishes a hierarchy of secondary methods for proving the content of public records. A copy can be used to prove the terms of the original if it is (1) certified in accordance with Rule 902(4) or (2) a witness attests that he has favorably compared the copy to the original.[3] Other secondary evidence is admissible to prove the terms of a public record only if a preferred copy "cannot be obtained by the exercise of reasonable diligence." Before other secondary evidence can be admitted the terms of Rule 1002 must be satisfied. Thus only if both the original and a Rule 1005 copy are unavailable may other evidence be used. Rule 1005 also does not specify what constitutes "other" evidence. Beyond the certified and compared copies which are mentioned in Rule 1005, the remaining general types of secondary evidence are: duplicates, copies which are uncertified or uncompared, oral

---

[2] An official record does not have to be available to the public. The Advisory Committee on Evidence, while it could have, deliberately chose not to strike "official record" and substitute a "record kept in a public office and available to public inspection."

[3] United States v. Rodriguez, 524 F.2d 485, 488 n.6 (5th Cir. 1975), *cert. denied,* 424 U.S. 972 (1976) (agent testified that he made Xerox copy of vehicle certificate of title; although he was not specifically asked whether it was a "correct" copy, failure to indicate otherwise was sufficient to satisfy Rule 1005).

testimony with memory refreshed by a previously written memorandum, and unrefreshed oral testimony.

Rule 1005 is designed to prevent the loss and damage of public records and to permit public business to be conducted with a minimum of inconvenience to those who use records. Requiring the original to be provided would deprive the public of the record while it was in court. Compared or certified copies are preferred because they are easily obtained and the persuasive nature of public records makes some degree of protection against fraud desirable.

The preference for compared or certified copies results in the preemption of Rule 1003 which in the non-public record context allows copies that were produced by a method insuring accuracy to be used to the same extent as originals. Yet some flexibility in being sensible about proof of public documents is permitted by Rule 1002 despite the apparent rigidity of Rule 1005. There is no inconsistency between Rule 1005, on the one hand, and Rules 1001, 1002, 1004, 1006, 1007 and 1008 on the other. Under any of these rules admissibility of a copy of an original not on file is permitted even though there may also be a copy on file as a public record. For example, deeds are often recorded and a photostat is kept in the public file. The original is returned to the owner. The contents of the original in the hands of the owner may be proved in any way permitted by Article X. Alternatively, Rule 1005 can be used to prove the contents of the deed even if the original is still extant. If, however, what is sought to be proved is the contents of the deed actually on file, then Rule 1005 must be followed because the original, for this purpose, will be considered the document on file. If there is a question about whether the deed on file was the one actually recorded, then the original in the hands of the owner—or a duplicate or copy when authorized by the rules—as well as the authenticated copy of the public record may be required.[4] In cases of serious dispute, the court is

---

[4] Amoco Prod. Co. v. United States, 619 F.2d 1383, 1390 (10th Cir. 1980) (in action to quiet title where there was dispute as to whether recorded deed accurately reflected original deed apparently no longer in existence, error for trial court to apply Rule 1005 to exclude all other evidence of the contents of the deed; original deed is not a public record and Rule 1004 rather than Rule 1005 applies to it).

justified in ordering the file of the public office produced in court, taking care to minimize inconvenience by returning the records as soon as possible.

These terms ought to be given the broadest possible interpretation for purposes of Rule 1005.[5] If not, the governmental agency will be disrupted by the necessity of bringing its original records to court instead of furnishing a certified copy. It is, after all, not the accuracy of the copy that is really being contested in most instances but the admissibility of contents. The main issue as to admissibility normally involves hearsay or relevancy rather than best evidence issues where public records are involved.

¶ 9.05 Summaries—Rule 1006

¶ 9.05[01] Scope[1]

Rule 1006 provides that the contents of voluminous writings, recordings, or photographs may be proven by secondary evidence in the form of charts, summaries, or calculations. The Rule states:

Rule 1006

SUMMARIES

The contents of voluminous writings, recordings, or photographs which cannot conveniently be examined in court may be presented in the form of a chart, summary, or calculation. The originals, or duplicates, shall be made available for examination or copying, or both, by other parties at [a] reasonable time and place. The court may order that they be produced in court.

Rule 1006 is premised on the theory that charts, summaries, or calculations are not only a convenient means of proving the

---

[5] United States v. Tombrello, 666 F.2d 485, 491–92 (10th Cir.), *cert. denied,* 456 U.S. 994 (1982) (certified exemplified copies of docket entries from state court were admissible pursuant to Rule 1005); Seese v. Volkswagenwerk A.G., 648 F.2d 833, 845 (3d Cir.), *cert. denied,* 454 U.S. 867 (1981) (computer printouts of fatal accidents maintained by National Highway Traffic and Safety Administration admissible as public records).

[1] *See* **Treatise** at ¶¶ 1006[01]–[02], [04].

contents of voluminous materials, but sometimes the only practicable method of doing so.[2] Materials admitted pursuant to Rule 1006 constitute the evidence of the contents of the writings or recordings sought to be proved. Whether or not the originals are introduced at the trial, the summaries may be relied upon as evidence in chief. The rule differs conceptually from other aspects of the best evidence rule in that charts, summaries, or calculations are introduced under Rule 1006 as other evidence of materials available to all parties rather than as other evidence of materials which are lost, destroyed, or otherwise unavailable. The jury need not see the originals, but they must be made available to the other parties.[3] Instances where summaries are utilized without reliance on Rule 1006 are discussed below.

Rule 1006 requires that the original or duplicate writings, recordings, or photographs be made available for examination or copying by other parties at a reasonable time and place. This provision acts as a condition precedent which must be fulfilled before a summary, chart, or calculation may be admitted as evidence. Rule 1006 does not give the judge discretionary power to waive this condition.[4] Implicit in this requirement is

[2] United States v. Shirley, 884 F.2d 1130, 1133 (9th Cir. 1989) ("summary evidence . . . 'can help the jury organize and evaluate evidence which is factually complex and fragmentally revealed in the testimony of the multitude of witnesses' "); United States v. Campbell, 845 F.2d 1374, 1381 (6th Cir.), *cert. denied,* 488 U.S. 908 (1988) (trial court did not err in admitting summary chart based on 36 patient files already admitted into evidence; jury would otherwise have had to review hundreds of pages of technical data); United States v. Stephens, 779 F.2d 232, 239 (5th Cir. 1985) (the documents need not be so voluminous that examination in court is impracticable; summary charts may be admitted as a more convenient method of accessing evidence already admitted).

[3] *See* Zayre Corp. v. S.M. & R. Co., 882 F.2d 1145, 1148–49 (7th Cir. 1989) (offer to make originals available for review at stores around country may have been inadequate but, absent objection, was adequate compliance with Rule 1006).

[4] *But cf.* Stich v. United States, 730 F.2d 115, 119 (3d Cir.), *cert. denied,* 469 U.S. 917 (1984) (plaintiff had no access to the data underlying a "table" or statistical summary relied on by expert in testifying; however, as plaintiff did not object to admission of said table into evidence at trial, the appellate court would not find error in its admission in the absence of a specific timely objection by plaintiff under Rule 103).

the opposing party's right to adequate time for the examination of the underlying documents in order to prepare a defense or challenge the accuracy of the summary. The problem of surprise should be minimized by the appropriate use of discovery procedures and pretrial hearings.

The final sentence of Rule 1006 gives the judge discretion to compel the production in court of the original or duplicate materials on which the chart, summary, or calculation is based.[5] For example, the originals may be needed when an opponent wishes to establish inaccuracies in the summary, or when he intends to challenge the authenticity, accuracy or admissibility of the originals.

¶ 9.05[02]   Admissibility[1]

Before the charts, summaries, or calculations may be submitted to the jury pursuant to Rule 1006, the court must find that there is a sufficient factual basis for admitting them and that possible prejudice or confusion does not outweigh their usefulness in clarifying the evidence. See discussion of Rules 401 and 403 in Chapter 6 *supra*.

Charts, summaries, or calculations are inadmissible, if, for any reason, the materials on which they are based are inadmissible.[2] Consequently, unless the parties are willing to stipulate to the admissibility of the underlying documents, the party offering the exhibit must lay a foundation enabling the court

---

[5] *See* United States v. Smyth, 556 F.2d 1179, 1184 n.11 (5th Cir.), *cert. denied,* 434 U.S. 862 (1977) (implicit in Rule 1006 is the notion that the trial judge may choose to admit the underlying documents in evidence).

[1] *See* **Treatise** at ¶ 1006[03].

[2] *See* United States v. Seelig, 622 F.2d 207, 215 (6th Cir.), *cert. denied,* 449 U.S. 869 (1980) (admission of chart purporting to summarize sales activities at other drugstores constituted reversible error because no showing that sales at other stores were comparable and, accordingly, relevant); United States v. Conlin, 551 F.2d 534, 538–39 (2d Cir.), *cert. denied,* 434 U.S. 831 (1977) (error for trial judge to have admitted summary based on information about which court had refused to allow witnesses to testify); Boyd v. Ozark Air Lines, Inc., 419 F. Supp. 1061, 1065 (E.D. Mo. 1976), *aff'd,* 568 F.2d 50 (8th Cir. 1977) (charts based on exhibits which were refused at trial are not admissible pursuant to Rule 1006).

to determine that the original or duplicate materials on which the exhibit is based are admissible. A chart, summary, or calculation is inadmissible if it is based on inadmissible hearsay,[3] on privileged matter, or on materials made inadmissible by the constitutional protection against self-incrimination. Nor will the summary satisfy Rule 1006 if it contains information not present in, or computed from, the original or duplicate materials on which it is based. This latter situation may arise if the preparer of the summary incorporates information drawn from his personal knowledge of the organization whose books he is summarizing, or statements made to him by knowledgeable persons to whom he has spoken in the process of preparing the exhibit.[4] Almost never will an exhibit prepared by an expert be excluded, since the expert will testify that the basis complies with Rule 703. See discussion in Chapter 13.

¶ 9.05[03] Preparation and Authentication of Summaries[1]

Rule 1006 does not require that charts, summaries, or calculations be prepared by persons with special expertise, although practical considerations may dictate the necessity of having technicians prepare the exhibits. Nor does Rule 1006 expressly require that summaries, charts, or calculations be authenticated on the witness stand by the person responsible for their

---

[3] Paddack v. Dave Christensen, Inc., 745 F.2d 1254, 1259–60 (9th Cir. 1984) (summary not admissible where it was impossible to separate the admissible and inadmissible hearsay on which it was based); United States v. Goss, 650 F.2d 1336, 1344 n.5 (5th Cir. 1981) (Rule 1006 does not authorize the admission of summaries of the testimony of out-of-court witnesses; error to allow agent to testify as a "summary witness" that checks were mailed based on his interviews with witnesses).

[4] *Cf.* United States v. Jennings, 724 F.2d 436, 441–42 (5th Cir. 1984), *cert. denied,* 467 U.S. 1227 (1984) (although conclusions in summary charts were based on assumptions by government, no error in admitting charts where assumptions were explored in cross-examination and jury was instructed to give charts their appropriate weight; court noted that the nexus between the summary and the supporting evidence was "close to being as attenuated as should be allowed . . . and that . . . the trial court's ruling approached the limits of its discretion.").

[1] *See* **Treatise** at ¶ 1006[06].

preparation. As a practical matter it would be very difficult to authenticate any exhibit being offered pursuant to Rule 1006, or to establish its accuracy, without calling as a witness the person who supervised its preparation.[2] Courts have facilitated the authentication process by allowing supervisory personnel to attest to the authenticity and accuracy of charts, summaries, or calculations in situations where many individuals, computers or other machines are used in the production of the exhibit.

A chart, summary, or calculation offered as evidence in civil cases without the testimony of the person responsible for its preparation should not be objectionable as violating the hearsay rule. Availability of the original or duplicate material on which the exhibit was based should adequately substitute for the absence of the person responsible for the exhibit's preparation. Failure by such person to testify where the chart, summary, or calculation is offered as evidence against a criminal defendant would raise the question of whether the defendant's constitutional right to confrontation is violated. As a tactical matter, it is almost inconceivable that a prosecutor would not use a witness to explain a chart unless the defendant stipulated to its admission in evidence.

¶ 9.05[04] Summaries Utilized Without Reliance on Rule 1006[1]

[a] Summaries as Evidence

The provisions and considerations of Rule 1006 are inapplicable to charts, summaries, and calculations admitted as evidence under Rule 1001(3), 1004 and 1005. Where the summary is printed by a computer and reflects data in the computer, the printout may be the original itself. Provided the requirements of Rule 1004 are fulfilled, charts, summaries, or calculations are admissible as other evidence of the contents of unavailable originals. Charts, summaries, and calculations are additionally

---

[2] United States v. Scales, 594 F.2d 558, 563 (6th Cir.), *cert. denied,* 441 U. S. 946 (1979) (person who supervised compilation of summary was the proper person to attest to authenticity and accuracy of chart).

[1] *See* **Treatise** at ¶¶ 1006[05], [07].

admissible to prove the contents of public records, provided the requirements of Rule 1005 are satisfied.

A more complicated situation exists where some portion of the original or duplicate materials on which a chart, summary, or calculation is based are produced, but where the balance of such materials is unavailable. The chart, summary, or calculation may then be admissible as other evidence of the contents of the unavailable original or duplicate materials under Rules 1004 and 1005, and also admissible as a summary of available materials under Rule 1006. All of the provisions and considerations of Rule 1006 are applicable to those elements of the chart, summary, or calculation which are based on unavailable original or duplicate materials, and which serve as other evidence of their contents under Rule 1004 and 1005.

[b] Summaries as Pedagogical Devices

Care must be taken to distinguish between the use of summaries or charts as evidence pursuant to Rule 1006, and the use of summaries, charts or other aids as pedagogical devices to summarize or organize testimony for documents which have themselves been admitted in evidence.[2] Courts permit the use of this latter type of exhibit as an aid to the fact-finder in cases involving complicated or voluminous evidence, provided that it does not mislead the jury by unfairly emphasizing parts of the proponent's proof or creating the impression that the facts

---

[2] Some courts have erroneously interpreted Rule 1006 to apply to such summaries and charts. *See, e.g.,* United States v. Nivica, 887 F.2d 1110, 1125–26 (1st Cir. 1989), *cert. denied,* 110 S. Ct. 1300 (1990); Gomez v. Great Lakes Steel Div., 803 F.2d 250, 257 6th Cir. 1986 (explaining difference between summaries admitted pursuant to Rule 1006 and pedagogical devices); United States v. Means, 695 F.2d 811 (5th Cir. 1983); United States v. Scales, 594 F.2d 558 (6th Cir. 1978), *cert. denied,* 441 U.S. 946 (1979); United States v. Evans, 572 F.2d 455, 491–92 (5th Cir. 1978), *cert. denied,* 439 U.S. 870 (1979). Some of these courts at the same time have recognized that these types of summaries may not be used as evidence. *See, e.g.,* United States v. Evans, 572 F.2d 455, 492 (5th Cir. 1978), *cert. denied,* 439 U.S. (1979) (no error in using testimony and charts summarizing evidence admitted at trial where trial court instructed jury that charts and summaries were not evidence; summaries admissible pursuant to Rule 1006).

underlying the summary or chart, if disputed, have been conclusively established.[3]

It should be made clear, through limiting instructions, that these pedagogical devices, unlike Rule 1006 summaries, are not evidence, but only the proponent's organization of the evidence presented.[4] They should be shown to opposing counsel and approved by the court or by stipulation before they are unveiled before the jury and should not be allowed into the jury room without the consent of all parties since they are more akin to argument than evidence.[5]

---

[3] *See, e.g.,* Holland v. United States, 348 U.S. 121, 128 (1954) (admonition against allowing summary charts into jury room, without limiting instructions, because "bare figures have a way of acquiring an existence of their own, independent of the evidence which gave rise to them."); United States v. Gardner, 611 F.2d 770, 776 (9th Cir. 1980) (tax evasion case; court rejects defendant's claim that use of chart summarizing his assets, liabilities and expenditures was unduly prejudicial; chart was "summary of facts and calculations which were in evidence . . . the use of the chart contributed to the clarity of the presentation to the jury, avoided needless consumption of time and was a reasonable method of presenting the evidence"; no error to ultimately admit chart as evidence pursuant to Rule 1006). *See also* United States v. Soulard, 730 F.2d 1292, 1300 (9th Cir. 1984).

[4] *See, e.g.,* United States v. Possick, 849 F.2d 332, 339 (8th Cir. 1988) (submission of purely demonstrative charts to jury during deliberations is disfavored; submission without limiting instructions was error, but harmless; cites **Treatise**); Gomez v. Great Lakes Steel Div., 803 F.2d 250, 257 (6th Cir. 1986) (error to admit plaintiff's "summary of actual damages" in employment discrimination suit without a limiting instruction; court held that the "summary" was merely a pedagogical device because the chart included predictions of future events and assumptions of unproven facts; citing **Treatise**); United States v. Evans, 572 F.2d 455, *reh. denied,* 576 F.2d 931 (5th Cir. 1978), *cert. denied,* 439 U.S. 870 (1979) (no error in admitting testimony of FBI agent summarizing evidence admitted at trial, using charts; "The record . . . establishes that the court properly charged the jury that the charts and summaries were not evidence, and their purpose was merely explanatory. The jury was instructed to disregard any summaries not comporting with the evidence"); United States v. Abbas, 504 F.2d 123, 125, *cert. denied,* 421 U.S. 988 (1975) (trial court should have marked charts for identification and allowed them to be used as testimonial aid or as visual summary of complex facts, but should not have allowed charts to go to jury; however, in view of court's instruction that exhibits were explanation of other evidence and not proof per se, admitted as a matter of convenience, and may be disregarded by jury if not accurate summaries; no prejudice).

[5] *See* United States v. Gardner, 611 F.2d 770, 776 n.3 (9th Cir. 1980) (better practice is not to submit charts summarizing admitted evidence to

Usually these pedagogical devices are introduced through an expert, such as an accountant or FBI agent. When utilized by an expert in explaining his opinion, they should be considered part of his testimony pursuant to Rules 702 and 703, and they may then be exhibited to the jury if the relevant testimony is read to the jury during its deliberations. Sometimes they are used in summations even when not referred to earlier by a witness.

¶ 9.06   Proof of Contents Through Testimonial or Written Admissions of Adverse Party—Rule 1007 [1]

Rule 1007 permits a party to prove the contents of an original by introducing evidence of an adverse party's testimony, deposition, or written admission, including answers to interrogatories and requests to admit. An adverse party's oral admission cannot be used pursuant to this Rule. The rule states:

Rule 1007

TESTIMONY OR WRITTEN ADMISSION OF PARTY

Contents of writings, recordings, or photographs may be proved by the testimony or deposition of the party against whom offered or by that party's written admission, without accounting for the nonproduction of the original.

Rule 1007 operates as an exception to Rule 1002 because it does not require a showing that the original material is lost, destroyed, or otherwise unavailable. When original materials are lost, destroyed, or unavailable, or constitute non-producible public records, a party may offer an adverse party's admissions of contents—even if oral and not made in a deposition or testimony—as other evidence of contents under Rule 1004 or Rule 1005. In such a case, the provisions and considerations of Rule 1007 are inapplicable. The distinction between use of an adverse party's admissions as proof of contents under Rule

---

jury; but no reversible error here, where chart did go to jury). *See also* United States v. Soulard, 730 F.2d 1292, 1300 (9th Cir. 1984) (Ninth Circuit's requirements for admitting summaries).

[1] *See* **Treatise** at ¶¶ 1007[01]–[05].

1007 and Rules 1004 and 1005 is important because an adverse party's oral extrajudicial admissions are acceptable evidence of contents when offered in place of absent original materials under Rules 1004 and 1005.

Rule 1007 is a rule of convenience which permits a party to use an adversary's admissions to prove contents of a writing, recording, or photograph in lieu of the more time-consuming process of introducing and authenticating the original material. Admissions by an adverse party are considered acceptable proof of contents because it is assumed that such admissions— usually, but not always against interest—will be accurate and honest. The purpose of the restriction in Rule 1007 limiting admissibility of an adverse party's oral admissions to those delivered as "testimony" is to protect the party against being misquoted or quoted out of context. Since a party's admission is assumed to be true, it is not necessary to require that the "testimony" be delivered under oath in order to prove contents. A guarantee of the accuracy of the report of what was admitted would exist where the statement is part of a transcript made at an official, but non-judicial hearing, such as one conducted by a legislative committee. It would also include grand jury testimony which is transcribed. Similarly, the term "written admission" as used in Rule 1007 should be interpreted to include any statement, including one made in a private conversation, that can be guaranteed to be accurately and completely recorded. A statement by an adverse party which is captured verbatim by a tape recorder or other recording process and which is introduced unedited should also suffice to satisfy the "writing" requirement of Rule 1007.

Use of an adverse party's admissions to prove contents should not be confused with use of an adverse party's admission to directly establish a fact also evidenced by a writing, recording, or photograph. In the latter situation, both admissions by the adverse party and documentary material are primary evidence. Where a criminal defendant admits the commission of a crime and subsequently confesses in writing to his act, the oral admission and written confession are both primary evidence that the defendant committed the act. Or, where a defendant to a charge of negligence admits negligence and also fills out an accident report containing statements which establish his negligence, both items are primary evidence of negligence. Where, however, the defendant fills out an accident report and subsequently admits the genuineness of such report and states what its contents are, his admissions as to contents are only other evidence of the report's contents so that Rule 1007 applies. In situations where an adverse party's admission is introduced as other evidence of contents, the provisions and considerations of Rules 1002 and 1007 apply. Use of admissions as evidence-in-chief is governed by Rule 801(d)(2).

Since the theory behind the rule rests on the reliability of admissions (see discussion of the hearsay rule in Chapter 15 *infra*), admissions given in a representative capacity should qualify to the same extent as provided in Rule 801(d)(2).

CHAPTER 10

Witnesses Generally

SYNOPSIS

(Pub.819)

¶ 10.01   General Rules of Competency—Rule 601

¶ 10.01[01]   Scope[1]

Under Rule 601, two standards of competency apply in federal courts. In civil cases where state law furnishes the rule of decision, state restrictions on competency govern. In criminal cases, and in civil cases where state law does not furnish the rule of decision, all persons—other than the presiding judge (Rule 605), or a member of the jury hearing the case (Rule 606)—will be competent to testify as ordinary witnesses unless they have no personal knowledge of the events to which they seek to testify (Rule 602), or refuse to declare that they will testify truthfully (Rule 603). The rule states:

Rule 601

GENERAL RULE OF COMPETENCY

Every person is competent to be a witness except as otherwise provided in these rules. However, in civil actions and proceedings, with respect to an element of a claim or defense as to which State law supplies the rule of decision, the competency of a witness shall be determined in accordance with State law.

Under the Federal Rules, except where State law furnishes the rule of decision, most grounds for automatically disqualifying a witness have been abolished, and converted into grounds for impeaching a witness.[2] Conviction of crime as a ground for impeaching a witness is treated in Rule 609. Evidence of bias, lack of mental capacity, and infancy is not afforded special treatment in the rules but is highly relevant and will be admissible as bearing on credibility.[3] Rule 610 assures that evidence of religious belief may not be used to impeach.

---

[1] See **Treatise** at ¶ 601[01]–[04].

[2] United States v. Villaita, 662 F.2d 1205 (5th Cir. 1981), *cert. denied*, 456 U.S. 916 (1982) (error for trial judge to rule witness incompetent as to matters which transpired in Spanish on the ground that his knowledge of Spanish was insufficient; credibility of witness' testimony as to Spanish conversations with defendant is subject to cross-examination and expert's opinion about his ability is admissible; jury will also be able to hear taped conversations between witness and defendant).

[3] United States v. Abel, 469 U.S. 45, 105 S.Ct. 465, 83 L.Ed.2d 450 (1984) ("it

A preliminary examination pursuant to Rule 104(a) for the purpose of determining competency is usually not required.[4] This does not mean, however, that the trial judge no longer has any power to keep a witness from testifying. A trial judge still has broad discretion to control the course of a trial (Rule 611) and to rule on relevancy (Rules 401 and 403). The trial judge may exclude all or part of the witness' testimony on the ground that no one could reasonably believe the witness could have observed, remembered, communicated or told the truth with respect to the event in question,[5] or on Rule 403 grounds that prejudice is greater than the probative force of the testimony. The judge may use the voir dire to make this determination. Particularly difficult

---

is permissible to impeach a witness by showing his bias under the Federal Rules of Evidence just as it was permissible to do so before their adoption").

[4] See, e.g., United States v. Raineri, 91 F.R.D. 159 (W.D. Wis. 1980), aff'd, 670 F.2d 702 (7th Cir. 1982) (defendant made pretrial motion asking for evidentiary hearing before magistrate pursuant to Rule 104 to determine whether prosecution witness was competent, or in the alternative asking court to order witness to undergo psychiatric examination; court concluded that it would be more appropriate to have trial judge conduct preliminary competency hearing or voir dire examination of the witness at the time of the trial, and denied request for psychiatric examination as unnecessary, since defendant already had sufficient information for impeachment, and unwise, since voir dire examinations are preferable).

[5] United States v. Odom, 736 F.2d 104, 109–16 (4th Cir. 1984) (under Rule 601 every witness is presumed to be competent, regardless of mental infirmities, since the question of competency has become one of credibility and jurors are simply to judge the testimony for what it is worth; the only grounds for disqualification, which are to be determined by the court, are when a party does not have knowledge of the matters of which he is to testify, does not have the capacity to recall or does not understand the duty to testify truthfully); United States v. Gutman, 725 F.2d 417, 420 (7th Cir.), cert. denied, 105 S.Ct. 244 (1984) (in prosecution for extortion, trial judge did not abuse discretion by allowing witness with history of mental illness to testify, where psychiatric reports did not suggest witness was incapable of telling truth or appreciating significance of oath; no error in not conditioning witness' testifying on submission to psychiatric examination, where defense already had seven psychiatric reports); United States v. Lightly, 677 F.2d 1027 (4th Cir. 1982) (in prosecution of inmate for assault of fellow inmate, reversible error to have excluded testimony of accomplice who had been found incompetent to stand trial and criminally insane; trial judge had erred in finding that accomplice was incompetent to testify without conducting an in camera examination where testimony of his treating physician indicated that he had sufficient memory, understood the oath and could communicate what he saw).

problems may arise where the witness was or is taking psychotropic medication,[6] is an infant, is brain injured, is an interested attorney, or has had memory affected through hypnotism. In 1987, the Supreme Court in *Rock v. Arkansas,*[7] a 5–4 decision, held that a criminal defendant could not be precluded from testifying in her own behalf on the basis of a *per se* rule excluding a defendant's hypnotically refreshed testimony.[8] "A State's legitimate interest in barring unreliable evidence does not extend to per se exclusions that may be reli-

---

[6] Falwell v. Flynt, 797 F.2d 1270, 1277 (4th Cir. 1986), *rev'd on other grounds,* 108 S.Ct. 1 (1988) (in emotional distress suit, trial court did not abuse its discretion by admitting a damaging video-taped deposition of defendant publisher Larry Flynt even though defendant argued that he was incapable of telling the truth at the time of the deposition due to medication he was taking for a broken leg; incapacity must be so extreme as to fail to meet the relevancy standards of Rules 104(a), 401 and 403; issue raised by Flynt's deposition is one of credibility, not competency); United States v. Hyson, 721 F.2d 856, 863–64 (1st Cir. 1983) (in drug prosecution, trial court did not err in recalling a government witness and advising jury that witness' prior testimony was to be stricken due to the fact that he had taken a drug when testifying which caused acute confusional state; under Rule 601, competency of witness goes to issue of credibility which is for trier of fact; here jury had all facts necessary for reasoned credibility determination of witness' testimony); United States v. Garner, 581 F.2d 481 (5th Cir. 1978) (testimony of a narcotics user is not incredible as a matter of law; use of narcotics goes to witness' credibility not his competency); United States v. Harris, 542 F.2d 1283, 1303 (7th Cir. 1976), *cert. denied sub nom.* Clay v. United States (1977) (on appeal, defendants argued that testimony of witness who was acknowledged heroin addict and who had received heavy dosage of Demerol on eve of his testimony should have been stricken because he was incompetent to testify; appellate court noted that the "facts necessary for the evaluation of the witness' competency were peculiarly within the knowledge of the trial judge," that the witness' competency had not been directly challenged, and that the witness' condition was a matter of credibility for evaluation by the jury); United States v. Van Meerbeke, 548 F.2d 415 (2d Cir. 1976), *cert. denied,* 430 U.S. 974 (1977) (witness who may have taken drug while on stand could testify where jury observed his actions).

[7] — U.S. —, 107 S.Ct. 2704, 97 L.Ed.2d 37 (1987).

[8] The defendant was charged with fatally having shot her husband. After she underwent hypnosis because she could not remember the details of the shooting, she recalled that she had had her finger on the hammer of the pistol, but not on the trigger, and that gun had fired when her husband grabbed her arm. A gun expert testified that the pistol was defective and prone to fire without the trigger being pulled. Defendant was not permitted to testify to her hypnotically refreshed memory of the shooting and was convicted of manslaughter.

able in an individual case." [9] The Court suggested that a state "would be well within its powers if it developed guidelines to aid trial courts in the evaluation of posthypnosis testimony," [10] and that in a given case hypnotically refreshed testimony might be excludable as too unreliable. The majority opinion contemplates a case by case analysis of the proffered testimony. The opinion does not purport to deal with non-party witnesses. [11]

¶ 10.01[02] Children; Brain Injured Persons[1]

The testimony of a plaintiff who suffered brain damage in the accident being sued on and who is one of only two eyewitnesses may perhaps be essential; the testimony of a congenitally brain-damaged child who was one of a number of uninvolved witnesses to an accident may be prejudicial, confusing and probably cumulative and a waste of time if all or some of the other witnesses are in court. Certainly the court has power under Rule 611 to hear the plaintiff and to postpone hearing the child until the other witnesses have testified so that it can better assess whether the testimony is needed. If the child is the only witness, the need for his or her testimony would obviously be much greater. Its high probative value would, in fact, under the rules as written, probably compel admission, subject to challenge by cross-examination and impeachment. The court may instruct the jury to treat such evidence with care (Standard 107) and it may refuse to consider the testimony in deciding whether a prima facie case has been established.

---

[9] — U.S. —, 107 S.Ct. at 2714, 97 L.Ed.2d at 52.

[10] *Id.* at —, 107 S.Ct. 2714, 97 L.Ed.2d at 52.

[11] Beck v. Norris, 801 F.2d 242 (6th Cir. 1986) (habeas corpus denied; good analysis of Tennessee requirements to ensure that hypnotism used to obtain composite sketch of defendant was not suggestive; good procedural protections including videotaping of witness before and during hypnosis). *Compare* United States v. Awkard, 597 F.2d 667 (9th Cir.), *cert. denied,* 444 U.S. 885 (1979) (hypnosis does not render witness incompetent, but expert may not testify that as a result of hypnosis witness will testify truthfully) *with* State *ex rel.* Collins v. Superior Court, 644 P.2d 1266, 1294 (Ariz. 1982) (testimony about posthypnotic memories is per se excludible). Where the basis for a state's denial of use of a hypnotized witness testimony is based upon policy, rather than purely on reliability, the state incompetency rule should be applied with respect to a claim to which State law supplies the rule of decision).

[1] See **Treatise** at ¶ 601[04].

Despite the strong pressure of the rules to compel admissibility of the testimony of any child who might conceivably testify truthfully about an event, the careful attorney for the proponent will bear in mind that federal judges have exercised—albeit frugally—their power to exclude testimony of very young children. Sometimes the child's age at the time of the event or testimony, or the period between the event and the testimony, is such as to make it almost certain the child is parroting what he has heard his elders say about the event. Even if the child can fairly accurately relate what happened shortly after the event, when the case comes to trial a year or more later it is almost hopeless to expect a clear recollection. The child's statement immediately after the event may be reported under one of the exceptions to the hearsay rule. See, *e.g.,* Rules 803(l), (2), (4) and 804(b)(5). In addition, a promptly taken deposition may be useful.

Current research suggests greater reliability than heretofore believed existed in child witnesses, when precautions are taken against suggestibility.[2] Particularly in view of the increase of child abuse cases in the state courts, various techniques have been approved by legislatures and courts for enhancing the conditions under which such testimony is given.[3] It has been proposed that Congress enact Uniform Rule 807 into law.[4] Rule 807 would liberalize the hearsay rule with regard to certain videotaped statements of child victims of sex abuse, and would authorize videotaped or live closed-circuit televised testimony from such a child under certain circumstances. Considerable controversy exists about the desirability of these changes; those opposed fear that it will be too easy to prove a case against an innocent accused.[5] The Supreme Court has held that placing a screen between the defendant and child victims blocking

---

[2] Melton, "Children's Competency to Testify," 5 L. & Human Behav. 73 (1981); Goleman, "Studies of Children as Witnesses Find Surprising Accuracy," N.Y. Times, November 6, 1984, at C1, C4.

[3] *Id.*

[4] See Committee on Federal Legislation, A Proposal for Federal Legislation to Facilitate the Testimony of Child Witnesses, 43 The Record 54 (1988).

[5] See *id.* at 69–71 (separate statement dissenting in part).

(Rel.1–9/88 Pub.819)

defendant from their sight violated the confrontation clause.[6] Two justices would have affirmed the convictions and two justices in a concurring opinion suggested that they might have ruled differently had the victims testified by closed-circuit television.

¶ 10.01[03]   Attorneys[1]

Although the modern trend has been to regard attorneys with a pecuniary interest in the subject of the litigation as competent to testify,[2] federal judges have felt empowered to prevent an attorney from doing so on ethical grounds.[3] One technique—that of conditioning

---

[6] Coy v. Iowa, — U.S. —, 108 S.Ct. —, — L.Ed.2d. — (1988).

[1] See **Treatise** at ¶ 601[04].

[2] United States v. West, 680 F.2d 652, 654–55 (9th Cir. 1982) (assistant U.S. Attorney seated in spectator section properly allowed to testify about alleged signalling between defendant and witness; only other alternate witness was F.B.I. agent seated at counsel's table whose testimony would have presented essentially the same risks; reversal because prosecutor's comments in closing argument concerning credibility of assistant U.S. Attorney constituted impermissible vouching); United States v. Trapnell, 638 F.2d 1016 (7th Cir. 1980) (no error in permitting Assistant U.S. Attorney to testify about a chain of custody of some letters, since this related to a formal uncontested matter, and assertedly testimony could not have been provided by any other witness); Universal Athletic Sales Co. v. American Gym Recreational & Athletic Equipment Corporation, Inc. 546 F.2d 530 (3d Cir. 1976), *cert. denied sub nom.* Super Athletics Corporation v. Universal Athletic Sales Co., 430 U.S. 984 (attorney testified as expert; while testimony may subject attorney to disciplinary action, he is competent to testify).

[3] The giving of material testimony by an attorney for his own client is generally considered to be a breach of professional ethics as well as detrimental to the client's case. See ABA Code of Professional Responsibility DR-5-101, 5-1021; ABA Canons of Professional Ethics No. 19; ABA Code of Professional Responsibility EC 5–9 ("If a lawyer is both counsel and witness, he becomes more easily impeachable for interest and thus becomes a less effective witness. Conversely, the opposing counsel may be handicapped in challenging the credibility of the lawyer when the lawyer also appears as an advocate in the case. An advocate who becomes a witness is in the unseemly and ineffective position of arguing his own credibility. The rules of an advocate and of a witness are inconsistent; the function of an advocate is to advance or argue the cause of another, while that of a witness is to state facts objectively."). But *cf.* United States v. Nyman, 649 F.2d 208, 211 (4th Cir. 1980) (a trial court's discretion as to the competency of an attorney's testimony does not extend to that of nonprofessional employees such as a law clerk investigator; reversible error to exclude such testimony on closely controverted issue of identity of defendant where he raised alibi defense).

the attorney's testimony on withdrawal from the case[4]—presumably
rests on the court's inherent control over attorneys or on the courts'
power to control a trial which is now expressed in Rule 611.[5]

The federal courts have also recognized that forcing or permitting
an attorney to withdraw may have serious repercussions on the trial
in progress.[6] Even where substitution occurs before the trial commences, adjournments and delays often result. In some cases it has
been suggested that the problem can be solved by not permitting the
attorney to testify unless a clear need for his testimony is shown.[7]

A pretrial conference before either a criminal or civil trial is commenced provides a useful means of resolving the problem of forseeable instances where attorneys may be needed as witnesses. Often
the matter can be resolved by stipulations or by calling other witnesses with knowledge of the events. In addition at trial a proffer of proof
(see Rule 103(a)(2)) will often show that the evidence is excludable
under Rule 403. In a bench trial a more relaxed attitude is often warranted. Often, the parties will permit that court to take the attorney's
statement without oath or cross-examination.[8]

---

[4] See, *e.g.,* United States v. Clancy, 276 F.2d 617, 636 (7th Cir. 1960), *rev'd on other
grounds,* 365 U.S. 312 (1961).

[5] See Travellers Insurance Company v. Dykes, 395 F.2d 747, 748–49 (5th Cir. 1968)
(court refused to permit defendant's co-counsel to testify in an attempt to impeach
one of plaintiff's witnesses; appellate court affirmed noting that "Much considered
and wise discretion must be accorded to a district judge as he deals with the infinite
variables of evidence"; testimony was offered to impeach one of plaintiff's witnesses;
no discussion in opinion of importance of witness or of testimony).

[6] See, *e.g.,* United States v. Brown, 417 F.2d 1068 (5th Cir. 1969), *cert. denied,* 397
U.S. 998 (1970) (attorney who wanted to contradict witness he had interviewed was
neither permitted to testify while representing defendant nor allowed to withdraw;
court notes that withdrawal at that stage of trial would have resulted in mistrial.
A change in counsel after trial has commenced rests in the court's discretion). See
United States v. Ellenbogen, 365 F.2d 982, 988–89 (2d Cir. 1966); United States
v. Denno, 348 F.2d 12, 15 (2d Cir. 1965).

[7] United States v. Bates, 600 F.2d 505 (5th Cir. 1979) (court was well within its discretion in not allowing defense counsel to take stand where cross-examination was
used to present the same story the attorney would have told).

[8] Bickford v. John E. Mitchell Co., 595 F.2d 540 (10th Cir. 1979) (not error to allow
attorney to testify in light of the facts that 1) he had not previously participated
in trial; 2) he withdrew from case before testifying; 3) trial to court and not to jury);
Universal Athletic Sales Co. v. American Gym, Recreational & Athletic Equipment

¶ 10.01[04]   Application of State Law Required[1]

In civil cases where state law furnishes the rule of decision, "The competency of the witness [is] determined in accordance with State law." This provision was added to Rule 601 primarily to ensure that Dead Man's Acts would be given effect in cases governed by state law.[2] Dead Man's Acts generally prohibit the party-witness and sometimes other interested persons from testifying to conversations, transactions or other dealings with a decedent or incompetent when the decedent's estate or the incompetent's representative is an adverse party.[3]

Where the Dead Man's Act permits both the interested party's testimony and the decedent's hearsay to be introduced, the effect in civil state-rule-of-decision cases should be to permit hearsay to be introduced which is not admissible under Article VIII of these Rules. In non-state-rule-of-decision cases, testimony rendered competent by Rule 601 will still have to clear the hearsay hurdle. Unlike some state statutes which have specific provisions making statements by a decedent an exception to the hearsay rule, the Federal Rules of Evidence do not cover this situation expressly. The categories in Rules 803

Corp., 546 F.2d 530 (3d Cir. 1976), *cert. denied,* 430 U.S. 984 (1977) (appellate court suggested that in non-jury trial where attorney testified as expert that trial judge could have adjourned the proceedings until defendants selected another expert or another law firm; court further suggested that it would be appropriate to consider incorporating into Federal Rules of Evidence the current disciplinary norm proscribing the testimony of an attorney).

[1] See **Treatise** at ¶ 601[03].

[2] See *e.g.,* Crumley v. Memorial Hospital, Inc., 509 F.Supp. 531 (E.D. Tenn. 1979), *aff'd,* 647 F.2d 164 (6th Cir. 1981) (in medical malpractice action competency of witness governed by state statute). But see McKenzie v. Harris, 679 F.2d 8, 11 & n.8 (3d Cir. 1982) (action seeking Social Security benefits for two children of applicant based on earnings record of deceased wage earner; court, in finding that common law marriage existed between applicant and decedent and that there is presumption of legitimacy for children in absence of overwhelming evidence of nonaccess, stated that under Pennsylvania law neither mother nor husband may testify to non-access and therefore their testimony would be inadmissible in federal court pursuant to Rule 601).

[3] Wagner v. Tucker, 517 F.Supp. 1248 (S.D.N.Y. 1981) (applies N.Y. Dead Man's statute as construed by N.Y. courts); Super Valu Stores, Inc. v. First National Bank of Columbus, Georgia, 463 F.Supp. 1183 (W.D. Ga. 1979) (Georgia's Dead Man's statute applied).

and 804, however, are sufficiently broad to permit a witness, in most instances, to testify to conversations or transactions with a person now dead.

When state law does furnish the rule of decision, Rule 601 does not specifically direct itself to the question of which State's competency rule is to apply. No problem is presented if the case is brought to the federal court of State X and all the operative facts occurred in X. But consider the situation in which an action is brought in X to recover for a wrongful death that occurred in Y. Obviously, state rather than federal law will furnish the rule of decision, and, according to *Klaxon Co. v. Stentor Electric Manufacturing Co.*[4] the federal court should look to the conflict-of-laws rule of X to determine whether X will apply the law of X or the law of Y in regard to wrongful death.

¶ 10.02   Opinion Testimony by Lay Witnesses—Rule 701

¶ 10.02[01]   Scope and Rationale[1]

Rule 701 is a rule of discretion. It replaces the orthodox rule excluding opinion evidence with a rule that requires the trial judge on the basis of the posture of the particular case to decide whether concreteness of detail in reported observations, abstraction, or a combination of both will be most effective in enabling the jury to ascertain the truth and reach a just result. The rule provides:

Rule 701

OPINION TESTIMONY BY LAY WITNESSES

If the witness is not testifying as an expert, the witness' testimony in the form of opinions or inferences is limited to those opinions or inferences which are (a) rationally based on the perception of the witness and (b) helpful to a clear understanding of the witness' testimony or the determination of a fact in issue.

---

[4] 313 U.S. 487, 61 S.Ct. 1020, 85 L.Ed. 1477 (1941).

[1] See **Treatise** at ¶¶ 701[01]–[02].

Like the hearsay and authentication rules, the lay opinion rule is at heart a form of best evidence rule. The orthodox opinion rule,[2] rejected by the drafters of Rule 701, sought to ensure reliability by insisting that witnesses state facts rather than opinions. Although the supposed distinction between facts and opinions was impossible to apply, the rule had a core of sense. It recognized that more

(*Text continued on page 10–11*)

---

[2] See discussion of the history of the opinion rule in **Treatise** at ¶ 701[01].

concrete descriptions are preferable because they are more reliable and because it is the trier's duty to draw inferences from observed data reported to it. The possibility of error probably increases with each level of abstraction by the witness. Requiring specificity exposes flaws in the witness' memory—instead of spouting forth generalities the witness is forced to give a detailed story that can be tested by cross-examination. Misconceptions can be exposed much more readily by examining the raw data on which the witness grounded his conclusion than by challenging the conclusion itself.

Contrary to the orthodox rule, Rule 701 assumes that the witness will give testimony by stating his observations in as raw a form as practicable, but permits resort to inferences and opinions when this form of testimony will be helpful. Rule 701 is in accord with modern trends in conditionally favoring opinions provided two requirements are satisfied: the opinion or inference (1) must be rationally based on the witness' own perception and (2) must be helpful to the trier of fact in the form used.

Through this formulation, Rule 701 seeks to balance the need for relevant evidence against the danger of admitting unreliable testimony. It recognizes that necessity and expedience may dictate receiving opinion evidence, but that a factual account insofar as feasible may further the values of the adversary system.

¶ 10.02[02]   Application[1]

In order to comply with the first requirement of Rule 701—that the opinion be rationally based on the witness' own perception—the testimony must initially pass the personal knowledge requirement of Rule 602 which is incorporated in Rule 701.[2] But even if

---

[1] See **Treatise** at ¶ 701[02].

[2] Joy Mfg. Co. v. Sola Basic Industries, Inc., 697 F.2d 104, 110–12 (3d Cir. 1982) (abuse of discretion for trial court to exclude testimony of plaintiff's supervisor of production control concerning percentage of plaintiff's losses due to hearth problems where witness had extensive personal knowledge of plaintiff's plants and the furnaces in question, and his opinion was rationally based on his personal knowledge; witness' inability to state precisely why a furnace was inoperable at a particular time was proper material for cross-examination rather than for rendering opinion inadmissible).

the witness does have the requisite personal knowledge, any inferences or opinions he expresses must thereafter pass the rational connection and "helpful" tests of Rule 701.

The rational connection test means only that the opinion or inference is one which a normal person would form on the basis of the observed facts. The witness may express the opinion or inference rather than the underlying observations if the expression would be "helpful to a clear understanding of the testimony or the determination of a fact in issue."[3] Sometimes the opinion without the underlying facts would be misleading.[4]

Even under the orthodox rule which sought to exclude all opinion evidence, testimony in the form of opinion was allowed if the witness could not "accurately, adequately and with reasonable facility describe the fundamental facts upon which the opinion is erected."[5] This type of opinion testimony is merely a shorthand

---

[3] *Compare* United States v. Borrelli, 621 F.2d 1092 (10th Cir. 1980), *cert. denied,* 449 U.S. 956 (1980) (admission of defendant's stepfather's testimony regarding defendant's resemblance to subject of bank surveillance photograph not error where defendant lived with stepfather for five years until a few days before robbery and defendant had significantly altered his appearance between robbery and trial making it difficult for jury to compare so that opinion of stepfather was helpful) *with* United States v. Calhoun, 544 F.2d 291, 295 (6th Cir. 1976) (testimony by lay witness acquainted with defendant identifying defendant as robber shown in bank surveillance photographs "teases the outer limits of Rule 701 . . . . Whether this testimony was 'helpful' . . . is not at all clear"; testimony should have been excluded pursuant to Rule 403). See also Young v. Illinois Central Gulf R.R. Co. 618 F.2d 332 (5th Cir. 1980) (in action to recover for wrongful death of decedent when struck by train at railroad crossing which widow claimed was caused in part by condition of crossing, error to have excluded testimony of lay witnesses about their observations of crossing and their impression of its general condition; trial court had excluded evidence because photographs of the crossing had been admitted but appellate court found that non-conflicting evidence which enhances and explains photographic evidence satisfied Rule 701).

[4] United States v. Phillips, 600 F.2d 535 (5th Cir. 1979) (in prosecution arising from defendant's failure to disclose that he was working while receiving social security disability benefits, agent's testimony that defendant "indicated" he "understood the meaning of disability" was insufficient to prove fraudulent intent; testimony did not reveal what defendant had said or done to convince agent he understood meaning of disability and her testimony gave jury no basis for making an independent judgment about defendant's state of mind).

[5] Morgan, *Basic Problems of Evidence* 194 (Weinstein ed. 1976) (relying on Professor John M. Maguire).

rendition of the witness' observations.[6]

But the helpfulness test goes further than allowing inferences and opinions to be expressed only when they are inextricably intertwined with the underlying observations. Rule 701 authorizes the judge to permit the witness to express an opinion when a statement of the underlying facts would be a waste of time. Of course, the judge's determination will depend on the relationship of the opinion to the issues of the case. The closer the subject of the opinion gets to critical issues the likelier the judge is to require the witness to be more concrete, not because of the outmoded ultimate issue doctrine abolished in Rule 704, but because the jury is not sufficiently helped in resolving disputes by testimony which merely tells it what result to reach.

Rule 701 authorizes a witness to testify in terms with which he is familiar rather than in artificial circumlocutions which may cause the jury to miss the point. Many witnesses can clarify what they mean only by sprinkling opinions and inferences among their detailed descriptions. A witness constantly interrupted by objections may lose track of what is being said, and the jury may be too distracted to evaluate the testimony properly. So long as the witness is being sufficiently concrete in the context of the trial, the court should not prohibit the witness from including conclusions unless it finds that they might mislead the jury. Obviously the court, at times, may be unable to determine whether an opinion is based on the witness' perception or is helpful without ascertaining the observed data. In that case the court has power pursuant to Rules 104(a), 611 (a)(l) and 614 (b) to require the witness to state the basis for the opinion. In other cases, where it feels the expression of an opinion could be neither misleading nor prejudicial, it

---

[6] See, *e.g.,* Kerry Coal Co. v. United Mine Workers, 637 F.2d 957, 967 (3d Cir.), *cert. denied,* 454 U.S. 823 (1981) (testimony that plaintiff's employees were "nervous and afraid" merely a shorthand report of witness' observations of employee reactions); Singletary v. Secretary of Health, Education and Welfare, 623 F.2d 217, 219 (2d Cir. 1980) ("the testimony of lay witnesses has always been admissible with regard to drunkenness"); United States v. Arrasmith, 557 F.2d 1093, 1094 (5th Cir. 1977) (not error for trial judge to have permitted border patrol agent to testify that marijuana smells like marijuana; "Describing odors is a task that can severely test the abilities of even the most accomplished wordsmith. Defense counsel remained free, moreover, to pose additional questions requiring the witness to describe the smell in greater detail.").

can be left to the adverse party to develop the basis on cross-examination. Loaded terms such as "stolen," "accident" and "assault " should be avoided by witnesses when they are the very issues to be decided.[7]

A party should not be allowed to prevail on an opinion objection on appeal when the thrust of the witness' testimony was clear and counsel deliberately refrained from asking for a more detailed statement. So long as the witness' statement is based on personal knowledge and might aid the trier of fact, the fact that he expresses qualifications about its accuracy does not convert the testimony into a matter of opinion barred by Rule 701.

In construing Rule 701, the trier will bear in mind that the aim of the rule is to eliminate time-consuming quibbles over objections that would not effect the outcome regardless of how they were decided. The emphasis belongs on what the witness knows and not on how he is expressing himself. The jury can normally be depended upon—with the aid of counsel—to pick up the non-verbal signals absent from the record, indicating fairly clearly to the observer when the witness is describing what he saw and when what he thinks happened.

One of the consequences of the liberalization of the lay witness rule has been to blur rigid distinctions that existed between lay witnesses and expert witnesses. As the discussion of Rule 702 in Chapter 13, *infra,* indicates, some issues are viewed as requiring expert testimony as a matter of substantive law. Others, however, may be susceptible of either expert or lay proof. The helpfulness test incorporated in both Rules 701 and 702 means that the court should take a flexible approach tailored to the facts of the case.[8]

---

[7] United States v. Skeet, 665 F.2d 983 (9th Cir. 1982) (in prosecution arising out of defendant's shooting of his brother, trial court did not err in refusing to permit victim and his wife to express opinion whether shooting was accidental); United States v. Baskes, 649 F.2d 471, 478–79 (7th Cir. 1980), *cert. denied,* 450 U.S. 1000 (1981) (no error in court refusing to allow defendant to ask witness whether the conduct in question was "unlawful" or "willful" or whether the defendants "conspired"); Scheib v. Williams-McWilliams Co., Inc., 628 F.2d 509 (5th Cir. 1980) (in Jones Act case claiming injuries resulted from fall caused by boat's excessively steep deck, not error for trial court to have excluded lay witnesses' opinions on "dangerous state" of boat where they were allowed to testify about slips and falls which had occurred).

[8] Ernst v. Ace Motor Sales, Inc., 550 F.Supp. 1220 (E.D. Pa. 1982), *aff'd,* 720

¶ 10.03   Lack of Personal Knowledge—Rule 602[1]

Rule 602 provides that a witness may testify only about matters of which he has first hand knowledge: the testimony must be based upon events perceived by the witness through one of the physical senses. The rule states:

Rule 602

LACK OF PERSONAL KNOWLEDGE

A witness may not testify to a matter unless evidence is introduced sufficient to support a finding that the witness has personal knowledge of the matter. Evidence to prove personal knowledge may, but need not, consist of the witness' own testimony. This rule is subject to the provisions of rule 703, relating to opinion testimony by expert witnesses.

Rule 602 permits evidence of the requisite personal knowledge to be provided either through the testimony of the witness or through extrinsic testimony. Expert witnesses are expressly exempted from the personal knowledge requirement of the rule.

Rule 602 is subject to the hearsay rule. A witness testifying to what he or she heard may do so unless what the witness heard is excluded under the hearsay rules of Article VIII.[2] The testimony may even contain hearsay within hearsay. See Rule 805. There is no inconsistency between Rule 602 and the hearsay rules since the "matter" the

---

F.2d 661 (3d Cir. 1983) (police officer who arrived at scene about 5 or 10 minutes after accident could testify with respect to the point of impact either as a lay or expert witness).

[1] See **Treatise** at ¶¶ 602[01]–[03].

[2] See, *e.g.,* Elizarraras v. Bank of El Paso, 631 F.2d 366 (5th Cir. 1980) (reversible error to admit plaintiff's testimony where he had no personal knowledge and hearsay rule barred his relating what he had been told); United States v. Mandel, 591 F.2d 1347, 1369 (4th Cir. 1979), *aff'd en banc on reh.,* 602 F.2d 653 (4th Cir.), *cert. denied,* 445 U.S. 961 (1980) (in prosecution of governor for mail fraud, if a Senator testified that he did not believe that governor wanted his veto overridden and that belief was based on inadmissible hearsay statements, witness lacked personal knowledge of the event and testimony should have been excluded); United States v. Brown, 548 F.2d 1194 (5th Cir. 1977) (IRS agent could not testify that over 90% of the returns which had been prepared by defendant contained overstated deductions where she was testifying on the basis of out-of-court statements made to her by taxpayers she had interviewed rather than on the basis of her personal knowledge).

witness is testifying to is what was heard rather than the event described by the hearsay declarant.

The personal knowledge requirement is also satisfied when non-expert witnesses summarize evidence previously admitted at trial. One court has admitted such testimony pursuant to a broad interpretation of Rule 1006, the rule providing for the admission into evidence of summaries of data which is too voluminous to be conveniently examined in court.[3] Admission may also be based on the well-established tradition of admitting summaries of evidence previously put before the jury. The admission of summary testimony is akin to the admission of pedagogical devices which are not evidence, but only the proponent's organization of the evidence admitted. See Rule 1006. Courts admitting summary testimony should take care that no inadmissible hearsay is admitted along with the summarizing testimony.

Rule 602 has a two-fold significance: (1) it empowers judges to reject inherently incredible testimonial evidence; and (2) its personal knowledge requirement is incorporated into Rule 701, the opinion rule governing testimony by lay witnesses. Under Rule 602, the judge has the power to reject the evidence if it could not reasonably be believed—*i.e.,* if as a matter of law no trier of fact could find that the witness actually perceived the matter testified to.[4]

The judge must admit the testimony even though the witness is not positive about what she perceived provided the witness had an opportunity to observe and obtained some impressions from her ob-

---

[3] United States v. Lemire, 720 F.2d 1327, 1347 (D.C. Cir. 1983), *cert. denied,* 467 U.S. 1226 (1984).

[4] United States v. Larry, 536 F.2d 1149 (6th Cir.), *cert. denied,* 429 U.S. 984 (1976) (witness not permitted to testify about victim's participation in drug activities since testimony was not based on personal knowledge); *In re* A.H. Robins Co., Inc., 575 F.Supp. 718, 725–26 (D. Kan. 1983) (in consolidated discovery proceedings in multidistrict litigation against manufacturer of an intra-uterine device, court stated that since defendant had a corporate structure where deponents all worked for same company on same project, and communicated freely with one another, objections by defendant to statements made by its employees on grounds of lack of personal knowledge would not be sustained).

servations.[5] In addition, the judge should admit the testimony if the jury could find that the witness perceived the event to which she is testifying, since credibility is a matter for the jury.

The requirement of personal knowledge may arise in two ways in conjunction with the lay opinion rule. Read with Rule 701, the witness is required to have first, made observations supporting the opinion and second, reported the observations by giving as much of the raw data as is practicable. In instances where a lay witness may appropriately render an opinion, the personal knowledge question is limited to whether the witness had the opportunity to observe the facts on which the opinion is based. Courts applying the personal knowledge requirement should require the witness to state the underlying observations, if they can be stated without difficulty. But where the witness encounters difficulty in disentangling the individual elements of his observation from the impression as a whole, the courts should not insist on the impossible chore of delineating the boundary line between personal knowledge and opinion.

¶ 10.04   Oath or Affirmation—Rule 603[1]

Rule 603 requires that before being allowed to testify, a prospective witness must declare that he or she will testify truthfully.[2] The rule states:

---

[5] United States v. Sorrentino, 726 F.2d 876, 886 (5th Cir. 1984) (affirming exclusion of witness' testimony on grounds that witness' personal knowledge was tenuous and no factual foundation had been laid); M.B.A.F.B. Federal Credit Union v. Cumis Insurance Society, 681 F.2d 930, 932 (4th Cir. 1982) (trial court did not err in admitting deposition in which deponent who defaulted on loan stated that it was possible that he had discussed purchase price with credit union's general manager and that he thought his attorney had told general manager about it; "Rule 602 . . . does not require that the witness' knowledge be positive or rise to the level of absolute certainty. Evidence is inadmissible under this rule only if in the proper exercise of the trial court's discretion it finds that the witness could not have actually perceived or observed that which he testifies to.").

[1] See **Treatise** at ¶ 603[01].

[2] United States v. Fowler, 605 F.2d 181 (5th Cir. 1979), *cert. denied,* 445 U.S. 950 (1980) (court properly refused to allow defendant to testify after he refused either to swear or affirm to tell the truth).

Rule 603

OATH OR AFFIRMATION

Before testifying, every witness shall be required to declare that the witness will testify truthfully, by oath or affirmation administered in a form calculated to awaken the witness' conscience and impress the witness' mind with the duty to do so.

Because the purpose of the oath is to impress upon the witness the solemnity of the occasion, no reference to religious belief is required. Rule 603 does not operate as a rule of competency authorizing a judge to reject testimony on the grounds that the witness is incapable of telling the truth. Such testimony should be excluded on the ground that it has no probative value.

Rule 603 requires that the oath or affirmation "be administered in a form calculated to awaken [the] conscience [of the witness] and impress his mind with his duty to testify truthfully." The clerk who administers the oath should take the task seriously. While the oath is taken the judge should put aside all other work and face the witness in a way that makes it clear the court expects the witness to tell the truth.

The judge may question the witness to determine whether he or she wishes to take the oath or affirmation and to ensure that the witness is impressed with the duty to testify truthfully. The judge must be careful to conduct this questioning outside the hearing of the jury where a possibility exists that some of the prospective witness' answers with respect to a belief in God or objections to an oath might lead to prejudice in the eyes of the jury.[3]

---

[3] United States v. Rabb, 394 F.2d 230, 233 (3d Cir. 1968) ("Where the defendant is a follower of a minority religion which is unpopular with many persons in the community, it is better practice to permit him to affirm and have any questions on the subject of his religion asked out of the presence of the jury.").

¶ 10.05 Writing Used to Refresh Memory—Rule 612

¶ 10.05[01] Evidentiary Doctrine and Scope and Rationale of Rule 612[1]

Rule 612 covers but a small portion of the law relating to the refreshing of recollections. A brief survey of some of the features of reviving memory is useful in understanding the rationale of the Rule and its scope even though these aspects will continue to be governed by case law.

(*Text continued on page 10–19*)

---

[1] See **Treatise** at ¶ 612[01].

Described below are the problems which generally arise from refreshment by the proponent of the witness. To be distinguished are the hostile kinds of "refreshment" by an opponent. It is normally in the form of an implied inconsistent statement—*e.g.*, "Now that you have examined the document and refreshed your recollection, is it not true that you were mistaken when you said . . . ."

1. No means of arousing recollection may be used until the witness has satisfied the trial judge that he lacks effective present recollection.[2] Of course in a properly prepared case, counsel will have interviewed the witness prior to calling him to the stand. Sound preparation requires counsel to try to obtain as spontaneous a statement as possible from the witness in the course of preparing for trial so that counsel can ascertain the facts as they are, rather than as he or his client would like them to be. But during the course of discussion it normally will be necessary, whether or not there is loss of memory, to ask the prospective witness leading questions and to show him documents or other objects. Consequently, it may often be impossible for the witness, let alone the judge, to differentiate between actual recollections independent of any memory juggling and recollections which owe their existence to pre-trial discussions with counsel and others. Although the trial judge "should in the first instance satisfy himself as to whether the witness testifies upon a record or upon his own recollection,"[3] the cases indicate that judges are likely to honor claims of loss of memory without extensive examination when considerable time has elapsed between the event and trial, or numerous details are involved,[4] or the witness is of a class that fre-

[2] See, *e.g.*, United States v. Morlang, 531 F.2d 183, 191 (4th Cir. 1975) (error for prosecution to examine witness by reading from his grand jury testimony when "there was not even a representation the witness' memory needed refreshing.").

[3] United States v. Riccardi, 174 F.2d 883, 889 (3d Cir. 1949), *cert. denied*, 337 U.S. 941 (1949).

[4] Bankers Trust Co. v. Publicker Industries, Inc., 641 F.2d 1361, 1363 (2d Cir. 1981) ("There is no required, ritualistic formula for finding exhaustion of memory"; no error in trial court's having permitted witness to use prepared chronology while testifying where events had occurred two years ago and there was no impermissible suggestiveness; comparison of chronology with testimony clearly dem-

quently testifies in like situations.[5]

2. Anything may be used to revive a memory—"a song, a scent, a photograph, all allusion, even a past statement known to be false."[6] Thus, a "writing" in Rule 612 includes sound recordings and pictures of all kinds. Compare Rule 1001. It does not matter whether a statement is written by the witness himself, was made contemporaneously with the event itself, is a copy rather than an original, or was obtained in violation of a constitutional or procedural rule.

3. The witness' recollection must be revived after he consults the particular writing or object offered as a stimulus so that his testimony relates to a present recollection. If his recollection is not revived, a memorandum may be read into evidence and admitted if it meets the test of recorded recollection set forth in Rule 803(5). See discussion in Chapter 16, *infra*. Obviously, however, particularly in light of pre-trial preparation, "the categories, present recollection revived and past recollection recorded are clearest in their extremes but they are, in practice, converging rather than parallel lines; the difference is frequently one of degree."[7]

Two safeguards have been adopted by the courts to temper the possibility of the witness putting before the court inaccurate, though perhaps unconscious, inventions which purport to be his present recollection. The first, which remains a matter of case law,

---

onstrated that witness was not reading a script); Kramer v. Commissioner of Internal Revenue, 389 F.2d 236 (7th Cir. 1968) (accountant's computation); United States v. Boyd, 606 F.2d 792 (8th Cir. 1979) (propriety of permitting refreshment lies largely within discretion of court; no abuse of discretion where witness assured court of need to refer to report summarizing his previous statements to FBI).

[5] See, *e.g.*, Taylor v. United States, 19 F.2d 813, 817 (8th Cir. 1927) ("it would be practically impossible for officers, making daily investigations of alleged violations of law, to remember the names, dates, and what took place, without referring to notes made by them at the time or immediately thereafter."); Goings v. United States, 377 F.2d 753, 761, n.11 (8th Cir. 1967) ("Generally, doctors, engineers, accountants and other lay witnesses testifying should be allowed continuously to refer to data on their reports, etc.").

[6] United States v. Rappy, 157 F.2d 964, 967 (2d Cir.), *cert. denied*, 329 U.S. 806 (1947).

[7] United States v. Riccardi, 174 F.2d 883 (3d Cir.), *cert. denied*, 337 U.S. 941 (1949).

is that the trial court has considered discretion at various points to reject the testimony. As already noted, it can hold that the witness is not lacking in memory, or that the writing does not refresh his memory, or the court can find as in the case of leading questions (see Rule 611(c)) that the danger of unfair suggestion outweighs any value the writings may have for refreshing the witness' recollection.[8]

The second safeguard is the subject of Rule 612. It ensures the adverse party a right to inspect the writing used for refreshing recollection, to use the writing as a basis for cross-examination, and to introduce into evidence those portions of the writing that relate to the testimony of the witness. The rule provides:

Rule 612

WRITING USED TO REFRESH MEMORY

Except as otherwise provided in criminal proceedings by section 3500 of title 18, United States Code, if a witness uses a writing to refresh memory for the purpose of testifying, either—

(1) while testifying, or

(2) before testifying, if the court in its discretion determines it is necessary in the interests of justice, an adverse party is entitled to have the writing produced at the hearing, to inspect it, to cross-examine the witness thereon, and to introduce in evidence those portions which relate to the testimony of the witness. If it is claimed that the writing contains matters not related to the subject matter of the testimony the court shall examine the writing in camera, excise any portions not so related, and order delivery of the remainder to the party entitled thereto. Any portion

---

[8] See, *e.g.*, Parliament Insurance Co. v. Hanson, 676 F.2d 1069, 1073 (5th Cir. 1982) (trial court did not abuse discretion in refusing to allow witness to testify on the basis of notes made in anticipation of litigation which were summaries of logs written substantially earlier and which were made while witness was working for or preparing to work for competitor of defendant); United States v. Shoupe, 548 F.2d 636 (8th Cir. 1977) (trial court clearly abused its discretion in permitting witness' recollection to be refreshed by prior, unsworn statements which had not been shown to be reliable and accordingly should not have been disclosed to jury even for a limited purpose; statements, which were directly probative of defendants' guilt in case in which there was very little other evidence implicating them, had been incorporated in memorandum prepared by law enforcement agent six days after he interviewed witness; court cited Rule 803(8)(B) as evincing Congress' reluctance to credit the accuracy of such documents).

withheld over objections shall be preserved and made available to the appellate court in the event of an appeal. If a writing is not produced or delivered pursuant to order under this rule, the court shall make any order justice requires, except that in criminal cases when the prosecution elects not to comply, the order shall be one striking the testimony or, if the court in its discretion determines that the interests of justice so require, declaring a mistrial.

By giving the adverse party the right to refer to the writing on cross-examination and to introduce into evidence those portions that relate to the testimony of the witness,[9] Rule 612 seeks to enhance the ability of the trier of fact to assess the credibility of the witness. When the adverse party exercises these options, the writing that had been used for refreshment becomes in effect a prior inconsistent statement. Consequently, it cannot be used substantively unless it satisfies the requirements of Rule 801 (d)(l)(A), and the jury should be instructed, if a request for such an instruction is made, to consider it only as to the credibility of the refreshed witness, and not as evidence-in-chief.

Rule 612 further recognizes that in order to explore the witness' credibility the jury may need to know what materials he used to refresh his recollection before appearing on the stand. Away from the courtroom the dangers attendant on refreshing recollection are even more pronounced: there is no bar on leading questions, no predetermined order in which questions must be asked, and no limitations on the kind of materials that a prospective witness may be shown. If the court in its discretion determines that it is necessary in the interests of justice for the jury to understand how the witness achieved his present testimonial knowledge, the cross-examiner will be accorded the right to have the writings which were

---

[9] While only the related portions have to be turned over pursuant to Rule 612, this may, at times, lead to the admissibility of other portions of the writing when demanded by the proponent of the witness, either on a theory of rehabilitation by prior consistent statements, or pursuant to the doctrine of completeness embodied in Rule 106. See United States v. Rubin, 609 F.2d 51 (2d Cir. 1979), *aff'd on other grounds,* 449 U.S. 424 (1981) (notes used to refresh prosecution witness could be introduced pursuant to Rule 106, because selective cross-examination by defense counsel, which focused on inconsistencies, may have left a confusing or misleading impression on jury).

used for pre-trial refreshment, produced, inspected and introduced.[10] The extent to which work product and privilege claims limit the production of materials consulted by a witness in preparing for a deposition is discussed below.

If the writing is not produced or not delivered after the court so orders, the court has considerable discretion in ordering appropriate sanctions. In criminal cases, Rule 612 provides that where the prosecution fails to comply, the court must either order a mistrial or order that the witness' testimony be struck. Obviously, however, there can be no production if the writing has been destroyed. In Jencks Act cases non-production in the case of destroyed writings has been excused without imposing sanctions where notes were destroyed after having been incorporated into statements which were produced. The Rule 612 situation is somewhat different since it is not the content or form of the writing that determines production but the fact that it was shown to the witness. But the Supreme Court has stated that a failure to produce pursuant to the Jencks Act does not always reach constitutional proportions, even when the non-produced notes are not available in some other form.

It would seem, therefore, that when the prosecution fails to comply with Rule 612, an appellate court may nevertheless find that a trial judge's failure to strike testimony or order a mistrial does not amount to reversible error in the context of the particular case. Except, however, in cases of inability to comply where the trial judge feels that the defendant's rights will not be prejudiced, the trial judge should order production without considering whether this failure to so order might ultimately be considered harmless error. Non-production will not be considered harmless where the defendant was prejudiced by the failure to produce, as, for example, when it is shown that the writing would almost certainly have served to impeach a crucial witness and no other impeaching evidence was available.

In other cases, Rule 612 does not limit the sanctions that are available. The Committee's Notes suggest that contempt, dismissal and finding issues against the offender are some of the techniques that might be employed. A mild sanction which may be

---

[10] See discussion in **Treatise** at ¶ 612[05].

useful is for the court to explain to the jury why the refreshment evidence is required to be revealed under the Federal Rules and then to give a strong charge on spoliation and the adverse inferences that may be drawn from such spoliation in assessing the witness's credibility.

¶ 10.05[02] Applying Rule 612 in Criminal Cases—the Jencks Act Problem[1]

The text of Rule 612 starts with a specific proviso: "Except as otherwise provided in criminal proceedings by section 3500 of title 18, United States Code . . . ." The statutory reference is to the so-called Jencks Act which at the time Rule 612 became effective provided that after a government witness testifies in court, the defense is entitled to demand delivery "of any statement of the witness" in the possession of the United States which "relates to the subject matter concerning which the witness has testified." The provision in Rule 612 therefore meant that Rule 612 could not be used to compel the production and inspection of writings that would be outside the scope of the Jencks Act. Even if a witness in a criminal trial had refreshed his recollection before testifying, the writings used would not be made available to the cross-examiner unless they independently qualified as Jencks Act material.

Since December 1, 1980, Rule 26.2 of the Federal Rules of Criminal Procedure which "place[s] in the criminal rules the substance of what is now 18 U.S.C. § 3500" has been in effect. Rule 26.2 mandates the production of statements made by a defense witness as well as statements made by prosecution witnesses. Rule 612 was not amended; no reference to Rule 26.2 has been substituted for the reference to 18 U.S.C. § 3500, the Jencks Act. Nor has § 3500 expressly been repealed although it arguably has been partly superseded by Rule 26.2, since rule recodifications intended to cover an entire subject should be deemed to supercede conflicting provisions on the same subject.[2]

---

[1] See **Treatise** at ¶ 612[02] for discussion of interrelationship between Rule 612 and the Brady doctrine and Rules 6(e) and 16 of the Federal Rules of Criminal Procedure.

[2] Rule 26.2 was left unchanged by Congress which did modify another aspect of the Rules promulgated by the Supreme Court, Pub. L. 96–42, 93 Stat. 326. See 18

In light of these events, what is now the current status of the provision in Rule 612? We prefer to believe that Rule 612 should be interpreted as though there were no reference to 18 U.S.C. § 3500. Rule 612 would then authorize production of all writings used in refreshing a witness at a criminal trial, and afford the court discretion "in the interests of justice," to order production of writings used prior to trial to refresh the witness. Adequate protection to the government is possible against revelation of investigative materials through in camera inspection and exercise of discretion.

¶ 10.05[03]   Work Product and Privilege Issues[1]

Although Rule 612 does not spell out the reasons why a party may refuse to produce or deliver a writing pursuant to order, the rule must be interpreted in light of Rule 501 which acknowledges the existence of privileges governed by the Constitution, Acts of Congress and the rules prescribed by the Supreme Court, as well as those rooted in the principles of the common law. The most troublesome issue for the courts in both civil and criminal cases has been to decide whether use of materials to refresh a witness' recollection prior to testifying at a deposition results in waiver of the attorney-client privilege[2] or a work product claim.

[a]   Attorney-Client Privilege

Imputing waiver whenever a witness uses a privileged document to refresh his recollection is theoretically unsound. Since a witness may refresh his recollection with statements other than his own, holding that the attorney as agent for the client has waived the client's privilege by using the statements dilutes the client's rights.

U.S.C. § 3771 ("All laws in conflict with such rules shall be of no further force . . .").

[1] See **Treatise** at ¶ 612[03].

[2] Privilege issues can also arise with regard to governmental privileges. Since governmental privileges are not viewed as absolute, except for the state secret privilege, the court in the usual non-state secret case can use a balancing test to decide whether the need for the material in order to assess the accuracy of the witness' testimony outweighs the need to protect the governmental information. See **Treatise** at ¶ 612[04] for discussion of the state secret privilege.

Furthermore, difficult problems can arise in the corporate context when the holder of the privilege is the corporation itself but the communicants are employees of the corporation. If employee A's communication to counsel would be privileged and so would employee B's statements, it is difficult to see why the corporation should be found to have waived its privilege if the attorney in the course of providing legal services to the corporation reveals B's statement to A. The adversary of the corporation is, of course, free to take the depositions of A and B; the desire for a short-cut is not enough: "considerations of convenience do not overcome the policies served by the attorney-client privilege."[3]

The court can avoid some problems by refusing to allow material subject to a claim of attorney-client privilege to be used for refreshing a witness' recollection at trial. This solution however, cannot be applied at a deposition, or when the witness consults the privileged material prior to testifying at a trial or deposition. Although some courts apparently assume that any material consulted by a witness prior to trial loses its privileged status,[4] waiver should be found only when the witness has consulted a writing embodying his own communication to counsel, and his testimony at the deposition, or at trial, discloses a significant part of the

---

[3] Upjohn Co. v. United States, 449 U.S. 383, 101 S.Ct. 677, 66 L.Ed.2d 584 (1981).

[4] See *e.g.,* Wheeling-Pittsburgh Steel v. Underwriters Laboratories, 81 F.R.D. 8 (N.D. Ill. 1978) (ex-employee of plaintiff had refreshed his recollection prior to deposition with file containing communications between representatives of the plaintiff, including witness when he was employed, and its counsel; court granted defendant access to files noting that "access is limited only to those writings which may fairly be said in fact to have an impact upon the testimony of [witness]." The court also stated that "[i]f the paramount purpose of the federal discovery rules is the ascertainment of the truth, the fact that a document was used to refresh one's recollection prior to his testimony instead of during his testimony is of little significance."). The court's reasoning would dispose of all privileges since they always operate to suppress the truth. A more fruitful inquiry would have been whether the effortless manner in which the witness obtained access to the file, apparently by asking a present employee, indicated a lack of confidentiality since the supposedly privileged information was being disseminated beyond those with a need-to-know. See discussion of attorney-client privileges, Chapter 18, *infra.* See also R.J. Hereley & Son Co. v. Stotler & Co., 87 F.R.D. 358 (N.D. Ill. 1980) (when at settlement conference attorney relies on memorandum supplied to him by client, attorney-client privilege "was waived by [attorney's] use of the memorandum to refresh his recollection.").

communication.[5] See discussion of Standard 511 in Chapter 18, *infra*.

[b]   Work Product Claim

The work product claim[6] is probably the one most commonly asserted to resist a request for the production of materials used in refreshing a witness' recollection. Work product is divided into two categories: (1) what may be referred to as core product embodies the attorney's mental impressions and is entitled to special protection—the Supreme Court has not yet decided whether it is ever subject to disclosure, (2) peripheral product, on the other hand, loses its protection upon a showing of need and inability to obtain the equivalent without undue hardship.[7]

Prior to the enactment of Rule 612 the federal cases do not seem to have considered whether a work product limitation must be applied. Of course, the kind of writing with which a witness re-

---

[5] See *e.g.*, Barrer v. Women's Nat'l Bank, 96 F.R.D. 202 (D.D.C. 1982) (where defendant's president consulted memorandum she had prepared at request of counsel prior to testifying at deposition about subject of memorandum, magistrate ordered memorandum to be produced for in camera examination, and stated that if discrepancies were found between deposition testimony and memorandum, disclosure would be ordered and the deposition would be reopened); Prucha v. M & N Modern Hydraulic Press Co., 76 F.R.D. 207 (W.D. Wis. 1977) (court ordered plaintiff to produce, for inspection and copying, statement which he had made to attorneys contemporaneously with accident sued on and which he had relied on in refreshing his recollection in preparation for deposition). See also Jos. Schlitz Brewing Co. v., Muller & Phipps (Hawaii), Ltd., 85 F.R.D. 118 (W.D. Mo. 1980) (court found that an otherwise privileged document should be given special discretionary safeguards against disclosure and absent showing that each document had been studied by witness prior to testifying, motion for production would be denied; court furthermore suggested its decision might have been the same even if attorney had testified that he had reviewed a particular document, as otherwise a coach might be interposed between witness and document).

[6] See **Treatise** at ¶ 612[04] for analysis of the Supreme Court's decisions regarding work product in Hickman v. Taylor, 329 U.S. 495, 67 S.Ct. 385, 91 L.Ed. 451 (1947) and United States v. Nobles, 422 U.S. 225, 95 S.Ct. 2160, 45 L.Ed.2d 141 (1975).

[7] See Upjohn v. United States, 449 U.S. 383, 101 S.Ct. 677, 66 L.Ed.2d 584 (1981).

freshed himself at trial—the only instance in which production was required—probably usually fell within the category of materials not embodying the attorney's thought processes, and would therefore in any case have been exempted from the operation of the doctrine. Resort to notes embodying an attorney's theories and mental impressions, for refreshment, could be barred at the trial on analogy to the prohibition against leading, without reaching the question of whether production of the notes would be barred by a work product rule.

[c] Trials

The enactment of Rule 612 poses a new question of whether waiver results when an attorney refreshes a witness' recollection with core work product materials, *i.e.,* those that embody the thought processes of the attorney. Waiver would mean that the opponent would then be entitled to production, inspection and use of the materials pursuant to Rule 612.

Certainly, bringing the refreshment process into the open at trial would better enable the trier of fact to assess the credibility of the witness. On the other hand, as the Supreme Court noted in *Hickman v. Taylor,* if none of an attorney's file is privileged, "much of what is now put down in writing would remain unwritten."[8] There may also be some advantages of an adversary system which would be lost if one's hand must always be shown to the opposing side.

In its opinions since *Hickman v. Taylor,* the Supreme Court has never permitted intrusion into work-product revealing the attorney's thought processes. Until there is further clarification by the Court, a party can argue either waiver or need in seeking production at trial of material used to refresh a witness which the proponent claims reflects the attorney's thought processes. If the Supreme Court decides that this sort of material is absolutely privileged, then the only possible avenue for production will be waiver, although this theory may be more tenable for material used for refreshment at trial than for material used in preparation

---

[8] 329 U.S. 495, 511, 67 S.Ct. 385, 91 L.Ed 451 (1947).

for trial.[9]

Until such time as the Supreme Court decides these issues, the following approach is suggested. If the adverse party demands material which the party producing the witness claims reflects solely the attorney's thought processes, the judge should examine the material in camera. Unless the judge finds that the adverse party would be seriously hampered in testing the accuracy of the witness' testimony, he should not order production of any writings which reflect solely the attorney's mental processes. If the adverse party would be seriously hampered, the court should apply Rule 612 on the theory that the lawyer who showed the witness his work product is estopped. In arriving at his decision, the judge must weigh the significance of the testimony, the availability of other evidence impeaching the testimony and the degree to which the witness apparently relied upon the writing. Just as in applying Rule 403, the judge will have to be governed in his decision by the facts of the particular case before him. See discussion of Rule 403, Chapter 6, *supra*.

[d] Depositions

It has been suggested that work-product protection should cease when a witness consults work-product material prior to testifying at a deposition "either on a theory of waiver or qualified privilege, where an attempt is made to exceed decent limits of preparation on the one hand and concealment on the other."[10] Al-

---

[9] See United States v. Nobles, 422 U.S. 225, 240 n.14, 95 S.Ct. 2160, 45 L.Ed.2d 141 (1975). ("What constitutes a waiver with respect to work-product materials depends, of course, upon the circumstances. Counsel necessarily makes use throughout trial of the notes, documents, and other internal materials prepared to present adequately his client's case, and often relies on them in examining witnesses. When so used, there normally is no waiver. But where, as here, counsel attempts to make a testimonial use of these materials the normal rules of evidence come into play with respect to cross-examination and production of documents.").

[10] Berkey Photo, Inc. v. Eastman Kodak Co., 74 F.R.D. 613, 617 (S.D.N.Y. 1977) (experts in antitrust litigation had consulted notebooks consisting of counsel's synthesis of facts and factual issues as background; court did not order disclosure since "counsel were not vividly aware of the potential for a stark choice between withholding the notebooks from the experts or turning them over to opposing counsel," but court said it was now giving fair warning for the future).

though some courts impose a rule of automatic disclosure to any materials consulted in preparation for a deposition,[11] such a rule does not comport with the policies underlying work product protection. It ignores the special protection that may have to be accorded the attorney's thought processes. In addition, the rationale for requiring production of peripheral work-product materials used for refreshment is considerably less compelling in the discovery stage context. At this point, the material is not needed in order for the trier of fact to assess the credibility of the witness, and complete disclosure undermines the anti-indolence rationale of the work-product rule. Perhaps most importantly, automatic disclosure whenever a witness prepares himself for a deposition by referring to pertinent materials may lead to the very practices which troubled the *Hickman* court: "Inefficiency, unfairness and sharp practices, would inevitably develop in the giving of legal advice in the preparation of cases for trial."[12] "[M]uch of what is now put down in writing would remain unwritten,"[13] or the attorney will coach the witness with the materials rather than allowing the witness to peruse them on his own, or the attorney will fail to prepare the witness adequately. None of these alternatives seems compatible with the rationale of the work product rule. Given the liberality of disclosure and the work product exception in the discovery rules, the opponent should be required to make a substantial showing of need in order to obtain materials which a witness reviewed before a deposition instead of achieving wholesale

---

[11] Boring v. Keller, 97 F.R.D. 404 (D. Colo. 1983) (attorney's opinion work product not protected from disclosure where used by expert to formulate his opinion; court holds no privilege exists for attorney's summary of his impressions of plaintiff's demeanor and appearance as witness or of plaintiff's substantive deposition testimony where summary was given to defendant's experts to aid them in preparing this testimony); James Julian, Inc. v. Raytheon Co., 93 F.R.D. 138, 146 (D.Del. 1982) (court relies on *Berkey*, 74 F.R.D. 613, in ordering that binder containing documents selected and arranged by counsel for use in preparing witnesses for deposition must be disclosed since without binders opposing counsel "cannot know or inquire into the extent to which the witness' testimony has been shaded by counsel's presentation of the factual background"; each case must be decided on own facts and court states that in a given case fact that documents sought contained attorney's mental impressions might cause court to strike balance against disclosure).

[12] 329 U.S. at 511.

[13] *Id.*

disclosure.[14]

In the present state of uncertainty, attorneys should not refresh prospective deponents or witnesses with material containing counsel's theories or thought processes. Not only may such documents ultimately fall into opposing counsel's hands if Rule 612 is satisfied, but there are too many risks of unethical suggestions to witnesses when they see such material.

¶ 10.06   Exclusion of Witnesses—Rule 615

¶ 10.06[01]   Scope and Rationale[1]

Rule 615 requires the exclusion of witnesses from the courtroom on demand by a litigant. The court may not deny the litigant's request unless the witness is (1) a party, or (2) a designated representative, or (3) a person whose presence is essential. The rule provides:

---

[14] Bogosian v. Gulf Oil Corp., 738 F.2d 587, 592–96 (3d Cir. 1984) (in anti-trust action, the court held that provisions of the Federal Rules of Civil Procedure which permit discovery of facts known or opinions held by an expert witness do not permit discovery of documents prepared by attorneys containing solely their mental impressions and thought processes relating to the legal theories of the case even though the expert may rely on the documents to some extent in formulating his own opinions; such documents represent core work product and are entitled to heightened protection; additionally, showing the material to the witnesses did not constitute a waiver of the protection for attorney work product); Al-Rowaishan Establishment Universal Trading & Agencies, Ltd. v. Beatrice Foods Co., 92 F.R.D. 779 (S.D.N.Y. 1982) (court used in camera procedure and concluded that it was difficult to see how defendant would be "hampered in testing the accuracy" of deponent's testimony by not being permitted to read digest prepared by plaintiff's attorney, and in any event found that the value to defendant was outweighed by the principles precluding disclosure of work product revealing the attorney's thought processes); *In re* Comair Air Disaster Litigation, 100 F.R.D. 350, 353–54 (E.D. Ky. 1983) (court ordered disclosure of internal accident report which had been used by deponent in preparing for deposition; court noted that opponent had less access to plane wreckage, and that no attorneys were involved in the preparation of the report).

[1] See **Treatise** at ¶¶ 615[01]–[02].

Rule 615

EXCLUSION OF WITNESSES

At the request of a party the court shall order witnesses excluded so that they cannot hear the testimony of other witnesses, and it may make the order of its own motion. This rule does not authorize exclusion of (1) a party who is a natural person, or (2) an officer or employee of a party which is not a natural person designated as its representative by its attorney, or (3) a person whose presence is shown by a party to be essential to the presentation of the party's cause.

The practice of excluding, separating, or sequestering witnesses is at least as old as the Bible. Almost from the beginning of recorded trials, the story of Susanna and the Elders has been relied upon to justify keeping witnesses from hearing each others'stories so that inconsistencies in their testimony will be revealed. Sequestration also seeks to prevent witnesses from unconsciously shaping their testimony to conform to that given by other witnesses. A rule such as Rule 615 therefore has a two-fold purpose: to prevent fabrication and to uncover fabrication that has already taken place.

[a]   A Party

A party who is a natural person may not be excluded from the courtroom. This provision, which operates automatically, is designed to eliminate problems of confrontation and due process which would otherwise arise.[2]

---

[2] *Cf.* Geders v. United States, 425 U.S. 80, 87–88, 96 S.Ct. 1330, 47 L.Ed.2d 592 (1976) (order preventing criminal defendant from consulting his counsel about anything during an overnight recess between his direct and cross-examination impinged upon his right to assistance of counsel guaranteed by the Sixth Amendment; court noted that trial judge has "broad power to sequester witnesses before, during and after their testimony . . . [b]ut the petitioner was not simply a witness; he was also the defendant."). See also Potashnick v. Port City Construction Co., 609 F.2d 1101 (5th Cir. 1980), *cert. denied,* 449 U.S. 820 (1980) (in civil case, judge's ruling which prohibited any conversations between counsel and a witness once witness' testimony commenced deprived defendant of its constitutional rights to effective assistance of counsel and right to retain counsel; witness was the president and sole shareholder of corporate defendant and court applied "control group" test of attorney-client privilege in determining that witness should be viewed as party constitutionally entitled to retain counsel).

[b] Designated Representative

Rule 615 prohibits exclusion of "an officer or employee of a party which is not a natural person designated as its representative by its attorney." Frequently this provision is relied upon by the government as the basis for having its case agent remain in the courtroom.[3] Exemption from sequestration should be automatic provided the government or other party makes a request for designation at the time the defendant or other opponent moves for an order of exclusion pursuant to Rule 615.

While the rule is phrased in the singular, the court should have discretion to allow more than one designated representative to remain in the courtroom as, for instance, when it is impossible to find one person within the structure of a large entity who has all the information needed to assist the attorney. Determining the sequence in which the case representative will testify remains a matter entrusted to the trial court's discretion by virtue of Rule 611.[4] In most instances, the court will not interfere with the parties' choice of the order in which evidence is to be introduced.

[c] A Person Whose Presence is Essential

Rule 615 has not eliminated all judicial discretion. The rule prohibits exclusion of "a person whose presence is shown by a party to be essential to the presentation of his cause." The burden is on the party opposing sequestration to convince the court to exercise its discretion to except a particular witness from its order.

---

[3] United States v. Jones, 687 F.2d 1265, 1268 (8th Cir. 1982) (nothing in cases or legislative history suggests that state or local officers should be treated differently than federal officers; no abuse of discretion in permitting municipal police officer who had searched car to remain in courtroom).

[4] United States v. Parodi, 703 F.2d 768, 774 (4th Cir. 1983) (no abuse of discretion in allowing case agent to testify at conclusion of government's case where only one part of agent's testimony could have been admitted at beginning of trial without confusing order of proof; court held that absolute rule conditioning agent's right to remain in courtroom on his testifying first would conflict with its decisions allowing witness who had disobeyed sequestration order to testify); United States v. Butera, 677 F.2d 1376 (11th Cir. 1982), *cert. denied*, 459 U.S. 1108 (1983) (sequential presentation of case agent's testimony—he took stand on four separate occasions—is a matter entrusted to district court's discretion).

This exception is probably most frequently invoked in the case of expert witnesses.[5] Certainly an expert who intends to base his opinion on "facts or data in the particular case" (Rule 703) will be unable to testify if he has been excluded. Experts needed to advise counsel on technical matters, as for instance in tax or patent litigation, or on how to cross-examine opposing experts, also qualify as essential persons.[6]

¶ 10.06[02]   Procedure Pursuant to Rule 615[1]

Rule 615 is silent on when a demand for exclusion must be made. The practice is to exercise judicial discretion to exclude prospective witnesses during openings and any arguments or proffers of proof where a witness' testimony may be summarized. The rule should be applied at hearings, as to suppress, and on other occasions when witnesses may be heard, as on sentencing.

The rule is also silent as to what instructions the court may give the witnesses when they are excluded. A number of cases have indicated that the court should direct the witnesses not to discuss the case with each other, but a failure to give such an instruction has not ordinarily been considered reversible error.[2] When an instruc-

[5] Morvant v. Construction Aggregates Corp., 570 F.2d 626, 629–30 (6th Cir. 1978) ("where a fair showing has been made that the expert witness is in fact required for the management of the case, and this is made clear to the trial court, we believe that the trial court is bound to accept any reasonable, substantiated representation to this effect by counsel."); Verlack v. SWC Caribbean, Inc., 550 F.2d 171 (3d Cir. 1977) (where corporation described person as former owner and did not designate him with sufficient clarity as corporate representative or indicate how he was essential to presentation of its case, sequestration was not violation of Rule 615 or due process). Cf. N.L.R.B. v. Pope Maintenance Corp., 573 F.2d 898, 906–07 (5th Cir. 1978) (unnecessary to determine the extent to which Rule 615 applies to NLRB proceedings—though court intimates that sequestration is a valuable device which should be used by administrative law judges—because failure to sequester did not amount to denial of due process where record indicates no resulting prejudice).

[6] United States v. Burgess, 691 F.2d 1146, 1157 (4th Cir. 1982) (in drug prosecution where defendant raised insanity defense, court did not err in ruling that psychiatrists for both parties might remain in courtroom, where written reports from experts were delayed, becoming available from defendant only two days before trial commenced and from government on second and last day of trial).

[1] See **Treatise** at ¶ 615[02].

[2] United States v. Smith, 578 F.2d 1227, 1235 (8th Cir. 1978) (within judge's dis-

tion is given, it should be worded in terms of a direction "not to discuss the case with anyone *other than counsel.*" Prohibiting contact between a party and his attorney may deprive a criminal defendant-witness of his Sixth Amendment right to effective assistance of counsel, and in a civil case might amount to a denial of due process.

¶ 10.06[03]   Consequences of Non-compliance[1]

Rule 615 does not mention the consequences of noncompliance with an order of exclusion. As under previous practice, the imposition of sanctions remains a matter of case law. Three methods of enforcement have been used by the courts (1) citing the witness for contempt, (2) permitting comment on the witness' noncompliance in order to reflect on his credibility and (3) refusing to let the witness testify or striking his testimony.

Each method has drawbacks. A contempt citation punishes the witness and may perhaps deter future misconduct but does not rid the case of testimony which the witness may have fabricated after listening to other witnesses. The comment, while useful, may have unwarranted repercussions where the witness remained in the courtroom but his testimony was unaffected. A derogatory comment on his credibility may actually distort the truth. Exclusion of the testimony deprives the jury of relevant evidence, a result which the Rules of Evidence do not ordinarily sanction. See discussion in Chapter 6, *supra.*

In most of the reported decisions, the witness who has disobeyed an order of exclusion by remaining in the courtroom is permitted to testify. In *Holder v. United States,*[2] the Supreme Court put its weight against disqualifying the witness:

If a witness disobeys the order of withdrawal, while he may be proceeded against for contempt, and his testimony is open to comment to

---

cretion to determine if segregated witnesses should be instructed not to communicate with each other, and in judge's discretion to determine whether order of sequestration has been violated). *Cf.* Miller v. Universal City Studios, Inc., 650 F.2d 1365 (5th Cir. 1981) (providing sequestered witness with daily copy violates Rule 615).

[1] See **Treatise** at ¶ 615[03].

[2] 150 U.S. 91, 14 S.Ct. 10, 37 L.Ed. 1010 (1893).

the jury by reason of his conduct, he is not thereby disqualified, and the weight of authority is that he cannot be excluded on that ground, merely, although the right to exclude under particular circumstances may be supported as within the sound discretion of the trial court.[3]

This more generous attitude to the parties is justified. Often a prospective witness will be confused or will not understand what the court said or he may come into the courtroom after the court has made its order. Counsel is often so busy and intent on trial problems that he will not be aware that one of his witnesses is in the courtroom. This possibility of confusion is one reason that courts are reluctant to order witnesses not to speak to each other. They inadvertently do from time to time and then the trial degenerates into ugly accusations of bad faith that becloud the central issues.

To be distinguished from situations where the trial court exercises its discretion to allow the disobedient witness to testify are cases where the trial court erroneously thought it had discretion to refuse to exclude witnesses despite a party's request. The Circuits have used a number of different approaches in dealing with a district court's erroneous denial of a sequestration request—automatic reversal, no reversal absent a showing of prejudice, or a presumption of prejudice requiring reversal unless harmless error is shown.[4]

---

[3] *Id.* at 92.

[4] See discussion in United States v. Ell, 718 F.2d 291 (9th Cir. 1983).

CHAPTER 11

Special Witness Rules

SYNOPSIS

(Pub.819)

¶ 11.01　Overview of Special Witness Rules

With few exceptions, there are no prior limits on types of witnesses and the degrees of probative force to be allotted to them. Except as substantive law, special rule or the circumstances of the case may require, all witnesses are considered competent and evaluation of credibility is for the trier. Among the references the reader may wish to consult are Rule 601 on competency generally, discussed in ¶ 10.01, *supra,* importing state dead person statutes; Rule 501, importing the federal spousal privilege-incompetency rule and similar state rules under some circumstances, discussed in ¶ 18.04, *infra;* the United States Constitution Article III, Section 3, requiring "testimony of two Witnesses to same overt Act, or . . . Confession in open Court," for conviction of treason; Rule 602, requiring personal knowledge of the witness, discussed in ¶ 10.03, *supra;* Rule 104(a) giving the court the power to exclude testimony where no reasonable jury could believe the witness, discussed in ¶ 3.01, *supra;* and Rules 702 and 703, permitting the court to exclude certain expert testimony, discussed in Chapter 13. There are also certain protections for limited classes of witnesses, as in Rule 412, covering victims of rape (discussed in ¶ 7.09, *supra*), Rule 704(b) on testimony of experts giving certain kinds of psychiatric evidence (discussed in ¶ 13.04, *infra*), and Rule 609(a) limiting some attacks on the credibility of criminal defendants (discussed in ¶ 12.04[03], *infra*).

This chapter covers three special witness rules which are less evidentiary than procedural and substantive in nature. It deals with interpreters, judges and jurors.

¶ 11.02　Interpreters—Rule 604[1]

Rule 604 imposes two requirements on interpreters: they must be qualified as experts in the skill of interpreting, and they must take an oath or affirm that they will interpret truthfully, *i.e.,* communicate to the court exactly what is being said by the witness. The rule must be read in conjunction with Rule 43 of the Federal Rules of Civil Procedure and Rule 28 of the Federal Rules of Criminal Proce-

---

[1] See **Treatise** at ¶ 604[01].

dure both of which provide that judges in their discretion may order the appointment and compensation of interpreters.[2] Rule 604 states:

Rule 604

INTERPRETERS

An interpreter is subject to the provisions of these rules relating to qualification as an expert and the administration of an oath or affirmation to make a true translation.

Interpreters in criminal cases should be instructed to not only interpret the questions directed to the witness and the witness' answers but, if the defendant does not speak English, also to interpret constantly all that is being said by the judge, other witnesses and attorneys. The defendant is entitled to know what is going on in the courtroom at all times.

The court and counsel should insure that the translator does his or her job properly. If there are long silences when the translator does nothing while proceedings are continuing, there should be a sharp reminder on the record that everything should be translated. The interpreter should not be permitted to hold long conversations with a witness in his native tongue, while the response is being shaped into a "yes" or "no" answer. He or she is to interpret, not advise.

The court should be sensitive to dialect problems that may make critical differences on subtle points. Wherever possible, counsel should be aware of these problems in advance so that continuances to obtain a different interpreter will not be required.

If at all possible official interpreters should be used. Use of relatives or others interested in the case often leads to sloppy and inadequate hearings. In civil cases the parties have the obligation to provide interpreters. In criminal cases the obligation is that of the court.

---

[2] See also the Court Interpreters Act, 28 U.S.C. § 1827 (1978). The Act provides a system for the use of interpreters in the federal court.

¶ 11.03   Competency of Judge as Witness—Rule 605

¶ 11.03[01]   Rationale and Scope[1]

Rule 605 prevents a judge presiding at a trial from testifying as a witness in that trial. The rule states:

Rule 605

COMPETENCY OF JUDGE AS WITNESS

The judge presiding at the trial may not testify in that trial as a witness. No objection need be made in order to preserve the point.

The rationale for a rule of incompetency is obvious. Permitting a judge to testify raises perplexing questions of who will rule on objections, who will compel answers, what will be the scope of cross-examination, and how counsel is to maintain a proper relationship with the court.

Rule 605 also applies when a judge assumes the role of a witness although he is neither called to testify nor voluntarily takes the stand.[2] Judicial testimony occurs when the judge refers to relevant facts of which he has personal knowledge in the guise of taking judicial notice.[3] Difficulties may also arise where the court purports to take judicial notice of prior proceedings in the case. Judicial notice may be proper if a record exists to which reference can be made and which the appellate court can review. But where the

---

[1] See **Treatise** at ¶¶ 605[01], [04].

[2] See, *e.g.*, Price Bros. Co. v. Philadelphia Gear Corp., 629 F.2d 444 (6th Cir. 1980) (plaintiff alleged that trial judge's law clerk had traveled to plaintiff's plant prior to trial and court remanded for evidentiary hearing to determine truth of allegation, noting that sending a law clerk to gather evidence in a non-jury trial would be destructive of the appearance of impartiality required of the presiding judge).

A trial judge does not "improperly testify" when making a preliminary determination of authenticity. See United States v. Sliker, 751 F.2d 477, 497–500 (2d Cir. 1984), *cert. denied*, 105 S.Ct. 1772 (1985) (identification of voices on tape recording).

[3] Furtado v. Bishop, 604 F.2d 80, 90 (1st Cir. 1979), *cert. denied*, 444 U.S. 1035 (1980) (error, though harmless, for trial judge to admit affidavit of dead lawyer after determining its trustworthiness on personal knowledge of the deceased).

judge relies on his own recollection of what previously occurred, the parties should have an opportunity to challenge the accuracy of the memory,[4] at least where the judge's statements are relevant to a material issue.

A judge may also be forced into the role of a witness by questions of counsel connecting him with events relevant to the trial. For example, if a prosecutor cross-examines a defendant as to whether she remembers certain statements previously made before the same judge, the judge has implicitly been made the guarantor of their accuracy. To avoid this uncomfortable position, the trial judge should use his powers under Rule 611 to curtail lines of questioning connecting him to the facts of the case.

The rule refers to trials. It does not cover such usual situations as the court's indicating on sentencing or a post-sentencing hearing what it saw in its presence.[5] On hearings of contempt that took place in the presence of the court, the judge is not disqualified by Rule 605. However, due process or statute[6] may require trial by another judge.

The rule does not create a privilege. Where the judge's testimony may be critical, he has no right to deny a party his aid. Refusal to testify may therefore create reversible error for exclusion of evidence. If the case is before the judge required as a witness a mistrial may be required unless the parties will stipulate to the facts in issue. Even when the judge does not testify, the mere knowledge that he has been sought as a witness may be prejudicial. The problem is alleviated to a great extent by statute.[7] A fed-

---

[4] *Cf.* Coley v. Star & Herald Co., 390 F.2d 364, 369 (5th Cir. 1968) (a judge's grant of summary judgment not sustained on basis of judicial notice of a case, that the judge had previously decided, where record did not indicate whether the judge had physically examined the record of the prior case or relied on his own recollection).

[5] *Cf.* United States v. Alberico, 453 F.Supp. 178, 186 (D. Colo. 1977), *aff'd,* 604 F.2d 1315 (10th Cir. 1979) (court refused to disqualify itself on motion made by defendant after conviction, which would have left case in limbo and staved off sentencing, because Rule 605 only applies to preclude judge's testimony at trial over which he presides). The limits on a judge's power to rely on recollections of what occurred a trial are discussed in the **Treatise** at ¶ 605[04].

[6] Fed. R. Crim. P. 42(b) disqualifies a judge from presiding at proceedings to punish contempts involving "disrespect" or "criticism" directed at himself.

[7] 28 U.S.C. § 455 (1982).

eral judge is required to disqualify himself in any proceeding in which his impartiality might reasonably be questioned. The effect of this statute is to require the parties to inform a judge of their intention to call him as a witness, enabling him to disqualify himself before trial, and before a question under Rule 705 arises.

¶ 11.03[02]   Judge Called or Testifying[1]

If the judge does not disqualify himself prior to trial and is thereafter called as a witness he has two options. In a civil case he can recuse himself or he can continue with the trial. If he adopts the first approach a new trial should be granted. If the judge continues with the trial and the verdict favors the proponent, the appellate court must examine the situation even if no objection was made at trial.

If the judge testified either formally or putatively to a material fact, the appellate court should generally reverse because of the likelihood of prejudice. Where the judge's testimony related solely to a formal, non-material matter the appellate court must weigh the facts of the particular case as it does whenever a claim of plain or substantial error is made.

Where the judge refused to testify, the reviewing court must decide on the facts of the particular case whether the mere seeking of the judge's testimony was sufficiently prejudicial to require a reversal. Precisely what was said in the jury's presence, the importance attached to the testimony by the proponent, and the other witnesses' knowledge of the event are all factors that should be considered. To determine how important the testimony would have been, a proffer of proof should be made outside the presence of the jury and the judge should cooperate fully in making a full record of how he would have testified.

In a criminal case, the problems attendant on calling a judge as a witness are considerably more complex because of the special constitutional guarantees to which a defendant in a criminal trial is entitled.[2] Where the judge disqualifies himself when he is called, a further complication arises since Federal Rule of Criminal Procedure

---

[1] See **Treatise** at ¶¶ 605[02]–[03].

[2] See **Treatise** at ¶ 605[03].

25(a) provides that if a judge is disabled and unable to proceed with a trial, any regularly sitting judge may be substituted. It is unclear whether a judge who withdraws when called to testify is "disabled" within the meaning of Rule 25(a).[3]

¶ 11.04   Competency of Juror as Witness—Rule 606

¶ 11.04[01]   Scope[1]

Rule 606 deals with a variety of situations in which a member of a jury is incompetent to testify. Subdivision (a) is concerned with the juror as a witness in the trial of the case in which the juror is empanelled. Subdivision (b) deals with the juror as a witness attacking or supporting the validity of a verdict or indictment.

¶ 11.04[02]   Juror as Witness at Trial[2]

Subdivision (a) of Rule 606 bars a juror from testifying as a witness in the case which he is trying. The subdivision states:

Rule 606

COMPETENCY OF JUROR AS WITNESS

(a) At the trial.—A member of the jury may not testify as a witness before that jury in the trial of the case in which the juror is sitting. If the juror is called so to testify, the opposing party shall be afforded an opportunity to object out of the presence of the jury.

The rule does not prevent the court from questioning jurors on issues such as the effect on them of publicity, attempted tampering and the like.[3] Jurors are prohibited from testifying because it is believed that counsel will be inhibited in cross-examination by fear of

---

[3] *Id.*

[1] See **Treatise** at ¶ 606[01].

[2] See **Treatise** at ¶ 606[02].

[3] United States v. Robinson, 645 F.2d 661 (8th Cir.), *cert. denied,* 451 U.S. 992 (1981) (juror who had seen defendant in custody of marshals could testify at mistrial motion).

offending the juror who has been sworn as a witness, and that the witness may lose his impartiality by identifying with the side for which he testified. Prohibiting the testimony does not solve the entire problem, for the possibility of prejudice arises as soon as the other jurors become aware that the testimony of one of their fellows is sought. Nor does Rule 606(a) indicate what the judge should do if the offer of proof indicates that the juror's testimony is important. In a criminal case, a refusal to permit a witness to testify for the defendant may raise constitutional problems.

In practice these unanswered questions are of little significance since persons having knowledge relevant to the facts in issue are far more likely to be challenged for cause and excused as jurors than sworn as witnesses. In the unlikely event that it comes to light during trial that a juror's testimony will be sought, the judge should determine if the offered testimony is excludable pursuant to Rule 403 or excludable pursuant to Rule 6ll.[4] If the testimony is excluded, whether the trial should be aborted depends on the circumstances of the particular case. The judge must consider whether the jurors were aware that the testimony was sought, whether the juror divulged the special case-specific information to the other jurors on the panel, and if so whether such divulgence would have prejudiced the jury, whether the case is civil or criminal, and whether alternate jurors are available.

If the court finds that the juror's testimony is required it should declare a mistrial in a civil as well as in a criminal case. Absent extraordinary circumstances, it should not continue the trial with an alternate juror and permit the ex-juror to testify since Rule 606 clearly expresses a determination that testimony by a juror is inherently prejudicial. To avoid the problem of double jeopardy in criminal cases, if possible, consent of the parties to the granting of the mistrial should be obtained or they should waive the point on the record.

Even if the existence of a juror-witness does not come to light at trial, the careful attorney assuming certain knowledge on the part of the jury of notorious facts in the community, should, where possible, meet the problem by testimony and argument explaining why it does not affect his theory of the case. The "secret juror wit-

---

[4] See discussion of "necessity test" in **Treatise** at ¶ 601[04].

ness" who does his work in the privacy of the jury room is much more dangerous than one who testifies in court where misconceptions and misinformation can be dealt with.[5] Primary reliance for preventing such abuses lies in the thorough jury *voir dire* which minimizes the chance of persons with special knowledge of the case being chosen as jurors.

11.04[03]   Juror Testimony as to Validity or Invalidity of Verdict[1]

Rule 606(b) is a rule of incompetency barring jurors from testifying to the motives, methods or mental processes by which they reached their verdict or failed to reach it.[2] The rule is equally applicable to testimony by grand jurors where the validity of an indictment is under attack.[3] Testimony by a juror in support of a verdict and testimony by non-juror witnesses as to statements by a juror, which would be barred if made by the juror, are disallowed.[4]

Rule 606(b) states:

(b) Inquiry into validity of verdict or indictment. Upon an inquiry into the validity of a verdict or indictment, a juror may not testify as to any

---

[5] Whether jurors become "witnesses" within the reach of the Confrontation Clause when they discuss extra-record factual matters is discussed in the **Treatise** at ¶ 606[02].

[1] See **Treatise** at ¶¶ 606[03]–[04], [07].

[2] *Cf.* Washington v. Strickland, 673 F.2d 879, 903–05 (5th Cir. 1982) (because defendant, "by waiving his right under [state] law to an advisory jury . . . , essentially substituted [state] judge for his jury," error to allow state judge to testify about his mental processes at habeas corpus proceedings), *rev'd on other grounds,* 466 U.S. 668 (1984). But see note 9 suggesting that in certain circumstances constitutional rights may require inquiry into jury deliberations in spite of Rule 606.

[3] See **Treatise** at ¶ 606[01].

[4] Roches v. J.J. Newberry Co., 549 F.2d 1166, 1169 (8th Cir. 1977) (statements by juror to fellow air passenger excluded). But see United States v. Eagle, 539 F.2d 1166 (8th Cir. 1976), *cert. denied,* 429 U.S. 1110 (1977) (witness permitted to testify that juror had told him he realized defendant was connected to other uncharged shootings; juror, however, could not testify because no extraneous influence was involved but only the mental process of the juror; consequently, motion for a new trial was properly denied, citing Rule 606(b)).

matter or statement occurring during the course of the jury's deliberations or to the effect of anything upon that or any other juror's mind or emotions as influencing the juror to assent to or dissent from the verdict or indictment or concerning the juror's mental processes in connection therewith, except that a juror may testify on the question whether extraneous prejudicial information was improperly brought to the jury's attention or whether any outside influence was improperly brought to bear upon any juror. Nor may a juror's affidavit or evidence of any statement by the juror concerning a matter about which the juror would be precluded from testifying be received for these purposes.

Rule 606(b) seeks to reach an accommodation between policies designed to safeguard the institution of trial by jury and policies designed to insure a just result in the individual case. It does so by drawing the dividing line between inquiry into the thought processes of the jurors on the one hand, and inquiry into the existence of conditions or the occurrence of events calculated to exert an improper influence on the verdict on the other. Since inquiry into the thought processes of any individual is at best speculative and the cases suggest that it is relatively easy to convince a juror that he acted mistakenly, a judge's ability to reconstruct the juror's thoughts at the time of his deliberation is doubtful and unverifiable. Where overt factors are present by which the verdict's validity can be objectively assessed, the law's commitment to a just result warrants receiving evidence as to the alleged acts of misconduct. But where the juror would testify solely to matters resting on his own consciousness, the dubious value of the testimony is outweighed by the need for stability in verdicts, and Rule 606(b) renders the testimony incompetent.[5]

The restrictions in Rule 606(b) apply only to inquiry after the verdict or indictment has been reached,[6] or after a partial verdict has

---

[5] United States v. Green, 523 F.2d 229, 235 (2d Cir. 1975) ("the protection of jurors from harassment requires that investigation into the subjective motivations and mental processes of jurors not be permitted"), *cert. denied,* 423 U.S. 1074 (1976). The prevention of fraud by individual jurors who could remain silent during trial and later claim that they were improperly influenced has also been asserted as a reason for a non-impeachment rule. See, *e.g.,* United States v. Eagle, 539 F.2d 1166 (8th Cir. 1976).

[6] Wilsmann v. Upjohn, 572 F.Supp. 242, 245 (W.D. Mich. 1983) (evidence concerning the method used by the jury to reach its damage award excluded). *Cf.* Bays v. Petan Co., 94 F.R.D. 587 (D. Nev. 1982) (Rule 606(b) does not apply to proceeding to determine whether juror should be held in contempt of court for alleged misconduct during deliberation).

been recorded.[7] They do not operate to bar a judge from questioning a jury that returns with an ambiguous or inconsistent verdict.

The question of which side of the line given behavior falls on is not without its difficulties.[8] It is further complicated by *Parker v. Gladden,* a Supreme Court decision which suggests that in criminal cases, at least, constitutional rights may require inquiry into the circumstances regarding a jury's deliberations regardless of the jurisdiction's rule on impeachment by jurors.[9]

Rule 606(b) operates to prohibit testimony as to certain conduct by the jurors which has no verifiable outward manifestations.[10] Excluded would be testimony that a juror misunderstood or disregarded evidence,[11] misunderstood or disregarded the judge's instruc-

---

[7] United States v. Hockridge, 573 F.2d 752, 760 (2d Cir.), *cert. denied,* 439 U.S. 821 (1978) (policy against inquiry into internal deliberations of jury and interest in verdict finality requires extending Rule 606(b) to partial verdicts followed by continuing deliberations; where jury had reached a partial verdict, it "ought not be disturbed absent a showing of the type which would permit impeachment of a complete verdict"); Vizzini v. Ford Motor Co., 72 F.R.D. 132 (E.D. Pa. 1976) (Rule 606 applied to bar statement by juror received after a verdict was accepted and before judgment had been entered), *rev'd on other grounds,* 569 F.2d 754 (3d Cir. 1977) (court reserved decision on whether partial verdicts are subject to Rule 606(b)).

[8] The courts have struggled over whether juror mental incompetency or juror physical disability can be subject to inquiry. See, *e.g.,* Government of Virgin Islands v. Nicholas, 759 F.2d 1073 (1985) (though stating that evidence of physical disability does not come within the exceptions to Rule 606 permitting inquiry into juror activity, the court indicated that inquiry into juror incompetence may be permitted if sufficiently strong showing of incompetence were made); *Cf.* Sullivan v. Fogg, 613 F.2d 465, 467 (2d Cir. 1980) (on appeal from denial of habeas corpus relief court stated "[o]nce a preliminary showing of incompetence or juror misconduct has been made there is a corresponding [due process] right to an inquiry into the relevant surrounding circumstances").

[9] 385 U.S. 363, 87 S.Ct. 468, 17 L.Ed.2d 420 (1966). For a discussion of the *Parker* case, see the **Treatise** at ¶ 606[04]. See also note 28, *infra.*

[10] Carson v. Polley, 689 F.2d 562, 580–82 (5th Cir. 1982) (letter to judge from juror indicating that he thought plaintiff had worthless case and that defendants and court were victims revealed only juror's internal mental processes and were beyond the scope of inquiry); United States v. Gerard, 586 F.2d 896 (1st Cir. 1978) (juror's vacillations and second thoughts did not inpugn validity of guilty verdict).

[11] Wilsmann v. Upjohn, 572 F.Supp. 242, 245 (W.D. Mich. 1983) (evidence that jury included interest as an element of the award of damages excluded). See also Libertelli v. Hoffman-LaRoche, Inc., 565 F.Supp. 234 (S.D.N.Y 1983).

tions,[12] thought that the jury would be kept out indefinitely until agreement was reached,[13] considered an election of the accused not to take the stand,[14] believed that recommending mercy would avoid the death penalty, was overcome by weariness[15] or was harassed by other jurors.[16] The Supreme Court, in a 5–4 opinion, has held that Rule 606(b) would also prohibit a juror from testifying about alcohol and drug use by jurors during the trial.[17] The case suggests a sharp shift towards protecting jurors and verdicts in balancing these objectives against that of verdicts arrived at fairly.

---

[12] Peveto v. Sears, Roebuck and Co., 807 F.2d 486, 488–89 (5th Cir. 1987) (in wrongful death action, Rule 606(b) precludes any inquiry into the decision making processes of the jurors even if they misunderstood the instructions of law; where there is no objection to the instruction, the judges's instruction was not an "extraneous influence" on the jury so as to come within an exception); United States v. Jelsma, 630 F.2d 778 (10th Cir. 1980) (prosecution for operating gambling business of five or more persons; Rule 606(b) precludes judicial inquiry into jury confusion as to number of persons involved in the gambling scheme); United States v. D'Angelo, 598 F.2d 1002, 1003 (5th Cir. 1979) ("The possibility that the jury misunderstood or even intentionally misapplied the law . . . does not warrant reversal of the conviction."); United States v. Neary, 552 F.2d 1184 (7th Cir. 1977) (statement by juror after completion of trial that she had served in "civil" case did not prove her ignorance of government's burden of proof in criminal case; in any event, juror may not impeach verdict by testimony concerning his misconception of court's instructions).

[13] United States v. Weiner, 578 F.2d 757 (9th Cir.) (testimony that juror had voted guilty with reservation barred), *cert. denied,* 439 U.S. 981 (1978).

[14] United States v. Falsia, 724 F.2d 1339, 1343 (9th Cir. 1983); United States v. Friedland, 660 F.2d 919 (3d Cir. 1981), *cert. denied,* 456 U.S. 989 (1982).

[15] Roches v. J.J. Newberry Co., 549 F.2d 1166, 1169 (8th Cir. 1977) (juror's statement indicating prejudice against husband of party and desire to complete case quickly were not received).

[16] United States v. Musto, 540 F.Supp. 318 (D. N.J. 1982); Simmons First Nat'l Bank v. Ford Motor Co., 88 F.R.D. 344 (E.D. Ark. 1980).

[17] Tanner v. United States, — U.S. —, 107 S.Ct. 2739, 2348, 97 L.Ed.2d 90, 107 (1987) (Court affirmed trial court's denial of criminal defendant's motion for leave to interview the jurors, and refusal to hold evidentiary hearing to inquire into allegations by two jurors that jurors had engaged in substantial drinking of alcohol and ingestion of marijuana during lunch breaks on a number of occasions; Court relied on legislative history in concluding that "[d]rugs or alcohol voluntarily ingested by a juror seems no more an 'outside influence' than a virus, poorly prepared food, or lack of sleep"; dissent, citing **Treatise,** found such conduct to lie clearly within the "outside influence exception.").

Rule 606(b) would not render a witness incompetent to testify to juror irregularities such as exposure to threats, acceptance of bribes, or possession of knowledge relevant to the facts in issue obtained not through the introduction of evidence but acquired prior to trial,[18] or during trial, through unauthorized views, experiments,[19] investigations,[20] news media,[21] books or documents,[22] or through consultation with parties, witnesses or others,[23] regardless of whether the jury misconduct occurred within or without the jury room.

Rule 606(b) would not bar testimony by a juror that all the jurors agree that through inadvertence, oversight or mistake the verdict an-

---

[18] Hard v. Burlington Northern R.R., 812 F.2d 482, 486 (9th Cir. 1987) (in a FELA action brought by a railroad worker in which plaintiff was awarded minimal damages, the trial court abused its discretion by not allowing an evidentiary hearing into juror's failure to disclose on voir dire that he had previously worked for the defendant and his subsequently telling other jurors that the defendant-railroad pays all medical expenses of injured employees; where juror's past personal experiences "are related to the litigation, as they are here, they constitute extraneous evidence which may be used to impeach the jury's verdict"; citing **Treatise**); United States v. Blair, 444 F.Supp. 1273 (D.C. Cir. 1978) (juror A allowed to testify that she heard juror B state that she had known the defendant; juror B then testified that she had known defendant in school and that she had heard he was hooked on drugs; court ordered new trial).

[19] United States v. Castello, 526 F.Supp. 847 (W.D. Tex. 1981) (ballistics experiment); Simon v. Kuhlman, 488 F.Supp. 59 (S.D.N.Y. 1979) (jury experimented with whether it was possible to identify person in stocking mask).

[20] *In re* Beverly Hills Fire Litigation, 695 F.2d 207 (6th Cir. 1982), *cert. denied,* 461 U.S. 929 (1983); United States v. Bagnarial, 665 F.2d 877 (9th Cir. 1981), *cert. denied,* 456 U.S. 962 (1982) (research in public library).

[21] United States v. Bruscino, 662 F.2d 450, 460 (7th Cir. 1981) (testimony that juror carried newspaper clippings regarding case into jury room), *rev'd on other grounds,* 687 F.2d 938 (7th Cir. 1982), *cert. denied,* 459 U.S. 1228 (1983).

[22] United States v. Bassler, 651 F.2d 600 (8th Cir.), *cert. denied,* 454 U.S. 1151 (1982); United States v. Pinto, 486 F.Supp. 578 (E.D. Va. 1980).

[23] United States v. Green, 620 F.2d 1383 (10th Cir. 1980) (marshal explained eligibility for sentencing under Youth Corrections Act which some jurors may have thought applied to defendant); United States v. Williams, 613 F.2d 573 (5th Cir.), *cert. denied,* 449 U.S. 849 (1980) (communication between trial judge and juror in which juror informed court that she was socially acquainted with defense character witness; appellate court found no abuse of discretion in refusal to grant new trial).

nounced was not the verdict on which agreement had been reached.[24] This situation must be distinguished from the case where a juror is incompetent to testify that he was mistaken or unwilling in giving assent to the verdict.[25]

Several types of jury conduct may present special difficulties. For instance, juror bias manifested in prejudiced comments during the deliberation may be viewed in a variety of ways. Where the comments indicate that the juror had preconceived notions of liability or guilt or personal knowledge about the facts in issue, the statements may be admissible not because they are not prohibited by Rule 606(b), but as tending to prove that the juror lied on the voir dire, a separate question from that of impeachment of verdicts.[26] But what should be done in terms of Rule 606(b)? Can

(*Text continued on page 11–15*)

---

[24] United States v. Dotson, 817 F.2d 1127, 1130 (5th Cir.), *vacated in part on other grounds,* 821 F.2d 1034 (5th Cir. 1987) (district court's ex parte correction of verdict, after jury had been polled and discharged, to acquit defendant on one of ten counts of tax evasion was proper where phone conversations with two jurors and foreman indicated that the jury had unanimously acquitted defendant on one count); Mount Airy Lodge, Inc. v. Upjohn Co., 96 F.R.D. 378 (E.D. Pa. 1982) (two jurors and foreman could be recalled for interviews where plaintiffs' attorneys represented that jurors had congratulated them after jury had answered special interrogatories indicating victory for defendant).

[25] McNulty v. Borden, Inc., 542 F.Supp. 655, 657 (E.D. Pa. 1982).

[26] Hard v. Burlington Northern R.R., 812 F.2d 482 (9th Cir. 1987) (juror's failure to reveal on voir dire that he had previously been employed by defendant not barred by Rule 606(b); citing **Treatise**). *Cf.* Brofford v. Marshall, 751 F.2d 845, 853 (6th Cir. 1985) (statement by juror that she did not put personal prejudices aside during deliberation not admissible to prove that juror lied on *voir dire*).

proof of a biased statement be separated from proof of the effect the statement has on the minds of the jurors, or are the two so inextricably interwoven that the entire testimony should be rejected under the Rule? The line may be very difficult to draw. Generally, it seems better to draw it in favor of juror privacy; in the heat of juror debate all kinds of statements may be made which have little effect on outcome, though taken out of context they seem damning and absurd.[27] However, "[t]here might be instances in which such testimony of the juror could not be excluded without 'violating the plain principles of justice.' "[28]

The question of when a juror is resorting to knowledge obtained outside the record also presents difficulties. If a jury conducted an experiment or read a book not introduced in evidence, a juror would be competent to testify about it, but may a juror testify that another juror reminisced about an experiment he had watched, or a book he had read during his high school days? Though exclusion would appear to be consistent with the rationale of the rule, in a criminal case it might be held to be inconsistent with the right of confrontation.[29]

Rule 606(b) is silent as to whether evidence should be permitted that the jurors reached a verdict by an improper method such as a majority vote, a quotient of the individual juror's awards, or a chance manner such as drawing lots. While it has been held that such behavior constitutes a provable objective irregularity,[30] in

---

[27] United States v. Brooks, 677 F.2d 907, 911 (D.C. Cir. 1982); United States v. Cuzac, 622 F.2d 911 (5th Cir.), *cert. denied*, 449 U.S. 1012 (1980).

[28] McDonald v. Pless, 238 U.S. 264, 268–69, 35 S.Ct. 783, 59 L.Ed. 1300 (1915). See Wright v. United States, 559 F.Supp. 1139, 1151–52 (E.D.N.Y. 1983), *aff'd on other grounds*, 732 F.2d 1048 (2d Cir. 1984), *cert. denied*, 105 S.Ct. 779 (1985) (court suggests that if accused can show by clear and convincing evidence that jury was racially biased, evidence could not be ignored and "[g]iven the potential constitutional difficulties in applying Rule 606(b) to all allegations of racial prejudice, the better rule . . . is to analyze each such claim on a case-by-case basis"; defendant must produce substantial evidence of bias before evidentiary hearings into allegations of juror bias will be held); Smith v. Brewer, 444 F.Supp. 482, 489 (S.D. Iowa); *aff'd*, 577 F.2d 466 (8th Cir.), *cert. denied*, 439 U.S. 967 (1978).

[29] See the discussion in **Treatise** at ¶ 606[04].

[30] Judge Learned Hand in Jorgenson v. York Ice Machinery Corporation, 160 F.2d 432, 435 (2d Cir.), *cert. denied*, 332 U.S. 764 (1947) held that an agreement

light of the rationale of Rule 606(b) and the legislative history, the better view would be to treat such evidence of jury misconduct in deliberations as incompetent. It is extremely unlikely that jurors would agree to be bound by an impermissible method of arriving at a verdict from the onset of their deliberations and never deliberate at all. Rather, the irregularity represents a mode of compromising after initial disagreement that should not be singled out from all the other instances where jurors adjust their initial positions in order to achieve unanimity.[31]

¶ 11.04[04] Role of Court When Misconduct Is Alleged[1]

In determining how a court should react to allegations of juror misconduct, a number of distinctions have to be drawn consonant with the rationale of Rule 606(b). If a party alleges the sort of misconduct about which testimony would be barred, the judge should conclude that further inquiry would be futile. Accordingly, the court should refuse to schedule a hearing, and will deny a motion for a new trial.

There is some uncertainty about whether a hearing must be held whenever a party asserts that there has been misconduct which is not on its face barred by Rule 606(b). While some courts require an evidentiary hearing whenever such misconduct is alleged,[2]

---

to abide by the vote of the majority is provable but does not require a new trial, pointing out that it represented "a no greater impropriety than a 'quotient' verdict."

[31] See Scogin v. Century Fitness, Inc., 780 F.2d 1316 (8th Cir. 1985) (testimony that juror told witness jury had used quotient verdict barred by Rule 606(b)); Multiflex, Inc. v. Samuel Moore & Co., 709 F.2d 980 (5th Cir. 1983), *cert. denied,* 465 U.S. 1100 (1984) (in an antitrust action, court properly ignored defendant's claim that jury awarded impermissible punitive damages or arrived at a "quotient verdict"); United States v. Marques, 600 F.2d 742 (9th Cir.), *cert. denied,* 444 U.S. 1019 (1979) (appellate court held that a claim of compromise verdict cannot be analogized to a verdict by lot and that the compromise verdict did not result from improper outside influence and therefore inquiry was precluded under Rule 606(b)).

[1] See **Treatise** at ¶ 606[05].

[2] United States v. Bagnariol, 665 F.2d 877, 885 (9th Cir. 1981), *cert. denied,* 456 U.S. 962 (1982) (trial court "must hold an evidentiary hearing to determine the precise nature of the extraneous information"); United States v. Phillips, 664 F.2d 971 (5th Cir. 1981), *cert. denied,* 457 U.S. 1136 (1982) (where jury miscon-

others require a preliminary "sufficient showing" of misconduct.[3] It has also been held that it is within the judge's discretion to determine if a hearing is warranted.[4]

When a hearing is held, the jurors may testify to those irregularities whose proof is not barred by the Rule. May they, however, testify to the effect such irregularities had on their minds? The language of Rule 606(b)—"a juror may not testify . . . to the effect of anything upon his or any other juror's mind or emotions"—can be read as meaning that even when the juror is testifying about extraneous information or outside influence, he may not be interrogated about its impact.[5] Or the language quoted above can be viewed as relevant solely to drawing the line between misconduct which is subject to inquiry, and misconduct which is not.[6]

---

duct concerns influence from outside sources, failure of court to hold hearing would constitute an abuse of discretion).

[3] United States v. Marques, 600 F.2d 742 (9th Cir.), *cert. denied,* 444 U.S. 1019 (1979) (affidavit by juror that unnamed juror had allegedly seen all four defendants, who supposedly did not know each other, get into one automobile, while competent, did not indicate prejudice where there was no allegation that the information was passed on to the other jurors, or discussed, or considered); United States v. Williams, 543 F.2d 47, 51 (8th Cir. 1976) (insufficient showing; court did not err in finding that no communication had occurred between witness and juror and in refusing to question the jury about incident).

[4] United States v. Wilson, 534 F.2d 375, 379 (D.C. Cir. 1976) (within judge's discretion "to determine what manner of hearing, if any, is warranted").

[5] Wiedeman v. Galiano, 722 F.2d 335 (7th Cir. 1983) (district court improperly considered and relied on inadmissible post-verdict juror testimony as to whether jury's deliberations were prejudiced by extraneous information); United States v. Greer, 620 F.2d 1383 (10th Cir. 1980) (marshal explained sentencing provisions of Youth Corrections Act to jury; trial judge held hearing and found no prejudice; majority reversed on ground that trial judge had received evidence as to effect of extraneous material on jury deliberations; dissent); United States v. Castello, 526 F.Supp. 847, 850 (W.D. Tex. 1981) (court may consider objective facts only: "(1) whether the extrinsic material was actually received, and if so, how it was received; (2) how long it was available to the jury; (3) the extent to which the jury discussed and considered the material; (4) whether the material intruded before or after the jurors reached a verdict and, if before verdict was reached, at what point in the deliberations it occurred; and (5) 'other matters as may bear on the issue of the reasonable possibility of whether they affected the verdict' ").

[6] Krause v. Rhodes, 570 F.2d 563, 570 (6th Cir. 1977), *cert. denied,* 435 U.S. 924 (1978) (court noted that Rule 606 would permit testimony as to threats to ju-

Since Rule 606(b) is designed to protect jury privacy, shielding the juror's thought processes from inquiry seems desirable. Consequently, a court should apply an objective test to determine prejudicial effect, rather than elicit testimony about the jurors' subjective reactions. In this area as elsewhere, the trial court must have discretion so that it can evaluate the prejudice in light of the facts of the case. While certain types of jury misbehavior may be so prejudicial that a new trial must be ordered if the allegations can be established as true, other types of misbehavior may not require any judicial action.[7]

¶ 11.04[05]   The Propriety of Counsel Interviewing Clients After Verdict[1]

Rule 606(b) is silent as to the propriety of counsel interviewing jurors after they have been discharged in an attempt to discover details of juror conduct which could be used to support or resist a motion to set aside a verdict. Whether all investigations of jurors need be under judicial control from the onset is debatable.[2] The

---

ror but stated that "the question of whether a juror may be interrogated after a verdict is rendered as to the effect of extraneous influences on him . . . is not settled by Rule 606.") The disagreement is in part attributable to uncertainty over whether the drafters of Rule 606(b) intended to overrule the Supreme Court's second decision in Remmer v. United States, 350 U.S. 377, 76 S.Ct. 425, 100 L.Ed. 435 (1955), in which the Court criticized the district court for taking an unduly restrictive view of the Supreme Court's mandate, in the first *Remmer* case, 348 U.S. 904, 75 S.Ct. 288, 99 L.Ed. 710 (1954), to investigate a communication with a juror. The Court stated: "It was our intention that the entire picture should be explored and the incident complained of and to be examined included Satterly's communication with the juror and the impact thereof upon him then, immediately thereafter, and during the trial." 350 U.S. at 379.

[7] United States v. Bagnariol, 665 F.2d 877, 885 (9th Cir. 1981), *cert. denied*, 456 U.S. 962 (1982) ("No bright line divides cases of juror misconduct that demand reversal from those that must be affirmed"); United States v. Bassler, 651 F.2d 600, 603 (8th Cir.), *cert. denied*, 454 U.S. 944 (1982) (in criminal case "whether such effects might be shown to affirm or negate the conclusion of actual prejudice, a presumption of prejudice is created and the burden is on the government to prove harmlessness"); Lanza v. Poretti, 537 F.Supp. 777, 782 (E.D. Pa. 1982) ("whether prejudice resulted . . . must be resolved by the court drawing reasonable inferences as to the probable effect of the jury's misconduct").

[1] See **Treatise** at ¶ 606[06].

[2] United States v. Moten, 582 F.2d 654, 665–66 (2d Cir. 1978) ("At a minimum

American Bar Association's Code of Professional Responsibility permits investigations without court supervision, but suggests that they be conducted with circumspection and restraint.[3] It is within the judge's power to order that all interviews be conducted under its supervision.[4]

To prevent harassment in cases which are notorious the court may prevent interviews by counsel. It should inform jurors that they are not obligated to speak to anyone. Protection against the press is warranted by arranging, at the jurors' request, for the jury to be taken out by back doors and furnished with limousine service to their homes.

... notice to opposing counsel and the court should be given" before post-verdict interviews of jurors are held).

[3] See **Treatise** at ¶ 606[06].

[4] See, *e.g.*, United States v. Cauble, 532 F.Supp. 804 (E.D. Tex. 1982), *aff'd*, 757 F.2d 282 (5th Cir. 1985).

CHAPTER 12

Credibility

SYNOPSIS

12–1

(Rel.3–9/90 Pub.819)

¶ 12.01　Overview of Impeachment and Rehabilitation[1]

The Federal Rules of Evidence do not comprehensively treat either impeachment or rehabilitation. Rather, a few aspects of each are expressly covered. Rules 608 and 609 govern impeachment by evidence of character and conviction of crime, respectively; Rule 613 establishes the foundation requirements for impeachment by prior inconsistent statements; Rule 610 abolishes impeachment by evidence of religious belief; and Rule 608 deals with some aspects of rehabilitating testimony.

At common law—apart from observed reaction in the courtroom—there were six modes of impeachment: by proof of bias, mental incapacity, contradiction, prior inconsistent statement, bad character including conviction, and religious belief. Because these matters originally related to competency and were only gradually and at different times converted into questions of credibility, each mode of impeachment was treated separately by the courts and developed its own unique distinctions and limitations. Such an approach is outmoded and should be discarded now that the Federal Rules are in effect. Technicalities submerge the basic aim of all credibility rules: evidence should be admitted if it better enables the trier of fact to determine when a witness is lying or telling the truth. Analysis of the proffered evidence in terms of its capacity to shed light on the particular witness' credibility eliminates the so-called "collateral" test insofar as it is mechanically applied, and simplifies many of the artificial rules and exceptions that evolved in connection with the use of prior statements. See discussion below.

Although the Federal Rules do not expressly cover all aspects of credibility, a recasting of the case law is appropriate because of the overriding mandate expressed in Rules 102, 401 and 403, emphasizing the need for relevant evidence that enhances the possibility of ascertaining the truth and doing justice. Evidence offered for impeachment should be analyzed in terms of the criteria of Rules 401 and 403—is its probative value on credibility assessment sufficiently high to warrant admission, taking into account the dangers specified in Rule 403?[2] Evidence that passes

---

[1] *See* **Treatise** at ¶ 607[02].

[2] *See, e.g.,* United States v. Robinson, 530 F.2d 1076, 1081 (D.C. Cir. 1976) ("[I]f the prejudice outweighs the benefit, the judge sometimes excludes the

these hurdles as to a particular theory of impeachment is admissible even if it would have to be excluded if offered on another theory.[3]

The Supreme Court has held that illegally obtained evidence may be used for impeachment.[4] It should, however, be excluded if it is unreliable, or otherwise incapable of passing a Rule 403 balancing test.[5]

¶ 12.01[01] Impeachment: Bias[1]

Impeachment by showing the witness to be biased rests on two assumptions: (1) that certain relationships and circumstances impair the impartiality of a witness and (2) that a witness who is not impartial may—sometimes consciously but perhaps

evidence with the conclusory comment that the case involves only 'collateral' character impeachment; while if high probative value offsets slight prejudice, he may say that the evidence is admissible impeachment for bias. To avoid the possibility that confusion may lurk in such labeling and shorthand, it would be preferable to confront the problem explicitly, acknowledging and weighing both the prejudice and the probative worth of impeachment in the spirit of balancing stressed in the newly effective Federal Rules.") (footnotes omitted). *Cf.* Rule 609(a), as amended in 1990, discussed at ¶ 12.04*infra* .

[3] United States v. Abel, 469 U.S. 45, 105 S. Ct. 465, 83 L. Ed. 2d 450 (1984) ("[T]here is no rule of evidence which provides that testimony admissible for one purpose and inadmissible for another purpose is thereby rendered inadmissible; quite the contrary is the case. It would be a strange rule of law which held that relevant, competent evidence which tended to show bias on the part of a witness was nonetheless inadmissible because it also tended to show that the witness was a liar.").

[4] *See* Michigan v. Harvey, — U.S. —, 110 S. Ct. 1176, — L. Ed. 2d — (1990) (statements taken in violation of defendant's sixth amendment right to counsel may be used to impeach the defendant); Harris v. New York, 401 U.S. 222, 91 S. Ct. 643, 28 L. Ed. 2d 1 (1971). *See* discussion of Impeachment By Illegally Obtained Evidence in **Treatise** at ¶ 607[09]. *But see* James v. Illinois, — U.S. —, 110 S. Ct. 643, — L. Ed. 2d — (1990) (holding that the *Harris* impeachment exception is limited to defendant's own testimony; prosecution may not use illegally obtained evidence to impeach defense witnesses).

[5] *See, e.g.,* discussion *infra* of limiting impeachment by contradiction even when it satisfies the constitutional test set forth by the Supreme Court in United States v. Havens, 446 U.S. 620, 100 S. Ct. 1912, 64 L. Ed. 2d 559, *reh'g denied,* 448 U.S. 911 (1980), *cert. denied,* 450 U.S. 995 (1981).

[1] *See* **Treatise** at ¶ 607[03].

unwittingly—shade testimony in favor of or against one of the parties.[2] Since bias is always significant in assessing the witness' credibility, the trier must be sufficiently informed of the underlying relationships, circumstances and influences operating on the witness so that, in the light of experience, the trier can determine whether a mistake or lie by the witness could reasonably be expected as a probable human reaction.

Courts are, therefore, very liberal in accepting testimony relevant to a showing of bias. The Supreme Court explained in *United States v. Abel*:

Proof of bias is almost always relevant because the jury, as finder of fact and weigher of credibility, has historically been entitled to assess all evidence which might bear on the accuracy and truth of a witness' testimony. The "common law of evidence" allowed the showing of bias by extrinsic evidence, while requiring the cross-examiner to "take the answer of the witness" with respect to less favored forms of impeachment.[3]

The exposure of a witness' motivation in testifying is so significant that in a criminal case curtailment of this right may amount to a denial of confrontation[4] or due process[5] rights. Even when

[2] United States v. Abel, 469 U.S. 45, 105 S. Ct. 465, 469, 83 L. Ed. 2d 450 (1984) ("Bias is a term used in the 'common law of evidence' to describe the relationship between a party and a witness which might lead the witness to slant, unconsciously or otherwise, his testimony in favor or against a party.").

[3] 105 S. Ct. at 469. *But cf.* Outley v. City of New York, 837 F.2d 587, 594 (2d Cir. 1988) (in civil rights action alleging police brutality, it was reversible error to permit cross-examination and argument concerning the plaintiff's prior lawsuits against law enforcement officers, when there was no evidence of a pattern of fraudulent lawsuits; the court distinguished *Abel;* the evidence was more of an attack on the plaintiff's character than a showing of bias).

[4] Davis v. Alaska, 415 U.S. 308, 316–17, 94 S. Ct. 1105, 39 L. Ed. 2d 347 (1974) (state's interest in protecting the confidentiality of juvenile offenders' records must yield when the witness' probationary status following a juvenile adjudication provides a basis for inferring undue prosecutorial pressures or a motive to lie because of possible concern at being suspected as the perpetrator of the charged crime); United States v. Lynn, 856 F.2d 430, 432–34 (1st Cir. 1988) (error to cut off questioning concerning polygraph test, which witness took as part of his plea agreement with the government); United States v. Anderson, 881 F.2d 1128, 1136–1139 (D.C. Cir. 1989) (defendant's right of confrontation violated when trial court refused to permit cross-examination of key prosecution witness about recent dismissal of murder charge against her).

there has been a restriction on cross-examination, however, the error may, at times, constitute only harmless constitutional error.[6]

Some limitations on introducing evidence for the purpose of establishing bias do exist. In the first place, the proffered evidence must meet the relevancy test of Rule 401—it must tend to show that the likelihood of bias that might affect the trier's evaluation of credibility is more probable than it would have been without the evidence.[7] Secondly, the trial court has a limited discretion pursuant to Rules 102, 104(b), 403, 611, 901(a) and 1008 to control the extent of the proof.[8] While the court will not cut off

---

[5] Giglio v. United States, 405 U.S. 150, 92 S. Ct. 763, 31 L. Ed. 2d 104 (1972) (where witness, upon whose testimony government's case depended almost entirely, has been promised immunity from prosecution, a failure to disclose promise amounted to a denial of due process).

[6] Delaware v. Van Arsdall, 106 S. Ct. 1431, 1438, 89 L. Ed. 2d 674 (1986) ("[T]he constitutionally improper denial of a defendant's opportunity to impeach a witness for bias, like other Confrontation Clause errors, is subject to *Chapman* harmless-error analysis. The correct inquiry is whether, assuming that the damaging potential of the cross-examination were fully realized, a reviewing court might nonetheless say that the error was harmless beyond a reasonable doubt. Whether such an error is harmless in a particular case depends upon a host of factors, all readily accessible to reviewing courts. These factors include the importance of the witness' testimony in the prosecution's case, whether the testimony was cumulative, the presence or absence of evidence corroborating or contradicting the testimony of the witness on material points, the extent of cross-examination otherwise permitted, and, of course, the overall strength of the prosecution's case."). *See* United States v. Towne, 870 F.2d 880, 886–87 (2d Cir.), *cert. denied,* 109 S. Ct. 2456 (1989) (although court should have allowed defense to question witness about state charges pending against him, error was harmless). *See also* United States v. Anderson, 881 F.2d 1128, 1140 (D.C. Cir. 1989).

[7] United States v. Williams, 875 F.2d 846, 852 (11th Cir. 1989) (no error in exclusion of evidence that defendant's secretary, who testified for prosecution, had borne child of man involved in litigation with defendant; defendant failed to demonstrate a connection between the affair, the prior litigation and the present case and mere assertion of relationship does not suffice).

[8] Delaware v. Van Arsdall, 106 S. Ct. 1431, 1435, 89 L. Ed. 2d 674 (1986) ("It does not follow, of course, that the Confrontation Clause of the Sixth Amendment prevents a trial judge from imposing any limits on defense counsel's inquiry into the potential bias of a prosecution witness. On the contrary, trial judges retain wide latitude insofar as the Confrontation Clause is concerned to impose reasonable limits on such cross-examination based on concerns about, among other things, harassment, prejudice, confusion of the

completely all inquiry into bias, it may limit the scope of the inquiry in order to protect a party from prejudice,[9] or a witness from unnecessary harassment or to further the policies of some other evidentiary rule.[10] The trial court may also limit the extent of cross-examination into bias if the witness invokes the constitutional privilege against self-incrimination.[11]

issues, the witness' safety, or interrogation that is repetitive or only marginally relevant."). *See* United States v. Candoli, 870 F.2d 496, 503–04 (9th Cir. 1989) (in prosecution for arson, trial court did not abuse its discretion in refusing to allow defense to cross-examine the federal agent in charge of the investigation, concerning his three-day suspension for releasing internal forms to the insurance companies that had insured the businesses in the building in which the arson occurred; evidence was cumulative because even without it the jury could reasonably infer that a law enforcement officer would be "biased" against the defendant).

[9] United States v. Abel, 469 U.S. 45, 105 S. Ct. 465, 470, 83 L. Ed. 2d 450 (1984) (where trial court properly allowed proof that defendant and witness belonged to same organization, and that organization was a secret prison sect sworn to perjury and self-protection, court did not err in excluding name of organization, and in sustaining defense objections to prosecutor's questions about the punishment meted out to unfaithful members: "These precautions did not prevent *all* prejudice to respondent . . . , but they did in our opinion ensure that the admission of this highly probative evidence did not *unduly* prejudice respondent."); United States v. Kopituk, 690 F.2d 1289, 1336–37 (11th Cir. 1982), *cert. denied,* 461 U.S. 928 (1983) (where defense was permitted to show witness' participation in plot to kill business associate, no error to have prohibited questioning about the proposed method of killing with ice-pick which court felt would only inflame jury).

[10] *See, e.g.,* United States v. Tracey, 675 F.2d 433, 437 (5th Cir. 1982) (no abuse of discretion in trial court refusing to allow defense to question only prosecution witness about incident in which then United States Attorney had come to bail him out after arrest for drunkenness; trial court excluded evidence out of concern that allowing the inquiry would result in testimony by United States Attorney; appellate court found that jury had heard considerable other evidence from which it could deduce relationship between government and witness, and that proffered evidence was cumulative).

[11] *See, e.g.,* Coil v. United States, 343 F.2d 573, 577–79 (8th Cir.), *cert. denied,* 382 U.S. 821 (1965) (court allowed witness to invoke privilege against self-incrimination when questioned about two unrelated crimes involving narcotics; theory of defense was that witness would steal, burglarize or lie to obtain narcotics). *But cf.* United States v. Kaplan, 832 F.2d 676 (1st Cir. 1987), citing **Treatise** (error, but harmless, for court to prohibit any questioning that would cause government witness to invoke the fifth amendment before the jury; the invocation of the privilege is a form of impeachment).

Except for the rare case where the evidence directly tends to establish that the witness admitted that his testimony would be affected by his feelings towards a party,[12] the existence of bias can only be demonstrated circumstantially by proof of relationships or conduct or utterances. While there can be no precise catalogue of the sources of bias, certain situations recur so frequently that they raise immediate suspicion of bias, which a careful advocate should look for in scrutinizing the background of prospective witnesses prior to trial to determine whether they are vulnerable to impeachment. If the witness is highly vulnerable, counsel should ascertain whether the same point could be made by another, less susceptible to attack. If the witness is essential, counsel will have no choice but to use the witness, but the witness must be prepared to withstand the attack and counsel should arrange for rehabilitating testimony when allowable.

Relationships between a party and a witness are always relevant to a showing of bias whether the relationship is based on ties of family, sex—heterosexual[13] or homosexual,[14]—money,[15] membership in organizations,[16] friendship,[17] enmity,[18] or fear.[19]

---

[12] There is no hearsay problem because the evidence is being used to show the witness' state of mind. *See* Rules 801(c), 803(3).

[13] *See, e.g.,* United States v. Willis, 647 F.2d 54 (9th Cir. 1981) (denial of defendant's right to confrontation necessitating reversal to have prohibited defendant from cross-examining narcotics agent about his alleged sexual relationship with defendant's live-in girlfriend who had been chief informant).

[14] But evidence of homosexuality may be so prejudicial as to warrant exclusion under Rule 403 if the prejudice substantially outweighs the probative value. *See, e.g.,* United States v. Wright, 489 F.2d 1181, 1186 (D.C. Cir. 1973) (proof of homosexual advances rejected despite relevancy where conduct was ambiguous and potentially prejudicial).

[15] *See, e.g.,* Collins v. Wayne Corp., 621 F.2d 777, 784 (5th Cir. 1980) (since pecuniary interest in outcome of case may bias witness, appropriate to cross-examine expert witness about fees earned in prior cases).

[16] *See* United States v. Abel, 469 U.S. 45, 105 S. Ct. 465, 83 L. Ed. 2d 450 (1984) (witness and defendant were members of secret prison organization).

[17] *See, e.g.,* United States v. Robinson, 530 F.2d 1076, 1080 (D.C. Cir. 1976) ("open to the government . . . to reveal aspects of [witness'] relationship evidencing a special partiality toward defendant and particular motive to testify falsely on his behalf").

[18] *See, e.g.,* Dick v. Watonwan County, 562 F. Supp. 1083 (D. Minn. 1983), *rev'd on other grounds,* 738 F.2d 939 (8th Cir. 1984) (not error to permit

The witness' relationship with the litigation, or another witness, is also significant. In a criminal case, bias may be manifested by the witness' legal status and treatment. Jurors may take into consideration that a witness was a paid informer,[20] was paid maintenance costs as a material witness in protective custody,[21] was a co-indictee,[22] was granted immunity,[23] hoped to have his sentence reduced,[24] or had received or expected other special treatment.[25] If the witness is crucial to the government's case, appellate courts are particularly careful to scrutinize the cross-examination in its entirety—a number of errors insufficient in

---

plaintiff's daughter to testify concerning her rebuff of sexual advances made by a defense witness).

[19] United States v. Bratton, 875 F.2d 439, 443–44 (5th Cir. 1989) (no error in government's showing that defendant had previously physically abused his wife and threatened her with a gun as this conduct of defendant could have induced wife to testify falsely out of fear of husband); United States v. Briggs, 457 F.2d 908 (2d Cir.), *cert. denied,* 409 U.S. 986 (1972) (threats by defendant).

[20] *See, e.g.,* United States v. Leja, 568 F.2d 493 (6th Cir. 1977) (reversible error to preclude defense from cross-examining informer about his rate of reimbursement for the entire period of his employment; trial court had only permitted questions about amounts informer had received in instant case).

[21] *See* United States v. Librach, 520 F.2d 550 (8th Cir. 1975), *cert. denied,* 429 U.S. 939 (1976) (new trial required where government failed to disclose that principal witness was in protective custody, had been granted immunity, and had been paid almost $10,000).

[22] *See, e.g.,* United States v. Musgrave, 483 F.2d 327, 338 (5th Cir. 1973), *cert. denied,* 414 U.S. 1023 (1973) (although witness had been acquitted, "prior status as coindictee certainly suggested a personal interest in the litigation, a potential lack of complete impartiality").

[23] *See, e.g.,* United States. v. Scharf, 558 F.2d 498 (8th Cir. 1977). Once the witness is impeached, questions may arise as to whether the entire immunity-for-testimony agreement becomes admissible. *See, e.g.,* United States v. Rubier, 651 F.2d 628 (9th Cir.), *cert. denied,* 454 U.S. 875 (1981).

[24] *See* United States v. Iverson, 648 F.2d 737 (D.C. Cir. 1981) (chief prosecution witness lied about sentencing status).

[25] *See, e.g.,* United States v. Garza, 574 F.2d 298 (5th Cir. 1978) (reduction of witness' bond); United States v. Wolfson, 437 F.2d 862 (2d Cir. 1970) (witness received no action letter from SEC). *See also* United States v. Anderson, 881 F.2d 1128, 1136–1139 (D.C. Cir. 1989) (defendant's right of confrontation violated when trial court refused to permit cross-examination of key prosecution witness about recent dismissal of murder charge against her); United States v. Lynn, 856 F.2d 430, 432–34 (1st Cir. 1988) (error to cut off questioning concerning polygraph test, which witness took as part of his plea agreement with the government).

themselves to warrant reversal may cumulatively convince the court that the jury was not afforded sufficient glimpses into the workings of the witness' mind for it to assess his motivation in testifying.

The identity and residence of the witness are also relevant to bias in two respects. In the first place, "[t]he witness' name and address open countless avenues of in-court examination and out-of-court investigation."[26] Secondly, the witness' residence may be directly relevant to bias by disclosing to the jury "the setting in which to judge the character, veracity or bias of the witness."[27] The witness may, for instance, be in federal custody.[28]

The two-fold significance of residence has led the Supreme Court to hold in a number of cases that counsel may cross-examine a witness as to his present address without a preliminary indication of the relevancy of the inquiry.[29] District judges have, however, been understandably reluctant to force divulgence of a witness' address in cases where the witness fears that he is signing his or his family's death warrant by testifying. If the trial judge concludes that the need to protect the witness precludes divulgence of his exact address or place of employment, defendant is entitled to ask all other relevant questions bearing on credibility that would not affect the witness' safety.[30] Where there

---

[26] Smith v. Illinois, 390 U.S. 129, 131, 88 S. Ct. 748, 19 L. Ed. 2d 956 (1968).

[27] United States v. Varella, 407 F.2d 735, 750 (7th Cir. 1969).

[28] Alford v. United States, 282 U.S. 687, 51 S. Ct. 218, 75 L. Ed. 624 (1931) (conviction reversed because defendant was not permitted to ascertain where witness lived).

[29] 282 U.S. at 693.

[30] United States v. Varella, 692 F.2d 1352, 1355–56 (11th Cir. 1982), *cert. denied,* 463 U.S. 1210 (1983) (after in camera hearing, court limited cross-examination of informants concerning their names, occupations, home and business addresses and names of other cases in which they had testified); United States v. Hughes, 658 F.2d 317 (5th Cir. 1981), *cert. denied,* 455 U.S. 922 (1982) (not plain error to sustain questions concerning witness' address where he was thoroughly cross-examined; extensive discussion). *See also* United States v. Palermo, 410 F.2d 468, 472–73 (7th Cir. 1969) ("government bears the burden of proving to the district judge the existence of such a threat" and must disclose the relevant information to the trial judge "in order that he could make an informed decision").

is hard evidence that the cross-examination is being conducted to punish, harass, or intimidate a witness or his family, the court is justified in taking strong steps to protect the witness by strictly controlling the examination.

[a] Foundation Requirements

There is some disagreement among courts as to whether a foundation has to be laid on cross-examination before a witness can be impeached by extrinsic evidence of utterances or conduct indicative of bias. Rule 613(b), which requires that a witness be afforded an opportunity to explain or deny when extrinsic evidence of a prior inconsistent statement is introduced, does not refer to impeachment by bias. Nor do the Advisory Committee's Notes to Rule 613 indicate whether the policy of the rule should be extended to the bias situation. Prior to the adoption of the Federal Rules, the federal courts did tend to require a foundation for utterances of bias. It is, therefore, reasonable and appropriate to continue the foundation requirement for statements of bias to the extent required by Rule 613—that is, in most instances, to afford the witness an opportunity to explain or deny.[31]

On the other hand, evidence of biased conduct arguably remains exempt from a foundation requirement, since the notes to Rule 613(b) state that "the rule [on inconsistent statements] does not apply to impeachment by evidence of prior inconsistent conduct." Pursuant to Rule 611, the court may require such a foundation, but it should make its ruling before the witness steps down to prevent inadvertent preclusion of the cross-examiner from producing extrinsic proof of the acts tending to show bias.

The court has discretion to waive the requirement of a foundation. *See* Rule 611(a). Careful counsel should either get an advance ruling on the court's position or actually lay the foundation to avoid the embarrassment of a ruling excluding the line of impeachment for failure to lay a foundation. In

[31] United States v. DiNapoli, 557 F.2d 962, 965 (2d Cir.), *cert. denied,* 434 U.S. 858 (1977) (impeachment by prior statement showing bias should be in accord with Rule 613(b)).

general it is desirable to ask the witness sought to be impeached about the statements or acts believed to show bias. If the witness forthrightly admits, that ends the matter with a considerable saving of time and inconvenience to other witnesses.

¶ 12.01[02]   Impeachment: Mental Incapacity[1]

Credibility can always be attacked by showing that the witness' capacity to observe, remember or narrate is impaired. Consequently, the witness' capacity at the time of the event, as well as at the time of trial, are significant. Since defects of this nature reflect on mental capacity for truth-telling rather than on moral inducements for truth-telling, Rule 608 does not apply. The rationale for permitting evidence of less than normal mental capacity is obvious. A witness who is incapable of accurate observation, recollection or communication is less capable than the average person of testifying truthfully regardless of intent.

Although the actual scope of cross-examination is within the trial judge's control, a witness' capacity to perceive the event to which he testifies may be tested on cross-examination or by courtroom experiment. Similarly, courtroom testing of a witness' memory, even as to circumstances unconnected with the trial is a recognized means of impeachment. Counsel needs particular latitude in cross-examining the very young[2] or the very old since extremes of age are known to affect the accuracy of a person's recollections. Particularly in the case of children, however, the court may have to take measures to obtain useful testimony, including examination in chambers or by video.

Under the orthodox rule predating the adoption of the Federal Rules, extrinsic evidence of a witness' mental incapacity was prohibited; such a rigid approach is unwarranted under

---

[1] *See* **Treatise** at ¶ 607[04].

[2] There are special problems in protecting young children testifying to sexual molestation. Special statutes and techniques, including the use of television, hearsay and limits on cross-examination may apply. *Cf.* also the limits in sex offense cases of Rule 412, discussed in Chapter 7 *supra*.

the Federal Rules. Mental incapacity has high probative value on the issue of credibility if it can be established.[3]

(Text continued on page 12–13)

---

[3] Technically Rule 704(b), limiting opinion on the ultimate issue of mental capacity, does not apply to the credibility issue. See discussion in Chapter 13 *infra*. Nevertheless, in deference to Congressional policy the courts are likely to apply a similar approach on credibility.

Admission, as is the case with non-extrinsic proof, should rest in the trial court's discretion. The factors of prejudice and confusion which the court must weigh in applying Rule 403 may frequently dictate exclusion of extrinsic evidence, but at times probative value may be so high as to warrant admission.

Particularly troublesome have been cases where the party seeking to impeach wishes to show that the witness suffers from an abnormal condition such as alcoholism, drug addiction or mental illness. Some courts assume that proof of the abnormality without more proves impairment of the witness' capacity to observe, remember or narrate.

Other courts require that the actual effect on testimonial capacity be shown, the court's conclusion often resting on the nature of the underlying infirmity. In these cases, the dangers of prejudice and confusion are inordinately high.

Although the capacity of witnesses to make accurate eyewitness identifications does not involve an abnormal condition, the courts have increasingly permitted expert psychological testimony on this question,[4] in recognition of the tendency of laypersons to overestimate the value of eyewitness testimony, and the risk of a miscarriage of justice as a result.

[a] Alcohol and Drug Use

Extrinsic evidence is always admissible to show that the witness was under the influence of drink or drugs at the time of the events being testified to, or at the time of testifying.[5] The courts generally exclude evidence of chronic alcoholism as not bearing on credibility.[6] While having the virtue of simplicity, this rule fails to accord

---

[4] *See, e.g.,* United States v. Downing, 753 F.2d 1224 (3d Cir. 1985); People v. McDonald, 37 Cal. 3d 351 (1984). *Cf.* the discussion of experts and mental illness, ¶ 12.03[02][b] *infra.*

[5] *See, e.g.,* Rheaume v. Patterson, 289 F.2d 611, 614 (2d Cir. 1961) (drinking at the time of the event); United States v. Holman, 680 F.2d 1340, 1352–53 (11th Cir. 1982) (use of controlled substances on date of charged offense); United States v. Van Meerbeke, 548 F.2d 415 (2d Cir. 1976), *cert. denied,* 430 U.S. 974 (1977) (opium ingestion while on witness stand).

[6] *See, e.g.,* Poppell v. United States, 418 F.2d 214, 215 (5th Cir. 1969) (general reputation for intemperance "wholly unrelated to the ability of the witness to observe, recall or testify").

with medical reality. Habitual alcoholism, some experts say, causes such extensive mental deterioration that if counsel can prove a long-standing alcoholism, the court should allow expert testimony that the witness' credibility is suspect. The general condition may also tend to establish the particular state at the time in question.

Although the physiological consequences of long-term alcohol use are far from clear, even less is known about the effects of drug addiction. The multiplicity of drugs, the varying reactions they cause, and the far greater odium attached to drug abuse have increased the complexity of a court's task in determining whether evidence of drug addiction should be admitted.

The court's decision should be governed by Rule 403 which rejects mechanical solutions in favor of determinations based on the facts of the case; neither routine rejection nor admission is warranted.[7] Counsel who wish to use evidence of drug addiction for impeachment purposes should furnish the court—outside the hearing of the jury—with specific information about the kind of drug, dosage, its probable effect on the witness, when the witness took it in relation to the chronology of the case, and how often and frequently he used it at other times. Counsel should also be prepared to substantiate the claim that the drugs adversely affected the witness' credibility by expert testimony or recognized literature to that effect.

In addition to assessing probative value, the court must consider the dangers specified in Rule 403. If, as may happen, there

---

[7] *See* United States v. Lochmondy, 890 F.2d 817, 824 (6th Cir. 1989) (court permitted some exploration of prosecution witness's heroin addiction); United States v. Ramirez, 871 F.2d 582 (6th Cir.), *cert. denied,* 110 S. Ct. 127 (1989) (not error for trial court to refuse psychiatric examination of chief prosecution witness who had been addicted to cocaine or to exclude testimony by a defense psychiatrist as to effect of drug usage, which would lead to battle of the experts on the credibility issue).

However, a number of federal courts permit proof of addiction even without requiring proof that the witness' testimonial capacities were impaired, usually on the theory that a user of drugs is a liar, a theory of impeachment that seems to rest more on the character of the witness than on his mental capacity. This theory should therefore be governed by Rule 608. *See, e.g.,* People of Territory of Guam v. Dela Rosa, 644 F.2d 1257, 1261 (9th Cir. 1981) (on retrial, addict instruction should be given if defendant develops testimony that chief prosecution witness is a heroin addict).

is no medical consensus about the effect narcotic usage had on a particular witness' ability to perceive, recall or narrate, the court must decide whether allowing this question to be debated by the experts would not confuse rather than enlighten the jurors. Furthermore, the court may foreclose reference to drugs if it feels that probative value would be substantially outweighed by the potential for prejudice.[8] The nature of the case[9] and the degree of the witness' involvement with drugs may be significant.[10] In a criminal case, for instance, the judge may be more lenient in allowing the narcotic issue to be explored in the impeachment of prosecution witnesses because of the special protection afforded criminal defendants.[11]

[b] Mental Illness

Federal courts recognize that a witness' prior commitment for mental illness has a bearing on credibility. Cross-examination about the witness' previous history is allowed,[1] though it may be curtailed.[2] A hospital record may be admitted if its probative

---

[8] United States v. Kizer, 569 F.2d 504 (9th Cir.), *cert. denied,* 435 U.S. 976 (1978) (potential prejudice of drug addiction evidence outweighed probative value). *Cf.* United States v. James, 576 F.2d 1121 (5th Cir. 1978), *cert. denied,* 442 U.S. 917 (1979) (where witness' addiction had been brought out on cross-examination, not error for trial court to have refused defense counsel the right to examine witness' arms for evidence of recent drug addiction).

[9] Drug use may be relevant to bias as indicating why the witness is cooperating with the government. *See* Government of Virgin Islands v. Hendricks, 476 F.2d 776 (3d Cir. 1973) (discusses dangers of testimony by addicts who are in pay of government).

[10] *Cf.* United States v. Leonardi, 623 F.2d 746, 757 (2d Cir.), *cert. denied,* 447 U.S. 928 (1980) (evidence that prosecution witness had met defendant at methadone clinic properly was excluded as site of meeting did not further impeach witness and posed some danger of prejudice to defendant).

[11] *See, e.g.,* United States v. Lochmondy, 890 F.2d 817, 824 (6th Cir. 1989).

[1] United States v. Lindstrom, 698 F.2d 1154, 1163 (11th Cir. 1983) (reversible error in trial court's restriction of cross-examination of chief prosecution witness where her medical records suggested history of psychiatric disorders; extensive discussion); United States v. Allegretti, 340 F.2d 254, 257 (7th Cir. 1964), *cert. denied,* 381 U.S. 911 (1965).

[2] United States v. Slade, 627 F.2d 293 (D.C. Cir.), *cert. denied,* 449 U.S. 1034 (1980) (no error in restricting cross-examination about details of witness' commitment to mental hospital where jury knew of commitment, drug habit, and witness' hope to avoid imprisonment by cooperation with government).

value outweighs prejudice, confusion, and the opening of this topic would not result in an undue consumption of court time.

When counsel suspects that a witness is not entirely normal even though he has never been formally diagnosed as having a mental illness, counsel can seek to suggest this hypothesis to the jury by adroit cross-examination. The scope of this cross-examination is subject to judicial control exercised in accordance with Rules 403 and 611.[3]

The federal courts have been hesitant in authorizing experts to observe or test witnesses and then relate their findings in the courtroom. The federal courts have generally declined to admit the results of lie detector tests and truth-serum interviews where they have been offered as relevant to the credibility of a witness.[4] The federal courts have also been reluctant to order psychiatric examinations of witnesses,[5] or to permit testimony by experts based on in-court observations of witnesses.[6] This reluctance

---

[3] *See* United States v. Lopez, 611 F.2d 44, 45–46 (4th Cir. 1979) (court prohibited counsel from cross-examining witness about psychiatric examination conducted in connection with his testifying in another prosecution; court applied Rule 403).

[4] United States v. Masri, 547 F.2d 932, 936 (5th Cir.), *cert. denied,* 431 U.S. 932, 97 S. Ct. 2640, 53 L. Ed. 2d 249, 434 U.S. 907, 98 S. Ct. 309, 54 L. Ed. 2d 195 (1977) (results of lie detector tests are inadmissible in federal criminal cases); Lindsey v. United States, 237 F.2d 893, 895 (9th Cir. 1956) ("the courts have not generally recognized the trustworthiness and reliability of such tests as being sufficiently well established to accord the results the status of competent evidence"; leading case). *See* United States v. Miller, 874 F.2d 1255, 1262 (9th Cir. 1989) (error to allow testimony as to actual questions and answers in lie detector test). *But cf.* United States v. Piccinonna, 885 F.2d 1529, 1536 (11th Cir. 1989) (polygraph evidence may be admitted to impeach or corroborate trial testimony, subject to certain preconditions).

[5] *See, e.g.,* United States v. Ramirez, 871 F.2d 582 (6th Cir.), *cert. denied,* 110 S. Ct. 127 (1989) (not error for trial court to refuse psychiatric examination of chief prosecution witness, who had been addicted to cocaine); United States v. Provenzano, 688 F.2d 194, 204 (3d Cir.), *cert. denied,* 459 U.S. 1071 (1982) (not abuse of discretion for trial court to refuse to order psychiatric examinations of two prosecution witnesses; "use of such evidence at trial to attack or support a witness' credibility has not generally been favored").

[6] United States v. Riley, 657 F.2d 1377, 1387 (8th Cir. 1981), *cert. denied,* 459 U.S. 1101 (1983) (not error to exclude psychiatric testimony based on in-court observation of witness). *But see* United States v. Hiss, 8 F. Supp. 559 (S.D.N.Y.), *aff'd,* 185 F.2d 822 (2d Cir. 1950), *cert. denied,* 340 U.S. 948

undoubtedly stems from judicial awareness that psychiatric testimony often confuses rather than enlightens because experts often disagree with each other, and are unclear and contradictory in their terminology. Psychiatrists may not readily be able to relate their diagnosis of the witness to his ability to give credible testimony since they are not geared to answering the questions in which a court is interested. This factor is observed in connection with Congressional action in adopting Rule 704(b), discussed in Chapter 13 *infra*.

Nevertheless, courts should maintain a flexible attitude to the admissibility of psychiatric or other expert testimony offered to impeach the credibility of a witness. Admissibility will depend on the judge's evaluation of whether the deleterious impact the psychiatric testimony might have on the course of the particular trial would be justified by the insight the jury might gain into the capacity of the witness to observe, recollect and relate truthfully and accurately. Variable factors affecting the probative value of the testimony would include the degree of consensus in the medical community about the diagnosis and significance of the particular symptoms presented by the witness, the degree of certainty with which the expert can testify—which depends partly on whether there has been an out-of-court examination or only in-court observation, and the posture of the credibility issue in the case. If credibility is crucial, the court should be more lenient in allowing the jury to hear testimony that may be helpful.

One procedural protection can be insisted upon by the court— notice in advance of trial.[7] The very real possibility of prejudice, confusion and undue consumption of time mandates pretrial exploration of these issues to the fullest extent possible. The opponent is entitled to know the names of the experts who will be called and, if available, to have their reports showing the theory on which they will testify, and the reports and records on which they will base their opinions. Insofar as possible, the court

---

(1951) (psychiatrist allowed to testify on basis of in-court observation of witness and study of witness' writings). Although the *Hiss* case is a leading case on the use of psychiatric testimony for impeachment, it is cited more frequently in the federal courts in distinguishing the case at hand than as a precedent.

[7] See discussion of other procedures for controlling expert testimony in Chapter 13 *infra*.

should make its ruling known as long before the trial as possible so that both sides can try the issue properly.

¶ 12.01[03] Impeachment: Contradiction[1]

Impeachment by contradiction rests on the inference that if a witness is mistaken as to one fact, perhaps he is mistaken as to others, and therefore all of the witness' testimony is suspect. Obviously, however, the strength of this inference will vary with the circumstances. A misstatement about the weather on the day the witness signed a petition in bankruptcy is not particularly conclusive on whether his denial that he sought to defraud creditors should be believed. On the other hand, a mistake about the weather may be probative both of a substantive issue and the witness' lack of credibility, if he is maintaining that he was in Tucson the day the prosecution claims he murdered his wife in Maine.[2] The danger exists that a persuasive trial attorney could use even a misstatement about the weather in the bankruptcy example to convince a jury that the witness is not worthy of belief.[3] In addition to confusing the jury, the contradiction may cause prejudice if it concerns events that have moral implications, particularly if the witness is a party whom the jury may consequently wish to punish.[4] Furthermore, proof of contradictions by extraneous evidence may consume a good deal of time.

---

[1] *See* **Treatise** at ¶ 607[05].

[2] United States v. Robinson, 544 F.2d 110, 114 (2d Cir. 1976), *cert. denied,* 435 U.S. 905 (1978) (defendant's alibi witness claimed he was with defendant on day of bank robbery and that he remembered day because he had picked up unemployment check; prosecution could properly attempt to impeach witness by proving that he had not received a check on that day).

[3] *See, e.g.,* United States v. Harris, 542 F.2d 1283, 1317 (7th Cir. 1976), *cert. denied,* 430 U.S. 934 (1977) (not error to exclude evidence that witness had lied to authorities concerning dates of her birth and marriage; evidence properly excluded that witness may have been in error in stating that defendant had received large sums of money where evidence was being offered as basis for inference that witness may also have been in error about defendant's participation in conspiracy).

[4] *See, e.g.,* United States v. Jaqua, 485 F.2d 193 (5th Cir. 1973) (conviction for interfering with border patrol guard reversed where after defendant denied having a temper, government questioned him about three prior assaults).

These factors of confusion, prejudice and waste of time are the ones which Rule 403 directs courts to consider in determining whether otherwise relevant evidence should be excluded. Historically, however, limitations on impeachment by contradiction were imposed not via a rule of discretion but rather by applying the so-called "collateral matter" test. A fact sought to be proved was not classified as collateral if (1) it was relevant in that it tended to prove or disprove a material proposition of fact, or (2) it was admissible for impeachment on some theory other than contradiction, such as bias, character for untruthfulness, or mental incapacity. Cases predating the Federal Rules indicate that discerning the boundary between direct and collateral issues is frequently a matter of difficulty and dispute. A Rule 403 approach which analyzes the probative strength of the evidence and assesses the dangers attendant on its admission seems more helpful in focusing on the primary truth-seeking function of the law.[5]

Recasting the "collateral matter" test into a rule of discretion also solves another problem on which courts are divided. In some jurisdictions, the bar against contradiction by extrinsic facts on collateral matters is applied only if the fact which is to be contradicted was elicited on cross-examination. If the witness volunteered the statement on direct, the bar is not applied. Other courts, however, refuse to admit extrinsic contradictory evidence on collateral matters regardless of whether the fact to be contradicted was introduced on direct or cross-examination.

The Supreme Court has held that it does not constitutionally matter whether the false statements which the extrinsic evidence rebuts were made on direct examination or on cross-examination that was within the scope of the direct.[6] The Court focuses on

---

[5] *See, e.g.,* United States v. Tarantino, 846 F.2d 1384, 1410 (D.C. Cir.), *cert. denied,* 109 S. Ct. 108, 174 (1988) (after prosecution witness testified that defendant had given her the deed to a house, in return for her services in drug conspiracy, testimony that witness told police officer that defendant owned the house, a statement that witness denied making, was properly excluded pursuant to Rule 403 as not sufficiently probative under the circumstances); Barrera v. E.I. Dupont de Nemours & Co., Inc., 653 F.2d 915 (5th Cir. 1981) (proper inquiry when ruling on impeaching evidence is balancing test of Rule 403); United States v. Pantone, 609 F.2d 675, 681 (3d Cir. 1979) (court endorsed balancing test).

[6] United States v. Havens, 446 U.S. 620, 100 S. Ct. 1912, 64 L. Ed. 2d 559, *reh'g denied,* 448 U.S. 911 (1980), *cert. denied,* 450 U.S. 995 (1981)

the propriety of the cross-examination rather than on when defendant made the statement. In the case before it, however, the rebutting evidence had high probative value; it was excluded and unusable substantively only because it had been obtained through an illegal search and seizure. When the proffered extrinsic evidence has no relevancy to a material proposition—*i.e.,* it is not being used as evidence-in-chief—it seems sound to take into account the fact that the testimony sought to be contradicted was elicited on cross rather than direct. Often the cross-examiner will frame his question so as "to lay a trap which will be sprung in rebuttal."[7] Prosecutors should not be permitted to escape the restrictions of Rules 404, 608, and 609 in the guise of impeachment by contradiction.[8]

(defendant, who was being tried for importing cocaine, testified on cross that he had nothing to do with cocaine or T-shirts; his traveling companion had been found with cocaine sewn into a makeshift pocket in T-shirt he was wearing; defendant's luggage, which was illegally searched, contained T-shirt from which pieces had been cut that matched pocket in which cocaine was found; Court held that trial court properly allowed introduction of T-shirt). *See* **Treatise** at ¶¶ 607[05], [09] for discussion of other decisions by the Supreme Court that may bear on the constitutionality of impeachment.

[7] United States v. Pantone, 609 F.2d 675, 683 (2d Cir. 1979) (defendant, a magistrate, was charged with conspiring to refer criminal defendants to a particular bonding agency in return for kickbacks; on direct, defendant made no denial of bribe-taking from other bonding agencies; on cross, when asked if he had ever charged any bondsman anything, he made a sweeping denial and the government then introduced evidence of kickbacks from other agencies; majority held that receipt of this evidence constituted reversible error: "If we were to construe Rule 611(b) as permitting cross-examination with respect to other crimes solely for the purpose of creating credibility issues we would present a defendant who takes the stand with the Hobson's choice of admitting prior uncharged acts of misconduct or of opening the door to presentation of evidence of such acts in rebuttal. The net effect of such a rule would be to permit the introduction of specific acts of prior misconduct whenever a defendant took the stand. That result could not be squared with the provisions of Rule 404(b).").

[8] *See* United States v. Pisari, 636 F.2d 855 (1st Cir. 1981) (defendant was charged with committing a robbery with a knife; on cross, defendant was asked if he had ever committed any robberies by knife in 1977; after denial, prosecution challenged an undercover agent who testified that defendant had told him of committing a robbery with a knife; court found that evidence was not admissible pursuant to Rule 404(b) as bearing on identity, and that it should have been excluded as impeachment evidence).

Where the evidence of another witness is relevant to a material proposition of fact it will be admissible as evidence-in-chief. Such evidence, of course, can also be used to impeach a witness who has given contradictory evidence. Obviously to the extent that the jury believes witnesses who support a material proposition, it will have to disbelieve a witness who supports the negative of the proposition.

¶ 12.01[04] Impeachment: Prior Inconsistent Statements [1]

Impeachment by prior inconsistent statements made before trial rests on the notion that a jury should not place much credence in a witness who is so unreliable as to contradict himself. The use of prior inconsistent statements for purposes of impeachment should be distinguished from the use of such statements as evidence in chief,[2] which under the Federal Rules is restricted to a limited class of statements made under oath. *See* Rule 801(d)(1)(A). When the statements are being used substantively rather than on credibility alone, counsel may argue as to the truth of the particular statements, rather then using the inconsistencies solely to shed light on the credibility of the witness.

Before a prior statement can be used for impeachment, an inconsistency has to be shown between the two statements. The courts have relied on two principal, but competing tests, to determine inconsistency: (1) the inconsistency has to be apparent on the face of the two statements and the prior statement is rejected unless the only possible inference is one of inconsistency, and (2) the setting and implications of the statements may be taken into consideration and the prior statement admitted as long as inconsistency is one of several possible inferences that may be drawn. Even before the adoption of the Federal Rules, the federal

---

[1] *See* **Treatise** at ¶ 607[06]. Rules 613 and 806 codify and modify the foundational requirements for prior inconsistent statements but are silent as to other prerequisites.

[2] *Cf.* United States v. Gossett, 877 F.2d 901, 906–07 (11th Cir. 1989), *cert. denied,* 110 S. Ct. 1141 (1990) (not error to exclude statements allegedly made by co-defendant to cellmate; "impeachment by prior inconsistent statement may not be permitted where it is used as a strategem to get before the jury otherwise inadmissible evidence.").

courts had generally rejected the first, mechanical test of inconsistency in favor of the more liberal and psychologically sounder second approach which admits the prior statement when the trial judge finds that one reasonable inference would be that of inconsistency. This approach is consistent with the emphasis in the Federal Rules on the admission of all relevant evidence.[3]

Admitting all prior inconsistent statements made by the witness would not, however, be satisfactory. Although all contradictory statements are relevant to credibility in the broad sense that a witness who has made a mistake before may again be mistaken, permitting an unlimited probe into the witness' past for evidence of self-contradiction may disclose inconsistencies of trifling probative significance which might prejudice or confuse the jury while unduly protracting the trial. At common law, as in the case of contradiction, discussed *supra,* exclusion was achieved by means of the "collateral" test. If the witness denied making a statement on a matter classified as collateral, the examiner had to take the answer—that is, the making of the statement could not be proved by extrinsic evidence.

The difficulty with a "collateral" test is that it looks to only one side of the equation governing admissibility—high probative value—and insists that this factor can be assayed mechanically. Actually it is often difficult to assess the probative effect of a proffered statement. Allowing the trial court to rationalize its decision solely by applying the "collateral" label deprives the reviewing court of an opportunity to assess the factors considered by the trial court. The better approach—and one in accord with the structure of the Federal Rules—is to eliminate mechanical application of the "collateral" test in favor of the balancing approach mandated by Rule 403. Evidence at which the collateral

---

[3] *See* United States v. Gravely, 840 F.2d 1156, 1163 (4th Cir. 1988); United States v. Williams, 737 F.2d 594, 606–10 (7th Cir. 1984), *cert. denied,* 470 U.S. 1003, 105 S. Ct. 1354, 1355, 84 L. Ed. 2d 377 (1985); United States v. Dennis, 625 F.2d 782, 795 (8th Cir. 1980) ("inconsistency is not limited to diametrically opposed answers but may be found in evasive answers, inability to recall, silence, or changes of position"); United States v. Rogers, 549 F.2d 490, 496 (8th Cir. 1976), *cert. denied,* 431 U.S. 918 (1977) (court found that trial judge could well infer from witness' equivocal answers that he was fully aware of the content of his prior statement but was trying not to implicate the defendant).

test is primarily directed, which is relevant solely because it suggests that the witness may have lied about something in the past, would generally be excluded because of its low probative value and its tendency to prejudice the jury. Evidence of higher probative value would be assessed in terms of its impact on the jury in light of the particular circumstances presented. The court should consider factors such as the availability of other evidence, the extent to which the particular witness' credibility is crucial to the case, the length of time that has elapsed since the underlying event, and the nature of the extrinsic evidence.[4] Usually the result under either approach would be the same, but the Rule 403 balancing test authorizes a flexible approach when the proffered statement has high probative value but is strongly prejudicial, or when the probative value of the statement is debatable.

A failure to assert a fact it would have been natural to affirm is usually admitted by the federal courts as inconsistent with a witness' assertion of the existence of the fact, provided there is no constitutional bar to allowing such impeachment.[5] In a series of cases, the Supreme Court has held that when the witness' silence was induced by implicit assurances that his silence could not be used against him, cross-examining the witness about his silence is fundamentally unfair and in violation of the Due Process Clause.[6] Except when silence is induced by governmental

---

[4] *See, e.g.,* United States v. Shoupe, 548 F.2d 636 (8th Cir. 1977) (due process violation requiring new trial where prosecutor had recited entire substance of witness' disavowed unsworn prior statement to jury in order to impeach witness; court noted that statements were directly probative of defendants' guilt, that there was very little other evidence, that statements had allegedly been made to government agent, but that no recording or transcript of interview had been prepared, that agent's notes were not dictated until six days after interview, that witness was never shown memorandum, that trial court never requested original notes or read memorandum and neither sought to determine reliability of the statements through independent evidence nor attempted to limit the scope of impeachment).

[5] *See, e.g.,* United States v. Vega, 589 F.2d 1149, 1150–52 (2d Cir. 1978) (pre-arrest silence at Kennedy Airport when defendant encountered DEA agent was probative of defendant's credibility since her counsel had suggested that defendant had not approached police in Chicago when she found out about narcotics transaction because she needed to return to New York).

[6] The leading case for this proposition is Doyle v. Ohio, 426 U.S. 610, 96 S. Ct. 2240, 49 L. Ed. 2d 91 (1976). The Court has explained its position in

action, the Court has held that impeachment by silence is an evidentiary rather than constitutional matter.[7] In many instances, even when there is no constitutional bar, silence is so ambiguous, and the possibility of prejudice so high, that the evidence should be excluded pursuant to Rule 403.

¶ 12.01[05]   Impeachment: Character

Impeachment by evidence of character and conduct is governed by Rule 608. Impeachment by conviction of crime is treated in Rule 609. See discussion below.

¶ 12.01[06]   Support or Rehabilitation[1]

Except insofar as practice permits an accused to insinuate evidence of good character for veracity prior to attack, the Federal Rules have in no way altered the general principle that a witness' credibility cannot be bolstered on direct or supported on rebuttal unless there has been an attack on the witness' veracity.[2] Some

---

Jenkins v. Anderson, 447 U.S. 231, 100 S. Ct. 2124, 65 L. Ed. 2d 86 (1980) (due process not violated by the impeachment use of pre-*Miranda* warnings silence before arrest); Anderson v. Charles, 447 U.S. 404, 100 S. Ct. 2180, 65 L. Ed. 2d 222, *reh'g denied,* 448 U.S. 912 (1980) (due process not violated by the impeachment use of voluntarily made post-*Miranda* statements); Fletcher v. Weir, 455 U.S. 603, 102 S. Ct. 1309, 71 L. Ed. 2d 490 (1982) (no violation of due process by impeachment use of silence after arrest where no *Miranda* warnings were given). *See also* Roberts v. United States, 445 U.S. 552, 100 S. Ct. 1358, 63 L. Ed. 2d 622 (1980); Wainwright v. Greenfield, 106 S. Ct. 634, 88 L. Ed. 2d 623 (1986).

[7] Jenkins v. Anderson, 447 U.S. 231, 100 S. Ct. 2124, 65 L. Ed. 2d 86 (1980) (defendant's failure to tell police authorities that he had killed in self-defense could be used to impeach him after he testified that he had acted solely in self-defense).

[1] *See* Treatise at ¶ 607[08].

[2] *See, e.g.,* United States v. Awkard, 597 F.2d 667 (9th Cir.), *cert. denied,* 444 U.S. 885 (1979) (since Ninth Circuit allows hypnotically refreshed evidence to be used, a foundation concerning the reliability of hypnosis is no longer necessary; consequently it was error (though harmless in context of case) for trial court to permit expert on hypnotism to testify prior to hypnotized witness since this had the effect of bolstering his credibility before it was attacked); United States v. Bursten, 560 F.2d 779 (7th Cir. 1977) (error, though harmless, for government to buttress the believability of its key witness by introducing evidence that witness was willing to submit to polygraph test).

leeway is offered in allowing the proponent of a witness to draw the sting of its witness' impeachment by bringing out on direct matters damaging to the witness' credibility which will inevitably be brought out on cross-examination.[3]

After impeachment by evidence of bias, interest or self-contradiction, evidence in denial or explanation is always available[4] subject to the judge's discretion to curtail proof which

---

[3] *See, e.g.,* United States v. Cosentino, 844 F.2d 30, 34 (2d Cir.), *cert. denied,* 109 S. Ct. 303 (1988) (cooperation agreement could be admitted on direct after defense attacked witness's credibility in the opening statement); United States v. Oxman, 740 F.2d 1298, 1302–03 (3d Cir. 1984) (not error for prosecution to disclose on direct that plea agreement obligated witness to testify truthfully where government could reasonably anticipate plea agreement would be used for impeachment); United States v. Singh, 628 F.2d 758 (2d Cir.), *cert. denied,* 449 U.S. 1034 (1980) (bias of witness towards defendant); *see* discussion in Rule 609 *infra* of revealing convictions on direct; *but cf.* United States v. Melia, 691 F.2d 672, 676 (4th Cir. 1982) (reversible error where government, in order to counter defense efforts to discredit government witnesses, presented direct evidence from five separate witnesses of death threats to prosecution witness, of government's concern for safety of witnesses, and of their participation in Witness Protection Program; no simple formula to determine how much evidence should be admissible but "trial court must exercise its discretion, bearing in mind the purpose of the evidence—to rebut, in appropriate circumstances, the appearance of special treatment and improper motivation or bias"; in instant case, too much likelihood that jury would infer that defendant was source of death threats).

[4] United States v. Mitchell, 556 F.2d 371, 379–80 (6th Cir.), *cert. denied,* 434 U.S. 925 (1977) (where defendant challenged government informant's motivation at great length, it was not error for the judge to permit further questioning of informant to show that many of the arrangements were conceived not so much to reward informant but to protect him and his family, even though the inference was that defendant was a dangerous criminal who would seek revenge); United States v. Holland, 526 F.2d 284 (5th Cir.), *rev'd on other grounds,* 537 F.2d 821 (5th Cir. 1976) (court admitted evidence that witness had corrected an earlier misstatement in grand jury testimony which had been used to impeach him); United States v. Cirillo, 468 F.2d 1233, 1240 (2d Cir. 1972), *cert. denied,* 410 U.S. 989 (1973) (impeached witness should have been permitted to explain his failure to mention meeting with defendant was prompted by fear of being killed); Russo v. Peikes, 71 F.R.D. 110 (E.D. Pa. 1976), *aff'd mem.,* 547 F.2d 1163 (3d Cir. 1977) (court permitted testimony by associate in law firm representing defendant to testify as to what expert had actually said after expert was impeached during cross-examination). *See also* United States v. Moreno, 649 F.2d 309 (5th Cir. 1981) (example of rehabilitation after impeachment showing poor memory).

confuses or consumes an undue amount of time.[5] The explanation must seek to show that the impeaching facts offered do not really indicate lies.[6] Rebutting evidence should be excluded when its only purpose is to show additional reasons justifying the witness' bias.[7] Reputation or opinion evidence testifying to the principal witness' good character for truthfulness may also be admitted pursuant to Rule 608(a) once the character of the witness for truthfulness has been attacked. See discussion of Rule 608 *infra*.

The most troublesome aspect of rehabilitation is the extent to which impeachment by prior inconsistent statements opens the door to support by prior consistent statements. Since the inconsistency remains even if the witness had made out-of-court statements consistent with his testimony, prior consistent statements are admitted "only in those few exceptional situations where, as

---

[5] United States v. Roberts, 618 F.2d 530, 536 (9th Cir. 1980) (discusses use by prosecution of plea agreement that contains promise to testify truthfully; court counsels trial judge to be alert to problem of vouching and whether it suggests "the unspoken message . . . that the prosecutor knows what the truth is and is assuring its revelation"; reviews cases); Bracey v. United States, 142 F.2d 85, 89 (D.C. Cir.), *cert. denied*, 322 U.S. 762 (1944)("[T]he admission or rejection of such evidence lies in the discretion of the trial judge. Generally speaking, it has been held that when bias is freely admitted without qualification, under circumstances which leave no doubt as to its existence or the reason for it, rebuttal evidence upon the point is unnecessary. Even under such circumstances the evidence is not inadmissible in the usual sense, but rather is excluded because its admission would unnecessarily expand the trial to include collateral issues, and thus confuse the jury. When, however, the impeachment of a witness is conducted in such manner as itself to confuse the jury concerning the existence of bias, or of its character if bias does exist, and thus to mislead the jury concerning the veracity and dependability of the witness, then the trial judge may properly permit an explanation to be made.").

[6] *Cf.* United States v. Arnold, 890 F.2d 825, 830 (6th Cir. 1989) (trial court did not commit reversible error in allowing prosecutor to bring out guilty pleas of co-defendants to restore the credibility of prosecution witnesses, after their testimony had been attacked as a fabrication; trial court had instructed jury that pleas were not substantive evidence of guilt).

[7] United States v. Pintar, 630 F.2d 1270, 1284 (8th Cir. 1981) (where defense elicited on cross-examination that prosecution witness disliked defendants, error in allowing prosecution to elicit on re-direct examination that witness thought defendants were engaged in kickback scheme).

experience has taught, they could be of clear help to the fact finder in determining whether the witness is truthful."[8]

Rule 801(d)(1)(B) states that a prior consistent statement is not hearsay when "offered to rebut an express or implied charge against . . . [the witness] of recent fabrication or improper influence or motive." Pursuant to Rule 801(d)(1)(B), then, a prior consistent statement may be used as substantive evidence to prove the truth of the matter asserted, and not merely to support the witness's credibility.[9] There has been some disagreement as to 801(d)(1)(B) whether the same standards of admissibility should be applied if a prior consistent statement is offered for rehabilitative purposes, as opposed to being offered as substantive evidence pursuant to Rule 801(d)(1)(B). The disagreement has centered on the question of whether the prior consistent statement must have been made before the motive to fabricate allegedly arose. Although some courts have drawn a distinction between rehabilitation and substantive use in this respect,[10] other courts have declined to do so.[11] In assessing probative value, "the issue ought to be whether the particular consistent statement sought to be used has some rebutting force beyond the mere fact that the witness has repeated on a prior occasion a statement consistent

[8] Coltrane v. United States, 418 F.2d 1131, 1140 (D.C. Cir. 1969) ("mere repetition does not imply veracity").

[9] *See* discussion of Rule 801(d)(1), Chapter 15 *infra* as to admissibility of prior consistent statements made after prior inconsistent statement.

[10] *See* United States v. Brennan, 798 F.2d 581 (2d Cir. 1986); United States v. Pierre, 781 F.2d 329 (2d Cir. 1986); United States v. Harris, 761 F.2d 394, 398–400 (7th Cir. 1985) (condition that the motive to fabricate must not have existed at the time the statement was made need not be met when statement is offered for rehabilitative purposes).

[11] *See* United States v. Miller, 874 F.2d 1255, 1273 (9th Cir. 1989); United States v. Lawson, 872 F.2d 179, 182 (6th Cir. 1989) ("[T]he trial judge [must] examine the circumstances under which the statement was made and make a determination of the statement's relevancy and probity. . . . While these factors are more likely to be found where the statement was made prior to the alleged discrediting influence, . . . where there are other indicia of reliability surrounding a prior consistent statement that make it relevant to rebut a charge of recent fabrication or improper motive, then the fact that the statement was made after the alleged motive to falsify should not preclude its admissibility. Of course, where the danger of unfair prejudice outweighs the probative value of the evidence Fed. R. Evid. 403 is available.").

with his trial testimony."[12] When the witness denies having made the inconsistent statement used for impeachment, a consistent statement would have significant rebutting force in diminishing the likelihood that the witness had made the inconsistent statement.[13]

Prior consistent statements also have high probative value when they shed light on whether the admitted prior inconsistent statement was truly inconsistent.[14] Some courts have suggested that allowing recourse to the prior consistent statement "when the consistent statement will amplify or clarify the allegedly inconsistent statement . . . is . . . only an invocation of the principle of completeness, though not a precise use of Rule 106."[15]

The question of admissibility of the prior consistent statement on credibility alone is one left almost entirely to the discretion of the trial court.[16] It must consider whether the jury will understand and follow an instruction—which must be given on demand—that the evidence is limited to the credibility issue.

---

[12] United States v. Pierre, 781 F.2d 329, 331 (2d Cir. 1986).

[13] *See, e.g.,* United States v. Corry, 183 F.2d 155, 156–57 (2d Cir. 1950).

[14] *See, e.g.,* United States v. Pierre, 781 F.2d 329 (2d Cir. 1986) (where agent who testified that defendant refused to make a controlled delivery was impeached by his notes containing no reference to such a refusal, court properly allowed agent to testify on direct that his formal report contained fact of refusal); United States v. Rubin, 609 F.2d 51 (2d Cir. 1979) (concurring opinion of Friendly, J.), *aff'd on other grounds,* 449 U.S. 424, 101 S. Ct. 698, 66 L. Ed. 2d 633 (1981); United States v. Juarez, 549 F.2d 1113 (7th Cir. 1977) (where government agents had been cross-examined in detail about reports they had written concerning transactions with defendant and had been questioned about omission of certain facts and one witness had admitted that report was a "generalization" which might be inaccurate in certain respects, trial judge did not err in admitting reports for the limited purpose of consideration with regard to the witnesses' credibility; court did not abuse discretion afforded it by Rule 403).

[15] United States v. Brennan, 798 F.2d 581 (2d Cir. 1986) (where key witness gave grand jury testimony inconsistent with part of his testimony at trial, important to admit whole grand jury testimony); United States v. Pierre, 781 F.2d 329, 333 (2d Cir. 1986). *See also* United States v. Rubin, 609 F.2d 51 (2d Cir. 1979) (majority and concurring opinions), *aff'd on other grounds,* 449 U.S. 424 (1981).

[16] United States v. Obayagbona, 627 F. Supp. 329 (E.D.N.Y. 1985); *cf.* United States v. Abel, 469 U.S 45, 105 S. Ct. 465, 83 L. Ed. 2d 450 (1984).

Another important factor for the court to consider in exercising its discretion is the amount of time that proof of the prior statements will take. If admission will introduce a substantial ancillary dispute about whether the statements were made and the surrounding circumstances, the court, after weighing that factor against the importance of the witness and the critical nature of the impeachment and rehabilitation effects, may well decide to close off or severely limit the inquiry.

¶ 12.02   Who May Impeach—Rule 607

¶ 12.02[01]   Impeaching One's Own Witness Allowed[1]

Rule 607 eliminates the traditional rule that a party may not impeach its own witness. The rule itself imposes no restriction whatsoever on the impeachment process it authorizes. The rule provides:

Rule 607

WHO MAY IMPEACH

The credibility of a witness may be attacked by any party, including the party calling the witness.

The only problem that has emerged in applying Rule 607 is in the use of prior inconsistent statements for impeachment when the statements are not admissible as evidence-in-chief pursuant to Rule 801(d)(1)(A). Since unsworn inconsistent statements are not excluded from the definition of hearsay in Rule 801, and such statements may usually be used only for impeachment,[2] there is

---

[1] *See* **Treatise** at ¶ 607[01] for discussion of previous practice, and the exceptions which had been developed to side-step the impact of the traditional rule.

[2] *See* United States v. Dietrich, 854 F.2d 1056, 1062 (7th Cir. 1988) (unsworn statement could still be used for impeachment). Also, an unsworn prior inconsistent statement would be admissible as substantive evidence if it satisfied one of the other hearsay exclusions or one of the exceptions to the hearsay rule. *See, e.g.,* United States v. Leslie, 542 F.2d 285 (5th Cir. 1976) (statement admitted pursuant to residual hearsay exception and for impeachment).

a danger that the jurors will misuse the evidence, and that Rule 607 could thus have the effect of creating a new route for the admission of hearsay evidence in the guise of impeachment. To insist on a showing of surprise and affirmative damage, as under prior law, before a party may impeach its own witness would mean a return to the unsatisfactory mechanical approach which led to the adoption of Rule 607. While such a mechanical solution is at odds with the Federal Rules which favor the admissibility of relevant evidence,[3] it is frequently properly used as a guide to prevent overreaching by prosecutors dealing with turncoat witnesses.

An approach consistent with the thrust of the rules is to analyze the problem in terms of Rule 403—is the probative worth of the impeaching evidence outweighed by its prejudicial impact? The trial judge needs to assess such factors as the likelihood the statement was made, ambiguities in the statement, and the possibility that the jury might use the statement either to infer defendant's guilt or to conclude that the defendant was an associate of a proven liar, and therefore, probably lying as well when he pleaded not guilty.[4] The court must also conclude that the jury is capable of following an instruction to use the evidence in assessing credibility and not for its truth in determining guilt directly.

In applying Rule 607, courts often reiterate as their guiding principle that "impeachment by prior inconsistent statement may not be permitted where employed as a mere subterfuge to get

---

[3] *See* United States v. Webster, 734 F.2d 1191, 1193 (7th Cir. 1984) ("a mistake to graft such a requirement to Rule 607, even if such a graft would be within the power of judicial interpretation of the rule").

[4] *See, e.g.,* United States v. DeLillo, 620 F.2d 939, 947 (2d Cir.), *cert. denied,* 449 U.S. 835 (1980) (court balanced probative value and prejudice and held that government was entitled to impeach its own witness where impeaching statement enabled jury to resolve conflicts in credibility, that evidence was admitted with limiting instruction, that there was no question but that witness made statement, and that defense could have cross-examined witness). *See also* United States v. Rogers, 549 F.2d 490 (8th Cir. 1976), *cert. denied,* 431 U.S. 918 (1977). *Cf.* United States v. Peterman, 841 F.2d 1474, 1480 (10th Cir. 1988), *cert. denied,* 109 S. Ct. 783 (1989) (no abuse of discretion in permitting impeachment of co-defendant, a government witness, by evidence of his prior conviction).

before the jury evidence not otherwise admissible."[5] This approach, dubbed the "good faith standard" by one court,[6] usually yields the same result as the Rule 403 test advocated above, since the courts are willing to find good faith even in instances where the profferer of the witness knows that the witness will give some unfavorable testimony, provided the witness also gives helpful testimony, so that the inconsistent statement is needed to nullify the harmful aspect of the testimony. Under a Rule 403 approach, the court's decision to permit impeachment would be appropriate because under these circumstances the probative value of the statement in shedding light on the credibility of the witness would exceed its prejudicial effect. Conversely, if the witness provides no helpful testimony on the stand, the "bad faith" in calling the witness (or the prejudice to the opposing party) is apparent.

The lawyer who knows the problem exists has the obligation to inform the court and his adversary in advance that his witness will probably testify to the contrary of a prior statement so that the court can make a ruling before the impeaching questions are asked in the presence of the jury. Circumventing an adverse ruling by seeking to shake a witness through use of "refreshment," reading "didn't you say . . ." questions and the like is not acceptable. To make the critical decisions required, the court will sometimes have to insist that the witness be questioned in part preliminarily outside the jury's presence so the court can judge the impact of the impeachment and the likelihood that it is designed primarily as an end-run around the hearsay barrier.

---

[5] United States v. Gossett, 877 F.2d 901, 906–07 (11th Cir. 1989), *cert. denied,* 110 S. Ct. 1141 (1990). *See* United States v. Morlang, 531 F.2d 183, 190 (4th Cir. 1975) (although Rule 607 was not yet in effect, court concluded that limitation it endorsed would have to be applied). In United States v. Webster, 734 F.2d 1191, 1192 (7th Cir. 1984), the court concluded that the *Morlang* limitation "has been accepted in all circuits that have considered the issue."

[6] *See* United States v. Webster, 734 F.2d 1191 (7th Cir. 1984) (court suggests that Rule 403 test should be superimposed on top of good faith test).

¶ 12.03   Impeachment by Evidence of Character and Conduct of Witness—Rule 608

¶ 12.03[01]   Scope[1]

Rule 608 governs impeachment by evidence of character or conduct, limiting admissibility to character evidence probative of truthfulness. The rule recognizes three different ways of proving character: (1) by testimony as to reputation, (2) by testimony in the form of opinion, and (3) by evidence of specific instances of conduct. Reputation or opinion evidence of bad character can come in either through the direct or cross-examination of a character witness. Good character can similarly be proved provided that the character of the witness for truthfulness has first been attacked. Specific acts of misconduct not culminating in a conviction, that are probative of veracity, cannot be proved by extrinsic evidence but can be inquired into on cross-examination. Misconduct that has been the basis of a conviction may be proved as provided in Rule 609. Evidence that is barred by Rule 608 may nevertheless be admissible if it is used in connection with some other technique of attacking or supporting the credibility of a witness.[2]

The Rule provides:

Rule 608

EVIDENCE OF CHARACTER AND CONDUCT OF WITNESS

(a) Opinion and reputation evidence of character. The credibility of a witness may be attacked or supported by evidence in the form of opinion or reputation, but subject to these limitations: (1) the evidence may refer only to character for truthfulness or untruthfulness, and (2) evidence of truthful character is admissible only after

---

[1] *See* **Treatise** at ¶¶ 608[01], [07].

[2] United States v. James, 609 F.2d 36, 45–48 (2d Cir. 1979), *cert. denied,* 445 U.S. 905 (1980) (specific acts of misconduct admissible to prove motive); United States v. Rios Ruiz, 579 F.2d 670 (1st Cir. 1978) (same). *But see* United States v. Sutherland, 656 F.2d 1181, 1198–99 (5th Cir. 1981), *cert. denied,* 455 U.S. 949 (1982) (court suggests that evidence not admissible pursuant to Rule 608(b) to show witness' truthfulness or untruthfulness is not admissible to show prejudice).

the character of the witness for truthfulness has been attacked by opinion or reputation evidence or otherwise.

(b) Specific instances of conduct. Specific instances of the conduct of a witness, for the purpose of attacking or supporting the witness' credibility, other than conviction of crime as provided in rule 609, may not be proved by extrinsic evidence. They may, however, in the discretion of the court, if probative of truthfulness or untruthfulness, be inquired into on cross-examination of the witness (1) concerning the witness' character for truthfulness or untruthfulness, or (2) concerning the character for truthfulness or untruthfulness of another witness as to which character the witness being cross-examined has testified.

The giving of testimony, whether by an accused or by any other witness, does not operate as a waiver of the accused's or the witness' privilege against self-incrimination when examined with respect to matters which relate only to credibility.

Rule 608 applies in civil[3] as well as criminal cases and makes no distinction between these types of cases or between principal witnesses and character witnesses. Because Rule 608 is subject to the overriding protection of Rule 403 (requiring the exclusion of evidence whose probative value is substantially outweighed by danger of prejudice, confusion or waste of time),[4] and Rule 611 (barring harassment and undue embarrassment of witnesses), the trial court has considerable discretion to vary admission of character evidence depending upon the type of case and the status of the witness.

The final sentence of Rule 608(b) states that a person who takes the witness stand does not thereby waive the right against self-incrimination with respect to matters relating solely to credibility.[5] The limitation on waiver of the privilege provided by the rule rarely applies. It does not curtail questions about convictions since such inquiry is not incriminating; it does not prohibit questions about misconduct so long past that all possibility of

---

[3] Sguyers v. Hilliary, 599 F.2d 918 (10th Cir. 1979).

[4] United States v. Haynes, 554 F.2d 231 (5th Cir. 1977) (trial court did not err in limiting defendant to one witness to attack prosecution witness' reputation for truth and veracity where testimony would have been the same and therefore cumulative).

[5] *See, e.g.,* Air Et Chaleur, S.A. v. Janeway, 757 F.2d 489, 496 (2d Cir. 1985).

prosecution has been barred; and it does not exclude evidence of prior misconduct if that conduct is relevant to something other than credibility.[6] In criminal cases, even if the privilege does apply, it is seldom relied upon by a defendant. Although the judge may instruct the jurors not to draw any adverse inferences from a claim of privilege by a criminal defendant, the jurors will have the feeling that the witness is not being wholly candid. Under such circumstances it is necessary for the defendant to seriously consider staying off the stand, even though there is a danger that the jurors will, despite the judge's instructions to the contrary, weigh the defendant's failure to testify against him.

¶ 12.03[02]   Attack on Character: Reputation and Opinion Evidence[1]

Rule 608(a) recognizes that a witness' credibility may be impeached by proof of his or her reputation or proof by opinion, and it has been held that exclusion of this line of attack may amount to reversible error.[2] Testimony must be relevant to non-truthfulness rather than to any other character trait.[3]

Reputation testimony must relate to the witness' reputation at or shortly before the time of trial.[4] Reputation testimony can be offered by first establishing the impeaching witness X's connection with the witness W, then by establishing that W has a general reputation for non-truthfulness in the community in which W

[6] United States v. Blankenship, 746 F.2d 233, 238 n.1 (5th Cir. 1984) (questioning about crime defendant was charged with); United States v. Panza, 612 F.2d 432 (9th Cir. 1979), *cert. denied,* 447 U.S. 925 (1980) (cross-examination within scope of direct).

[1] *See* **Treatise** at ¶¶ 608[03]–[04].

[2] United States v. Davis, 639 F.2d 239 (5th Cir. 1981) (exclusion of two character witnesses called by the defense to impeach key government witnesses reversible error). The court can reasonably limit the size of a parade of pro and con character witnesses.

[3] United States v. Greer, 643 F.2d 280 (5th Cir.), *cert. denied,* 454 U.S. 854 (1981) (inquiry as to witness' general reputation properly excluded). *See also* United States v. Dotson, 799 F.2d 189, 194 (5th Cir. 1986).

[4] United States v. Watson, 669 F.2d 1374, 1382–85 (11th Cir. 1982).

works[5] or lives,[6] and that X is in a position to know that reputation.

Opinion evidence is obtained by asking impeaching witnesses to directly state their opinion of the principal witness' character for non-truthfulness. There are no prerequisites of long acquaintance or recent information about the witness;[7] cross-examination can be expected to expose defects of lack of familiarity and to reveal reliance on isolated or irrelevant instances of misconduct, or the existence of feelings of personal hostility towards the principal witness. Nevertheless, if the court finds the witness lacks sufficient information[8] to have formed a reliable opinion, or that the witness' testimony would be inherently prejudicial,[9] it can exclude, relying on Rules 403 and 602. The courts have usually declined to permit expert testimony concerning a witness' veracity.[10]

---

[5] United States v. Mandel, 591 F.2d 1347, 1370 (4th Cir. 1979) (reputation or character in law office in which witness worked).

[6] United States v. Truslaw, 530 F.2d 257, 265 (4th Cir. 1975).

[7] United States v. Watson, 669 F.2d 1374, 1382 (11th Cir. 1982) (reversible error for district court to have excluded testimony for failure to meet a foundation requirement; defendant was seeking to impeach critical prosecution witness).

[8] United States v. Dotson, 799 F.2d 189, 194 (5th Cir. 1986) (reversible error to allow FBI agents to give opinion as to defendant's veracity since there was no showing of how long agents knew defendant or the basis for their opinion; mere fact that agents had conducted an investigation was not a sufficiently reliable basis for the testimony; in addition, it was not error to admit testimony of IRS agent about truthfulness of defendant's mother because he had interviewed her four times, had investigated her tax returns, and had studied her grand jury testimony); United States v. Watson, 669 F.2d 1374, 1382 (11th Cir. 1982) (no error in excluding testimony where impeachment witness only knew person whose reputation she was seeking to impeach for a short period and at a time remote from both the time of the conspiracy and the time of trial).

[9] United States v. Bruscino, 666 F.2d 450, 463 (7th Cir. 1981), rev'd on other grounds, 687 F.2d 938 (7th Cir. 1982), *cert. denied,* 459 U.S. 1228 (1983) (court refused to hold as a matter of law that an F.B.I. agent's opinion as to the lack of credibility of a defense witness is as inherently prejudicial as that of a prosecuting attorney).

[10] *See* Bastow v. General Motors Corp., 844 F.2d 506, 510–11 (8th Cir. 1988) (trial court did not abuse discretion in excluding testimony of clinical psychologist that plaintiff had a behavior disorder giving him a character for untruthfulness); United States v. Azure, 801 F.2d 336, 340 (8th Cir. 1986) (error to allow expert to testify that victim was telling the truth); United States

In qualifying the impeachment witness, a proponent should not be allowed to inquire whether the witness is aware of specific instances of misconduct.[11] Although such questioning within limits is permissible on cross-examination of a witness testifying to truthfulness (see discussion below), permitting evidence of specific instances of misconduct to be introduced on direct examination of a reputation witness in the guise of qualifying the witness by showing the basis for his knowledge of the character of the person whom he is attacking would undermine the prohibition against the use of specific instances of conduct in the first sentence of subdivision (b) of Rule 608.

¶ **12.03[03]** **Attack on Character: Cross-examination of Witness as to Specific Instances of Previous Conduct**[1]

Rule 608(b) authorizes inquiry into specific instances of misconduct on cross-examination but requires that they must be clearly "probative of truthfulness or untruthfulness." Misconduct not culminating in a conviction cannot be proved by extrinsic evidence pursuant to Rule 608.[2] Courts often summarize the no extrinsic evidence rule by stating that "the examiner must take his answer."[3] This phrase is descriptive of federal practice in the sense that the cross-examiner cannot call other witnesses to prove the misconduct after the witness' denial;[4] it is misleading insofar

---

v. Awkard, 597 F.2d 667, 671 (9th Cir.), *cert. denied,* 444 U.S. 885, 969, 100 S. Ct. 179, 460, 62 L. Ed. 2d 116, 383 (1979) (harmless error to receive expert testimony); United States v. Barnard, 490 F.2d 907 (9th Cir. 1973), *cert. denied,* 416 U.S. 959, 94 S. Ct. 1976, 40 L. Ed. 2d 310 (1974). *Cf.* United States v. Earley, 505 F. Supp. 117 (S.D. Iowa), *aff'd,* 657 F.2d 195 (8th Cir. 1981) (opinion testimony of polygraphist not permitted since witness would not express opinion on the subject's character for truthfulness).

[11] United States v. Manglameli, 668 F.2d 1172 (10th Cir.), *cert. denied,* 456 U.S. 918 (1982); United States v. Hoskins, 628 F.2d 295 (5th Cir.), *cert. denied,* 449 U.S. 987 (1980).

[1] *See* **Treatise** at ¶¶ 608[05]–[06].

[2] United States v. Dimatteo, 716 F.2d 1361, 1366–67 (11th Cir. 1983) (admission of extrinsic evidence to attack a witness' credibility was reversible error); United States v. Bosley, 615 F.2d 1274 (9th Cir. 1980) (same).

[3] *See, e.g.,* United States v. Cohen, 631 F.2d 1223, 1226 (5th Cir. 1980).

[4] *See, e.g.,* United States v. Ling, 581 F.2d 1118 (4th Cir. 1978) (reversible error for prosecutor to ask defendant if he had ever discharged firearm on public street and then after defendant's denial introduce extrinsic evidence about defendant's arrest for such act).

as it suggests that the cross-examiner cannot continue pressing for an admission so long as the examiner does not in effect become an unsworn witness to the incidents being inquired about.[5]

The Rule 608 bar to the admissibility of extrinsic character evidence does not prevent such evidence from being admitted[6] to attack the witness' credibility on some theory[7] other than impeachment by prior misconduct. Nor is extrinsic evidence barred when offered to prove a material fact[8] or when the witness admits prior misconduct.[9]

Counsel and courts sometimes have difficulty in distinguishing between Rule 608 impeachment and impeachment by

[5] *See* People v. Sorge, 301 N.Y. 198 (1950), disapproved by the Advisory Committee.

[6] United States v. Abel, 469 U.S. 45, 105 S. Ct. 465, 83 L. Ed. 2d 450 (1984) (evidence which tends to show bias on the part of a witness is admissible although it also tends "to show that the witness [is] a liar.").

[7] United States v. Ray, 731 F.2d 1361, 1363–64 (9th Cir. 1984) (bias); United States v. Banks, 520 F.2d 627, 630 (7th Cir. 1975) (drug use relevant to capacity to observe or remember).

[8] United States v. Calle, 822 F.2d 1016, 1021 (11th Cir. 1987) (reversible error to exclude testimony that would have contradicted main prosecution witness; extrinsic evidence should be admitted to disprove a specific fact material to the defendant's case); United States v. Vaglica, 720 F.2d 388, 393–94 (5th Cir. 1983) (evidence admissible to prove intent); United States v. Opager, 589 F.2d 799, 802 (5th Cir. 1979) (Rule 608(b) is "inapplicable in determining the admissibility of relevant evidence introduced to contradict a witness' testimony as to a material issue"); United States v. Liopowski, 423 F. Supp. 864 (D.N.J. 1976) (evidence bore on authenticity of tapes).

[9] Carter v. Hewitt, 617 F.2d 961, 969–73 & n.11 (3d Cir. 1980) ("reasons for barring extrinsic evidence lose their force when the witness whose credibility is challenged concedes the alleged acts. No issues are confused or time wasted through a trial of a collateral matter."); *See also* United States v. Jackson, 882 F.2d 1444, 1448–49 (9th Cir. 1989) (no error in showing defendant, a disbarred attorney, a written statement signed by him in which he admitted misappropriating funds from former client after defendant denied misappropriating funds; statement was never admitted into evidence; citing **Treatise**); United States v. Simpson, 709 F.2d 903 (11th Cir.), *cert. denied,* 464 U.S. 942 (1983). *Cf.* United States v. Bosley, 615 F.2d 1274 (9th Cir. 1980) (court reserved decision on whether there is exception to no extrinsic evidence rule when defendant makes an unelicited statement on cross-examination).

contradiction.[10] The troublesome kind of case arises when the witness—usually the defendant—makes a claim on direct examination inconsistent with bad conduct. Extrinsic evidence may not be admitted pursuant to Rule 608 to rebut the claim. Whether extrinsic evidence may be admitted on a theory of impeachment by contradiction would depend on the circumstances of the case. The trial judge should apply a Rule 403 balancing test, hinging admissibility on a finding that the probative value of the extrinsic evidence, in showing lack of credibility through inconsistency, outweighs the dangers of prejudice and surprise guarded against by Rule 608.[11]

Inquiry into specific instances of misconduct on cross-examination is within the discretion [12] of the trial judge who can rule in advance to limit such attack.[13] The judge has the power to apply the overriding safeguards of Rule 403 (excluding evidence if its probative value is substantially outweighed by dangers of prejudice, confusion, or delay) [14] and Rule 6ll (barring harassment and undue embarrassment of witnesses).[15] When

---

[10] *See, e.g.,* United States v. Tejada, 886 F.2d 483, 487–88 (1st Cir. 1989) (court assumes that Rule 608(b) bars extrinsic evidence to impeach witness by contradiction).

[11] *See* United States v. Phillips, 888 F.2d 38, 40–41 (6th Cir. 1989) (prosecution witnesses denied using drugs after they started working for the FBI; court upheld trial judge's exclusion of extrinsic evidence of cocaine use, since evidence would not affect probability that defendant sold drugs or that he was entrapped); United States v. Vaglica, 720 F.2d 388 (5th Cir. 1983); Perel v. Vanderford, 547 F.2d 278, 281 (5th Cir. 1977) (where record indicates trial judge had "painstakingly weighed any prejudicial impact against its probative force . . . we are not inclined to tip the scales in the opposite direction from where they came to rest").

[12] United States v. Tarantino, 846 F.2d 1384, 1409–11 (D.C. Cir.), *cert. denied,* 109 S. Ct. 108, 174 (1988), citing **Treatise.**

[13] United States v. Ray, 731 F.2d 1361, 1363–64 (9th Cir. 1984) (trial court can require a threshold level of evidence of witness misconduct in order to prevent bootstrapping of inadmissible evidence into court).

[14] United States v. Tarantino, 846 F.2d 1384, 1405–07 (D.C. Cir.), *cert. denied,* 109 S. Ct. 108, 174 (1988), citing **Treatise** (trial court did not err in refusing to allow defense counsel to cross-examine government witness about his involvement in plot to kill government witness to keep him from testifying).

[15] United States v. Leake, 642 F.2d 715, 719 (4th Cir. 1981) (reversible error for court not to have permitted cross-examination where trial court failed to balance the proper factors).

determining whether to permit Rule 608(b) cross-examination it is appropriate for a trial judge to distinguish between the non-party witness, and the witness who is also a party, particularly in a criminal case, since the possibility of prejudice will be the greatest when the witness is the accused.[16] In a criminal case there is a substantial danger that the jury will believe the defendant is a bad person deserving of punishment even if the accused did not do the particular act charged.[17] If attack on a criminal defendant through bad acts is restricted, the trial court can prevent the defendant from appearing in a false light compared to other witnesses, by asking that similar attacks be limited against the people's main witness.

The trial judge also has discretion over what type of conduct can be inquired into on cross-examination. The character of the previous conduct, the recency of the conduct,[18] the importance of the testimony,[19] and the probable effect on the jury if the misconduct is divulged are all factors a judge must consider in deciding whether to allow inquiry about past conduct. The rule specifies that the inquiry must be limited to those specific modes of conduct that are probative of a lack of truthfulness.[20]

---

[16] United States v. Pintar, 630 F.2d 1270 (8th Cir. 1980) (reversible error to permit questions whose prejudice exceed their probative value, particularly because the witness being cross-examined was the defendant).

[17] *See* United States v. DeGeratto, 876 F.2d 576, 583–584 (7th Cir. 1989) (in prosecution for receiving stolen property, cross-examination of defendant about prostitution ring constituted prejudicial error, since government did not have basis for good faith belief that defendant knowingly helped prostitution operation and government's emphasis on prostitution was excessive).

[18] *Compare* United States v. Jackson, 882 F.2d 1444, 1448 (9th Cir. 1989) (no error in admitting evidence of misappropriation of client's funds fourteen years previously, since evidence was particularly relevant to show lack of credibility) *with* United States v. Kennedy, 714 F.2d 968, 973 (9th Cir. 1983) (trial court properly foreclosed cross-examination about conduct that was more than ten years old and detracted only minimally from witness' credibility).

[19] *See* United States v. Sullivan, 803 F.2d 87, 91 (3d Cir. 1986), *cert. denied,* 107 S. Ct. 889 (1987) (defendant could be cross-examined about filing inaccurate income tax and fiancial disclosure forms since his credibility was the central issue); United States v. Fortes, 619 F.2d l08 (1st Cir. 1980) (broad cross-examination of principal witness should be allowed when credibility of witness is central issue).

[20] *See* United States v. Covelli, 738 F.2d 847, 856–57 (7th Cir.) *cert. denied,* 469 U.S. 867 (1984) (testimony that defendant had previously faked insanity

Questions about behavior that indicates a disregard for the rights of others should not be allowed on the theory that such an attitude might reasonably be expected to express itself in giving false testimony whenever it would be to the advantage of the witness.[21] Such an approach paves the way to an exception that would swallow the rule. It is but a small step from there to the hypothesis that all bad people are liars, an unverifiable conclusion that runs counter to the doctrine that the defendant is innocent of the particular crime until proven guilty.

Inquiry about prior arrests or charges that did not result in a conviction may not be made pursuant to Rule 608,[22] although questions may be asked about the underlying conduct if it is probative of truthfulness and survives Rule 403 balancing. Arrests do not constitute "specific instances of conduct" as required by the rule. Futhermore, such evidence is extremely prejudicial because it suggests to the jury that the witness, even if he was acquitted, has been under suspicion by police authorities and that such suspicion is usually based upon fact.

The Second Circuit has held in a case of first impression that a prosecutor may not ask the defendant whether he had committed tax fraud and perjury when the first charge resulted in an

defense admissible); United States v. Sperling, 726 F.2d 69, 75 (2d Cir.), *cert. denied,* 467 U.S. 1243 (1984) (cross-examination regarding false credit card applications permitted); United States v. O'Malley, 707 F.2d 1240 (11th Cir. 1983) (cross-examination about defendant's failure to report political cash contributions permitted); United States v. Cole, 617 F.2d 151 (5th Cir. 1980) (cross-examination proper concerning false excuse for being absent from work). *See also* United States v. Tarantino, 846 F.2d 1384, 1405–07 (D.C. Cir.), *cert. denied,* 109 S. Ct. 108, 174 (1988) (although government witness' involvement in plot to kill another witness to keep him from testifying was relevant as to credibility, trial court did not err in refusing to allow defense counsel to cross-examine on this issue since it would have been highly prejudicial to a co-defendant who was also implicated in the plot).

[21] United States v. Rubin, 733 F.2d 837 (11th Cir. 1984) (drug use cannot be the subject of cross-examination); United States v. Mausaw, 714 F.2d 785, 789 (8th Cir.), *cert. denied,* 464 U.S. 964 (1984) (witness' prostitution not a proper subject for Rule 608 cross-examination); United States v. Bocra, 623 F.2d 281 (3d Cir.), *cert. denied,* 449 U.S. 875 (1978) (trial court properly held that fact that defendant solicited bribes was not a proper subject for Rule 608(b) cross-examination).

[22] *Cf.* United States v. Reed, 715 F.2d 870, 875–76 (5th Cir. 1983).

acquittal and the second in a dismissal.[23] The court explained that "[t]o permit the inquiry risks unfair prejudice, which is not justified by the theoretical possibility that the witness, though acquitted, will admit to the misconduct."[24]

¶ 12.03[04]   Attack on Character: Cross-examination of Character Witness as to Specific Acts of a Principal Witness[1]

Character witnesses, called pursuant to Rule 608(a), being witnesses themselves, are subject to impeachment and may be examined about their acts relevant to truthfulness. On cross-examination they may also be asked whether they had heard or had known of specific acts committed by the principal witness in order to ascertain the basis and standard for their testimony as to reputation or opinion. The courts should limit the scope of character inquiry on cross-examination of character witnesses to those specific acts of the main witness demonstrably probative of veracity even when the purpose of the examination is to attack the credibility of the character witness. The fact that character witnesses can be cross-examined about a principal witness' previous conduct is of particular importance where the principal witness was called by the defendant after his credibility was attacked. If defendant's witness can be asked about defendant's prior bad acts unrelated to lack of truthfulness, the jury may misuse defendant's past misdeeds against him regardless of the substantive evidence at hand.

The criminal defendant must consider whether his right to introduce evidence of good character for veracity is advantageous, or whether it might instead open the door to revelations about

---

[23] United States v. Schwab, 886 F.2d 509 (2d Cir. 1989), *cert. denied,* 110 S. Ct. 1136 (1990) (court noted that Rules 608(b) and 403 both require the exercise of discretion with respect to impeachment by prior acts of misconduct and that an acquittal normally alters the balance between probative force and prejudice).

[24] *Id.* at 513 (court also noted that charge resulting in acquittal had arisen eighteen years prior to trial, and that dismissed charge was made twenty-three years before trial; under these circumstances prosecutor should have made offer of proof outside hearing of jury before instituting inquiry).

[1] *See* **Treatise** at ¶ 608[06].

past misdeeds which the prosecutor could not otherwise bring to the jury's attention. Where it is apparent that the issue will arise, the defendant is entitled to an advance ruling on what will be permitted on the cross-examination of a character witness. This will permit an intelligent tactical decision on whether to call such a witness.

¶ 12.03[05]   Rehabilitating Character: Proof by Reputation or Opinion[1]

Rule 608(a)(2) provides that rehabilitation or opinion[2] evidence may be used to sustain a witness' character for truthfulness. First the witness' veracity must have been attacked.[3]

The courts of appeals have not agreed on whether a promise to testify truthfully as part of a plea agreement with the government (inadmissible on direct) is rehabilitating evidence.[4] Generally such evidence should not be permitted since it has the effect of putting the prosecution in the position of vouching for the witness.[5] The trial court has the power to limit the admissibility of cumulative rehabilitating evidence.

---

[1] *See* **Treatise** at ¶ 608[08].

[2] *But cf.* United States v. Azure, 801 F.2d 336, 340 (8th Cir. 1986) (error to allow expert to testify that witness/victim was believable and that there was no reason to believe she was not telling the truth).

[3] United States v. Hicks, 748 F.2d 854, 859 (4th Cir. 1984) (error, but harmless, to allow the government to prove in its direct examination of government witness, whose character for truthfulness had not yet been attacked, that he had no prior criminal record).

[4] *Compare* United States v. Edwards, 631 F.2d 1049, 1051–52 (2d Cir. 1980) ("bolstering" portions of plea agreement not admissible on direct examination); United States v. Roberts, 618 F.2d 530, 536 (9th Cir. 1980), *cert. denied,* 452 U.S. 942 (1981) (promise of truthfulness not admissible on direct), *with* United States v. Cosentino, 844 F.2d 30, 34 (2d Cir.), *cert. denied,* 109 S. Ct. 303 (1988) (cooperation agreement could be admitted on direct after defense attacked witness's credibility in the opening statement); United States v. Winter, 663 F.2d 1120, 1133–34 (1st Cir. 1981), *cert. denied,* 460 U.S. 1011 (1983) (permitting witness to testify that he was immunized in exchange for his complete and truthful testimony does not allow government improperly to vouch for witness' credibility); United States v. Craig, 573 F.2d 513, 519 (7th Cir. 1978), *cert. denied,* 439 U.S. 820 (1978) (same).

[5] By using other portions of a plea agreement in attacking credibility, the cross-examiner may provide a basis for admission of the entire agreement under Rule 106 as a related writing.

Before rehabilitating evidence is admitted, the trial court must decide whether the witness' character for truthfulness has been attacked. Attack in some circumstances is easy to discern. A witness may offer evidence of his good character for truth if reputation or opinion evidence of his bad character for veracity has been admitted. The introduction of evidence of convictions pursuant to Rule or the elicitation on cross-examination of the witness' acknowledgment of misconduct not the subject of conviction (Rule 608(b)) will open the door to evidence in support of truthfulness. A trial judge can also find that a witness' credibility was attacked in the trial attorney's opening statement.[6]

When the witness denies misconduct but insinuations have been conveyed to the jury by an accusatory cross-examination, rehabilitation should be allowed in the court's discretion if it finds the witness' denial has not erased the jury's doubts.[7] While evidence of corrupt conduct on the part of a witness should be regarded as an attack on truthfulness warranting supporting evidence, evidence of bias by facts not indicating corruption, such as evidence of family relationships, should not be. The court should admit rehabilitating evidence following impeachment by proof of prior inconsistent statement[8] or by proof of contradiction, if it finds that in the circumstances of the particular case the contradiction amounted to an attack on veracity.[9]

[6] United States v. Cosentino, 844 F.2d 30, 34 (2d Cir.), *cert. denied,* 109 S. Ct. 303 (1988) (cooperation agreement could be admitted on direct after defense attacked witness's credibility in the opening statement); United States v. Maniego, 710 F.2d 24 (2d Cir. 1983) (not error to allow the elicitation of direct examination testimony that government witness would receive immunity "if they told truth" where the credibility issue was joined by counsel for co-defendant in opening argument).

[7] United States v. Scholle, 553 F.2d 1109, 1122–23 (8th Cir.), *cert. denied,* 434 U.S. 940 (1977).

[8] Beard v. Mitchell, 604 F.2d 485 (7th Cir. 1979) (prior inconsistent statements may be used to impeach credibility and reputation evidence for truthfulness was properly admitted).

[9] *See* Stokes v. Delacambre, 710 F.2d 1120 (5th Cir. 1983) (court properly excluded evidence of deputy's reputation for truthfulness where plaintiff had not attacked his reputation; proffer, consisting only of another assault victim attributing a statement to defendant which he denied making); United States

¶ 12.04   Impeachment by Evidence of Conviction — Rule 609

¶ 12.04[01]   Scope[1]

Rule 609 governs the use of criminal convictions for impeachment. There is no entirely satisfactory solution to the use of convictions to impeach.

The version of Rule 609 that was originally enacted had a complicated legislative history, as extensively explored by the Supreme Court in *Green v. Bock Laundry Machine Co.*[2] In reaction to the opinion in *Green,* subdivision (a) of the rule was extensively revised, effective December 1, 1990.[3] The 1990

---

v. Angelini, 678 F.2d 380, 382 n.1 (1st Cir. 1982) (mere fact that defendant takes the stand or is contradicted does not require admission of evidence for truthfulness; no error in exclusion where cross-examination of defendant "could hardly be characterized as so 'slashing' . . . as to constitute an attack on credibility"). *But see* United States v. Jackson, 588 F.2d 1048, 1055 (5th Cir. 1979) (court without discussion adhered to the pre-Federal Rules of Evidence rule that impeachment by contradiction does not constitute an attack).

[1] *See* **Treatise** at ¶ 609[01] for a discussion of the legislative history of the rule, and ¶ 609[03] for its historical antecedents. The admissibility for impeachment purposes of tainted convictions is discussed in the **Treatise** at ¶ 609[11].

[2] 490 U.S. —, 109 S. Ct. 1981, 104 L. Ed. 2d 557 (1989). The *Green* case is discussed further at ¶ 12.04[03][a] *infra.*

[3] Pursuant to 28 U.S.C. § 2074(a), the amendment is scheduled to take effect on December 1, 1990, "unless otherwise provided by law." It is not anticipated that Congress will take any action with respect to this amendment, and the amendment should take effect as indicated and as scheduled.

Until the effective date of the 1990 amendment, Rule 609(a) reads as follows:

(a) General rule. — For the purpose of attacking the credibility of a witness, evidence that the witness other than an accused has been convicted of a crime shall be admitted if elicited from the witness or established by public record during cross-examination but only if the crime (1) was punishable by death or imprisonment in excess of one year under the law under which the witness was convicted, and the court determines that the probative value of admitting this evidence outweighs its prejudicial effect to the defendant; or (2) involved dishonesty or false statement, regardless of the punishment.

amendment represents the latest in a series of long-fought-over compromises designed to achieve a workable and reasonably fair set of rules.

(Text continued on page 12–45)

(Matthew Bender & Co., Inc.)

(Rel.4–8/91   Pub.819)

As amended in 1990, subdivision (a) treats criminal defendants differently from other witnesses in criminal cases and witnesses in civil cases. Subdivision (b) imposes time restrictions on the use of convictions. Subdivision (c) considers when a pardon or its equivalent renders the conviction inadmissible. Subdivision (d) governs the use of juvenile adjudications, and subdivision (e) regulates the use of convictions that are up on appeal. Each of these subdivisions is discussed separately below.

The Rule states:

Rule 609

IMPEACHMENT BY EVIDENCE OF CONVICTION OF CRIME

(a) General rule.—For the purpose of attacking the credibility of a witness,

(1) evidence that a witness other than an accused has been convicted of a crime shall be admitted, subject to Rule 403, if the crime was punishable by death or imprisonment in excess of one year under the law under which the witness was convicted, and evidence that an accused has been convicted of such a crime shall be admitted if the court determines that the probative value of admitting this evidence outweighs its prejudicial effect to the accused; and

(2) evidence that any witness has been convicted of a crime shall be admitted if it involved dishonesty or false statement, regardless of the punishment.

(b) Time limit.— Evidence of a conviction under this rule is not admissible if a period of more than ten years has elapsed since the date of the conviction or of the release of the witness from the confinement imposed for that conviction, whichever is the later date, unless the court determines, in the interests of justice, that the probative value of the conviction supported by specific facts and circumstances substantially outweighs its prejudicial effect. However, evidence of a conviction more than 10 years old as calculated herein, is not admissible unless the proponent gives to the adverse party sufficient advance written notice of intent to use such evidence to provide the adverse party with a fair opportunity to contest the use of such evidence.

(c) Effect of pardon, annulment, or certificate of rehabilitation.— Evidence of a conviction is not admissible under this rule if (1) the conviction has been the subject of a pardon, annulment, certificate of rehabilitation, or other equivalent procedure based on a finding of the rehabilitation of the person convicted, and that person has not been convicted of a subsequent crime which was punishable by death or imprisonment in excess of one year, or (2) the conviction has been the subject of a pardon, annulment, or other equivalent procedure based on a finding of innocence.

(d) Juvenile adjudications.— Evidence of juvenile adjudications is generally not admissible under this rule. The court may, however, in a criminal case allow evidence of a juvenile adjudication of a witness other than the accused if conviction of the offense would be admissible to attack the credibility of an adult and the court is satisfied that admission in evidence is necessary for a fair determination of the issue of guilt or innocence.

(e) Pendency of appeal.— The pendency of an appeal therefrom does not render evidence of a conviction inadmissible. Evidence of the pendency of an appeal is admissible.

¶ 12.04[02]   Rationale[1]

At common law all felony convictions were usable for impeachment on the theory that a person with a criminal past has a bad general character, and a person with a bad general character is more likely to lie on the witness stand. The assumption that there is a link between credibility and committing crimes has been questioned since the time of Bentham,[2] especially in the case of crimes of violence. Doubts have also been expressed about admitting evidence of a single criminal act that may be atypical of the witness, and may have occurred in the distant past.

Aside from the low probative value of some convictions, the divulgence of a criminal past exposes the witness to the hazards of jury prejudice. The jurors may discount the testimony because of dislike rather than disbelief. If the witness is the complainant, the jurors may "acquit a man plainly guilty of crime because of their distaste for the victim."[3] Fear of public degradation may make the possessors of a criminal record reluctant to testify, or

[1] See **Treatise** at ¶ 609[02].

[2] Bentham, Rationale of Judicial Evidence 406 (Browning's ed. 1827) (Bentham pointed out the absurdity of labeling a liar someone who had killed someone for calling him a liar).

[3] Davis v. United States, 409 F.2d 453, 457 (D.C. Cir. 1969).

even to complain of criminal acts, to the detriment of the judicial system's interest in obtaining useful testimony.

When the witness is a party, the jury's antipathy may be translated into findings of guilt or liability without regard to whether the witness committed the charged acts. This danger is particularly acute in the case of a criminal defendant with a record. The jury may wish to punish regardless of present guilt, or it may assume guilt if the prior conviction was for a similar crime. If the defendant does not testify, statistics indicate that jurors are likely to infer guilt.[4] The defendant is, therefore, caught in the same type of dilemma against which the propensity rule embodied in Rule 404 seeks to protect. Rule 609 extends the policies of the propensity rule to the impeachment process. It responds to both criticisms of the common law rule: the low probative value of some prior convictions, and the high possibility of prejudice, particularly in the case of criminal defendants. In subdivisions (a), (b) and (c), the rule restricts the use of convictions with the least amount of relevance and affords extra protection to the criminal defendant through the balancing test in subdivision (a)(1).

¶ 12.04[03]   Rule 609(a)—Overview[1]

As originally enacted, Rule 609(a) allowed the credibility of a witness to be impeached either by eliciting the fact of the conviction from the witness[2] or by establishing the public record of the conviction.[3] As amended in 1990, however, the rule

---

[4] Note, "To Take the Stand or Not to Take the Stand: The Dilemma of the Defendant with a Criminal Record," 4 Colum. J.L. & Soc. Probs. 213 (1968).

[1] *See* **Treatise** at ¶¶ 609[04], [06].

[2] United States v. Nevitt, 563 F.2d 406 (9th Cir. 1977) (Rule 609(a) does not require a public record of the conviction to lay the foundation for a cross-examination of the witness). *See also* United States v. Scott, 592 F.2d 1139 (10th Cir. 1979) (although "rap sheet" is not admissible as public record of the conviction, it may be used as a basis for cross-examining defendant about his record).

[3] United States v. Bovain, 708 F.2d 606 (11th Cir.), *cert. denied,* 464 U.S. 898 (1983) (in prosecution for drug-related offenses, credibility of non-testifying hearsay declarant was properly impeached with certified records of his prior convictions for narcotics and stealing money orders).

recognizes that the usual practice is for counsel to bring out the witness' conviction on direct in order to remove some of the force of the cross-examination. Following the amendment, the requirement of eliciting the conviction during cross-examination no longer applies. The Advisory Committee explained the change as follows:

> The amendment does not contemplate that a court will necessarily permit proof of prior convictions through testimony, which might be time-consuming and more prejudicial than proof through a written record. Rules 403 and 611(a) provide sufficient authority for the court to protect against unfair or disruptive methods of proof.

For impeachment purposes, a conviction that results from a guilty plea is equivalent to a determination of guilt following trial.[4] A nolo contendere plea[5] or an *Alford* plea[6] is treated like any other conviction for purposes of Rule 609.

Subject to the restrictions of subdivisions (b)–(e) of the rule, any witness may be impeached by evidence of any conviction involving dishonesty or a false statement. Rule 609(a), as amended in 1990, imposes further restrictions on the use of other felony convictions for impeachment. If the witness is the defendant in a criminal trial, the burden rests on the prosecutor to demonstrate that "the probative value of admitting this evidence outweighs its prejudicial effect to the accused." For all other witnesses, felony convictions shall be admitted "subject to Rule 403."

The restrictions of Rule 609 do not apply if evidence of a conviction is offered for a purpose other than attacking the credibility of a witness.[7] For example, evidence of a conviction

---

[4] United States v. Pardo, 636 F.2d 535, 545–46 n.32 (D.C. Cir. 1980).

[5] United States v. Dennis, 532 F. Supp. 625 (E.D. Mich. 1982).

[6] United States v. Lipscomb, 702 F.2d 1049, 1069 (D.C. Cir. 1983) (en banc).

[7] United States v. Leavis, 853 F.2d 215, 220 (4th Cir. 1988) (where defendant made statements on direct examination implying that he had had no prior contact with drugs or drug dealers, prosecution was entitled to bring out a more than ten-year-old conviction for possession of marijuana even if it would ordinarily have been barred by Rule 609(b); Roshan v. Ford, 705 F.2d 102, 104 (4th Cir. 1983) (trial court erred in excluding evidence that defendant was an informant for DEA who had been instrumental in securing convictions of plaintiff, since evidence was offered primarily to demonstrate motive and only incidentally to attack credibility).

may be admitted to contradict the defendant's testimony on a material issue in the case.[8]

[a] Prosecution Witnesses and Witnesses in Civil Proceedings

Rule 609(a) was amended in 1990 in response to the Supreme Court's opinion in *Green v. Bock Laundry Machine Co.*[9] In the *Green* case, the Court resolved a conflict among the circuits as to whether a court may exclude a felony conviction offered to impeach a witness in a civil case on the ground of undue prejudice. Conceding that the text of Rule 609 is ambiguous,[10] the Court relied on legislative history[11] and the overall structure of the Federal Rules[12] to conclude that Congress "intended that only the accused in a criminal case should be protected from unfair prejudice by the balance set out in Rule 609(a)(1),"[13] and that furthermore "Rule 403 balancing should not pertain" to Rule 609.[14] Consequently, all felony convictions and all misdemeanor

---

[8] *See* United States v. Gaertner, 705 F.2d 210, 216 (7th Cir. 1983), *cert. denied,* 464 U.S. 1091 (1984) (in a prosecution for possession of cocaine, after trial court initially ruled that it would exclude, as overly prejudicial, evidence of defendant's prior conviction for possession of marijuana, defendant testified that he was not involved with drugs; the court reversed its ruling and properly admitted the marijuana conviction, since defendant's testimony had specifically raised the issue). *But cf.* United States v. Shapiro, 879 F.2d 468, 471–72 (9th Cir. 1989) (after prosecution stipulated that it would not offer evidence of defendant's prior convictions unless defense were to imply that he had no prior record, it was reversible error for prosecution to cross-examine defendant about his prior convictions, claiming they were relevant to his motive and intent under Rule 404(b)).

[9] 490 U.S. −, 109 S. Ct. 1981, 104 L. Ed. 2d 557 (1989) (plaintiff who lost his arm while working in a laundry on work release program had been impeached by his prior convictions).

[10] *Id.* at −, 109 S. Ct. at 1985, 104 L. Ed. 2d at 565 (the majority pointed to the language in subdivision (a)(1) permitting the court to consider the "prejudicial effect to the defendant" as on its face not distinguishing between a defendant in a criminal or civil case, but then suggested that a rule that treated plaintiffs differently than civil defendants is constitutionally suspect and therefore could not mean what it said.

[11] *Id.* at −, 109 S. Ct. at 1985, 104 L. Ed. 2d at 565.

[12] *Id.* at −, 109 S. Ct. at −, 104 L. Ed. 2d at −.

[13] *Id.* at −, 109 S. Ct. at 1992, 104 L. Ed. 2d at 573.

[14] *Id.* at −, 109 S. Ct. at 1993, 104 L. Ed. 2d at 574.

convictions involving dishonesty and false statement were usable for impeachment against all witnesses in civil proceedings regardless of the prejudice to the witness or the party.[15] Prosecution witnesses were subject to the same broad impeachment since the same reasoning with regard to the inapplicability of Rule 403 would apply.

The 1990 amendment to Rule 609(a)[16] specifically overturned the holding in *Green* that the balancing provisions of Rule 403 did not pertain to Rule 609. As amended in 1990, the rule states that all witnesses other than the accused may be impeached by any felony conviction (for a crime other than one involving dishonesty or false statement) subject to a Rule 403 balancing test. Convictions involving dishonesty or false statement are automatically admissible. *See infra.*

The Advisory Committee explained the purpose of the change as follows:

> The amendment reflects the view that it is desirable to protect all litigants from the unfair use of prior convictions, and that the ordinary balancing test of Rule 403, which provides that evidence shall not be excluded unless its prejudicial effect substantially outweighs its probative value, is appropriate for assessing the admissibility of prior convictions for impeachment of any witness other than a criminal defendant.

The Advisory Committee also indicated that it is undesirable "to admit convictions in civil cases that have little, if anything to do with credibility." On the other hand, the Advisory Committee suggested that convictions of prosecution witnesses should be admitted more readily:

> The probability that prior convictions of an ordinary government witness will be unduly prejudicial is low in most criminal cases.

---

[15] The Court acknowledged "longstanding and widespread" dissatisfaction with the rule but stated that it was not its task "to fashion the rule we deem desirable." *Id.* at —, 109 S. Ct. at 1984, 104 L. Ed. 2d at 564. In footnote 29, the majority opinion sets forth some proposed amendments to Rule 609 that would give the court discretion to exclude a conviction in a civil case. *Id.* at —, 109 S. Ct. at 1992, 104 L. Ed. 2d at 573.

[16] Pursuant to 28 U.S.C. § 2074(a), the amendment is scheduled to take effect on December 1, 1990, "unless otherwise provided by law." It is not anticipated that Congress will take any action with respect to this amendment, and the amendment should take effect as indicated and as scheduled.

Since the behavior of the witness is not the issue in dispute in most cases, there is little chance that the trier of fact will misuse the convictions offered as impeachment evidence as propensity evidence. Thus, trial courts will be skeptical when the government objects to impeachment of its witnesses with prior convictions. Only when the government is able to point to a real danger of prejudice that is sufficient to outweigh substantially the probative value of the conviction for impeachment purposes will the conviction be excluded.

[b]   Accused

A two-pronged test governs the admissibility of the convictions of the accused. Clause (2) of Rule 609(a) provides for automatic admission of evidence of all prior convictions of any crime—felony or misdemeanor—involving dishonesty or false statement. While Clause (1) covers felonies not involving dishonesty or false statement; it conditions the admissibility of convictions of lesser probative value on a balancing test (where prejudice to the defendant, not the government, is put on the scale) to be administered by the trial judge. This two-pronged test of admissibility requires consideration of Rule 609(a)(2) first, because a conviction that may not automatically be admitted under the second prong may still be admitted in the court's discretion if it meets the criteria of the first.

[c]   Rule 609(a)(2)—Convictions for Crimes Involving Dishonesty or False Statement

Rule 609(a)(2) requires the admission of evidence of all prior convictions of any crime—felony or misdemeanor—involving dishonesty or false statement.[17] While the Supreme Court has not ruled on whether a conviction involving dishonesty or false statement can nevertheless be excluded in the exercise of the judge's discretion pursuant to Rule 403 on grounds of confusion, waste of time, or extreme prejudice, "[t]he current weight of authority is that Rule 609(a)(2) crimes cannot be excluded under

---

[17] United States v. O'Connor, 635 F.2d 814 (10th Cir. 1980) (misdemeanor conviction for crime involving false statement admitted).

Rule 403."[18] This conclusion has been strengthened by the 1990 amendment to Rule 609, which specifically provided in subdivision (a)(1) for balancing of Rule 403 factors with respect to the felony conviction of a witness other than an accused, but made no change in subdivision (a)(2).

While characterization for purposes of Rule 609 is a federal, not a state matter,[19] the exact state definition will need to be considered.[20] A lesser plea may take a conviction out of the rule even though the details of the criminal act underlying the charge showed extreme dishonesty or involved use of false statements. Though a number of courts have suggested looking to the underlying criminal act rather than the definition of the offense in ascertaining admissibility,[21] it is a mistake for the trial court to be forced to look behind the conviction to determine its details.[22]

---

[18] United States v. Lipscomb, 702 F.2d 1049, 1057. n.28 (D.C. Cir. 1983) (en banc) (court intimates no view on question). A number of circuits have concluded that the court has no discretion to exclude. *See* United States v. Kiendra, 663 F.2d 349 (1st Cir. 1983); United States v. Wong, 703 F.2d 65, 68 (3d Cir.), *cert. denied,* 464 U.S. 842 (1980); United States v. Kuecker, 740 F.2d 496, 501–02 (7th Cir. 1984); United States v. Leyva, 659 F.2d 118 (9th Cir. 1981), *cert. denied,* 454 U.S. 1156 (1982).

[19] United States v. Cameron, 814 F.2d 403, 405 (7th Cir. 1987) (not error to exclude witness' state conviction for possession of a switchblade, a misdemeanor, even if state law would characterize crime as one involving dishonesty).

[20] *See* United States v. Rogers, 853 F.2d 249, 252 (4th Cir.), *cert. denied,* 109 S. Ct. 375 (1988) (defendant's convictions under state worthless check statutes were automatically admissible since the statutes themselves characterized crime as involving dishonesty or false statement); *See* United States v. Wright, 564 F.2d 785 (8th Cir. 1977) (since prostitution is a misdemeanor under Illinois law, conviction would not be usable for impeachment pursuant to Rule 609).

[21] United States v. Lipscomb, 702 F.2d 1049, 1064–68 (D.C. Cir. 1983) (en banc) (court notes that "[a]ll circuits that have considered the question, including our own, have held that the prosecution may adduce specific facts to bring a prior conviction within Rule 609(a)(2)."). *See also* United States v. Grandmont, 680 F.2d 867, 871 (1st Cir. 1982) (robberies); United States v. Hayes, 553 F.2d 824, 827 (2d Cir.) (narcotics conviction), *cert. denied,* 434 U.S. 867 (1977); United States v. Papia, 560 F.2d 827, 845–48 (7th Cir. 1977) (misdemeanor theft conviction).

[22] United States v. Pandozzi, 878 F.2d 1526, 1533–34 (1st Cir. 1989) (underlying details excluded); United States v. Lewis, 626 F.2d 940, 946 (D.C. Cir. 1980) ("we do not perceive that it is the manner in which the offense is

In this area convenience requires a rather mechanical rule. It is better to arbitrarily classify crimes one way or the other and not get into details of a particular conviction, such as whether the witness testified at the prior trial and was not believed or whether the particular assault was based on a dishonest trick luring the victim into an alley.[23]

The courts have had no difficulty in finding that bribery,[24] perjury, subornation of perjury, false statement,[25] embezzlement, false pretense[26] or crimes involving fraud[27] fall within Rule

committed that determines its admissibility.. . . [W]e interpret Rule 609(a)(2) to require that the crime involved dishonesty or false statement' as an element of the statutory offense"). *See also* Altobello v. Borden Confectionary Prods., Inc., 872 F.2d 215, 217 (7th Cir. 1989) ("the trial judge must not allow himself to be sidetracked into the details of the earlier conviction, but where as in this case the deceitful nature of the crime is admitted or is plain on the face of the indictment or other official record, the fact that the same type of offense can be committed in a manner not involving deceit does not make the conviction inadmissible." Crime in question was misdemeanor of tampering with electric meter which court states "is *necessarily* a crime of deception" as "the goal is *always* to deceive the meter reader."). *But cf.* United States v. Perry, 857 F.2d 1346, 1352 (9th Cir. 1988) (defendant's attempt to explain away conviction by offering his own version of the underlying facts will open door to detailed cross-examination).

23 *But see* United States v. Bogers, 635 F.2d 749 (8th Cir. 1980) (no error in trial court permitting inquiry into specific facts about underlying crime and inquiry into term of defendant's sentence for conviction used for impeachment, that shotgun was involved, that defendant was currently in penitentiary, and effect federal conviction would have on state parole); United States v. Barnes, 622 F.2d 107, 110 (5th Cir. 1980) (shoplifting does not involve dishonesty and false statement; some petty larceny offenses may and "therefore it is necessary to look at the basis of the conviction to determine whether the crime embraced dishonesty.").

24 United States v. Williams, 642 F.2d 136 (5th Cir. 1981) (bribery is a crimen falsi).

25 United States v. Klein, 438 F.Supp 485 (S.D.N.Y. 1977) (misdemeanor conviction for willful failure to file income tax withholding returns was admissible although such a conviction does not require proof of an intention to defraud, since "saying nothing" in this instance is tantamount to a false statement). *See also* United States v. Gellman, 677 F.2d 65 (11th Cir. 1982) (failure to file federal income tax return).

26 Shingleton v. Armour Velvet Corp., 621 F.2d 180 (5th Cir. 1980) (evidence of conviction related to a false pretense scheme admissible pursuant to Rule 609(a)(2)).

27 United States v. Hans, 738 F.2d 88, 93 (3d Cir. 1984) (prior conviction for interstate transportation of forged securities); United States v. Harris, 738

609(a)(2), while crimes solely involving force do not.[28] The conference committee report to original Rule 609(a) explained that "dishonesty and false statement" includes "any other offense in the nature of crimen falsi, the commission of which involves some element of deceit, untruthfulness, or falsification bearing on the accused's propensity to testify truthfully."[29] An uncertain area exists, due in part to the vagaries of state practice. Courts have differed, especially in their treatment of crimes involving the taking of property. Some courts view property crimes as involving dishonesty,[30] while others stress that this category of crime had not historically been included in the crimen falsi category.[31] If the crime is a felony, it is more in keeping with the spirit of the rule to treat it as one not involving dishonesty or a false statement,

---

F.2d 1068, 1073 (9th Cir. 1984), *cert. denied,* 105 S. Ct. 1771, 2335 (1985); (conviction for passing counterfeit money); United States v. Whitman, 665 F.2d 313 (10th Cir. 1982) (land fraud scheme); United States v. Apuzzo, 555 F.2d 306, 307–08 (2d Cir. 1977), *cert. denied,* 435 U.S. 916 (1978) (possession and transportation of untaxed cigarettes (a misdemeanor); "a crime which involves defrauding the revenue stands high in the category of crimes affecting veracity").

[28] Carlsen v. Javurek, 526 F.2d 202, 210 (8th Cir. 1975) (evidence of assault and battery conviction should have been excluded); United States v. Bianco, 419 F. Supp. 507 (E.D. Pa. 1976), *aff'd mem.,* 547 F.2d 1164 (3rd Cir. 1977). *Cf.* United States v. Jackson, 405 F. Supp. 938, 943 (E.D.N.Y. 1975) (defendant's assault conviction excluded at pretrial hearing on condition that defense counsel not use assault convictions of any government witnesses without specific advance authorization from the court).

[29] Conf. Rep. No. 93–1597, 93d Cong., 2d Sess. 9, reprinted in (1974) U.S. Cong. & Ad. News 7098.

[30] United States v. Kinslow, 860 F.2d 963, 968 (9th Cir. 1988) (armed robbery involves "dishonesty"); United States v. Del Toro Soto, 676 F.2d 13, 18 (1st Cir. 1982) (grand larceny); United States v. Wilson, 536 F.2d 883 (9th Cir.) *cert. denied,* 429 U.S. 982 (1976) (receiving stolen property and attempted robbery); United States v. Carden, 529 F.2d 443 (5th Cir.), *cert. denied,* 429 U.S. 848 (1976) (petty larceny).

[31] United States v. Scisney, 885 F.2d 325, 326 (6th Cir. 1989) (shoplifting is not a crime involving dishonesty or false statement); United States v. Yeo, 739 F.2d 385 (8th Cir. 1984) (theft); United States v. Glenn, 667 F.2d 1269 (9th Cir. 1982) (burglary and grand theft); United States v. Entrekin, 624 F.2d 597 (5th Cir. 1980) (shoplifting). *Cf.* United States v. Grandmont, 680 F.2d 867 (1st Cir. 1982) (robbery per se is not a crime of dishonesty or false statement; in absence of showing that prior robberies in question (purse snatchings) were committed by deceitful or fraudulent means, convictions not admissible).

so that the trial court can exercise its discretion to exclude the conviction under Rule 609(a)(1). However, if a felony conviction is erroneously admitted under Rule 609(a)(2), the error will be harmless if the trial court properly balanced the pertinent factors.**32**

The 1990 amendment to Rule 609 did not make any substantive change in subdivision (a)(2). The Advisory Committee's note explained:

> the Conference Report provides sufficient guidance to trial courts and . . . no amendment is necessary, notwithstanding some decisions that take an unduly broad view of "dishonesty," admitting convictions such as for bank robbery or bank larceny.

[d] Rule 609(a)(1)—Balancing Test

Rule 609(a)(1) provides that the credibility of a criminal defendant may be attacked by evidence of the defendant's prior felony (not misdemeanor)**33** convictions, subject to the time limit in Rule 609(b), provided "the court determines that the probative value of admitting this evidence outweighs its prejudicial effect to the accused." The 1990 amendment to the rule makes it clear that this particular balancing test is applicable only to the impeachment of a criminal defendant.**34**

---

32 *See, e.g.,* United States v. Provenzano, 620 F.2d 985, 1002–03 (3d Cir.), *cert. denied,* 449 U.S. 899 (1980) (appellate court declined to decide if convictions were admissible pursuant to subdivision (a)(2), since the trial court implicitly found that probative value exceeded prejudice).

33 United States v. Slade, 627 F.2d 293, 308 (D.C. Cir. 1980), *cert. denied,* 101 S. Ct. 608 (1980) (reversible error to impeach defendant with misdemeanor conviction for possessing a pistol especially where curative instruction not given until day later); United States v. Harvey, 588 F.2d 1201 (8th Cir. 1978) (an assault conviction does not involve dishonesty or false statement and therefore error to admit evidence of conviction of a misdemeanor). *Cf.* United States v. Lane, 708 F.2d 1394 (9th Cir. 1983) (court did not err in excluding evidence of witness' prior arson conviction where original felony was withdrawn and witness had pleaded guilty to lesser included misdemeanor offense).

34 As interpreted by the Supreme Court, the original rule provided that a balancing of prejudice to the defendant must be conducted only in criminal cases. The prior convictions of witnesses for the prosecution, or witnesses in a civil case, were to be admitted without regard to the potential for prejudice. Green v. Bock Laundry Machine Corp., 490 U.S. —, 109 S. Ct. 1981, 104

The courts have endorsed the consideration of a number of factors in balancing probative value against prejudice to the accused.[35] The trial court should consider (1) the relationship the crime has to veracity,[36] (2) the recency of the conviction,[37] and (3) the similarity between the past crime and the charged crime. The more similar the two are the more likely it is that admitting evidence of the past crime will prejudice the defendant because the jurors are likely to believe that "if he did it before he probably did so this time."[38]

L. Ed. 2d 557 (1989), discussed in subhead [a] *supra.* The 1990 amendment added a provision that evidence of a felony conviction of a witness other than an accused "shall be admitted, subject to Rule 403." *See* subhead [a] *supra.*

[35] *See, e.g.,* United States v. Jackson, 627 F.2d 1198 (D.C. Cir 1980) (listing factors trial court should consider); United States v. Mahone, 537 F.2d 922, 929 (7th Cir.), *cert. denied,* 429 U.S. 1025 (1976) (same).

[36] *See, e.g.,* United States v. Halbert, 668 F.2d 489, 495 (8th Cir.), *cert. denied,* 456 U.S. 934 (1982) (armed robbery probative of credibility); United States v. Fountain, 642 F.2d 1083 (7th Cir.), *cert. denied,* 451 U.S. 999 (1981) (premeditated murder does bear on credibility); United States v. Larsen, 596 F.2d 347 (9th Cir. 1979) (admission of child molesting convictions, which bore only nominally on credibility, plain error); United States v. Hayes, 553 F.2d 824, 828 (2d Cir.), *cert. denied,* 434 U.S. 867 (1977) (smuggling "ranks relatively high on the scale of veracity-related crimes").

[37] The more remote in time a conviction is the less likely it will be considered probative of credibility. *See, e.g.,* United States v. Jackson, 696 F.2d 578 (8th Cir. 1982), *cert. denied,* 460 U.S. 1073 (1983) (recent firearm conviction admissible); United States v. Beahm, 664 F.2d 414 (4th Cir. 1981) (error in admitting 9

year old conviction for child molesting because of remoteness and odious nature of crime). *See also* United States v. Jones, 647 F.2d 696, 700 (6th Cir.), *cert. denied,* 454 U.S. 898 (1981) (not abuse of discretion to admit 9 year old conviction for grand larceny which took place when defendant was 20 years old although court noted that district court could well have excluded). Rule 609(b) presumes that evidence of a conviction that is more than 10 years old is inadmissible.

[38] *See, e.g.,* United States v. Bagley, 772 F.2d 482, 488 (9th Cir.), *cert. denied,* 475 U.S. 1023 (1986) (in prosecution for bank robbery, it was an abuse of discretion to admit evidence of two prior convictions for bank robbery, when two forgery convictions could have been used instead); United States v. Hans, 738 F.2d 88, 93 (3d Cir. 1984) (when making Rule 609(a)(1) determination, trial court properly excluded conviction for similar crime); United States v. Martinez, 555 F.2d 1273, 1276 (5th Cir. 1977) (abuse of discretion for trial judge to allow defendant to be impeached by prior conviction arising out of identical factual circumstances and involving many of the identical elements as offense with which he was presently charged).

Even if the trial court finds that evidence of the conviction is probative of truthfulness, it should evaluate (4) the importance of the defendant's testimony, considering the consequences of the defendant being kept from the stand by the fear of having prior convictions divulged. Thus, the court may exclude the conviction if it finds that the defendant's testimony will aid the jury in ascertaining the truth, and refuse to exclude when there is no real need for the defendant's testimony because it would be substantially the same as that of other witnesses.[39] This consideration may, however, be at odds with yet another factor, (5) the centrality of the credibility issue. When the defendant's credibility is the dispositive issue in the case, a court may favor admitting anything, including convictions, that might possibly shed light on whose version should be believed.[40]

Prior to the 1990 amendment, this balancing test was also applied to the impeachment of defense witnesses other than the accused. Under the amendment, the impeachment of such witnesses will now be subject to Rule 403 balancing, as discussed above. The Advisory Committee note to the amendment points out that this provision continues to protect the accused "when the witness bears a special relationship to the defendant such that the defendant is likely to suffer some spill-over effect from impeachment of the witness." For instance, if the witness is a close relative or associate of the defendant, the jury's distrust of the witness if informed of prior convictions may wash off on the defendant. In deciding whether to permit the convictions of the witness to be used, the trial judge should take into consideration the degree of prejudice likely because of the relationship, as well as the significance of the witness' testimony, the similarity between witness' crime and defendant's crime, and the probative value of the prior conviction on the witness' credibility.[41]

---

[39] *See, e.g.,* United States v. Fountain, 642 F.2d 1083 (7th Cir.), *cert. denied,* 451 U.S. 993 (1981) (no abuse of discretion where, inter alia, defendant was able to present his defense without testifying).

[40] *See, e.g.,* United States v. Murray, 751 F.2d 1528, 1533 (9th Cir.), *cert. denied,* 106 S. Ct. 381 (1985) (witness credibility was highly probative in order to resolve conflict between defendant and government's chief witness); United States v. Ortiz, 553 F.2d 782 (2d Cir.), *cert. denied,* 434 U.S. 897 (1977) (same).

[41] *See* United States v. Peterman, 841 F.2d 1474, 1480 (10th Cir. 1988), *cert. denied,* 109 S. Ct. 783 (1989) (no abuse of discretion in permitting

[e] Procedure

In all but rare instances, a motion to exclude pursuant to Rule 609(a) is won or lost at the trial level. Appellate courts are loath to reverse the court below when the trial judge examined the pertinent factors and applied them to the facts presented.[42]

While the rationale of the rule—protecting defendants from the prejudicial impact of admitting convictions not probative of truthfulness—is better served if the trial court makes its Rule 609 determination before the defendant takes the stand, the appellate courts afford the district court discretion to defer ruling until after the evidence is offered.[43] Generally, however, the question of which convictions will be usable to attack credibility should be determined prior to trial.[44] Counsel need to know what the ruling will be on this matter so that they can make appropriate tactical decisions. For example, the opening of defense counsel or the decision of the defendant to take the stand may be affected.

The Supreme Court has held that a trial judge's decision to admit a defendant's prior conviction for impeachment purposes is not subject to review unless the defendant takes the stand.[45] Thus an adverse ruling in limine must be followed up by preserving the matter at trial. The Second Circuit has held, however, that this limitation does not apply when defendant objects to the

impeachment of co-defendant, a government witness, by evidence of his prior conviction).

[42] *See, e.g.,* United States v. Lewis, 626 F.2d 940, 950 (D.C. Cir. 1980) ("When the trial court explicitly balances probative value and prejudicial effect, his decision will be reviewed only for an abuse of discretion."). *Cf.* United States v. Mehrmanesh, 689 F.2d 822, 834 (9th Cir. 1982) (abuse of discretion standard does not apply when court fails to make any inquiry into relevant 609(a)(1) considerations).

[43] *See, e.g.,* United States v. Kennedy, 714 F.2d 968 (9th Cir.), *cert. denied,* 465 U.S. 1034 (1983); United States v. Burkhead, 646 F.2d 1283 (8th Cir.), *cert. denied,* 454 U.S. 898 (1981); United States v. Pfingst, 477 F.2d 177 (2d Cir.), *cert. denied,* 412 U.S. 941 (1973).

[44] United States v. Cook, 608 F.2d 1178, 1186, 1189 (9th Cir. 1979) (en banc) (matter should be left to discretion of trial judge with a reminder that advance planning helps both parties and the court); United States v. Oakes, 565 F.2d 170, 172 (1st Cir. 1977) (same).

[45] Luce v. United States, 469 U.S. 38, 105 S. Ct. 460, 83 L. Ed. 2d 443(1984).

conviction which the trial court refused to exclude on the ground that it is constitutionally invalid.[46]

The trial court should make its determination after a hearing on the record pursuant to Rule 104, explicitly identifying and weighing the pertinent factors.[47] In a criminal case, the prosecution has the burden of showing that the accused's prior conviction should be admissible to impeach him.[48] However, defense counsel should also be prepared to analyze and argue the pertinent considerations.[49] In civil cases and for witnesses in criminal trials other than the accused, the proponent of the witness will have to demonstrate that the factors of unfair prejudice, confusion or misleading the jury, as specified in Rule 403, substantially outweigh the probative value of the conviction.

If the trial judge admits a conviction, counsel for the government should not be allowed to prejudice the defendant by

---

[46] Biller v. Lopes, 834 F.2d 41 (2d Cir. 1987) (habeas corpus; *Luce* does not apply where in limine ruling depends on legal and not factual considerations). *See* **Treatise** at ¶ 609[11] for discussion of use of tainted convictions for impeachment.

[47] United States v. Cook, 608 F.2d 1175, 1186 (9th Cir. 1979) (en banc) ("In future cases, the court and counsel confronting Rule 609 problems should turn to Fed.R.Evid. 103 for guidance."); United States v. Prestan, 608 F.2d 626, 639 (5th Cir. 1979) (trial judge must make on the record finding); United States v. Seamaster, 568 F.2d 188 (10th Cir. 1978) (urging trial judges to make determinations on the record); United States v. Mahone, 537 F.2d 922, 929 (7th Cir.), *cert. denied,* 429 U.S. 1025 (1976) (same). *But see* United States v. Key, 717 F.2d 1206, 1208–09 (8th Cir. 1983) (no reversible error where at bench conference, counsel were able to make arguments in terms of prejudice and probative value); United States v. Lipscomb, 702 F.2d 1049, 1070 & n.77 (D.C. Cir. 1983) (en banc) (explanation of the trial judge's reasoning is important but may not always be essential); United States v. Grandmont, 680 F.2d 867, 872 (1st Cir. 1982) (no error where government's memorandum discussed in detail factors bearing upon balancing).

[48] *See, e.g.,* United States v. Hendershot, 614 F.2d 648, 652 (9th Cir. 1980) (reversible error where not clear whether trial court properly applied Rule 609(a)(1) which requires prosecution to bear the burden of establishing that probative value outweighs prejudice).

[49] United States v. Reed, 572 F.2d 412, 427 (2d Cir.), *cert. denied,* 439 U.S. 913 (1978) (trial court could not "be faulted for failing to make extensive findings in response to a mere inquiry at a pre-trial hearing, unaccompanied by either facts or argument").

(Rel.3–9/90 Pub.819)

bringing out details of the crime.[50] Nor should insinuations about any other crimes be countenanced.[51]

The witness may make a brief statement in explanation or mitigation.[52] The scope of the statement lies in the trial judge's discretion subject to the general policy of Rule 403 dictating exclusion of prejudicial, confusing and time-consuming evidence unredeemed by substantial probative value.

¶ 12.04[04] Time Limit[1]

If more than ten years has elapsed from the date of conviction, or the witness' release, whichever is later, the conviction is ordinarily not usable for impeachment.[2] A conviction which is

---

[50] United States v. Callison, 577 F.2d 53 (8th Cir.), *cert. denied,* 439 U.S. 873 (1978) (trial judge properly excluded questions relating to fact that previous robbery was of same bank at same time as charged robbery).

[51] United States v. Tumblin, 551 F.2d 1001 (5th Cir. 1977) (reversible error for government on cross-examination to not only have reaffirmed existence of prior convictions conceded on direct, but also to have emphasized that defendant had been released for only a few weeks when he was again arrested, and that he had held no regular job because he was almost always in jail).

[52] *Cf.* United States v. Wolf, 561 F.2d 1376 (10th Cir. 1977) (where the defendant on direct examination attempts to explain away the effect of the conviction or to minimize his guilt, the defendant may be cross-examined on any facts which are relevant to the direct examination, and prosecutor could question defendant as to the details of the count to which he pleaded guilty and the remaining counts which were dismissed).

[1] *See* **Treatise** at ¶ 609[07].

[2] Lenard v. Argento, 699 F.2d 874, 895 (7th Cir.), *cert. denied,* 464 U.S. 815 (1983) (court, noting that convictions older than ten years should only be admitted in exceptional circumstances, found that trial court had not erred in concluding that twenty-four-year-old conviction, which was possibly a juvenile adjudication, for a crime unrelated to truth telling should have been excluded); Harbin v. Interlake Steamship Co., 570 F.2d 99 (6th Cir.), *cert. denied,* 437 U.S. 905 (1978) (civil case; court excluded two convictions of plaintiff); United States v. Carpio, 547 F.2d 490 (9th Cir. 1976) (use of eleven-year-old felony conviction of chief prosecution witness properly prohibited pursuant to Rule 609(b)). *But see* United States v. Mullins, 562 F.2d 999 (5th Cir.), *cert. denied,* 435 U.S. 906 (1978) (where defendant's voluntary flight after he was charged resulted in his not being tried until more than ten years had elapsed since his prior conviction, the ten-year limitation in Rule 609(b) was tolled and defendant could be impeached by the prior conviction).

more than ten years old is admissible in a criminal or civil action[3] if the proponent gives advance written notice[4] of intent to use and convinces the trial judge that because of specific facts and circumstances the probative value of the conviction outweighs its prejudicial effect. When the conviction is more than ten years old but the witness' parole or probation for that conviction was revoked within ten years of the trial, the court may use the date of the revocation rather than the conviction, if the reason for the revocation is related to the original conviction.[5] In the case of a prosecution witness, the pressures of the Confrontation Clause may, at times, require admission of convictions that are more than ten years old.

Some courts interpreting Rule 609(b) have expressed uncertainty about whether the applicable period should be measured up to the date when the trial commences, or the witness testifies, or the date of the charged crime.[6] The time of testimony is more appropriate since the jury must determine credibility at that moment.[7]

---

[3] Czaijka v. Hickman, 703 F.2d 317 (8th Cir. 1983); Tussel v. Witco Chem. Corp., 555 F. Supp. 979 (W.D. Pa. 1983).

[4] Powell v. Levit, 640 F.2d 239 (9th Cir.), *cert. denied,* 454 U.S. 845 (1981) (failure to give notice and to make finding constituted reversible error where credibility of witnesses was chief issue); United States v. Gilliland, 586 F.2d 1384 (10th Cir. 1978) (convictions 14 to 34 years before crime charged could not be used where no notice of intent to use had been given and court had not found that probative value exceeded prejudicial effect).

[5] United States v. McClintock, 748 F.2d 1278 (9th Cir. 1984), *cert. denied,* 474 U.S. 822 (1985) (probation was revoked for violation of condition related to the original crime). *See* United States v. Gray, 852 F.2d 136, 139 (4th Cir. 1988) (ten year limt not applicable when parole had been revoked, and defendant was still incarcerated at time of trial). *But cf.* United States v. Wallace, 848 F.2d 1464, 1472 (9th Cir. 1988) (revocation of parole for 1970 heroin conviction did not make conviction admissible, since probation was revoked because of a 1977 perjury conviction, which was not related to the original crime).

[6] United States v. Cathey, 591 F.2d 268, 274 n.13, 278 n.2 (5th Cir. 1979).

[7] *But see* United States v. Foley, 683 F.2d 273, 277 n.5 (8th Cir.), *cert. denied,* 459 U.S. 1043 (1982) (court measures up to date of charged crime).

¶ 12.04[05] Pardon or Equivalent[1]

Rule 609(c) considers the effect of a pardon, annulment, or certificate of rehabilitation on the admissibility of a conviction. It provides that evidence of a conviction is not admissible if the pardon, annulment, certificate of rehabilitation or other equivalent procedure[2] was (1) based on innocence or (2) required a showing of rehabilitation and the witness has not subsequently been convicted of a felony.[3]

The burden rests on counsel proffering the pardoned witness to show that the prior conviction may not be used for impeachment. It is the attorney's obligation to gather the pertinent facts underlying the pardon or certificate of rehabilitation and to demonstrate to the court outside the hearing of the jury that the use of the conviction is barred pursuant to Rule 609(c).[4]

---

[1] *See* **Treatise** at ¶ 609[08].

[2] United States v. Pagan, 721 F.2d 24, 28–31 (2d Cir. 1983) (certificate setting aside defendant's prior youthful offender conviction and unconditionally discharging him from further probation prior to expiration of maximum term of probation implied finding of rehabilitation, which constituted an "other equivalent procedure" under Rule 609(c)(1)).

[3] *Compare* United States v. Thorne, 547 F.2d 56 (8th Cir. 1976) (trial court properly exercised its discretion in concluding that prosecution witness had been rehabilitated although this was not evidenced by any certificate; subsequent to drug conviction, witness had received master's degree in guidance and counseling and was now director of drug rehabilitation program) *with* United States v. Jones, 647 F.2d 696 (6th Cir.), *cert. denied,* 454 U.S. 898 (1981) (pardon which restored civil rights did not prove defendant's rehabilitation and did not make evidence of prior conviction inadmissible); United States v. Hall, 588 F.2d 613 (8th Cir. 1978) (use of convictions for which suspended sentences were received is permissible); United States v. DiNapoli, 557 F.2d 962 (2d Cir.), *cert. denied,* (1977) (issuance of New York Certificate of Relief does not require a determination that convict has been rehabilitated and consequently New York conviction is admissible for impeachment use because certificate is beyond scope of Rule 609(c)); United States v. Moore, 556 F.2d 479 (10th Cir. 1977) (not error for trial judge to deny defendant's motion to exclude evidence of prior California felony conviction where conviction had been expunged but California statute specifically provided that expunged conviction might be used in a subsequent criminal proceeding involving the same party). *See also* Brown v. Frey, 889 F.2d 159, 171 (8th Cir. 1989), *cert. denied,* 110 S. Ct. 1156 (1990) (court has no discretion to allow use of conviction when pardon states that it was based on rehabilitation).

[4] United States v. Trejo-Zambrano, 582 F.2d 460 (9th Cir.), *cert denied,* 439 U.S. 1005 (1978) (no error where conviction was used for impeachment

¶ 12.04[06]   Juvenile Adjudications[1]

In criminal proceedings,[2] subdivision (d) of Rule 609 authorizes impeachment use of a juvenile adjudication[3] of a witness other than the defendant if "the judge is satisfied that admission in evidence is necessary for a fair determination of the issue of guilt or innocence."[4] The burden is on the side wishing to use the adjudication to show that the particular factors of the case excuse compliance with the usual rule of exclusion.[5]

¶ 12.04[07]   Pendency of Appeal[1]

Subdivision (e) provides that pendency of an appeal does not bar use of the conviction. The rule rests on the assumption of correctness which ought to attend judicial proceedings. The same rationale permits use of convictions even though post-trial motions following sentencing are still under consideration by the trial court.[2] Rule 609(e) specially provides that evidence of the

---

because defense counsel overlooked entry on rap sheet provided by government; Rule 609 does not shift burden to government to discover whether a prior conviction was vacated; dissent found that government had responsibility to show that conviction had not been expunged).

[1] See **Treatise** at ¶ 608[09].

[2] Powell v. Levit, 640 F.2d 239 (9th Cir.), *cert. denied,* 454 U.S. 845 (1981) (error to have admitted inquiry about juvenile record in civil case).

[3] United States v. Ashley, 569 F.2d 975 (5th Cir.), *cert. denied,* 439 U.S. 853 (1978) (conviction under the Federal Youth Corrections Act is a conviction of a crime not rendered inadmissible by Rule 609(d) which refers only to adjudications of delinquency). *But cf.* United States v. Mothershed, 859 F.2d 585, 591 (8th Cir. 1988), in which the court reserved decision on whether adjudication under the Federal Youthful Offenders Act is a "juvenile adjudication" under Rule 609(d).

[4] United States v. Ciro, 753 F.2d 248 (2d Cir.), *cert. denied,* 105 S. Ct. 2025 (1985) (given the ample opportunity for cross-examination of witness, excluded evidence was not necessary for a fair trial).

[5] See United States v. Decker, 543 F.2d 1102, 1104–05 (5th Cir. 1976), *cert. denied sub nom.* Vice v. United States, 431 U.S. 906 (1977) (where defendants proffered no evidence concerning prosecution witness' juvenile adjudication they could not complain of the trial court's failure to admit evidence of the adjudication).

[1] See **Treatise** at ¶ 609[10].

[2] United States v. Bianco, 419 F. Supp. 507, 509 (E.D. Pa. 1976), *aff'd mem.,* 547 F.2d 1164 (3d Cir. 1977). *Cf.* United States v. Collins, 552 F.2d

appeal's pendency may be admitted to reduce the impact of the conviction.[3] It is silent about a somewhat related but rarer situation: the propriety of attacking a witness' credibility by showing a verdict of guilty on which no judgment has been entered or sentence passed. Under federal practice, a judgment of conviction requires setting forth the sentence.[4]

However, in some cases the trial court's acceptance of the jury's verdict is a sufficient predicate to use the conviction for impeachment in a subsequent trial.[5]

¶ 12.05 Impeachment by Evidence of Religious Belief Prohibited — Rule 610[1]

Rule 610 bars evidence of religious adherence[2] when offered for the purpose of showing that the witness' credibility is thereby impaired or enhanced.[3] Exclusion rests on grounds of relevancy,

243, 247 (8th Cir.), *cert. denied,* 434 U.S. 870 (1977) (using conviction on which sentence had been suspended is substantially analogous to using conviction which is pending on appeal; citing Rule 609(c); Missouri law that a suspended sentence is not a final judgment of conviction is not applicable in federal prosecution).

[3] United States v. Shaver, 511 F.2d 933 (4th Cir. 1975) (citing Rule 609(c) and suggesting that instruction to jury to disregard conviction pending appeal might be desirable). *Cf.* United States v. Klayer, 707 F.2d 892 (6th Cir.), *cert. denied,* 464 U.S. 858 (1983) (the only generally recognized exception to Rule 609(e) involves the credibility impeachment of a defendant convicted without representation of counsel).

[4] Fed. R. Crim. P. Rule 32(b)(1).

[5] *See* United States v. Mitchell, 886 F.2d 667, 670–71 (4th Cir. 1989) (although defendant had not been sentenced with regard to prior federal conviction at time he was impeached, district court had denied post-trial motions, and defendant was properly impeached on this basis).

[1] *See* **Treatise** at ¶ 610[01].

[2] United States v. Sampol, 636 F.2d 621, 666 (D.C. Cir. 1980) ("scope of the prohibition includes unconventional or unusual religions.").

[3] Government of Virgin Islands v. Peterson, 553 F.2d 324 (3d Cir. 1977) (Rule 610 prohibits testimony that alibi witness' religious beliefs reject violence; such testimony cannot be used to enhance credibility); United States v. Kalaydjian, 784 F.2d 53 (2d Cir. 1986) (defendant may not question witnesses as to why they refused to swear on the Koran; right to make affirmation under Rule 603 rather than take oath would be meaningless if cross-examination were allowed). *Cf.* People v. Wood, 66 N.Y. 2d 374, 497

prejudice, and constitutional considerations.◄

The Rule provides:

Rule 610

RELIGIOUS BELIEFS OR OPINIONS

Evidence of the beliefs or opinions of a witness on matters of religion is not admissible for the purpose of showing that by reason of their nature the witness' credibility is impaired or enhanced.

Evidence probative of something other than veracity is not within the prohibition of the rule. For example, disclosure of affiliation with a church which is a party to the litigation may be admitted as relevant to bias, and adherence to a particular religious sect may have bearing on whether expenditures had been made for medical care in a personal injury case.

¶ 12.06   Prior Statements of Witnesses—Rule 613

¶ 12.06[01]   Scope[1]

Rule 613 governs foundational requirements for the introduction of a witness' prior inconsistent statements, written or oral, made out of court. Foundation requirements for statements inconsistent with hearsay testimony are prescribed by Rule 806.

Rule 613 provides:

Rule 613

PRIOR STATEMENTS OF WITNESSES

(a) Examining witness concerning prior statement.—In examining a witness concerning a prior statement made by the witness, whether written or not, the statement need not be shown nor its contents

---

N.Y.S. 2d 340, 488 N.E.2d 86 (1985) (prosecutor's questioning of primary defense witness about religious beliefs and decision to affirm, rather than swear, to the truth of his testimony, deemed sufficiently prejudicial to require a new trial).

◄ *See* **Treatise** at ¶ 610[01].

[1] *See* **Treatise** at ¶ 613[01].

disclosed to the witness at that time, but on request the same shall be shown or disclosed to opposing counsel.

(b) Extrinsic evidence of prior inconsistent statement of witness.— Extrinsic evidence of a prior inconsistent statement by a witness is not admissible unless the witness is afforded an opportunity to explain or deny the same and the opposite party is afforded an opportunity to interrogate the witness thereon, or the interests of justice otherwise require. This provision does not apply to admissions of a party-opponent as defined in rule 801(d)(2).

Rule 613 liberalizes foundation requirements in two ways: (1) It rejects the so-called Rule of the Queen's case which requires a witness to be shown a prior written statement before impeachment on the statement can proceed, and (2) it eliminates mandatory foundational questions directing the attention of the witness to the time when, place where, and person to whom the alleged inconsistent statement was made.

The main impact of the changes from the orthodox rule is to give greater weight to surprise than to warning as a technique for ferreting out the truth. In civil cases where discovery has been fully utilized, only rarely will a critical witness not have been apprised of any important inconsistent statements. The liberalization of the traditional rule is, therefore, most likely to have an impact in criminal cases.

Rule 613 should be applied to inconsistent statements used to impeach even though the statements would be admissible as evidence-in-chief pursuant to Rule 801(d)(1).[2] As explicitly provided in subdivision (b), however, Rule 613 does not apply to inconsistent statements of a party opponent as defined in Rule 801(d)(2), since the statements of a party qualify as admissions without regard to whether the party takes the stand. It should be noted that the Federal Rules extend the concept of party admissions considerably beyond a party in an individual capacity.

Rule 613, under principles of expressio unius, does not apply to impeachment by evidence of prior inconsistent conduct. The court, however, has the power to require inquiring counsel to

---

[2] *See* United States v. International Business Machines Corp., 432 F. Supp. 138 (S.D.N.Y. 1977) (although Rule 613(b) has no direct application where evidence may be used substantively as well as for impeachment, standards of fairness contemplated by the rule are apposite).

reveal to the court and opposing counsel, outside the hearing of the jury, the basis for any question to the witness designed to show inconsistent conduct. Attorneys should not be permitted to insinuate by innuendo that something has occurred which in fact has not.

¶ 12.06[02]   Impeachment by Proof of Prior Inconsistent Statement[3]

Rule 613 considerably simplifies the foundational requirements for impeachment by prior inconsistent statements. A witness need not be shown or made aware of the contents of a prior statement at the time the witness is being examined about the statement. Nor must the witness be asked on the stand, while under cross-examination, whether he or she made the supposed inconsistent statement as a condition precedent to impeachment by extrinsic evidence of the statement. There are only two conditions that Rule 613 imposes: (1) subdivision (a) requires that on request, the statement "shall be shown or disclosed to opposing counsel,"[4] and (2) subdivision (b) provides that when extrinsic evidence of a prior inconsistent statement is introduced, the witness must, at some time, either before or after the contents of the statement are made known to the jury, be afforded a chance to explain, while the opposite party must be given an opportunity to examine on the statement.

Unlike the common law rule, Rule 613 does not specify a particular sequence for impeachment by prior inconsistent statements.[5] Impeachment satisfies the requirements of Rule 613 if the witness is ultimately given an opportunity to explain, and the opposite party is given an opportunity to examine.

---

[3] *See* **Treatise** at ¶ 613[03], [04].

[4] United States v. Lawson, 683 F.2d 688, 694 (2d Cir. 1982) (error not to have disclosed report used in cross-examining witness where request had been made; "Rule 613(a) does not allow for the exercise of discretion. It flatly commands disclosure . . . ." On retrial, if witness is cross-examined either by report used in first trial, or by testimony at first trial, report must be disclosed.).

[5] *See, e.g.,* United States v. McLaughlin, 663 F.2d 949 (9th Cir. 1981) (reversible error to have excluded statement on the ground that witness had not had opportunity to deny or explain on direct examination; Rule 613(b) requires no more than allowing proponent of witness to recall witness to explain or deny).

Notions of fairness underlie the requirements set forth in subdivisions (a) and (b). Allowing counsel to see the statement protects the witness from unfair insinuations, and gives counsel the opportunity to protest the authenticity of the statement. Insistence upon the witness' right to explain protects the witness who has something to say in extenuation: a denial that the statement was made, or an explanation, which undercuts the supposed inconsistency.

Although the traditional rule provides more of a shield against unfairness because it always gives the witness an opportunity to explain before the inconsistent statement is introduced, the drafters of Rule 613 found a diminution in protection justified. Allowing the statement to be introduced before the witness is asked for an explanation, guards against the tailoring of testimony that may occur when dishonest witnesses are forewarned about the terms of a statement, thereby enabling them to thwart the efficacy of cross-examination as a truth-testing device.

Rule 613 does not make the party that uses the prior inconsistent statement for impeachment responsible for affording the witness an opportunity to explain. The rule merely states that the witness must be afforded that opportunity. Thus neither side has the burden of recalling the witness; normally the impeaching party will not wish to do so.[6] To obviate the necessity of having the witness wait to see whether inconsistent statements will be introduced and whether the witness will be asked to explain them, the court may require impeachment while the witness is on the stand or immediately thereafter. The proponent of the witness should then be entitled to recall the witness at once so that the witness is free to depart from the courthouse.

Rule 613 permits a court to dispense with the witness' right to explain or deny in "the interests of justice." A court might rely on this provision when the statement was made after cross-examination, or came to counsel's attention after the witness testified, and the witness, through no fault of counsel, is not available for recall. Beyond such situations, the court's discretion

---

[6] *See, e.g.,* Wilmington Trust Co. v. Manufacturers Life Insurance Co., 749 F.2d 694, 699 (11th Cir. 1985) (waiver where proponent of witness failed to request that witness be allowed to testify in surrebuttal about impeaching statement, or that case be reopened).

under subdivision (b) should rarely be exercised. Prior inconsistent statements that relate to crucial testimony should almost never be admitted if foundational requirements can be, but have not been, met.[7]

Despite the liberalization of foundation requirements in Rule 613, the court or counsel may still choose to follow traditional practice.[8] The pressures of the best evidence and authentication rules may force counsel to cross-examine the witness about the statement before offering it for impeachment, since proof of authenticity or originality may be much easier or, in some instances, possible only if the witness is available. These requirements should normally be met before the statement is introduced or read to the jury. Permitting the statement to be revealed to the jury subject to a later limiting instruction to disregard may be highly prejudicial where the improperly admitted statement relates to a crucial point.

When a prior inconsistent statement is drawn to a witness' attention, the witness may admit, deny or explain the statement. Under traditional practice, some courts would refuse to allow extrinsic evidence of the statement once the witness admitted having made it.[9] If counsel suspects the witness may admit, there may be an incentive to dispense with the preliminary laying of a foundation since the statement may have more of an impact if it is read in its entirety or testified to by another witness.

In a criminal case, there is some uncertainty about whether a prior statement may be used for impeachment where the witness

---

[7] *See* Wammock v. Celotex Corp., 793 F.2d 1518, 1522 (11th Cir. 1986), citing **Treatise** (trial judge properly refused to admit prior inconsistent statements made by plaintiff's expert, when they were offered at the close of the trial and the expert was no longer available).

[8] *See* United States v. Marks, 816 F.2d 1207, 1211 (7th Cir. 1987) (trial judge did not err in requiring defense counsel to show an FBI report containing prior statements to government witnesses, before conducting impeachment of the witnesses; Rule 613 does not eliminate judge's discretion to manage the trial to promote accuracy and fairness).

[9] *See, e.g.,* United States v. Greer, 806 F.2d 556, 558 (5th Cir. 1986) (affirming exclusion of witness' tape-recorded statement, which contradicted his trial testimony, when he had admitted making the prior statement); Dillen v. Chesapeake & Ohio Ry. Co., 327 F.2d 249 (6th Cir. 1964), *cert. denied,* 379 U.S. 824 (1964).

not only denies having made the statement, but also denies all knowledge of the underlying event. A constitutional issue may be posed if counsel for the prosecution introduces the statement and subsequently discovers that the witness claims an inability to remember.[10] Allowing the witness to explain immediately after the statement has been used for impeachment is rarely likely to lead to error.

The cross-examiner's choice of when to ask the foundational questions will hinge on such tactical concerns as, for instance, whether delay will increase the likelihood that the jury will discount the explanation, or whether the explanation will have a "spill-over effect" destructive to the cross-examiner's theory of the case. The court's choice will normally be to require foundational questions while the witness is cross-examined, since this will often speed up the trial and prevent confusion on the part of the jury.

---

[10] *See* **Treatise** at ¶¶ 613[04], 801(d)(1)(A)[05].

CHAPTER 13

Expert Witnesses

SYNOPSIS

(Rel.2–9/89 Pub.819)

¶ 13.01 Overview of Expert Witness Rules

Rules 702 through 705 of the Federal Rules of Evidence represent an integrated approach to the subject of expert testimony which differs in a number of significant ways from the common law approach to this subject. The drafters of the rules deliberately sought to eliminate many of the restrictions which had blocked the admissibility of useful expert testimony, such as requiring the expert's opinion to be rendered in response to a hypothetical question containing an assumed set of circumstances grounded in admissible evidence; refusing to permit experts to state their opinions on ultimate issues of fact; prohibiting experts from relying upon hearsay, including the opinions of other experts; and imposing a "general acceptance" test when the witness sought to testify about a new principle which had not previously been accorded judicial recognition. Rule 705 eliminated mandatory reliance on a hypothetical question; Rule 704 abolished the ultimate issue rule (although it was reinstated in part in 1984 for testimony relating to a criminal defendant's mental state); and Rule 703 greatly expanded the data on which an expert may rely.

Additional rules have made it easier to introduce expert testimony. Among them are hearsay definitions and exceptions for raw data often required by experts, including Rules 801(a), 803(3), 803(4), 803(6) and 803(8). The 803(6) and 803(8) exceptions themselves include diagnoses and opinions, so that an expert's opinion can theoretically come in without the expert ever appearing. Tactical pressures to produce the most persuasive evidence result in most instances in the use of experts' live testimony rather than of their hearsay reports.

The learned treatise exception, Rule 803(18), and such exceptions as Rule 803(17) on market and commercial reports, are also important. They make it easier for expert witnesses to educate the trier about a body of knowledge that may be unfamiliar to the layperson.

Rule 1006 allows summaries of voluminous data to be introduced into evidence despite the traditional "best evidence" rule. This rule provides expert witnesses such as accountants and analysts with an additional convenient and understandable way to present their data.[1]

---

[1] For a discussion of the interplay of Rules 803(6), 803(8) and 1006, *see Manual on Complex Litigation 2d* § 21.446 n.80.

The Federal Rules of Evidence and their state counterparts have thus produced an enormous loosening up of the restrictions on the admission of expert testimony, on its basis, on its form and on the effective utilization of such testimony once admitted. This relaxation was needed to give the trier of fact convenient access to the reliable technical knowledge that is available in our modern society. As might be expected, the modification of the old rules demands more attention by counsel to pretrial stages and requires the court to exercise greater control before and during trial through *in limine* rulings and control of discovery.[2]

The primary actions taken to date involve supervision of the preparation of expert testimony in the pretrial stage. If local practice does not require each party to identify the experts that it will use at trial and to provide a summary of those experts' expected testimony, a party may request such aid.

Similarly, parties may be required to provide a glossary of terms that their experts will use at the trial. Intended primarily to assist the reporters to take testimony accurately, the definition of terms—particularly if the experts can agree on them—can be used by the judge in preparing for the trial. A list of exotic terms with definitions can be furnished for each of the jurors as part of his or her notebook in a complex case.

Joint pretrial meetings between the judge and key expert witnesses need to be encouraged. The presence of each side's experts at the other side's experiments is also encouraged.

Some courts properly require that each side list before each trial those learned treatises admissible under Rule 803(18) and other hearsay that it intends to rely upon at trial. A party intending to offer statistical data and analysis at trial should be required to provide the opposing party with all the underlying records from which the data were collected; make available for conferences with other parties the personnel that compiled the data; attempt to agree on a database well before trial; and be required to object to an opponent's experts' analysis before trial.

Questioning and comment by the judge may be needed to help in-

---

[2] *See* Weinstein, *Improvement of Expert Testimony,* 31 Richmond L. Rev. 1 (1986), for further development of these views.

form the jury. Even the summary judgment and directed verdict powers may need more expansive exercise to prevent spurious theories from being relied upon in emotional cases.[3]

¶ 13.02   Testimony By Experts—Rule 702

¶ 13.02[01]   The Helpfulness Test[1]

Most important of the new rules is Rule 702, which focuses on helpfulness to the trier as the essential condition of admissibility. Rule 702 provides:

Rule 702

TESTIMONY BY EXPERTS

If scientific, technical, or other specialized knowledge will assist the trier of fact to understand the evidence or to determine a fact in issue, a witness qualified as an expert by knowledge, skill, experience, training, or education, may testify thereto in the form of an opinion or otherwise.

In deciding whether the expert testimony will "assist the trier of fact to understand the evidence or to determine a fact in issue," the court has to pass on two intertwined issues, and may have to determine a third: (1) will expert testimony help resolve a controverted issue and (2) does this particular expert possess sufficient specialized knowledge to enable him or her to assist the trier of fact? When a novel form of expertise is being offered, the court must also decide (3) is the proffered expert's expertise of a kind that will be helpful?

¶ 13.02[02]   When Is Expert Testimony Helpful?[2]

The average juror will have no basis for evaluating certain kinds

---

[3] *Id.*

[1] *See* **Treatise** at ¶ 702[01].

[2] *See* **Treatise** at ¶ 702[02].

of evidence without the assistance of expert testimony.[3] Certain issues are so universally acknowledged by the courts to be amenable only to expertise that as a matter of substantive law the plaintiff loses if it fails to provide expert testimony.[4] Medical malpractice is a prime example.[5] Other subjects, however, lie within the comprehension of the average juror. Prior to the enactment of the Federal Rules, courts might reject expert testimony unless it related to an issue "not within the common knowledge of the average layman."[6] Such a rigid approach is incompatible with the standard of helpfulness expressed in Rule 702. It assumes wrongly that there is a bright line separating issues within the comprehension of jurors from those that are not,[7] and it ignores the possibility that even when jurors are well equipped to make judgments based on their common experience, experts may be able to add specialized knowledge that would be helpful.[8]

---

[3] *See, e.g.,* Shad v. Dean Witter Reynolds, Inc., 799 F.2d 525, 529–30 (9th Cir. 1986) (in suit against brokerage firm for engaging in excess trading for the purpose of generating commissions, expert testimony about various components of churning was essential; reversible error to have excluded); United States v. Winters, 729 F.2d 602 (9th Cir. 1984) (in Mann Act prosecution, expert testimony on post-traumatic stress disorder and forced prostitution would assist jurors in understanding why the young women in question failed to escape despite opportunities to do so); United States v. Riccobene, 709 F.2d 214 (3d Cir.), *cert. denied,* 464 U.S. 849 (1983) (terms "La Cosa Nostra," "capo," and "consigliere" were not generally known, and there was considerable value in having expert testimony define them). *Cf.* Little v. Armontrout, 835 F.2d 1240, 1244–45 (8th Cir. 1987), *cert. denied,* 108 S. Ct. 2857 (1988) (en banc) (violation of due process of law for state court to refuse to appoint expert in hypnosis for indigent defendant to aid defense in countering rape victim's post hypnotic identification of defendant).

[4] *See, e.g.,* Huddell v. Levin, 537 F.2d 726, 736 (3d Cir. 1976) ("[w]here the issue concerns a product's *design* . . . expert opinion is the only available method to establish defectiveness, at least where the design is not patently defective").

[5] Rule 803(18) may provide a way of circumventing this barrier.

[6] Bridger v. Union Railway Co., 355 F.2d 382, 387 (6th Cir. 1966).

[7] United States v. Sickles, 524 F.Supp. 506 (D. Del. 1981), *aff'd,* 688 F.2d 827 (3d Cir. 1982) (although expert conceded on cross-examination that no specialized knowledge was needed to draw conclusion, court refused to strike testimony, holding that it was helpful under either Rule 701 or 702). *See also* Weinstein, *Improvement of Expert Testimony,* 31 Richmond L. Rev. 1 (1986), on using Rules 701 and 702 interchangeably in some areas.

[8] *See* cases permitting expert testimony on whether the defendant is the person portrayed in a surveillance photograph, *e.g.,* United States v. Alexander, 816 F.2d 164, 167–68 (5th Cir. 1987) (in bank robbery prosecution of physician solely on the basis

The helpfulness test also embodies the principles set forth in Rules 401 and 403.[9] Expert testimony that is not relevant is not helpful. Nor will such evidence assist the trier of fact if it is overly confusing,[10] more prejudicial than probative, or needlessly time-consuming. The court, as with all relevancy determinations, will have to proceed on a case-by-case basis. Its conclusions will depend on (1) the court's evaluation of the state of knowledge presently existing about the subject of the proposed testimony and (2) on the court's appraisal of the facts of the case.[11]

---

of surveillance film and eyewitness testimony, reversible error to prohibit defense from calling (1) an orthodontist specializing in cephalometry (scientific measurement of dimensions of the head) to testify as to differences in the facial features of the defendant and the person in the photograph; and (2) a former FBI agent, with expertise in photographic comparison, to testify to the distortion produced by bank surveillance cameras); United States v. Barrett, 703 F.2d 1076, 1084 n.14 (9th Cir. 1983) (expert permitted to testify about similarities between clothing seized from defendant and that worn by robber in surveillance photograph; testimony about tonal condition, style and placement of buttons, stripes, and stains satisfied helpfulness test); United States v. Snow, 552 F.2d 165 (6th Cir.), *cert. denied*, 434 U.S. 970 (1977).

[9] Scott v. Sears, Roebuck & Co., 789 F.2d 1052, 1055 (4th Cir. 1986) (testimony is prejudicial pursuant to Rule 403 "when the evaluation of the commonplace by an expert witness might supplant a jury's independent exercise of common sense.").

[10] United States v. Kupau, 781 F.2d 740, 745 (9th Cir.), *cert. denied*, 107 S. Ct. 93 (1986) (although the testimony of one linguist was properly admitted to explain technical terms in taped conversations, testimony of other linguist who sought to interpret language in ordinary usage would have confused, rather than assisted, the jury).

[11] United States v. St. Pierre, 812 F.2d 417, 420 (8th Cir. 1987) (clinical psychologist who had evaluated victim in child sex abuse case was permitted to compare traits and characteristics of sexually abused children with those of victim; "the common experience of the jury may represent a less than adequate foundation for assessing the credibility of a young child who complains of sexual abuse"). *Compare* United States v. Azure, 801 F.2d 336, 340-41 (8th Cir. 1986) (in prosecution for carnal knowledge of a female under age sixteen, trial court committed reversible error by allowing prosecution's expert to testify that victim of sexual abuse was believable and that expert could see no reason why victim was not telling the truth; no reliable test for truthfulness existed. *But cf.* United States v. Anderson, 851 F.2d 384, 392-94 (D.C. Cir. 1988), *cert. denied*, 109 S. Ct. 801 (1989) (in Mann Act prosecution, testimony of government's expert witness on pimping patterns and the pimp-prostitute relationship could have aided jury in determining whether defendant was a pimp or a gambler, and could have helped the jury in determining the credibility of the government's prostitute-witnesses whose credibility had been undermined on cross-

Because the trial court's analysis must necessarily be case specific, federal appellate courts have long recognized that "the trial judge has broad discretion in the matter of the admission or exclusion of expert evidence, and his action is to be sustained unless manifestly erroneous."[12] The trial court must be given wide latitude in rulings excluding or admitting expert testimony in the exercise of its responsibility under Rules 102, 403 and 611.[13] Special problems in criminal cases are discussed at ¶ 13.03[03], *infra*.

Because the thrust of the Federal Rules is to relax the common law restrictions, doubts about the usefulness of proffered testimony should generally be resolved in favor of admissibility unless there are strong factors such as incredibility, time or surprise favoring exclusion.[14] The jury, aided by counsel, is generally intelligent enough to ignore what is unhelpful in its deliberations.

---

examination). *See also* United States v. Scop, 846 F.2d 135, 142–44 (2d Cir.), *rev'd in part on other grounds,* 856 F.2d 5 (2d Cir. 1988) (in securities fraud prosecution, majority held that "expert witnesses may not offer opinions on relevant events based on their personal assessment of the credibility of another witness's testimony"; expert in securities trading had stated on cross-examination that he believed other government witnesses, and had relied on their testimony; concurring judge questioned whether majority's conclusion "is consistent with Rules 703 and 705 of the Federal Rules of Evidence and the Advisory Committee Notes."); United States v. Shorter, 809 F.2d 54, 60–61 (D.C. Cir.), *cert. denied,* 108 S.Ct. 71 (1987) (lawyer charged with tax evasion; applying the *Frye* test, the court held that expert testimony that defendant suffered from a pathological or compulsive gambling disorder had been properly excluded; court also suggested that this was topic that jury could comprehend without expert assistance).

[12] Salem v. United States Lines, 370 U.S. 31, 82 S. Ct. 1119, 8 L. Ed. 2d 313 (1962). *But see* United States v. Acres of Land, More or Less, Situated in the City of Birmingham, Jefferson County, Ala., 837 F.2d 1036, 1039–1042 (11th Cir. 1988) (in eminent domain proceeding, abuse of discretion for trial court to have excluded testimony of expert economist who had spent over 200 hours researching 145 land sales in area in which condemnation occurred).

[13] United States v. Anderson, 851 F.2d 384, 393–94 (D.C. Cir. 1988), *cert. denied,* 109 S. Ct. 801 (1989) (court conceded that in Mann Act prosecution, testimony by government expert about pimping patterns and the pimp-prostitute relationship raised legitimate concerns about unfair prejudice because of testimony's "aura of special reliability and trust" heightened by sordid and disturbing nature of subject matter; nevertheless, court found that in light of "large quantity of uncontested, particularized evidence," expert testimony was at worst harmless error).

[14] United States v. Nersesian, 824 F.2d 1294, 1307–08 (2d Cir.), *cert. denied,* 108 S.Ct. 357 (1987) (DEA agent permitted to testify as expert about meaning of wire-

¶ 13.02[03] When Is a Witness Qualified To Testify as an Expert?[15]

Rule 702 recognizes that it is the actual qualifications, rather than the title, of the witness that count.[16] An expert may be qualified by virtue of "knowledge, skill, experience, training or education," or any combination of these attributes. In each instance the court must decide, pursuant to Rule 104(a), whether the witness is competent to form an opinion that would assist the trier in resolving particular disputed issues. Cases decided pursuant to the Federal Rules support a liberal standard in evaluating qualifications.[17]

Initially, the trial court must make a relevancy determination that expertise will assist the trier in resolving or understanding an issue. Then the court has to decide if the expert has appropriate qualifications given the facts of the case. Just as the wrong title may mean that the witness is nevertheless qualified, the right title will not suffice if the witness does not have the qualifications required by the facts of the case. In making this determination, the courts are called upon to resolve a number of recurring and often interrelated questions: may an expert testify who is qualified by practical experience rather than education, and the reverse, may an expert testify who is qualified by education rather than practical experience; how much

---

tapped conversation; since terms such as "cheese, land, room, house, car, horse, and stick-shift" could carry a hidden meaning related to narcotics, expert testimony was helpful; appellate court "acknowledge[d] some degree of discomfiture in cases such as the instant one in which this practice is employed, since, uncontrolled, such use of expert testimony may have the effect of providing the government with an additional summation by having the expert interpret the evidence"; court found no abuse of discretion where trial judge gave extensive limiting instructions). *See also* United States v. Hoffman, 832 F.2d 1299, 1310 (1st Cir. 1987) (DEA agent properly permitted to state opinion about meaning of intercepted conversations; "[l]ay jurors cannot be expected to be familiar with the lexicon of the cocaine community"). *Compare* United States v. Dicker, 853 F.2d 1103, 1108–1110 (3d Cir. 1988) (error to allow undercover agent to testify to his understanding of recorded conversations where statements made were perfectly clear without agent's "interpretations").

[15] *See* **Treatise** at ¶ 702[04].

[16] Tagatz v. Marquette University, 861 F.2d 1040, 1042 (7th Cir. 1988) (Rule 702 does not bar plaintiff from testifying as his own expert witness).

[17] United States v. 10,031.98 Acres of Land, 850 F.2d 634 (10th Cir. 1988) (landowner as expert).

training, whether academic or practical, is required; does a person generally qualified in a field have sufficient specific knowledge to deal with the particular issues in the case at hand; does the witness have sufficient expertise about local, as compared to national, conditions; and did the witness have the requisite expertise at the relevant time.

Voir dires at trial should be discouraged, since these matters should be resolved before trial. Cross-examination about basic qualifications may assist the juror in evaluating credibility, particularly if the expert has done some puffing, or if his or her background is not impressive compared to other experts, or if the expert's specialized knowledge lies in a field not directly related to the issues in the case.

¶ 13.02[04]   When Is Testimony About a Novel Form of Expertise Admissible?[18]

The court faces a difficult task when the proffered expert testimony rests on a scientific hypothesis that has not previously been accorded judicial recognition as an appropriate basis for expert testimony.[19] Even though the court will almost never have sufficient personal expertise to evaluate the new technique or principle, it must rule on whether this development will assist the jury in resolving disputed issues.

Prior to the enactment of the Federal Rules, courts encountering this problem often relied on a test having its genesis in *Frye v. United States.*[20] The court in *Frye,* in the course of considering and rejecting the admissibility of evidence derived from a crude precursor of the polygraph, stated:

---

[18] *See* **Treatise** at ¶ 702[03].

[19] *See* The majority, concurring and dissenting opinions in United States v. Kozminski, 821 F.2d 1186 (6th Cir.), *aff'd on other grounds,* 108 S.Ct. 2751 (1988) (defendants were prosecuted for willfully holding two retarded farm workers in involuntary servitude; psychologist testified that given the victims' low mentality, psychological pressures exerted on them created an "involuntary conversion" to complete dependency akin to "captivity syndrome"; majority concluded that "involuntary conversion" theory was not scientifically recognized; extensive discussion).

[20] 293 Fed. 1013 (D.C. Cir. 1923).

Just when a scientific principle or discovery crosses the line between the experimental and demonstrable stages is difficult to define. Somewhere in this twilight zone the evidential forces of the principle must be recognized, and while courts will go a long way in admitting expert testimony deduced from a well-recognized scientific principle or discovery, the thing from which the deduction is made must be sufficiently established to have gained general acceptance in the particular field in which it belongs.[21]

The same decision excluding polygraph evidence on the issue of credibility would be made today, but it would be based upon a balancing standard and policies against introducing this potentially abusive technique routinely into trials.[22]

Rule 702 does not use the term "general acceptance." Although commentators[23] and courts[24] are still somewhat divided about the inference to be drawn, the clear trend is a movement away from *Frye* both in the federal courts[25] and in states which have adopted a ver-

---

[21] *Id.* at 1014.

[22] Brown v. Darcy, 783 F.2d 1389 (9th Cir. 1986) (reviews cases).

[23] *See* United States v. Downing, 753 F.2d 1224 (3d Cir. 1985). *See also, e.g.,* Graham, "Relevancy and the Exclusion of Relevant Evidence: Admissibility of Evidence of a Scientific Principle or Technique—Application of the Frye Test," 19 Crim. L. Bull. 51 (1983).

[24] *Compare* United States v. Gillespie, 852 F.2d 475, 480–81 (9th Cir. 1988) (court concluded that *Frye* test had to be used to determine admissibility of expert testimony in child sex abuse case based on play therapy with anatomically correct dolls; district court's failure to consider evidence as to scientific reliability of technique constituted reversible error.); United States v. Christophe, 833 F.2d 1296, 1299 (9th Cir. 1987) (court held that proffered testimony on the unreliability of eyewitnesses was properly excluded because it "does not conform to a generally accepted explanatory theory"); United States v. Tranowski, 659 F.2d 750 (7th Cir. 1981); United States v. Kilgus, 571 F.2d 508, 510 (9th Cir. 1978); United States v. Brown, 557 F.2d 541, 557 (6th Cir. 1977) (all applying *Frye* test) *with* cases listed in note 6, *infra.*

[25] *See, e.g.: Second Circuit:* United States v. Williams, 583 F.2d 1194 (2d Cir. 1978), *cert. denied,* 99 S. Ct. 1025 (1979); *Third Circuit:* United States v. Downing, 753 F.2d 1224 (3d Cir. 1985); *Fourth Circuit:* United States v. Baller, 519 F.2d 463 (4th Cir.), *cert. denied,* 96 S. Ct. 456 (1975). *Cf.* Kropinski v. World Plan Executive Council-US, 853 F.2d 948, 956–57 (D.C. Cir. 1988) (court noted that a less demanding standard than "general acceptance" might be appropriate in civil case but declined to decide issue in case in which trial judge had erroneously admitted expert

sion of the Federal Rules.[26] This repudiation of the "general acceptance" test is justified because it is inconsistent with the policies expressed in the rules dealing with opinion evidence.[27] A restrictive
standard in addition to the "helpfulness" test mandated by Rule 702
would undercut the emphasis on admissibility which was a central
concern underlying the revision of the rules on expert testimony.[28]

If general scientific acceptance is not a prerequisite to admissibility, how then, consonant with the mandate of Rule 702, should a
court determine the reliability of novel scientific evidence? As with
other kinds of expert testimony, the helpfulness, probative force and
prejudice standards implicated in Rules 702 and 403 must be utilized. Initially, the court must assess the probative value of the proffered evidence, a difficult determination since the court will only
rarely have any personal scientific expertise. Whether or not the scientific principles involved have been generally accepted by experts
in the field may still have a bearing on reliability and consequent
probative value of the evidence.[29] "[A] technique unable to garner

---

testimony on thought reform; proponent had failed to introduce any evidence that
theory had a significant following, let alone general acceptance).

[26] *See, e.g.,* State v. Shaw, 369 N.W.2d 772 (Wis. App. 1985); State v. Walstad, 119
Wis.2d 483, 351 N.W.2d 469 (1984); State v. Hall, 297 N.W.2d 80 (Iowa 1980);
State v. Williams, 388 A.2d 500 (Me. 1978). *See* Rossi, *Modern Evidence and the
Expert Witness,* 12 Litigation 18, 21 (1985) (survival of *Frye* test "seems unlikely.
Too many courts in too many different jurisdictions have abandoned *Frye* in too
short a time.").

[27] *See* United States v. Downing, 753 F.2d 1224, 1236 (3d Cir. 1985) ("its vagueness
and its conservatism;" extensive discussion).

[28] Clinchfield Railroad Co. v. Lynch, 784 F.2d 545, 553–54 (4th Cir. 1986) (in a
civil, non-jury suit, the court affirmed the admission of expert testimony from an
experienced economist concerning the total market value of all the personal property located in each county involved based on census data even though the expert
admitted that he was the only economist using this method; "[a] court should not
exclude expert testimony simply because it involves a new method or novel theory";
court noted that expert had been deposed, that adversaries had received copy of
his report well in advance of trial, and that he had been extensively cross-examined
at trial).

[29] *See* United States v. Downing, 753 F.2d 1224, 1238 (3d Cir. 1985) ("The reliability inquiry that we envision is flexible and may turn on a number of considerations,
in contrast to the process of scientific 'nose-counting' that would appear to be compelled by a careful reading of *Frye.* . . . The district court in assessing reliability

any support, or only minuscule support, within the scientific community would be found unreliable by a court."[30] Other factors to be weighed include: the expert's qualifications and stature;[31] the use which has been made of the new technique;[32] the potential rate of error;[33] the existence of specialized literature;[34] the novelty of the new invention;[35] the degree to which the opinion is based on subjective analysis;[36] the verifiability of the data bases the expert relies upon; the extent to which there are other experts who can testify on the matter; the ability of laypersons to understand the testimony and integrate it successfully with nonscientific anecdotal evidence and general knowledge, and the fit between the testimony proffered and the particular, controverted issues in the case[37] can be considered.

---

may examine a variety of factors in addition to scientific acceptance. In many cases, however, the acceptance factor may well be decisive, or nearly so.").

[30] United States v. Williams, 583 F.2d 1194, 1198 (2d Cir. 1978), *cert. denied,* 439 U.S. 1117 (1979).

[31] United States v. Luschen, 614 F.2d 1164 (8th Cir.), *cert. denied,* 446 U.S. 939 (1980) (education, long career as public health chemist); United States v. Baller, 519 F.2d 463 (4th Cir.), *cert. denied,* 423 U.S. 1019 (1975) (pioneer of technique and qualified practitioner).

[32] United States v. Hendershot, 614 F.2d 648 (9th Cir. 1980) (used by other police departments); State v. Hall, 297 N.W.2d 80 (Iowa 1980) (expert had conducted seminars on subject for crime investigators).

[33] United States v. Williams, 583 F.2d 1194, 1198 (2d Cir. 1978), *cert. denied,* 439 U.S. 1117 (1979) (rate and type of error).

[34] State v. Hall, 297 N.W.2d 80 (Iowa 1980).

[35] State v. Bullard, 322 S.E.2d 370 (N.C. 1984) (footprint comparisons admitted; court noted use of established procedures and independent research).

[36] Such opinions could have less probative value because it may be difficult to evaluate the skill of the expert in extrapolating a judgment from the scientific data. *See* United States v. Williams, 583 F.2d 1194 (2d Cir. 1978), *cert. denied,* 439 U.S. 1117 (1979) ("Spectrography is qualitatively different from polygraph evidence. In spectrography, the examiner merely compares spectrograms reflecting the purely physical characteristics of a voice. In polygraph analysis, the examiner must go on, to extrapolate a judgment of something not directly measured by the machine *i.e.,* the credibility of the person examined.").

[37] United States v. Dowling, 855 F.2d 114, 118–19 (3d Cir. 1988), *cert. granted,* 109 S. Ct. 1309 (1989) (court held that expert testimony on unreliability of eyewitness testimony was properly excluded where the factors which the expert wished to testify about as affecting a witness' testimony were not present in case).

Lastly, there may be extrinsic and intrinsic public policy issues, such as those concerning the use of polygraph evidence, should be evaluated.

After assessing probative value, the court must also assess the dangers posed by this particular kind of expert scientific evidence.[38] Some of the factors duplicate those already referred to in the prior paragraph. The court will have to evaluate the degree to which the jurors might be overimpressed by the aura of reliability surrounding the evidence, thereby leading them to abdicate their role of critical assessment.[39] In making this determination the nature of the evidence may be significant. Some scientific evidence merely guides the jury in making its own assessment of the evidence;[40] in other instances, the jury may be incapable of estimating the accuracy of the expert's conclusions by reference to the data on which the expert relies. Confusion of the jury, and the consumption of inordinate trial time are other dangers for the court to consider.[41] See Rule 403.

---

[38] *Cf.* Giannelli, *The Admissibility of Novel Scientific Evidence: Frye v. United States, A Half-Century Later,* 80 Colum. L. Rev. 1197, 1237 (1980) ("[F]actors, such as undue prejudice, confusion of issues, and waste of time, may be associated with scientific evidence, but often these factors overlap with the danger of misleading the jury or are of only secondary importance. Here, unlike the assessment of the probative value of novel scientific evidence, the trial judge appears to be on familiar turf; evaluating the misleading aspects of evidence is a problem judges face in admitting or excluding nonscientific evidence.") (footnote omitted).

[39] United States v. Addison, 498 F.2d 741, 744 (D.C. Cir. 1974) (scientific evidence may "assume a posture of mystic infallibility in the eyes of a jury of laymen").

[40] *See, e.g.,* People v. Marx, 54 Cal. App. 3d 100, 111, 126 Cal. Rptr. 350, 356 (1975) (in comparing analysis of bite-marks with polygraph evidence, court noted: "[T]he trier-of-fact . . . was shown models, photographs, x-rays and dozens of slides of the victim's wounds and defendant's teeth. It could see what we have seen in reviewing the exhibits to determine the admissibility of the evidence. . . . Thus, the basic data on which the experts based their conclusions were verifiable by the court. . . . In short, in admitting the evidence, the court did not have to sacrifice its independence and common sense in evaluating it.").

[41] United States v. Hearst, 412 F. Supp. 893 (N.D. Cal. 1976), *aff'd,* 563 F.2d 1331 (9th Cir. 1977), *cert. denied,* 435 U.S. 1000 (1978) (court rejected testimony of expert in psycholinguistics because the field had not achieved general acceptance, because the relevance of the proffered testimony under the circumstances of the case was questionable, and because an inordinate amount of time would be consumed by the testimony and the rebuttal testimony to which the government would be entitled).

In balancing the probative worth of the novel scientific evidence against the dangers specified in Rule 403, the court must also consider such factors as the significance of the issue to which the evidence is directed, the availability of other proof, and the utility of limiting instructions. The court may also be influenced by the extent to which the issues posed by this novel evidence were explored prior to trial, and whether the party opposing admissibility is adequately prepared.[42] The availability of competent experts to explore the limitations of the novel technique may also enter into the court's calculus.[43]

¶ 13.03   Bases of Opinion Testimony By Experts—Rule 703

¶ 13.03[01]   Scope and Rationale[1]

Rule 703 governs the permissible bases upon which experts may ground their opinions. The first sentence of the rule codifies the traditional and universally accepted view that an expert may base an opinion on (1) first hand information, or (2) facts or data made known to the expert in court. The second sentence expands the permissible bases for the expert's opinion beyond that usually permitted at common law. It allows the expert to base an opinion on facts or data which could not be admitted in evidence, provided they are of the type reasonably relied upon by experts in forming opinions in their particular field of competence. In broadening the basis for admissibility, Rule 703 operates as one of the cornerstones of the liberal approach the Federal Rules of Evidence take to expert testimony. The rule provides:

---

[42] United States v. Baller, 519 F.2d 463, 466 (4th Cir.), *cert. denied,* 423 U.S. 1019, (1975) (in criminal case, appellate court stressed that defendant's "attorney demonstrated thorough knowledge of the subject in a detailed cross-examination that developed the possibility of error in both the general technique and the specific identification of the defendant").

[43] *Id.* ("Competent witnesses were available to expose its limitations, and the defense was furnished with the names of other experts who could conduct their own analysis of the tapes.").

[1] *See* **Treatise** at ¶ 703[01].

Rule 703

BASES OF OPINION TESTIMONY BY EXPERTS

The facts or data in the particular case upon which an expert bases an opinion or inference may be those perceived by or made known to the expert at or before the hearing. If of a type reasonably relied upon by experts in the particular field in forming opinions or inferences upon the subject, the facts or data need not be admissible in evidence.

The second sentence of Rule 703 recognizes that data which is not admissible because it does not pass hearsay rule scrutiny may nevertheless be considered by an expert in reaching his or her conclusion. Experts, after all, are allowed to testify precisely because they have training or skills which the ordinary juror lacks. Consequently, when experts rely upon data in order to function effectively in their area of expertise, guarantees of trustworthiness are present that compensate for the hearsay nature of the underlying data. Rule 703 assumes that experts' testimony will be more useful when they are allowed to function in the courtroom the same way they operate in their respective fields.

¶ 13.03[02]   The Three Bases for Expert Testimony[2]

[a]   Personal Knowledge

The first sentence of Rule 703 codifies prior practice in permitting an expert to state an opinion based on personal observation. Often the testimony of an expert with firsthand knowledge is particularly credible and convincing. When testimony is offered on this basis, the court, pursuant to Rule 104(a), may have to decide such issues as whether the testimony was based on personal observation, whether the witness had a sufficient opportunity to observe,[3] and whether the

---

[2] *See* **Treatise** at ¶¶ 703[02], [03].

[3] *Cf.* United States v. Hill, 655 F.2d 512 (3d Cir. 1981) (majority found trial court had erred in excluding psychologist's testimony about entrapment on the ground that expert had not heard defendant or informant testify; majority pointed out that testimony need not have been based solely on personal observation but could also have rested on psychological profiles, intelligence tests and other data relating to

witness' observation was relevant to a material fact in issue.[4] The Supreme Court has held, in a *per curiam* decision, that there is no violation of the Confrontation Clause when an expert bases his opinion on personal observation, but is then unable to recall the theory underlying his conclusion.[5]

[b] Facts or Data Made Known to Expert at Trial

Before the enactment of the Federal Rules of Evidence, when experts relied upon data not personally known to them as the basis for an opinion, a hypothetical question was customarily used to bring the data to the experts' attention. The alternative—having experts attend the trial to hear testimony which would then become the basis for their opinions—was often impracticable in terms of expense and time, and presented problems when conflicts in the evidence made it difficult to determine on what testimony the experts relied. These theoretical obstacles to the expert's attendance at the trial continue to exist. Nevertheless, it is usual for an expert to attend in order to prepare to testify as well as to assist counsel in meeting the opponent's case. The expert who misses part of the trial may even depend upon counsel's filling in with a summary.

The Federal Rules allow use of the hypothetical question and it still is a convenient way of presenting evidence in some cases. However, hypothetical questions are considerably less significant than under former practice. Not only does Rule 703 greatly expand the sources on which experts may base their opinions by allowing them to rely on materials they customarily consult outside the courtroom, but, in addition, Rule 705 permits experts to state an opinion without first disclosing the underlying data on which it is based. See discussion below.

---

defendant; dissent objected that the opinion expert sought to express could only have been based on testimony of informant).

[4] *See, e.g.,* United States v. Busic, 592 F.2d 13 (2d Cir. 1978) (evidence relevant to specific intent was properly excluded when offense charged involved only a showing of general criminal intent).

[5] Delaware v. Fensterer, 106 S.Ct. 292, 88 L.Ed.2d 15 (1985) (Court noted that in this case lapse of memory did not frustrate opportunity for cross-examination).

[c] Reasonable Reliance on Data Presented Outside the Courtroom

The most controversial aspect of Rule 703 is its second sentence which authorizes experts to base their opinions upon non-admissible data if they would reasonably rely upon such data in reaching conclusions in their respective fields of expertise.[6] When there is a factual dispute over the issue of reliance, it is the court, pursuant to Rule 104(a), that must determine whether such reliance is justified.[7] In making this finding, the trial judge may wish to hold a hearing outside the presence of the jury at which the expert can be examined, and at which the proponent may introduce textbooks or other evidence indicating that experts in the field customarily rely upon the material in question in performing their work. Since Rule 703 is concerned with the trustworthiness of the resulting opinions, the proponent of the expert must establish that experts other than the proposed witness would act upon the information relied upon, and would do so for purposes other than testifying in a lawsuit.

It is apparent from the reported decisions that the courts are loosely divided into two camps in interpreting the reasonable reliance test. The difference between the two groups is one of emphasis. Unlike their more liberal-minded colleagues, judges who take a restrictive

---

[6] *See, e.g.,* International Adhesive Coating Co., Inc. v. Bolton Emerson Int'l, Inc., 851 F.2d 540, 545 (1st Cir. 1988) (expert on damages relied on interviews with plaintiff's personnel); United States v. Bramlet, 820 F.2d 851, 856 (7th Cir. 1987), *cert. denied,* 108 S.Ct. 175 (1987) (reliance on recorded observation of psychiatric hospital staff); United States v. Kail, 804 F.2d 441, 447–48 (8th Cir. 1986) (coin expert could rely on the American Numismatic Association's official grading standards and the Coin Dealer's Newsletter—the "grey sheet"—as a basis for his opinion of the worth of the coins in question because such publications enjoyed industry-wide acceptance); Stevens v. Cessna Aircraft Co., 634 F. Supp. 137, 142–43 (E.D. Pa.), *aff'd mem.,* 806 F.2d 252 (3d Cir. 1986) (reliance on associates of airplane pilot); Lewis v. Rego Co., 757 F.2d 66, 74 (3d Cir. 1985) (testifying expert could rely on conversation with other expert); United States v. Bilson, 648 F.2d 1238 (9th Cir. 1981) (reliance on psychological tests); *In re* Swine Flu Immunization Products Liability Litigation, 533 F.Supp. 567, 578 (D. Colo. 1980) (reliance on laboratory findings); Bauman v. Centex Corp., 611 F.2d 1115, 1120 (5th Cir. 1980) (library research).

[7] Faries v. Atlas Truck Body Mfg. Co., 797 F.2d 619, 623–24 (8th Cir. 1986) (expert in accident construction could not reasonably rely upon eyewitness in forming opinion about cause of accident).

view of Rule 703 undertake an independent assessment of the reliability of the materials on which the expert relied. The expert's opinion will be admitted only if the judge, rather than the expert, is persuaded of the trustworthiness of the underlying data.

The two approaches are reflected in the trial and court of appeals opinions in the *Matsushita Electric Industries, Ltd. v. Zenith Radio Corp.* case.[8] The trial judge, who had already ruled that many of the documents proffered by plaintiff were insufficiently trustworthy to satisfy the business or public records hearsay exceptions, extended his hearsay analysis to the Rule 703 situation. He refused to admit the opinions of experts who had relied on the excluded hearsay even though those experts had sworn in uncontested affidavits that the data on which they had relied was of a type customarily relied upon by experts in their fields.[9] The court of appeals found that the trial court had erred:

> The proper inquiry is not what the court deems reliable, but what experts in the relevant discipline deem it to be. . . . In substituting its own opinion as to what constitutes reasonable reliance for that of the experts in the relevant fields the trial court misinterpreted Rule 703. . . . [O]nce the court finds that the data relied on is such as experts in the field reasonably rely upon, the rigorous examination should be conducted in the cross-examination for which Rule 705 makes explicit provision.[10]

The difficulty with the restrictive approach lies not so much in the actual results, but in the assumption that trustworthiness of the underlying data is an independent factor which Rule 703 requires the judge to verify in order for the expert's testimony to pass the threshold of admissibility. Were that so, the hearsay rules would be determinative and the second sentence of Rule 703 would be mean-

---

[8] 505 F.Supp. 1313 (E.D. Pa. 1981), *aff'd in part and rev'd in part,* 723 F.2d 238 (3d Cir. 1983), *rev'd,* 106 S.Ct. 1348 (1986) (on substantive rather than evidential grounds, but the dissent gave greater weight to an expert's opinion than did the majority).

[9] The trial judge explained: "it is plain that the 'reasonable reliance' requirement of F.R.E. 703 grew from and is cognate with the requirement that information admitted as an exception to the hearsay rule have some circumstantial degree of reliability or trustworthiness. We see the reasonable reliance language built into Rule 703 as essentially a short-hand translation of the hearsay rules' trustworthiness element." 505 F.Supp. at 1324.

[10] 723 F.2d at 276–77.

ingless, except for saving the proponent of the expert the inconvenience of having to offer the underlying data into evidence. The dangers feared by courts espousing a restrictive view of Rule 703 can, in many cases, be avoided through effective pretrial discovery, detailed consideration of expert testimony issues at the pretrial conference, and extensive cross-examination of the expert at trial. Some courts hold that Rule 703 does not dictate admission of evidence upon which an expert reasonably relied if the evidence is excludable by reason of another rule of evidence.[11]

Espousal of the liberal view does not mean that a motion for summary judgment is precluded whenever the plaintiff's case is dependent on expert testimony, and the plaintiff submits affidavits from experts supporting the plaintiff's claim for relief. In some cases, examination of the basis of an expert's opinion reveals that it is not supported by any reliable evidence.[12] In these cases, exclusion of the

---

[11] Nachtsheim v. Beech Aircraft Corp., 847 F.2d 1261, 1270 (7th Cir. 1988) (in a products liability action arising from an airplane crash, the district court did not err in holding that plaintiffs could not elicit from their expert that he had relied on other accidents involving the same aircraft. The evidence of other accidents was barred by Rule 403 and Rule 703 "does not necessarily mean that materials independently excluded by the court by reason of another rule of evidence will automatically be admitted . . . .").

[12] See, e.g., Evers v. General Motors Corp., 770 F.2d 984 (11th Cir. 1985) (summary judgment granted despite affidavit from plaintiff's expert stating that "air bag" restraint system would have prevented or reduced severity of plaintiff's injuries and that defendant's failure to incorporate "air bag" constituted design defect; court found that affidavit made conclusory allegations without providing specific facts, contradicted earlier deposition testimony of plaintiff's witness, and failed to show how "air bag" would have aided in side-impact collision); Merit Motors, Inc. v. Chrysler Corp., 569 F.2d 666, 673 (D.C. Cir. 1977) (Rule 703 "was intended to broaden the acceptable bases of expert opinion, but it was not intended, as appellants seem to argue, to make summary judgment impossible whenever a party has produced an expert to support its position"). See also Almonte v. National Union Fire Insurance, 787 F.2d 763, 769–70 (1st Cir. 1986) (court draws distinction between expert relying on statements by defendant's former business partner to prove that fire was incendiary and relying on statements to prove who started fire); Fontenot v. Upjohn Co., 780 F.2d 1190 (5th Cir. 1986) (summary judgment granted for defendant where after discovery plaintiff failed to produce any affidavit by expert alleging that progesterone manufactured by defendant could cause birth defects). Compare Bulthuis v. Rexall Corp., 789 F.2d 1315, 1318 (9th Cir. 1985) (plaintiff claimed her mother had taken DES; defendant disputed claim; trial court granted summary judgment for defendants; appellate court reversed, finding that plaintiff's experts' opinions that mother had taken DES were based on tissue changes in the mother;

expert's opinion under Rule 703 and a grant of summary judgment to the opposing party might be appropriate. In other cases, an expert's opinion is supported by some credible evidence, but further investigation reveals that there is other, much more important evidence available which cuts against the expert's opinion and which the expert is ignoring.[12a] In these cases, the court might exclude the expert's opinion either under Rule 702, as not helpful to the trier of fact, or under Rule 403, as likely to mislead the jury.[13] The reasoning and the result are much the same regardless of which rule is used.

¶ 13.03[03] Problems in Criminal Cases[14]

It is not clear to what extent the constitutional right of confrontation may entitle an accused to the opportunity to cross-examine persons who prepared the underlying data on which an expert relied. Potentially troublesome are cases in which a government agent testifies on the basis of hearsay statements or reports generated through

---

majority found that although plaintiff's experts' affidavits "did not describe in detail how they arrived at their opinions, they sufficiently disclosed the basis for their conclusions absent any indication from the court that greater detail was desired"; dissent concluded that experts' opinions were based on hearsay statements of mother rather than tissue changes and that summary judgment should have been granted).

[12a] *See, e.g.,* Lynch v. Merrell-National Laboratories, Div. of Richardson-Merrell, Inc., 830 F.2d 1190 (1st Cir. 1987) (Bendectin); Viterbo v. Dow Chemical Co., 826 F.2d 420 (5th Cir. 1987) (herbicide); *In re* "Agent Orange" Product Liability Litigation, 611 F.Supp. 1223, 1250, 1255–56 (E.D.N.Y. 1985); *In re* "Agent Orange" Product Liability Litigation, 611 F.Supp. 1267, 1281–83 (E.D.N.Y. 1985).

[13] See, *e.g.,* Shatkin v. McDonnell Douglas Corp., 727 F.2d 202, 208 (2d Cir. 1984) ("here the district court, in ruling on the admissibility of the proposed testimony, possessed not only the power under Fed.R.Evid. 403 to determine whether it had a propensity for misleading or confusing the jury [citations omitted], but also the discretionary right under Fed.R.Evid. 703 to determine whether the expert acted reasonably in making assumptions of fact upon which he could base his testimony"). Richardson By Richardson v. Richardson-Merrell, Inc., 857 F.2d 823 (D.C. 1988) (in products liability action to recover for birth defects allegedly caused by drug, appellate court affirmed judgment n.o.v. that district court had granted for defendant on the ground that there was no basis for plaintiff's expert's conclusion about causation).

[14] *See* **Treatise** at ¶ 703[04].

a governmental investigation.[15] When a case agent testifies as an expert, the jury may conclude that the agent's opinion about the defendant's criminal activity is firmly grounded in knowledge beyond the evidence introduced at trial.[16] A strong instruction by the court should obviate the Confrontation Clause problem except in instances

---

[15] See, e.g., United States v. Angiulo, 847 F.2d 956, 974–75 (1st Cir.), cert. denied, 109 S. Ct. 314 (1988) (no error in having agent testify without disclosing identitites of informants; court found that agent's testimony was not based on informants but on tape recordings played at trial and non-confidential sources of information); United States v. Lundy, 809 F.2d 392, 395–96 (7th Cir. 1987) (arson detection expert could rely on eyewitnesses in combination with circumstantial evidence in concluding that fire was not accidental); United States v. Ginsberg, 758 F.2d 823 (2d Cir. 1985) (expert in drug prosecution testified that arrested narcotics dealers had told him of the use of codes and beepers; court finds that testimony properly admitted under Federal Rules of Evidence; no discussion of confrontation); United States v. Genser, 582 F.2d 292, 298–99 (3d Cir. 1978) (IRS agent could testify on the basis of IRS audits not admitted into evidence); United States v. Brown, 548 F.2d 1194 (5th Cir. 1977) (majority, over strong dissent, reversed where IRS agent had based her testimony on interviews with other taxpayers).

[16] See, e.g., United States v. Scop, 846 F.2d 135, 143 (2d Cir.), rev'd in part on other grounds, 856 F.2d 5 (2d Cir. 1988) (in securities fraud prosecution, investigator for the SEC, who had spent four years investigating the case and who was qualified to testify as an expert on securities trading practices, purported to base his opinions solely on the evidence introduced at trial; in the course of holding that his testimony should not have been admitted because it was based on a positive assessment of the credibility of the chief prosecution witness, the majority stated: "[S]uch testimony by an investigator and opinions based thereon are clearly prejudicial when offered to a jury . . . . Certainly, the risk of a jury believing that an opinion offered as to credibility by an agent such as Whitten was based on his investigation as a whole rather than solely on evidence adduced at trial is particularly great."); United States v. Alvarez, 837 F.2d 1024, 1030–1031 (11th Cir.), cert. denied, 108 S. Ct. 2003, 2004 (1988) (prosecution for conspiracy to possess with intent to distribute marijuana and cocaine which coast guard found in secret compartment on boat stopped on the high seas; in order to prove that four men on board had knowledge of presence of drugs, DEA agent was permitted to testify that it would be riskier to use unknowing participants in drug smuggling scheme than those who knew about the contraband; defendants failed to object and court held that there was enough other evidence of knowledge so that admission of agent's testimony did not render trial fundamentally unfair, but court stated that it was "troubled" by the effect which such evidence may have on a jury and the risk of undue prejudice. But cf. United States v. Kinsey, 843 F.2d 383, 387–88 (9th Cir.), cert. denied, 109 S. Ct. 99 (1988) (police narcotics officer could testify that in his opinion the large stash of cocaine to which defendant had access meant that defendant was involved in the distribution of cocaine).

where the expert's opinion is so permeated with hearsay that the opinion is worthless unless the hearsay is accepted as true.[17] In the latter cases the expert's testimony should be excluded. Nevertheless, it must be recognized that the opinions of many experts routinely accepted are based upon assumptions and data-bases that are hearsay: fingerprint evidence, blood analysis, psychiatric testimony, for example, are all in this category. No expert can rely entirely on his or her own research and experimentation; there must be resort at least to standard texts.

¶ 13.04   Opinion on Ultimate Issue—Rule 704

¶ 13.04[01]   Scope and Rationale[1]

Until it was amended by Congress in 1984, Rule 704 expressly abolished the ultimate opinion doctrine. The amendment reinstated

---

[17] In Delaware v. Fensterer, 106 S. Ct. 292, 88 L.Ed.2d 15 (1985), the Supreme Court, in a per curiam decision, held that the Confrontation Clause was not violated when an expert who had based his opinion on personal observations was unable to recall the theory on which he relied in reaching his conclusion. The Court noted that the case did not involve any out-of-court statements. *See also* United States v. Daly, 842 F.2d 1380, 1387–89 (2d Cir.), *cert. denied,* 109 S. Ct. 66 (1988) (not abuse of discretion to have admitted expert testimony about the existence and operation of the Gambino crime family; expert described requirements for membership, explained meaning of certain jargon, and described how organized crime has infiltrated labor unions; expert also identified various persons named on surveillance tapes; court noted that for the most part expert's testimony was general and did not relate to elements of offenses charged, and that this evidence was admissible as background information, even if it was based on hearsay, provided experts reasonably rely on such information in forming opinions and drawing inferences); United States v. Rollins, 862 F.2d 1282, 1292–93 (7th Cir. 1988) (in narcotics prosecution, agent could testify about meanings of code words even though agent testified that he relied in part on what informant told him certain words meant; although court agreed with defense that government could not use government agent to avoid putting informant on stand by substituting agent to sanitize informant's testimony, court found no error in this case because agent's opinion was based also on his extensive training and experience and because defendants were able to cross-examine agent extensively; court found no confrontation clause violation because of extensive cross-examination and because defense had been provided with all FBI reports regarding information informant had given agent).

[1] *See* **Treatise** at ¶ 704[01].

the doctrine to a limited extent: an expert testifying in a criminal case may not express an opinion on the ultimate issue of the defendant's insanity.

The Rule provides:

Rule 704

OPINION ON ULTIMATE ISSUE

(a) Except as provided in subdivision (b), testimony in the form of an opinion or inference otherwise admissible is not objectionable because it embraces an ultimate issue to be decided by the trier of fact.

(b) No expert witness testifying with respect to the mental state or condition of a defendant in a criminal case may state an opinion or inference as to whether the defendant did or did not have the mental state or condition constituting an element of the crime charged or of a defense thereto. Such ultimate issues are matters for the trier of fact alone.

In its most extreme form, the ultimate opinion rule held that no expert—whether lay or skilled—could express his or her opinion on the ultimate issue in the case. The usual reason offered was the shorthand phrase that such an opinion would invade the province of the jury. It had, however, been recognized long before the enactment of the Federal Rules that distinctions between ultimate issues and non-ultimate issues were often difficult to draw, and that the expressed rationale for the rule made little sense because jurors remain free to draw their own conclusions. The core of the doctrine—that jurors cannot ascertain what happened if they are merely told how to decide—was often eclipsed by wrangling over how to apply the rule. By the time Rule 704 was drafted, the federal courts had taken account of the condemnation of the rule voiced by other courts and legal scholars,[2] and had "long tolerated violation"[3] of the ultimate opinion rule. Rule 704, as enacted, thus did little more than proclaim actual practice.

---

[2] Wigmore had termed the rule "a mere bit of empty rhetoric" and "one of those impracticable and misconceived utterances which lack any justification in principle." 7 Wigmore, *Evidence* §§ 1920 and 1921 at 17–18 (3d ed. 1940).

[3] Harried v. United States, 389 F.2d 281, 285 n.3 (D.C. Cir. 1967) (opinion by then Circuit Judge Burger).

The treatment of the ultimate rule problem in the federal rules has numerous advantages over previous practice. It eliminates quibbles over the meaning of ultimate fact, and the distinction between fact and law. Abolition of the rule ends the spectacle of courts endorsing a principle which they cite only as a precursor to applying an exception. It stops the resort to indirect means to bring the prohibited matter to the jury's attention, and most importantly, it allows the jury to receive the full benefit of a witness' judgment. Both lay and expert witnesses may testify in a more natural, straightforward manner uninterrupted by technical objections interfering with the flow of the trial. Abolition of the ultimate issue rule was seen by the drafters as an adjunct to the helpfulness approach expressed in Rule 702; an opinion that merely tells jurors what result to reach is not helpful.[4] This consistency of treatment has now been somewhat undercut by the 1984 addition of subdivision (b), discussed below.

¶ 13.04[02]   Problems in Applying Rule 704[5]

Even in its original unamended form, Rule 704 did not mean that all proffered opinions by experts would be admissible. Aside from the helpfulness standard expressed in Rule 702, Rule 705 minimizes the impact of too broad an opinion by authorizing the judge to require preliminary disclosure of the data underlying the opinion so that the jury will have adequate material with which to evaluate an opinion. The judge will often require the expert to testify in more concrete terms that the jury will find helpful in deciding the ultimate issue. The power continues to exist to require the expert to avoid the ultimate issue.[6] Except to the extent indicated below, it is such

---

[4] *See, e.g.,* Kostelecky v. NL Acme Tool/NL Industries, Inc., 837 F.2d 828, 830 (8th Cir. 1988) (error, but harmless, to have admitted accident report made by plaintiff's co-worker stating that accident was caused by plaintiff's conduct, and could have been avoided if plaintiff listened to warnings; "in the context of this case, the opinion as to causation served to do nothing more than tell the jury what result it should reach.").

[5] See **Treatise** at ¶¶ 702[02], [03].

[6] Harris v. Pacific Floor Machine Manufacturing Co., 856 F.2d 64, 67–68 (8th Cir. 1988) (not error for district court to allow expert to explain criteria by which he would judge adequacy of warning but not allow him to give opinion on ultimate question of adequacy; concurring judge, quoting **Treatise** expressed "hope that our

considerations— rather than Rule 704 or the ultimate opinion rule— which the courts rely upon when they limit expert testimony.[7]

[a] Legal Standard

One troublesome issue arises when the opinion is couched in terms of a legal standard. Often the difficulty with this evidence is a lack of helpfulness: a statement by a physician that plaintiff is disabled within the meaning of the Social Security Act would have much less meaning than an opinion that plaintiff's incapacities would prevent him from doing certain types of work.[8] Sometimes, the court fears

---

holding will not be considered a precedent to exclude expert testimony in the form of an opinion on whether a product may be defective and unreasonably dangerous absent adequate warning. Such knowledge is not within the general knowledge of a lay jury and should ordinarily be admissible as expert opinion.").

[7] *See, e.g., In re* Japanese Electronic Products Litigation, 505 F.Supp. 1313, 1331 (E.D. Pa. 1981), *rev'd,* 723 F.2d 238 (3d Cir. 1983), *rev'd,* 106 S.Ct. 1348 (1986) (although district court took a markedly restrictive view of the admissibility of expert testimony, it acknowledged the untenability of exclusion because an opinion was expressed on an ultimate issue; instead it examined the proffered testimony pursuant to Rules 702 and 705).

[8] *See* Specht v. Jensen, 853 F.2d 805, 808 (10th Cir. 1988), *cert. denied,* 109 S. Ct. 792 (1989) (en banc) (majority found that legal expert should not have been allowed to testify in civil rights action under § 1983 as to whether a legally valid search had been conducted; the expert's testimony "supplant[ed] both the court's duty to set forth the law and the jury's ability to apply this law to the evidence"; dissent criticizes majority opinion for not demonstrating how defendant was prejudiced since court's instruction on applicable law did not materially differ from expert's testimony, and court directed jury to follow judge's instructions; both majority and dissent quote **Treatise**); United States v. Scop, 846 F.2d 135, 140 (2d Cir.), *rev'd in part on other grounds,* 856 F.2d 5 (2d Cir. 1988) (convictions in securities fraud prosecution reversed where SEC investigator, testifying as government's expert on securities trading practices "made no attempt to couch the opinion testimony at issue in even conclusory factual statements but drew directly upon the language of the statute and accompanying regulations concerning 'manipulation' and 'fraud' . . . they could not have been helpful to the jury in carrying out its legitimate functions."); United States v. Kelly, 679 F.2d 135 (8th Cir. 1982) (police officer could testify that amount of cocaine possessed by defendant was a quantity that would be possessed "with intent to distribute"; no danger of confusing jury as words are commonly used and their plain meaning matches their legal meaning); Strong v. E.I. DuPont de Nemours Co., Inc., 667 F.2d 682 (8th Cir. 1981) (not abuse of discretion to exclude expert's opinion that communications from defendant about

confusion; the conclusion may convey different information to jurors than to lawyers, a danger which does not exist when there is no conflict between the expert's definition and the legal definition.[9] Closely related is the apprehension that the jurors will turn to the expert, rather than to the judge, for guidance on the applicable law.[10] Many of these problems could be alleviated by admitting the expert testimony with appropriate instructions.[11] In nonjury cases, exclusion

---

product did not constitute proper warning where trial judge found that question was too broadly and simplistically phrased under Rule 704).

[9] United States v. Johnson, 637 F.2d 1224 (9th Cir. 1980) (in prosecution for assault resulting in serious bodily injury, not error for treating physician to give expert opinion that victim had suffered serious bodily injury; court drew distinction between expert opinions about legal terms which are reasonably clear to laymen, as in instant case, and opinions offered about legal terms which are not reasonably clear to lay persons; court found no misleading conflict between expert's medical definition of serious bodily injury and the proper legal definition; court noted that testimony was likely to assist jury and that defendant was free to probe expert's conclusion under Rule 705). *See* also First Nat'l State Bank of New Jersey v. Reliance Electric Co., 668 F.2d 725 (3d Cir. 1981) (expert on Uniform Commercial Code permitted to testify about bank and industry practices, but court barred opinion as to the resulting legal duties).

[10] United States v. Zipkin, 729 F.2d 384, 387 (6th Cir. 1984) (bankruptcy judge should not have been permitted to testify about bankruptcy law; "jury . . . would be expected to give special credence to such testimony . . . sole function of the trial judge to instruct the jury on the law"). Stoler v. Penn Central Transportation Co., 583 F.2d 896, 899 (6th Cir. 1978) (railroad crossing collision; no abuse of discretion in refusal to permit plaintiff's expert witness to testify that he believed crossing was extra hazardous; judge has wide discretion to exclude, "In the circumstances here, plaintiff's civil engineer was being asked for what amounted to a legal opinion as to what constitutes an "extra hazardous" crossing under Ohio law"); Marx & Co., Inc. v. Diner's Club, Inc., 550 F.2d 505, 510, 511–12 (2d Cir.), *cert. denied,* 434 U.S. 861 (1977) (court found that trial judge had erred in admitting testimony which amounted to expert's conclusions on the applicable rules of domestic law which governed a contract; court stated that while "[r]ecognizing that an expert may testify to an ultimate fact, and to the practices and usage of a trade, we think care must be taken lest, in the field of securities law, he be allowed to usurp the function of the judge"; cites Advisory Committee Note on Proposed Rule 704; "It is for the jury to evaluate the facts in light of the applicable rules of law, and it is therefore erroneous for a witness to state his opinion on the law of the forum"; expert in a securities case "may tell the jury whether he thinks the method of trading was normal, but not, in our view, whether it amounted to *illegal* manipulation under Section 9 of the Securities Exchange Act of 1934.").

[11] *See, e.g.,* United States v. Fogg, 652 F.2d 551 (5th Cir. 1981), *cert. denied,* 456 U.S. 905 (1982) (in tax evasion case no error in agent's stating a legal conclusion

on 704 grounds is almost never justified. Nevertheless, some courts continue to take a narrow view when the expert's opinion relates to a legal standard.

[b] Defendant's Mental State in a Criminal Case

A specialized instance of experts rendering opinions couched in terms of a legal standard occurs when a psychiatrist or other mental health expert testifies about a criminal defendant's mental state. The subjectiveness of much psychiatric testimony, and the sensitive criminal context in which issues of mental state are at times determinative of life or death, may have contributed to some courts' uneasiness about allowing this type of testimony.[12] When these fears interacted with criticisms of the insanity defense that erupted as an aftermath of the assassination attempt upon President Reagan, Congress responded by amending Rule 704 to prohibit expert testimony on the ultimate legal issue of whether or not a criminal defendant possessed "the mental state or condition constituting an element of the crime charged or of a defense thereto."[13]

---

where court's instructions placed statements in proper perspective and where testimony was not couched as instructions to jury).

[12] *See* United States v. Ingredient Technology Corp., 698 F.2d 88, 96–98 (2d Cir.), *cert. denied,* 462 U.S. 1131 (1983) (in tax fraud prosecution defendant argued that district court's exclusion of proffered expert testimony thwarted defense that defendants could not have formed a willful intent; appellate court stated that "[q]uestions of law are for the court," and explained "that it would be very confusing to a jury to have opposing opinions of law admitted into evidence as involving a factual question for them to decide"); Suggs v. LaVallee, 570 F.2d 1092, 1115 n.58 (2d Cir.), *cert. denied,* 439 U.S. 915 (1978) (in review of whether district judge has been entitled to consider petitioner's competency in evidentiary hearing in proceeding on petition for habeas corpus, appellate court noted that "If the judge can be faulted at all it is that he, like so many other courts before him . . . did not limit psychiatric testimony to psychiatric findings. He also permitted psychiatric experts to express the legal conclusions to be drawn from those findings. . . . However, the Federal Rules of Evidence permit experts to testify on the ultimate issue for factual resolution.").

[13] United States v. Alexander, 805 F.2d 1458, 1462–63 (11th Cir. 1986) (Rule 704 does not violate equal protection clause); United States v. Mest, 789 F.2d 1069, 1071–72 (4th Cir.), *cert. denied,* 107 S.Ct. 163 (1986) (court held that Rule 704(b) is purely a procedural change that does not alter the elements of the offense or lessen

As the Report of the Senate Judiciary Committee notes, the amendment was intended to eliminate the "confusing spectacle of competing expert witnesses testifying to directly contradictory conclusions" as to the ultimate legal issue of a defendant's sanity.[14] How drastic a change will be effected by the amendment remains unclear. As the Report indicates, the amended rule still permits experts to present their opinions concerning a defendant's diagnosis, mental state and motivation at the time of the act.[15] Thus, the amended rule may only result in experts resorting to a variety of indirect means in order to bring the defendant's sanity to the attention of the jury. It will be obvious in most cases what the expert's view is on the ultimate issue. The Senate Report also provides that the rationale for precluding ultimate opinion psychiatric testimony extends beyond the insanity defense to any ultimate mental state of the defendant that is relevant to the legal conclusion sought to be proven.[16] Accord-

---

the government's burden of proof and therefore does not violate prohibition against ex post facto laws).

[14] Report of the Committee on the Judiciary, Senate, 98th Cong., 1st Sess., 225–30 [hereinafter *Report*].

[15] *Id.* at 231. *See* United States v. Gipson, 862 F.2d 714, 715–16 (8th Cir. 1988) (in prosecution of inmate for attempted escape, prosecution expert could express opinion as to whether or not defendant was suffering from a mental defect, but could not be asked whether defendant had the requisite mental state to have willfully or intentionally attempted to escape; appellate court stated that it would affirm even if district court had erred in admitting evidence, because defendant's expert had "opened door" by testifying that defendant suffered from "depersonalization"). United States v. Dubray, 854 F.2d 1099, 1102 (8th Cir. 1988) (psychiatrist's testimony that defendant was not psychotic was limited to the medical question of psychosis "and did not state an opinion whether Dubray was able to appreciate the wrongness of his actions."); United States v. Edwards, 819 F.2d 262, 265–66 (11th Cir. 1987) (testimony by psychiatrist explaining why the defendant's frantic behavior over a financial crisis did not necessarily indicate an active manic state was properly admitted; "Every actual fact concerning the defendant's mental condition is still as admissible after the enactment of Rule 704(b) as it was before."); United States v. Dotson, 817 F.2d 1127, 1132 (5th Cir.), *vac. in part on other grounds,* 821 F.2d 1034 (5th Cir. 1987) (in a prosecution for income tax evasion, court agreed that Rule 704(b) would bar testimony that defendant had requisite state of mind but found no error, where, with one possible exception, government expert's testimony merely explained his analysis of the facts indicating willful evasion).

[16] *Report, supra* note 10, at 231. United States v. Alvarez, 837 F.2d 1024, 1031 (11th Cir.), *cert. denied,* 108 S. Ct. 2003, 2004 (1988) (where knowledge of the presence of narcotics constituted an element of the crime charged, testimony by DEA expert

ingly, amended Rule 704 reaches all such "ultimate" issues, such as premeditation in a homicide case, or lack of predisposition in entrapment.[17]

¶ 13.05   Disclosure of Bases Underlying Expert Opinion— Rule 705

¶ 13.05[01]   Operation of Rule at Trial[1]

Rule 705 permits experts to express their opinions without first disclosing the underlying facts or data, unless the court orders otherwise. A hypothetical question is no longer required, even when the experts are relying on facts beyond their personal knowledge, as authorized by Rule 703. A full exploration of the underlying data by the cross-examiner is available.[2] Rule 705 provides:

---

that unknowing participants in smuggling schemes would jeopardize smuggling operation was offered as the basis for an inference that defendants knew of presence of drugs and therefore constituted testimony "with respect to the mental state or condition of a defendant"; no violation of Rule 704(b), however, because agent left inference for jury to draw);United States v. Cox, 826 F.2d 1518, 1523–25 (6th Cir. 1987) (in bank robbery prosecution where defendant raised issue of intent, government psychiatrist's opinion that defendant was not prevented by his mental illness from conforming his conduct to the dictates of the law did not directly state an opinion on intent and was therefore admissible; defendant did not claim insanity and therefore to the extent testimony expressed an opinion about sanity it did not transgress Rule 704(b) because insanity was not an issue in the case).

[17] *Report, supra,* note 10, at 231.

[1] *See* **Treatise** at ¶ 703[01].

[2] *Cf.* United States v. Cecil, 836 F.2d 1431, 1439–1441 (4th Cir.) (en banc), *cert. denied,* 109 S. Ct. 2846 (1988) (court held in a 7-3 decision that trial court did not err in refusing to admit a 1981 psychiatric report about the mental condition of an important prosecution witness; because the psychiatrist did not testify in person, admission of the report would have deprived the government of the opportunity to cross-examine him about the bases of his opinion as guaranteed by Rule 705).

Rule 705

DISCLOSURE OF FACTS OR DATA UNDERLYING EXPERT OPINION

The expert may testify in terms of opinion or inference and give reasons therefor without prior disclosure of the underlying facts or data, unless the court requires otherwise. The expert may in any event be required to disclose the underlying facts or data on cross-examination.

The objective of Rule 705 is to enhance the progress of the trial. It enables experts to communicate their conclusions to the jury without the risk of confusion posed by artificial and belabored hypothetical questions. In practice, however, the pressures of orderly presentation will usually lead to divulgence of the critical supporting data on direct.

The proponent of the witness will want to present that data and the opinion in the most persuasive fashion, using charts, summaries and documents presented to the trier to convince it that the opinion is well founded. Expert witnesses with firsthand knowledge may be asked about the facts underlying their opinions because the facts themselves are needed to satisfy the proponent's burden of proof. A witness' familiarity with certain data may have to be shown in qualifying the witness as an expert pursuant to Rule 702. And the necessity of making the evidence understandable to the jury will often result in the posing of some foundational questions before the expert states an opinion. Rule 705 does not prevent disclosure of the bases of an expert's opinion on direct.[3] It gives the proponent of the expert the choice of describing the underlying data on direct, or waiting to see if the opponent will require disclosure on cross-examination.

Nor is the use of hypotheticals prohibited—it is only made optional. When, however, an attorney persists in asking confusing or repetitious or unnecessary hypothetical questions, the court has the power pursuant to Rule 403 to exclude them if it finds that their probative

---

[3] See, e.g., Lewis v. Rego Co., 757 F.2d 66, 74 (3d Cir. 1985) (error to have prevented expert from testifying on direct that he had relied on conversation with other expert who had modified his opinion after writing a report, the contents of which were made known to jury). But see Nachtsheim v. Beech Aircraft Corp., 847 F.2d 1261, 1270–71 (7th Cir. 1988) (see discussion in text at ¶ 13.03[02], supra).

value is outweighed by the dangers of prejudice, confusion or waste of time.

Because of the broad scope of discovery in civil cases,[4] a well-prepared attorney should know enough about the subject of the expert's testimony to decide whether it would be fruitful to require the expert to amplify the underlying data on cross-examination. Obviously, if further testimony would only solidify the expert's conclusions, an adversary will refrain from further questioning.[5] But if the cross-examiner concludes that the expert has omitted pertinent facts in arriving at an opinion, or has misconstrued them, or is accepting disputed facts as true, or is basing an opinion on someone else's opinion which is in conflict with the established facts, then the attorney will probe the expert's premises.

In a criminal case because of the much narrower scope of discovery, an attorney will be less likely to have sufficient advance knowledge for effective cross-examination. Consequently, the trial court should more frequently exercise its discretion to require a detailed preliminary disclosure of the data on which the expert relied. It is even more important in criminal cases than in civil cases to require that experts' reports be shown to defense counsel before trial. Defense counsel should, in exchange for this privilege, be required to show the government its experts' reports before trial. Surprise by experts should not be permitted.

¶ 13.05[02]   Operation of Rule in Conjunction with Motion for Summary Judgment

There is somewhat of a tension between Rule 56(e) of the Federal Rules of Civil Procedure and Rule 705. Rule 56(e) requires that affidavits in opposition to summary judgment "must set forth specific facts." Rule 705 permits an expert to state an opinion "and give his

---

[4] In addition to the exchange of information about experts through interrogatories, many courts permit depositions of experts who will be testifying at trial. Reports or summaries of the experts' opinions may be exchanged at the pretrial conference.

[5] Studiengesellschaft Kohle, m.b.H. v. Dart Industries, Inc., 862 F.2d 1564, 1568 (Fed. Cir. 1988) (but nothing in Rule 705 requires trier of fact to credit the testimony of an expert who has not revealed or been asked about the basis underlying the opinion).

reasons therefore without prior disclosure of the underlying facts or data." The court has to reconcile these two rules when the opposition to a motion for summary judgment is based on the affidavit of an expert. A number of courts have held "that Rules 703 and 705 do not alter the requirement of Fed.R.Civ.P. 56(e) that an affidavit must set forth specific facts in order to have any probative value."[6]

Restricting the operation of Rule 705 to the trial context is consistent with the rationale for the rule. It was designed to lead to more effective and efficient trials, and should not be allowed to undermine the efficacy of summary judgment procedures.

¶ 13.06 Court Appointed Experts—Rule 706[1]

Rule 706 authorizes a judge to appoint expert witnesses. It applies in civil and criminal cases. A court would have the right of appointment as part of its general authority to appoint masters, even in the absence of this rule, as a specific instance of a court's inherent power to call witnesses expressed in Rule 614.[2] Rule 706 operates to restrict the judge's common law powers in that subdivision (a) mandates procedures that must be followed. The rule provides:

Rule 706

COURT APPOINTED EXPERTS

(a) Appointment. The court may on its own motion or on the motion of any party enter an order to show cause why expert witnesses should not be appointed, and may request the parties to submit nominations. The court may appoint any expert witnesses agreed upon by the parties, and may appoint expert witnesses of its own selection. An expert witness shall not be appointed by the court unless the witness consents to act.

---

[6] Evers v. General Motors Corp., 770 F.2d 984 (11th Cir. 1985). *Compare* Bulthuis v. Rexall Corp., 789 F.2d 1315, 1318 (9th Cir. 1986) ("Expert opinion is admissible and may defeat summary judgment if it appears the affiant is competent to give an expert opinion and the factual basis for the opinion is stated in the affidavit, even though the underlying factual details and reasoning upon which the material is based are not.").

[1] *See* **Treatise** at ¶¶ 706[01]–[03].

[2] *See* Hart v. Community School Board of Brooklyn, 383 F.Supp. 699 (E.D.N.Y. 1974), *aff'd,* 512 F.2d 37 (2d Cir. 1975) (full discussion of use of masters as experts).

A witness so appointed shall be informed of the witness' duties by the court in writing, a copy of which shall be filed with the clerk, or at a conference in which the parties shall have opportunity to participate. A witness so appointed shall advise the parties of the witness' findings, if any; the witness' deposition may be taken by any party; and the witness may be called to testify by the court or any party. The witness shall be subject to cross-examination by each party, including a party calling the witness.

(b) Compensation. Expert witnesses so appointed are entitled to reasonable compensation in whatever sum the court may allow. The compensation thus fixed is payable from funds which may be provided by law in criminal cases and civil actions and proceedings involving just compensation under the fifth amendment. In other civil actions and proceedings the compensation shall be paid by the parties in such proportion and at such time as the court directs, and thereafter charged in like manner as other costs.

(c) Disclosure of appointment. In the exercise of its discretion, the court may authorize disclosure to the jury of the fact that the court appointed the expert witness.

(d) Parties' experts of own selection. Nothing in this rule limits the parties in calling expert witnesses of their own selection.

¶ 13.06[01]   Rationale

Rule 706 provides an alternative not intended to be used routinely in run-of-the-mill litigation. In some cases it is a useful corrective to the unsatisfactory process of party-controlled expert testimony which often leaves the trier of fact grappling with highly technical, diametrically opposed testimony that it finds exceedingly difficult to evaluate. By summoning its own witness where expert testimony is critical and the parties' experts are at loggerheads, the court seeks to procure a higher caliber and less venal expert, and to assist the court and parties in reaching a settlement, or the jurors in arriving at a justified verdict.

Despite these advantages which may flow from the court's appointment of an expert, judges have not exercised their power to call experts frequently, either pursuant to Rule 706 or under prior practice. Concern that a court expert will "usurp" the jury's function because jurors would defer to a court sponsored witness, the difficulty in finding a neutral expert, problems of cost, and a commitment to adversarial responsibility for presenting evidence are the principal reasons why courts do not appoint experts more often.

Some of the provisions in subdivision (a) of Rule 706 were designed to overcome these objections. The appointment need not be divulged to the jury if the court fears it would be overimpressed by the status of the witness. The judge may ask the parties for their recommendations and act upon them. Since the parties have an absolute right to the expert's report and to call their own witnesses, they are able to cross-examine the expert effectively, thereby satisfying the goals of the adversary system.

¶ 13.06[02] Procedure

Subdivision (a) of Rule 706 provides that before a court-appointed expert can act, there must be (1) a hearing on an order to show cause why the expert should not be appointed, (2) consent by the expert, and (3) the expert must be notified of his or her duties either in writing or at a conference. The subdivision also requires the expert to communicate his or her findings to the parties. While the rule speaks of an expert, the court may appoint more than one expert and, at times, may find a panel or committee useful as an adjunct to the court in its fact-finding role.[3] Because time is needed to comply with these provisions, Rule 706 will ordinarily be invoked considerably before trial,[4] although the rule does not contain any time restrictions. Additional time may also be required if the court exercises its option to request the parties to submit nominations or the parties exercise their right to subject the expert to deposition procedures. The process should be set in motion at a pretrial conference pursuant to Rule 16 of the Federal Rules of Civil Procedure or Rule 17.1 of the Federal Rules of Criminal Procedure.

The trial court has broad discretion to appoint or to refuse to ap-

---

[3] Lora v. Board of Educ. of City of New York, 587 F.Supp 1572 (E.D.N.Y. 1984) (committee of national experts to draft standards for students with emotional problems, used as basis for settlement).

[4] United States v. Weathers, 618 F.2d 663 (10th Cir.), *cert. denied,* 446 U.S. 956 (1980) (expressing serious doubt about whether post-trial employment of psychiatric expert comported with rule; but harmless error).

point an expert.[5] While Rule 706 makes it optional with the court whether to appoint experts on whom the parties agree, in practice, the judge should accede to the parties' wishes to the extent practicable since their agreement reduces the likelihood of the abuses in utilizing Rule 706.

A reluctant witness usually presents too great a hazard to justice. Subdivision (a) therefore provides that an expert appointed pursuant to Rule 706 must consent to act. This provision does not bar the subpoenaing of non-court appointed experts who otherwise would be unwilling to testify.[6]

Rule 706 gives the trial judge the option of informing the expert of his or her duties orally at a conference which the parties attend, or in writing, a copy of which is to be filed with the clerk. A telephone conference will sometimes prove useful. Such a conference may facilitate a settlement, especially if it is held after discovery is complete and the parties know the position of the non-court appointed experts who will testify. The parties' experts may be required to attend so that a joint decision of all experts can limit disagreement and focus the controversy. If the court feels that discussions among all the experts would be fruitful in simplifying or terminating the case, it could ask the non-court appointed experts to attend the con-

---

[5] Georgia-Pacific Corp. v. United States, 640 F.2d 328, 334 (Ct. Cl. 1980)United States v. St. John, 851 F.2d 1096, 1098 (8th Cir. 1988) (discussion of why defendant in child sex abuse prosecution was not entitled to appointment of expert); ("Divergence of opinions among the experts of the parties does not require that the court appoint experts to assist it in resolving such conflicts.").

[6] Kaufman v. Edelstein, 539 F.2d 811, 820 (2d Cir. 1976) ("[T]here is no constitutional or statutory privilege against the compulsion of expert testimony, and we perceive no sufficient basis in principle or precedent for holding that the common law recognizes any general privilege to withhold his expert knowledge." A concurring opinion indicated that this was dictum.). *See* Comment, "Supervisory Mandamus Threatens the Finality Rule—Unequivocal Discretionary Power to Compel Expert Testimony in the District Courts," 43 Bklyn L. Rev. 1149 (1977); Note, "Compelling Experts to Testify: A Proposal," 44 U. of Chi. L. Rev. 851 (1977). *See also* Wright v. Jeep Corp., 547 F.Supp. 871 (E.D. Mich. 1982) (upholding subpoena duces tecum to expert); Fitzpatrick v. Holiday Inns, Inc., 507 F.Supp. 979 (E.D. Pa. 1981) (plaintiff allowed to subpoena expert engaged by defendant whom defendant does not intend to call as witness in order to have him authenticate his report which plaintiff wishes to introduce).

ference.[7]

The conference will also give the parties a foretaste of how the court appointed expert will react to the theories advanced by the parties' experts. For example, if in a personal injury action it becomes evident that the court's medical expert considers plaintiff's theory of causality utterly at odds with reputable medical thought, the parties may be impelled to reach a settlement. Even if no settlement ensues, the conference may be useful in narrowing the issues and resolving what might otherwise be time-consuming disputes at trial about terminology and methodology.

A useful provision in subdivision (a) allows the witness' deposition to be taken by any party. Rule 706 provides the only instance where a deposition may be taken as of right by any party in a criminal case. Rule 706 is silent on what use may be made of the depositions at trial. Presumably the restrictions of Rule 32 of the Federal Rules of Civil Procedure and Rule 15 of the Federal Rules of Criminal Procedure would apply. In a criminal case, the use of a deposition taken by the government may raise as yet unresolved questions on the scope of defendant's rights under the Confrontation Clause of the Sixth Amendment. If the expert is available he should be called as a witness.

Unresolved issues still remain about the interrelationship between Rule 706 and procedural provisions governing examinations by experts. For instance, to what extent, if any, must the limitations and notice provisions of Rule 706 be applied to mental examinations of a criminal defendant ordered pursuant to § 4244 of title 18 or Rule 12.2(c) of the Federal Rules of Criminal Procedure?[8]

Other provisions of Rule 706 should provoke little difficulty. Each party's right to cross-examine is recognized, carrying with it the right to ask leading questions and to develop relevant material beyond the scope of the expert's direct testimony. See Rule 611. This right exists even if a party exercises its right under Rule 706(a) to call the court appointed expert itself. In any event, subdivision (d) states that the

---

[7] *See* United States v. Articles ... Provimi, etc., 74 F.R.D. 126 (D.N.J. 1977) (court advised counsel that it would schedule a conference with the court-appointed expert and counsel and any expert of their own which counsel wished to bring at which the directions to be given the expert would be decided on).

[8] *See* discussion in **Treatise** at ¶ 706[02].

parties' right to call experts of their own choosing is in no way limited by Rule 706.

Subdivision (c) of Rule 706 gives the trial court discretion to authorize disclosure of the expert's status as a court appointed witness to the jury. The trial court may forbid revelation of the expert's role, if, for instance, it discovers after the appointment that two responsible schools of thought do exist on the subject of the expert's testimony and it suspects that divulgence of the expert's status may cause the jury to favor his position. In other cases, not to identify the court appointed expert as such would deprive the jury of information it needs to evaluate the witness' testimony.

¶ 13.06[03]   Compensation

Subdivision (b) of Rule 706 sets forth two different modes of compensation for the court appointed expert. If the expert has been employed in a criminal case or a civil proceeding involving just compensation under the fifth amendment, the judge determines the amount in whatever sum he deems reasonable, and it is payable "from funds which may be provided by law." The Comptroller General has determined that the Department of Justice must pay the expert's compensation.[9] In civil cases, the judge has discretion to tax the expert's compensation against the parties in such proportions as he deems proper.[10] The judge's determination will turn on the nature of the case, why the need for a court appointed expert arose, the status of the parties, and the decision and its consequences.[11] Assessment of

---

[9] Decision of the Comptroller General B-139703 (March 21, 1980) (same rule applies in condemnation cases).

[10] *But cf.* Webster v. Sowders, 846 F.2d 1032, 1038–39 (6th Cir. 1988) (in class civil rights action by inmates for damages resulting from exposure to asbestos, court found that district judge should have made findings of fact and conclusions of law to justify continuing employment of court expert to monitor compliance with asbestos removal regulations, and to support imposition of costs on state where only preliminary injunction had been granted).

[11] United States v. R.J. Reynolds Tobacco Co., 416 F.Supp. 313 (D.N.J. 1976) (United States as plaintiff asserted that no part of fees of court-appointed experts was chargeable to United States; trial court held that United States as plaintiff had no special or different status than any other party and that it would have to comply with court orders for payment). *See also* Leesona Corp. v. Varta Batteries Inc., 522

the cost may be deferred to abide the event of ultimate disposition of the controversy, with one or both sides advancing fees. The provision for compensation in Rule 706(b) makes it clear that court-appointed experts in federal civil cases can realistically expect adequate compensation. That compensation may include reasonable expenses, including costs of testing and acquiring data.

F.Supp. 1304 (S.D.N.Y. 1981) (expert's compensation to be shared equally in patent infringement case).

CHAPTER 14

Hearsay: Definition, Organization and Constitutional Concerns

SYNOPSIS

(Pub.819)

¶ 14.01   Overview of Hearsay

¶ 14.01[01]   The Risks Involved[1]

The Anglo-American tradition has evolved three conditions for testimony which it is assumed will cause witnesses to try their best to be accurate and will expose any inaccuracies in perception, memory or narration, deliberate or otherwise, which nevertheless persist: oath, personal presence at the trial, and cross-examination.

[a]   Oath

While the oath perhaps exerts less influence than formerly when witnesses had a greater fear of divine punishment, it still marks the solemnity of the occasion and paves the way for prosecutions for perjury. See discussion under Rule 603, Chapter 11, *supra.*

[b]   Personal Presence at Trial

It traditionally has been thought that the trier can more accurately evaluate credibility if he can observe the witness' demeanor while he is testifying, though it has proved virtually impossible to articulate what the trier looks for. The requirement of personal presence in a public forum also undoubtedly makes it more difficult to lie against someone, particularly if that person is an accused, present at trial, who is looking the witness "in the eye." The constitutional right of confrontation, discussed below rests in part on this assumption.

[c]   Cross-Examination

While all may not endorse Wigmore's characterization of cross-examination as "beyond doubt the greatest legal engine ever invented for the discovery of truth," all would concur with him in calling it a "vital feature" of the Anglo-American system. Cer-

---

[1] See discussion in **Treatise** at ¶ 800[01].

tainly cross-examination has the potential of shedding light on all the elements of credibility—the witness' perception, memory, accuracy in narration and sincerity. It can expose inconsistencies, incompletenesses, and inaccuracies in the testimony. Anxiety about what cross-examination will reveal probably creates a stimulus to truth-telling even though in practice deliberate perjury is rarely exposed.

The triers are less likely to reach a correct conclusion with respect to the credibility of the observers of the event in question if they cannot observe the declarant making his statement when he is (1) under oath, and the stress of a judicial hearing, (2) being observed by an adverse party, and (3) subject to almost immediate cross-examination to test the various elements of his credibility. The dangers against which the hearsay rule is directed are that evidence which is not subject to these three conditions will be less reliable and less likely to be properly evaluated by the trier because faults—or strengths—in the perception, memory and narration of the declarant will not be exposed.

Despite these hazards of hearsay, all judges and lawyers are aware that the value of a particular out-of-court statement varies from case to case. Some persons speak truthfully and for the most part accurately no matter where they are; others lie or distort or misapprehend even if they are under oath in a courtroom. In between, and probably most typical, is the person whose credibility depends upon the circumstances under which he made the observation attributed to him, those surrounding his statement and those affecting his relationship to the case. Insistence on the exclusion of all evidence which does not meet the three ideal conditions would frequently make it impossible to prove any material proposition of fact and legal relief or a defense would be unobtainable by the party who bears the burden of proof. The loss of relevant evidence increases the likelihood of erroneous determinations. Despite the thousands of pages devoted to proposals for reform of the hearsay rule, no one suggests that a possible solution is to bar all hearsay. Even when hearsay is erroneously admitted, or admitted because no objection is made, verdicts based on such evidence are usually sustained and affirmed if the evidence appears sufficiently reliable or the trier was likely to have evaluated it properly.

¶ 14.01[02]   Design of the Federal Rules[1]

The drafters of the Federal Rules declined to abolish all restrictions on the use of hearsay. They believed that the hearsay rule does serve to exclude evidence too unreliable to be evaluated accurately by the trier of fact. They also concluded, however, that under the traditional scheme, evidence of high probative value is too often excluded. To lessen the possibility of this occurring, a number of changes were made: (1) the definition of hearsay was reworked to exclude from its scope certain types of utterances and conduct that pose few hearsay dangers (see Rule 801(a)–(c)); (2) certain types of highly probative prior statements were defined as not constituting hearsay (see Rule 801(d)(1)); (3) admissions were treated as non-hearsay and expanded to include vicarious, as well as authorized admissions (see Rule 801(d)(2)); and (4) the scope of some of the class exceptions was significantly enlarged (see, *e.g.,* Rule 803(8)—official records and Rule 803(18)—learned treatises). Finally, the basic structure of the hearsay rule was significantly altered. Instead of limiting the doctrine to a statement of the rule and enumerated class exceptions, the drafters added open-ended provisions in Rules 803(24) and 804(b)(5). These permit the admission of trustworthy hearsay that does not fit into a class exception. The operation of these residual, non-class exceptions is discussed after the definition of hearsay, and before the consideration of the class exceptions, so as to serve as a reminder that evidence that is defined as hearsay may nevertheless be admissible even though it does not satisfy a category in Rules 801(d), 803 or 804.

Hearsay which is untrustworthy even though it is not technically excludable under the hearsay rules may be excluded under Rule 403 on grounds of prejudice, confusion or waste of time.[2] The discretionary aspect of admissibility of hearsay is made explicit in a few rules such as 804(b)(3) on statements against interest and Rules 803(24) and 804(b)(5), the open-ended exceptions. Trustworthiness as the touchstone of admissibility is coming to be a central concept of the

---

[1] See discussion in **Treatise** at ¶ 800[02].

[2] But see United States v. DiMaria, 727 F.2d 265, 270–72 (2d Cir. 1984) (reversible error to exclude statement that falls into Rule 803(3) category even if it is of dubious reliability).

Confrontation Clause as interpreted by the Supreme Court, as indicated in the following discussion.

¶ 14.02   The Definition of Hearsay—Rule 801(a)–(c)[1]

Rule 801(c) follows conventional practice in defining hearsay in terms of the use of a statement. Subdivision (c) must, however, be read in conjunction with subdivision (a) which ensures that only statements intended as assertions are included in the hearsay definition. Consequently, evidence of out-of-court conduct—either verbal or non-verbal—does not constitute hearsay if it was (1) not intended as an assertion, *or* (2) if it was so intended, it is not being offered to prove the truth of the matter asserted. Rule 802 provides that evidence that is not excluded from the hearsay definition is inadmissible unless admission is mandated by some provision in the Federal Rules of Evidence themselves, other rules adopted by the Supreme Court pursuant to its rule-making authority, or by Act of Congress.[2]

Subdivisions (a)–(c) of Rule 801 state:

RULE 801

DEFINITIONS

The following definitions apply under this article:

(a) Statement.—A "statement" is (1) an oral or written assertion or (2) nonverbal conduct of a person, if it is intended by the person as an assertion.

(b) Declarant.—A "declarant" is a person who makes a statement.

(c) Hearsay.—"Hearsay" is a statement, other than one made by the

---

[1] See discussion in **Treatise** at ¶¶ 801(a)[01]–[02], 801(c)[01].

[2] Rule 802 provides:

Rule 802

HEARSAY RULE

Hearsay is not admissible except as provided by these rules or by other rules prescribed by the Supreme Court pursuant to statutory authority or by Act of Congress.

See discussion in **Treatise** at ¶¶ 802[01]–[02].

declarant while testifying at the trial or hearing, offered in evidence to prove the truth of the matter asserted.

¶ 14.02[01]   Statement

Subdivision (a) provides that a declarant's out-of-court utterance or conduct does not constitute a "statement" unless it is intended as an assertion. "Assertion" is defined nowhere in the rule. To comprehend the meaning of this term, and why it was inserted into both halves of the definition of "statement," requires some understanding of the history and analytical framework of the hearsay rule.

Most words cause few problems of definition. They obviously constitute a statement—that is they are intended as a communication about the matter sought to be proved. The communicator frames his words deliberately so that the communicant will receive information that the speaker wishes to transmit about an event the speaker observed. This is the testimonial situation. Whether the speaker is to be believed depends upon assessment of the credibility elements: observational capacity and opportunity, memory, veracity and skill in communication. Where the communicant repeats the statement to the trier we have the typical hearsay statement since both the credibility of the witness and of the original communicator, or declarant,[3] must be assessed.

It has never been doubted that some conduct other than verbal is testimonial, the equivalent of a verbal statement in its communicative intent. For instance, when the issue is whether X owed Y money, evidence that X nodded when asked if he was indebted to Y is as much a statement about the obligation as an express oral or written declaration by X acknowledging the debt. Both kinds of conduct are statements under Rule 801(a)(1) because X by either nodding or speaking was intending to make an assertion about the matter in issue. There are a large number of non-verbal signs that are the equivalent of words for purposes of deliberate communication.

But words and actions are not always expressly intended as com-

---

[3] Subdivision (b) provides: "Declarant. A 'declarant' is a person who makes a statement."

municative of the fact in question. Sometimes their relevance to a particular fact depends on drawing an inference that a person would not have spoken or acted in the way sought to be shown unless he believed a relevant proposition of fact to be true. For instance, on the issue of X's sanity, proof that he was elected to a public office is relevant on the theory that a voter would not have voted for X unless he believed him to be sane. At the time of the election, however, the voter (the declarant for hearsay purposes) is not intending to make an assertion about his belief in the candidate's sanity; he is interested in getting him elected. Whether such an implied assertion should be analogized to an express allegation about X's sanity has been the subject of an enormous scholarly debate,[4] although judicial treatment of the problem has remained scant.

The exception to the dearth of judicial attention, and the starting point for all discussions of implied assertions is the famous English case, usually referred to as *Wright v. Doe d. Tatham,*[5] which entailed no less than four separate trials, hundreds of pages of published transcript, numerous appeals, vast amounts of money, and the participation of most of England's high judiciary, before it was finally concluded in 1838. The issue in this will contest was whether the testator was mentally competent at the time he executed his will. If he was, his steward was the principal beneficiary under that will. If he was not, his cousin, who instituted the attack on the will, would inherit as his sole heir-at-law. In order to prove the testator's sanity, several letters were proffered which had been written to the testator by persons now deceased. One, from a cousin, told about his trip to America, another from a vicar dealt with a legal controversy in which the testator was involved, a third from a curate expressed thanks for past favors. The theory underlying their offer was that the writers would not have written in this vein unless they believed the testator to be sane. Baron Parke held

---

[4] See References to Rule 801(a) in **Treatise.**

[5] The official captions and citations are as follows: Tatham v. Wright, 2 Russ. & M. 1, 39 Eng. R. 295 (1830, 1831) (first trial and subsequent motions); Wright v. Doe d. Tatham, 1 Ad. & El. 3, 110 Eng. Rep. 1108 (1833, 1834) (second trial and subsequent appellate stage); Wright v. Doe d. Tatham, 7 Ad. & El. 313, 112 Eng. R. 488 (1834, 1836, 1837) (third and fourth trials and subsequent appellate stages); Wright v. Doe d. Tatham, 5 Cl. & Fin. 670, 7 Eng. R. 559 (1838) (final appellate stage in House of Lords).

that receipt of the letters was barred by the rule against hearsay because the admissibility of evidence of the letter writers' conduct should stand on the same basis as an explicit declaration by them that the testator was sane. Additional instances were suggested by the *Tatham* judges as examples of implied assertions that would be barred by the hearsay rule: (1) proof that underwriters paid the amount of the policy, as evidence of the loss of the insured ship; (2) proof of payment of a wager, as evidence of the happening of the event which was the subject of the bet; (3) precautions of the family to show the person involved was a lunatic; (4) on the question of seaworthiness, proof that the deceased captain, after examining every part of the vessel, embarked on her with his family.[6] Implicit in the Tatham approach is the underlying assumption that express and implied assertions pose the same hearsay dangers.

By the time the federal rules were being drafted, this basic assumption was being questioned. Two principal arguments were made in support of removing implied assertions from the scope of the hearsay rule. First, when a person acts in a way consistent with a belief but without intending by the act to communicate that belief, the declarant's sincerity is not implicated, and consequently it does not matter that the declarant's veracity will not be tested by cross-examination. In the second place, the underlying belief is in some instances self-verifying because the declarant has acted on his belief, as in the case of the ship captain who takes his family on board after inspecting the vessel. The drafters of the Federal Rules of Evidence agreed with this analysis. By defining statement in terms of "assertion," they removed from the coverage of the hearsay rule all verbal or non-verbal out of-court conduct that was not intended by the declarant as a communication about the matter sought to be proved.

The innovation in Rule 801(a) does not mean that all conduct— other than that obviously equivalent to words like pointing, nodding, or sign language—is removed from the hearsay classification. According to the rule, the conduct still must be treated as hearsay if it was intended as an assertion of the matter sought to be proved.[7] Pursuant to Rule 104(a), the court makes this determination in ascertaining admissibility.

---

[6] Wright v. Doe d. Tatham, 7 Ad. & El. 313, 386–89, 112 Eng. R. 488, 515–17.

[7] See, *e.g.*, United States v. Barash, 365 F.2d 395, 399 (2d Cir. 1966), *cert. de-*

Ascertaining the declarant's intent may often prove difficult. In making determinations about borderline hearsay, the court must keep in mind that the drafters removed implied assertions from the coverage of the hearsay rule because they believed that hearsay dangers were minimal. The court should analyze the proffered evidence to see whether there is a substantial risk of placing unreliable evidence before the trier of fact.

For example, in a prosecution for illegal bookmaking the court should admit evidence that the agents conducting a search of the gambling premises received a number of telephone calls seeking to place bets while they were searching the premises.[8] Allowing this evidence to be used to show that the callers believed that the premises were used for gambling, the fact in issue, does pose dangers of insincerity. Yet, the declarants were calling to place bets and not to convey to the police the proposition that the premises were used for gambling.[9] Of course, the defendants would not have placed bets unless they believed that they were calling a bookmaking operation, and there is objective verification of this conclusion because the declarants had paid the price of a phone call to act on their belief.

Other cases are more difficult. For instance, in *United States v. Oaxaca*,[10] the court held that photographs of an FBI agent wearing defendant's clothing which were admitted for purposes of comparison with bank surveillance photographs did not constitute hearsay. The photographs are, however, the equivalent of a state-

---

nied, 396 U.S. 832 (1969) (statement by witness that he had expected pay-off because defendant had been introduced to him by a fellow employee who "never introduced me to anyone except someone who was going to pay me off"; introduction by fellow employee is irrelevant unless it is intended as an assertion, and would therefore constitute hearsay under Rule 801(a)).

[8] See, *e.g.*, United States v. Zenni, 492 F. Supp. 464 (E.D. Ky. 1980).

[9] See also United States v. Hensel, 699 F.2d 18, 34–35 (1st Cir.), *cert. denied*, 461 U.S. 958 (1983) (to show defendants' participation in conspiracy evidence was introduced that when arrested conspirator was in possession of list containing names of three defendants; court found that possession of list could not have been intended as an assertion about defendant's role "unless Duke had been staging an elaborate charade to implicate the defendants. If defendants believed that to be the case, however, they bore the burden of proving that the conduct was indeed intended as an assertion, . . . and they offered no such proof.").

[10] 560 F.2d 518, 525 (9th Cir. 1978).

ment by the agent giving an opinion of what was worn at a critical time which may in part be based on what other witnesses told him. It is less clear than in the gambling situation that cross-examination is not needed to explore the declarant's sincerity. Admission of the photographs may still be warranted because of the rules' preference for the admission of indirect hearsay, but the jurors should be warned about the hearsay dangers present.

¶ 14.02[02]   To Prove the Truth of the Matter Asserted

A second major category of statements is excluded from the scope of the hearsay rule by the definition of hearsay in subdivision (c) of Rule 801 which excludes assertive verbal or non-verbal conduct when it is offered as a basis for inferring something other than the matter asserted. Utterances may be offered for a variety of reasons not entailing their truth; when they are, there is no need to assess the credibility of the declarant because the value of the utterance does not depend on whether it is true. Three of the more common categories of non-hearsay are verbal acts, parts of verbal acts, and utterances offered to show their effect on the hearer. Implied assertions, discussed below, also fall outside the hearsay definition.

The term "verbal act" is applied when the utterance is an operative fact that gives rise to legal consequences. The fact that the words were spoken (or written) is significant regardless of their truth.[11] Examples are evidence of the utterance of words constituting a contract, or a defamatory statement,[12] or a threat,[13] or a misrepresentation,[14] or the giving of notice.[15] When non-verbal

---

[11] Tennessee v. Street, 471 U.S. 409, 105 S.Ct. 2078, 85 L.Ed.2d 425 (1985) (where defendant claimed that his confession was a coerced imitation of confession previously given by accomplice, accomplice's confession was properly admitted for the nonhearsay purpose of allowing the jurors to compare the differences in the confessions).

[12] Luster v. Retail Credit Co., 575 F.2d 609 (8th Cir. 1978).

[13] United States v. Jones, 663 F.2d 567 (5th Cir. 1981) (threats to judge).

[14] United States v. Wellington, 754 F.2d 1457, 1464 (9th Cir. 1985), *cert. denied*, 106 S.Ct. 592 (1985) (false representations to potential investors).

[15] *In re* Fidelity America Mortgage Co., 15 B.R. 622, 623 (Bankr. E.D. Pa. 1981) (notice of default).

conduct is ambiguous, the accompanying verbal conduct that characterizes and defines the transaction is not hearsay.[16] The utterance then is merely the *verbal part of the act*. For instance, when a person transfers money to another, the accompanying words he uses determine whether the transaction will be characterized as a gift, a loan, or the repayment of a debt, regardless of the intent of the speaker. This situation must be differentiated from the case where words which clarify an ambiguous situation are relevant only because they are offered for their truth.[17] In such a case, the words constitute hearsay.

When relevant, an utterance or a writing may be admitted to show the *effect on the hearer* or reader. The statement will be used to prove such states of mind as knowledge,[18] motive,[19] fear,[20] or

---

[16] United States v. Romano, 684 F.2d 1057, 1066 (2d Cir.), *cert. denied,* 459 U.S. 1016 (1982) (evidence of requests to give money to the "boys in the union" admissible as utterances contemporaneous with independently admissible non-verbal act of picking up the money); United States v. Jackson, 588 F.2d 1046, 1049 n.4 (5th Cir.), *cert. denied,* 442 U.S. 941 (1979) (witness, considered by prosecution to be innocent participant in heroin distribution scheme, permitted to testify that stranger came to her apartment in Los Angeles with airfare for Birmingham, and small canvas bag to take with her, and told her that defendant would pick her up; court classified statements of stranger as non-hearsay statements under Rule 801(c), *i.e.* utterances made contemporaneously with a non-verbal act for the purpose of throwing light on it).

[17] See, *e.g.,* Flores v. United States, 551 F.2d 1169 (9th Cir. 1977) (letters from bank stating that money which had been seized by Internal Revenue Service constituted a loan from the bank to the taxpayer were hearsay; could not be used for their testimonial value).

[18] See United States v. Tamura, 694 F.2d 591, 598 (9th Cir. 1982) (where defendant in bribery prosecution claimed that he unwittingly carried out instructions of his superiors, telexes setting forth details of bribery scheme were properly admitted for the non-hearsay purpose of showing his knowledge where he had testified that he routinely read telexes); United States v. Jackson, 621 F.2d 216, 219 (5th Cir. 1980) (in prosecution of bank president for making alleged false entry as to purpose of loan, conversation in which defendant was told purpose of loan should not have been excluded as hearsay since it was offered to establish defendant's lack of knowledge that entry was false); United States v. Sackett, 598 F.2d 739, 742 (2d Cir. 1979) (in prosecution for obtaining loan by making false statements where loan application was made on behalf of defendant's mother, government sought to show that defendant obtained life insurance on mother's life as part of loan without medical examination at time he knew she was dying; hospital record of mother stating that family felt she was probably pre-terminal was properly ad-

reasonableness[21] on the part of the recipient. The hearsay rule does not apply because the utterance is not being offered to prove the truth or falsity of the matter asserted. For example, when plaintiff in a products liability action alleges that defendant failed in its duty to warn, evidence that the defendant received a complaint about the product may be admitted, not as proof of a defect, but to show that the recipient was on notice that the product might be injurious.[22] Or, an accused may proffer statements consistent with good faith on his part to rebut the inference of criminal intent which might otherwise be drawn from his actions.[23]

Because of the definition in subdivision (c), *implied assertions,* that is, statements offered to show the state of mind of the declarant, are not analytically hearsay since they are not directly assertive of the state of mind in issue.[24] When a statement such as "I am

---

mitted as non-hearsay not to show that she was dying but that the family thought she was).

[19] United States v. Reed, 639 F.2d 896, 907 (2d Cir. 1981) (letter to defendant from bank indicating he was in serious financial difficulty not hearsay where offered to show defendant believed he was in such difficulty and thus had a reason for participating in unlawful scheme).

[20] United States v. Lynn, 608 F.2d 132, 135 (5th Cir. 1979) (in extortion case, testimony as to what was said to victim to produce fear not hearsay).

[21] Callon Petroleum Co. v. Big Chief Drilling Co., 548 F.2d 1174 (5th Cir. 1977) (where plaintiff oil company claimed that drilling company moved site location for its own advantage, conversations between representative of driller and contractor hired by oil company indicating that oil company consented to move were properly admitted as non-hearsay to explain the driller's course of conduct). In homicide or assault cases where accused claims self-defense, accused should be allowed to introduce evidence of communicated threats as bearing on the reasonableness of his belief that his alleged victim intended to carry out the threat).

[22] See, *e.g.,* Worsham v. A.H. Robins Co., 734 F.2d 676, 687 (11th Cir. 1984).

[23] United States v. Leake, 642 F.2d 715, 720 (4th Cir. 1981) (in prosecution involving misappropriation of federal funds, held, prejudicial error to exclude defendant's proffered evidence recounting a statement made to him, offered to show he believed funds were being used legitimately; statement served as circumstantial evidence of defendant's state of mind and would have been evidence negating his specific intent to aid and abet illegal payment).

[24] United States v. Bobo, 586 F.2d 355, 371–77 (5th Cir. 1978), *cert. denied,* 440 U.S. 976 (1979) (in narcotics conspiracy trial, prosecution witness' testimony that ringleader had told him that defendant had been arrested on drug charge and that search warrant presented by arresting officer stated that he had been told by reliable informant that defendant was carrying drugs did not constitute hearsay;

Napoleon" is being offered to prove that the declarant is mentally abnormal, the statement is not being offered for its truth. There may, however, be a genuine issue as to whether the declarant is feigning insanity.

The chief rationale offered for the hearsay rule is the need to test out-of-court statements by cross-examination in order to assess the credibility of the declarant. Rather than focusing on the technical question of whether a given statement lies outside the hearsay rule's scope or qualifies as an exception, it is more often fruitful to concentrate on the hearsay dangers posed, and on whether admission of the statement would satisfy the policies underlying the rule.[25] The central question is whether the trier of fact will accurately evaluate the probative force of the out-of-court statement. This approach is the basis for admitting hearsay bearing guarantees of trustworthiness (pursuant to the residual exceptions in Rules 803(24) and 804(b)(5)).[26]

In many instances a declaration may have both a hearsay and a non-hearsay use. The court, when requested, should explain why the declaration is usable for only limited purposes (pursuant to Rule 105 on limited admissibility). Total exclusion may be justified if it is unlikely that the jury will use the evidence only for non-hearsay purposes (pursuant to Rule 403). In general, it has been our experience that jurors can and will respond to instructions on lim-

---

statement was not admitted for truth of whether defendant had actually been arrested but to show ringleader's state of mind; it indicates that he was concerned about existence of informers which tended to prove the existence of a conspiracy).

[25] See Park v. Huff, 493 F.2d 923, 927–28 (5th Cir. 1974), *cert. denied,* 423 U.S. 824 (1975) (habeas corpus review of murder conviction; witness testified that he was warned by third party that if witness did not go through with killing, defendant would have something done to his family; while out-of-court statement of defendant was not being offered to prove the truth of the matter asserted—that something would be done to witness' family—it clearly implied that defendant was involved in murder conspiracy, and the truth of the implication depended on the credibility and the trustworthiness of a declarant not subject to cross-examination; consequently the hearsay dangers of insincerity or untrustworthiness were as great in this case of an implied assertion as if there had been a direct assertion and the statement had to be classified as hearsay).

[26] See detailed analysis in United States v. Muscato, 534 F.Supp. 969 (E.D.N.Y. 1982).

ited admissibility). Total exclusion may be justified if it is unlikely that the jury will use the evidence only for non-hearsay purposes (pursuant to Rule 403). In general, it has been our experience that jurors can and will respond to instructions on limited admissibility or to the need to carefully evaluate hearsay dangers, if the court explains its ruling in a way that makes it appear reasonable.

¶ 14.03   The Confrontation Clause[1]

The Confrontation Clause of the Sixth Amendment provides "that in all criminal prosecutions, the accused shall enjoy the right . . . to be confronted with the witnesses against him." Taken literally this clause could mean that no evidence falling within a hearsay exception may be admitted against an accused unless the declarant is available to testify, or that no extra-judicial statements may be admitted unless an opportunity for cross-examination has been afforded. At no time, however, has either personal presence of the witness or cross-examination been insisted upon as indispensible.[2] At its narrowest, the provision could also mean only that the defendant has a constitutional right to cross-examine those witnesses who actually testify against him at trial, so that the Confrontation Clause and the hearsay rule are simultaneously satisfied when evidence is admitted pursuant to a hearsay exception although the declarant does not testify. This theory, however, has been expressly rejected by the Supreme Court, which has on numerous occasions repudiated the notion that the hearsay rule and the right to confrontation are fully congruent, although the Court concedes that both protect similar values.[3]

---

[1] See discussion in **Treatise** at ¶ 800[04].

[2] See Mattox v. United States, 156 U.S. 237 (1895) (Court admitted the former testimony of a now unavailable witness and pointed out that a dying declaration, as to which there could never have been cross-examination, could also meet Confrontation Clause challenge). In United States v. Inadi, — U.S. —, 106 S.Ct. 1121, 89 L.Ed.2d 251 (1986), the majority held that the Confrontation Clause does not require unavailability to be demonstrated before a co-conspirator's statement may be introduced).

[3] United States v. Inadi, 106 S.Ct. 1121, 1125–26, n.5 ("overlap is not complete"); California v. Green, 399 U.S. 149, 155, 90 S.Ct. 1930, 26 L.Ed.2d 489 (1970) ("While it may readily be conceded that hearsay rules and the Confrontation Clause

What then does the Confrontation Clause mean? As recently as 1986, the Supreme Court "disclaimed any intention of proposing a general answer to the many difficult questions arising out of the relationship between the Confrontation Clause and hearsay."[4] Taken together, however, the latest Supreme Court pronouncements on the Confrontation Clause in *United States v. Inadi,*[5] *Bourjaily v. United States,*[6] and *United States v. Owens,*[7] which are discussed below, suggest that the Sixth Amendment will not operate independently to exclude evidence permitted under the hearsay rules except in rare instances where the confrontation issue has placed the defendant at a severe disadvantage in challenging the apparent probative force of the hearsay declaration. Despite the Court's insistence on noncongruence between the hearsay rules and the Confrontation Clause, evidence that is admissible pursuant to Rules 801, 803 or 804 of the Federal Rules of Evidence will in virtually every instance automatically satisfy the Confrontation Clause. Extreme cases, as for example, where the prosecution hides a witness to take advantage of hearsay rules could, of course, still bring into play due process as well as confrontation rights.

The hearsay rules in Article VIII of the Federal Rules of Evidence are extremely liberal in admitting evidence and have been so construed by the courts over the past decade. The Supreme Court's in-

---

are generally designed to protect similar values, it is quite a different thing to suggest that the overlap is complete and that the Confrontation Clause is nothing more or less than a codification of the rules of hearsay and their exceptions as they existed historically at common law."); Dutton v. Evans, 400 U.S. 74, 86, 91 S.Ct. 210, 27 L.Ed.2d 213 (1970) ("It seems apparent that the Sixth Amendment's Confrontation Clause and the evidentiary hearsay rule stem from the same roots. But this Court has never equated the two, and we decline to do so now."). See also, Lee v. Illinois, — U.S. —, 106 S.Ct. 2056, 2064, n.5, 90 L.Ed.2d 514 (1986) ("[W]e reject respondent's categorization of the hearsay involved in this case as a simple 'declaration against penal interest.' That concept defines too large a class for meaningful Confrontation Clause analysis."). The Court has held that the nonhearsay use of an out-of-court statement does not implicate the Confrontation Clause. Tennessee v. Street, 471 U.S. 409, 105 S.Ct. 2078, 85 L.Ed.2d 425 (1985).

[4] United States v. Inadi, 106 S.Ct. 1121, 1125 (1986) (Court was referring to its decision in Ohio v. Roberts, 448 U.S. 56, 100 S.Ct. 2531, 65 L.Ed.2d 597 (1980)).

[5] 475 U.S. 387, 106 S.Ct. 1121, 89 L.Ed.2d 390 (1986).

[6] 483 U.S. —, 107 S.Ct. 2775, 97 L.Ed.2d 144 (1987).

[7] 484 U.S. —, 108 S.Ct. 838, 98 L.Ed.2d 951 (1988).

creasing synchronization of hearsay and confrontation puts greater pressure on the trial court to exclude prejudicial evidence pursuant to Rule 403. The tests in the hearsay articles and Rule 403 are completely independent. Because hearsay evidence is difficult for a jury to assess, the trial judge should make a point of identifying the hearsay that has been admitted and of instructing the jurors on why they should be especially skeptical and careful in evaluating such evidence.

The interaction between the hearsay rule and the Confrontation Clause is most easily seen by viewing the Supreme Court's decisions in the context of the organization of hearsay in the Federal Rules of Evidence: (1) declarant testifying and subject to cross examination (Rule 801(d)(1)); (2) declarant's availability immaterial (Rule 803 and Rule 801(d)(2)(C)–(E)); (3) declarant must be unavailable (Rule 804).

¶ 14.03[01] Declarant Testifying and Subject to Cross-Examination

When the declarant is present at trial, under oath, and subject to cross-examination about his extra-judicial statement, the statement is not hearsay if the other requirements of Rule 801(d)(1) are met. See discussion in Chapter 15. According to *California v. Green,*[1] and *United States v. Owens,*[2] the Confrontation Clause is satisfied as well.

In *Green,* the majority phrased the applicable constitutional test as "whether subsequent cross-examination at the defendant's trial will still afford the trier of fact a satisfactory basis for evaluating the truth of the prior statement."[3] It reserved decision on whether a declarant's lack of memory of the underlying event so affects the defendant's right to cross-examine as to impair his right to confrontation.[4]

---

[1] 399 U.S. 149, 90 S.Ct. 1930, 26 L.Ed.2d 489 (1970).

[2] — U.S. —, 108 S.Ct. 838, 98 L.Ed.2d 951 (1988).

[3] *Id.* at 161.

[4] *Id.* at 168–69. *Cf.* Delaware v. Fensterer, — U.S. —, 106 S.Ct. 292, 88 L.Ed.2d 15 (1985) (per curiam) (in murder prosecution, no violation of Confrontation Clause where expert testified that hair on murder weapon was similar to the victim's hair and had been forcibly removed, and admitted that he could no longer recall the

In 1988, however, in *United States v. Owens*,[5] the Supreme Court resolved this issue by holding that the Confrontation Clause is satisfied by the production of the declarant rather than by effective cross-examination.[6] So long as the declarant takes the witness stand and is subject to unrestricted cross-examination, his or her inability to remember giving the prior statement or to recall the underlying event has no Sixth Amendment consequences. Since "afford[ing] the trier of fact a satisfactory basis for evaluating the truth of the prior statement"[7] has been rejected as the constitutional test, it also follows that no constitutional rights of the defendant are violated when a declarant denies the underlying event without giving any details that can be questioned by cross-examination. According to the majority of the Court, the inability through cross-examination to ascertain the basis for the declarant's present belief does not amount to a denial of the constitutionally requisite *opportunity* for cross-examination. The defendant's remedy, which satisfies constitutional requirements, is the opportunity to impeach the declarant on the witness stand by bringing out such matters as the fact that he or she is biased, or has a bad memory, or poor eyesight or is inattentive.[8] The Court explicitly noted that the testimony need not be examined for "indicia of reli-

---

basis for his opinion; Court noted that trial court did not limit scope or nature of defense counsel's cross-examination, and that the defense was able to suggest to the jury through its own expert witness that the prosecution witness had relied on a theory which the defense witness considered to be baseless; Court again reserved decision on whether there are circumstances in which a witness' inability to recall would so frustrate the opportunity for cross-examination as to violate the Confrontation Clause).

[5] 484 U.S. —, 108 S.Ct. 838, 98 L.Ed.2d 951 (1988) (the declarant Foster, a correctional counselor at a federal prison, had identified the defendant as his assailant to an FBI agent who interviewed Foster while he was hospitalized with severe head injuries; at trial, Foster remembered identifying the defendant, but could not remember seeing his assailant, and could not remember who, other than the FBI agent, had visited him in the hospital).

[6] The Court explicitly adopted the reasoning of Justice Harlan concurring in *California v. Green*. Justice Harlan repudiated this approach in Dutton v. Evans, 400 U.S. 74, 94, 91 S.Ct. 210, 222, 27 L.Ed.2d 213 (1970).

[7] See note 3, *supra.*

[8] United States v. Owens, 484 U.S. —, 108 S.Ct. 838, 842, 98 L.Ed.2d 951, 958 (1988).

ability" or "particularized guarantees of trustworthiness," [9] factors which the Court had previously stressed when ruling on other categories of hearsay discussed below.

The Court in *Owens* rests its ruling on an interpretation of the language of Rules 801(d)(1)(C) and 802. While supportable on this ground, there is no analysis of the problem of the cross-examiner who meets the solid barrier of "I don't remember anything of the event or the statement." This kind of practical problem must be evaluated by the trial court pursuant to Rule 403 to determine whether the jury is in a position to evaluate effectively the hearsay's probative force. The appealing circumstances of the hearsay declarant in *Owens* made overvaluation of the hearsay by jurors likely.

¶ 14.03[02]   Declarant's Availability Immaterial

In *United States v. Inadi,*[1] a majority of the Supreme Court refused to require the prosecution to show that a nontestifying co-conspirator is unavailable to testify, as a condition for admission of the declarant's statements under the co-conspirator exception. The analysis of the Court in rejecting an unavailability requirement would seemingly extend to the specific Rule 803 exceptions as well.[2]

In *Inadi,* the majority noted that reliability of the out-of-court statement was not at issue, and the dissent concluded that defendant "is thus free to return to the Court of Appeals and argue that the

---

[9] *Id.* at —, 108 S.Ct. at 843, 98 L.Ed.2d at 958.

[1] 106 S.Ct. 1121, 89 L.Ed.2d 251 (1986).

[2] The Court differentiated co-conspirators' statements from former testimony (which requires a showing of unavailability) on the ground that former testimony is a weaker version of live testimony while co-conspirator statements cannot be replicated, "even if the declarant testifies to the same matters in court . . . [because they] derive much of their value from the fact that they are made in a context very different from trial, and therefore are usually irreplaceable as substantive evidence."*Id.* at 1126–27. The same could certainly be said of the most frequently used Rule 803 exceptions. Subdivisions (1)–(4) deal with spontaneous statements, subdivision (5) authorizes the admission of statements which declarant could not make at trial because of a lack of memory, and subdivisions (6)–(10) govern statements made in the course of employment that frequently could not be duplicated in court because of the passage of time and the lack of independent recollection by all the persons in the chain creating the record.

co-conspirator declarations admitted against him lack the 'indicia of reliability' demanded by the Confrontation Clause."[3] The Court returned to this issue in *Bourjaily v. United States*[4] and held that a statement admitted under the co-conspirator exemption in Rule 801(d)(2)(E) automatically satisfies Sixth Amendment reliability requirements. Since, as discussed below, the admissibility of co-conspirators' declarations is generally seen to rest on an agency rationale rather than on considerations of trustworthiness,[5] the holding in *Bourjaily* suggests that statements admitted pursuant to the Rule 803 exceptions, which all hinge on reliability, would automatically satisfy the Confrontation Clause.[6] The need for such statements is much less, however, than in the case of Rule 804 exceptions grounded on the unavailability of the declarant.[7] Accordingly, a particularized showing of reliability should be required.[8]

The opinion in *Dutton v. Evans*[9] is the only opinion to date in which the Supreme Court analyzed indicia of reliability in a case where the prosecution failed to produce the declarant for cross-examination or to show why he was unavailable. In analyzing the co-conspirator's statement in question, the four-man plurality pointed to the fact that it was spontaneous, that it was against the declar-

---

[3] *Id.* at 1129.

[4] — U.S. —, 107 S.Ct. 2775, 97 L.Ed.2d 144 (1987).

[5] This was the position of the dissent in *Bourjaily, id.* at —, 107 S.Ct. at 2785, 97 L.Ed.2d at 161 (1987) (citing **Treatise**).

[6] Puleio v. Vose, 830 F.2d 1197, 1207 (1st Cir. 1987) (habeas corpus review; under principles of *Bourjaily* and *Roberts,* an excited utterance is a firmly rooted hearsay exception that obviates the need for a separate assessment of indicia of reliability).

[7] See discussion below of *Lee v. Illinois* in which a bare majority held in a case not involving the Federal Rules of Evidence that a declaration against penal interest does not automatically possess adequate indicia of reliability.

[8] In Ohio v. Roberts, 448 U.S. 56, 66, 100 S.Ct. 2531, 65 L.Ed.2d 597 (1980), the Court, speaking of a declarant not present at trial, noted that usually a showing of unavailability is required and that, in addition, indicia of reliability must be shown, but that "[r]eliability can be inferred without more in a case where the evidence falls within a firmly rooted hearsay exception." *Inadi* and Lee v. Illinois, — U.S. —, 106 S.Ct. 2056, 90 L.Ed.2d 514 (1986), appear to limit *Roberts* to situations where the declarant is required to be unavailable, or is in fact unavailable, so that "the firmly rooted hearsay exception" language may be inapplicable in a Rule 803 situation.

[9] 400 U.S. 74, 91 S.Ct. 210, 27 L.Ed.2d 213 (1970).

ant's penal interest, that it was corroborated, that it was unlikely to have been based on faulty memory, and that it "contained no express assertion about past fact."[10] The plurality also suggested that in addition to reliability, the court must consider the conduct of the prosecution and the significance of the evidence in the setting of the case when determining whether production of the declarant should be excused.[11] Whether the declarant must be produced when the evidence is crucial even though indicia of reliability are present has not yet been decided. This is, however, the situation par excellence where the right to confrontation should prevail if confrontation is viewed as a prophylactic rule.

¶ 14.03[03]   Declarant Must Be Unavailable

At this time it is not clear to what extent the Supreme Court would be willing to hold that any statement that satisfies Federal Rule 804 also satisfies the Confrontation Clause. Though it has found that former testimony and dying declarations which were admitted pursuant to state evidentiary law satisfy the Confrontation Clause,[1] in *Lee v. Illinois*[2] five members of the Court refused to approve admission of a statement against penal interest[3] where indicia of reliability had

---

[10] *Id.* at 88. Critics of the plurality's analysis point to the ambiguity of the statement, "If it hadn't been for that dirty son-of-a-bitch Alex Evans, we wouldn't be in this now." *Id.* at 77, in the context of a case in which the defense had offered evidence that the murder prosecution may have been instituted because of enmity stirred up by Evans. Furthermore, a concurring opinion found harmless error because it doubted whether a reasonable jury would believe that the statement had ever been made. *Id.* at 91.

[11] "This case does not involve evidence in any sense 'crucial' or devastating . . . . It does not involve the use, or misuse, of a confession made in the coercive atmosphere of official interrogation. . . . It does not involve any suggestion of prosecutorial misconduct or even negligence . . . ." *Id.* at 87.

[1] Ohio v. Roberts, 448 U.S. 56, 100 S.Ct. 2531, 65 L.Ed.2d 597 (1980) (former testimony); Mattox v. United States, 156 U.S. 237, 15 S.Ct. 337, 39 L.Ed. 409 (1895) (dying declarations).

[2] — U.S. —, 106 S.Ct. 2056, 90 L.Ed.2d 514 (1986).

[3] The majority refused to characterize the hearsay involved as a "simple 'declaration against penal interest.' That concept defines too large a class for meaningful Confrontation Clause analysis. We decide this case as involving a confession by an accomplice which incriminates a criminal defendant." *Id.* at 2064 n.5.

not been demonstrated by the prosecution. The statement in question was an in custody confession to the police by an accomplice in a murder case inculpating the defendant. The admissibility of the statement as a matter of Illinois evidentiary law was, of course, not before the Court. Had the statement been offered in a federal prosecution, the Court could have dealt with the issue in evidentiary terms. If it then held, as some lower federal courts do,[4] that an inculpatory, in custody confession is not against penal interest in the absence of special guarantees of trustworthiness, the majority in *Lee* might be willing to adopt the view, apparently acceptable to the dissenters,[5] that any hearsay statement admitted pursuant to a class exception[6] in the Federal Rules of Evidence satisfies the Confrontation Clause if the declarant is unavailable.

Until such time as the Court considers a declaration against interest in a federal case, or until such time as the majority in *Lee* changes, Rule 804(b)(3) statements will have to be scrutinized on a case by case basis to see if they are sufficiently reliable to withstand Confrontation Clause challenge. The majority is apparently unwilling at this time to hold that in custody confessions can never satisfy constitutional requirements.[7] Except on the most extraordinarily clear showing of reliability and need, allowing confessions over confrontation

---

[4] See discussion, *infra,* of declarations against penal interest.

[5] "[S]tatements squarely within established hearsay exceptions possess the 'imprimatur of judicial and legislative experience' . . . and that fact must weigh heavily in our assessment of their reliability for constitutional purposes." Lee v. Illinois, — U.S. —, 106 S.Ct. 2056, 2068, 90 L.Ed.2d 514 (1986).

[6] Whether evidence that is admitted pursuant to the residual hearsay exception in Rule 804(b)(5) automatically satisfies the Confrontation Clause as well is more problematic because the factors of reliability in each case have not been developed through legislative or judicial experience. See United States v. Woolbright, 831 F.2d 1390, 1397 (8th Cir. 1987) (court declines to decide whether statement satisfying Rule 804(b)(5) would always satisfy Confrontation Clause requirements, but finds requisite indicia of reliability in instant case).

[7] See New Mexico v. Earnest, 106 S.Ct. 3332 (1986) (per curiam) (state court had excluded accomplice's in custody confession, that apparently was the only evidence against the defendant, on the ground that such confessions had to be excluded on the authority of Douglas v. Alabama, 380 U.S. 415, 85 S.Ct. 1074, 13 L.Ed.2d 934 (1965); Court remanded on authority of *Lee*).

objections runs counter to long held assumptions of the profession.[8]

The Court may also draw a distinction between the different types of hearsay exceptions insofar as proving unavailability is concerned. In *Ohio v. Roberts,*[9] where the preliminary hearing testimony was highly reliable, having been subjected to the equivalent of cross-examination, the Court sanctioned its admission, even though the prosecution did not pursue all possible leads to determine the whereabouts of the now absent witness.

¶ 14.04   Residual Hearsay Exceptions—Rules 803(24) and 804(b)(5)[1]

Rules 803(24) and 804(b)(5), the residual hearsay exceptions, were designed to ensure flexibility in the application of the hearsay rule. By building a situation-specific non-class exception into the two rules that set forth the hearsay exceptions, the drafters recognized that detailed rules cannot anticipate every contingency, and that in a particular case, hearsay evidence that does not fall within one of the exceptions may have greater probative value than evidence that does.

Rule 804(b)(5) differs from Rule 803(24) in that it can be utilized only when the declarant is unavailable. In language and purpose, the two rules are identical, although Rule 804(b)(5) will apply more frequently, for only when cross-examination would not enhance the reliability of the evidence, or the guarantees of trustworthiness are inordinately high, should hearsay be admitted pursuant to Rule 803(24) when the declarant is available but does not appear as a witness.[2]

---

[8] Bruton v. United States, 391 U.S. 123, 88 S.Ct. 1620, 20 L.Ed.2d 476 (1968) suggests the court's skepticism about the jury's ability to properly evaluate a confession of a third party as hearsay. In Cruz v. New York, — U.S. —, —, 107 S.Ct. 1714, 1719, 95 L.Ed.2d 162, 172 (1987), the Court in rejecting an "interlocking confession" exception to *Bruton,* acknowledged that a statement of a co-defendant might be admissible directly against the defendant, in which case there is no *Bruton* issue. See discussion in Chapter 3 and **Treatise** at ¶ 105[04].

[9] 448 U.S. 56, 100 S.Ct. 2531, 65 L.Ed.2d 597 (1980).

[1] See discussion in **Treatise** at ¶¶ 803(24)[01], 804(b)(5)[01].

[2] United States v. Renville, 779 F.2d 430, 440 (8th Cir. 1985) (in finding that statement was properly admitted pursuant to Rule 803(24), court stressed fact that declarant testified).

Rule 803(24) and Rule 804(b)(5) each state:

Other exceptions. A statement not specifically covered by any of the fore-going exceptions but having equivalent circumstantial guarantees of trustworthiness, if the court determines that (A) the statement is offered as evidence of a material fact; (B) the statement is more probative on the point for which it is offered than any other evidence which the proponent can procure through reasonable efforts; and (C) the general purposes of these rules and the interests of justice will best be served by admission of the statement into evidence. However, a statement may not be admitted under this exception unless the proponent of it makes known to the adverse party sufficiently in advance of the trial or hearing to provide the adverse party with a fair opportunity to prepare to meet it, the proponent's intention to offer the statement and the particulars of it, including the name and address of the declarant.

The residual exceptions require five findings by the trial court, which should be made on the record, unless there is an explicit waiver, or the basis for the ruling is obvious.

¶ 14.04[01]   Circumstantial Guarantees of Trustworthiness

The statement must have circumstantial guarantees of trustworthiness equivalent to the other exceptions in either Rules 803 or

(*Text continued on page 14–23*)

804. Since, on the whole, Rule 804 exceptions rest more on need than reliability when compared with Rule 803 exceptions, this formula suggests that a lesser showing of trustworthiness may suffice when admission is sought pursuant to Rule 804(b)(5). Even in applying Rule 803(24), however, the trial court has broad discretion because of the enormous variations in trustworthiness among the twenty-three exceptions encompassed by the rule. If the declarant is available, the trial court may condition admissibility on the declarant being called as a witness.

In order to determine reliability, the trial court must assess the circumstances and context in which the statement was made. Such factors as the nature of the statement,[3] the relationship between the declarant and the witness,[4] the knowledge and qualifications of the declarant,[5] the probable motivation of the declarant in making the statement,[6] and the type of case[7] will enter into the court's evaluation.

---

[3] See, *e.g.,* Dartez v. Fibreboard Corp., 765 F.2d 456, 462–63 (5th Cir. 1985) (sworn testimony of physician given at prior proceeding in which parties with same motives as present defendants had cross-examined).

[4] See, *e.g.,* United States v. Mandel, 591 F.2d 1347, 1369 (4th Cir. 1979), *cert. denied,* 445 U.S. 96 (1980) (in prosecution of governor for mail fraud, testimony by state senators that other unidentified state senators had told them that the governor did not care whether his veto was overridden should not have been admitted pursuant to Rule 803(24) since it did not possess guarantees of trustworthiness; court noted that the setting from which the testimony was drawn had to be taken into account and that it was dealing "with a purely legislative political scene" where many of the most damaging hearsay statements were repeated by long-time political foes of the defendant).

[5] See, *e.g.,* Huff v. White Motor Corp., 609 F.2d 286, 292 (7th cir. 1979) (remand to district judge for determination as to whether declarant possessed requisite mental capacity).

[6] See, *e.g,* Robinson v. Shapiro, 646 F.2d 734 (2d Cir. 1981) (in wrongful death action court admitted testimony by witness that decedent had told him that the building's superintendent had refused to allow work crew to have access to the work site through his apartment or to take down the fence which crashed down on decedent; appellate court found there was little motive to dissemble by decedent, and that other evidence corroborated his explanation of why superintendent had limited work crew's access to roof; court also noted party's good faith effort to locate superintendent and his ex-employer's lack of diligence in locating him, and that trial judge did not abuse discretion in admitting).

[7] A court may apply different standards in a non-jury case, a civil jury case, and

¶ 14.04[02]   Offered as Evidence of Material Fact

The court would in any event be required to make this finding by Rules 401 and 402. The provision seems to mean that the residual hearsay exceptions should not be used "for trivial or collateral matters."[8]

¶ 14.04[03]   More Probative on the Point

The statement must be "more probative on the point for which it is offered than any other evidence which the proponent can procure through reasonable efforts." What is "reasonable" depends upon such matters as the importance of the evidence, the means at the command of the proponent and the amount in controversy.[9] The good sense of the trial judge must be relied upon. Even though the evidence may be somewhat cumulative, it may be important in evaluating other evidence and arriving at the truth so that the "more probative" requirement cannot be interpreted with cast-iron rigidity.

¶ 14.04[04]   Interests of Justice

Admissibility must accord with "the general purposes of these rules and the interests of justice." This is a restatement of Rule 102.

¶ 14.04[05]   Notice

The adverse party must be notified of the proponent's intention to offer the statement, and the particulars of the statement, "suffi-

---

in a criminal case, and depending on whether the prosecution or the defendant offers the evidence.

[8] United States v. Iaconetti, 406 F.Supp. 554, 559 (E.D.N.Y.), aff'd, 540 F.2d 574 (2d Cir. 1976), cert. denied, 429 U.S. 1041 (1977).

[9] United States v. Parker, 749 F.2d 628, 633 (11th Cir. 1984) (in prosecution for possession of Scotch whiskey knowing it to be stolen from foreign shipment, testimony about information received from unknown employee at distillery about marking of bottles was admissible; witnesses with direct information on the issue all resided in Scotland).

ciently in advance of the trial or hearing to provide the adverse party with a fair opportunity to prepare to meet it." Generally, notice should be given in writing at or before the pretrial conference if the proponent is aware of the problem. When it is questionable whether another exception applies, the safer course is to give notice so that the statement can also be proffered pursuant to the residual hearsay exceptions.

If the proponent becomes aware of the evidence during trial—something bound to occur from time to time, no matter how thorough the discovery—the court can comply with the rule by granting a continuance.[10] A few courts have interpreted the notice requirement with absolute and unwarranted rigidity, unmindful of Rule 102 and trial realities, and have refused to apply the residual exceptions in the absence of notice before the commencement of trial.[11]

Congress did not wish to see the courts create new, formal exceptions to the hearsay rule except by the formal method of promulgation by the Supreme Court subject to Congressional veto. Nevertheless, it had no intention to deny justice in individual cases; the residual hearsay exceptions authorize individual case decisions admitting hearsay not within the precise bounds of a recognized exception. However, one situation has arisen with sufficient frequency to suggest that some circuits are developing a

---

[10] United States v. Bailey, 581 F.2d 341, 348 (3d Cir. 1978) ("We believe that the purpose of the rules and the requirement of fairness to an adversary contained in the advance notice requirement of Rule 803(24) and Rule 804(b)(5) are satisfied when, as here, the proponent of the evidence is without fault in failing to notify his adversary prior to trial and the trial judge has offered sufficient time, by means of granting a continuance, for the party against whom the evidence is to be offered to prepare to meet and contest its admission"; reviewing court should examine adequacy of notice and time allowed to determine whether adverse party had a "fair opportunity" to prepare to contest statement); United States v. Iaconetti, 540 F.2d 574, 578 (2d Cir. 1976), *cert. denied*, 429 U.S. 1041 (1977) ("some latitude [in giving notice] must be permitted in situations like this in which the need does not become apparent until after the trial has commenced. The fact that defendant did not request a continuance or in any way claim that he was unable adequately to prepare to meet the rebuttal testimony further militates against a finding that he was prejudiced by it.").

[11] United States v. Oates, 560 F.2d 45, 72–73 n.30 (2d Cir. 1977) ("There is absolutely no doubt that Congress intended that the requirement of advance notice be rigidly enforced.").

class exception pursuant to Rule 804(b)(5).[12] Some circuits allow a witness' grand jury testimony to be admitted against a defendant when the witness is unavailable at trial, finding that both the hearsay rule and the Confrontation Clause are satisfied.[13] Other circuits have refused to find sufficient "circumstantial guarantees of trustworthiness" to satisfy the evidentiary standard of Rule 804(b)(5) in this situation.[14] When, however, there is evidence indicating that the defendant caused the unavailability of the grand jury witness, courts admit the grand jury testimony on the ground that defendant's conduct waived his right to confrontation and a fortiori his right to raise a hearsay objection.[15]

¶ 14.05   Hearsay Within Hearsay—Rule 805[1]

Rule 805, which deals with hearsay within hearsay, or multiple hearsay as it is frequently termed, makes hearsay within hearsay admissible if each of the statements involved falls within an exception to the hearsay rule. The rule provides:

---

[12] See, *e.g.,* Garner v. United States, 439 U.S. 936, 939, n.3, 99 S.Ct. 333, 58 L.Ed.2d 333 (1978) (dissent from denial of certiorari) ("It seems to me open to serious doubt whether Rule 804(b)(5) was intended to provide case-by-case hearsay exceptions, rather than only to permit expansion of the hearsay exceptions by categories.").

[13] See, *e.g.,* United States v. West, 574 F.2d 1131 (4th Cir. 1978); United States v. Garner, 574 F.2d 1141 (4th Cir. 1978), *cert. denied,* 439 U.S. 936 (1978); United States v. Barlow, 693 F.2d 954 (6th Cir. 1982), *cert. denied,* 461 U.S. 945 (1983); United States v. Carlson, 547 F.2d (8th Cir. 1976), *cert. denied,* 431 U.S. 914 (1977).

[14] See, *e.g,* United States v. Gonzalez, 559 F.2d 1271 (5th Cir. 1977).

[15] See, *e.g,* United States v. Thevis, 665 F.2d 616 (5th Cir.), *cert. denied,* 459 U.S. 825 (1982) ("clear and convincing" standard must be used to determine whether defendant caused the unavailability); United States v. Balano, 618 F.2d 624 (10th Cir.), *cert. denied,* 449 U.S. 840 (1980) (preponderance standard); United States v. Mastrangelo, 693 F.2d 269 (2d Cir. 1982), *on remand,* 561 F. Supp. 1114 (E.D.N.Y.), *aff'd,* 722 F.2d 13 (2d Cir. 1983), *cert. denied,* 467 U.S. 1204 (1984) (preponderance standard).

[1] See discussion in **Treatise** at ¶ 805[01].

Rule 805

HEARSAY WITHIN HEARSAY

Hearsay included within hearsay is not excluded under the hearsay rule if each part of the combined statements conforms with an exception to the hearsay rule provided in these rules.

Rule 805 places no restriction on the number of levels of hearsay that a statement may contain.[2] Theoretically, there would be no objection to the number, provided each conformed to an exception. It must be remembered, however, that "[m]ultiple hearsay is, of course, even more vulnerable to all the objections which attach to simple hearsay[.]"[3] With each additional level of hearsay, there is a greater possibility of unreliability. Even if each included portion meets the requirements of an exception, the trial court has discretion to exclude a statement of multiple hearsay pursuant to Rule 403 when it finds the statement so untrustworthy that its probative value is substantially outweighed by the dangers of confusion and prejudice.

The problem of multiple hearsay arises with some frequency with regard to the admissibility of business records when the entrant has no personal knowledge of the underlying event and has based the entry on information supplied by someone outside the business entity. Rule 805 makes the record admissible if the statement of the informant independently satisfies a hearsay exception, or if the infor-

---

[2] See, *e.g.,* United States v. Portsmouth Paving Corp., 694 F.2d 312 (4th Cir. 1982) (court admitted two level and three level hearsay; a statement which witness testified secretary had said her employer, the defendant, had made was admissible as a vicarious admission coupled with an admission; a second statement, which witness testified X told witness that the secretary had said, that her employer had made, was also admissible because X's statement satisfied Rule 803(1)).

[3] Naples v. United States, 344 F.2d 508, 511 (D.C. Cir. 1964) (quoting McCormick, Evidence § 225 at 461 (1954); murder conviction reversed; D made statement to police lieutenant claiming he had no memory of hurting victim; lieutenant in D's presence repeated D's story to police captain but added that D said he struck victim; captain testified that lieutenant told him that D told him he struck woman; court held that this was double hearsay and that lieutenant's statement could not come in as an adoptive admission through D's silence [See ¶ 801(d)(2)(B)[01], *supra*] because it could not be found that the accused understood and unambiguously assented to the statement).

mant's statement was exempted from the hearsay rule by Rule 801.[4] Thus, for example, the record is admissible if it records an excited utterance, or an admission, or a co-conspirator's statement. Situations may also arise where one of the statements does not fully qualify as a hearsay exception but nevertheless possesses sufficient assurances of trustworthiness to bring it within Rule 803(24) or Rule 804(b)(5).[5]

¶ 14.06 Attacking and Supporting Credibility of Declarant—Rule 806[1]

Rule 806 provides that the credibility of a declarant may be attacked, and then supported, as though the declarant had been a witness, whenever the declarant's statement is admitted pursuant to a Rule 803 or 804 exception, or as an authorized or vicarious admission, or as a co-conspirator's declaration. The rule specifically eliminates the need to lay a foundation for impeachment by a prior inconsistent statement, and allows a party against whom a hearsay statement has been admitted to examine the declarant as under cross-examination if the party calls him as a witness. The rule provides:

Rule 806

ATTACKING AND SUPPORTING CREDIBILITY OF DECLARANT

When a hearsay statement, or a statement defined in Rule 801(d)(2), (C), (D), or (E), has been admitted in evidence, the credibility of the declarant may be attacked, and if attacked may be supported, by any evidence which would be admissible for those purposes if declarant had testified as a witness. Evidence of a statement or conduct by the declarant at any time, inconsistent with the declarant's hearsay statement, is not subject to any requirement that the declarant may have been afforded an oppor-

---

[4] United States v. Dotson, 821 F.2d 1034, 1035 (5th Cir. 1987) (per curiam) ("For the purposes of the hearsay-within-hearsay principle . . . 'non-hearsay' statements under Rule 801(d) . . . should be considered in analyzing a multiple-hearsay statement as the equivalent of a level of the combined statement 'that conforms with an exception to the hearsay rule.'").

[5] See, *e.g.*, Herdman v. Smith, 707 F.2d 839, 842 (5th Cir. 1983).

[1] See discussion in **Treatise** at ¶ 806[01].

tunity to deny or explain. If the party against whom a hearsay statement
has been admitted calls the declarant as a witness, the party is entitled
to examine the declarant on the statement as if under cross-examination.

CHAPTER 15

Hearsay Exclusions

SYNOPSIS

15–1

¶ 15.01   Prior Statement By Witness—Rule 801(d)(1)

¶ 15.01[01]   In General[1]

The orthodox view rejects all prior statements offered substantively because their value depends on the credit of a declarant who was not subject to cross-examination at the time the statement was made.[2] Critics of the traditional approach question the underlying assumption that the reliability of a statement cannot be assessed unless it is tested contemporaneously. So long as the statement is ultimately thoroughly explored and examined, they argue, it is not decisive when this occurs. When the declarant becomes a witness who can be examined about the prior statement, the purpose of the hearsay rule is satisfied because all the ideal conditions for giving testimony are met. The witness is under oath, subject to cross-examination, and his demeanor can be observed by the trier of fact. Some opponents of the orthodox approach would, accordingly, treat as nonhearsay all prior statements of a witness. A third group takes an intermediate position. While it agrees that cross-examination can be conducted successfully after the statement is made, it also believes that other dangers exist with regard to some prior statements, and that only certain kinds are sufficiently trustworthy to be admitted despite the hearsay rule.

Rule 801(d)(1) adopts this compromise position towards classifying a prior statement of a witness as hearsay. It does not characterize all prior statements as hearsay, as required by the orthodox approach; nor does it exempt all prior statements from the hearsay rule, or even all prior inconsistent statements as was originally proposed by the Advisory Committee. Instead it accords substantive value to three kinds of prior statements that have been defined to possess characteristics that ensure a high degree of reliability. The three categories of statements exempted from the hearsay definition if they meet certain specified requirements are prior inconsistent statements (subparagraph (A)), prior consistent statements (subparagraph (B)) and statements of identification (subparagraph (C)). As the discus-

---

[1] See discussion in **Treatise** at ¶ 801(d)(1)[01].

[2] See State v. Saporen, 205 Minn. 358, 285 N.W. 898 (1939) (classic statement of orthodox rule).

sion below indicates, another reason for admitting these kinds of statements is their relevancy to the credibility of the witness; they are likely to be of great assistance in enabling the trier to evaluate the evidence properly.

¶ 15.01[02]   Prior Inconsistent Statements[1]

The first category of prior statement made admissible by Rule 801(d)(1) is a statement inconsistent with the witness' testimony that the witness had previously given under oath at a trial, deposition or other proceeding. By requiring that the statement have been given in circumstances where there normally will be a transcript, the rule eliminates the danger that witnesses will fabricate prior statements.[2] The rule's limitations also make unusable substantively many types of statements which are given in response to subtle and sometimes severe pressures, as, for instance, statements elicited by an insurance agent or an FBI agent; statements made before the Grand Jury, where leading is the norm, are admissible, however. The rule provides:

Rule 801

DEFINITIONS

(d) Statements which are not hearsay.—A statement is not hearsay if—

(1) Prior statement by witness.—The declarant testifies at the trial or hearing and is subject to cross-examination concerning the statement, and the statement is (A) inconsistent with the declarant's testimony, and was given under oath subject to the penalty of perjury at a trial, hearing, or other proceeding, or in a deposition . . ..

[a]   Oath

According to Rule 801(d)(1), a prior statement cannot be accorded substantive use unless it was given under "oath." Federal

---

[1] See discussion in **Treatise** at ¶¶ 801(d)(1)(A)[01]–[08].

[2] This is, however, a non-hearsay danger since the witness is present in court.

law[3] provides, however, that certain unsworn declarations made under penalty of perjury may be used in lieu of statements under oath, and such declarations satisfy Rule 801(d)(1).

[b] Trial, Hearing, Other Proceeding or Deposition

In order for the statement to satisfy Rule 801(d)(1), it must have been made at some kind of judicial or quasi-judicial proceeding,[4] in addition to having been given under oath. For example, testimony before a grand jury or before an administrative board would be treated as a "hearing." The solemnity of the official occasion and oath, plus a stenographic record, reduce possibilities of overreaching by the questioner and carelessness by the witness. Consequently, an affidavit does not qualify for substantive use. The absence of cross-examination at the prior proceeding is irrelevant.

The oath and hearing requirement ensure that there will be no dispute about whether the prior statement was made.

[c] Inconsistent

To be admissible, the prior statement must be inconsistent with

---

[3] 28 U.S.C. § 1746 (an unsworn written declaration given under penalty of perjury may not be substituted for 1) a deposition, 2) an oath of office, or 3) a document required to be signed before a specified official other than a notary public).

[4] *Compare* United States v. Castro-Ayon, 537 F.2d 1055 (9th Cir.), *cert. denied,* 429 U.S. 983 (1976) (sworn tape-recorded statement given by aliens at a Border Patrol station could be admitted pursuant to Rule 801(d)(1)) *with* United States v. Livingston, 661 F.2d 239, 242 (D.C. Cir. 1981) (reversible error to have admitted sworn statement to postal inspector; court distinguished *Castro-Ayon* on grounds that questioning was not held before independent officer, no recordings were made, interrogation was held at witness' home, and no rights were afforded to witness so that there were less formalities than those " 'which surround a first hand appearance at an on the record proceeding.' "). See also United States v. Day, 789 F.2d 1217, 1221–23 (6th Cir. 1986) (court excluded sworn taped statement given to IRS agents analogizing it to a "station house interrogation, which is not an 'other proceeding' within the meaning of Rule 801(d)(1)(A)"; court based absence of reliability on factors such as: agents characterized meeting with witness as an interview and not a formal proceeding, statement was not given under oath, and witness' motivation, shown by his tone and pattern of self-serving statements, disclaimed statement's reliability and truthfulness).

the testimony given by the witness. The rule is silent about what test of inconsistency should be used, and whether courts should look to case law dealing with impeachment by prior inconsistent statements. When used for impeachment, the usual test applied by the federal courts is whether a reasonable person could infer on comparing the whole effect of the two statements that they had been produced by inconsistent beliefs. In other words, the keystone for impeachment use is relevancy—would the prior statement of the witness help the trier of fact evaluate the credibility of the witness, taking into account the dangers specified in Rule 403 which mandate exclusion if they substantially outweigh the probative value of the evidence? The approach under Rule 801 should be the same. Here the question is not whether the statement is helpful in evaluating credibility, but whether it is helpful in resolving a material fact in issue.[5]

Is the in-court testimony inconsistent with the prior statement when the witness denies all recollection of the underlying event rather than testifying to an inconsistent version of what occurred? Courts rarely focused on this issue, preferring instead to analyze whether a witness could be "subject to cross-examination concerning the statement" as required by Rule 801(d) if he lacked all recollection of the underlying event.

The prototypical case was *California v. Green.*[6] In that case, a sixteen year old boy arrested for selling marijuana had made oral statements to an undercover police officer naming the defendant as his supplier. At trial, the witness was evasive. While he admitted making the prior statements, and remembered that he possessed a bag of marijuana shortly after receiving a telephone call from the defendant, he claimed not to remember whether he had obtained the marijuana from the defendant because he had taken LSD just before the call. The Supreme Court, after stating that the Confrontation Clause permits substantive use of prior statements when the witness can be adequately cross-examined, remanded for a determination of wheth-

---

[5] See, *e.g.,* United States v. Williams, 737 F.2d 594, 606–10 (7th Cir. 1984), *cert. denied,* 105 S.Ct. 1354 (1985) (to be inconsistent, statements need not be "diametrically opposed or logically incompatible"; inconsistency may be found in evasive answers, silence, a change in positions or even a purported change in memory).

[6] 399 U.S. 149, 90 S.Ct. 1930, 26 L.Ed.2d 489 (1970) (the California Evidence Code admits all prior inconsistent statements whether or not made under oath at a prior proceeding).

er there had been an opportunity for effective cross-examination in light of the witness' claimed memory impairment.[7] In *United States v. Owens,*[8] however, the Supreme Court interpreted the "subject to cross-examination" requirement in Rule 801(d) as necessitating only that the "witness is placed on the stand, under oath, and responds willingly to questions."[9] By eliminating the need to examine the effectiveness of the declarant-witness' cross-examination, the opinion in *Owens* may lead courts to pay more attention than previously to whether the prior statement was inconsistent with the in-court testimony.

¶ 15.01[03] Prior Consistent Statements[1]

Prior consistent statements are given substantive effect by Rule 801(d)(1)(B) if they are admitted to rebut charges of recent fabrication or improper influence or motive,[2] the two situations

---

[7] *Id.* at 168–69. On remand, the California state court examined the trial transcript and concluded that the trial court could properly disbelieve the witness' claim that he could not remember how the marijuana came into his possession. Accordingly, his evasions constituted an implied denial that defendant had furnished the marijuana, thereby making his testimony inconsistent with his prior statement, and satisfying both evidentiary and constitutional requirements. People v. Green, 92 Cal. Rptr. 494, 3 Cal.3d 981, 479 P.2d 998 (1971) (en banc).

[8] 484 U.S. —, 108 S.Ct. 838, 98 L.Ed.2d 951 (1988).

[9] *Id.* at —, 108 S.Ct. at 844, 98 L.Ed.2d at 959 (1988). While the statement in question was a statement of identification admitted pursuant to Rule 801(d)(1)(C), the Court was construing the "subject to cross-examination" language which applies to all the subparagraphs of Rule 801(d). Furthermore, the Court specifically stated that "It would seem strange, for example, to assert that a witness can avoid introduction of testimony from a prior proceeding that is inconsistent with his trial testimony, see Rule 801(d)(1)(A), by simply asserting lack of memory of the facts to which the prior testimony related." *Id.* at —, 108 S.Ct. at 845, 98 L.Ed.2d at 960 (1988) (citing **Treatise**).

[1] See discussion in **Treatise** at ¶ 801(d)(1)(B)[01].

[2] United States v. Reed, 887 F.2d 1398 (11th Cir. 1989); United States v. Rodriquez-Cardenas, 866 F.2d 390, 395 (11th Cir. 1989); United States v. Red Feather, 865 F.2d 129 (8th Cir. 1989) (child sex abuse victim's diary entries permitted as prior consistent statements where defendant charged that her testimony resulted from suggestion of social worker); United States v. Tarantino, 846 F.2d 1384, 1411 (D.C. Cir. 1988); United States v. Khan, 821 F.2d 90, 93–94 (2d Cir. 1987); United States v. Gwaltney, 790 F.2d 1378, 1384 (9th Cir. 1986), *cert. denied,* 479 U.S. 1037, 107 S. Ct. 1337, 94 L. Ed. 2d 187 (1987).

where the prior statement is most likely to have high probative value. Evidence that counteracts a suggestion that the witness changed his story in response to some threat or scheme or bribe, by showing that his story was the same prior to the alleged external pressure, is highly relevant in shedding light on the witness' credibility. Evidence that merely shows that the witness said the same thing on other occasions when his motive was the same does not have much probative force, "for the simple reason that mere repetition does not imply veracity."[3]

Unlike prior inconsistent statements, the prior consistent statement need not be made under oath or at a previous trial, hearing, or other proceeding.

The rule provides:

(d) Statements which are not hearsay.—A statement is not hearsay if—

(1) Prior statement by witness.—The declarant testifies at the trial or hearing and is subject to cross-examination concerning the statement, and the statement is . . . (B) consistent with the declarant's testimony and is offered to rebut an express or implied charge against the declarant of recent fabrication or improper influence or motive . . . .

[a] To Rebut an Express or Implied Charge

Rule 801(d)(1)(B) provides that the prior consistent statement may be accorded substantive use only if it is used to rebut an express[4] or implied[5] suggestion that the witness changed his story

---

[3] United States v. McPartlin, 595 F.2d 1321, 1351 (7th Cir.), *cert. denied,* 444 U.S. 833, 100 S. Ct. 65, 62 L. Ed. 2d 43 (1979).

[4] *See* United States v. Reed, 887 F.2d 1398 (11th Cir. 1989) (in opening statement, defense counsel indicated that the witness had fabricated his testimony; witness's prior statement was properly admitted); United States v. Obayagbona, 627 F. Supp. 329, 332–38 (E.D.N.Y. 1985) (defense directly charged that agent had fabricated testimony in order to convict defendant because of a lack of physical evidence).

[5] United States v. Martin, 798 F.2d 308 (8th Cir. 1986); United States v. De Peri, 778 F.2d 963, 977 (3d Cir. 1985), *cert. denied,* 475 U.S. 1109, 476 U.S. 1159, 106 S. Ct. 1518, 2277, 89 L. Ed. 2d 916, 90 L. Ed. 2d 720 (1986); United States v. Doyle, 771 F.2d 250, 256–57 (7th Cir. 1985); United States v. Albert, 595 F.2d 283, 289 (5th Cir. 1979).

because of a motive to lie. The Advisory Committee's notes do not indicate whether the rule extends to situations where the prior consistent statement is admitted to refute an imputation of inaccurate memory on the part of the witness. However, the ordinary meaning of the words "fabrication," "influence" and "motive" suggests that the Rule is intended to cover only those situations where the witness consciously alters his testimony.[6]

[b] To Rebut Recent Fabrication

In determining whether the proffered consistent statement rebuts the "express or implied charge" of "recent fabrication or improper influence or motive," some circuits have held that the prior consistent statement must have been made before the declarant had a motive to fabricate his story.[7] Other courts have held that the statement was admissible under the circumstances of the case if it might aid the jury in determining which version of the events represented the truth.[8] As discussed in ¶ 12.01[06]

---

[6] *See* Mayoza v. Heinold Commodities, 871 F.2d 672, 675 (7th Cir. 1989); United States v. Pendas-Martinez, 845 F.2d 938, 942–43 (11th Cir. 1988); United States v. Brantley, 733 F.2d 1429, 1438 (11th Cir. 1984), *cert. denied,* 470 U.S. 1006, 105 S. Ct. 1362, 84 L. Ed. 2d 383 (1985); United States v. Herring, 582 F.2d 535, 541 (10th Cir. 1978). *See also* McGowan v. Cooper Industries, 863 F.2d 1266, 1274 (6th Cir. 1988) (in products liability action, prior statements of deponent were excluded in the absence of any charge that deponent fabricated the deposition testimony). *But see* United States v. Coleman, 631 F.2d 908, 914 (D.C. Cir. 1980) (stating in dictum that prior consistent statement admissible even where impeachment is only an imputation of inaccurate memory).

[7] *See* United States v. Vest, 842 F.2d 1319, 1330 (1st Cir. 1988); United States v. Bowman, 798 F.2d 333, 338 (8th Cir. 1986), *cert. denied,* 479 U.S. 1043, 107 S. Ct. 906, 93 L. Ed. 2d 856 (1987) (although admission of statements was harmless error in this case); United States v. Henderson, 717 F.2d 135, 138 (4th Cir. 1983) (a witness's prior consistent statements, offered for rehabilitation purposes, where properly admitted were made after witness' arrest but before the time he entered into a plea agreement).

[8] United States v. Miller, 874 F.2d 1255, 1271–74 (9th Cir. 1989) ("the requirement of no motive to fabricate . . . should not be applied as a rigid *per se* rule barring all such prior consistent statements . . . without regard to other surrounding circumstances that may give them significant probative value."); United States v. Lawson, 872 F.2d 179, 182 (6th Cir. 1989); United States v. Pendas-Martinez, 845 F.2d 938, 942 n.6 (11th Cir. 1988) ("the consistent statement need not have been made prior to the time that the

above, some circuits have distinguished between the substantive use of prior statements and a more limited use of prior statements for purposes of rehabilitation only, where the requirement is not strictly applied.⁹

¶ 15.01[04]   Statement of Identification¹

Rule 801(d)(1)(C) makes admissible an out-of-court statement by the witness identifying a person. Subparagraph (C) operates independent of the impeachment process. There is neither a requirement of inconsistency as in subparagraph (A), nor a condition of previous impeachment as in subparagraph (B). Statements of identification are admitted because the earlier identification has greater probative value than an identification made in the suggestive atmosphere of the courtroom, after the witness' memory has started to fade.² "Protection against identifications of questionable certainty is afforded by the requirement that the declarant be available for cross-examination; questions of the probative value of the testimony are thus for the jury."³ Instead of relying on the hearsay rules or the Confrontation Clause, the Supreme Court has imposed constitutional requirements designed to increase the reliability of out-of-court identifications.⁴

---

alleged motive to fabricate arose"); United States v. Williams, 573 F.2d 284, 289, & n.3 (5th Cir. 1978). *See also* United States v. Rios, 611 F.2d 1335, 1349 (10th Cir. 1979), *cert. denied,* 452 U.S. 918, 101 S. Ct. 3054, 69 L. Ed. 2d 422 (1981).

⁹ United States v. Brennan, 798 F.2d 581, 587–89 (2d Cir. 1986) (witness' grand jury testimony was inadmissible under Rule 801(d)(1)(B) since the witness had a motive to lie at that time, but the government was allowed to use the testimony to rehabilitate him); United States v. Harris, 761 F.2d 394, 398–400 (7th Cir. 1985), citing **Treatise.**

¹ See discussion in **Treatise** at ¶ 801(d)(1)(C)[01].

² See Gilbert v. California, 388 U.S. 263, 87 S.Ct. 1902, 16 L.Ed.2d 1003 (1967).

³ United States v. Marchand, 564 F.2d 983, 996 (2d Cir. 1977), *cert. denied,* 434 U.S. 1015 (1978).

⁴ See, *e.g.,* United States v. Wade, 388 U.S. 218, 87 S.Ct. 1926, 18 L.Ed.2d 1149 (1967); Gilbert v. California, 388 U.S. 263, 87 S.Ct. 1902, 16 L.Ed.2d 1003 (1967); Stovall v. Denno, 388 U.S. 293, 87 S.Ct. 1967, 18 L.Ed.2d 1199 (1967); Foster v. California, 394 U.S. 440, 89 S.Ct. 1127, 22 L.Ed.2d 902 (1979).

The rule provides:

(d) Statements which are not hearsay.—A statement is not hearsay if—

(1) Prior statement by witness.—The declarant testifies at the trial or hearing and is subject to cross-examination concerning the statement, and the statement is . . . (C) one of identification of a person made after perceiving the person.

Rule 801(d)(1)(C) applies regardless of when the prior identification was made—whether at the scene of the crime, at a later chance

(Text continued on page 15–11)

encounter, or at a police line-up. The rule has also been interpreted to authorize testimony that the witness had made an out-of-court identification of a photograph[5] or sketch[6] of a person, rather than the person himself.

The rule does not bar persons other than the witness who made the out-of-court identification from testifying to the statement. For instance, a police officer who heard the witness identify the defendant at the line-up may testify concerning the witness' identification, provided both the witness and the police officer are subject to cross-examination.[7] In *United States v. Owens,*[8] the Supreme Court held that the declarant-witness' inability to remember anything about the circumstances of the identification, or about the defendant at the time of the crime, does not prevent the statement from satisfying Rule 801(d)(1)(C) as well as the Confrontation Clause. The majority interpreted the "subject to cross-examination concerning the statement" language in Rule 801(d)(1) as requiring no more than placing the witness on the stand, subject to oath, and having the witness willing to answer questions.[9] Effectiveness of cross-examination, enabling the trier of fact to have some basis for determining the truth of the statement, is, according to the Court, not required by the Sixth Amendment either, which demands only that defendant be furnished with an "opportunity" for cross-examination. If the declarant-witness is produced, and is subject to unrestricted examination, no inquiry is required into the trustworthiness of his prior statement. See discussion at ¶ 15.01[02][c], *supra.*

---

[5] See, *e.g.,* United States v. Fosher, 568 F.2d 207, 210 (1st Cir. 1978).

[6] See, *e.g,* United States v. Moskowitz, 581 F.2d 14 (2d Cir. 1978).

[7] United States v. Jarrad, 754 F.2d 1451, 1456 (9th Cir.), *cert. denied,* 106 S.Ct. 96 (1985) (FBI agent permitted to testify to witness' tentative identification of photograph of defendant after witness denied that any of photographs she viewed resembled defendant, defense cross-examined agent, but did not recall witness; court stated that purpose of rule was to solve problem of eyewitness who identifies defendant before trial but refuses to acknowledge identification at trial for fear of reprisal); United States v. Elemy, 656 F.2d 507 (9th Cir. 1981) (testimony by police officer about witness' prior identification at line-up would be admissible even if witness refused to acknowledge previous identification).

[8] 484 U.S. —, 108 S.Ct. 838, 98 L.Ed.2d 951 (1988).

[9] *Id.* at —, 108 S.Ct. at 844, 98 L.Ed.2d at 959.

¶ 15.02 Admissions—Rule 801(d)(2)

¶ 15.02[01] In General[1]

Rule 801(d)(2) is in accord with the traditional view that admissions of party-opponents and their agents may be admitted as substantive evidence despite the hearsay rule. Rather than characterize admissions as exceptions to the hearsay rule, the Federal Rules of Evidence provide that admissions by a party-opponent are not hearsay, thereby recognizing that admissions differ from other hearsay exceptions. Unlike other exceptions which are grounded upon a probability of trustworthiness, the circumstances in which an admission was made do not furnish the trier of fact with the means of evaluating the reliability of the statement. Rather, admissions are admitted on an estoppel notion, or as the product of the adversary system, or as a matter of precedent because the reception of this type of evidence predates the development of the hearsay rule. Wigmore's view that admissions are not hearsay because a party does not need to cross-examine himself is not persuasive since so many admissions are made vicariously. We are dealing here with out-of-court statements presenting hearsay and confrontation dangers that require open-eyed caution.

Rule 801(d)(2) represents an accommodation to the common view that statements of a principal actor should generally be received rather than excluded per se. Because of their value, they are receivable whether or not the declarant is available or appears as a witness.

¶ 15.02[02] By Party in Individual or Representative Capacity[1]

Rule 801(d)(2)(A) provides that the statement of a party made in either an individual or representative capacity is not hearsay when it is offered in evidence against the party. The rule provides:

(d) Statements which are not hearsay.—A statement is not hearsay if—

. . .

---

[1] See discussion in **Treatise** at ¶ 801(d)(2)[01].

[1] See **Treatise** at ¶ 801(d)(2)(A)[01].

. . .

(2) Admission by party-opponent.—The statement is offered against a party and is (A) the party's own statement, in either an individual or a representative capacity . . . .

The party's statement may have been self-serving when made, need not be based on personal knowledge,[2] and may be in the form of an opinion. The rule does not require that the statement must have been made in the party's representative capacity in order for it to be offered against the party in a representative capacity; the fact that the statement is relevant to representative affairs is sufficient.

The rule makes no attempt to categorize the myriad ways in which an admission can be made. Admissions can be in the form of explicit statements or may be inferred from conduct. They may be made orally or in writing. The statement may have been made in connection with no case, the instant case, or some other completely independent litigation. All that is required is that a statement made by a party is offered into evidence by an adverse party.

¶ 15.02[03]   Admissions: Adoptive[1]

Rule 801(d)(2)(B) recognizes that an admission may be made by acquiescing in the statement of another. The rule provides:

(d) Statements which are not hearsay.—A statement is not hearsay if—

. . .

(2) Admission by party-opponent.—The statement is offered against a party and is . . . (B) a statement of which the party has manifested an adoption or belief in its truth . . . .

The rule is clearly satisfied when a party verbally and unambiguously adopts the statement of another.[2] A judge may, however, reject

---

[2] United States v. Matlock, 415 U.S. 164, 172 n.8, 94 S.Ct. 988, 39 L.Ed.2d 242 (1974) (statement that party was married).

[1] See discussion in **Treatise** at ¶ 801(d)(2)(B)[01].

[2] See, *e.g.,* Zenith Radio Corp. v. Matsushita Electric Industrial Co., Ltd., 505 F.Supp. 1190, 1243 (E.D. Pa. 1980), *rev'd on other grounds,* 723 F.2d 238 (3d Cir. 1983), *rev'd on other grounds,* 106 S.Ct. 1348 (1986) (documents written by someone else but signed by party). The courts frequently admit tapes of conversations between a party and another person on the theory that the statements of the party

evidence of verbal or non-verbal behavior if it is susceptible to more than one interpretation.[3] A statement of another may also be adopted by the conduct of a party.[4] For instance, the use[5] or possession[6] of documents may constitute an adoption. In all cases, the burden is on the proponent of the evidence to show that the behavior, verbal or otherwise, was intended as an adoption.[7]

The most troublesome cases—because they involve the most ambiguous response—are those where the party remains silent after hearing a damaging statement. When silence is offered pursuant to Rule 801(d)(2)(B), the burden is on the proponent to convince the judge[8] that in the circumstances of the case, a failure to respond is

qualify as party admissions under Rule 801(d)(2)(A), and the statements of the other person qualify as adoptive admissions under Rule 801(d)(2)(B). See, *e.g.,* United States v. Kenny, 645 F.2d 1323, 1340 (9th Cir.), *cert. denied,* 452 U.S. 920 (1981); United States v. Murray, 618 F.2d 892, 900 (2d Cir. 1980) (court noted that jury had been instructed not to consider statements for their truth except to extent that defendant adopted them).

[3] See, *e.g.,* National Bank of N. America v. Cinco Investors, Inc., 610 F.2d 89 (2d Cir. 1979) (court held that evidence should not be considered where it was not clear that person who allegedly adopted statement had made up his mind about the truth or falsity of the statement).

[4] An adoption by conduct is possible because the definition of statement in Rule 801(a) embraces "nonverbal conduct . . . if . . . intended . . . as an assertion."

[5] See, *e.g.,* Wagstaff v. Protective Apparel Corp. of America, 760 F.2d 1074 (10th Cir. 1985) (defendants manifested adoption of inflated representations about their financial situation contained in newspaper articles when they reprinted the articles and distributed them to their customers).

[6] See, *e.g.,* United States v. Marino, 658 F.2d 1120 (6th Cir. 1981) (airline ticket found in defendant's possession usable to prove that defendants traveled in interstate commerce).

[7] See, *e.g,* United States v. Giese, 569 F.2d 527, 543–44 (9th Cir.), *cert. denied,* 439 U.S. 876 (1978) (court admitted testimony that defendant nodded and smiled when an attorney for an unindicted co-conspirator stated in presence of witness and defendant that defendant was the leader of all illegal activities; at trial, attorney testified that defendant had denied being ringleader but was impeached with prior grand jury testimony in which he had stated that defendant had failed to deny accusation; court found that evidence was strong enough to permit a reasonable inference that defendant had admitted guilt).

[8] See Rule 104(a). But *cf.* United States v. Barletta, 652 F.2d 218 (1st Cir. 1981) (court held that task for trial judge is to determine whether a reasonable jury could find that there had been an adoptive admission, but also found that trial judge could

so unnatural that it supports the inference that the party acquiesced in the statement. The theory underlying admission is that the normal human reaction would be to deny such a statement if untrue. In order to evaluate the truth of this generalization when applied to the particular case before it, the court must assess such factors as the circumstances in which an accusation was made,[9] the nature of the statement,[10] by whom it was made,[11] and the physical[12] and psychological state of the party against whom the statement is being offered. Although there is no requirement in Rule 801(d)(2)(B) that the party have knowledge of the contents of the statement which is being proffered as an adoptive admission, a court may find, after evaluating the type of statement and by whom it was made, that the party could not have been expected to deny the statement because of a lack of information that would permit the verity of the statement to be assessed.[13] In cases of a continuing commercial relationship, a response

---

exclude tape offered as adoptive admission pursuant to Rule 403 as unduly prejudicial). Once admitted, the jury must also decide whether silence betokened acknowledgement of truth in determining probative force.

[9] See, *e.g.,* United States v. Jenkins, 779 F.2d 606, 612 (11th Cir. 1986) (statement in the presence of defendant that declarant had to "get some money up" for the defendant to finish paying for a cocaine shipment while defendant said nothing was admissible because an innocent person would have probably denied the statement under such circumstances; witness testified that declarant was not whispering); United States v. Carter, 760 F.2d 1568, 1579–80 (11th Cir. 1985) (parties sitting in back seat of car directly behind declarant); United States v. Caballero, 712 F.2d 126, 130 (5th Cir. 1983) (party and declarant in close proximity).

[10] See, *e.g.,* United States v. Fortes, 619 F.2d 108, 116 (1st Cir. 1980) ("an inquiry of two persons as to whether they had 'done a bank robbery,' followed by an affirmative response by one of them describing his participation with the other in the crime, is the type of exchange to which the silence of the unresponsive accomplice, assuming he is present and conscious of the conversation 'gives consent' ").

[11] A court in the exercise of its discretion pursuant to Rule 104(a) may find that a party did not manifest adoption of a damaging statement made in the party's presence by, for instance, a drunk, an unknown bystander, or a child.

[12] See, *e.g.,* United States v. Sears, 663 F.2d 896 (9th Cir. 1981), *cert. denied,* 455 U.S. 1027 (1982) (question whether defendant actually heard statement because of her hearing disability).

[13] See, *e.g.,* United States v. Dellaro, 99 F.2d 781, 783 (2d Cir. 1938) (conspiracy to unlawfully possess still; declarant, in the presence of D, the owner and lessor of house where still was found, stated that "boss" said to call D in case of trouble; conviction reversed; "how could [D] answer as to what the 'boss' had told [declarant]?").

is normally expected.[14] In other kinds of civil cases, the court's view of what would be normal under the circumstances will control.[15]

In criminal cases, Rule 801(d)(2)(B) must be considered in conjunction with consitutional developments. The Supreme Court has recognized that no adverse inference may be drawn from defendant's failure to deny accusations while in custody once *Miranda* warnings have been given.[16] An inference from the defendant's silence may theoretically be possible if the accusation was made before *Miranda* warnings had to be given.[17] Since any well-advised prospective defendant will know enough to say nothing about possible criminal activities even at the hint of a possible official investigation, silence should almost invariably be excluded as non-probative of defendant's guilt in a criminal trial. If no law enforcement agents were present directly or through an intermediary when defendant failed to deny an accusation, the court will have to evaluate the factors discussed above to determine whether the silence was probative under the circumstances of the case.

---

[14] See, *e.g.,* Megarry Brothers, Inc. v. United States, 404 F.2d 479 (8th Cir. 1968) (failure to respond to two invoices was evidence tending to show that amount owed was not in dispute).

[15] See, *e.g.,* Southern Stone Co., Inc. v. Singer, 665 F.2d 698, 702–03 (5th Cir. 1982) (no adoptive admission where circumstances surrounding the letter do not support a reasonable expectation of a response).

[16] Doyle v. Ohio, 426 U.S. 610, 617, 96 S.Ct. 2240, 49 L.Ed.2d 91 (1976) (silence following receipt of *Miranda* warnings "insolubly ambiguous"); Wainwright v. Greenfield, 474 U.S. —, 106 S.Ct. 634, 88 L.Ed.2d 623 (1986) (unfair to use silence to overcome insanity plea). See also United States v. Hale, 422 U.S. 171, 95 S.Ct. 2133, 45 L.Ed.2d 99 (1975) (rejecting use of silence on the evidentiary ground of lack of probative value).

[17] Fletcher v. Weir, 455 U.S. 603, 102 S.Ct. 1309, 71 L.Ed.2d 490 (1982) and Jenkins v. Anderson, 447 U.S. 231, 100 S.Ct. 2124, 65 L.Ed.2d 86 (1980) hold that when no *Miranda* warnings were given, neither due process nor the privilege against self-incrimination prohibits use of the defendant's silence for impeachment purposes. Two justices, concurring in *Jenkins,* would have allowed the silence to be used substantively as well. But *cf.* United States v. Caro, 637 F.2d 869, 876 (2d Cir. 1981) ("[w]hatever the future impact of *Jenkins* may be, we have found no decision permitting the use of silence, even the silence of a suspect who has been given no *Miranda* warnings and is entitled to none, as part of the Government's direct case").

¶ 15.02[04]   Admissions: Authorized[1]

Rule 801(d)(2)(C) restates the orthodox proposition that a statement by a person authorized by a party to make a statement is treated as though the statement had been made by the party, *i.e.,* as an admission.[2] The rule provides:

> (d) Statements which are not hearsay.—A statement is not hearsay if—
>
> . . .
>
> (2) Admission by party-opponent. The statement is offered against a party and is . . . (C) a statement by a person authorized by the party to make a statement concerning the subject . . . .

Whether a given statement satisfies this rule is resolved by applying agency doctrine, rather than evidentiary principles such as trustworthiness. By evidence independent of the statement seeking admission, the proponent must show agency,[3] and the fact that the agent had "speaking authority" to make the statement in question on behalf of the party against whom the statement is being offered.[4] In a civil case, the Federal Rules of Civil Procedure greatly simplify the proponent's task of showing that a person deposed on behalf of a corporation is the corporation's authorized agent.[5]

---

[1] See discussion in **Treatise** at ¶ 801(d)(2)(C)[01].

[2] See, *e.g.,* Michaels v. Michaels, 767 F.2d 1185, 1201 (7th Cir. 1985), *cert. denied,* 106 S.Ct. 797 (1986) (broker); United States v. Da Silva, 725 F.2d 828, 831–32 (2d Cir. 1983) (interpreter); B-W Acceptance Corp. v. Porter, 568 F.2d 1179, 1182 (5th Cir. 1978) (branch manager).

[3] See, *e.g.,* City of New York v. Pullman Inc., 662 F.2d 910, 915 (2d Cir. 1981), *cert. denied,* 454 U.S. 1164 (1982) (fact that federal government had provided funding for purchase of subway cars was not sufficient to create agency relationship between federal agency and the New York City Transit Authority so as to make government report admissible as authorized admission); *In re* Japanese Electronic Products Litigation, 723 F.2d 238, 300 (3d Cir. 1983), *rev'd on other grounds,* 106 S.Ct. 1348 (1986) (statements did not qualify since declarant was no longer employed by defendant when statement was made).

[4] Donovan v. Local 738, 575 F.Supp. 52, 53–54 (D. Md. 1983) (statement of administrative assistant excluded where although he may have been authorized to speak on behalf of international union, that union was not a party, and there was no evidence that the assistant was authorized to speak for the Local, the party-opponent).

[5] Rules 30(b)(6) and 31(a) of the Federal Rules of Civil Procedure allow the party seeking discovery to name the corporation as deponent, and the corporation is then required to designate a natural person to testify on its behalf. Rule 32(a)(2) gives

Rule 801(d)(2)(C) treats as admissions statements made by the agent to his principal as well as statements made to a third person.[6] The drafters believed that this type of evidence is highly reliable and often extremely helpful to a trier of fact.

Intra-company reports do pose a danger, however, when the declarant lacks personal knowledge. The lack of a personal knowledge requirement in the case of party admissions can perhaps be justified on the ground that admissions which become relevant in litigation usually concern some matter of substantial importance to the declarant, upon which he would probably have informed himself, so that they possess greater reliability than the usual run of hearsay, even when they are not grounded in personal perception. This rationale becomes suspect when extended to the declarations of an agent, particularly when the agent is making statements to the principal. In the case of statements to third persons, it can perhaps be argued that an employee will not make a false statement damaging his employer because he has a stake in the employer's welfare and does not wish to risk his job, though even this argument is somewhat suspect in an era of widespread disaffection. An employee well-disposed to his employer is, however, apt to report rumors to his employer, not because of their truth, but because he thinks the employer will be interested in hearing the rumors.

Permitting the witness to testify to a statement of the agent, based on hearsay that cannot be evaluated, is contrary to the philosophy of Rule 403 and Rule 805, which allows hearsay within hearsay only if both statements conform to the requirements of a hearsay exception. While Rule 805 does not literally apply, because it is drafted in terms of a hearsay statement that contains another hearsay statement, and authorized admissions are by definition not hearsay at all, the rationale of the rule is to ensure that each portion of a combined statement will possess assurances of accuracy. The rationale of Rule 805 would authorize receipt of an admission by an agent who lacks personal knowledge only if the declarant obtained his information

---

the resulting deposition the status of an admission by providing that it "may be used by an adverse party for any purpose."

[6] See, *e.g.,* Reid Brothers Logging Co. v. Ketchian Pulp Co., 699 F.2d 1292, 1306–07 n.25 (9th Cir.), *cert. denied,* 464 U.S. 916 (1983); Kingsley v. Baker/Beech-Nut Corp., 546 F.2d 1136 (5th Cir. 1977).

from a reliable source, such as records made in the course of a regularly conducted activity.

Rule 403 compels the same result, since the trial court in its discretion would have to exclude an agent's statements if it found that their probative value was substantially outweighed by the dangers of prejudice or confusion. Such a conclusion seems warranted where the statements refer to a crucial issue and are based on nothing more than office rumor.

¶ 15.02[05] Admissions: Vicarious[1]

Rule 801(d)(2)(D) makes admissible statements by agents made within the scope of their employment regardless of whether they have "speaking authority." The drafters favored this rule, whose effect is to permit the reception of all statements by an agent or employee that are relevant to his employment, because they found that the restricted "speaking authority" formula embodied in the orthodox authorized admissions rule frequently resulted in the rejection of highly probative evidence. Rule 801(d)(2)(D) provides:

> (d) Statements which are not hearsay.—A statement is not hearsay if—
>
> . . .
>
> (2) Admission by party-opponent.—The statement is offered against a party and is . . . (D) a statement by the party's agent or servant concerning a matter within the scope of the agency or employment, made during the existence of the relationship . . . .

The proponent of a statement offered as a vicarious admission need only show agency,[2] the making of the statement while the relationship continues,[3] and that the statement relates to a matter within

---

[1] See discussion in **Treatise** at ¶ 801(d)(2)(D)[01].

[2] See, *e.g.,* United States v. Mandel, 591 F.2d 1347, 1368 (4th Cir. 1979), *cert. denied,* 445 U.S. 961 (1980) (in prosecution of governor for mail fraud, statements of governor's legislative aides, but not of members of senate, were admissible).

[3] See, *e.g.,* S.E.C. v. Geon Industries, Inc., 531 F.2d 39, 43 n.3 (2d Cir. 1976) (court declined to admit testimony pursuant to Rule 801(d)(2)(D) where employee had been suspended by employer).

the scope of the agency.[4] The relationship between the agent and the principal need not be investigated and analyzed to determine the scope of the agent's authority as precisely as it must be when a statement is offered pursuant to Rule 801(d)(2)(C).[5] Statements made by the agent to his principal, as well as statements to third persons, are admissible.

Rule 801(d)(2)(D) does not contain an express requirement of personal knowledge. As was pointed out above, however, in connection with the discussion of authorized admissions, such a requirement should be read into the rule in order to fulfill the objectives of Rules 805 and 403. Gossip does not become reliable merely because it is heard in the workplace rather than at home. Not all courts agree that a lack of trustworthiness is a factor to be considered.[6]

Rule 801(d)(2)(D) rejects privity as a ground of admissibility by

---

[4] See, *e.g.,* Wright v. Farmer's Co-op of Ark. & Okla., 681 F.2d 549, 553 (8th Cir. 1982) (statement given to insurance adjuster by employee of service station about filling propane tank was admissible since it concerned matter within scope of his employment).

[5] See, *e.g.,* Hoptowit v. Ray, 682 F.2d 1237, 1262 (9th Cir. 1982) (rule does not require showing that statement is within the scope of the declarant's agency, but only that it relates to a matter within the scope of the agency). But see United States v. Valencia, 826 F.2d 169 (2d Cir. 1987) (statements made by counsel to prosecutor during informal plea discussions not admissible where statements could be used only for impeachment and not substantively, statements had not been transcribed or in writing, and use of statements might chill prospects for plea negotiations; dissent found that all the requirements of Rule 801(d)(2)(D) were met). *Compare* United States v. McKeon, 738 F.2d 26 (2d Cir. 1984) (opening statement admitted to counter a position taken by the defense at retrial). *Cf.* RAD Services, Inc. v. Aetna Casualty and Surety Co., 808 F.2d 271 (3d Cir. 1986) (ex-employee's invocation of Fifth Amendment at depositions admissible against employer).

A complete failure to lay a foundation will lead to exclusion of the statement. See Mitroff v. Xomox Corp., 797 F.2d 271, 276 (6th Cir. 1986) (in age discrimination suit, reversible error to admit statements by assistant personnel manager where there was no showing of basis for declarant's statements, or whether they were within scope of employment).

[6] See, *e.g.,* Mahlandt v. Wild Canid Survival & Research Center, Inc., 588 F.2d 626 (8th Cir. 1978) (employee's statement about an alleged attack by wolf owned by employer should have been admitted, even though employee had not seen attack and based his statement on conversations with persons who had not seen attack, because there is no personal knowledge requirement).

making no provision for it.[7] Most declarations of predecessors in interest will, however, be admissible as against interest when made if the declarant is unavailable or will come in under a residual clause.[8]

¶ 15.02[06]   Admissions: Co-conspirators' Statements[1]

Rule 801(d)(2)(E) provides that a statement of a co-conspirator is not hearsay if it is made (1) during the course and (2) in furtherance (3) of a conspiracy (4) of which declarant is a member. The rule applies in both civil and criminal cases, although it is most frequently invoked in criminal litigation. When conspiracy is charged, the statements may be admissible even though the trial court could properly direct a verdict on the conspiracy charge.[1a] There need not be a conspiracy count in the indictment to make this provision applicable. The rule provides:

(d) Statements which are not hearsay.—A statement is not hearsay if—

. . .

(2) Admission by party-opponent.—The statement is offered against a party and is . . . (E) a statement by a coconspirator of a party during the course and in furtherance of the conspiracy.

[a]   Theory

The drafters of the Federal Rules of Evidence refused to expand the co-conspirators exception by adopting a relevancy approach in-

---

[7] See, *e.g.*, Calhoun v. Baylor, 646 F.2d 1158, 1163 (5th Cir. 1981) (declarations of agents of bankrupt could not be considered admissions by trustee in bankruptcy, as successor in interest).

[8] See, *e.g.*, Huff v. White Motor Corp., 609 F.2d 286, 291 (7th Cir. 1979) (while privity-based admissions are not admissible as such, they may be admitted pursuant to residual hearsay exception).

[1] See discussion in **Treatise** at ¶ 801(d)(2)(E)[01].

[1a] United States v. Dworken, 855 F.2d 12, 23-24 (1st Cir. 1988) (in narcotics case where government sought to prove one over-arching conspiracy as to which jury acquitted, defendants argued on appeal that trial court should have directed verdict on conspiracy charge and therefore should have excluded co-conspirators' statements; appellate court found that statements were properly admitted since trial judge could have found by a preponderance of the evidence that there were several separate conspiracies).

stead of an agency approach as was done in the case of vicarious admissions. Even though the Advisory Committee considered "the agency theory of conspiracy . . . at best a fiction," it was adjudged a useful device for imposing some limits on the dangers posed by conspiracy prosecutions.

The agency theory holds that when persons enter into an agreement to commit a joint venture, they become agents for each other, so that each authorized statement made by a conspirator in the course of the conspiracy is attributable to all parties to the agreement. The goal or objective of the common enterprise or joint venture need not be illegal in order for the coconspirators exception to apply.[1b] Only those statements that tend to advance the objectives of the conspiracy are authorized because the acts of an agent bind his principal only when the agent acts within the scope of his authority. Rule 801(d)(2)(E) compels this result by making admissible only those statements of a conspirator that are made "in furtherance of the conspiracy." Although the requirement may exclude some relevant statements made by conspirators, it was inserted in order to strike a balance between the great need for co-conspirators' statements in combating undesirable criminal activity, which is inherently secretive and difficult to prove, and the need to protect the accused against the idle chatter and boasting of criminal partners, and inadvertently misreported or deliberately fabricated evidence.

[b]   Preliminary Questions for the Court

In 1987, in *Bourjaily v. United States,*[2] the Supreme Court resolved a number of issues about how Rule 801(d)(2)(E) should be interpreted. The Court confirmed, consonnant with the approach which had gradually been adopted by all of the circuits, that it is the trial court, rather than the jury, that must determine whether the four require-

---

[1b] United States v. Layton, 855 F.2d 1388, 1397-1400 (9th Cir. 1988), *cert. denied,* 109 S. Ct. 1178 (1989) (the critical question is whether the confederate was acting as an agent of the defendant when he made the statement sought to be admitted; in prosecution for murder of congressman in Guyana, statements made in furtherance of conspiracy to prevent congressman from learning truth of conditions in Jonestown would qualify as co-conspirators' statements whether the enterprise was legal or illegal).

[2] 483 U.S. —,107 S.Ct. 2775, 97 L.Ed.2d 144 (1987).

ments of the rule have been satisfied.[3] To ask the jurors to consider highly prejudicial statements of co-conspirators only if they first find the existence of the conspiracy and the defendant's participation in it is to present them with too tricky a task. Consequently, judges should refrain from advising juries about the admissibility of co-conspirator's statements, though they may be instructed that such evidence should be treated with caution.[4]

In *Bourjaily*, the Supreme Court also held "that when the preliminary facts relevant to Rule 801(d)(2)(E) are disputed, the offering party must prove them by a preponderance of the evidence." [5] Consequently, the government must prove by a preponderance of the evidence that there was a conspiracy involving the declarant and the defendant and that the statement seeking admission was made during the course of the conspiracy and in furtherance of the conspiracy.[6]

The *Bourjaily* Court also resolved the issue of what evidence the trial court may consider in making its preliminary determinations. The majority of the circuits had concluded that the court could look only to evidence independent of the co-conspirator's statement seeking admission.[7] The result, which was justified on an "anti-bootstrapping" rationale expressed initially by the Court in 1942 in *Glasser v. United States,*[8] seemed to a few of the circuits to be con-

---

[3] *Id.* at —, 107 S.Ct. at 2778, 97 L.Ed.2d at 152.

[4] United States v. Peters, 791 F.2d 1270, 1285–86 (7th Cir.), *cert. denied,* 107 S.Ct. 168 (1986) (although the district judge's comments on the admissibility of co-conspirator's statements was "ill-advised," there was no prejudice to defendants because the court later withdrew its comments and told the jury it could disregard them, citing **Treatise**).

[5] 483 U.S. —, —, 107 S.Ct. 2775, 2779, 97 L.Ed.2d 144, 153 (1987).

[6] Prior to *Bourjaily,* a number of courts had permitted the defendant's connection to the conspiracy to be proved by a lesser, slight evidence standard, once the existence of the conspiracy had been established by the preponderance of evidence standard. See, *e.g.,* United States v. Provenzano, 620 F.2d 985, 999 (3d Cir.), *cert. denied,* 449 U.S. 889 (1980). The defendant's involvement in the conspiracy must now be proved by the preponderance standard.

[7] Bourjaily v. United States, 483 U.S. —, —, 107 S.Ct. 2775, 2780, 97 L.Ed.2d 144, 154 (1987).

[8] 315 U.S. 60, 74–75, 62 S.Ct. 457, 467, 86 L.Ed. 680, 701 (1942) (in rejecting the admissibility of a co-conspirator's statement, the Court had said: "[S]uch declara-

trary to the mandate of Rule 104(a) which authorizes a court to use hearsay in determining preliminary questions. In *Bourjaily,* the Court agreed with the minority; it found that the bootstrapping rule of *Glasser* had not survived the enactment of the Federal Rules of Evidence: "Rule [104] on its face allows the trial judge to consider any evidence whatsoever, bound only by the rules of privilege." [9] A trial court may, therefore, examine the hearsay statements sought to be admitted in making a preliminary factual determination pursuant to Rule 104(a). The Court reserved decision on "whether the courts below could have relied solely upon [the] hearsay statements to determine that a conspiracy had been established by a preponderance of the evidence." [10]

While some circuits have endorsed preferred orders of proof that require trial courts, whenever possible, to determine the admissibility of co-conspirator statements before the statements are admitted in order to avoid jury prejudice,[11] all appellate courts recognize that the trial court must have considerable discretion to control the order of a trial.[12] To the extent possible, the admissibility of co-conspirator

---

tions are admissible over the objection of an alleged co-conspirator, who was not present when they were made, only if there is proof *aliunde* that he is connected with the conspiracy . . . . Otherwise, hearsay would lift itself by its own bootstraps to the level of competent evidence.").

[9] Bourjaily v. United States, 483 U.S. —, —, 107 S.Ct. 2775, 2780, 97 L.Ed.2d 144, 154 (1987) (Court relied on plain meaning of Rule 104(a).).

[10] *Id.* at —, 107 S.Ct. at 2781–82, 97 L.Ed.2d at 156. United States v. Silverman, 861 F.2d 571 (9th Cir. 1988) (all members of the court agree that the government must produce some evidence corroborating the coconspirator's statements but majority reverses on the ground that the additional evidence consisted of wholly innocuous conduct and statements by the defendant which were completely consistent with defendant's unawareness of the conspiracy, while the dissent argues that the majority's approach reinstates the pre-*Bourjaily* no bootstrapping rule).

[11] See, *e.g.,* United States v. James, 590 F.2d 575, 581–82 (5th Cir.) (en banc), *cert. denied,* 442 U.S. 917 (1979); United States v. Petersen, 611 F.2d 1313, 1330 (10th Cir. 1979), *cert. denied,* 447 U.S. 905 (1980).

[12] See, *e.g.,* United States v. Marquardt, 695 F.2d 1300, 1304–05 (5th Cir.), *cert. denied,* 460 U.S. 1093 (1983) (failure to hold *James* hearing not error where trial court determines that hearing would be duplicative of trial and waste time); United States v. Kaatz, 705 F.2d 1237, 1244 (10th Cir. 1983) ("[i]n a complex case such as this, the failure to make the finding until the close of the government case does not justify reversal").

statements should be discussed at the pre-trial conference, or if at trial, outside the hearing of the jury.[12a] In most cases, the court will be able to make its determination on the basis of colloquy, documents marked in advance of trial, proof from the pre-trial or suppression hearings, and the testimony of one or two witnesses. The court should rule conditionally on admissibility as soon as possible. Delay will inhibit the government in putting in its proof in the most desirable order, and may inconvenience witnesses who may have to return to tell the part of their story dealing with the co-conspirator's statement. In *Bourjaily,* the Court declined to "express an opinion on the proper order of proof that trial courts should follow in concluding that the preponderance standard has been satisfied in an on-going trial." [13]

[c]   In Furtherance

The adoption of Rule 801(d)(2)(E) should be viewed as mandating a construction of the "in furtherance" requirement protective of defendants, particularly since the Advisory Committee was concerned lest relaxation of this standard lead to the admission of less reliable evidence.[14] In view of the drafting history, it is inappropriate to treat co-conspirators' statements analogously to vicarious admissions by admitting statements that relate to the conspiracy but do not further its objectives.[15] Narrative declarations should not be admitted as a

---

[12a] United States v. Lance, 853 F.2d 1177, 1184 (5th Cir. 1988) (conspiracy conviction need not be reversed merely because jury heard judge's preliminary finding that a conspiracy existed for purposes of the coconspirator exception).

[13] Bourjaily v. United States, 483 U.S. —, —, n.1, 107 S.Ct. 2775, 2779, n.1, 97 L.Ed.2d 144, 153, n.1 (1987).

[14] *Cf.* United States v. Lieberman, 637 F.2d 95 (2d Cir. 1980) (court re-analyzed co-conspirator's statement that did not satisfy the "in furtherance" requirement as a declaration against penal interest; statement in question—that defendant had told declarant not to open the warehouse door at night—was found to be against interest because it indicated the declarant's knowledge of the furtive nature of his activities). Decisions such as *Lieberman* allow inculpatory declarations against penal interest to overcome the protections for the defendant supposedly built into Rule 801(d)(2)(E).

[15] But see United States v. Peacock, 654 F.2d 339, 350 (5th Cir. 1981) (*quoting* United States v. Patton, 594 F.2d 444, 447 (5th Cir. 1979); arson; statement about insurance fraud techniques that was made immediately after fire admitted; "[w]e have

matter of course,[16] and statements of confession should be carefully scrutinized.[17] Whether a particular statement tends to advance the objectives of the conspiracy can be determined only by examining the context in which the statement was made.[17a] In light of the policy of the rule, "in furtherance" should not be construed mechanically to authorize admission whenever the proponent or court is able to suggest a possible motive.[18]The statements need not be made to a

previously noted that the concept of furthering a conspiracy 'must not be applied too strictly or the purpose of the exception would be defeated.' ").

[16] See, e.g., United States v. Urbanik, 801 F.2d 692, 698 (4th Cir. 1986) ("casual aside" to buyer of marijuana concerning defendant's "connection" in Florida made while declarant and witness were weight-lifting was not in furtherance of the conspiracy because the statement did nothing to further the conspiracy; reversible error to have admitted; dissent found no error because it concluded that declarant was at gym to carry out drug transaction); United States v. Means, 695 F.2d 811, 818 (5th Cir. 1983) ("mere idle conversation" while driving to airport excluded); United States v. Eubanks, 591 F.2d 513, 520 (9th Cir. 1979) (casual admissions of culpability made to someone declarant had decided to trust were excluded).

[17] Compare Battle v. Lubrizol Corp., 673 F.2d 984, 990 (8th Cir. 1982) (boasts excluded) with United States v. Miller, 664 F.2d 94, 98 (5th Cir. 1981), cert. denied, 459 U.S. 854 (1982) ("Puffing, boasts, and other conversation . . . are admissible when used by the declarant to obtain the confidence of one involved in the conspiracy . . . (or) to allay suspicions.").

[17a] United States v. Caraza, 843 F.2d 432, 437 (11th Cir. 1988) (statement to captain of boat used in drug smuggling operations identifying person who had visited the boat as a principal in the operation was in furtherance of the conspiracy because captain's knowledge of person's status could affect future dealings between captain and declarant); United States v. Blackmon, 839 F.2d 900, 912-13 (2d Cir. 1988) (statement indicating that continued funding would be available if needed was "in furtherance;" such statements "promote cooperation among coconspirators by emphasizing the availability of essential prerequisites for the success of the criminal enterprise.").

[18] See, e.g., United States v. Mason, 658 F.2d 1263, 1270 (9th Cir. 1981) (agent, in order to elicit information about narcotics deal, concocted story about passing car and said he hoped source had not been scared off; statement by declarant that his source could not have been scared off as he left earlier admitted as statement of reassurance); United States v. Trotter, 529 F.2d 806 (3d Cir. 1976) (statement to owner of storage space that goods belonged to co-conspirator but that declarant was thinking of buying them can be construed as attempt to secure storage space). See also United States v. Dorn, 561 F.2d 1252, 1256-57 n.6 (7th Cir. 1977) (statements made by conspirator to wife telling her what was going on and who was doing what were properly admitted as she could not have been enlisted into conspiracy "without knowing at least minimally what each conspirator's duties were."). But

member of the conspiracy to be admissible.[18a]

[d] During the Course

Rule 801(d)(2)(E) requires that the statement have been made "during the course" of the conspiracy. Statements made before the conspiracy came into being, or after it terminated, do not qualify. Measuring the duration of a conspiracy often poses difficult issues for the trial court, particularly since it is sometimes hard to distinguish a long-term comprehensive conspiracy with intermittent activity from a series of discreet ventures.[19] RICO prosecutions have enormously increased the temporal scope as well as the substantive width of conspiracies for both substantive and evidentiary purposes. In *Krulewich v. United States,*[20] the Supreme Court refused to find

---

see United States v. Shoffner, 826 F.2d 619, 628 (7th Cir. 1987) ("statement need not have been exclusively, or even primarily, made to further the conspiracy"; reasonable basis or plausible interpretation is all the government must show); United States v. Magee, 821 F.2d 234, 244 (5th Cir. 1987) ("Ordinarily, a statement that identifies the role of one co-conspirator to another is in furtherance of the conspiracy.").

[18a] United States v. Zavala-Serra, 853 F.2d 1512, 1516 (9th Cir. 1988) (statements to person who was someone to whom declarant turned for assistance even though he was not actual member of the conspiracy were statements made "in furtherance").

[19] See, *e.g.,* United States v. Smith, 833 F.2d 213, 220–21 (10th Cir. 1987) (defendant argued that there was a conspiracy to sell two computers that ended with sale of second; government argued that there was a long-term conspiracy to sell computers; court found for government, stating: "When conspiratorial activity takes place for some two months, as true here, a hiatus of less than three months may support an inference of a breathing spell rather than a termination of the conspiracy.").

[20] 336 U.S. 440, 69 S.Ct. 716, 93 L.Ed. 790 (1949) (Mann Act prosecution; statement that it would be better if girls should take the blame was made after trip ended and conspirators had been arrested). United States v. Persico, 832 F.2d 705, 715–16 (2d Cir. 1987) (in RICO prosecution, statements by co-conspirator while in hiding, and after the announcement of an indictment and the arrests of several members of the conspiracy, were made during the course of the conspiracy; court concluded that the conspiracy lasted at least until the time of trial, since facts indicated that "some members of the conspiracy found prison no obstacle to continuing their association with the enterprise").

that the duration of a conspiracy covers all attempts to evade punishment; instead it held that termination occurs once the "main aim" of the conspiracy has been achieved. This test requires the trial court

(*Text continued on page 15–27*)

to decide how far beyond the actual commission of the crime[21] the objectives of the conspiracy extend, to acts such as the destruction of incriminating evidence,[22] or the obstruction of justice,[23] or the disposal of the illegally obtained proceeds.[24]

It is usually held, as a concomitant of agency rationale, that by joining a conspiracy the new member ratifies all prior action, thereby making admissible against him all statements that satisfy Rule 801(d)(2)(E), even though they were made before he became a member.[25] On the other hand, statements made by members of the conspiracy after a particular member has made a legally sufficient withdrawal[26] are not admissible against the person who has terminated his relationship with the conspiracy.[27] Nor can the declarations of

---

[21] United States v. Xheka, 704 F.2d 974, 986 (7th Cir.), *cert. denied,* 464 U.S. 993 (1983) (arson conspiracy continued while conspirators waited for insurance proceeds).

[22] See, *e.g.,* United States v. Medina, 761 F.2d 12, 16–18 (1st Cir. 1985) (kidnapping; statements about burning the ransom pickup car admitted). See also United States v. Carter, 760 F.2d 1568, 1581 (11th Cir. 1985) (arriving undetected or escaping is a primary objective in every drug-smuggling operation).

[23] See, *e.g.,* United States v. Carter, 721 F.2d 1514, 1524 (11th Cir.), *cert. denied,* 105 S.Ct. 89 (1984) (prosecution for drug smuggling encompassed further objective of obstructing justice).

[24] See, *e.g.,* United States v. Fortes, 619 F.2d 108, 117 (1st Cir. 1980) (admitting statement made while unloading loot from bank robbery).

[25] See, *e.g.,* United States v. United States Gypsum Co., 333 U.S. 364, 393, 68 S.Ct. 525, 92 L.Ed. 746 (1948) ("With the conspiracy thus fully established, the declarations and acts of the various members, even though made or done prior to the adherence of some to the conspiracy, become admissible against all as declarations or acts of co-conspirators in aid of the conspiracy."); United States v. Heater, 689 F.2d 783, 788 (8th Cir. 1982) ("[o]ne who joins a conspiracy after its inception, knowing its unlawful purpose, is charged with the same responsibility as if he had been one of its instigators").

[26] See **Treatise** at ¶ 801(d)(2)(E) for cases discussing the effect a conspirator's arrest has on the admissibility of his statements against the other conspirators, and the admissibility of their statements against him.

[27] See, *e.g.,* United States v. Walker, 796 F.2d 43, 49 (4th Cir. 1986) (mere cessation of activity insufficient to terminate conspiracy; conspiracy presumed to continue unless or until defendant affirmatively shows "acts inconsistent with the object of the conspiracy and that his intent to withdraw from the conspiracy was communicated in a manner reasonably calculated to reach his co-conspirators"); United States v. Mardian, 546 F.2d 973, 978 n.5 (D.C. Cir. 1976) (*quoting* United States

a person who is no longer a member of the conspiracy—because of arrest or voluntary withdrawal—be admitted against the remaining participants.[28]

[e] Confrontation

The Supreme Court has held that the requirements for complying with Rule 801(d)(2)(E) are identical to those which satisfy the Confrontation Clause. Consequently, once a co-conspirator's statement is admitted, it automatically complies with the dictates of the Sixth Amendment, regardless of whether the declarant is unavailable or whether the statement has been examined for indicia of reliability. See discussion of confrontation in ¶ 14.03[02].

Because of these recent developments, consideration should be given by the Advisory Committee on the Federal Rules of Criminal Procedure to the problem of disclosure of the statements of conspirators which the government intends to offer into evidence. The courts have interpreted Rule 16(a) of the Criminal Procedure Rules narrowly to authorize disclosure only of the statement of the defendant himself.[29] This approach overlooks that:

> [B]road discovery contributes to the fair and efficient administration of criminal justice by providing the defendant with enough information to make an informed decision as to plea, by minimizing the undesirable effect of surprise at trial; and by otherwise contributing to an accurate determination of the issue of guilt or innocence.[30]

---

v. Borelli, 336 F.2d 376, 388 (2d Cir. 1964), *cert. denied,* 379 U.S. 960 (1965); withdrawal requires "either the making of a clean breast to the authorities . . . or communication of the abandonment in a manner reasonably calculated to reach coconspirators").

[28] See, *e.g.,* United States v. Taylor, 802 F.2d 1108, 1117 (9th Cir. 1986), *cert. denied,* 107 S.Ct. 1309 (1987) (statements are admissible against a co-conspirator even though he had been arrested before the statement was made if the unarrested declarant believed conspiracy was still in progress); United States v. Smith, 578 F.2d 1227 (8th Cir. 1978).

[29] See, *e.g., In re* United States, 834 F.2d 283 (2d Cir. 1987), *rev'g* United States v. Gallo, 654 F.Supp. 463 (E.D.N.Y. 1987); United States v. Percevault, 490 F.2d 126 (2d Cir. 1974), *rev'g* 61 F.R.D. 338 (E.D.N.Y. 1973).

[30] Notes of Committee on the Judiciary, House Rept. No. 247, 94th Cong., 1st Sess.

In a complex case, such as a RICO prosecution, co-conspirators' statements may have enormous impact. If these statements are to be immune to hearsay and Confrontation Clause challenge, defendants should at least be protected from the prejudical effect of surprise. Even if the trial court does not have the inherent power to order disclosure, it can exclude unreliable co-conspirators' statements pursuant to Rule 403.

13, reprinted in 1975 U.S. Code Cong. & Ad. News 674, 685 (quoting Notes of the Advisory Committee on Rules, 62 F.R.D. 271, 307, 308 (1974)).

CHAPTER 16

Hearsay Exceptions—Availability of Declarant Immaterial

SYNOPSIS

(Pub.819)

¶ 16.01   Present Sense Impression—Rule 803(1)[1]

Rule 803 governs those exceptions to the hearsay rule that, unlike Rule 804 exceptions, do not require the declarant to be unavailable. Twenty-three of the provisions in Rule 803 set forth class exceptions; Rule 803(24) establishes a non-class, or residual, exception for hearsay that does not fit into any of the foregoing categories but possesses equivalent guarantees of trustworthiness. Rule 803(24) and the corresponding exception in Rule 804(b)(5) are discussed in Chapter 14, *supra*.

The exceptions in Rule 803 can be grouped into a number of major categories around which the discussion below is organized: spontaneous statements (Rules 803(1)–(4)), written documents and records of both a private and a public nature (Rules 803(5)–(16), (22)–(23)), publications (Rules 803(17) and (18)) and reputation (Rules 803(19)–(21)).

Though advocated by Thayer,[2] and acknowledged to exist by a few courts prior to 1975,[3] the hearsay exception for statements of present sense impression was rarely utilized until it was codified as Rule 803(1) of the Federal Rules of Evidence. The rule provides:

Rule 803

HEARSAY EXCEPTIONS; AVAILABILITY OF DECLARANT IMMATERIAL

The following are not excluded by the hearsay rule, even though the declarant is available as a witness:

(1)–Present sense impression.—A statement describing or explaining an event or condition made while the declarant was perceiving the event or condition, or immediately thereafter.

---

[1] See discussion in **Treatise** at ¶ 803(2)[01].

[2] See Thayer, "Bedingfield's Case—Declarations as a Part of the Res Gestae," 15 Am. U.L. Rev. 71, 82–83 (1881).

[3] See, *e.g.*, Houston Oxygen Co. v. Texas, 139 Tex, 1 (1942); Emens v. Lehigh Valley R.R. Co., 223 Fed. 810 (N.D.N.Y. 1915), *cert. denied*, 242 U.S. 627 (1916).

¶ 16.01[01]   Rationale

Underlying Rule 803(1) is the assumption that statements of perception substantially contemporaneous with an event are highly trustworthy because there is no memory problem, and little or no opportunity to fabricate.[4] Furthermore, the witness who testifies frequently had the same opportunity to perceive the event as the declarant, thereby providing a check on the veracity of the declarant.[5]

A number of requirements must be met for the statement to be admissible pursuant to Rule 803(1). A discussion of these requirements follows.

¶ 16.01[02]   Time

The statement must be made while the event or condition is being perceived by the declarant or "immediately thereafter." Precise contemporaneity is not always possible, and a slight lapse of time should not result in the loss of valuable evidence.[6] The trial court must exercise its discretion pursuant to Rule 104(a) to decide whether the lapse of time is justified by the circumstances of the particular case, or whether it undermines the reliability of the evi-

---

[4] United States v. Peacock, 654 F.2d 339, 350 (5th Cir. 1981), *modified on other grounds,* 686 F.2d 356 (5th Cir. 1982) (statements by witness about comments her husband had made to her immediately after telephone conversation with defendant satisfied Rule 803(1) because there was no time for husband to consciously manipulate the truth).

[5] Robinson v. Shapiro, 484 F.Supp. 91, 95 (S.D.N.Y. 1980), *aff'd on other grounds,* 646 F.2d 734 (2d Cir. 1981) (statement trustworthy because witness could independently observe the condition to which the statement referred).

[6] See, *e.g.,* United States v. Portsmouth Paving Corp., 694 F.2d 312, 323 (4th Cir. 1982) (admitting statement made within few seconds after event described); Hilyer v. Howat Concrete Co., Inc., 578 F.2d 422 (D.C.Cir. 1978) (statement made 15 to 45 minutes after accident did not qualify as present sense impression); United States v. Obayogbona, 627 F.Supp. 329 (E.D.N.Y. 1985), *aff'd,* — F.2d — (2d Cir. 1986) (15 minutes after event permitted under special circumstances), Wolfson v. Mutual Life Ins. Co. of N.Y., 455 F.Supp. 82 (M.D.Pa.), *aff'd,* 588 F.2d 825 (3d Cir. 1978) (statement about meeting made immediately after meeting might qualify; statements made several hours afterwards would not) (dictum).

dence. The lapse of time may mean that the witness will not be able to corroborate the declarant's statement. Although corroboration is not a requirement, it is a factor that a court may consider in determining whether a statement not exactly contemporaneous qualifies for admission.[7]

¶ 16.01[03]   Perception

While the declarant must have perceived the event or condition about which the statement was made, Rule 803(1) does not require the declarant to have participated in the event described. Consequently, the remarks of a bystander and even of an unidentified bystander are admissible provided the requirements of the exception are met.[8] The less contact the declarant has with the event in question, the more difficult it becomes to infer that it was perceived by the declarant.[9] An unidentified declarant's capacity to perceive can neither be substantiated nor attacked (*cf.* Rule 806); accordingly a court may be more likely to find that the danger of fabrication is too great to justify admission.

It is immaterial according to Rule 803(1) whether declarant is available or present as a witness. When the declarant fails to testify, the court's suspicion of the witness' testimony may lead it to find that the declarant's perception was not established. On the

---

[7] United States v. Blakey, 607 F.2d 779, 785 (7th Cir. 1979) (tape recorded statement of victim, deceased by time of trial, made between several minutes and 23 minutes after defendants left victim's shop admitted as present sense impression where several witnesses could testify to all the events leading up to and following the brief meeting between victim and defendants so that there was substantial corroboration).

[8] United States v. Medico, 557 F.2d 309 (2d Cir.), *cert. denied,* 434 U.S. 986 (1977) (bank employee testified that after bank robbery he wrote down license plate number which was called out to him by unidentified bystander to whom it was being relayed by other unidentified bystander; majority found that both statements satisfied Rule 803(1); according to dissent only the statement by person perceiving the license plate was covered by Rule 803(1)).

[9] See Meder v. Everest & Jennings, Inc., 637 F.2d 1182, 1186 (8th Cir. 1981) (portion of policeman's accident report regarding cause of accident did not qualify as present sense impression where officer was unable to specify source of the information, making it impossible to determine whether the maker of the statement had perceived the accident).

other hand, since the witness can be cross-examined, the court may conclude that the witness' credibility and the declarant's derived credibility can safely be left to the jury. Much will depend on the type of case, the availability of other evidence, the verifying details in the statement, and the setting in which the statement was made.

¶ 16.01[04]   Subject Matter

Rule 803(1) requires that the statement be one "describing or explaining" the event or condition. Narratives of past events or statements on other subjects are meant to be excluded by this phraseology because they lack the required contemporaneity that guards against fabrication. A statement evoked by the event but which does not describe or explain it would not be admissible. This limitation may be decisive in a case where it is questionable whether the event is sufficiently exciting to qualify under Rule 803(2), the excited utterance exception, which does not impose this limitation. The "describing or explaining" limitation should not, however, be interpreted as meaning that the statement must relate directly to the proposition. The statement should be admitted if it might aid the jury in determining what happened, and satisfies the contemporaneity test. [10]

¶ 16.02   Excited Utterances—Rule 803(2) [1]

The hearsay exception for excited utterances, unlike the exception for present sense impressions, had been well-recognized in the federal courts prior to the enactment of the Federal Rules of Evidence. Many of the earlier cases used res gestae terminology, a practice no longer appropriate. Rule 803(2) provides:

The following are not excluded by the hearsay rule, even though the declarant is available as a witness:

---

[10] See cases in which courts have admitted statements about telephone conversations, *e.g.*, United States v. Portsmouth Paving Corp., 694 F.2d 312, 322 (4th Cir. 1982) (statement described contents of telephone conversation); United States v. Earley, 657 F.2d 195 (8th Cir. 1981) (declarant victim, after receiving call two days before her murder, said it sounded like defendant).

[1] See discussion in Treatise at ¶ 803(2).

. . .

(2) Excited utterance.—A statement relating to a startling event or condition made while the declarant was under the stress of excitement caused by the event or condition.

¶ 16.02[01]   Rationale

The assumption underlying this exception is that a person under the sway of excitement precipitated by an external event will be bereft of the reflective capacity essential for fabrication, so that any statements made while the excitement lasts will be spontaneous and trustworthy. Although some criticism has been voiced about the reliability of statements made under stress, the drafters of Rule 803(2) opted not to lose the relevant evidence that may be admitted pursuant to this exception.

A number of requirements must be met in order for a statement to qualify for admission pursuant to the excited utterance exception.

¶ 16.02[02]   Startling Event or Condition

In order for the exception to apply, there must be proof that an event occurred and that it was startling. Ordinarily, proof that the event occurred is furnished either by testimony of witnesses other than the declarant, or by circumstantial evidence that something out of the ordinary occurred. If there is no proof of the startling event other than the statement itself, it may still be admitted pursuant to the last sentence of Rule 104(a) which provides that a court is not bound by rules of evidence, other than privilege, in making preliminary determinations. Consequently, a court may use the hearsay statement to establish the foundation for a hearsay exception.

The court must also determine whether the event was startling. The presence of blood, caused by either accident or assault, seems to create an automatic assumption of excitement. Whether non-sanguinary events qualify depends on the judge's assessment of the shock value of the event in question.[2] Statements about non-

---

[2] See, *e.g.*, David By Berkeley v. Pueblo Supermarket, 740 F.2d 230, 233 (3d

startling events may be admissible pusuant to Rule 803(1) if they are sufficiently contemporaneous.

¶ 16.02[03]   Perception

Rule 803(2) does not expressly state that declarant must have seen the event. Observation is, however, mandated by the requirement that the declarant's excitement be "caused" by the event or condition. Despite the difference in wording, the requirement of perception is identical in Rules 803(1) and (2). The perception need not be proved directly, but may be inferred from the nature of the statement and surrounding circumstances, and the declarant need not be a participant in the event. Suspicion of the statement's reliability may lead to exclusion, particularly when the risk of fabrication is high because the declarant is an unidentified bystander.[3]

¶ 16.02[04]   Under the Stress of Excitement

Analytically, the court must find (1) that because of the event the declarant was excited, and (2) that declarant was still excited when making the statement. Courts rarely analyze the first factor separately; they assume that a reasonable person viewing a startling event will be excited, and do not attempt to evaluate the impact of the event on the particular declarant's mind.

¶ 16.02[05]   Time

When evidence is presented as to declarant's state or behavior, it is usually because considerable time has elapsed between the event and the statement, and the proponent is seeking to establish

---

Cir. 1984) (fall by eight months pregnant plaintiff onto her stomach was a startling occasion); United States v. Napier, 518 F.2d 316 (9th Cir.), *cert. denied,* 423 U.S. 895 (1975) (assault victim suddenly confronted with photograph of assailant).

[3] See, *e.g.,* Miller v. Keating, 754 F.2d 507 (3d Cir. 1985) (statement by unidentified declarant excluded where external circumstances failed to demonstrate that declarant was in a position to have seen what happened and that he spoke under stress of excitement).

that defendant was still under nervous stress while making the statement. Since lack of capacity, rather than lack of time, to fabricate is the justification for this exception, the period of acceptable time will frequently be considerably longer than when the statement is being offered as a present sense impression, an exception that rests on the latter rationale.

No particular period of elapsed time is decisive. The crucial point is that the court must be able to find that the declarant's state at the time of making the statement ruled out the possibility of conscious reflection. In making this determination, the court must assess all the factors in the case,[4] including the nature of the startling event,[5] the character of the statement,[6] the condition of the declarant,[7] the identity of the declarant, and the availability of other evidence.

¶ 16.03   Then Existing Mental, Emotional, or Physical Condition—Rule 803(3)

Rule 803(3) combines in one provision what are really two exceptions of markedly different characteristics. Statements of then existing physical condition are among the least troubling and complex exceptions to the hearsay rule; statements of mental or emo-

---

[4] See, *e.g.*, United States v. Golden, 671 F.2d 369 (10th Cir.), *cert. denied*, 456 U.S. 919 (1982) (court admitted statement made by victim 15 minutes after assault after driving from scene at 120 miles an hour).

[5] United States v. Iron Shell, 633 F.2d 77, 85–87 (8th Cir. 1980), *cert. denied*, 450 U.S. 1001 (1981) (intent to rape prosecutrix where defendant had pulled down 9 year-old declarant's jeans).

[6] See United States v. Knife, 592 F.2d 472, 481 n.10 (8th Cir. 1979) (defendant's statement, "you didn't think we'd just let him off for killing one of our friends in the jail the other night, did you?" by its very nature constituted a reflection on the part of the declarant and could not qualify as an excited utterance).

[7] Physical factors, such as shock, unconsciousness or pain, may prolong the period in which the risk of fabrication is reduced to an acceptable minimum. See, *e.g.*, Haggins v. Warden, Fort Pillow State Farm, 715 F.2d 1050, 1057–58 (6th Cir. 1983), *cert. denied*, 464 U.S. 1071 (1984) (statement by four year old made one to one and a half hours after rape admissible); Hilyer v. Howat Concrete Co., Inc., 578 F.2d 422 (D.C. Cir. 1978) (statement made between 15 and 45 minutes after accident admissible where declarant testified that he was so excited that he didn't recall making statement).

tional condition, on the other hand, pose some of the most difficult issues that have to be faced in applying the hearsay rule. The rule provides:

> The following are not excluded by the hearsay rule, even though the declarant is unavailable as a witness: . . .
>
> (3) Then existing mental, emotional, or physical condition.—A statement of the declarant's then existing state of mind, emotion, sensation, or physical condition (such as intent, plan, motive, design, mental feeling, pain, and bodily health), but not including a statement of memory or belief to prove the fact remembered or believed unless it relates to the execution, revocation, identification, or terms of declarant's will.

The joint treatment of these conditions is explicable because, historically, the exception for statements of a presently existing mental state or emotion grew out of the exception for declarations of bodily pain or feeling, and because the basic rationale underlying both exceptions is the same. Both types of statement are considered trustworthy because their spontaneous nature makes them more reliable (or at least no less reliable) than declarations made on the stand at a time when memory may be impaired and external pressures have been brought to bear. As with statements of present sense impressions, of which the instant statements are but a specialized application, the factor of contemporaneousness provides some assurance against fabrication. Furthermore, the genuine need for evidence of an individual's physical or mental state might otherwise be unmet since a person's feelings are not directly cognizable by anyone else. Consequently, evidence of such statements is admissible regardless of whether the declarant is available.

¶ 16.03[01]   Then Existing Physical Condition[1]

Proof of pain and suffering is frequently called for in personal injury litigation both to establish damages and to show the nature and extent of the injury. While objective conditions may give some indication of the degree of pain involved, the sufferer's own contemporaneous description is often a decidedly superior form of proof.

Rule 803(3) does not require the statement to be made to a phy-

---

[1] See discussion in **Treatise** at ¶ 803(3)[01].

sician. It may be testified to by "members of the family, friends or other persons." The rule does not differentiate between words of complaint and gestures or non-verbal sounds of pain. The latter, if instinctive and involuntary, do not fall within the hearsay definition in Rule 801 since they constitute non-assertive conduct, but there is no need to draw this line since they would in either case be admissible.

Since contemporaneity is the guarantee of trustworthiness, statements indicative of reflection rather than spontaneity must be excluded. Consequently, descriptions of past pain or symptoms, and explanations of how the injury occurred, may not be admitted pursuant to Rule 803(3). Such statements may, however, satisfy other hearsay rules: they may qualify as admissions or prior inconsistent statements pursuant to Rule 801, as excited utterances pursuant to Rule 803(2), as statements for purposes of medical diagnosis or treatment pursuant to Rule 803(4), or under Rule 703 as the basis for testimony by a medical or other expert if "of a type reasonably relied upon by experts in the particular field."

The declaration must be contemporaneous with the physical feeling, not the precipitating event. While it is irrelevant for the purposes of admissibility whether the statement was made after the claim or controversy arose, the trier of fact may assess this factor in deciding how much weight the statement should be given.

¶ 16.03[02]   Then Existing Mental or Emotional Condition

[a]   In General[1]

Before turning to a discussion of the scope of the exception for statements of mental or emotional condition, it is useful to consider the ways in which mental state can be proved, since some of the confusion and complexity stem from a failure to identify hearsay dangers and to distinguish between hearsay and non-hearsay use.

1. The hearsay rule is not involved when a witness testifies about his own state of mind at a particular time.

---

[1] See discussion in **Treatise** at ¶ 803(3)[02].

2. A state of mind can be proved circumstantially by statements or conduct which are not intended to assert the truth of the fact being proved. Technically, pursuant to the definitions in Rule 801, proof of such statements or non-verbal conduct does not raise a hearsay problem at all under the Federal Rules of Evidence. Nevertheless, further discussion is warranted under Rule 803(3) because courts frequently do not distinguish between the two uses, and because even statements that are technically non-hearsay may pose hearsay dangers.

3. Mental state is sometimes proved as part of a so called "verbal act." See discussion, in Chapter 14, *supra*. The statement is not hearsay because it is not being used assertively; it is admitted to shed light on an otherwise ambiguous relevant act, such as handing over money.

4. A statement may be proffered on the theory that it is probative of declarant's then existing state of mind, such as fear, knowledge, or belief, and this state of mind is the issue to be proved. This is a hearsay use, but Rule 803(3) applies.

5. A statement may be proffered to prove declarant's then existing state of mind not as an end in itself but as the basis for an inference that the declarant subsequently acted in accordance with the earlier expressed intent. This again is a hearsay use, but the statement is admissible pursuant to Rule 803(3).

6. A statement may be proffered to prove the declarant's then existing state of mind as the basis for an inference that declarant had previously acted in a particular way. Rule 803(3) admits such statements only if they relate to the execution, revocation, identification or terms of declarant's will.

[b] Mental State in Issue[2]

The least complicated situation involving mental state to which Rule 803(3) applies is when the statement is used to evidence a state of mind in issue—that is to say where the state of mind is the material proposition or is used to infer the truth or falsity of a material proposition. The declarant's state of mind may be relevant in

---

[2] See **Treatise** at ¶ 803(3)[03].

a wide variety of contexts. For example, statements have been admitted to show such matters as the state of mind of customers on the issue of good will,[3] motive to prove guilt,[4] competency to enter into legal transactions,[5] intent as a material proposition,[6] and fear as a material proposition on a charge of extortion.[7]

Rule 803(3) restates the traditional requirement that the statement must relate to a then existing state of mind. However, courts generally admit some statements indicative of the mental state in issue even if they were made before or after the moment in question on the assumption that states of mind have a certain degree of continuity. The trial court must decide whether a given statement falls within or without this period of continuous mental process.[8] In making this determination, the court should consider the hearsay dangers involved, as well as the availability of the declarant as a witness.

---

[3] See, *e.g.,* Morris Jewelers v. General Electric Credit Corp., 714 F.2d 32 (5th Cir. 1983) (where damages were claimed for loss of good will, statements showing angered state of mind of plaintiff's customers properly admitted); Hydrolevel Corp. v. American Society of Mechanical Engineers, Inc., 635 F.2d 118, 128 (2d Cir. 1980), *aff'd,* 456 U.S. 556, (1982) (reasons for not dealing with a supplier).

[4] See, *e.g.,* United States v. Harvey, 526 F.2d 529 (2d Cir. 1975), *cert. denied,* 424 U.S. 956 (1976) (conspiracy to murder eyewitness; statements by victim indicative of his knowledge were relevant to showing conspirator's motive).

[5] See, *e.g.,* Seattle-First National Bank v. Randall, 532 F.2d 1291 (9th Cir. 1976) (diaries of customer of bank admitted on issue of whether customer was competent at time of loan).

[6] See, *e.g.,* United States v. DiMaria, 727 F.2d 265, 270–72 (2d Cir. 1984) (reversible error to have excluded defendant's statement at time of arrest which revealed his then existing state of mind); United States v. Taglione, 546 F.2d 194, 200–01 (5th Cir. 1977) (extortion; defendant claimed he had merely been negotiating for reward; error to have excluded testimony of defendant's former attorney as to conversation in which defendant asked if it would be legal to negotiate for reward).

[7] See, *e.g.,* United States v, Kelly, 722 F.2d 873, 878 (1st Cir. 1983), *cert. denied,* 465 U.S. 1070 (1984) (testimony that victim of extortion was afraid of defendant).

[8] See United States v. Ponticelli, 622 F.2d 985, 991 (9th Cir.), *cert. denied,* 449 U.S. 1016 (1980) (in applying Rule 803(3) court must consider contemporaneousness, chance for reflection and relevance).

[c]   State of Mind to Show Subsequent Act[9]

The starting point for all discussions of statements of intention to prove a subsequent act is the fascinating case of *Mutual Life Insurance Co. v. Hillmon.*[10] The crucial issue in *Hillmon* was whether a man fatally shot at Crooked Creek, Kansas on March 17, 1879, was Hillmon, who was heavily insured, or a man called Frederick Walters. Neither Hillmon nor Walters was ever seen again after the shooting. In order to prove that the body was that of Walters rather than their insured, the insurance companies in question offered in evidence letters from Walters to his sister and fiancee indicating his intention to leave with "a certain Mr. Hillmon, a sheep trader, for Colorado, and parts unknown to me" in early March, 1879. The Supreme Court held that the letters should have been admitted, in language which forms the basis for all further discussions of the admissibility of statements of intention to prove a subsequent act:

> The existence of a particular intention in a certain person at a certain time being a material fact to be proved, evidence that he expressed that intention at that time is as direct evidence of the fact, as his own testimony that he then had that intention would be. After his death there can hardly be any other way of proving it; and while he is still alive, his own memory of his state of mind at a former time is no more likely to be clear and true than a bystander's recollection of what he then said, and is less trustworthy than letters written by him at the very time and under circumstances precluding a suspicion of misrepresentation.

> The letters in question were competent, not as narratives of facts communicated to the writer by others, nor yet as proof that he actually went away from Wichita, but as evidence that, shortly before the time when other evidence tended to show that he went away, he had the intention of going, and of going with Hillmon, which made it more probable both that he did go and that he went with Hillmon, than if there had been no proof of such intention.[11]

Rule 803(3) codifies *Hillmon* by classifying a statement of intent as a statement of the declarant's then existing state of mind to

---

[9] See **Treatise** at ¶ 803(3)[04].

[10] 145 U.S. 285, 36 L.Ed. 706 (1892).

[11] Mutual Life Insurance Co. v. Hillmon, 145 U.S. 285, 295–96, 36 L.Ed. 706 (1892).

which the hearsay rule does not apply. Whether the statement may be used to prove a subsequent event is a question of relevancy governed by Rule 401. Both the hearsay and relevancy hurdles must be passed in order for the statement to be admissible. Even relevancy does not guarantee admissibility if probative value is substantially outweighed by the dangers of prejudice, confusion or waste of time specified in Rule 403.

A frequently occurring instance of low probative value and prejudice arises when declarant's statement implicates a second person's intention to commit a future act as well as his own. In the *Hillmon* case itself, proof that Walters was willing to go with Hillmon did not prove that Hillmon was willing to go with Walters. The House Judiciary Committee would have limited the Hillmon doctrine "so as to render statements of intent by a declarant admissible only to prove his future conduct, not the future conduct of another person." The Senate Report and the Conference Report are silent on this point.

Cases decided pursuant to Rule 803(3) indicate that although statements of intent have been admitted in joint action situations,[12] the federal judiciary has been extremely circumspect about relying on Rule 803(3) when the action of a person other than the declarant is at issue.[13] At times, the statement in question has been admitted instead as a statement of a co-conspirator pursuant to Rule 801(d)(2)(E).[14]

[d] State of Mind to Show Previous Act[15]

Although Rule 803(3) permits a statement of state of mind to

---

[12] See, *e.g.,* United States v. Pheaster, 544 F.2d 353, 374–80 (9th Cir.), *cert. denied,* 429 U.S. 1099 (1977) (pre-Rules case admitting statement that victim was going to meet defendant); United States v. Astorga-Torres, 682 F.2d 1331, 1335–36 (9th Cir.), *cert. denied,* 459 U.S. l040 (1982) (relies on *Pheaster*).

[13] See, *e.g.,* United States v. Cicale, 691 F.2d 95, 103–04 (2d Cir. 1982), *cert. denied,* 460 U.S. 1082 (1983) (imposing requirement that independent non-hearsay evidence corroborate statement); United States v. Mangan, 575 F.2d 32, 43 n.12 (2d Cir.), *cert. denied,* 439 U.S. 931 (1978) (court refused to rely on Rule 803(3) to admit statement by declarant about his plans with another).

[14] See, *e.g.,* United States v. Moore, 571 F.2d 76 (2d Cir. 1978).

[15] See discussion in **Treatise** at ¶ 803(3)[05].

prove subsequent conduct, it specifically excludes "a statement of memory or belief to prove the fact remembered or believed" except in will cases.[16] A contrary rule would annihilate the hearsay rule.[17] From the standpoint of relevance, a memory of an event makes it more likely that the event did occur. If the hearsay hurdle could be overcome, an out-of-court statement, such as "I went to the movies yesterday," could be reformulated into a statement "I have a present belief that I went to the movies yesterday," which would then be relevant to show that declarant had gone to the movies.

The blanket exclusion of statements of memory or belief is justified on the ground that the dangers of improper perception, faulty memory and deliberate misstatement are far greater when the statement is being used to prove a past act rather than a future act. This is particularly so when the statement implicates the past acts of third parties, as in the leading case of *Shepard v. United States*,[18] in which the Supreme Court considered the admissibility of the victim's statement that "Dr. Shepard has poisoned me." Rejecting the argument that the statement was admissible as evidence of declarant's state of mind to rebut the defense of suicide, Justice Cardozo wrote for the Court:

> The testimony now questioned faced backward and not forward. This at least it did in its most obvious implications. What is even more important, it spoke to a past act, and more than that, to an act by some one not the speaker.[19]

---

[16] Statements of memory or belief may be admitted to prove the fact remembered or believed if they relate to the execution, revocation, identification, or terms of declarant's will. Will matters arise infrequently in federal jurisdictions. Whether statements made in somewhat similar situations such as in suits about life insurance policies should be treated analogously is discussed in the **Treatise** at ¶ 803(3)[05].

[17] Shepard v. United States, 290 U.S. 96, 105–06, 54 S.Ct. 22, 78 L.Ed. 196 (1933) ("Declarations of intention, casting light upon the future, have been sharply distinguished from declarations of memory, pointing backwards to the past. There would be an end, or nearly that, to the rule against hearsay if the distinction were ignored.").

[18] 290 U.S. 96, 54 S.Ct. 22, 78 L.Ed. 196 (1933).

[19] *Id.* at 106. See also United States v. Day, 591 F.2d 861, 882–83 (D.C. Cir. 1978) (prophecy by victim as to what might happen to him had too great a potential for unfair prejudice as jury might draw inference about defendants' past con-

When, however, the statement of memory or belief would be used circumstantially to prove conduct on the part of the declarant which produced the mental state, the dangers of faulty perception or memory, and deliberate fabrication are minimal when only a small amount of time elapsed between the event and statement, and the statement was made before a motive to falsify arose. Despite Rule 803(3), such a statement should qualify for admission pursuant to Rule 803(24) as a "statement having equivalent circumstantial guarantees of trustworthiness." See discussion, *infra*.

Frank recognition that some statements of memory and belief are reliable would encourage consideration of the actual dangers presented by the facts of the particular case. It would moderate the highly theoretical discussions in which some courts indulge in seeking to implement *Hillmon* and *Shepard,* and effectuate the policy of the Federal Rules of Evidence in promoting accurate fact-finding.

The most difficult cases are those in which the past, present and future are intertwined in the statement seeking admission. In *United States v. Annunziato,*[20] for instance, a prosecution for receiving bribes, a son testified that his father told him that he had received a call from defendant asking for money on a particular construction project. In response to his son's question about what he intended to do, the father stated that he had agreed to send money to the defendant. The Second Circuit found that the "most obvious implications" of the father's statement looked forward— he was going to send the money. Arguably, however, the evidence was much more powerful and probative in looking backwards—to show that the defendant had requested the payment as a bribe. In difficult cases such as these, in the ultimate analysis, the principles expressed in Rule 403 must be applied.[21]

---

duct towards victim); United States v. Brown, 490 F.2d 758, 766 (D.C. Cir. 1974) (prejudicial error in allowing victim's wife to testify that her husband was afraid he would be murdered by defendant).

[20] 293 F.2d 373 (2d Cir.), *cert. denied*, 368 U.S. 919 (1961).

[21] See, *e.g.,* United States v. Mandel, 437 F.Supp. 262 (D. Md. 1977) (court refused to admit testimony by wife of co-defendant that her husband had told her that he and other co-defendant were going to acquire race track but that she was not to reveal this to anyone including the defendant; court noted that statement implied 1) that co-defendants had an agreement, entered into in the past, to con-

In any event, in a case like *Annunziato* it would no longer be necessary to press the *Hillmon* doctrine so far. Under the subsequently enacted Federal Rules of Evidence, such a statement of a past event may be admissible as a declaration against interest pursuant to Rule 804(b)(3), since the declarant had died by the time of trial, or pursuant to Rule 803(24), if the court is satisfied that sufficient guarantees of trustworthiness are present. No matter what the category, probative force and prejudice must be weighed.

¶ 16.04 Statements for Purposes of Medical Diagnosis or Treatment—Rule 803(4)[1]

Rule 803(4) provides an extremely broad exception for statements made for purposes of medical diagnosis or treatment. The rule excludes from the hearsay rule statements relating to present or past pain, symptoms and sensations, as well as statements which describe the inception and cause of these conditions, insofar as they bear on treatment or diagnosis. The rule does not differentiate between statements made to treating physicians and those made to physicians consulted solely for diagnosis, even if the consultation was solely with a view to having the physician testify in court as an expert on behalf of the declarant. Nor is the rule limited to statements relating to bodily conditions; statements pertaining to mental health are covered by the rule, although as the discussion below indicates, they may at times be excluded.

Rule 803(4) provides:

The following are not excluded by the hearsay rule, even though the declarant is available as a witness:

. . .

(4) Statements for purposes of medical diagnosis or treatment.—

---

ceal their interests from defendant and 2) that co-defendants intended to keep their interests secret in the future; court excluded because it found that the probative value and weight of the statement was outweighed by prejudice, since unlike the *Annuziato* situation, the declaration did not qualify as a declaration against interest or a co-conspirators' statement, and there was no need for this hearsay since the declarant could testify and receipt of the hearsay could lead to widespread fabrication).

[1] See discussion in **Treatise** at ¶ 803(4)[01].

Statements made for purposes of medical diagnosis or treatment and describing medical history, or past or present symptoms, pain, or sensations, or the inception or general character of the cause or external source thereof insofar as reasonably pertinent to diagnosis or treatment.

The reliability of statements made for the purpose of medical treatment is ensured by the declarant's motive to be truthful since treatment hinges largely on the accuracy of the information imparted to the physician or other person involved in providing medical care. The need for such statements is great since there frequently will be no other evidence available concerning subjective symptoms. Since the declarant's motive to promote effective treatment is crucial, the Advisory Committee's notes indicate that statements to hospital attendants, ambulance drivers, or even members of the family are also admissible provided they were made in order to obtain treatment.

Nor does the rule require the statements to refer to the declarant's physical condition. Statements relating to someone else's physical condition, such as a child, are admissible, provided again, that they were made for purposes of treatment. The relationship between declarant and patient will usually determine admissibility. In the case of a child, a court would undoubtedly assume the absence of any motive to mislead on the part of parents. As the relationship becomes less close, the statement becomes less reliable, both because the motive to tell the truth becomes less strong, and because even a stranger in good faith may not be able to describe another's physical pain and suffering as infallibly as an intimate. The court in its discretion pursuant to Rule 403 will have to assess the probative worth of the statement, which will depend on its significance, its contents, by whom it was made, and in what circumstances it was made, and decide whether admission is warranted despite the dangers of prejudice, confusion and waste of time. Statements made for the purposes of medical diagnosis to a non-treating physician rest on a somewhat different rationale. Although some courts and commentators have expressed apprehension that in the absence of a motive to foster treatment, a declarant has no motive to speak truthfully, the Advisory Committee felt that exclusion of such statements would be inconsistent with the overall scheme of the Federal Rules. Rule 803(6) authorizes the admission of hospital and medical office records that contain diagnoses and opinions, and Rule 703 permits a physician to express an opinion based on the patient's statements. These rules assume that the particular facts relied upon by the physician will be trustworthy because the integrity and specialized skill of the expert will bar reliance on questionable matter. As a matter of policy, a fact reliable enough to serve as the basis for a diagnosis is also reliable enough to escape hearsay proscription. The test for statements made for purposes of medical diagnosis under Rule 803(4) is the same as that in Rule 703—is this particular fact one that an expert in this particular field would be justified in relying upon in rendering an opinion? Furthermore, to allow jurors to consider the patient's statement in evaluating the basis for the expert's opinion but not to admit the statement itself sets up a meaningless distinction that jurors are unlikely to apply.

The reliability of medical testimony is enhanced by procedural rules such as Rule 35 of the Federal Rules of Civil Procedure and Rule 16 of the Rules of Criminal Procedure which entitle the parties to obtain copies of their adversaries' medical reports prior to trial. Effective cross-examination can bring out weaknesses in the diagnosis stemming from an uncritical willingness to accept the patient's story. In a civil case, the threat of one-sided medical testimony is further obviated by provisions authorizing the court to order a party to submit to a physical or mental examination.

The rationales underlying statements made for treatment and statements made for diagnosis converge when the issue is whether statements "describing medical history . . . or the inception or general character of the cause or external source thereof" should be admitted. Even in the case of a statement made for treatment, the test is not only whether the declarant thought it relevant (thereby establishing reliability), but also whether a doctor would reasonably have relied upon such a statement in deciding upon a course of treatment. Since doctors may be assumed not to want to waste their time with unnecessary history, the fact that a doctor or other trained medical personnel took the information is prima facie evidence that it was pertinent. Courtroom practice has tended to let in medical records and statements to nurses and doctors fairly freely, leaving it to the jury to decide probative force.

Each case will have to be determined on its own facts to determine which statements, or which portion of a statement pertains to treatment. In *United States v. Iron Shell*,[2] the statements in question had been made by the nine-year-old female victim of the alleged assault with intent to rape to the doctor who examined her on the night of the assault. The statements concerning the cause of the victim's injuries were testified to by the physician at trial, over the defendant's objection that the doctor had been acting in an investigatory rather than in a treating or diagnostic capacity. The Eighth Circuit explained why the statements had been properly received:

> . . . There is nothing in the content of the statements to suggest that Lucy was responding to the doctor's questions for any reason other than promoting treatment. It is important to note that the statements concern what happened rather than who assaulted her. The former in most cases is pertinent to diagnosis and treatment while the latter would seldom, if ever, be sufficiently related . . . .. The age of the patient also mitigates against a finding that Lucy's statements were not within the traditional rationale of the rule . . . .. It is not dispositive that Dr. Hopkins' examination would have been identical to the one he performed if Lucy had been unable to utter a word . . . .. It is enough that the information eliminated potential physical problems from the doctor's examination in order to meet the test of 803(4). Discovering what is not injured is equally as pertinent to treatment and diagnosis as finding what is injured. Dr. Hopkins also testified, in response to specific questions from the court, that most doctors would have sought such a history and that he relied upon Lucy's statements in deciding upon a course of treatment.[3]

---

[2] 633 F.2d 77 (8th Cir. 1980), *cert. denied*, 450 U.S. 1001 (1981).

[3] *Id.* at 84–85. See also United States v. Renville, 779 F.2d 430, 435–39 (8th Cir. 1986) (in child abuse case, physician properly permitted to testify to statements victim made during physical examination identifying her step-father as her abuser; statements of this kind are reasonably relied upon by physician because there is psychological component in child abuse cases, and physician has obligation under state law not to return victim to harmful environment; in this case doctor had explained to victim that questions he was asking were necessary in order for him to obtain information to treat her). *Compare* Roberts v. Hollocher, 664 F.2d 200, 204 (8th Cir. 1981) (in civil right action against police seeking damages for injuries, district court excluded hospital record entry which read, "Multiple contusions and hematoma, consistent with excessive force"; appellate court affirmed, distinguishing *Iron Shell* as case where there was no improper motive behind dec-

A criminal case such as *Iron Shell* is, of course, subject to Confrontation Clause and Rule 403 analyses. As the court noted, these issues were blunted by the availability of the victim for cross-examination.[4]

Some statements of causation that do not qualify under Rule 803(4) may meet the requirements of Rule 803(1) or (2) and come in as present sense impressions or excited utterances. Others may be admissible pursuant to Rule 801(d)(1) or (2) as prior inconsistent statements or admissions.

Statements made to a psychiatrist or to someone like a psychologist, who would relay them to a medical doctor, fall within Rule 803(4)'s category of "statements made for purposes of medical diagnosis or treatment." As a general rule all statements made in this context, regardless of their content, are relevant to diagnosis or treatment since experts in the field view everything relating to the patient as relevant to his personality.[5] Nevertheless, the statements may be extremely unreliable as evidence of the facts related, since the condition for which the patient is consulting the psychiatrist may have impaired his perception, memory or veracity. The trial judge has discretion pursuant to Rules 401 and 403 to admit the statements only as proof of the patient's condition and not as proof of the occurrence of the recited events. In an automobile accident case, for instance, if a claim of mental damage is made, the court may allow proof of irrational, incoherent statements of the victim to his physician without, however, allowing any statements directly relating to the accident to be used as proof of how it occurred.

The judge also has discretion to limit statements dealing with the patient's condition. Extensive details covering many years of treatment may be excluded if the court finds their probative value is substantially outweighed by the danger of prejudice, confusion or waste of time. See commentary to Rule 403 in ¶ 6.05, *supra*.

---

laration, where statements aided physician in limiting his examination, and where age of child assured trustworthiness).

[4] 633 F.2d at 87.

[5] United States v. Lechoco, 542 F.2d 84 (D.C. Cir. 1976) (statements made to defense psychiatrists by defendant fall within the exception embodied in Rule 803(4)).

¶ 16.05   Recorded Recollection—Rule 803(5)[1]

Rule 803(5) excludes from the operation of the hearsay rule a written memorandum concerning a matter about which the witness once had personal knowledge but as to which the witness "now has insufficient recollection to enable him to testify fully and accurately," provided certain requirements are met. The rule provides:

> The following are not excluded by the hearsay rule, even though the declarant is available as a witness:
>
> . . .
>
> (5) Recorded recollection.—A memorandum or record concerning a matter about which a witness once had knowledge but now has insufficient recollection to enable the witness to testify fully and accurately, shown to have been made or adopted by the witness when the matter was fresh in the witness' memory and to reflect that knowledge correctly. If admitted, the memorandum or record may be read into evidence but may not itself be received as an exhibit unless offered by an adverse party.

¶ 16.05[01]   Insufficient Recollection to Testify Fully and Accurately

Two theories have been advanced to justify admission of recorded recollection despite the hearsay rule: (1) that use of the memorandum is necessary because the witness is "unavailable" as a result of lack of memory of the event in question, and (2) that a contemporaneous, accurate record is inherently superior to a present recollection subject to the fallibility of human memory. Rule 803(5) seeks to accomodate both rationales. It recognizes that requiring some demonstration of impaired memory discourages the use of self-serving statements especially prepared for litigation by insurance adjusters, investigators and the like.[2] On the other hand, memory need not be wholly exhausted before the memorandum can be used.

By providing for admission of the memorandum if the witness "now has insufficient recollection to enable him to testify fully and

---

[1] See discussion in **Treatise** at ¶ 803(5)[01].

[2] United States v. Felix-Jerez, 667 F.2d 1297, 1300 (9th Cir. 1982) (marshall's memorandum based on notes of an interview with defendant should not have been admitted where there was no showing that marshall had insufficient recollection to testify).

accurately," Rule 803(5) decrees that admission of the memorandum should not be on an all or nothing basis. If the witness answers some questions without hesitation, but then becomes vague or evasive or claims an inability to remember a particular aspect of the event in question even after being shown the memorandum for refreshment purposes, the trial court should admit at least those portions of the memorandum which failed to restore the witness' memory.[3] Admissibility should be determined on a question by question basis rather than by viewing the witness' testimony as a whole. Determining whether the witness is not testifying fully and accurately rests in the discretion of the trial court, and is often so dependent on the witness' demeanor that its determination should rarely be overturned on appeal.

The memorandum may be admissible pursuant to other rules of evidence even if the witness retains a memory of the underlying event. For instance, admission may be mandated as a prior inconsistent statement (Rule 801(d)(l)(A)), as an admission (Rule 801(d)(2)), or as a record of regularly conducted activity (Rule 803(6)). If the memorandum was made in circumstances guaranteeing its trustworthiness it may qualify for admission pursuant to Rules 803(24) or 804(b)(5). See Chapter 14(d), *supra*.

¶ 16.05[02]   Witness Once Had Knowledge

Rule 803(5) follows conventional doctrine in requiring the memorandum to concern a matter "about which a witness once had knowledge." This means that the memorandum is not admissible pursuant to this rule unless the witness had sufficient personal knowledge of the underlying events to meet the personal knowledge requirement of Rule 602 were he testifying about these matters. If, for instance, the witness was not present at the event recorded and the memorandum was based on information supplied by persons who do not testify, the memorandum cannot be admitted. But the memorandum may be of an event which is itself

(*Text continued on page 16–27*)

---

[3] See, *e.g.,* United States v. Williams, 571 F.2d 344 (6th Cir.), *cert. denied,* 439 U.S. 841 (1978) ("selective memory" with regard to critical question is sufficient predicate for admissibility).

hearsay. If this other hearsay would be admissible under some exception so is the memorandum. See Rule 805. For example, if the writing constituted a recording of a statement made by a party it would be an admission and the writing would come in to prove the event—*i.e.,* the admission.

¶ 16.05[03] Freshness and Accuracy of Memorandum

Since the witness does not remember the recorded facts, testimony about the perception cannot be obtained either on direct or cross-examination.[4] Instead, Rule 803(5) imposes two requirements to ensure that the witness correctly recorded his knowledge at a time when he still remembered what he had perceived: (1) to ensure that the past recollection is worth trusting, Rule 803(5) requires the memorandum "to have been made or adopted by the witness when the matter was fresh in [the witness'] memory" and (2) to guarantee that the memory was properly transcribed, the rule requires that the memorandum "reflect that knowledge correctly."

The concept of "freshness" is intended to be more flexible[5] than the traditional formula which required the memorandum to be made "at or near the time of the events in question." In determining whether the matter was sufficiently fresh to guarantee the memory's trustworthiness, the trial court will probably wish to take into account such factors as the time when the memorandum was made, the quality of the memory embodied in the memorandum, whether it was made before the litigation commenced, whether it was made spontaneously or in answer to a request by an interested party, and other circumstances.

To ensure that the witness or someone else transcribed his

---

[4] Despite the inability to test the witness' perception by cross-examination, the courts have upheld the use of recorded recollection in criminal cases against Confrontation Clause challenge. See, *e.g.,* United States v. Cambindo-Valencia, 609 F.2d 603, 633 (2d Cir. 1979), *cert. denied,* 446 U.S. 940 (1980). Memoranda of recorded recollection have had a long history of substantive use predating the development of the hearsay rule and the adoption of the Confrontation Clause.

[5] See, *e.g.,* United States v. Patterson, 678 F.2d 774, 778 (9th Cir.), *cert. denied,* 459 U.S. 911 (1982) (court has broad discretion pursuant to Rule 803(5); memory fresh 10 months after conversation with defendant).

knowledge correctly, the witness must either testify (1) that he recalls having made an accurate memorandum or checking it for accuaracy or (2) that though he now does not recollect his state of mind when making the record, he would not have made it unless it were correct. Proof in the first instance consists of testimony by the witness relating the circumstances in which the memorandum was made and his statement that he knew it to be true.[6] In the second case, it is sufficient if the witness testifies that he knows that a record of this type is correct because it was his habit or practice to record such matters accurately. Or he can testify that he recognizes his handwriting and would not have written, signed, initialed or marked the memorandum unless he had been convinced that it was correct.

¶ 16.05[04] Multiple Participants

The witness need not himself have been the person who actually wrote the memorandum.[7] It is admissible if the witness can testify that he saw the memorandum when the matter it concerned was fresh in his memory, and that he then knew it to be correct. Only the witness who adopted the memorandum need be called.

A more complicated situation arises when a person perceives an event and reports it to another who records it. Both participants must ordinarily testify, the reporter vouching for the accuracy of his oral report and the recorder for the accuracy of his transcription. The recorder need not be the actual writer. If he has seen the memorandum and approved it, and so testifies, the person who physically wrote the memorandum need not be

---

[6] See, *e.g.,* United States v. Patterson, 678 F.2d 774, 779 (9th Cir.), *cert. denied,* 459 U.S. 911 (1982) (witness testified that "he did not think he had lied to the grand jury"); United States v. Edwards, 539 F.2d 689, 692 (9th Cir.), *cert. denied,* 429 U.S. 984 (1976) (conceded fact that declarant was drunk at time he made statement bears heavily on weight to be given statement but not on its admissibility where declarant testified that he believed statement accurately reflected his recollection at the time it was made, statement was signed and acknowledged by declarant, and agent who was present at interview testified that answers of declarant "were not monosyllabic, but rather consisted of fairly detailed narrations.").

[7] United States v. Williams, 571 F.2d 344 (6th Cir.), *cert. denied,* 439 U.S. 841 (1978) (witness adopted memorandum by signing and swearing to it).

produced.[8] So long as accuracy is vouched for by each participant in the chain, a memorandum compiled through the efforts of more than two persons satisfies the requirements of Rule 803(5). There is no need for the original viewer to testify if the statement qualifies as an exception to the hearsay rule.[9]

¶ 16.05[05]   Admissibility of Memorandum

Rule 803(5) provides that a memorandum that satisfies the conditions of the rule may be read into evidence but may not be treated as an exhibit which goes to the jury room unless offered by an adverse party. This limitation was added because the memorandum is viewed as a substitute for oral testimony, and it was feared that it might be given undue weight in relation to other oral testimony which is not normally taken into the jury room. Upon stipulation the document may be sent to the jury.

Since the contents of the writing are being proved, even if the writing itself does not qualify as an exhibit, the best evidence rule applies. The original memorandum, or duplicate to the extent permitted by Rule 1003, must be produced unless failure to produce the original is satisfactorily explained.

¶ 16.06   Records of Private Entities

Rule 803 contains a number of provisions that make the records of private entities admissible despite the hearsay rule. By far the most frequently used of these exceptions, contained in Rule 803(6), is the exception for records of regularly conducted activity, which is discussed in detail below. Rules 803(7), the exception for evidence of the absence of a record, 803(16), the statements in ancient documents exception, and 803(17), the exception for market reports and commercial publications, are also discussed below. In

---

[8] For example, if the recorder dictates the record to a stenographer, the stenographer need not testify if the recorder states that the memorandum accurately reproduces the dictation.

[9] See United States v. Steele, 685 F.2d 793, 809 (3d Cir. 1982) (objection that maker of memorandum lacked personal knowledge is irrelevant where notes were introduced to prove declarations of co-conspirators).

addition, there are a number of other provisions in Rule 803, much less frequently used, that exempt particular types of written records of private entities from being barred by the hearsay rule. Records of religious organizations are specifically governed by Rule 803(11).[1] Statements in family records such as Bibles are treated in Rule 803(13).[2] Rule 803(14)[3] provides an exception for records of documents affecting an interest in property, and Rule 803(15)[4] covers statements in documents affecting an interest in property.

---

[1] Rule 803(11) provides:

The following are not excluded by the hearsay rule, even though the declarant is available as a witness:

. . .

Records of religious organizations.—Statements of births, marriages, divorces, deaths, legitimacy, ancestry, relationship by blood or marriage, or other similar facts of personal or family history, contained in a regularly kept record of a religious organization.

See discussion in **Treatise** at ¶ 803(11)[01].

[2] Rule 803(13) provides:

The following are not excluded by the hearsay rule, even though the declarant is available as a witness:

. . .

Family records.—Statements of fact concerning personal or family history contained in family Bibles, genealogies, charts, engravings on rings, inscriptions on family portraits, engravings on urns, crypts, or tombstones, or the like.

See discussion in **Treatise** at ¶ 803(13)[01].

[3] Rule 803(14) provides:

The following are not excluded by the hearsay rule, even though the declarant is available as a witness:

. . .

Records of documents affecting an interest in property.—The record of a document purporting to establish or affect an interest in property, as proof of the content of the original recorded document and its execution and delivery by each person by whom it purports to have been executed, if the record is a record of a public office and an applicable statute authorizes the recording of documents of that kind in that office.

See discussion in **Treatise** at ¶ 803(14)[01].

[4] Rule 803(15) provides:

The following are not excluded by the hearsay rule, even though the declarant is available as a witness:

. . .

Statements in documents affecting an interest in property.—A statement contained in a document purporting to establish or affect an interest in property if

¶ 16.06[01]   Records of Regularly Conducted Activity— Rule 803(6)

[a]   In General

The hearsay exception for records of regularly conducted activity, frequently termed the business records exception, relieves the proponent of the record from having to produce in court each person in the chain which produced the record, provided the requirements discussed below are met. Although the exception is of fairly recent origin,[1] owing its existence to legislation adopting a Model Act reported in 1927, it is probably the most frequently used of the hearsay exceptions.

Rule 803(6) provides:

The following are not excluded by the hearsay rule, even though the declarant is available as a witness:

. . .

(6) Records of regularly conducted activity.—A memorandum, report, record, or data compilation, in any form, of acts, events, conditions, opinions, or diagnoses, made at or near the time by, or from information transmitted by, a person with knowledge, if kept in the course of a regularly conducted business activity, and if it was the regular practice of that business activity to make the memorandum, report, record, or data compilation, all as shown by the testimony of the custodian or other qualified witness, unless the source of information or the method or circumstances of preparation indicate lack of trustworthiness. The term "business" as used in this paragraph includes business, institution, association, profession, occupation, and calling of every kind, whether or not conducted for profit.

---

the matter stated was relevant to the purpose of the document, unless dealings with the property since the document was made have been inconsistent with the truth of the statement or the purport of the document.

See discussion in **Treatise** at 803(15)[01].

[1] Although there were some common law antecedents, the shop book rule and the regular entries rule, these were far more limited in their scope. See discussion in **Treatise** at ¶ 803(6)[01].

[b] Rationale[2]

As is the case with other hearsay exceptions, the exception for records of regularly conducted activity is justified on the grounds of reliability and need. Guarantees of reliability are present because: (1) such records are customarily checked; (2) the regularity and continuity of such records produce habits of precision in the record keeper; (3) businesses function in reliance on such records; and (4) employees are required to make accurate records as part of their job or risk embarrassment and censure if they blunder. Need exists because without the exception all participants in the creation of the record would have to be produced, a burden which would not only disrupt the business entity, but would often amount to a futile gesture because of the improbability that many of the participants would remember the details of the complex records which they helped create.

[c] Foundation Requirements[3]

Unlike public records governed by Rule 803(8), records of regularly conducted activity are not normally self proving. Rule 803(6) states that satisfaction of all the requirements of the rule must be "shown by the testimony of the custodian or other qualified witness." There is no requirement that the records have been prepared by the party which now has custody and seeks to introduce them; the proponent must, however, be able to establish that the requirements of the Rule have been satisfied.[4]

A custodian who testifies as the foundation witness need not have personal knowledge of the actual creation of the document,[5]

---

[2] See discussion in **Treatise** at ¶ 803(6)[01].

[3] See discussion in **Treatise** at ¶ 803(6)[02].

[4] See United States v. Veytua-Bravo, 603 F.2d 1187, 1191 (5th Cir. 1979), *cert. denied*, 444 U.S. 1024 (1980) (where records of firearms dealer who was no longer in business were in custody of Bureau of Alcohol, Tobacco, and Firearms, testimony by ATF agent that record was made and kept in regular course of business sufficed).

[5] Itel Capital Corp. v. Cups Coal Co., Inc., 707 F.2d 1253, 1259 (11th Cir. 1983); United States v. Rose, 568 F.2d 1246 (5th Cir. 1977) (no requirement that custodian have personal knowledge of the particular evidence contained in the record).

nor have been in the employ of the business at the time of the making of the record.[6] The phrase "other qualified witness" should be given the broadest possible interpretation. Such a witness need not be an employee of the entity whose records are being offered so long as the witness understands the system that created the records.[7]

At times it may be possible to lay a foundation for the admission of business records without resort to the testimony of a custodian or other qualified witness through stipulations, judicial notice, admissions, circumstantial evidence or the residual hearsay exception.[8]

[d]   Regular Practice; Scope of Business[9]

Rule 803(6) requires that the record seeking admission have been "kept in the course of a regularly conducted business activity," and that "it was the regular practice of that business activity to make" the record in question.

The "regularly conducted business activity" requirement is intended to ensure that the rationale for the exception is satisfied. There are no guarantees of reliability when records are kept for purely personal reasons[10] because of the usual absence of factors such as systematic checking, habits of precision on the part of the record keeper, reliance by others on the records, or a duty and motive to record accurately.

The second sentence of Rule 803(6) defines "business" ex-

---

[6] United States v. Smith, 609 F.2d 1294, 1301 (9th Cir. 1979).

[7] See, e.g., United States v. Phillips, 515 F.Supp. 758, 762 (E.D. Ky. 1981) (psychiatrist could lay foundation for nursing notes both from hospital at which he was employed and another institution at which defendant had been confined since he was familiar with how records were kept).

[8] See discussion in Zenith Radio Corp. v. Matsushita Elec. Indus. Co., Ltd., 503 F.Supp. 1190, 1236 (E.D. Pa. 1980), rev'd on other grounds, 723 F.2d 238 (3d Cir. 1983), rev'd on other grounds, 106 S.Ct. 1348 (1986).

[9] See discussion in **Treatise** at ¶ 803(6)[03].

[10] See, e.g., Clark v. City of Los Angeles, 650 F.2d 1033, 1037 (9th Cir. 1981), cert. denied, 456 U.S. 927 (1982) (in civil rights action, plaintiff's diary of his encounters with police should not have been admitted as business record).

tremely broadly as a "business, institution, association, profession, occupation, and calling of every kind, whether or not conducted for profit." Personal records kept for business reasons,[11] and records of illicit organizations,[12] may be able to qualify for admission pursuant to Rule 803(6).

Governmental records, such as police records and reports, clearly meet the definition of business in Rule 803(6), as well. Nevertheless, there is some tendency to rely upon the public records exception in Rule 803(8), since the more particular rule usually controls. The latter rule, however, contains some restrictions upon the use of police reports in criminal cases that are not found in Rule 803(6). The discussion of Rule 803(8), *infra*, considers to what extent the limitations in Rule 803(8) can be avoided by offering police reports as the records of a regularly conducted activity.

The "regular practice" requirement was added by Congress. The Advisory Committee had eliminated this factor because it found that even though a virtually identical requirement was mandated by the Federal Business Records Act, which predated the Federal Rules of Evidence, records were customarily admitted if made in the course of business without regard to routineness, except when a court was concerned with trustworthiness.

Since Congress did not intend to make the business record ex-

---

[11] When diaries are offered, the court will have to determine whether they satisfy a business purpose or are purely personal. The burden is on the proponent to make the appropriate showing. See, *e.g., In re* Japanese Elec. Prods. Litigation, 723 F.2d 238, 291 (3d Cir. 1983), *rev'd on other grounds,* 106 S.Ct. 1348 (1986) (diary entries purporting to describe what transpired at business meetings properly excluded where there was no evidence that keeper of diaries attended meetings, no evidence of keeper's source of information, and no evidence of keeper's purpose in making the entries; other entries not suffering from these infirmities were admissible); Keogh v. Commissioner of Internal Revenue, 713 F.2d 496, 499–500 (9th Cir. 1983) (diary showing income of casino dealer was admitted where it showed every indication of being kept in the regular course of business activity); United States v. Hedman, 630 F.2d 1184, 1197 (7th Cir. 1980), *cert. denied,* 450 U.S. 965 (1981) (diary listing pay-offs to building inspectors admitted where recorder kept diary because he felt he might have to account for payments). See also Clark v. City of Los Angeles, 650 F.2d 1033 (9th Cir. 1981), *cert. denied,* 456 U.S. 927 (1982).

[12] See, *e.g.,* United States v. Foster, 711 F.2d 871, 882 (9th Cir. 1983), *cert. denied,* 465 U.S. 1103 (1984); United States v. Kasvin, 757 F.2d 887, 892–93 (7th Cir.), *cert. denied,* 106 S.Ct. 592 (1985).

ception more restrictive than it previously had been, Rule 803(6) should be interpreted so that the absence of routineness does not result in exclusion of the record when all other requirements of the rule are satisfied unless "the sources of information or other circumstances indicate lack of trustworthiness." This latter condition, which is discussed in detail below, operates not as a blanket exclusion, but only when the facts of the case indicate unreliability.

[e]   Transmitting with Personal Knowledge and in the Regular Course[13]

For Rule 803(6) to be satisfied, the record seeking admission must be based on "information transmitted by a person with knowledge."[14] The knowledge requirement means that the informant whose data is embodied in the business record must have personally perceived the matter which is the subject of the record.[15] The recorder of the information need not have firsthand knowledge.

Rule 803(6) also requires that the record be "made . . . by, or from information transmitted by, a person with knowledge, if kept in the course of a regularly conducted activity . . . ." This requirement, which has its counterpart in prior law,[16] has been inter-

---

[13] See discussion in **Treatise** at ¶ 803(6)[04].

[14] See, *e.g.*, City of Cleveland v. Cleveland Elec. Illuminating Co., 538 F.Supp. 1257, 1269–70 (N.D. Ohio 1980) (reports compiled by city explaining why customers had decided to terminate electric power service from the city did not satisfy Rule 803(6) since the former customers were not acting "in the course of a regularly conducted business activity").

[15] The legislative history of the rule indicates that Congress intended a liberal interpretation of the phrase "person with knowledge." The name of the person whose firsthand knowledge was the basis of the entry need not even be known as long as the business regularly gets information from such a person. See, *e.g.*, Stone v. Morris, 546 F.2d 730 (7th Cir. 1976) (admissibility not affected because memorandum does not reveal the source of the information contained within it).

[16] The leading case is the New York case Johnson v. Lutz, 253 N.Y. 124 (1930), which held that entries in a policeman's accident report based upon information supplied by a bystander were inadmissible because each participant must be acting in the course of business, and the initial informant must have firsthand knowledge.

preted to mean that each participant in the chain producing the event—from the initial observer-reporter to the final entrant—must be acting in the course of a regularly conducted business activity,[17] or must meet the test of some other hearsay exception. The guarantees of reliability underlying the business records exception are absent if any one of the participants is outside the pattern of regularity of activity.

The two requirements—the informant's personal knowledge and that the record be made and kept in the regular course of business—lead to exclusion when the supplier of the data is not acting within the course of a regular business. A recurring situation is that of a "volunteer" offering information to persons conducting an inquiry or investigation. The person to whom the information is offered cannot qualify as the initial person in the chain, because the initial person furnishing the information must have personal knowledge of the underlying event; the transmitter who has knowledge is not a part of the chain because he or she is not acting under a business duty.

Cases which at first glance appear aberrant are explicable on the ground of multiple hearsay. Rule 805 authorizes the admission of hearsay within hearsay if both statements conform to the requirements of an exception. Consequently, business records incorporating statements made by persons outside the business entity may be admissible under a two-step analysis. For instance, if the informant's statement qualifies as an admission, or as an excited utterance, or as a statement for purposes of medical diagnosis or treatment, the record embodying the statement is admissible if the recording was done in the course of a regularly conducted business activity.

In addition, Rules 803(24) and 804(b)(5) allow statements to be admitted that fulfill requirements of trustworthiness even if they

---

[17] *Compare* United States v. Lieberman, 637 F.2d 95, 100 (2d Cir. 1980) (hotel registration card cannot be used to prove identity of guest where employee had not verified information provided) *with* Matter of Olag Constr. Corp., 665 F.2d 43, 46 (2d Cir. 1981) (financial statements prepared by debtors at bank's request on bank's own form were admitted as business records on the ground that guarantees of trustworthiness surrounding financial statements are greater than for hotel registrations since they are relied upon in day-to-day operations, and criminal sanctions apply when false information is furnished).

fail to meet the tests of a particular exception. A judge, therefore, has some discretion to admit the statements of non-participants in the regular activity if the facts remove the taint of unreliability.[18]

[f]   Contemporaneity of Recording and Form of Record[19]

Rule 803(6) requires the record to be "made at or near the time" of the events recorded. The purpose of the provision is to increase the probability of accuracy. It should not, however, be applied mechanically. The circumstances of the particular case must be taken into consideration in determining whether the persons compiling the record had a fresh recollection of the matter sought to be proved at the time the entry was made.[20]

Rule 803(6) broadly describes the form the record must assume as a "memorandum, report, record or data compilation." This provision is intended to mandate the admission of any form of writing so long as the tests of the business record exception are satisfied.

The term "data compilation" was added to ensure the admissibility of records not kept in conventional written form, including audio tapes and electronic, magnetic and other types of computer data storage. If the data was entered into the computer "at or near the time" of the events recorded, and the court is convinced of the trustworthiness of the information produced, it should admit printouts even if they were made in preparation for litigation and not in the ordinary course of business long after the events in question.[21] A mechanical insistence on having the printouts satisfy

---

[18] See, *e.g.,* United States v. Ullrich, 580 F.2d 765, 772 (5th Cir. 1978) (court admitted, through testimony of manager of automobile agency, inventory schedule prepared by Ford Motor Company); United States v. Flom, 558 F.2d 1179, 1182 (5th Cir. 1977) (invoices prepared by one company and held in regular course of defendant's business admitted even though they were offered through the testimony of official of receiving rather than preparing entity; circumstances demonstrate trustworthiness and "trial judge has a broad zone of discretion").

[19] See discussion in **Treatise** at ¶ 803(6)[05].

[20] See, *e.g.,* United States v. Lemire, 720 F.2d 1327 (D.C. Cir. 1983), *cert. denied,* 467 U.S. 1226 (1984) (one-year and ten-month lapse between events and memorandum made memorandum untimely, and, in addition, not regular practice to make this type of memorandum).

[21] See, *e.g.,* United States v. Sanders, 749 F.2d 198–99 (5th Cir. 1984) (where

the contemporaneity requirement would undermine the usefulness of computerized record-keeping.[22] The court has the power
under the discretion afforded it by the last clause of Rule 803(6),
authorizing exclusion for a "lack of trustworthiness," to determine the amount and kind of information that must be furnished,
and by whom, in laying the foundation for data compilations.[23]
Expert testimony on the type of software programs used and modifications in the data after original entry may be required.

[g] Acts, Events, Conditions, Opinions or Diagnoses; Hospital Records[24]

To lay to rest the recurring dispute under prior law as to whether
records containing "opinions" rather than facts are embraced by
the business records exception, Rule 803(6) unequivocally states
that records of "acts, events, conditions, opinions or diagnoses"
are admissible.

The admissibility of statements of opinion under the business
records exception had been especially troublesome in the area of
medical records. From the standpoint of the opinion rule, all statements by physicians incorporated in a hospital record or in a report concerning the patient's condition or its cause consist of opinion except for recordation of facts directly observed, such as
temperature, blood pressure and other objective factors. While
the relevancy of medical records is apparent, advocates of a re-

---

testimony established that data was prepared and kept pursuant to procedures
designed to assure accuracy, fact that data was summoned in a readable form
shortly before trial did not require exclusion where data had been entered contemporaneously with the events recorded and no further modifications had been
made).

[22] United States v. Russo, 480 F.2d 1228, 1240 (6th Cir. 1973), *cert. denied,* 414
U.S. 1157 (1974).

[23] *Cf.* United States v. Vela, 673 F.2d 86, 89 (5th Cir. 1982) (no abuse of discretion in admitting computerized telephone bills; computers were used at two
stages: 1) in recording initial dialing, and 2) in preparation of bills; custodian of
records explained precise manner in which data were compiled but was unable to
identify the brand, type and model of each computer or to vouch for proper operating conditions; court held these factors might at best go to weight but not
admissibility).

[24] See discussion in **Treatise** at ¶ 803(6)[06].

strictive rule feared that when opinions are admitted, the jury is unable to assess the qualifications of their authors or the accuracy of their conclusions because records cannot be cross-examined. In contrast, proponents of the admissibility of medical records containing diagnostic opinions pointed to the need for such evidence, the reputability of physicians and medical institutions, the uncertain line between fact and opinion and, above all, the adversary's right to subpoena the reporting physician in order to bring out any weaknesses of the diagnosis.

Prior to the enactment of the Federal Rules of Evidence, most federal courts reached an accommodation between the need for relevant information and the fear of uncross-examined opinion. They drew a distinction between diagnoses involving "conjecture and opinion" and diagnoses upon which "competent physicians would not differ."[25]

While Rule 803(6) rejects any attempt to exclude a particular class of hospital records, and does not distinguish between the routine and the conjectural, the last phrase of Rule 803(6) authorizes the trial judge to exclude a particular record where indications of trustworthiness are shown to be lacking. The court may choose to exercise this power if the record or other evidence indicates that the author of the record is unqualified, or the diagnostic opinion is of a type about which competent experts disagree. If the expert is available, the judge may require the expert to testify, particularly if the medical issue is crucial.[26]

Records of patients who were examined for diagnosis only in connection with pending litigation may, at first, seem to be lacking in requisite trustworthiness since the diagnoses will not be relied upon by persons responsible for treatment. While this may be true

---

[25] New York Life Ins. Co. v. Taylor, 147 F.2d 297, 300 (D.C. Cir. 1945) (leading case).

[26] See, e.g., Petrocelli v. Gallison, 679 F.2d 286, 291 (1st Cir. 1982) (in medical malpractice action, trial court did not err in excluding two entries in hospital record which stated that a nerve had been severed, the most critical issue in the case, where it was impossible to determine whether patient or physicians were the source of the information, and plaintiff apparently made no attempt to depose or otherwise seek clarification from the physicians so that the trial court could "entertain legitimate doubts as to whether the doctors who recorded these statements were actually rendering professional judgments.").

in a particular case, wholesale exclusion is unwarranted as incompatible with Rule 803(4), which admits statements made with a view to diagnosis alone. As the discussion under Rule 803(4) indicates, the statements would in any event be available under Rule 703 to show the basis of the physician's diagnosis, and experts can generally be relied upon to consider trustworthy facts in arriving at professional conclusions. These reasons apply equally to Rule 803(6). There is no more reason to expect a physician to render an unreliable diagnosis than there is to expect him to base it on untrustworthy facts. Nevertheless, there may be instances where the court feels that the particular facts of the case warrant excluding the records unless the physician appears as a witness.

Non-medical opinions in business records are also admissible pursuant to Rule 803(6) provided they meet the requirements of the rule. Since the transmitter of the information on which the record is based must have had personal knowledge of the matter on which he expressed an opinion, some guarantee of reliability is present, but other problems of trustworthiness may arise similar to those posed by the proffer of intracompany reports as admissions.[27]

The trial judge has discretion, pursuant to Rule 803(6), as well as Rules 403 and 805, to assess the particular factors present to determine whether a more accurate determination could probably be obtained by admitting or excluding the record.[28] Such determi-

---

[27] See discussion in **Treatise** at ¶ 801(d)(2)(C)[01], *supra,* and see ¶ 15.02[04], *supra.*

[28] Forward Communications Corp. v. United States, 608 F.2d 485, 510–11 (Ct. Claims 1979) (in action for recovery of federal taxes, plaintiff sought to prove valuation by proffering report by appraiser pursuant to Rule 803(6); court held that report could not be admitted where record failed to disclose qualifications or identity of appraiser and the opinions were not incident to or part of factual reports of contemporaneous events or transactions; for report to be admitted, preparer must be present to testify and to be cross-examined pursuant to Rule 702 and 705); United States v. Licavoli, 604 F.2d 613, 622–23 (9th Cir. 1979), *cert. denied,* 446 U.S. 935 (1980) (record of appraisal of value of painting properly admitted even though proponent of record did not establish qualifications of appraiser; court refused to adopt inflexible rule of exclusion in absence of demonstration of untrustworthiness; since opponent raised no specific facts raising doubts about appraiser's qualification and insurance company relied on appraisal in making payment, trial judge did not abuse discretion in admitting).

nations should, wherever possible, be made at the pretrial stages so that counsel can be prepared to obtain other evidence by live witnesses, normal depositions or videotape depositions. Failure to rule in advance may require continuances during the trial to avoid a miscarriage of justice.

[h]   Lack of Trustworthiness; Accident Reports[29]

The Advisory Committee was unwilling to mandate a hearsay exception for anything recorded in the course of a regularly conducted activity. It recognized that a motive to misrepresent rather than the regular course of business leads to the creation of some records,[30] which consequently are not sufficiently reliable to escape the proscription of the hearsay rule. Because of the impossibility of formulating a provision specific enough to apply to all situations, Rule 803(6) provides that records made in the course of a regularly conducted activity are admissible "unless the sources of information or other circumstances indicate lack of trustworthiness."

The "lack of trustworthiness" formula directs courts to consider the context in which the record was created. In order to evaluate motivation, the court may have to consider factors such as: whether the material was prepared specifically for litigation,[31]

---

[29] See **Treatise** at ¶ 803(6)[07].

[30] The paradigm case preceding the enactment of the Federal Rules was Palmer v. Hoffman, 318 U.S. 109, 63 S.Ct. 477, 87 L.Ed. 645 (1943), *aff'g* 129 F.2d 976 (2d Cir. 1942) in which both the circuit court and the Supreme Court held that the report made by a railroad engineer, deceased by the time of trial, about the railroad collision in which he had been involved, could not be admitted as a business record. The Second Circuit excluded the report on the ground that it was "dripping with motivations to misrepresent" (129 F.2d at 991); the Supreme Court affirmed on the theory that the report was not "in the regular course of business," since the business of a railroad is "railroading," not litigating (318 U.S. at 114). Despite the Supreme Court's rationale for exclusion, subsequent cases stressed that the motive to misrepresent rather than the regular course of business lies at the heart of the *Palmer v. Hoffman* situation. The Advisory Committee approved this view in its Notes to Rule 803(6).

[31] See, *e.g.*, United States v. Williams, 661 F.2d 528, 531 (5th Cir. 1981) (error to have admitted statement that trailer was worth $5,600 where "[a]ll too clearly" declarant prepared statement for purposes of trial only and $5,000 was the minimum jurisdictional amount).

whether non-litigation purposes were served by the report,[32] who prepared the report in question,[33] and who is offering the report.[34] Whenever possible, the assessment of probative force should be left to the jury. The jury's function should not be reduced by excluding relevant evidence unless the court is reasonably assured that the result of the litigation will be less reliable were the evidence to be revealed to the jury.

Even when the facts disclose the possibility of a motive to misrepresent, the court may be able to devise measures that will diminish the dangers posed by the record without depriving the factfinder of relevant evidence. When the declarant is available, the court may condition admissibility of the record on the declarant's being called as a witness so that his or her credibility can be examined. When the declarant is unavailable, the court may take into account what evidence would be available, pursuant to Rule 806, to attack the credibility of the declarant if the record is admitted. The significance of the evidence contained in the record, the availability of other evidence on the point,[35] the degree to which the declarant's bias would be self-evident to the jury, and the circumstances in which the record was made,[36] are all factors which the

---

[32] See, *e.g.*, Abdel v. United States, 670 F.2d 73, 75 (7th Cir. 1982) (Department of Agriculture reports were sufficiently reliable where they were completed regardless of whether violations were found, and litigation did not necessarily ensue even when violations were found); United States v. Grossman, 614 F.2d 295, 296 (1st Cir. 1980) (catalogue properly admitted to identify lighters in question since a catalogue is a compilation for business purposes that has its own guarantee of trustworthiness).

[33] See, *e.g.*, Lewis v. Baker, 526 F.2d 470 (2d Cir. 1975) (railroad accident report; no motive to misrepresent where preparers of report were not involved in lawsuit and could not have been target of lawsuit by plaintiff; reports were made pursuant to ICC requirements and were relied upon by employer in preventing accidents).

[34] See, *e.g.*, United States v. Smith, 521 F.2d 957, 967 (D.C. Cir. 1975), *quoting* Bracey v. Herringa, 466 F.2d 702, 705 n.9, (7th Cir. 1972) (" 'Police reports are ordinarily excluded when offered by the party at whose instance they were made,' . . . but may still be admitted as business records when, as here, they are offered against . . . the prosecution.").

[35] See, *e.g.*, United States v. Cincotta, 689 F.2d 238, 243 (1st Cir.), *cert. denied,* 459 U.S. 991 (1982) (notebook admitted where its entries were corroborated, although it would have been "untrustworthy standing alone").

[36] See, *e.g.*, United States v. Davis, 542 F.2d 743 (8th Cir.), *cert. denied,* 429

court should consider in determining whether the need for the evidence outweighs the dangers stemming from its admission.

Statements by professionals, such as physicians, expressing their opinions on a relevant matter should be excluded only in rare instances, particularly if the expert is independent of any party, and especially if the reports had been made available to the other side through discovery so that rebuttal evidence can be prepared.

The "lack of trustworthiness" language of Rule 803(6) is broad enough to encompass other aspects of unreliability besides the declarant's motive to misrepresent. For instance, records may be excluded because of untrustworthiness if the type of record does not satisfy the rationale for the exception, or the entry was made or kept improperly,[37] or the declarant-expert did not have sufficient qualifications. See discussion, *supra*.

[i]   Criminal Cases

Rule 803(8) prohibits the use of investigative reports, and reports of matters observed by police and other law enforcement officers, as evidence against an accused. As is discussed more fully below in the treatment of Rule 803(8), a number of courts have held that a report barred by Rule 803(8) cannot be admitted even though it satisfies another hearsay exception such as Rule 803(6).[38] Most courts, however, have held that Congress did not

---

U.S. 1004 (1976) (list of serial numbers of bait money admitted where list remained unchanged until bait money was removed, list was periodically checked and audited, and kept in regular course of business at all teller windows in accordance with regular practice of bank).

[37] See, *e.g.*, United States v. Houser, 746 F.2d 55, 56–63 (D.C. Cir. 1984) (error to have admitted Bureau of Alcohol, Tobacco and Firearms tracer form to show weapon's movement in interstate commerce; Special Agent had given serial number of weapon to BATF clerk over the phone, and clerk had then phoned manufacturer and filled out the form; neither clerk nor manufacturer's representative was identified; court found that the possibility of error in passing on the number from the agent to the clerk to the manufacturer's employee and then passing the information back to the clerk was too great to satisfy the trustworthiness requirement); Lloyd v. Professional Realty Servs., Inc., 734 F.2d 1428, 1433 (11th Cir. 1984), *cert. denied*, 105 S.Ct. 908 (1985) (draft minutes excluded as untrustworthy where draft was marked and edited and quite different from the final copy of the minutes that had previously been admitted).

[38] See United States v. Oates, 560 F.2d 45 (2d Cir. 1977).

intend to exclude records of routine, nonadversarial matters either under Rules 803(6) or 803(8).[39] Furthermore, a number of courts have held that the restrictions in Rule 803(8) will not bar resort to some other hearsay exception, provided the declarant takes the stand and is subject to cross-examination.[40]

The circuits have split on whether records admitted pursuant to the business records exception automatically satisfy a Confrontation Clause challenge.[41]

¶ 16.06[02]   Absence of Entry in Records of Regularly Conducted Activity—Rule 803(7)[1]

When evidence of the failure to mention a matter which would ordinarily be mentioned is offered to prove the nonoccurrence or nonexistence of the matter, Rule 803(7) authorizes the admission of such evidence as an exception to the hearsay rule. For instance, the absence of any records indicating that freight cars were inspected and cleaned may be used to prove the nonoccurrence or nonexistence of any cleaning or inspection of the cars.[2] The rule provides:

> The following are not excluded by the hearsay rule, even though the declarant is available as a witness:
>
> . . .
>
> (7) Absence of entry in records kept in accordance with the provisions of paragraph (6).—Evidence that a matter is not included in the memoranda, reports, records, or data compilations, in any form, kept in accordance with the provisions of paragraph (6), to prove the nonoccur-

---

[39] See, e.g., United States v. Orozco, 590 F.2d 789 (9th Cir.), cert. denied, 442 U.S. 920 (1979).

[40] See, e.g., United States v. King, 613 F.2d 670 (7th Cir. 1980) (Social Security forms relating to interview with defendant admissible pursuant to Rule 803(6) where author testified).

[41] Compare United States v. Haili, 443 F.2d 1295 (9th Cir. 1971) and United States v. Leal, 509 F.2d 122 (9th Cir. 1975) (holding in the affirmative) with United States v. Smith, 521 F.2d 957 (D.C. Cir. 1975) and McDaniel v. United States, 343 F.2d 785 (5th Cir. 1965) (holding in the negative).

[1] See discussion in **Treatise** at ¶ 803(7)[01].

[2] See Kaiser Aluminum & Chemical Corp. v. Illinois Central Gulf R.R. Co., 615 F.2d 470 (5th Cir.), cert. denied, 449 U.S. 890 (1980).

rence or nonexistence of the matter, if the matter was of a kind of which a memorandum, report, record, or data compilation was regularly made and preserved, unless the sources of information or other circumstances indicate lack of trustworthiness.

Demonstrating that the records were kept in such a way that the matter would have been recorded had it occurred, is, of course, crucial.[3]

The last phrase of Rule 803(7)—which mandates exclusion if "the sources of information or other circumstances indicate lack of trustworthiness"—is identical to the concluding phrase of Rule 803(6), and should receive the same interpretation. The motivation and qualification of the entrant, and the manner in which the records were made and stored are some of the questions that may be raised pursuant to this provision. See discussion, *supra*.

¶ 16.06[03]   Statements   in   Ancient   Documents—Rule 803(16)[1]

Rule 803(16) recognizes that statements in a document at least twenty years old whose authenticity is established may be admitted as evidence of the truth of the facts recited. The rule provides:

The following are not excluded by the hearsay rule, even though the declarant is available as a witness:

. . .

---

[3] See, *e.g.,* Fury Import Inc. v. Shakespeare Co., 554 F.2d 1376, 1381 (5th Cir. 1977), *cert. denied,* 450 U.S. 921 (1981) (error for judge to conclude on basis of Rule 803(7) that there were no orders because there was no documentary evidence thereof where there had been testimony that orders were not always in written form). *Cf.* United States v. DeGeorgia, 420 F.2d 889, 895–96 (9th Cir. 1969) (Ely, J., concurring) (evidence that computer records showed no transaction; "[i]f a machine is to testify against an accused, the courts must, at the very least, be satisfied with all reasonable certainty that both the machine and those who supply its information have performed their functions with utmost accuracy. Therefore, it is essential that the trial court be convinced of the trustworthiness of the particular records before admitting them into evidence. And it should be convinced by proof presented by the party seeking to introduce the evidence rather than receiving the evidence upon the basis of an inadequate foundation and placing the burden upon the objector to demonstrate its weakness.").

[1] See discussion in **Treatise** at ¶ 803(16)[01].

(16) Statements in ancient documents.—Statements in a document in existence twenty years or more the authenticity of which is established.

This exception must be viewed in tandem with the ancient document rule of authentication which is set forth in Rule 901(b)(8). The authentication rule ensures that the document is in writing, that it was produced from proper custody and that it is unsuspicious in appearance. These factors point to reliability, which is further enhanced because the age of the document virtually ensures that the statement was made before the controversy resulting in the present litigation arose, and before any motivation to misrepresent was present.

Rule 803(16) does not expressly contain a requirement of personal knowledge, although the notes to Rule 803 indicate that this condition applies to all declarants. While it would usually be impossible to prove actual knowledge on the part of the declarant after the lapse of so many years, the court should require a showing from the circumstances that declarant could have had the requisite knowledge. If not, the statement should be excluded.

¶ 16.07   Records of Public Entities

The exceptions for public records are treated analogously to the exceptions for private records. There is one principle rule, Rule 803(8), which is by far the most frequently used. Rule 803(10), which is the exception for evidence of the absence of a public record, corresponds in the public sphere to Rule 803(7) in the private. Both of these rules are discussed below, as is Rule 803(9), which makes admissible records of vital statistics, and Rule 803(22), which governs judgments of convictions. Rule 803(23)[1] allows a

---

[1] Rule 803(23) provides:

The following are not excluded by the hearsay rule, even though the declarant is available as a witness:

. . .

(23) Judgment as to personal, family, or general history, or boundaries.— Judgments as proof of matters of personal, family or general history, or boundaries, essential to the judgment, if the same would be provable by evidence of reputation.

See discussion in **Treatise** at ¶ 803(23)[01].

judgment to be admitted as prima facie evidence of a fact essential to the determination, if the fact is concerned with a matter of personal, family or general history or boundaries, and would be provable by evidence of reputation pursuant to Rules 803(19) or (20).[2]

¶ 16.07[01]   Public Records—Rule 803(8)

[a]   Scope and Rationale[1]

Rule 803(8) recognizes three categories of public records that generally will be admissible despite the hearsay rule: (1) records of the office's or agency's own activities,[2] (2) records of "matters observed pursuant to duty imposed by law,"[3] and (3) evaluative reports. Rule 803(8) does not distinguish between federal and nonfederal offices—the sole criterion is whether the record is that of a public body.[4]

Rule 803(8) differs from the business records exception set forth in Rule 803(6) in two important respects. First, because the assurances of accuracy are even greater for public records than for business records, a public record is admitted as proof of the facts to

---

[2] See text of rules, *infra*, at ¶ 16.09.

[1] See discussion in **Treatise** at ¶ 803(8)[01].

[2] This category found ample support in previous law. See, *e.g.*, Chesapeake & Delaware Canal Co. v. United States, 250 U.S. 123, 39 S.Ct. 407, 63 L.Ed.889 (1919) (Treasury records); Howard v. Perrin, 200 U.S. 71, 26 S.Ct. 195, 50 L.Ed. 374 (1906) (records of the general land office to show disposition of land).

[3] This category also had been recognized under law predating the Federal Rules of Evidence. See, *e.g.*, La Porte v. United States, 300 F.2d 878, 879–80 (9th Cir. 1962) (observation of defendant's failure to comply with selective service regulations).

[4] United States v. Torres, 733 F.2d 449, 455 n. 5 (7th Cir.), *cert. denied*, 105 S.Ct. 204 (1984) (Indian Tribal Roll); *In re* Agent Orange Litigation, 611 F.Supp. 1223, 1239–41 (E.D.N.Y. 1985) (epidemiological studies of federal, state and Australian governments). See also United States v. Regner, 677 F.2d 754, 757, 762–64 (9th Cir.), *cert. denied*, 459 U.S. 911 (1982) (majority found that records of state-run Hungarian taxicab company were properly admitted without testimony of foundation witness; dissent objected that records of foreign entities that would be private in United States should not be treated as public for purposes of hearsay exception, because indicia of reliability are not greater for such records than for private records).

which it relates without foundation testimony by a custodian or other qualified witness. Authentication is required.[5] Eliminating the need for a foundation also furthers the exception's goal of not disrupting governmental work by forcing officials into court. Second, the rule recognizes that in criminal cases the Confrontation Clause may impose limits on the use of investigative and police reports against an accused. See discussion below of the restrictions built into subdivisions (B) and (C).

The public records exception—which should be interpreted as broadly as Rule 803(6)—is like the business records exception in providing the trial judge with discretion to determine admissibility on a case by case basis. A lack of trustworthiness mandates exclusion unless the difficulty can be obviated by measures such as testimony by a custodian or the author of the report in question.[6]

Rule 803(8) provides:

The following are not excluded by the hearsay rule, even though the declarant is available as a witness:

. . .

(8) Public records and reports.—Records, reports, statements, or data compilations, in any form, of public offices or agencies, setting forth (A) the activities of the office or agency, or (B) matters observed pursuant to duty imposed by law as to which matters there was a duty to report, excluding, however, in criminal cases matters observed by police officers and other law enforcement personnel, or (C) in civil actions and proceedings and against the Government in criminal cases, factual findings resulting from an investigation made pursuant to authority granted by law, unless the sources of information or other circumstances indicate lack of trustworthiness.

[b]   Personal Knowledge Requirement[7]

Rule 803(8) is silent about a requirement of personal knowl-

---

[5] The record will be self-authenticating if it meets the requirements of Rule 902(4). See also Rule 1005 on use of copies of public records.

[6] See, *e.g.*, Givens v. Lederle, 556 F.2d 1341, 1346 (5th Cir. 1977) (documents prepared by Center for Disease Control listing vaccine-induced polio cases were admissible pursuant to Rule 803(8) where editor of reports identified reports and was subject to cross-examination).

[7] See discussion in **Treatise** at ¶ 803(8)[02].

edge, although the introductory note to Rule 803 states that "neither this rule nor Rule 804 dispense with the requirement of first hand knowledge." In the case of Rule 803(8) this requirement must be interpreted flexibly, bearing in mind that the primary objective of the hearsay rule is to bar untrustworthy evidence.

In the case of records of activities performed or facts observed (Rule 803(8)(A),(B)), the personal knowledge requirement should be enforced.[7a] The initial person in the chain creating the report must have personal knowledge of the transaction; the official who prepares the actual report may rely on a government colleague or subordinate with personal knowledge. The history of subdivisions (A) and (B) of Rule 803(8) indicates that the drafters intended the initial informant to be an official, but some courts interpret Rule 803(8) rather broadly as authorizing the admission of reports made by a private person pursuant to a statutory duty.[8] Courts that take a more restrictive view of the personal knowledge requirement of subdivisions (A) and (B) may nevertheless find the reports of ad hoc officials sufficiently trustworthy to be admitted pursuant to Rules 803(6)[9] or 803(24).

In the case of investigative reports, the subject of Rule 803(8)(C), the official has a duty other than to record or certify facts ascertained through an official's personal observation. The reports are admissible because they satisfy the requirement of reliability in other ways. Therefore, when this kind of record seeks admissibility, the personal knowledge requirement must be liberally construed. See discussion, *infra*. Reports filled by outside consultants that are incorporated in

---

[7a] Nachtsheim v. Beech Aircraft Corp., 847 F.2d 1261, 1271–1273 (7th Cir. 1988) (court did not abuse discretion in excluding statement appended to government report made by unknown author since plaintiffs were unable to establish that the official who reported the disputed statement had firsthand knowledge of the condition observed; cites **Treatise**).

[8] See, *e.g.,* United States v. Central Gulf Lines, Inc., 747 F.2d 315, 319 (5th Cir. 1984) (survey conducted by independent surveyor with a duty to report to a public official).

[9] See, *e.g.,* United States v. Neal, 509 F.2d 122 (9th Cir. 1975) (Hong Kong hotel registration forms were admitted as business records despite lack of testimony by custodian; court noted that analogy with official records was not inappropriate since forms were required by Hong Kong law).

an agency report will not qualify if the court finds that they do not embody the findings of the agency.[9a]

[c] Investigative Reports: Civil Cases[10]

The officials involved in the preparation of an investigative report need not have firsthand knowledge about the events sought to be proved through the report, since the reliability of an investigative report stems from the ability of an experienced investigator to determine which facts are sufficiently trustworthy to be relied upon in reaching conclusions.[10a] The trial court has discretion, however, to exclude the report if it finds a lack of trustworthiness, such as an improper motive or insufficient qualifications or diligence on the part of the investigator.[11] Through resort to discovery, the opponent of

---

[9a] Brown v. Sierra Nevada Memorial Miners Hosp., 849 F.2d 1186, 1189–90 (9th Cir. 1988). *See also* City of New York v. Pullman Inc., 662 F.2d 910, 915 (2d Cir. 1981), *cert. denied,* 454 U.S. 1164, 102 S. Ct. 1038, 71 L. Ed. 2d 320 (1982) (interim staff report not admitted because it embodied "tentative results of an incomplete staff investigation."); Zenith Radio Corp. v. Matsushita Elec. Ind. Co., 505 F. Supp. 1125 (E.D. Pa. 1980).

[10] See discussion in **Treatise** at ¶ 803(8)[03].

[10a] Trustees of University of Pa. v. Lexington Insurance Co., 815 F.2d 890, 905 (3d Cir. 1987) (judicial findings not within scope of rule).

[11] See, *e.g.,* Faries v. Atlas Truck Body Mfg. Co., 797 F.2d 619, 623 (8th Cir. 1986) (in strict liability action, reversible error to admit police accident report prepared by state trooper who expressed opinion about cause of action without having conducted full physical examination, and who relied largely upon the statements of an interested eyewitness); Baker v. Firestone Tire and Rubber Co., 793 F.2d 1196, 1199 (11th Cir. 1986) (on an appeal from a jury verdict finding defendant not liable for punitive damages as a result of injuries caused by defendant's tire "blowing out," the court affirmed the exclusion of a congressional subcommittee's investigation of defendant's tires because the report "did not contain the factual findings necessary to an objective investigation, but consisted of the rather heated conclusions of a politically motivated hearing"); Matthews v. Ashland Chemical, Inc., 770 F.2d 1303, 1309–10 (5th Cir. 1985) (fire report excluded where court was uncertain of author's special skills or expertise, and report was based on cursory investigation). *Compare* Fraley v. Rockwell Int'l Corp., 470 F.Supp. 1264, 1267 (S.D. Ohio 1979) (in action against plane manufacturer arising out of crash of Navy plane, court found that report prepared by Naval Rework Facility satisfied Rule 803(8)(C), but excluded report prepared for Judge Advocate General's office by an inexperienced investigator) *with* Sage v. Rockwell Int'l Corp., 477 F.Supp. 1205, 1209 (D.N.H. 1979) (com-

the report can investigate the author's qualifications, and may be able to take his or her deposition. The trial court has discretion to condition admission of the report upon having the author produced for examination.

Rule 803(8)(C) makes admissible "reports . . . setting forth . . . factual findings." Although the meaning of "factual findings" was not entirely clear when the rule went into effect, due in part to a somewhat inconclusive legislative history,[12]the Supreme Court has now unanimously endorsed the view, which already had been adopted by a clear majority of the Circuits,[13] that the phrase must be given an expansive meaning. In *Beech Aircraft Corp. v. Rainey,*[13a] the Court held that

". . . portions of investigatory reports otherwise admissible under Rule 803(8)(C) are not inadmissible merely because they state a conclusion

---

panion case arising out of same crash as in *Fraley;* court admitted both reports holding that lack of experience of JAG investigator went to weight, not admissibility).

[12] While the House Judiciary Committee stated that it "intends that the phrase 'factual findings' be strictly construed and that evaluations or opinions contained in public reports shall not be admissible under this Rule," the Senate Committee on the Judiciary took "strong exception to this limiting understanding." See House Comm. on Judiciary, H.R. Rep. No. 650, 93d Cong., 1st Sess., p. 14 (1973); Senate Comm. on Judiciary, S. Rep. No. 1277, 93d Cong., 2d Sess., p. 18 (1974). No reference to the differing approaches was made in the Conference Report. A broader conception of the phrase is consonant with the Advisory Committee's Note, which accepted "evaluative reports" as being within the scope of Rule 803(8)(C).

[13] All circuits other than the Fifth and Eleventh that had considered the issue had adopted the broader interpretation. *See, e.g.,* Zenith Radio Corp. v. Matsushita Elec. Indus. Co., Ltd., 505 F.Supp. 1125, 1144–45 (E.D. Pa. 1980), *aff'd in part and rev'd in part,* 723 F.2d 238 (3d Cir. 1983), *rev'd on other grounds,* 106 S.Ct. 1348 (1986) (court concluded after extensive review of the decided cases that "it is now generally accepted (and settled in this circuit) that under the aegis of 803(8)(C) evaluative reports of public agencies (*i.e.,* those rendering normative judgments or opinions, not just reciting facts) are admissible."). Ellis v. International Playtex, Inc. 745 F.2d 292, 299-304 (4th Cir. 1984) (wrongful death action; studies of toxic shock syndrome conducted by the Center for Disease Control); Robbins v. Whelan, 653 F.2d 47, 50 (1st Cir.), *cert. denied,* 454 U.S. 1123 (1981) (error to exclude report of Transportation on maximum stopping distances of different model cas); Lloyd v. American Export Lines, Inc., 580 F.2d 1179, 1183 (3rd Cir.), *cert. denied,* 439 U.S. 969 (1978) (decision and order of Coast Guard hearing examiner that there was no evidence that seaman involved in altercation was intoxicated or first aggressor).

[13a] — U.S. —, 109 S. Ct. 439, 102 L.Ed.2 445 (1988) (citing **Treatise**).

or opinion. As long as the conclusion is based on a factual investigation and satisfies the Rule's trustworthiness requirement, it should be admissible along with other portions of the report."[13b]

Accordingly, the Court found that the trial judge had not erred in admitting conclusions in a report concerning the probable cause of the crash of a Navy training aircraft.[13c] The Court noted that a broad interpretation of "factual findings" is consistent with the plain meaning of Rule 803(8), furthers the intent of the Advisory Committee to make evaluative reports admissible, and is in accord with "the liberal thrust of the Federal Rules"[13d] and their "general approach of relaxing the traditional barriers to 'opinion' testimony."[14]

A report which simply reaches a conclusion without any factual underpinnings is useless to fact-finders because it simply tells them how to decide a case without giving them sufficient information upon which to reach an informed decision. In this sense, the opinion must be factual. If, however, the report states an opinion that is helpful, it should be admitted, provided the report does not suffer from a lack of trustworthiness.[15] The Supreme Court approved of this approach in *Rainey*.[15a]

[13b] 13b *Id.* at —, 109 S. Ct. at 450, 102 L.Ed.2d at 463.

[13c] The only seriously contested issue in the litigation was whether pilot error or malfunctioning equipment had caused the crash.

[13d] — U.S. at —, 109 S.Ct. at 450, 102 L.Ed.2d at 463.

[14] *Id.*

[15] See, *e.g.*, *In re* Japanese Elec. Prods. Litigation, 723 F.2d 238, 272–73 (3d Cir. 1983), *rev'd on other grounds,* 106 S.Ct. 1348 (1985) (court found abuse of discretion in exclusion of records and findings of Japanese Fair Trade Commission since investigation and hearing which produced them were conducted in thorough timely fashion by experienced staff); Anderson v. City of New York, 657 F.Supp. 1571, 1579–80 (S.D.N.Y. 1987) (congressional subcommittee report, which discovered abusive conduct by white New York City police toward minorities, was not admissible because the report lacked "the ordinary indications of reliability . . . not based on the personal knowledge of the reporter, and contains the testimony of interested parties, not experts"; cites **Treatise**).

[15a] — U.S. —, —, 109 S.Ct. 439, 499, 102 L.Ed.2d 445, 463 (1988) ("The Rule's limitations and safeguards lie elsewhere: First, the requirement that reports contain factual findings bars the admission of statements not based on factual investigation. Second, the trustworthiness provision requires the court to make a determination as to whether the report, or any portion thereof, is sufficiently trustworthy to be admitted.").

Trustworthiness must be determined by the trial court on a case by case basis. Many courts have followed the suggestion in the Advisory Committee's notes to Rule 803(8)(C) that the following factors should be evaluated in deciding whether a lack of reliability has been shown: (1) the timeliness of the investigation; (2) the skill or experience of the official conducting the investigation; (3) whether a hearing has been held in connection with the investigation; and (4) possible motivational problems on the part of the preparer of the report.[16] The burden is on the opponent of the report to demonstrate untrustworthiness.

[d]   Criminal Cases[17]

The language in Rule 803(8)(C), which authorizes the admission of investigative reports in civil actions and against the Government in criminal cases, operates to prohibit investigative reports from being admitted against an accused under this hearsay exception. Rule 803(8)(B) was amended in Congress to exclude "in criminal cases matters observed by police officers and other law enforcement personnel." There was no discussion, either in Congress, or in the legislative reports, about whether this amendment read in conjunction with the limitation in Rule 803(8)(C) was designed to exclude all reports made by a government employee and offered against a criminal defendant, or whether the addition served the narrower function of excluding only those reports that would enable the prosecution to prove directly the elements of the offense charged without

---

[16] See, *e.g.,* Baker v. Elcona, 588 F.2d 551 (6th Cir.), *cert. denied,* 441 U.S. 933 (1979) (state highway patrolman's report concluding that plaintiff's car had entered intersection against red light properly admitted because there was an immediate investigation by an independent investigator with special skills; formal hearing is not a sine qua non of admissibility; court noted that patrolman had testified and had been cross-examined, though not about traffic light, probably because of trial strategy); City of New York v. Pullman, Inc., 662 F.2d 910, 914 (2d Cir. 1981), *cert. denied,* 454 U.S. 1164 (1982) (action to recover damages for subway trains which developed cracks; appellate court found that trial court did not abuse its broad discretion in excluding investigative report by federal Urban Mass Transit Administration because 1) report was an interim report subject to revision, 2) "findings" were based on hand-outs by the parties rather than on independent testing by the UMTA, or derived from administrative hearings, and 3) report was prepared for different purpose).

[17] See discussion in **Treatise** at ¶ 803(8)[01].

having the perception and credibility of its police and investigative officers tested by cross-examination.

The courts have split on two issues: (1) do subdivisions (B) and (C) operate to exclude all reports by police or other law enforcement personnel from being admitted against a criminal defendant pursuant to Rule 803(8), and (2) may a report barred by Rule 803(8) be admitted against an accused if it satisfies some other hearsay exception?

The most restrictive approach has accorded enormous scope to the limitations on using reports against an accused contained in Rule 803(8)(B) and (C) by defining "other law enforcement personnel" as including "any officer or employee of a governmental

(Text continued on page 16–53)

agency which has law enforcement responsibilities," and extending the limitations to all reports, regardless of their nature.[18] Other courts, after considering the underlying policies of the hearsay rule, have been less inflexible in interpreting Rule 803(8). They have accorded a narrower definition to "other law enforcement personnel,"[19] and have been willing to admit records of routine, nonadversarial matters.[20] Furthermore, although the restrictive view holds that a report barred by Rule 803(8) must be excluded even if it satisfies some other hearsay exception,[21] courts

---

[18] In the first case of this series, United States v. Oates, 560 F.2d 45 (2d Cir. 1977), a narcotics prosecution, the government sought to prove that the seized substance was heroin by introducing the report of the chemist who had done the analysis, instead of calling the chemist. Although the exhibit on its face raised questions about the heroin's chain of custody and about the accuracy with which the reports had been prepared, the appellate court declined to rest on a "lack of trustworthiness," but instead found that a full-time chemist of the United States Customs Service is included within the category of "law enforcement personnel," that his report fell within the ambit of both Rule 803(8)(B) and (C), and that such a report "cannot satisfy the standards of any hearsay exception if those reports are sought to be introduced against the accused." *Id.* at 84. See also United States v. Ruffin, 575 F.2d 346, 355–56 (2d Cir. 1978) (computer print-out of an IRS record inadmissible).

[19] See, *e.g.*, United States v. Hansen, 583 F.2d 325, 333 (7th Cir.), *cert. denied*, 439 U.S. 912 (1978) (does not include building inspector).

[20] United States v. Quezada, 754 F.2d 1190, 1193–95 (5th Cir. 1985) (documents recording routine, objective observations are inherently reliable; warrant of deportation containing information proving defendant's prior arrest and deportations); United States v. Orozco, 590 F.2d 789 (9th Cir.), *cert. denied*, 442 U.S. 920 (1979) (computer data (TECS) cards bearing license plate information furnished by customs inspectors used to show that car in which drugs found had been recorded as crossing Mexican border at the same time as defendant claimed to have been driving in Los Angeles; no motive to fabricate); United States v. Grady, 544 F.2d 598 (2d Cir. 1976) (police records of Northern Ireland recording serial numbers and receipt of certain weapons admitted in prosecution for unlawful export of firearms; Congressional purpose was to prevent proof of government's case by reports of observation of crime). Finger-print records, mug shots, arrest records and the like are routinely admitted without objection.

[21] United States v. Oates, 560 F.2d 45 (2d Cir. 1977); United States v. Quinto, 582 F.2d 225 (2d Cir. 1978). But see United States v. Metzger, 778 F.2d 1195, 1201 (6th Cir. 1985) ("nothing . . . would even remotely suggest that the restrictions of Rule 803(8)(C) should be grafted onto Rule 803(10)."); United States v. Yakabov, 712 F.2d 20, 25–26 (2d Cir. 1983) (holding that conclusion in *Oates* should not be extended to bar receipt of a certificate meeting the requirements of

will now admit the report if its author takes the stand and is subject to cross-examination. [22]

The less restrictive view is amply justified by the legislative history of Rule 803(8) which indicates no intention on the part of Congress to bar the admissibility of those records which prior to the enactment of the Federal Rules of Evidence had been admitted pursuant to the business records exception to the hearsay rule. When the circumstances surrounding the creation of a report demonstrate the likelihood of inaccurate observation or misrepresentation, exclusion is warranted because of a "lack of trustworthiness," regardless of whether the report is being offered pursuant to Rules 803(6) or (8).

The language of subdivision (C) clearly contemplates that a criminal defendant may use an investigatory report against the prosecution. Subdivision (B), on its face, prohibits the use in all criminal cases of reports of matters observed by police and other law enforcement personnel. It has, however, been held that there is no reason for interpreting subdivisions (B) and (C) differently: subdivision (B) "should be read in accordance with the obvious intent of Congress to authorize the admission of the reports of police officers and other law enforcement personnel at the request of the defendant in a criminal case." [23] In any event, most such documents would constitute admissions under Rule 801(d)(2) and there is no confrontation problem.

¶ 16.07[02]   Absence of Public Record or Entry—Rule 803(10) [1]

Rule 803(10) provides that the nonoccurrence of an event may be proved by evidence that there is no public record or entry of the event if a public record or entry of the event would have been

---

Rule 803(10) because a statement "envisaged by Rule 803(10) is normally a step removed from any element of the offense charged" and does not have evaluative aspects necessitating cross-examination).

[22] See, *e.g.*, United States v. King, 613 F.2d 670 (7th Cir. 1980); United States v. Sawyer, 607 F.2d 1190 (7th Cr. 1979), *cert. denied*, 445 U.S. 943 (1980).

[23] United States v. Smith, 521 F.2d 957, 969 n.24 (D.C. Cir. 1975).

[1] See discussion in **Treatise** at ¶ 803(10)[01].

"regularly made and preserved."[2] The rule is analogous to Rule 803(7). The rule states:

> The following are not excluded by the hearsay rule, even though the declarant is available as a witness:
>
> . . .
>
> (10) Absence of public record or entry.—To prove the absence of a record, report, statement, or data compilation, in any form, or the nonoccurrence or nonexistence of a matter of which a record, report, statement, or data compilation, in any form, was regularly made and preserved by a public office or agency, evidence in the form of a certification in accordance with rule 902, or testimony, that diligent search failed to disclose the record, report, statement, or data compilation, or entry.

Rule 803(10) allows the absence of a record or entry to be proved by a certificate complying with Rule 902,[3] or testimony, that there was a diligent search for the record whose absence is sought to be shown. "The diligence requirement is one of substance, not form."[4] The rule "is not satisfied merely by a ritual incantation . . . ."[5]

---

[2] See, *e.g.,* United States v. Johnson, 577 F.2d 1304 (5th Cir. 1978) (no record of tax return to prove that none filed).

[3] Rule 902(4) provides for certification complying with any rule adopted by the Supreme Court and also authorizes certification in accordance with state statutes. See Rule 44(b) of the Federal Rules of Civil Procedure and Rule 27 of the Federal Rules of Criminal Procedure. See United States v. Wilson, 732 F.2d 404, 413 (5th Cir.), *cert. denied,* 105 S.Ct. 609 (1984) (to counter defendant's contention that he was affiliated with CIA, court admitted affidavit of executive director of CIA, attested to by general counsel of CIA); United States v. Herrera-Britto, 739 F.2d 551 (11th Cir. 1984) (certificate by Honduran officials that no registration was found for vessel in question).

[4] United States v. Yakobov, 712 F.2d 20, 24 (2d Cir. 1983) (conviction for unlawfully engaging in business of dealing in firearms reversed because of trial court's erroneous admission of certificate prepared by the United States Treasury Department's Bureau of Alcohol, Tobacco and Firearms to prove that defendant was not licensed as a dealer).

[5] United States v. Yakobov, 712 F.2d 20 (2d Cir. 1983) (certificate indicated that search had been made for license bearing misspelled versions of defendant's name, and that since his name was misspelled with a "J" instead of a "Y," it would be likely that license or application for defendant would not be found even if it existed). See also United States v. Robinson, 544 F.2d 110, 114–15 (2d Cir. 1976), *cert. denied,* 435 U.S. 905 (1978) (casual or partial search is not a diligent search).

¶ 16.07[03]   Records of Vital Statistics—Rule 803(9)[1]

Records of vital statistics present a specialized instance of reports to public officials made by private citizens who are performing an official duty. The reports, of births, deaths and marriages, are usually made by ministers, physicians and undertakers. Because of the great need for this type of proof, and the usual disinterestedness and personal knowledge of the reporter, the reports are specifically made admissible by Rule 803(9), which provides:

> The following are not excluded by the hearsay rule, even though the declarant is available as a witness:
>
> . . .
>
> (9) Records of vital statistics.—Records or data compilations, in any form, of births, fetal deaths, deaths, or marriages, if the report thereof was made to a public office pursuant to requirements of law.

The rule is silent about a requirement of firsthand knowledge, as are the notes to this exception, although the general notes to Rule 803 state that "neither this rule nor Rule 804 dispenses with the requirement." The issue is most likely to arise in connection with statutes that require the reporter of a death to answer detailed questions about the circumstances surrounding the demise. The result may be a statement by a physician that reports not only that the deceased died of carbon monoxide poisoning, but also that he committed suicide, a fact of which the physician has no personal knowledge. Rule 803(9) should be interpreted flexibly to admit statements containing conclusions not based on firsthand knowledge, despite the suggestion in the notes to Rule 803 that this requirement applies to all the exceptions. This interpretation is in accord with the rationale underlying the creation of a system of vital statistics and recognizes that the persons required by statute to make reports on death are usually professionals who presumably perform their duties scrupulously and impartially. If, in a particular case, the trial court finds that the prejudice resulting from the admission of a certificate outweighs its probative value, exclusion pursuant to Rule 403 would be appropriate.

---

[1] See discussion in **Treatise** at ¶ 803(9)[01].

¶ 16.07[04] Marriage, Baptismal, and Similar Certificates —Rule 803(12)[1]

Rule 803(12) provides for the admission of statements of fact contained in a certificate issued by an authorized person attesting that he performed a marriage or other ceremony or administered a sacrament. To the extent that the authorized person is required to file a report of his action, Rule 803(12) offers an alternative to proof pursuant to Rule 803(9). Instead of obtaining a copy of the record of vital statistics, the proponent can offer the certificate which the presiding official had given to the participants. However, some acts, such as baptism or confirmation, are not required or even authorized to be recorded. Certificates or records of the religious organizations (see Rule 803(11)) are the only ways in which the facts supplied in connection with these ceremonies can be admitted as acceptable evidence. The rule provides:

> The following are not excluded by the hearsay rule, even though the declarant is available as a witness:
>
> . . .
>
> (12) Marriage, baptismal, and similar certificates.—Statements of fact contained in a certificate that the maker performed a marriage or other ceremony or administered a sacrament, made by a clergyman, public official, or other person authorized by the rules or practices of a religious organization or by law to perform the act certified, and purporting to have been issued at the time of the act or within a reasonable time thereafter.

Rule 803(12) requires preliminary proof that the clergyman, public official or other person was authorized to perform the certified act either by the rules or practices of a religious organization or by law. Rule 803(12) also requires that the certificate "purport" to have been issued at the time of the act or within a reasonable time thereafter. The evidence furnished by the certificate is not conclusive; it can be controverted by any other relevant evidence.

---

[1] See discussion in **Treatise** at ¶ 803(12)[01].

¶ 16.07[05]   Judgment   of   Previous   Conviction—Rule 803(22)[1]

Rule 803(22) allows evidence of certain kinds of criminal judgments to be admitted in subsequent criminal or civil proceedings "to prove any fact essential to sustain the judgment." The rule provides:

> The following are not excluded by the hearsay rule, even though the declarant is available as a witness:
>
> . . .
>
> (22) Judgment of previous conviction.—Evidence of a final judgment, entered after a trial or upon a plea of guilty (but not upon a plea of nolo contendere), adjudging a person guilty of a crime punishable by death or imprisonment in excess of one year, to prove any fact essential to sustain the judgment, but not including, when offered by the Government in a criminal prosecution for purposes other than impeachment, judgments against persons other than the accused. The pendency of an appeal may be shown but does not affect admissibility.

Rule 803(22) applies only to prior criminal judgments offered in subsequent proceedings.[2] Because the lesser applicable burden of proof makes them less reliable, prior civil judgments are inadmissible, except to the limited extent provided by Rule 803(23), or as given effect by the non-evidential substantive doctrines of res judicata and collateral estoppel.

The judgment of conviction must have been entered after trial or have been based upon a plea of guilty. Judgments of conviction based upon pleas of nolo contendere are not included consistently with Rule 410. Rule 803(22) does not apply to judgments of acquittal because of a lack of relevancy. Such judgments do not necessarily prove innocence; instead, they may indicate that the prosecution failed to meet its burden of proof beyond a reasonable doubt as to at least one element of the crime, or that the jury exercised its inherent mercy dispensing function. In either event, the

---

[1] See discussion in **Treatise** at ¶ 803(22)[01].

[2] Lloyd v. American Export Lines, Inc., 580 F.2d 1179, 1189 (3d Cir. 1978), *cert. denied,* 439 U.S. 969 (1979) (court held that trial court had erred in excluding Japanese judgment; the "test of acceptance . . . of foreign judgments . . . is whether the foreign proceedings accord with civilized jurisprudence, and are stated in a clear and formal record").

defendant cannot claim that the contrary of the material propositions of fact now being urged must have been found. The pendency of an appeal may be shown for the jurors to evaluate as they wish; it does not make the conviction inadmissible.[3]

The offense of which the defendant was guilty must be one "punishable by death or imprisonment in excess of one year." This limitation to convictions of felony grade, measured by federal standards, recognizes that motivation to defend at a lower level may be lacking. In this type of case, particularly if a traffic violation is concerned, the accused typically pleads guilty, often without consulting counsel, as a matter of convenience. To effectuate the policy of Rule 803(22) barring evidence of convictions punishable by imprisonment for less than one year, a court ought generally to be cautious about admitting evidence of guilty pleas in nonfelony cases on a theory other than Rule 803(22) as, for instance, an admission under Rule 801(d)(2), or as a declaration against interest pursuant to Rule 804(b)(3), because the plea may not be fully trustworthy.[4] Rule 803(22) allows the criminal judgment to be admitted in subsequent criminal as well as civil proceedings. Rule 803(22) does distinguish between civil and criminal litigation to the extent of excluding judgments of conviction of a third person offered by the government against the accused in a criminal case for purposes other than impeachment.[5]

While Rule 803(22) makes the prior conviction admissible, it does not prescribe the effect the judgment will have once it is ad-

---

[3] See also Rule 609(e).

[4] But *cf.* United States v. Gotti, 641 F.Supp. 283 (E.D.N.Y. 1986) (special reasons for allowing misdemeanor convictions in this RICO case).

[5] This limitation is dictated by constitutional considerations. See Kirby v. United States, 174 U.S. 47, 60, 19 S.Ct. 574, 43 L.Ed. 890 (1899) ("one accused of having received stolen goods with intent to convert them to his own use, knowing at the time that they were stolen, is not within the meaning of the Constitution confronted with the witnesses against him when the fact that the goods were stolen is established simply by the record of another criminal case with which the accused had no connection and in which he was not entitled to be represented by counsel."). See also United States v. Crispin, 757 F.2d 611 (5th Cir. 1985) (in prosecution for conspiracy to move within United States an alien present in violation of the law, error to have admitted judgments of conviction offered to prove the illegal status of some of the aliens, but harmless in light of overwhelming evidence of the aliens' illegal status).

mitted. Whether or not the conviction will be given a conclusive effect depends on substantive considerations such as the type of case,[6] whether the impact would be to bar a criminal from profiting by the act for which he was convicted,[7] and the existence of state policies that have to be implemented in a diversity case pursuant to the *Erie* doctrine.

A judgment of conviction can be used "to prove any fact essential to the judgment." Determining what facts were essential may be a laborious task for the trial judge when the antecedent litigation was complex and ended in a general verdict.[8] In some instances the judgment may be inadmissible because it will be impossible to determine whether the facts sought to be proved in the second case were necessarily determined in the first.[9]

¶ 16.08   Publications

Rule 803 contains two subdivisions that make particular types of publications admissible: Rule 803(18) recognizes a hearsay exception for particular types of published works that are termed "learned treatises"; Rule 803(17) provides a hearsay exception for published compilations of a commercial nature.

---

[6] See, *e.g.*, Standefer v. United States, 447 U.S. 10, 100 S.Ct. 1999, 64 L.Ed.2d 689 (1980) (Court refused to apply nonmutual collateral estoppel against the government in a criminal case).

[7] See, *e.g.*, Ruth v. First Nat'l Bank of N.J., 410 F.Supp. 1233 (D.N.J. 1976) (where plaintiff had been convicted of illegally having funds credited to corporation's account, court gave conclusive effect to judgment in action where plaintiff claimed that funds had been wrongly turned over to the United States).

[8] See Emich Motors Corp. v. General Motors Corp., 340 U.S. 558, 569, 71 S.Ct. 408, 95 L.Ed 534 (1951) ("A general verdict of the jury or judgment of the court without special findings does not indicate which of the means charged in the indictment were found to have been used in effectuating the conspiracy. And since all of the acts charged need not be proved for conviction . . . such a verdict does not establish that defendants used all of the means charged or any particular one. Under these circumstances what was decided by the criminal judgment must be determined by the trial judge hearing the treble-damage suit, upon an examination of the record, including the pleadings, the evidence submitted, the instructions under which the jury arrived at its verdict, and any opinions of the courts").

[9] See also Columbia Plaza Corp. v. Security Nat'l Bank, 676 F.2d 780, 790 (D.C. Cir. 1982) (court concluded that Rule 803(22) was not satisfied where it could not determine for what reasons the jury convicted the defendants).

¶ 16.08[01]   Learned Treatises—Rule 803(18)[1]

Rule 803(18) provides that statements contained in certain publications may be admitted to prove the facts asserted once certain requirements are satisfied. The rule provides:

> The following are not excluded by the hearsay rule, even though the declarant is available as a witness:
>
> . . .
>
> (18) Learned treatises.—To the extent called to the attention of an expert witness upon cross-examination or relied upon by the expert witness in direct examination, statements contained in published treatises, periodicals, or pamphlets on a subject of history, medicine, or other science or art, established as a reliable authority by the testimony or admission of the witness or by other expert testimony or by judicial notice. If admitted, the statements may be read into evidence but may not be received as exhibits.

According to Rule 803(18), a learned treatise must be "published." It can be a treatise, periodical or pamphlet on a "subject of history, medicine, or other science or art."[2] The opening phrase of the rule, "[t]o the extent called to the attention of an expert witness upon cross-examination or relied upon by him in direct examination," limits admissibility to those treatises whose existence is disclosed while an expert is on the stand, thereby guaranteeing that the trier of fact will have the benefit of expert evaluation and explanation of how the published material relates to the issues in the case. This requirement, as well as the prohibition in the last sentence on taking treatises into the jury room, guard against the danger that jurors will misuse the texts in question. When the statement in a treatise contains an undisputed fact, there may be some overlap with Rule 803(17). If the trial court finds that the data in question do not require elucidation, it should allow admission pursuant to Rule 803(17) so that an expert witness need not be called.

The treatise may not be admitted unless its authority is established to the satisfaction of the trial court. The profferor of the evidence

---

[1] See discussion in **Treatise** at ¶¶ 803(18)[01]–[02].

[2] See, *e.g.*, Johnson v. William C. Ellis & Sons Iron Works, Inc., 609 F.2d 820 (5th Cir. 1980) (safety codes); Connecticut Light & Power Co. v. Federal Power Comm'n, 557 F.2d 349, 356 (2d Cir. 1977) (historical treatises).

can satisfy this requirement in a number of different ways: by eliciting testimony about the treatise's reliability from an expert on direct,[3] by eliciting a concession of reliability from the opponent's expert on cross, or by persuading the court to take judicial notice that the publication is a "reliable authority."

The court has discretion to exclude pursuant to Rule 403 if the probative value of the statement in the treatise is substantially outweighed by the dangers of prejudice, confusion or waste of time.[4] Depending on the nature of the fact sought to be proved, its significance to the case, and the availability of other evidence on the point, the trial judge may elect to have the question of the admissibility of the treatise explored outside the presence of the jury. In a civil case, the trial judge may wish to deal with this issue at a Rule 16 conference. In all cases, the trial court may require notice to be given before trial of this type of hearsay so that there will be no surprises and experts will be prepared to deal with it without the need for continuances.

Since the objective of the rule is to make valuable information available to the trier of fact, trial judges should use a liberal standard in determining whether the treatise's authoritativeness has been established. For example, in a medical malpractice case, a court might take judicial notice that the proffered text appears on the reading list of a medical school, or that the book in question was admitted in the course of some other litigation.

---

[3] See, *e.g.,* Burgess v. Premier Corp., 727 F.2d 826 (9th Cir. 1984) (plaintiff's witness testified that author of books on cattle investments was the preeminent industry expert, and that defendant required its salesmen to read the books and to recommend them).

[4] Schneider v. Revici, 817 F.2d 987, 991 (2d Cir. 1987) (even if defense in medical malpractice action had laid proper foundation for introduction of defendant's text as a learned treatise, admission would remain subject to Rule 403 and balancing would favor exclusion).

¶ 16.08[02] Market Reports, Commercial Publications— Rule 803(17)[1]

Rule 803(17) is designed to allow published compilations generally used to be admitted into evidence, provided they are relied upon either by the public or by persons in a particular trade or business. The rule provides:

> The following are not excluded by the hearsay rule, even though the declarant is available as a witness:
>
> . . .
>
> (17) Market reports, commercial publications.—Market quotations, tabulations, lists, directories, or other published compilations, generally used and relied upon by the public or by persons in particular occupations.

The only difficulty with the exception is determining how narrowly it should be interpreted. Publications such as market quotations in newspapers, life expectancy tables, pink security sheets, animal pedigrees, and directories state readily ascertained facts about which there can be no real dispute. Admitting them without the possibility of cross-examining the persons who supplied the data makes little difference. On the other hand, there are publications upon which the public or persons in particular occupations rely, such as price lists, mercantile credit reports and safety codes, which fit within the literal language of the rule, but which are not concerned with simple objective facts. When it cannot be shown that the information was obtained and compiled in a manner consistent with trustworthiness, the judge should exclude. Requiring advance notice of intention to rely on this material is desirable and usually leads to stipulations since there has been an opportunity to check for accuracy.

¶ 16.09 Evidence of Reputation—Rules 803(19), (20), (21)

Three different subdivisions of Rule 803 authorize the reception of reputation evidence. Rule 803(19)[1] allows reputation evidence to

---

[1] See discussion in **Treatise** at ¶ 803(17).

[1] Rule 803(19) provides:

The following are not excluded by the hearsay rule, even though the declarant is available as a witness:

be used to prove facts of personal or family history, Rule 803(20)[2] creates a hearsay exception for evidence of reputation to prove the location of boundaries and matters of general history, and Rule 803(21)[3] was added to the Federal Rules to ensure that the hearsay rule would not bar the use of reputation evidence to prove character in those instances in which character evidence can be used substantively. See Rules 404 and 405.

---

(19) Reputation concerning personal or family history.—Reputation among members of a person's family by blood, adoption, or marriage, or among a person's associates, or in the community, concerning a person's birth, adoption, marriage, divorce, death, legitimacy, relationship by blood, adoption, or marriage, ancestry, or other similar fact of personal or family history.

See discussion in **Treatise** at ¶ 803(19).

[2] Rule 803(20) provides:

The following are not excluded by the hearsay rule, even though the declarant is available as a witness:

(20) Reputation concerning boundaries or general history.—Reputation in a community, arising before the controversy, as to boundaries of or customs affecting lands in the community, and reputation as to events of general history important to the community or State or nation in which located.

See discussion in **Treatise** at ¶ 803(20).

[3] Rule 803(21) provides:

The following are not excluded by the hearsay rule, even though the declarant is available as a witness:

(21) Reputation as to character.—Reputation of a person's character among associates or in the community.

See discussion in **Treatise** at ¶ 803(21).

CHAPTER 17

Hearsay Exceptions Requiring Unavailability— Rule 804

SYNOPSIS

(Pub.819)

¶ 17.01 Definition of Unavailability—Rule 804(a)[1]

Subdivision (a) of Rule 804 governs the definition of unavailability, the factor which subdivision (b) makes the condition precedent for admitting hearsay statements under the exceptions there specified. Rule 804(a) provides:

Rule 804

HEARSAY EXCEPTIONS; DECLARANT UNAVAILABLE

(a) Definition of unavailability.— "Unavailability as a witness" includes situations in which the declarant—

(1) is exempted by ruling of the court on the ground of privilege from testifying concerning the subject matter of the declarant's statement; or

(2) persists in refusing to testify concerning the subject matter of the declarant's statement despite an order of the court to do so; or

(3) testifies to a lack of memory of the subject matter of the declarant's statement; or

(4) is unable to be present or to testify at the hearing because of death or then existing physical or mental illness or infirmity; or

(5) is absent from the hearing and the proponent of a statement has been unable to procure the declarant's attendance (or in the case of a hearsay exception under subdivision (b)(2), (3), or (4), the declarant's attendance or testimony) by process or other reasonable means.

A declarant is not unavailable as a witness if exemption, refusal, claim of lack of memory, inability, or absence is due to the procurement or wrongdoing of the proponent of a statement for the purpose of preventing the witness from attending or testifying.

By insisting on the unavailability of the declarant's testimony, Rule 804(a) expresses a rule of preference. When a declarant is available, personal testimony in court, subject to the safeguards of an oath and cross-examination, is preferred. But when the declarant's testimony is unobtainable,[2] an extra-judicial statement that falls within

---

[1] See discussion in **Treatise** at ¶ 804(a)[01].

[2] The crucial factor is the unavailability of the declarant's testimony, rather than the unavailability of the declarant as a witness. The declarant's presence on the witness stand will not block use of the extra-judicial statement if the witness refuses to answer, exercises a privilege not to answer, or is suffering from a mental disability

the categories specified in Rule 804(b) is preferable to losing all evidence from that source. By using the word "includes" instead of the phrase "restricted to" in its introduction, subdivision (a) suggests that the definition is open-ended even though it appears to be comprehensive. A hierarchy of hearsay is created by the unavailability requirement because of the drafters' belief that statements made in the circumstances specified in Rule 804(b) are not as inherently trustworthy—except for prior testimony—as statements that conform to the requirements of Rule 803.

Rule 804(a) provides that a declarant is not unavailable if the unavailability was "due to the procurement or wrongdoing of the proponent of [the] statement for the purpose of preventing the witness from attending or testifying."[3] A statement will be admitted if the declarant's unavailability was caused by the party against whom the statement is being offered.[4]

¶ 17.01[01]   Privilege

Rule 804(a)(1) states that a declarant is unavailable when the court upholds a claim of privilege with regard to the subject matter of the statement. This species of unavailability occurs most frequently in connection with former testimony, and is most commonly invoked by claims of spousal privilege, or the privilege against self-incrimination. If the witness makes no formal claim of privilege, but refuses to testify, unavailability may result pursuant to paragraph (2) of Rule 804(a).

---

or impairment of memory. See, *e.g.,* Walden v. Sears, Roebuck & Co., 654 F.2d 443, 446 (5th Cir. 1981) (deposition of injured minor should have been admitted where he suffererd loss of memory and nine years had lapsed since testimony).

[3] See, *e.g.,* United States v. Pizarro, 756 F.2d 579, 582–83 (7th Cir.), *cert. denied,* 105 S.Ct. 2686 (1985) (prior testimony of witness who had testified at previous trial that defendant was not the source of heroin could not be admitted at second trial when witness refused to testify because of intimidation by defendant). The Second Circuit has held that this provision does not apply unless it can be concluded that the unavailability was caused to prevent the declarant from testifying. United States v. Seijo, 595 F.2d 116 (2d Cir. 1979) (government should have been allowed to introduce depositions of aliens who had been deported by INS).

[4] See, *e.g.,* Steele v. Taylor, 684 F.2d 1193, 1202 (6th Cir. 1982), *cert. denied,* 460 U.S. 1053 (1983).

¶ 17.01[02]   Refusal to Testify

If despite judicial orders to answer, the declarant refuses to testify about the subject matter of the hearsay statement by erroneously relying on a privilege, or by disregarding a grant of immunity, or by simply remaining silent, the declarant is unavailable pursuant to Rule 804(a)(2). The court should normally exercise some of its coercive power, as by threatening contempt outside the presence of the jury before concluding that the witness will not testify.

¶ 17.01[03]   Lack of Memory

Rule 804(a)(4) recognizes unavailability when a witness testifies to a lack of memory. Since the witness must testify, and is, therefore, subject to cross-examination about his claim, the trial judge has a good opportunity for assessing the witness' credibility, and the danger of a perjurious claim of forgetfulness is lessened. If the trial judge disbelieves the witness and finds that unavailability has not been established on this ground, the extra-judicial statement may nevertheless be admissible as a prior inconsistent statement if the requirements of Rule 801(d)(1)(A) are met. Moreover, a feigned failure to recollect may be treated as a refusal to testify pursuant to Rule 804(a)(2).

¶ 17.01[04]   Death or Infirmity

Rule 804(a)(4) states that unavailability exists when the declarant "is unable to be present or testify at the hearing because of . . . then existing physical or mental illness or infirmity." Death and severe permanent disabilities clearly satisfy this formula. In other instances, the trial court will have to consider such factors as the nature of the disability and its expected duration, the length of time the case has been pending, whether delays, if any, are attributable to the proponent of the hearsay, the nature of the case, the significance of the disabled witness' testimony, the availability of other evidence on the same point, and the need for cross-examination given the nature of the expected testimony and the subject of the hearsay statement.

Disability due to such temporary conditions as pregnancy or fractures may have to be handled by a continuance, particularly in a criminal case where the declarant is a prosecution witness whose testimony is crucial.[5] Given calendar pressures and the demands of speedy trial rules, the trial court must be given great discretion to decide on adjournments, continuances or mistrials because of the unavailability of witnesses. In a civil case, or in a criminal case where the defendant offers the hearsay statement, it is easier to find unavailability even when the disability is only temporary.

The trial judge's task is often more difficult when the claimed disability is mental rather than physical, since there may be greater disagreement and uncertainty about the patient's prognosis and treatment. A further complication is the possibility that the declarant may have been incompetent at the time the statement was made, a factor which would detract considerably from the statement's reliability.

Questions of a declarant's physical or mental infirmity are best explored at a pretrial hearing before a jury is picked that will be unable to act if a continuance is ordered. The court may order depositions to be taken or remove the court, including jurors, to the bedside of the witness.[6]

¶ 17.01[05]   Absence

When absence from the hearing is relied upon as the basis for unavailability, Rule 804(a)(5) requires the proponent of the declarant's hearsay statement to make a showing that it has not been possible to procure the declarant's attendance, or to take his deposition (if admission of the statement is sought pursuant to the exceptions in Rules 804(b)(2), (3), (4)) "by process or other reasonable means." The rule thus requires the proponent to show either

---

[5] See, e.g., United States v. Faison, 679 F.2d 292, 297 (3d Cir. 1982) (abuse of discretion not to grant continuance but instead to admit former testimony of crucial prosecution witness whom trial judge had found unavailable because he was about to undergo surgery which would disable him from testifying for at least 4 to 5 weeks).

[6] *In re* Application to Take Testimony in Criminal Case Outside District, 102 F.R.D. 521 (E.D. N.Y. 1985) (court may try part of case outside district in order to take the testimony of a sick witness).

that the declarant is beyond the reach of process, or that the declarant cannot be found or made to attend despite a good faith effort.

The differences in procedural rules for compelling the attendance of witnesses result in non-identical definitions of unavailability in civil and criminal cases. In federal civil cases, Rule 45(e) of the Federal Rules of Civil Procedure provides that a subpoena may be served anywhere within the district or anywhere without the district within 100 miles of the place of hearing or trial. In a civil case, therefore, a declarant more than 100 miles away from the place of the proceeding will usually be unavailable, unless he was subject to process by virtue of some other provision,[7] or unless no attempt was made to take his deposition, and admission of his statement is sought pursuant to Rules 804(b)(2), (3), or (4).[8]

In criminal cases, "a subpoena requiring the attendance of a witness at a hearing or trial may be served at any place within the United States." United States nationals and residents may also be reachable by process when they are outside the United States.[9]

A declarant who cannot be found obviously cannot be served with process. The language in Rule 804(a)(5), that the declarant's attendance could not be procured by "reasonable means," incorporates into the evidentiary rule the constitutional requirement that the prosecution may not use the declarant's hearsay statement unless it shows that it made a good-faith effort to produce the missing declarant.[10]

---

[7] Rule 45(e) also provides that "when a statute of the United States provides therefor, the court upon proper application and cause shown may authorize the service of a subpoena at any other place."

[8] The requirement relating to the taking of a deposition should, however, be interpreted flexibly in instances in which it is impracticable but not legally impossible to depose the declarant. When a relatively small claim would be overbalanced by the cost of a foreign deposition, or where the evidence comes to light during the trial and a continuance is not possible, the proponent should be found to be "unable" to procure the deposition.

[9] 28 U.S.C. ¶ 1783 authorizes a court of the United States to issue a subpoena to a national or resident who is in a foreign country "if the court finds that particular testimony . . . by him is necessary in the interest of justice, and, in other than a criminal action or proceeding, if the court finds, in addition, that it is not possible to obtain his testimony in admissible form without his personal appearance . . . ."

[10] Barber v. Page, 390 U.S. 719, 88 S.Ct. 1318, 20 L.Ed.2d 255 (1966) (state

¶ 17.02   Former Testimony—Rule 804(b)(1)

¶ 17.02[01]   In General[1]

Rule 804(b)(1) makes admissible, as an exception to the hearsay rule, former testimony or a deposition, given in the course of the same or a different proceeding, provided the party (or a predecessor in interest in a civil case) against whom the testimony or deposition is now offered, had the opportunity and motive to develop the testimony at the prior proceeding.[2]

Rule 804(b)(1) provides:

. . . (b) Hearsay exceptions.— The following are not excluded by the hearsay rule if the declarant is unavailable as a witness:

(1) Former testimony.— Testimony given as a witness at another hearing of the same or a different proceeding, or in a deposition taken in compliance with law in the course of the same or another proceeding, if the party against whom the testimony is now offered, or, in a civil action or proceeding, a predecessor in interest, had an opportunity and similar motive to develop the testimony by direct, cross, or redirect examination.

The proffer of a deposition or testimony given at another trial presents a hearsay question because the evidence is not being offered through the in-court testimony of a witness who perceived

---

prosecutor could not use preliminary hearing testimony of witness presently in federal penitentiary without making effort to persuade federal authorities to produce witness at trial). See also Ohio v. Roberts, 448 U.S. 56, 100 S.Ct. 2531, 65 L.Ed.2d 597 (1980) (Court held that good-faith requirement was satisfied where five subpoenas had been issued for declarant at her parents' home, and mother testified at hearing that she knew no way to reach declarant; three dissenters would have required the prosecution to initiate an investigation into declarant's whereabouts).

[1] See discussion in **Treatise** at ¶ 804(b)(1).

[2] The character of the tribunal before which the former trial was held is immaterial provided that the tribunal was empowered to conduct cross-examination. See, *e.g.,* Lloyd v. American Export Lines, Inc., 580 F.2d 1179 (3d Cir.), *cert. denied,* 439 U.S. 969 (1979) (Coast Guard hearing); Matter of Sterling Navigation Co., Ltd., 444 F.Supp. 1043, 1046 (S.D.N.Y. 1977) (testimony at hearing held pursuant to local Bankruptcy Rules could not be admitted since such hearings are "non-adversary fact-finding proceedings" which "cannot be said to give rise to the type of adversarial cross-examination contemplated by Rule 804(b)").

the events reported. The trier's inability to observe the witness' demeanor is, however, the only one of the ideal conditions for giving testimony that is lacking. The testimony or deposition was given under oath, under circumstances impressing upon the witness the need for care and accuracy, and was subject to the opportunity to cross-examine. It is, therefore, somewhat of an anomaly that prior testimony, which is undoubtedly more reliable than many of the statements encountered in Rule 803, is made admissible by virtue of Rule 804, the rule that deals with less reliable hearsay. Unavailability was retained as a requirement in deference to traditional practice.

When a transcript exists, the trial court should insist upon its production as the most reliable means of proving prior testimony. The certified transcript is admissible pursuant to Rule 803(8) as a public record. The former testimony may, however, also be proved (1) through the testimony of a firsthand observer of the former proceedings who can satisfy the court that he is able to remember the purport of all the witness said on direct and cross even if he cannot remember the exact words; (2) by the testimony of a first-hand observer whose memory has been refreshed with a memorandum, such as the stenographer's notes or transcript; or (3) by notes taken by an observer at the trial that qualify as a memorandum of recorded recollection pursuant to Rule 803(5). These alternative methods of proof are available since the matter sought to be proved is the former testimony rather than the contents of the official transcript; consequently the best evidence rule does not apply. The writing is required in the case of depositions because of special rules.

¶ 17.02[02]   Opportunity and Similar Motive[1]

Rule 804(b)(1) requires that the party against whom the testimony is now offered, or in a civil action a predecessor in interest, must have had "an opportunity and similar motive to develop the testimony." Actual cross-examination is not necessary, and the party need not have been represented by the same counsel at both proceedings.[2] The rule is grounded on the assumption that it is fair

---

[1] See discussion in **Treatise** at ¶ 804(b)(1)[02],[04].

[2] Ohio v. Roberts, 448 U.S. 56, 71–72, 100 S.Ct. 2531, 65 L.Ed.2d 597 (1980);

to make a party who had the opportunity and motive to explore testimony at a prior proceeding bear the consequences of a failure to cross-examine adequately or an election not to do so.

The "opportunity and similar motive" test is designed to ensure that the party against whom the testimony is being offered had a meaningful opportunity to expose its deficiencies at the first proceeding "in view of the realities of the situation."[3] A shift in the theory of the case,[4] or a change of tribunal,[5] will not defeat admis-

United States v. Amaya, 533 F.2d 188 (5th Cir. 1976), *cert. denied*, 429 U.S. 1101 (1977).

[3] United States v. Franklin, 235 F.Supp. 338, 341 (D.D.C. 1964) (at second trial, government sought to introduce testimony of codefendants at first trial; defendant had not cross-examined at first trial because testimony was exculpatory; court found that there had not been a meaningful opportunity to cross-examine); United States v. Atkins, 618 F.2d 366 (5th Cir. 1980) (where government at hearing to determine admissibility of co-conspirators' statement did not have motivation to make declarant acknowledge that the "Robert" of whom he spoke was defendant, declarant's testimony could not be admitted when offered by defendant); United States v. Wingate, 520 F.2d 309, 316 (2d Cir. 1975), *cert. denied*, 423 U.S. 1074 (1976) (defendant sought to introduce co-defendant's suppression hearing testimony which had been exculpatory as to him; court excluded on the ground that government had "no meaningful opportunity to cross-examine" co-defendant since the issue had not been guilt or innocence but whether co-defendant's confession was voluntary).

[4] See, *e.g.*, Matter of Johns-Manville/Asbestosis Cases, 93 F.R.D. 853 (N.D. Ill. 1982) (depositions of deceased physician taken in earlier suit in which plaintiffs sought recovery on theories of negligence, breach of warranty and misrepresentation admissible in second suit alleging intentional and fraudulent activity); Lyon v. United States, 413 F.2d 186, 189 (5th Cir. 1969) (change in indictment at second trial does not make testimony at first trial inadmissible if purpose for which testimony was originally offered does not change so that incentive and motive to cross-examine are substantially the same); Mid-City Bank & Trust Co. v. Nording Co., 3 F.R.D. 320 (D.N.J. 1944) (former testimony admitted where death of plaintiff converted negligence action into one for wrongful death).

[5] See, *e.g.*, United States v. Licavoli, 725 F.2d 1040, 1048–49 (6th Cir.), *cert. denied*, 467 U.S. 1252 (1984) (prior state court testimony of unavailable witness properly admitted; charges in state case were predicate acts for federal conviction so that motive to cross-examine was same in both cases); DeLuryea v. Winthrop Laboratories, 697 F.2d 222 (8th Cir. 1983) (in products liability action in which plaintiff claimed that she had never been advised to discontinue drug, error to exclude deposition of now/deceased physician taken in connection with plaintiff's workers compensation claim, in which physician had described plaintiff's abuse of drug and his warning her to stop).

sibility, provided the motivation to cross-examine remains substantially the same. Rule 804(b)(1) is not satisfied, however, when the motive of the party against whom the evidence is offered was substantially affected by differences in the cause of action,[6] or the presence of additional issues, or the addition of parties.

Despite the "similar motive" test courts have for the most part been unwilling to exclude prior testimony given at preliminary hearings, at least when offered by the government, even though tactical considerations often dictate little or no cross-examination so as not to tip the defendant's plan for trial.[7] Nor have the federal courts accorded any significance to the slight incentive for cross-examination that exists when a deposition is taken solely for discovery. Admitting such depositions is in accord with Rule 32(a)(3) of the Federal Rules of Civil Procedure, which creates a hearsay exception for depositions given by unavailable deponents independent of Rule 804, and which accords no significance to the fact that the deposition was taken for discovery.

¶ 17.02[03]   Develop the Testimony[1]

Most commonly former testimony is offered against the party who was the cross-examiner when the evidence was offered in the first proceeding. Rule 804(b)(1) recognizes that former testimony may also be offered against the party by whom it was originally offered, provided the party had an opportunity to develop the testimony "by direct . . . or redirect examination."[2]

In *Ohio v. Roberts*,[3] the Supreme Court found no violation of the Confrontation Clause when preliminary hearing testimony

---

[6] See, *e.g.*, Oberlin v. Marlin American Corp., 596 F.2d 1322 (7th Cir. 1979) (different theory lead to different motivation to cross-examine on crucial issue of agency).

[7] See, *e.g.*, Glen v. Dallman, 635 F.2d 1183 (6th Cir. 1980), *cert. denied*, 454 U.S. 843 (1981). The Supreme Court declined to reach this issue in Ohio v. Roberts, 448 U.S. 56, 70, 100 S.Ct. 2531, 65 L.Ed.2d 597 (1980).

[1] See **Treatise** at ¶¶ 804(b)(1)[02],[03].

[2] See, *e.g.*, United States v. Henry, 448 F.Supp. 819 (D.N.J. 1978) and United States v. Driscoll, 445 F.Supp. 864 (D.N.J. 1978) (defendant may offer grand jury testimony of now unavailable witness).

[3] 448 U.S. 56, 100 S.Ct. 2531, 65 L.Ed.2d 597 (1980).

given by a witness called by the defense was offered against the defendant at trial. The Court characterized the questioning by the defense as "cross-examination as a matter of form," noting that the presentation "was replete with leading questions," and "comported with the principal purpose of cross-examination: to challenge whether the defendant was sincerely telling what he believed to be the truth, whether the declarant accurately perceived and remembered the matter he related, and whether the declarant's intended meaning is adequately conveyed by the language he employed."[4]

In *Roberts,* the Supreme Court declined to impose a further "effectiveness" test once it found that the former testimony had been tested by the equivalent of cross-examination, at least in the absence of extraordinary circumstances, such as the denial of counsel or ineffective cross-examination at the first proceeding. In virtually every case, therefore, of actual cross-examination, direct examination or redirect examination, the former testimony exception will be satisfied, provided the motivation requirement, discussed above, is met.

¶ 17.02[04]   Party or Predecessor in Interest[1]

Rule 804(b)(1) provides that former testimony may be admitted "if the party against whom the testimony is now offered, or, in a civil action or proceeding, a predecessor in interest, had an opportunity and similar motive to develop the testimony . . . ."

The rule distinguishes between civil and criminal cases; absolute identity of parties is required in criminal cases. While this rule eliminates the constitutional concerns that would arise were former testimony offered against an accused who was not a party to the prior proceeding, it may be of questionable constitutional validity when it is the accused who seeks to use prior testimony against the United States even though it was not the prosecuting agency in the prior case.[2] In civil cases, Rule 804(b)(1) permits the

---

[4] *Id.* at 70, 71.

[1] See discussion in **Treatise** at ¶¶ 804(b)(1)[04], [05].

[2] *Cf.* Chambers v. Mississippi, 410 U.S. 284, 93 S.Ct. 1038, 35 L.Ed.2d 97 (1973). But *cf.* United States v. Barrett, 766 F.2d 609, 618–19 (1st Cir.), *cert. denied,* 106 S.Ct. 258 (1985) (not error to exclude transcript of coroner's testimony

former testimony to be admitted when a "predecessor in interest" of the party against whom the testimony is being offered had the opportunity and motive to develop the testimony. For the most part the cases indicate a reluctance to interpret "predecessor in interest" in its old, narrow, substantive law sense of privity,[3] which would require the party in the second action to share a property interest with the person who developed the testimony in the first proceeding. Even if a court feels compelled to give a narrower reading to Rule 804(b)(1), it should admit the testimony under Rule 804(b)(5), the residual exception, when the previous party had a like motive and opportunity to develop the testimony as the present party against whom the testimony is being offered.[4]

¶ 17.03   Statement Under Belief of Impending Death—Rule 804(b)(2)[1]

Rule 804(b)(2) is a reworking of the common law hearsay excep-

---

given at trial 20 years previously where government had not been a party to earlier prosecution as required by Rule 804(b)(1) and admission of transcript would have led to an ancillary and time-consuming inquiry).

[3] See Lloyd v. American Export Lines, Inc., 580 F.2d 1179, 1187 (3d Cir. 1978), *cert. denied*, 439 U.S. 969 (1979) (in action by crewman against shipowner for injuries sustained in fight with fellow crewman who was made a third-party defendant, court held that testimony given at Coast Guard hearing, at which both crewmen appeared and testified, could be admitted at subsequent trial because there was a sufficient community of interest between the Coast Guard investigating officer and crewman; "[u]nder these circumstances, the previous party having like motive to develop the testimony about the same material facts, is in the final analysis, a predecessor in interest to the present party."). See also Clay v. Johns-Manville Sales Corp., 722 F.2d 1289, 1294–95 (6th Cir. 1983), *cert. denied*, 467 U.S. 1253 (1984) (defendants in prior case had similar motive to confront witness' testimony as current defendant); *In re* Master Key Antitrust Litigation, 72 F.R.D. 108, 109 (D. Conn. 1976), *aff'd without opinion*, 551 F.2d 300 (2d Cir. 1976) (United States government in antitrust enforcement action found predecessor in interest of plaintiffs in subsequent private antitrust action).

[4] See, *e.g.*, *In re* Screws Antitrust Litigation, 526 F.Supp. 1316, 1319 (D. Mass. 1981) (refused to find earlier criminal defendants predecessors in interest of later civil defendants but admitted testimony pursuant to Rule 804(b)(5)). See also Lloyd v. American Export Lines, Inc., 580 F.2d 1179, 1190 (3d Cir.), *cert. denied*, 439 U.S. 969 (1979) (concurring opinion relied on Rule 804(b)(5)).

[1] See discussion in **Treatise** at ¶ 804(b)(2)[01].

tion for dying declarations. It broadens the traditional exception by allowing it to be used in all civil cases, as well as homicide cases, and in not confining unavailability to death. It is the declarant's belief at the time the statement is made that death will occur that furnishes a guarantee of reliability, rather than death at the time the statement is offered. The rule continues the common law restriction of admissibility to statements concerning the cause or circumstances of what declarant believed to be his impending death.

The rule provides:

. . . (b) Hearsay exceptions. The following are not excluded by the hearsay rule if the declarant is unavailable as a witness: . . .

(2) Statement under belief of impending death.— In a prosecution for homicide or in a civil action or proceeding, a statement made by a declarant while believing that the declarant's death was imminent, concerning the cause or circumstances of what the declarant believed to be impending death.

The exception for dying declarations was originally held to rest on the religious belief that a dying person would be unwilling to face his maker with a lie on his lips; it is now frequently justified on the secular, psychological ground that a declarant no longer has self-serving purposes to be furthered in the shadow of death. Critics of the exception disagree: they believe that the desire for revenge or self-exoneration or to protect one's loved ones often continues until the moment of death, that the accuracy of a dying declaration is dubious because the declarant's ability to perceive, remember or communicate may have been clouded by the condition causing his demise, and that a statement is additionally suspect if it was made in response to the prompting and questioning of interested bystanders such as policemen, insurance agents, or investigators.

Belief in the certainty of death—the factor which reduces the motive for falsification—must be shown in order for the exception to apply. Justice Cardozo explained what this entails:

Fear or even belief that illness will end in death will not avail of itself to make a dying declaration. There must be "a settled hopeless expectation" . . . that death is near at hand, and what is said must have been spoken in the hush of its impending presence . . . . The patient must have spoken with the consciousness of a swift and certain doom.[2]

---

[2] Shepard v. United States, 290 U.S. 96, 100, 54 S.Ct. 22, 78 L.Ed.2d 196 (1933).

The declarant's belief in the imminence of his death may be shown by his own statements,[3] or through circumstantial evidence,[4] such as the nature of the wounds, opinions of the attending physicians, statements made by others in the declarant's presence, or the fact that last rites were administered. It must be inferable from the evidence presented that declarant had personal knowledge of the facts contained in the statement seeking admission. The statement of a declarant shot in the back by an unseen assailant naming the defendant as his murderer cannot be admitted.

¶ 17.04   Statement Against Interest—Rule 804(b)(3)

¶ 17.04[01]   Scope and Rationale[1]

Rule 804(b) makes admissible statements against the pecuniary, proprietary or penal interest of the declarant provided certain requirements are met. The exception rests on the assumption that persons will not make damaging statements about themselves unless they are true. As a psychological generalization, this conclusion rings true; in the individual case, the diversity of the human personality makes generalizations suspect.

The addition of declarations against penal interest, which were not traditionally admitted, has greatly increased the significance of this exception, and has caused numerous difficult problems of interpretation which are discussed below.

The rule provides:

. . . (b) Hearsay exceptions.— The following are not excluded by the hearsay rule if the declarant is unavailable as a witness . . .

(3) Statement against interest.— A statement which was at the time of its making so far contrary to the declarant's pecuniary or proprietary interest, or so far tended to subject the declarant to civil or criminal liability, or to render invalid a claim by the declarant against another, that a

---

[3] See, *e.g.*, United States v. Kearney, 420 F.2d 170, 174–75 (D.C. Cir. 1969).

[4] Shepard v. United States, 290 U.S. 96, 100 (1933) ("Despair of recovery may indeed be gathered from the circumstances if the facts support the inference . . . . There is no unyielding ritual of words to be spoken by the dying.").

[1] See discussion in **Treatise** at ¶ 804(b)(3)[01].

reasonable person in the declarant's position would not have made the statement unless believing it to be true. A statement tending to expose the declarant to criminal liability and offered to exculpate the accused is not admissible unless corroborating circumstances clearly indicate the trustworthiness of the statement.

¶ 17.04[02]   Requirements[1]

A number of requirements apply to all statements offered pursuant to Rule 804(b)(3) regardless of the type of interest involved.

[a]   Unavailability

Rule 804(b)(3) retains unavailability as a condition of admissibility of statements against interest.

[b]   First-hand Knowledge

While Rule 804(b)(3) does not expressly require the declarant to have perceived the matter to which the statement relates, personal knowledge has always been considered an inherent condition of the exception, and is assured by Rule 602.[2]

[c]   Reasonable Person Test

Rule 804(b)(3), by providing that the statement would not have been made by a reasonable man unless he believed it to be true, purports to adopt an objective test for whether the statement was against interest when made. Such an objective test is designed to eliminate inquiries into the declarant's actual state of mind. Nevertheless, primarily with regard to declarations against penal interest, there is a real danger that confessions by liars, crackpots,

(*Text continued on page 17–17*)

---

[1] See discussion in **Treatise** at ¶ 804(b)(3).

[2] United States v. Lang, 589 F.2d 92 (2d Cir. 1978) (error to have admitted statement that declarant had supplied counterfeit notes to defendant through defendant's girl friend where statement also acknowledged that declarant had never met defendant).

and publicity seekers to acts they never committed would satisfy this definition. In the case of statements exculpating the accused, the reasonable person test is expressly tempered by the last sentence of Rule 804(b)(3), which requires corroboration of the trustworthiness of the statement. Since many courts insist on a corroboration requirement in the case of inculpatory statements as well, see discussion below, the consequence is that courts frequently evaluate the particular circumstances surrounding the proffered declaration against penal interest despite the reasonable person standard.[3]

[d]   Belief in Statement's Truth

The rationale for the exception fails if the declarant does not believe the statement to be against interest, since the rule rests on the notion that reasonable persons do not make false statements that expose them to liability.[4] In applying Rule 804(b)(3), the courts have been willing to assume that a reasonable person would be aware of the deserving nature of his or her remarks even when they were made to a supposed friend or family member.[5] More suspicion has been voiced when the statement, although against interest on its face, may actually have been made to gain an advantage, as when a person in custody makes a confession as part of a

---

[3] See, *e.g.,* United States v. Tovar, 687 F.2d 1210 (8th Cir. 1982) (exculpatory statement properly excluded where declarant knew he was going to prison for an unrelated crime and may have wished to help out friend); United States v. White, 553 F.2d 310, 313 (2d Cir.), *cert. denied,* 431 U.S. 972 (1977) (statements made after declarant's arrest as prostitute admissible despite defense argument that she may have been trying to curry favor with prosecution; court noted that she was not in custody and would have had little to gain from her admission of a state crime to a federal officer).

[4] *Compare* Pink Supply Corp. v. Hiebert, Inc., 612 F.Supp. 1334, 1345 (D. Minn. 1985) (conversation inadmissible; no indication that declarant had understanding of "vertical price-fixing") *with* Brennan v. Braswell Motor Freight Lines, Inc., 396 F.Supp. 704, 708 n. 9 (N.D. Tex. 1975) (court relies on expertise of declarant in labor matters in finding statement admissible).

[5] United States v. Mock, 640 F.2d 629 (5th Cir. 1981) (former wife); United States v. Goins, 593 F.2d 88 (8th Cir.), *cert. denied,* 444 U.S. 827 (1979) (daughter); United States v. Barrett, 539 F.2d 244, 251 (1st Cir. 1976) (conversation with acquaintances over cards); United States v. Bagley, 537 F.2d 162, 165 (5th Cir.), *cert. denied,* 429 U.S. 1075 (1977) (friend and cellmate).

plea bargain.[6]

[e]   Contrary to Interest

Rule 804(b)(3) is silent about how to handle self-serving or neutral statements that accompany a statement against interest. The decided cases indicate that the courts are assessing the statement as a whole to determine whether the rationale for the exception is satisfied, rather than excising the non-disserving parts.[7] The statement must be against interest at the time it is made, rather than at the time it is offered, in order for the rationale for the exception to be satisfied.

¶ 17.04[03]   Statements Against Penal Interest[1]

When the drafters of the Federal Rules of Evidence expanded the traditional against interest exception by adding declarations against penal interest, they were primarily contemplating a case in which the defense wished to offer a statement by a third person exculpating the accused. Once the rule went into effect, however, it became a vehicle for admitting inculpatory statements against the defendant. Fears of trumped-up confessions by a professional criminal or some person with a strong motive to lie resulted in the addition of the second sentence to Rule 804(b)(3), which makes declarations against penal interest offered to exculpate the accused inadmissible "unless corroborating circumstances clearly indicate the trustworthiness of the statement." Due to the preoccupation with exculpatory statements and the drafters' belief that inculpatory statements would be limited by constitutional doc-

---

[6] See, *e.g.,* United States v. Atkins, 618 F.2d 366 (5th Cir. 1980) (declarant was contemplating deal with government).

[7] See, *e.g.,* United States v. Barrett, 539 F.2d 244, 252 (1st Cir. 1976) (while part of statement exculpating defendant which accompanied declarant's inculpatory statement was not directly prejudicial to declarant, though "it strengthened the impression that he had an insider's knowledge," court found that entire statement was against interest since it does not appear "that Congress intended to constrict the scope of a declaration against interest to the point of excluding 'collateral' material that, as here, actually tended to fortify the statement's disserving aspects.").

[1] See **Treatise** at ¶ 804(b)(3)[04].

trine, no corroboration requirement for inculpatory statements appears in the rule, although some courts find that it is constitutionally required. See discussion below.

[a]   Exculpatory Statements

The chief question that arises with regard to exculpatory declarations against penal interest is the meaning and magnitude of the corroboration requirement. It is the hearsay statement that must be corroborated, not the trustworthiness of the witness who testifies to the statement. The witness' testimony presents no hearsay dangers and can be evaluated by the jury, taking into account the witness' demeanor and any impeaching evidence.[2]

The court should only ask for sufficient corroboration to "clearly" permit a reasonable person to believe that the statement might have been made in good faith and that it could be true. Imposing a higher burden on the defendant is constitutionally suspect; it should not be easier for the government to introduce a co-conspirator's statement than for the defendant to introduce an exculpatory statement, yet Rule 801(d)(2)(E), the coconspirators exception, contains no corroboration requirement. Furthermore, the defendant has rights under the fifth and sixth amendments to produce exculpatory evidence.[3] Nevertheless, in a number of cases

---

[2] But see United States v. Bagley, 537 F.2d 162, 165–68 (5th Cir. 1976), *cert. denied*, 429 U.S. 1075 (1977) (three of the four factors cited by court as demonstrating that statement offered by defense had not been made relate to credibility of witness).

[3] See, *e.g.*, Chambers v. Mississippi, 410 U.S. 284, 302, 93 S.Ct. 1038, 35 L.Ed.2d 297 (1973) (conviction reversed for lack of due process where defendant had neither been able to impeach witness who had several times confessed to charged crime (because of the prohibition against impeaching his own witness), nor had been able to call other witnesses to testify to out-of-court statements made by the confessing third party; the Court stated: "The testimony rejected by the trial court here bore persuasive assurances of trustworthiness and thus was well within the basic rationale of the exception for declarations against interest. That testimony was also critical to Chambers' defense. In these circumstances, where constitutional rights directly affecting the ascertainment of guilt are implicated, the hearsay rule may not be applied mechanistically to defeat the ends of justice."). *Cf.* Green v. Georgia, 442 U.S. 95, 97, 99 S.Ct. 2150, 60 L.Ed.2d 738 (1979) (violation of due process to exclude statement against interest at penalty

the corroboration requirement of Rule 804(b)(3) has been interpreted so stringently that it is difficult to conceive of the rule having much utility for an accused.[4]

[b]   Inculpatory Statements

Statements against penal interest offered to inculpate the accused are particularly troublesome. As an evidentiary matter, the
portion of the statement inculpating the accused is at best neutral
rather than disserving, and the danger exists that it may be self-
serving if the declarant is seeking to curry favor with the authorities. Some courts have reacted to these dangers by reading a corroboration requirement for inculpatory statements into Rule
804(b)(3);[5] others have adopted a per se rule of exclusion for
statements made in custody.[6] At the very least, a trial court should
not admit an inculpatory statement until it has carefully scrutinized the circumstances in which declarant allegedly made the
statement, and the relationship between the witness and
declarant.[7] In determining whether the statement is sufficiently
reliable to admit, the court should consider such factors as the role

---

stage). See also Davis v. Alaska, 415 U.S. 308, 94 S.Ct. 1105, 39 L.Ed.2d 347
(1974) (Sixth Amendment right to present evidence).

[4] See, *e.g.,* United States v. MacDonald, 688 F.2d 224 (4th Cir. 1982), *cert. denied,* 459 U.S. 1103 (1983) (murder prosecution; court held that trial court had
not abused discretion in excluding for lack of corroboration seven statements by
declarant admitting culpability; defense argued that his description of assailant
matched declarant, that declarant had no motive to fabricate, that defendant and
declarant had not been acquainted, that declarant's statements were spontaneous, and that she could not account for her whereabouts on night of crime; trial
court had focused on declarant's vacillation between admissions and denials of
complicity and her pervasive involvement with narcotics); United States v. Bagley, 537 F.2d 162, 165–68 (5th Cir. 1976), *cert. denied,* 429 U.S. 1075 (1977).

[5] See, *e.g.,* United States v. Alvarez, 584 F.2d 694, 701 (5th Cir. 1978).

[6] United States v. Sarmiento-Perez, 633 F.2d 1092, 1104 (5th Cir. 1980), *cert.
denied,* 459 U.S. 834 (1982).

[7] See, *e.g.,* United States v. Katsougrakis, 715 F.2d 769, 774–75 (2d Cir. 1983),
cert. denied, 464 U.S. 1040 (1984) (court found admissible affirmative nod by critically burned arsonist in response to hospital visitor's inquiry as to whether he
had been paid by defendants; reliability ensured because arsonist was communicating with friend, not police, and other evidence corroborated truth of
statement).

of the declarant, whether he was in custody, the resolution of the charges pending against him, whether the declarant was being tried jointly with the accused, and the significance of the declarant's testimony.

The constitutional test for inculpatory statements against interest is far from clear. In *New Mexico v. Earnest,* [8] the state appealed from a decision of New Mexico's highest court. The state court had found that although an in-custody inculpatory statement passed evidentiary muster under a rule which is identical to Federal Rule 804(b)(3), admission of the statement violated the defendant's right of confrontation, as interpreted by the Supreme Court in *Bruton v. United States* and *Douglas v. Alabama.* The majority of the Supreme Court, in a per curiam opinion, remanded to the state court. By refusing to affirm, the majority indicated that *Bruton* and *Douglas* do not demand exclusion of a statement admitted pursuant to the penal interest exception, and that in-custody statements do not automatically violate the Confrontation Clause. By citing to *Lee v. Illinois,* [9] the majority seems to have indicated that an inculpatory statement may be admitted despite a Confrontation Clause challenge if it is sufficiently reliable. See discussion in Chapter 14, *supra.*

¶ 17.05 Statement of Personal or Family History—Rule 804(b)(4)[1]

Rule 804(b)(4) broadens what has traditionally been termed the "pedigree" exception by extending the exception to the entire area of family history instead of merely matters of genealogy, by eliminating the ante litem motam requirement, by rejecting the view that only death suffices to establish unavailability, and by making declarations of nonfamily members admissible, provided their association with family members was sufficiently intimate.

The rule provides:

. . . (b) Hearsay exceptions.— The following are not excluded by the hearsay rule if the declarant is unavailable as a witness . . .

---

[8] 106 S.Ct. 2734, 91 L.Ed.2d 539 (1986).

[9] 106 S.Ct. 2056, 90 L.Ed.2d 514 (1986).

[1] See discussion in **Treatise** at ¶ 804(b)(4).

(4) Statement of personal or family history.— (A) A statement concerning the declarant's own birth, adoption, marriage, divorce, legitimacy, relationship by blood, adoption, or marriage, ancestry, or other similar fact of personal or family history, even though declarant had no means of acquiring personal knowledge of the matter stated; or (B) a statement concerning the foregoing matters, and death also, of another person, if the declarant was related to the other by blood, adoption, or marriage or was so intimately associated with the other's family as to be likely to have accurate information concerning the matter declared.

CHAPTER 18

Privileges

SYNOPSIS

18–1

¶ 18.01 Overview of Legislative History of Privilege Rules

The article on privileges promulgated by the Supreme Court contained thirteen separate rules on privilege. As finally enacted by Congress, Article V consisted of one rule, Rule 501, which differed radically from the Advisory Committee's position on privileges.[1]

The Advisory Committee had viewed as its paramount goal the admission of all relevant evidence in order to further the likelihood of accurate determinations. Since privileges hamper the truth-determining process by keeping evidence from the court and jury, the Advisory Committee concluded that they should be limited to the minimum scope needed to support clearly desirable public policy. The Advisory Committee sought to achieve this end by (1) not applying in federal court privileges created by state law, (2) reducing further expansion of new privileges by recognizing only privileges required by the Constitution, Acts of Congress or Federal Rules, and (3) narrowing the scope of the privileges that were incorporated in the new evidence rules. As the discussion below of Rule 501 indicates, Congress disagreed with each of these three principles.

Although Congress declined to enact specific evidentiary privileges, a number of the rules that had been promulgated by the Supreme Court have been cited by the courts as Standards, since they represent codifications of the law of privilege in the federal courts, and are reflective of "reason and experience." Particularly useful as black letter law are Standard 503 dealing with the attorney-client privilege (*see* ¶ 18.03); Standard 509 (*see* ¶ 18.05), covering secrets of state and other official information; and Standard 510 (*see* ¶ 18.06), describing the identity of informer privilege. They are still, in the main, reliable descriptions of present law, as are Standards 506 (communications to clergymen), 507 (political vote), and 508 (trade secrets) which are discussed below.

Other privilege rules promulgated by the Supreme Court and then rejected by Congress are not a dependable statement of present law. In addition to Standard 505 (the husband-wife

---

[1] *See* **Treatise** at ¶ 501[06] for a discussion of the Advisory Committee's proposal.

privilege, *see* ¶ 18.04), they are Standards 502 (required reports privileged by statute), 504 (psychotherapist-patient privilege), and 513 (comment upon or inference from claim of privilege; instruction). These proposed Rules are described in the commentary following the Rule 501 discussion.

Standards 511 and 512 deal respectively with waiver and disclosure under compulsion or without opportunity to claim the privilege. They are dealt with separately since they are reliable only in part as statements of the current law.

¶ 18.02   The Law of Privileges in the Federal Courts— Rule 501

¶ 18.02[01]   Scope

As discussed in ¶ 18.01, in enacting the Federal Rules of Evidence, Congress declined to adopt any rules dealing with specific privileges.[1] Rule 501 was the only rule on privileges adopted by Congress, and it contains only general provisions concerning the sources of the law of privileges to be applied in the federal courts. The rule provides:

Rule 501

GENERAL RULE

Except as otherwise required by the Constitution of the United States or provided by Act of Congress or in rules prescribed by the Supreme Court pursuant to statutory authority, the privilege of a witness, person, government, State, or political subdivision thereof shall be governed by the principles of the common law as they may be interpreted by the courts of the United States in the light of reason and experience. However, in civil actions and proceedings, with respect to an element of a claim or defense as to which State law supplies the rule of decision, the privilege of a witness, person,

---

[1] As submitted to Congress, Article V contained thirteen rules, nine of which concerned specific privileges while the balance dealt with matters common to all enumerated privileges. *See* **Treatise** at ¶ 501[01] and discussion of Congressional Action on Rule 501 for extensive treatment of why Congress rejected rules promulgated by Supreme Court.

government, State, or political subdivision thereof shall be determined in accordance with State law.

Rule 501 generally leaves the law of privileges to case by case development in the federal courts, except for privileges created by the Constitution, an Act of Congress, or the Supreme Court under its statutory rule-making authority.[2] The common law power of the federal courts over privileges is subject to two further qualifications. First, the Supreme Court has said that the courts should be hesitant to create a privilege that would conflict with a clear statutory policy. For example, a qualified work product privilege could not be applied to accountants' tax accrual papers, since it would conflict with the Congressional policy favoring disclosure of all information relevant to an I.R.S. inquiry.[3] The Court has also ruled that the policy objectives of Title VII of the Civil Rights Act of 1964, which empower the E.E.O.C. to obtain relevant evidence in investigating a charge of discrimination, prevent the courts from creating a privilege against disclosure of peer review documents, in proceedings alleging that university tenure appointments were discriminatory.[4] Second, as discussed in ¶ 18.02[02], the applicable state law of privileges must be applied in accordance with the *Erie* doctrine.

---

[2] As amended in 1988, the Rules Enabling Act, 28 U.S.C. § 2074(b), provides that any "rule creating, abolishing, or modifying an evidentiary privilege shall have no force or effect unless approved by Act of Congress." Although the Supreme Court has the final word on the common law development of privileges, Congress has, in effect, eliminated the Court's independent rule-making powers with respect to privileges.

See **Treatise** at ¶ 501[04] for a discussion of rules adopted by the Supreme Court that contain provisions relating to privileges.

[3] United States v. Arthur Young & Co., 465 U.S. 805, 104 S. Ct. 1495, 79 L. Ed. 2d 826 (1984) (summons enforcement proceedings under 26 U.S.C. § 7602).

[4] University of Pennsylvania v. E.E.O.C., 110 S. Ct. 577 (1990). *See also* E.E.O.C. v. General Telephone Co. of Northwest, 885 F.2d 575, 578 (9th Cir. 1989) (even if there is a qualified privilege against disclosure of self-critical portions of an employer's affirmative action plan, the employer waives it by using the plan as evidence of lack of discrimination).

¶ 18.02[02] Privileges: When Must State Law Be Applied?[1]

The second sentence of Rule 501 provides that state law shall apply "with respect to an element of a claim or defense as to which State law supplies the rule of decision." The far simpler formula, that in diversity cases state law applies and in federal question cases federal law applies, was apparently rejected because it does not completely comport with the *Erie* test which Congress was seeking to incorporate. Theoretically, therefore, a state privilege may control in a federal question case. In criminal cases, Rule 501 requires the application of federal privilege law even when a state definition of a crime is relied upon.[2]

The privilege rules submitted to Congress contained a proposed Rule 502,[3] which would have required the federal courts to apply state privileges for required reports even in criminal proceedings or actions arising solely under federal law. Although this rule was not enacted by Congress, and Rule 501 contemplates that state privileges will be ignored in these types of proceedings, to avoid unnecessary frustration of state policy courts should show deference to those state created privileges that reflect strong substantive policies. Unless it appears that the information can come from no other source and that a federal substantive policy or justice will be frustrated, the evidence should not be admitted.[4] Comity

---

[1] *See* **Treatise** at ¶ 501[01].

[2] United States v. Gillock, 445 U.S. 360, 100 S. Ct. 1185, 63 L. Ed. 2d 454 (1980) (Court noted that state privileges might be relevant in determining whether a particular privilege should be retained as a federal privilege).

[3] The proposed rule stated:

Supreme Court Standard 502—Required Reports Privileged By Statute

A person, corporation, association, or other organization or entity, either public or private, making a return or report required by law to be made has a privilege to refuse to disclose and to prevent any other person from disclosing the return or report, if the law requiring it to be made so provides. A public officer or agency to whom a return or report is required by law to be made has a privilege to refuse to disclose the return or report if the law requiring it to be made so provides. No privilege exists under this rule in actions involving perjury, false statements, fraud in the return or report, or other failure to comply with the law in question.

See discussion in **Treatise** at ¶¶ 502[01]–[04].

[4] *See* United States v. King, 73 F.R.D. 103, 105 (E.D.N.Y. 1976) (four factors must be balanced to determine whether state policy should be recog-

between state and federal sovereigns is desirable under our system of federalism.

The legislative history of Rule 501 indicates that the applicable state law of privileges was intended to govern, regardless of where in a line of proof the privileged information is utilized, so long as state law controls the particular claim or defense.[5] This policy may be impossible to implement when, under principles of concurrent or pendent jurisdiction, a civil federal proceeding includes claims based both on federal and state law. If a particular piece of evidence relates to both claims, it makes no sense to apply conflicting state and federal privileges, because "[o]nce confidentiality is broken, the basic purpose of the privilege is defeated."[6] The usual solution by the courts has been a refusal to follow the state rule of privilege when there is an irresolvable conflict with a federal policy.[7] While this solution accords with the general policies of the Federal Rules favoring truth, uniformity, and simplicity, it denigrates the substantive policy behind the state privilege.

Rule 501 is silent about which state's privilege to apply when state law controls and there are multi-state contacts. Prior to the enactment of the Federal Rules of Evidence, the federal courts held that under *Klaxon Co. v. Stentor Electric Mfg. Co.,*[8] they

---

nized: "first, the federal government's need for the information being sought in enforcing its substantive and procedural policies; second, the importance of the relationship or policy sought to be furthered by the state rule of privilege and the probability that the privilege will advance that relationship or policy; third, in the particular case, the special need for the information sought to be protected; and fourth, in the particular case, the adverse impact on the local policy that would result from non-recognition of the privilege.").

[5] Conference Report, Fed. R. Evid., 93rd Congress, 2d Session, Rep. No. 93-1597, p. 7 (Dec. 14, 1974). *See, e.g.,* Scott v. McDonald, 70 F.R.D. 568, 571 (N.D. Ga. 1976) (Georgia statute providing for confidentiality of certain records applied in discovery proceedings in diversity action).

[6] Perrignon v. Bergen Brunswig Corp., 77 F.R.D. 445, 458 (N.D. Calif. 1978) (court applied federal common law of privileges in federal question case with pendent state claims).

[7] *See, e.g.,* Wm. T. Thompson Co. v. General Nutrition Corp., Inc., 671 F.2d 100 (3d Cir. 1982) (court refused to apply state accountant-client privilege in action alleging federal antitrust violations and state pendent claims, holding that federal rule favoring admissibility should govern).

[8] 313 U.S. 487, 61 S. Ct. 1020, 85 L. Ed. 1477 (1941).

were constrained to apply the choice-of-law rule that the forum state would apply. Consequently, a satisfactory evidentiary solution could not be obtained in federal court unless it was attainable in state court.[9] Most courts continue to apply *Klaxon,*[10] although an argument can be made that Rule 501, as an Act of Congress, should be viewed as a federal choice-of-law rule that authorizes the federal courts to give privileges the effect they were designed to have.[11] When the privilege claim is raised at a deposition taken in a forum other than the one in which the trial is pending, the courts usually consider the state where the deposition is being taken as the forum whose privilege conflict-of-law rule applies.[12]

---

[9] *See, e.g.,* Hare v. Family Publications Serv., Inc., 342 F. Supp. 678 (D. Md. 1972), 334 F. Supp. 953 (D. Md. 1971) (New York accountant, sued in Maryland, simultaneously insisted that Maryland had no jurisdiction over him and refused to answer interrogatories on ground of Maryland accountant-client privilege; court applied Maryland privilege because it concluded state court would have done so even though the communication was made in New York which does not recognize the privilege).

[10] *See, e.g.,* Samuelson v. Susen, 576 F.2d 546 (3d Cir. 1978) (court looked to forum's conflict-of-laws rule).

[11] *See* **Treatise** at ¶ 501[02] *and see* Mitsui & Co. v. Puerto Rico Water Resources Auth., 79 F.R.D. 72, 78 (D.P.R. 1978) (in the majority of cases, "the state in which the assertedly privileged relationship was entered and exclusively sited should be deemed to have the most significant interest in determining whether or not that relationship is privileged"; court refused to apply forum's accountant-client privilege to depositions being taken in New York of New York accountants). *See* Restatement of the Law Second, Conflicts of Laws, 1986 Revisions 163 (April 15, 1986) (the black letter favors admissibility since it provides:

Privileged Communication

(1) Evidence that is not privileged under the local law of the state which has the most significant relationship with the communication will be admitted, even though it would be privileged under the local law of the forum, unless the admission of such evidence would be contrary to the strong public policy of the forum.

(2) Evidence that is privileged under the local law of the state which has the most significant relationship with the communication but which is not privileged under the local law of the forum will be admitted unless there is some special reason why the forum policy favoring admission should not be given effect.).

[12] *See, e.g., In re* Westinghouse Electric Corp. Uranium Contracts Litigation, 76 F.R.D. 47 (W.D. Va. 1977). *But see* Restatement (Second) of Conflict of Laws, n.11 supra, comment f, suggesting that privilege law of the state of most significant relationship to the communication should govern. This is a sensible proposal.

¶ 18.02[03] Privileges: The "Common Law Interpreted in the Light of Reason and Experience" Standard[1]

Instead of the detailed rules on privilege promulgated by the Supreme Court, Congress substituted a flexible standard which requires the courts to deal with privileges on a case-by-case basis in all criminal cases and most federal question cases. The formula adopted by Congress, that "the privilege of a witness . . . shall be governed by the principles of the common law as they may be interpreted by the courts of the United States in the light of reason and experience," had its origin in a 1934 Supreme Court decision dealing with the marital communications privilege.[2] It was subsequently incorporated into Rule 26 of the Federal Rules of Criminal Procedure, as the standard for handling all evidentiary matters, including questions of privilege, prior to the enactment of the Federal Rules of Evidence.

Adoption of this flexible standard has had a number of important consequences for the development of privileges in the federal courts. In the first place, instead of freezing the law of privileges, as was proposed by the Advisory Committee, the Rule 501 formula makes possible the evolution through case law of new, heretofore unrecognized privileges in response to changing conditions.[3] In *Trammel v. United States,* the Court explained:

> In rejecting the proposed Rules and enacting Rule 501, Congress manifested an affirmative intention not to freeze the law of privilege. Its purpose rather was to "provide the courts with the flexibility to develop rules of privilege on a case-by-case basis" and to leave the door open to change.[4]

Second, the Rule contemplates that existing privileges may have to be modified over time.[5] In justification of its decision to

---

[1] *See* **Treatise** at ¶ 501[03].

[2] Wolfle v. United States, 291 U.S. 7, 54 S. Ct. 279, 78 L. Ed. 617 (1934).

[3] *See, e.g.,* United States v. Green, 670 F.2d 1148 (D.C. Cir. 1981) (qualified governmental privilege not to disclose police secret surveillance point).

[4] 445 U.S. 40, 47, 100 S. Ct. 906, 63 L. Ed. 2d 186 (1980). *But cf.* University of Pennsylvania v. E.E.O.C., 110 S. Ct. 577 (1990) (although Rule 501 is intended to give the courts flexibility to develop new rules of privilege, "we are disinclined to exercise this authority expansively.").

[5] *See, e.g.,* Upjohn v. United States, 449 U.S. 383, 101 S. Ct. 677, 66 L. Ed. 2d 584 (1981) (control group test for attorney-client privilege is inconsis-

modify the privilege for adverse spousal testimony (see discussion below), the Court in *Trammel* relied on trends in state law[6] and changing concepts of the marital relationship, and rejected rationales offered in support of the existing rule.

Third, except for the attorney-client and marital privileges, the mandate to develop privilege rules "on a case-by-case basis"[7] has been interpreted to mean that the courts should look at privilege claims in the context of the particular case, balancing the usual need for all relevant evidence against the countervailing demand for confidentiality required to achieve the objectives of the privilege in question.[8] The new privileges that have evolved pursuant to Rule 501 are therefore often regarded as qualified rather than absolute, with the courts looking at factors such as the type of case—criminal or civil, the probative value of the evidence as to which the privilege claim is asserted, the availability of other evidence, and the societal interests at stake.[9] Standard 508,[10] which requires a weighing of competing interests when an

---

tent with the standard expressed in Rule 501; *see* further discussion of case in ¶ 18.03, *infra*); Trammel v. United States, 445 U.S. 40, 47, 100 S. Ct. 906, 63 L. Ed. 2d 186 (1980) ("Congress manifested an affirmative intention not to freeze the law of privilege.") *See* further discussion of case in ¶ 18.04, *infra*.

[6] *See* United States v. King, 73 F.R.D. 103, 105 (E.D.N.Y. 1976) ("[a] strong policy of comity between state and federal sovereignties impels federal courts to recognize state privileges where this can be accomplished at no substantial cost to federal substantive and procedural policy.").

[7] Statement by Representative Hungate, 120 Cong. Rec. 40891 (1974), quoted by Supreme Court in Trammel v. United States, 445 U.S. at 47.

[8] *See, e.g.,* University of Pennsylvania v. E.E.O.C., 110 S. Ct. 577 (1990) (rejecting a privilege against disclosure of peer review documents, in proceedings alleging that university tenure appointments were discriminatory); although Rule 501 is intended to give the courts flexibility to develop new rules of privilege, "we are disinclined to exercise this authority expansively."); E.E.O.C. v. General Tel. Co. of Northwest, 885 F.2d 575, 578 (9th Cir. 1989) (even if there is a qualified privilege against disclosure of self-critical portions of an employer's affirmative action plan, the employer waives it by using the plan as evidence of lack of discrimination); In re Grand Jury Subpoena Dated Jan. 4, 1984, 750 F.2d 223 (2d Cir. 1984) (in some cases, limited scholar's privilege may be appropriate); In re Zuniga, 714 F.2d 632 (6th Cir.), *cert. denied,* 464 U.S. 983 (1983) (court declined to apply psychotherapist-patient privilege in the instant case, although it noted that it had authority to recognize privilege pursuant to Rule 501).

[9] *See* discussion of the reporter's privilege in **Treatise** at ¶ 501[03].

[10] Standard 508 provides:

Supreme Court Standard 508—Trade Secrets

objection to revealing trade secrets is voiced, is consistent with this approach, and may be applied.[11]

Fourth, some of the proposed rules submitted to Congress remain a convenient and useful starting point for examining questions of privilege. These Standards are reflective of "reason and experience";[12] they are the culmination of three drafts prepared by an Advisory Committee consisting of judges, practicing lawyers and academicians, and were adopted by the Judicial Conference and the Supreme Court. For example, both before and since the enactment of Rule 501, the federal courts have uniformly refused to recognize a general physician-patient privilege except to the extent that state law applies.[13] The same result would have been reached under the proposed rules. Proposed Rule 504[14] would, however, have recognized a psychotherapist-

---

A person has a privilege, which may be claimed by him or his agent or employee, to refuse to disclose and to prevent other persons from disclosing a trade secret owned by him, if the allowance of the privilege will not tend to conceal fraud or otherwise work injustice. When disclosure is directed, the judge shall take such protective measure as the interests of the holder of the privilege and of the parties and the furtherance of justice may require.

For a discussion of this Standard, *see* **Treatise** at ¶¶ 508[01]–[04].

[11] Wearly v. F.T.C., 462 F. Supp. 589, 595 (D.N.J. 1978) ("court is satisfied, and finds, that the formulation of proposed Rule 508 adequately reflects the principles of the common law in the sense required by Fed.Ev.Rule 501").

[12] In United States v. Gillock, 445 U.S. 360, 367–68, 100 S. Ct. 1185, 63 L. Ed. 2d 454 (1980), in rejecting a new federal privilege for state legislators, the Court stated: "Neither the Advisory Committee, the Judicial Conference, nor this Court saw fit, however, to provide the privilege sought by *Gillock.* Although that fact standing alone would not compel the federal courts to refuse to recognize a privilege omitted from the proposal, it does suggest that the claimed privilege was not thought to be either indelibly ensconced in our common law or an imperative of federalism."

[13] *See, e.g.,* Robinson v. Magovern, 83 F.R.D. 79 (W.D. Pa. 1979) (no doctor-patient privilege).

[14] Standard 504 states:

Supreme Court Standard 504—Psychotherapist-Patient Privilege

(a) Definitions.

(1) A "patient" is a person who consults or is examined or interviewed by a psychotherapist.

(2) A "psychotherapist" is (A) a person authorized to practice medicine in any state or nation, or reasonably believed by the patient so to be, while engaged in the diagnosis or treatment of a mental or emotional condition,

patient privilege. Pursuant to the flexibility accorded them by
Rule 501, some federal courts have acknowledged their authority
to develop a psychotherapist privilege, and have looked to proposed Rule 504 as a standard to be consulted in sculpting the
contours of the privilege.[15] Clearly, however, the Standards are

including drug addiction, or (B) a person licensed or certified as a psychologist under the laws of any state or nation, while similarly engaged.

(3) A communication is "confidential" if not intended to be disclosed to
third persons other than those present to further the interest of the patient
in the consultation, examination, or interview, or persons reasonably
necessary for the transmission of the communication, or persons who are
participating in the diagnosis and treatment under the direction of the
psychotherapist, including members of the patient's family.

(b) General rule of privilege. — A patient has a privilege to refuse to disclose
and to prevent any other person from disclosing confidential communications, made for the purposes of diagnosis or treatment of his mental or
emotional condition, including drug addiction, among himself, his psychotherapist, or persons who are participating in the diagnosis or treatment
under the direction of the psychotherapist, including members of the
patient's family.

(c) Who may claim the privilege. — The privilege may be claimed by the
patient, by his guardian or conservator, or by the personal representative
of a deceased patient. The person who was the psychotherapist may claim
the privilege but only on behalf of the patient. His authority so to do is
presumed in the absence of evidence to the contrary.

(d) Exceptions.

(1) Proceedings for hospitalization. — There is no privilege under this rule
for communications relevant to an issue in proceedings to hospitalize the
patient for mental illness, if the psychotherapist in the course of diagnosis
or treatment has determined that the patient is in need of hospitalization.

(2) Examination by order of the judge. — If the judge orders an examination
of the mental or emotional condition of the patient, communications made
in the course thereof are not privileged under this rule with respect to the
particular purpose for which the examination is ordered unless the judge
orders otherwise.

(3) Condition an element of claim or defense. — There is no privilege under
this rule as to communications relevant to an issue of the mental or
emotional condition of the patient in any proceeding in which he relies upon
the condition as an element of his claim or defense, or, after the patient's
death, in any proceeding in which any party relies upon the condition as
an element of his claim or defense.

[15] See, e.g., In re Zuniga, 714 F.2d 632, 639 (6th Cir.), cert. denied, 464
U.S. 983 (1983) (court, after looking at Standard 504 "conclude[s] that a
psychotherapist-patient privilege is mandated by 'reason and experience' " but

subject to considerably more flexibility in construction than is vouchsafed to courts construing formally adopted Rules.

Some of the principles embodied in the Standards have been substantially modified by the judicial development of the law of privilege pursuant to Rule 501.[16] For example, the Supreme Court's decision in *Trammel v. United States,*[17] defining the husband-wife privilege, departed significantly from the rule proposed in Standard 505, as discussed below at ¶ 18.04. Standard 513,[18] which prohibits a comment or inference upon an assertion of a privilege, has had a mixed reception in the courts particularly in civil cases.[19]

---

declined to apply it when subpoena sought only patients' identities, dates and lengths of treatment which court found did not negate confidentiality; extensive review of applicability of privilege in the federal courts). *But see In re* Grand Jury Proceedings, 867 F.2d 562, 564–65 (9th Cir.), *cert. denied,* 110 S. Ct. 265 (1989) (court refused to recognize psychotherapist-patient privilege in criminal case; Congress rather than courts must define such a privilege); United States v. Layton, 90 F.R.D. 520 (N.D. Calif. 1981) (no psychotherapist-patient evidentiary privilege—court ignores Standard 504—but conversations between patient and psychiatrist may be protected when constitutional privacy interest outweighs need for disclosure). *See* discussion in **Treatise** at ¶¶ 504[01]–[07].

[16] Although Standard 502, requiring courts to defer to state privileges in purely federal law cases, is not formally consistent with Rule 501, it should, for reasons discussed, *supra,* be considered by a court when it determines on a "case-by-case" basis whether a privilege is warranted in the particular litigation.

[17] 445 U.S. 40, 100 S. Ct. 906, 63 L. Ed. 2d 186 (1980).

[18] The text of the proposed rule was as follows:

(a) Comment or inference not permitted.—The claim of a privilege, whether in the present proceeding or upon a prior occasion, is not a proper subject of comment by judge or counsel. No inference may be drawn therefrom.

(b) Claiming privilege without knowledge of jury.—In jury cases, proceedings shall be conducted, to the extent practicable, so as to facilitate the making of claims of privilege without the knowledge of the jury.

(c) Jury instruction.—Upon request, any party against whom the jury might draw an adverse inference from a claim of privilege is entitled to an instruction that no inference may be drawn therefrom.

See discussion in **Treatise** at ¶¶ 513[01]-513[02].

[19] *See, e.g.,* Brink's, Inc. v. City of New York, 717 F.2d 700 (2d Cir. 1983) (court refused to apply Standard 513 to prohibit inference from being drawn from assertion of privilege against self-incrimination in civil case). *See* **Treatise** at ¶ 513[02].

Standard 507,[20] which provides that a person has a right not to reveal how he or she voted, may well be redundant as it would in any case probably be constitutionally required. The existence of a priest-penitent or communications to clergymen privilege, provided for in Standard 506,[21] has been acknowledged by the Supreme Court in dictum.[22]

The discussion below considers in detail the extent to which Standards 503, 505, 509, 510, 511 and 512 remain a reliable statement of the law.

---

[20] Supreme Court Standard 507—Political Vote

Every person has a privilege to refuse to disclose the tenor of his vote at a political election conducted by secret ballot unless the vote was cast illegally.

[21] Standard 506 provides:

Supreme Court Standard 506—Communications to Clergymen

(a) Definitions—As used in this rule:

(1) A "clergyman" is a minister, priest, rabbi, or other similar functionary of a religious organization, or an individual reasonably believed so to be by the person consulting him.

(2) A communication is "confidential" if made privately and not intended for further disclosure except to other persons present in furtherance of the purpose of the communication.

(b) General rule of privilege.—A person has a privilege to refuse to disclose and to prevent another from disclosing a confidential communication by the person to a clergyman in his professional character as spiritual adviser.

(c) Who may claim the privilege.—The privilege may be claimed by the person, by his guardian or conservator, or by his personal representative if he is deceased. The clergyman may claim the privilege on behalf of the person. His authority so to do is presumed in the absence of evidence to the contrary.

See Treatise at ¶¶ 506[01]–[03].

[22] Trammel v. United States, 445 U.S. 40, 51, 100 S. Ct. 906, 63 L. Ed. 2d 186 (1980) ("The priest-penitent privilege recognizes the human need to disclose to a spiritual counselor, in total and absolute confidence, what are believed to be flawed acts or thoughts and to receive priestly consolation and guidance in return.").

¶ 18.03   The Attorney-Client Privilege—Standard 503

¶ 18.03[01]   The Applicability of Standard 503

Standard 503 remains a useful starting point for the examination of the attorney-client privilege in the federal courts. At this time, it is an accurate restatement of actual practice that is cited frequently.[1] Even had the Standard been enacted, it would have required supplementation by case law since the Advisory Committee deliberately chose not to deal with certain issues.[2] The discussion below indicates how the gaps in coverage have been handled by the courts. Standard 503 provides:

Supreme Court Standard 503

LAWYER-CLIENT PRIVILEGE

(a) Definitions. As used in this rule:

(1) A "client" is a person, public officer, or corporation, association, or other organization or entity, either public or private, who is rendered professional legal services by a lawyer, or who consults a lawyer with a view to obtaining professional legal services from him.

(2) A "lawyer" is a person authorized, or reasonably believed by the client to be authorized, to practice law in any state or nation.

(3) A "representative of the lawyer" is one employed to assist the lawyer in the rendition of professional legal services.

(4) A communication is "confidential" if not intended to be disclosed to third persons other than those to whom disclosure is in furtherance of the rendition of professional legal services to the client or those reasonably necessary for the transmission of the communication.

(b) General rule of privilege.—A client has a privilege to refuse to disclose and to prevent any other person from disclosing confidential communications made for the purpose of facilitating the rendition of professional legal services to the client, (1) between himself

---

[1] *See, e.g., In re* Feldberg, 862 F.2d 622, 626 (7th Cir. 1988) (comment to Standard 503(d)(1) "captures well the common law of the crime/fraud exception"); Citibank, N.A. v. Andros, 666 F.2d 1192, 1195 and n.6 (8th Cir. 1981) (Standard 503(c) is "a source for defining the federal common law of attorney-client privilege"); United States v. McPartlin, 595 F.2d 1321 (7th Cir. 1979) (Standard 503(b) a useful guide).

[2] *See* **Treatise** at ¶ 503[01].

or his representative and his lawyer or his lawyer's representative, or (2) between his lawyer and the lawyer's representative, or (3) by him or his lawyer to a lawyer representing another in a matter of common interest, or (4) between representatives of the client or between the client and a representative of the client, or (5) between lawyers representing the client.

(c) Who may claim the privilege.—The privilege may be claimed by the client, his guardian or conservator, the personal representative of a deceased client, or the successor, trustee, or similar representative of a corporation, association, or other organization, whether or not in existence. The person who was the lawyer at the time of the communication may claim the privilege but only on behalf of the client. His authority to do so is presumed in the absence of evidence to the contrary.

(d) Exceptions.—There is no privilege under this rule:

(1) Furtherance of crime or fraud. —If the services of the lawyer were sought or obtained to enable or aid anyone to commit or plan to commit what the client knew or reasonably should have known to be a crime or fraud; or

(2) Claimants through same deceased client.—As to a communication relevant to an issue between parties who claim through the same deceased client, regardless of whether the claims are by testate or intestate succession or by inter vivos transaction; or

(3) Breach of duty by lawyer or client.—As to a communication relevant to an issue of breach of duty by the lawyer to his client or by the client to his lawyer; or

(4) Document attested by lawyer.—As to a communication relevant to an issue concerning an attested document to which the lawyer is an attesting witness; or

(5) Joint clients.—As to a communication relevant to a matter of common interest between two or more clients if the communication was made by any of them to a lawyer retained or consulted in common, when offered in an action between any of the clients.

¶ 18.03[02] Rationale and Nature[1]

The lawyer-client privilege embodied in Standard 503 is the oldest of the privileges for confidential communications. The privilege now is justified primarily on the theory that encouraging clients to communicate fully with their attorneys enables the

---

[1] *See* **Treatise** at ¶ 503[02].

latter to act more effectively, justly and expeditiously, and that the consequent public benefits that stem from fully informed legal advice outweigh the harm caused by the loss of relevant information.[2]

In applying the attorney-client privilege the courts have usually held that if the purpose of the privilege is to be served, both attorney and client must be able to discern with some degree of predictability whether the communication will be protected. Generally, therefore, the courts do not analyze attorney-client privilege claims on a case-by-case basis.[3] Nor do courts, except in rare instances,[4] use a balancing test to determine whether the privilege should be honored; when the factors giving rise to the privilege are present, the privilege is absolute in the absence of an exception or waiver.

¶ 18.03[03] Definitions

Subdivision (a) of Standard 503 sets forth four definitions which are then used in subdivision (b) in stating the general rule of privilege.

---

[2] *See, e.g.,* Upjohn Co. v. United States, 449 U.S. 383, 389, 101 S. Ct. 677, 66 L. Ed. 2d 584 (1981) ("Its purpose is to encourage full and frank communication between attorneys and their clients and thereby promote broader public interests in the observance of law and administration of justice. The privilege recognizes that sound legal advice or advocacy serves public ends and that such advice or advocacy depends upon the lawyer's being fully informed by the client.").

[3] It should be noted, however, that in Upjohn Co. v. United States, 449 U.S. 383, 393, 396–97, 101 S. Ct. 677, 66 L. Ed. 2d 584 (1981), although the majority acknowledged the need for predictability, it nevertheless did not set out the parameters of the privilege in the corporate context, explaining that "such a 'case-by case' basis . . . obeys the spirit of the Rules." A concurring opinion by the Chief Justice criticized the majority for failing to articulate a standard.

[4] *See, e.g.,* Garner v. Wolfinbarger, 430 F.2d 1093 (5th Cir. 1970), *cert. denied,* 401 U.S. 974 (1971) (using balancing test for privilege claims in shareholders' suits). *See* **Treatise** at ¶ 503(b)[05].

[a] Client[1]

The definition in the Standard acknowledges that a client need not be an individual. Artificial entities, public or private, are also considered clients for purposes of the attorney-client privilege. The extent to which communications in the corporate context are privileged is discussed below.

A client is one who is rendered legal services by a lawyer, or who consults a lawyer[2] with a view to obtaining such services.[3] There is no requirement that the services have been rendered in conjunction with litigation or that a fee will be charged. The services must, however, be legal services.

The privilege does not apply when an attorney acts as a friend, co-conspirator, accountant, or business adviser, or in any capacity other than as a lawyer.[4] Difficult problems are posed when a lawyer mixes legal advice with business, as often happens when the attorney serves in the dual function of counsel and officer or

---

[1] See **Treatise** at ¶ 503(a)(1)[01].

[2] See United States v. Layton, 855 F.2d 1388, 1406 (9th Cir. 1988), cert. denied, 109 S. Ct. 1178 (1989) (fact that attorney was representing a religious cult to which defendant belonged did not establish that defendant was his client; burden of establishing requisite relationship rests on claimant of the privilege); United States v. Dennis, 843 F.2d 652, 657 (2d Cir. 1988) (initial statements made by co-defendant to defendant's attorney, while co-defendant was seeking legal representation, would be privileged, but privilege may have ended when attorney informed co-defendant that he could not represent him).

[3] United States v. Bay State Ambulance & Hospital Rental Service, Inc., 874 F.2d 20, 27–29 (1st Cir. 1989) (no attorney-client privilege relationship existed between hospital official and in-house counsel for ambulance service although official sent an outline to counsel; court noted that official had retained separate counsel, never paid attorney, and never asked attorney to take any action on his behalf); United States v. Wilson, 798 F.2d 509, 513 (1st Cir. 1986) (privilege did not apply when defendant was merely using attorney to convey information to attorney's clients, and not for purpose of obtaining legal advice).

[4] See, e.g., United States v. Huberts, 637 F.2d 630, 640 (9th Cir. 1980), cert. denied, 451 U.S. 975 (1981) (business agent); United States v. Stern, 511 F.2d 1364, 1367 (2d Cir.), cert. denied, 423 U.S. 829 (1975) (no privilege where communications made to attorney as potential co-defendant); Olender v. United States, 210 F.2d 795, 806 (9th Cir. 1954) (privilege inapplicable when communication made solely for preparation of tax returns and net worth statements).

director of a corporation. The burden in all such cases is on the claimant to prove that the attorney was acting in a professional legal capacity.[5] The attorney-client privilege does not bar questions about the nature of the legal services rendered.

[b]   Lawyer[6]

For purposes of the privilege, a lawyer satisfies the definition if authorized to practice anywhere in the world.[7] Bar membership is not essential. The test is subjective, rather than objective, since it is sufficient if the client reasonably believed that the person consulted was a lawyer. Reasonableness will depend on the particular circumstances of the case, and has to be shown by the person claiming the privilege.[8]

[c]   Representative of the Lawyer[9]

Office personnel such as secretaries and paralegals are clearly considered representatives of the lawyer. More difficult is determining who else is "employed to assist the lawyer in the rendition of professional legal services." The problem typically arises with respect to accountants, administrative practitioners, experts and employees of insurance companies. Unless they are considered representatives of the lawyer, communications made to them by a client in confidence will not be privileged.[10] In each instance the claimant bears the burden of showing that the person in question worked at the direction of the lawyer, and performed

---

[5] *See, e.g., In re* Sealed Test, 737 F.2d 94, 99 (D.C. Cir. 1984); United States v. Kelly, 569 F.2d 928, 938 (5th Cir. 1978).

[6] *See* **Treatise** at ¶ 503(a)(2)[01].

[7] Renfield Corp. v. E. Remy Martin & Co., S.A., 98 F.R.D. 442 (D. Del. 1982) (French in-house counsel).

[8] *See* United States v. Boffa, 513 F. Supp. 517 (D. Del. 1981), *modified on other grounds,* 688 F.2d 919 (3d Cir. 1982), *cert. denied,* 460 U.S. 1022 (1983) (extensive discussion in case in which court held that defendants failed to satisfy burden of proving reasonable belief).

[9] *See* **Treatise** at ¶ 503(a)(3)[01]. ¶ 503(b)[07] in the **Treatise** discusses communications from an insured to agents of the insurance company.

[10] United States v. El Paso Co., 682 F.2d 530 (5th Cir. 1982), *cert. denied,* 466 U.S. 944 (1984) (no federal accountant-client privilege).

tasks relevant to the client's obtaining legal advice, while responsibility remained with the lawyer.[11] If the expert has been hired to testify at trial, the attorney-client privilege cannot be invoked to prohibit pretrial discovery, though the work-product rules may limit some answers at the experts' deposition.

[d] Confidentiality[12]

Ordinarily the presence of a third person negates the confidentiality which lies at the heart of privilege.[13] Confidentiality is not lost, however, if the third person was present "in furtherance of the rendition of legal services," or was "reasonably necessary for the transmission of the communication."[14]

The communication also loses its privileged status if the client intended the matter to be made public.[15] For example, communications that a client knew would be disclosed in legal documents,

[11] *See, e.g.,* United States v. Kovel, 296 F.2d 918 (2d Cir. 1961) (communications to accountant hired by lawyer protected); Mendenhall v. Barber-Greene Corp., 531 F. Supp. 951 (N.D. Ill. 1982) (privilege exists with respect to patent agent when patent agent acts primarily as functionary of lawyer); United States v. Alvarez, 519 F.2d 1036 (3d Cir. 1975) (when defense counsel hires psychiatrist for advice about possible insanity defense, assertion of insanity defense does not waive attorney-client privilege with respect to psychiatric consultations made in preparation for trial). *Compare* United States *ex rel.* Edney v. Smith, 425 F. Supp. 1038 (E.D.N.Y. 1976), *aff'd,* 556 F.2d 556 (2d Cir. 1977) (acknowledges that *Alvarez* represents majority view but refuses to declare New York statute in question unconstitutional).

[12] *See* **Treatise** at ¶¶ 503(a)(4)[01]–[02], 503(b)[03].

[13] *See, e.g.,* United States v. Furst, 886 F.2d 558, 574–76 (3d Cir. 1989), *cert. denied,* 110 S. Ct. 878 (1990) (presence of third party destroyed expectation of confidentiality at meeting that otherwise might have been characterized as a joint consultation); United States v. Palmer, 536 F.2d 1278, 1281 (9th Cir. 1976) ("communication was not confidential since a third party was involved").

[14] *See, e.g.,* Kevlik v. Goldstein, 724 F.2d 844, 849 (1st Cir. 1984) (presence of client's father did not destroy confidentiality). *See also* United States v. Dennis, 843 F.2d 652, 657 (2d Cir. 1988) (initial statements made by co-defendant to defendant's attorney, while co-defendant was seeking legal representation, would be privileged, but privilege may have ended when attorney invited co-defendant's father into the room).

[15] *See, e.g.,* United States v. Mierzwicki, 500 F. Supp. 1331 (D. Md. 1980) (tax returns).

such as complaints, or in settlement negotiations, are not privileged.[16] Because the intent to keep the communication confidential is crucial, the privilege may be asserted to prevent an eavesdropper from disclosing confidential communications,[17] provided sufficient reasonable precautions were taken to ensure confidentiality. In the absence of adequate precautions, a court may find that the requisite intent to maintain confidentiality was lacking.[18]

Facts observable by anyone, such as whether the client was depressed, are excluded from the privilege. Acts are within the ambit of the privilege if the client intended to utilize them in making a confidential statement in connection with receiving legal services.

¶ 18.03[04]   Scope of Privilege[1]

Subdivision (b) of Standard 503 states the general rule that a confidential communication "made for the purpose of facilitating the rendition of professional legal services to the client" is privileged.

[a]   Whose Communications are Privileged?

Communications meeting the test of Standard 503 are privileged if they are between the client or the client's representative and the lawyer or the lawyer's representative. So are communications between the lawyer and the lawyer's representative, between

---

[16] *See, e.g.,* United States v. Tellier, 255 F.2d 441, 447 (2d Cir.), *cert. denied,* 358 U.S. 821 (1958) ("[C]ommunications between an attorney and his client, though made privately, are not privileged if it was understood that the information communicated in the conversation was to be conveyed to others." Client expected communication to be incorporated in letter.).

[17] *Cf.* United States v. Valenica, 541 F.2d 618 (6th Cir. 1976) (where attorney's secretary was revealed to be government informant, remand to give defendants an opportunity to show that evidence produced against them was obtained through government's intrusion into privilege).

[18] *See* Suburban Sew 'N Sweep, Inc. v. Swiss-Bernia, 91 F.R.D. 254 (N.D. Ill. 1981) (court refused to sustain defendant's privilege claim where plaintiff had retrieved confidential correspondence between defendant and its counsel from a garbage receptacle used exclusively by defendant).

[1] *See* **Treatise** at ¶¶ 503(b)[03], 503(a)(4)[02].

the client and the client's representative, and between lawyers representing the client. The privilege also attaches to communications made by the client or lawyer to another lawyer representing a person "in a matter of common interest."[2] The presence of more than one client at a joint conference does not destroy the privilege when "disclosure is in furtherance of the rendition of professional legal services to the client." See discussion of "confidential," *supra*. Nevertheless, it is safer not to have clients at such conferences because of the danger that they may make extraneous statements which can be taken as admissions.

Joint conferences frequently occur in criminal cases in which co-defendants retain separate counsel,[3] in class actions, in a number of non-litigated situations such as labor or commercial negotiations, and in general corporate and securities practice. "Common interest" is not defined in the Standard. Case law indicates that courts tend to construe the doctrine somewhat narrowly[4] especially in the criminal context.[5] The consequence of the common interest doctrine is that when separate counsel have been retained, the privilege continues to apply if litigation ensues between any of the parties who had engaged in joint consultations. When, however, clients who have retained the same counsel have a later falling out, there is no privilege for

---

[2] *See* **Treatise** at ¶ 503(b)[06].

[3] *See, e.g.,* United States v. McPartlin, 595 F.2d 1321, 1336 (7th Cir. 1979), *cert. denied,* 44 U.S. 833 (1980) (communication by co-defendant to investigator who was agent for defendant's attorney).

[4] *See, e.g., In re* Bevill, Bresler & Schulman Asset Mgmt, Corp., 805 F.2d 120, 125 (3d Cir. 1986) (party asserting privilege has burden of showing that parties agreed to pursue joint defense).

[5] *See, e.g.,* United States v. Bay State Ambulance & Hosp. Rental Serv., Inc., 874 F.2d 20, 28–29 (1st Cir. 1989) (in Medicare fraud prosecution, hospital official claimed that he had provided information to in-house counsel for ambulance service as part of common defense; court found that official failed to meet burden of showing that document was prepared as part of joint defense and also noted as significant official's failure to provide his own attorney with the information until months later); Government of Virgin Islands v. Joseph, 685 F.2d 857, 861–62 (3d Cir. 1982) (no common purpose or joint defense where defendant confessed to attorney for another suspect in order to exonerate latter); United States v. Cariello, 536 F. Supp. 698 (D.N.J. 1982) (statement by co-defendant to his attorney in presence of defendant was in furtherance of his individual defense). *See also* United States v. Furst, 886 F.2d 558, 574–76 (3d Cir. 1989), *cert. denied,* 110 S. Ct. 878 (1990).

communications made by any of them (see discussion below). The divergence in result is justified because the client who has retained separate counsel has taken all necessary steps to ensure the protection of the privilege. Consequently, in a multi-party situation, an attorney has an ethical obligation to suggest at the outset of the representation that each party may need separate counsel.[6]

[b] Communications[7]

A number of consequences follow from the fact that only "communications" are protected by the attorney-client privilege. A client's knowledge is not protected.[8] The client may, therefore, be questioned about what he knows, though not about what he told his attorney.

A communication in writing between the persons specified in the Standard is accorded the same protection as an oral communication. Transferring a pre-existing document or an object to an attorney is not a communication that will immunize the document from disclosure pursuant to the attorney-client privilege, although under some circumstances the fifth amendment prohibition against compelled self-incrimination will prevent disclosure connecting the object to the client. If the document or object could be compelled by process if it were in the hands of the client, it must be produced even though it is now in the possession of the attorney.[9]

---

[6] *See* discussion in **Treatise** at ¶ 503(b)[06] of the related problem of when an attorney must be disqualified because of information previously acquired in a professional capacity.

[7] *See* **Treatise** at ¶ 503(b)[03].

[8] Upjohn Co. v. United States, 449 U.S. 383, 395, 101 S. Ct. 677, 66 L. Ed. 2d 584 (1981) ("The privilege only protects disclosure of communications; it does not protect disclosure of the underlying facts by those who communicated with the attorney.").

[9] Fisher v. United States, 425 U.S. 391, 403–04, 96 S. Ct. 1569, 48 L. Ed. 2d 39 (1976) ("pre-existing documents which could have been obtained by court process from the client when he was in possession may also be obtained from the attorney by similar process following transfer by the client in order to obtain more informed legal advice"). *See, e.g.,* United States v. Clark, 847 F.2d 1467 (10th Cir. 1988).

As long as the communication is made for the purpose of rendering legal services, it does not matter pursuant to Standard 503 whether the communication is by the client to the attorney or by the attorney to the client. This is the usual rule in the federal courts,[10] although some cases suggest that communications from the attorney to the client are not within the privilege unless they would reveal the client's confidences.[11]

[c] Identifying Facts About the Client, Lawyer or Representation[12]

The general rule in the federal courts is that identifying facts about the client or attorney or the scope or objective of the employment are not treated as confidential communications to which the privilege applies.[13] Usually this does not create a problem. Rarely does a client want to keep these facts secret, but situations do arise in which clients desire their whereabouts, or identity, or fee information to be protected against disclosure. Standard 503 is silent about this problem.

In resolving these issues, the courts have divided into two major camps. One group would almost always require disclosure on the theory that these facts are "different from communications intended by the client to explain a problem to a lawyer in order to obtain legal advice."[14] Other courts have taken a more

---

[10] See, e.g., United States v. Amerada Hess Corp., 619 F.2d 980, 986 (3d Cir. 1980) ("Legal advice or opinion from an attorney to his client, individual or corporate, has consistently been held by the federal courts to be within the protection of the attorney-client privilege.").

[11] See In re LTV Securities Litigation, 89 F.R.D. 595, 602 (N.D. Tex. 1981) (review of cases and criticism of this view).

[12] See Treatise at ¶ 503(a)(4)[02].

[13] See Ramseur v. Chase Manhattan Bank, 865 F.2d 460 (2d Cir. 1989) (in employment discrimination action in which plaintiff claimed her discharge was pretextual, although content of memorandum of meeting between plaintiff's superiors and the legal department would be privileged, date of meeting would not be, and date might lead to inference that other employees were not treated similarly until after meeting); United States v. Pape, 144 F.2d 778, 782 (2d Cir.), cert. denied, 323 U.S. 752 (1944).

[14] In re Grand Jury Subpoenas United States v. Hirsch, 803 F.2d 493, 497–98 (9th Cir. 1986) (identity of third-party beneficiary paying defendant's attorney's fees is not privileged; privilege applies only where disclosure would

protective view and upheld the privilege claim where the information sought "would implicate the client in the very criminal act for which legal advice is sought,"[15] or more narrowly, where disclosure would be "the last link in an existing chain of incriminating evidence likely to lead to the client's indictment."[16]

¶ 18.03[05]   Corporate Clients: Attorney-Client Privilege and Work-Product[1]

Standard 503 did not deal with the scope of the privilege in the corporate context because the Supreme Court was evenly divided on this question at the time the proposed rule was drafted by the Advisory Committee.[2] It was not then clear whether a corporation, which can act only through its employees and agents, was entitled to claim privilege whenever any corporate employee, regardless of rank, communicated with counsel for the purpose of securing legal advice for the corporation, or whether the communicating employee had to be in a position of control within the corporation.[3]

convey the substance of a confidential professional communication between attorney and client); *In re* Shargel, 742 F.2d 61, 63 (2d Cir. 1984) (identity of client, of benefactor who paid legal fee, and details about fees not privileged; court leaves open possibility that privilege will be applied when there are special circumstances under which identification of the client would amount to disclosure of the confidential communication). *See also In re* Grand Jury Investigation No. 83-2-35, 723 F.2d 447 (6th Cir. 1983), *cert. denied sub nom.* Durant v. United States, 467 U.S. 1246 (1984) (identity of client not protected; exceptions discussed).

[15] *In re* Special Grand Jury No. 81-1 (Harvey), 676 F.2d 1005, 1009 (4th Cir. 1982), *vacated on other grounds,* 697 F.2d 112 (4th Cir. 1982) (special protections when attorney subpoenaed); matter of Grand Jury subpoenas served upon Field, 408 F. Supp. 1169 (S.D.N.Y. 1976) (location of client privileged; limitations discussed).

[16] *In re* Grand Jury Proceedings (Pavlick), 680 F.2d 1026, 1027 (5th Cir. 1982) (en banc); *In re* Grand Jury Proceedings (Twist), 689 F.2d 1351 (11th Cir. 1982) (adopting *Pavlick*).

[1] *See* **Treatise** at ¶¶ 503(b)[04]–[05].

[2] *See* **Treatise** at ¶ 503[01].

[3] The so-called control group test had first been enunciated in City of Philadelphia v. Westinghouse Electric Corp., 210 F. Supp. 483 (E.D. Pa.), *mandamus and prohibition denied sub nom.* General Electric Co. v. Kirkpatrick, 312 F.2d 742 (3d Cir. 1962), *cert. denied,* 372 U.S. 943 (1963).

In 1981, in *Upjohn Co. v. United States,*[4] the Supreme Court partially answered this question. Upjohn's claim of privilege was asserted when the Internal Revenue Service issued a summons for documents which had come into being as a consequence of an internal investigation into "questionable payments" conducted by Upjohn's general counsel. As part of this investigation, questionnaires had been sent to "all foreign and area managers" over the signature of the Chairman of the Board informing them that counsel had been asked to conduct an investigation, which was to be treated as "highly confidential," and asking for detailed information to be returned directly to the general counsel, who also, with the assistance of outside counsel, interviewed the recipients, as well as other Upjohn employees.

The district court rejected Upjohn's claim of privilege and concluded that the IRS summons should be enforced. On appeal, the Sixth Circuit found that only communications made by those within the "control group" would be privileged; it remanded for a determination of who was within this group.

The Supreme Court unanimously rejected the "control group test" as inconsistent with the standard for privileges expressed in Rule 501.[5] The Court explained that the "control group test"

> overlooks the fact that the privilege exists to protect not only the giving of professional advice to those who can act on it but also the giving of information to the lawyer to enable him to give sound and informed advice.
>
> . . .
>
> In the case of the individual client the provider of information and the person who acts on the lawyer's advice are one and the same. In the corporate context, however, it will frequently be employees beyond the control group as defined by the court below—"officers and agents . . . responsible for directing [the company's] actions in response to legal advice"—who will possess the information needed

---

[4] 449 U.S. 383, 101 S. Ct. 677, 66 L. Ed. 2d 584 (1981).

[5] The majority wrote: "the narrow 'control group test' sanctioned by the Court of Appeals in this case cannot, consistent with 'the principles of the common law as . . . interpreted . . . in light of reason and experience,' Fed.Rule.Evid. 501, govern the development of the law in this area." *Id.* at 397. Chief Justice Burger, concurring, agreed "fully with the Court's rejection of the so-called 'control group' test, its reasons for doing so, and its ultimate holding that the communications at issue are privileged." *Id.* at 402.

by the corporation's lawyers. Middle-level—and indeed lower-level—employees can, by actions within the scope of their employment, embroil the corporation in serious legal difficulties, and it is only natural that these employees would have the relevant information needed by corporate counsel if he is adequately to advise the client with respect to such actual or potential difficulties.

. . .

The narrow scope given the attorney-client privilege by the court below not only makes it difficult for corporate attorneys to formulate sound advice when their client is faced with a specific legal problem but also threatens to limit the valuable efforts of corporate counsel to ensure their client's compliance with the law.[6]

After noting that the information from Upjohn's employees "was needed to supply a basis for legal advice," a fact of which "the employees themselves were sufficiently aware," and that the communications "have been kept confidential," the Court held that "these communications must be protected against compelled disclosure."[7]

While rejecting the "control group test," the majority of the Court refused to do more than decide the case before it. The opinion does cite *Diversified Industries, Inc. v. Meredith*[8] a number of times, a case in which the Eighth Circuit, sitting en banc, held that the attorney-client privilege would be applicable when five requirements are satisfied:

(1) the communication was made for the purpose of securing legal advice; (2) the employee making the communication did so at the direction of his corporate superior; (3) the superior made the request so that the corporation could secure legal advice; (4) the subject matter of the communication is within the scope of the employee's corporate duties; and (5) the communication is not disseminated beyond those persons who, because of the corporate structure, need to know its contents. We note, moreover, that the corporation has the burden of showing that the communication in issue meets all of the above requirements.[9]

Expressly left open by the Court's decision in *Upjohn* is the question of whether the attorney-client privilege applies to

[6] *Id.* at 390–92.

[7] *Id.* at 394–95.

[8] 572 F.2d 596 (8th Cir. 1978).

[9] *Id.* at 609.

communications by former employees concerning activities during their period of employment.[10] Numerous other questions remain, such as: may a parent corporation assert a privilege as to communications by employees of a subsidiary, who can waive the privilege, and to what extent may a privileged communication be circulated within the corporate entity without losing its privileged status? *Upjohn* also raises a host of ethical problems for the corporate lawyer. To what extent may counsel interview a corporate employee (whose interests may be somewhat antithetical to those of the corporation) without warning the employee that counsel does not represent the employee, and that the employee has a right not to talk to corporate counsel and to obtain separate counsel?[11] Such warnings would, of course, undercut *Upjohn's* rationale of enabling corporate attorneys to obtain as much information as possible in order to function most effectively.

Aside from rejecting a narrow view of the attorney-client privilege in *Upjohn,* the Court also took an expansive approach to the work product doctrine. The Supreme Court stressed that the material sought by the government—notes and memoranda of witnesses' statements—has been accorded special protection, both by the decision in *Hickman v. Taylor*[12] and by Rule 26 of the Federal Rules of Civil Procedure, because such material "tends to reveal the attorney's mental processes."[13] Noting that "some courts have concluded that no showing of necessity can overcome protection of work product which is based on oral statements from witnesses," while other courts in "declining to adopt an absolute rule have nonetheless recognized that such material is entitled to special protection," the Supreme Court refused to "decide the issue at this time."[14]

---

[10] Upjohn Co. v. United States, 449 U.S. at 394 n.3.

[11] *Cf. In re* Coordinated Pretrial Proceedings in Petroleum Products Antitrust Litigation, 402 F. Supp. 1092, 1096 (C.D. Cal. 1980) (in antitrust action by Attorneys General of several states against major oil companies, court ordered that counsel be precluded from simultaneously representing a defendant and individual nonparty deponents who are employees or retired employees of a defendant corporation).

[12] 329 U.S. 495, 67 S. Ct. 385, 91 L. Ed. 451 (1947).

[13] Upjohn Co. v. United States, 449 U.S. 383, 400, 101 S. Ct. 677, 66 L. Ed. 2d 584 (1981).

[14] *Id.,* 449 U.S. at 401. ("While we are not prepared at this juncture to say that such material is always protected by the work-product rule, we think a

Since *Upjohn,* it appears that some of the circuit courts are curbing the potential sweep of the opinion by strict enforcement of the concept of waiver, and application of the crime-fraud exception.[15] See discussion below.

Another issue in the corporate context about which Standard 503 is silent is the extent to which shareholders and other beneficiaries of a fiduciary relationship may have access to what would otherwise qualify as privileged communications. The question has most frequently arisen in derivative suits brought by minority stockholders. Since such an action is theoretically for the benefit of the corporation, the corporation should have no objection to divulging the requested information to its representative, the minority stockholder. In actuality, there is mutual antagonism between those who bring the suit and those who run the corporation.

Instead of treating the privilege as absolute under these circumstances, a number of courts have adopted a flexible rule that permits disclosure of otherwise privileged matter if the plaintiff can demonstrate "good cause." In the seminal case of *Garner v. Wolfinbarger,*[16] the Fifth Circuit suggested weighing the following factors in determining good cause:

> [T]he number of shareholders and the percentage of stock they represent; the bona fides of the shareholders; the nature of the shareholders' claim and whether it is obviously colorable; the apparent necessity or desirability of the shareholders having the information and the availability of it from other sources; whether, if the shareholders' claim is of wrongful action by the corporation, it is of action criminal, or illegal but not criminal, or of doubtful legality; whether the communication related to past or to prospective actions; whether the communication is of advice concerning the litigation itself; the extent to which the communication is identified versus the extent to which the shareholders are blindly fishing; the risk of revelation of trade secrets or other information in whose

---

far stronger showing of necessity and unavailability by other means than was made by the Government or applied by the Magistrate in this case would be necessary to compel disclosure." *Id.* at 401–02.).

[15] *See, e.g., In re* Sealed Case, 676 F.2d 793 (D.C. Cir. 1982) and *In re* John Doe Corp., 675 F.2d 482 (2d Cir. 1982), discussed in **Treatise** at ¶ 503(b)[04].

[16] 430 F.2d 1093 (5th Cir. 1970), *cert. denied,* 401 U.S. 974 (1971).

confidentiality the corporation has an interest for independent
reasons.[17]

¶ 18.03[06]   Who May Claim the Privilege[1]

Standard 503(c) vests the privilege in the client. The privilege
may be claimed by the client regardless of whether or not the
client is a party to the proceeding in which disclosure of the
privileged communication is sought. If the client is present when
the privileged information is sought, the client or the attorney
must assert the privilege or it will be deemed waived. During a
period of disability, a guardian or conservator may assert the
privilege.

Standard 503 acknowledges that the privilege survives the
death of an individual client. In the corporate context, the
Standard provides that the successor of a dissolved corporation
may claim the privilege. The Supreme Court has held in *Commodity Futures Trading Commission v. Weintraub*[2] that the
power to waive, and presumably to assert, the attorney-client
privilege passes to the trustee in bankruptcy, who has the power
with respect to communications that took place before the filing
of the bankruptcy petition.

A lawyer who no longer represents a client will be presumed
to have authority to claim the privilege until evidence to the
contrary is offered. A lawyer currently representing a client may
assert a claim of privilege even though the communications in
question were made prior to the lawyer's representation of the

---

[17] *Id.* at 1104. *See* Ward v. Succession of Freeman, 854 F.2d 780, 784 (5th
Cir. 1988) (court declined to find "good cause" for production in non-
derivative stockholders' suit, where plaintiffs failed to show that information
was not available from other sources; requirement was not satisfied by
pleading of fraud claim and need for proof of scienter). *See also* Quintel Corp.,
N.V. v. Citibank, N.A., 567 F. Supp. 1357 (S.D.N.Y. 1983) (*Garner* applied
to limited partnership); *In re* LTV Sec. Litig., 89 F.R.D. 595, 608 (N.D. Tex.
1981); Valente v. Pepsico, Inc., 68 F.R.D. 361 (D. Del. 1975).

[1] *See* **Treatise** at ¶ 503(c)[01].

[2] 471 U.S. 343, 105 S. Ct. 1986, 85 L. Ed. 2d 372. *See also In re* Bevill,
Bresler & Schulman Asset Mgmt. Corp., 805 F.2d 120, 125 (3d Cir. 1986)
(where corporation has waived the privilege through the trustee, the assertion
of an individual privilege on behalf of a corporate official will not prevent
disclosure).

client. If former and present attorneys differ in their view of the client's position, the current attorney's position should be followed.[3]

¶ 18.03[07] Exceptions to the Privilege

Standard 503 recognizes a number of exceptions to the attorney-client privilege.

[a] Furtherance of Crime or Fraud [1]

Standard 503(d)(1) is in accord with the view "accepted by all courts today . . . that a client's communication to his attorney in pursuit of a criminal or fraudulent act yet to be performed is not privileged in any judicial proceeding."[2] This exception rests on the realization that the privilege's policy of promoting the administration of justice would be undermined if the privilege could be used as "a cloak or shield for the perpetration of a crime or fraudulent wrongdoing."[3] The privilege is lost regardless of whether the attorney was aware of the client's plans. It is the client's intention to use the attorney's services in aid of what the client knew, or reasonably should have known to be a crime or fraud, that controls. A few courts have extended the exception to embrace intentional or reckless torts.[4]

Advice obtained from an attorney by one who is already a wrongdoer and is seeking legal counsel in aid of a legitimate defense is privileged.[5] While it may at times be difficult to ascertain the boundaries between past and present wrongdoing, it is clear that an attorney should never directly or indirectly assist in the destruction of evidence,[6] or acquiesce in perjury.[7]

---

[3] United States v. DeLillo, 448 F. Supp. 840, 842 (E.D.N.Y. 1978).

[1] See **Treatise** at ¶ 503(d)(1)[01].

[2] In re Sawyer's Petition, 229 F.2d 805, 808–09 (7th Cir. 1956).

[3] SEC v. Harrison, 80 F. Supp. 226, 230 (D.D.C. 1948) (fraudulent underwriting); United States v. Gordon-Nikkar, 518 F.2d 972, 975 (5th Cir. 1975) (plans to commit perjury).

[4] See, e.g., Diamond v. Stratton, 95 F.R.D. 503, 505 (S.D.N.Y. 1982).

[5] See United States v. White, 887 F.2d 267, 271–72 (D.C. Cir. 1989).

[6] See, e.g., In re Ryder, 263 F. Supp. 360 (E.D. Va.), aff'd per curiam on opinion below, 381 F.2d 713 (4th Cir. 1967).

The Advisory Committee's notes to Standard 503(d)(1) explicitly state that the court need not make a preliminary finding that there is sufficient evidence aside from the communication to warrant a finding that the legal services were sought to enable the commission of the crime or fraud. The absence of any test has the advantage of leaving the question to the good sense of the trial judge. Certainly some crimes by their very nature suggest that there must have been legal guidance, and consequently a judge may, without more, conclude that the communication was in furtherance of crime or fraud. In many cases, the question of how much proof is needed to show unlawful purpose is purely theoretical.[8]

In *United States v. Zolin,*[9] the Supreme Court held that upon a proper showing the district court may conduct an in camera review to determine whether an allegedly privileged communication comes within the crime-fraud exception to the privilege. The Court ruled that in camera review could be obtained only if the party seeking disclosure makes a factual showing sufficient to support a reasonable belief that the in camera review would reveal evidence that would establish the crime-fraud exception.[10] "[T]he threshold showing to obtain *in camera* review may be met by using any relevant evidence, lawfully obtained, that has not been adjudicated to be privileged."[11]

[b] Claimants Through Same Deceased Claimant[12]

Standard 503(d)(2) is an exception to the general rule expressed in subdivision (c), *supra,* that the lawyer-client privilege survives the death of the client. There is no privilege "[a]s to a communication relevant to an issue between parties who claim through the

---

[7] *See* Nix v. Whiteside, 106 S. Ct. 988, 996, 89 L. Ed. 2d 123 (1986) ("under no circumstance may a lawyer either advocate or passively tolerate a client's giving false testimony").

[8] *See, e.g., In re* Grand Jury Subpoena Duces Tecum Dated September 15, 1983, 731 F.2d 1032, 1039 (2d Cir. 1984).

[9] 491 U.S. —, 109 S. Ct. 2619, 105 L. Ed. 2d 469 (1989).

[10] *Id.,* at —, 109 S. Ct. at 2631, 105 L. Ed. 2d at 490 (1989).

[11] *Id.,* at —, 109 S. Ct. at 2632, 105 L. Ed. 2d at 492.

[12] *See* **Treatise** at ¶ 503(d)(2)[01].

same deceased client, regardless of whether the claims are by testate or intestate succession or by inter vivos transaction."

In cases in which two or more parties claim through the same deceased, the very issue to be determined is who steps into the decedent's shoes. Since this cannot be determined until the end of the litigation, the question of who is entitled to claim the privilege must also be held in abeyance. Rather than allowing all to assert the privilege, the better choice is to hold that where all the parties claim under the client, the privilege does not apply. In will cases this approach furthers the public interest in having an estate distributed promptly in accordance with the decedent's intent.

When the contest is between a "stranger" and a person claiming through the deceased client, the party claiming through the decedent may invoke the privilege if he comes within the definition of Standard 503(c). If two or more parties claim through a client who is not deceased, the privilege continues unless the client waives it pursuant to Standard 511.

[c] Breach of Duty By Lawyer or Client[13]

Standard 503(d)(3) states the generally accepted view that when the attorney and client become opponents in a subsequent controversy, the attorney may reveal privileged communications to the limited extent necessary to establish the attorney's rights.[14]

[d] Document Attested By Lawyer[15]

Standard 503(d)(4) states that when an attorney acts as an attesting witness, the attorney-client privilege does not bar the disclosure of any communication relevant to an issue concerning

---

[13] See Treatise at ¶ 503(d)(3)[01].

[14] See, e.g., Tasby v. United States, 504 F.2d 332 (8th Cir.), cert. denied, 419 U.S. 1125 (1975) (claim of ineffective assistance of counsel claim waived protection of attorney-client privilege); In re Featherworks Corp., 25 B.R. 634, 644–45 (Bkrtcy E.D.N.Y. 1982), aff'd, 36 B.R. 460 (D.C.N.Y. 1984) (attorney of bankrupt who was unsecured creditor could testify as to validity of claim of secured creditor).

[15] See Treatise at ¶ 503(d)(4)[01].

the document. This exception permits the attorney to testify to such matters as the intent and competence of the client and the execution or attestation of the document.

Where the lawyer drew the document after receiving confidential communications, the lawyer should suggest that someone else act as the attesting witness so as not to reduce the privilege's protection.

[e]   Joint Clients[16]

Standard 503(d)(5) states the generally accepted principle that when "the same attorney acts for two or more parties having a common interest, neither party may exercise the privilege in a subsequent controversy with the other."[17] Communications with the attorney are still privileged in any action between one or all of the clients and a third person.

¶ 18.04   The Marital Privileges

At the time the Advisory Committee was drafting its detailed rules on privilege, the federal courts recognized two privileges affecting the marital relationship: a testimonial privilege which prevented adverse testimony by a spouse in a criminal case, and a communications privilege which immunized confidential communications between spouses against disclosure. The Advisory Committee made two decisions in drafting proposed Rule 505 as the only rule which would govern privileges pertaining to the marital relationship: (1) it continued the testimonial privilege in its common law form in which the accused is the holder of the privilege, and (2) it eliminated the privilege for confidential communications entirely. As discussed above in ¶ 18.02[01], Congress rejected the proposed detailed rules of privilege in favor of the formula embodied in Rule 501, which generally leaves the federal law of privilege to development on a case by case basis.

In *Trammel v. United States*,[1] the Supreme Court undertook a redefinition of the marital testimonial privilege, pursuant to the

---

[16] *See* **Treatise** at ¶ 503(d)(5)[01].

[17] Garner v. Wolfinbarger, 430 F.2d 1093, 1103 (5th Cir. 1970), *cert. denied*, 401 U.S. 974 (1971).

[1] 445 U.S. 40, 100 S. Ct. 906, 63 L. Ed. 2d 186 (1980).

mandate of Rule 501 for the federal courts to develop common law principles of privilege "in the light of reason and experience." In so doing, the Court departed substantially from the provisions of proposed Rule 505, with respect both to spousal testimony and to confidential communications. While strongly suggesting in dictum that the privilege for confidential marital communications remains valid, the Court significantly modified the privilege against spousal testimony by making the witness spouse the holder of the privilege. As a result, the proposed Rule 505 is of little assistance in outlining the principles of the marital privileges as currently applied in the federal courts. The discussion below considers the two marital privileges separately.

¶ 18.04[01] The Privilege Against Adverse Spousal Testimony[2]

The privilege against adverse spousal testimony is the only vestige of the now defunct common law rule that prohibited one spouse from testifying both for or against the other in any type of proceeding. By the time proposed Rule 505 was drafted, the federal courts had limited the privilege to criminal proceedings, and to testimony against the other spouse. The rationale for such a privilege had been explained by the Supreme Court in *Hawkins v. United States:*[3]

> The basic reason the law has refused to pit wife against husband or husband against wife in a trial where life or liberty is at stake was a belief that such a policy was necessary to foster family peace, not only for the benefit of husband, wife and children, but for the benefit of the public as well. Such a belief has never been unreasonable and is not now.[4]

In *Hawkins,* the Supreme Court had reaffirmed that the holder of the privilege is the accused, and the Advisory Committee had drafted proposed Rule 505[5] accordingly. When Congress rejected

---

[2] *See* **Treatise** at ¶¶ 505[01]–[05].

[3] 358 U.S. 74, 79 S. Ct. 136, 3 L. Ed. 2d 125 (1958).

[4] *Id.,* 358 U.S. at 77.

[5] Rule 505, as promulgated by the Supreme Court, provided:

Husband-Wife Privilege

(a) General Rule of privilege.—An accused in a criminal proceeding has a

the detailed rules on privilege, including proposed Rule 505, all questions of privilege became subject to resolution pursuant to Rule 501. When called upon in *Trammel v. United States*[6] to rule on a claim of testimonial spousal privilege, the Supreme Court modified its decision in *Hawkins:* "the witness spouse alone has a privilege to refuse to testify adversely; the witness may be neither compelled to testify nor foreclosed from testifying."[7]

In *Trammel,* the defendant's wife, an unindicted co-conspirator in a heroin importation prosecution, had testified against her husband after she had been granted use immunity. Her testimony concededly constituted virtually the entire government case against the defendant. The Court explained why the "reason and experience" formula of Rule 501 requires vesting the privilege in the witness spouse:

> When one spouse is willing to testify against the other in a criminal proceeding—whatever the motivation—their relationship is almost certainly in disrepair; there is probably little in the way of marital harmony for the privilege to preserve. In these circumstances, a rule of evidence that permits an accused to prevent adverse spousal testimony seems far more likely to frustrate justice than to foster family peace. Indeed, there is reason to believe that vesting the privilege in the accused could actually undermine the marital relationship. For example, in a case such as this, the Government is unlikely to offer a wife immunity and lenient treatment if it knows that her husband can prevent her from giving adverse testimony.

---

privilege to prevent his spouse from testifying against him.

(b) Who may claim the privilege.—The privilege may be claimed by the accused or by the spouse on his behalf. The authority of the spouse to do so is presumed in the absence of evidence to the contrary.

(c) Exceptions.—There is no privilege under this rule (1) in proceedings in which one spouse is charged with a crime against the person or property of the other or of a child of either, or with a crime against the person or property of a third person committed in the course of committing a crime against the other, or (2) as to matters occurring prior to the marriage, or (3) in proceedings in which a spouse is charged with importing an alien for prostitution or other immoral purpose in violation of 8 U.S.C. § 1328, with transporting a female in interstate commerce for immoral purposes or other offense in violation of 18 U.S.C. §§ 2421–2424, or with violation of other similar statutes.

[6] 445 U.S. 40, 100 S. Ct. 906, 63 L. Ed. 2d 186 (1980).

[7] *Id.,* 445 U.S. at 53.

If the Government is dissuaded from making such an offer, the privilege can have the untoward effect of permitting one spouse to escape justice at the expense of the other. It hardly seems conducive to the preservation of the marital relation to place a wife in jeopardy solely by virtue of her husband's control over her testimony.[8]

As defined in *Trammel,* the privilege for spousal testimony bars only the actual giving of testimony.[9] However, it applies at all stages of a criminal proceeding, and must, therefore, be given effect in a grand jury investigation. All testimony is prevented to the extent the rule applies, not merely statements that the spouses had made in confidence.

Pursuant to Rule 501, the courts, as under previous law, have applied the privilege only to the testimony of a spouse[10] —there is no privilege if the marriage is sham,[11] or has been terminated by divorce, annulment, or death. A number of courts have also refused to allow the assertion of the privilege despite the existence of a legal marriage when all the facts and circumstances demonstrate that in fact the marriage is moribund at the time of the testimony.[12]

---

[8] *Id.* at 52–53.

[9] *Id.* at n.12. *See* United States v. Chapman, 866 F.2d 1326, 1332 (11th Cir.), *cert. denied,* 110 S. Ct. 321 (1989) (hearsay statements by spouse claiming privilege are not barred by spousal privilege); *In re* Grand Jury 85-1 (Shelleda), *appeal dismissed,* 848 F.2d 200 (10th Cir. 1988) (spouse could be compelled to provide handwriting and fingerprint exemplars).

[10] *See, e.g., In re* Grand Jury Proceedings Witness Ms. X, 562 F. Supp. 486 (N.D. Calif. 1983) (no privilege for woman in non-formalized marriage relationship); United States v. Pensinger, 549 F.2d 1150 (8th Cir. 1977) (no privilege after divorce); United States v. Mathis, 559 F.2d 294 (5th Cir. 1977) (no privilege where defendant had coerced wife into remarriage).

[11] *In re* Grand Jury Proceedings (Emo), 777 F.2d 508, 509 (9th Cir. 1985) (marriage not sham where partners had lived together for two years and entered into marriage shortly after service of grand jury subpoena; "mere suspicious timing of a marriage does not support a finding of a sham marriage, especially when other evidence, such as living together or intentions of living together as husband and wife,indicates that the marriage was entered into in good faith").

[12] *See, e.g.,* United States v. Brown, 605 F.2d 389 (8th Cir.), *cert. denied,* 444 U.S. 972 (1979) (lengthy separation); United States v. Cameron, 556 F.2d 752 (5th Cir. 1977) (no common residence; husband was living with another person who had borne his child).

A number of unsettled questions remain in the wake of the *Trammel* decision.

[a] Is There a Joint Participation Exception?

At this point the circuits are split on whether the privilege is abrogated when the spouses are partners in crime.[13] Courts that apply a joint participation exception refuse to uphold a claim of privilege in a case like *Trammel*, even when the witness spouse refuses to testify, on the theory that the marital relationship is not entitled to protection when it is being used to foster acts inimical to the public interest. The circuits that reject the joint participation exception find that "it is not entirely beyond doubt that such marriages are not deserving of protection . . . . [T]he marriage may well serve as a restraining influence on couples against further antisocial acts and may tend to help future integration of the spouses back into society."[14] Furthermore, abrogating the privilege when the partners are engaged in crime may give prosecutors an unwarranted incentive to accuse the spouse of conspiracy in order to obtain the testimony of one who does not wish to testify.[15]

[b] Are There Other Exceptions?[16]

Proposed Rule 505 set forth three exceptions that should be looked to as indicative of "reason and experience" in analyzing a claim based on the adverse marital testimony privilege. These exceptions are no longer necessary after *Trammel* unless the

[13] *See, e.g., Second Circuit: In re* Koecher, 755 F.2d 1022 (2d Cir.), *cert. granted,* 106 S. Ct. 56 (1985), *cert. vacated as moot,* 106 S. Ct. 403 (1986) (no exception); *Third Circuit: In re* Malfitano, 633 F.2d 276 (3d Cir. 1980) (no exception); *Fifth Circuit:* United States v. Harrelson, 754 F.2d 1153, 1167–68 (5th Cir.), *cert. denied,* 106 S. Ct. 599 (1985) (exception applies); *Seventh Circuit:* United States v. Clark, 712 F.2d 299 (7th Cir. 1983) (exception applies); *Tenth Circuit:* United States v. Trammel, 583 F.2d 1166, 1169 (10th Cir. 1978), *aff'd on other grounds,* 445 U.S. 40 (1980).

[14] *In re* Malfitano, 633 F.2d 276, 278–79 (3d Cir. 1980).

[15] United States v. Trammel, 583 F.2d 1166, 1173 (10th Cir. 1978) (McKay, J., dissenting), *aff'd on other grounds,* 445 U.S. 40 (1980).

[16] *See* **Treatise** at ¶ 505[05].

witness spouse refuses to testify. The first exception allows a spouse to testify when the other is charged with a crime against the person or property of the other,[17] or child of either,[18] or when the spouse is charged with a crime against the person or property of a third person, committed in the course of committing a crime against the other spouse.

The second exception, which eliminates the privilege as to matters occuring prior to the marriage, represented a judgment by the Advisory Committee that the policies which underlie the husband-wife privilege are outweighed in such an instance by the undesirability of encouraging marriage in order to suppress relevant testimony. This exception continues to be of significance after *Trammel*. Courts which apply the exception consequently compel testimony regardless of the reason for the marriage;[19] others uphold the privilege unless the marriage is shown to be sham.[20]

The final exception in proposed Rule 505 abrogates the privilege when the defendant spouse has been charged with violating the Mann Act or similar statutes.[21] The exception is grounded in the common law view that sexual offenses with a third person are a crime against the spouse.

[c] How is the Privilege Applied in Multi-Party Situations?

In a number of post-*Trammel* cases, the witness whose testimony is sought has had information relevant to the criminal

---

[17] *See, e.g.,* United States v. Smith, 533 F.2d 1077 (8th Cir. 1976) (wife could testify that husband had planted heroin on her against her will).

[18] *See, e.g.,* United States v. Allery, 526 F.2d 1362 (8th Cir. 1975) (rape of daughter).

[19] *See, e.g.,* United States v. Clark, 712 F.2d 299 (7th Cir. 1983) (no requirement that evidence of collusion be presented).

[20] *In re* Grand Jury Proceedings (Emo), 777 F.2d 508 (9th Cir. 1985) (court reversed finding of civil contempt against wife who refused to testify before grand jury; subpoena served before parties married); United States v. Owens, 424 F. Supp. 423 (E.D. Tenn. 1976) (court concluded that "reason and experience" do not warrant allowing spouse to testify about events before marriage).

[21] *See* United States v. Ahern, 612 F.2d 507 (10th Cir. 1980) (privilege abrogated in Mann Act prosecution).

activities of third parties as well as the witness' spouse. At the trial stage, a severance of the spouse's case from that of the other defendants solves the problem of how to honor the witness' privilege not to testify against the spouse without losing the testimony against the third parties. When the matter is pending before a grand jury, however, judges have disagreed on how to handle the situation.[22]

[d] Are Hearsay Statements Barred By the Privilege?

Are a spouse's hearsay statements admissible when the spouse is unwilling to testify? The courts that have addressed the problem after *Trammel* have taken the view that the spouse's extra-judicial statements are not barred by the testimonial privilege, since the privilege only protects the spouse from testifying in court.[23]

¶ 18.04[02] The Privilege for Confidential Marital Communications[1]

The privilege for confidential marital communications is separate and distinct from the testimonial privilege discussed in

[22] *See, e.g., In re* Malfitano, 633 F.2d 276 (3d Cir. 1980) (majority and concurring judges disagreed on power of court to confer use-fruits immunity); *In re* Grand Jury Matter, 673 F.2d 688 (3d Cir.), *cert. denied,* 459 U.S. 1015 (1982) (disagreement about court's power to grant immunity; court held that witness could not be compelled to testify in grand jury proceedings about the criminal activities of third persons when the government acknowledges that such persons will be asked to testify against the spouse in a separate grand jury proceedings); Grand Jury Subpoena of Ford v. United States, 756 F.2d 249 (2d Cir. 1985) (court upheld contempt citation against husband who refused to testify because wife was target of grand jury investigation even after government had promised not to use testimony of witness directly or indirectly against wife, and to erect a "Chinese Wall" to insulate wife from effect of testimony).

[23] United States v. Chapman, 866 F.2d 1326, 1332 (11th Cir.), *cert. denied,* 110 S. Ct. 321 (1989) (hearsay statements by spouse claiming privilege are not barred by spousal privilege); United States v. Archer, 733 F.2d 354 (5th Cir.), *cert. denied,* 469 U.S. 861, 195 S. Ct. 196, 83 L. Ed. 2d 128 (1984) (extra-judicial statements do not come within testimonial privilege). *See also* United States v. Bond, 847 F.2d 1233, 1242 (7th Cir. 1988) (privilege does not apply when spouse is not compelled to testify; dictum).

[1] *See* **Treatise** at ¶ 505[05a].

subhead [01] above. It was not incorporated in proposed Rule 505, but was recognized, albeit in dictum, by the Supreme Court in *Trammel v. United States*.[2] The *Trammel* opinion therefore suggests that this privilege has continuing validity under the "reason and experience" test of Rule 501.

Unlike the testimonial privilege, the communications privilege may be asserted by a party to bar the testimony of a spouse who is willing to testify about the communication. It is intended to encourage the sharing of confidences between spouses. In a much earlier case, the Supreme Court said that the

> basis of the immunity given to communications between husband and wife is the protection of marital confidences, regarded as so essential to the preservation of the marital relationship as to out-weigh the disadvantage to the administration of justice which the privilege entails.[3]

Moreover, some commentators and at least one court have suggested that the communications privilege may have a constitutional underpinning stemming from the right of privacy which would preclude its complete abolition.[4]

There are three basic prerequisites to the assertion of the communications privilege. First, at the time of the communication, there must have been a marriage recognized as valid by state law.[5] Although some courts refuse to allow the testimonial privilege when a marriage is deteriorating on the grounds that marital harmony—the objective of the privilege—has already been destroyed,[6] such an approach is less justified in the case of

---

[2] 445 U.S. 40, 51, 100 S. Ct. 906, 63 L. Ed. 2d 186 (1980) (Court stated that testimonial privilege "is not needed to protect information privately disclosed between husband and wife in the confidence of the marital relationship—once described by the Court as 'the best solace of human existence.' . . . Those confidences are privileged under the independent rule protecting confidential marital communications.").

[3] Wolfle v. United States, 291 U.S. 7, 14, 54 S. Ct. 279, 78 L. Ed. 617 (1933).

[4] United States v. Neal, 532 F. Supp. 942 (D. Colo. 1982), *cert. denied*, 105 S. Ct. 1848 (1985).

[5] *See, e.g.,* United States v. Lustig, 555 F.2d 737 (9th Cir. 1977), *cert. denied*, 434 U.S. 926 (1978) (privilege claim denied in part because common law marriage of defendant not recognized as valid under Alaska law).

[6] United States v. Frank, 869 F.2d 1177, 1179 (8th Cir.), *cert. denied*, 110 S. Ct. 121 (1989) (no privilege; permanent separation and defunct marriage);

the communications privilege which is intended to encourage confidences that might conceivably strengthen a faltering marriage.[7]

The second prerequisite for the assertion of the communications privilege is that there must have been a communication with respect to which the privilege is asserted. Although some federal courts have acknowledged in dicta that "interspousal communications are not limited to speaking and writing,"[8] the federal courts have generally stated that the privilege "applies only to utterances or expressions intended by one spouse to convey a message to the other"[9] and have not recognized, under the facts of the cases before them, observations made of a spouse's activities or appearance as communications covered by the privilege.[10]

United States v. Roberson, 859 F.2d 1376 (9th Cir. 1988) (declining to adopt a categorical test for applicability of the privilege in failing marriages, court of appeals held that trial court should consider existence of separation and other circumstances bearing on possibility of reconciliation; in instant case, finding that marriage was defunct was not clearly erroneous, and thus wife could testify to statement by husband admitting crime); United States v. Fulk, 816 F.2d 1202, 1205 (7th Cir. 1987) (no privilege claim where defendant and his wife were permanently separated at the time of communication).

[7] United States v. Byrd, 750 F.2d 585 (7th Cir. 1984) (deterioration of the marriage or absence of marital peace irrelevant unless the spouses are permanently separated); United States v. Sims, 755 F.2d 1239, 1244 n.3 (6th Cir.) cert. denied, 105 S. Ct. 3533 (1985) (rejecting notion that marital problems eliminate privilege). See also United States v. Roberson, 859 F.2d 1376 (9th Cir. 1988).

[8] United States v. Brown, 605 F.2d 389, 396 n.6 (8th Cir.), cert. denied, 444 U.S. 972 (1979) (admission of testimony regarding husband's departure from residence, if departure was a communication, may have been error, but harmless). See also United States v. Lewis, 433 F.2d 1146, 1151 (D.C. Cir. 1970) (return of defendant at 3 a.m. with sawed-off shotgun not viewed as communication in absence of record indicating whether activities were open or clandestine or whether defendant was aware of wife's observation); United States v. Lefkowitz, 618 F.2d 1313, 1318 (9th Cir.), cert. denied, 449 U.S. 824 (1980) (removal of business records might have been communication but not confidential because of presence of third persons).

[9] United States v. Lustig, 555 F.2d 737, 748 (9th Cir. 1977), cert. denied, 434 U.S. 1045 (1978).

[10] See, e.g., United States v. Bolzer, 556 F.2d 948 (9th Cir. 1977), cert. denied, 449 U.S. 824 (1980) (testimony of wife that pants matched those worn by ex-husband); United States v. Smith, 535 F.2d 1077 (8th Cir. 1976) (act of placing heroin on wife's person not a communication).

This approach is consistent with the view that privileges should be narrowly construed. There is some disagreement as to whether the criminal participation exception should be applied to the initial communication in which one spouse advises the other about the intended crime.[11]

The final prerequisite to the assertion of the privilege is that the communication be made in confidence. The federal courts apply a presumption that communications between spouses are intended to be confidential.[12] The presumption may be overcome by a showing that the communication occurred in the presence of a third party[13] or that the communicating spouse intended to convey the information, or have it conveyed, to a third party.[14] The fact that third parties may have the same knowledge that was communicated to the witness spouse does not destroy the privilege. As long as the communication itself was private and was intended to remain so, the spouse cannot be compelled to

[11] *Compare* United States v. Estes, 793 F.2d 465, 467–68 (2d Cir. 1986) (exception does not apply to wife's testimony that defendant had come home with bags of money and told her that he had taken it from a Purolator truck; wife could not become joint participant until after this communication and therefore admission of testimony concerning defendant's initial disclosure of theft constituted reversible error), *with* United States v. Parker, 834 F.2d 408, 413 (4th Cir. 1988) ("the policy considerations that support the joint criminal participation exception are equally implicated where from the very outset—as in this case—the spouse is told about the intended kidnapping and murder and she agrees to assist her husband").

[12] *See, e.g.,* Pereira v. United States, 347 U.S. 1, 6, 74 S. Ct. 358, 98 L. Ed. 435 (1954).

[13] *See, e.g.,* Wolfle v. United States, 291 U.S. 7, 54 S. Ct. 279, 78 L. Ed. 617 (1934) (no privilege for letter to wife dictated to stenographer); United States v. Crouthers, 669 F.2d 635, 642 (10th Cir. 1982) (presence of third parties destroys confidentiality). *See also* New England Mut. Life Ins. Co. v. Anderson, 888 F.2d 646, 651 (10th Cir. 1989) (trial court properly applied marital privilege to bar husband's testimony about defendant's statements made in interview with newspaper reporter, at which husband was present, where husband stated that he could not recall interview sufficiently to distinguish wife's statements at interview from those she made to him in confidence).

[14] *See, e.g.,* Pereira v. United States, 347 U.S. 1, 6, 74 S. Ct. 358, 98 L. Ed. 435 (1954) (intention that information be transmitted to a third person negatives presumption of confidentiality).

testify as to its contents, although others may testify about the same subject.[15]

[a] Exceptions

Certain exceptions may apply which preclude reliance on the privilege even when the three prerequisites of valid marriage, communication, and confidential intent are met. Some courts permit an eavesdropper to testify on the ground that such testimony has no effect on one spouse's trust in the other.[16] By analogy to Standard 503, however, it would probably be best to exclude eavesdropper testimony, particularly if it is of a type difficult to guard against. Even courts that apply an eavesdropper exception might bar testimony where the eavesdropper learns "of a marital confidence through a spouse's betrayal or connivance."[17] In such a case, where one spouse actively assists the eavesdropper in obtaining the information in order to use it against the other spouse, the privilege should apply because the consequence of permitting the testimony is the very undermining of marital trust which the rule of privilege seeks to prevent.

Most circuits have held pursuant to Rule 501 that the government may compel testimony about confidential communications involving future or ongoing crimes in which the spouses were joint participants at the time of the communications.[18] These courts

---

[15] *See, e.g.,* Hipes v. United States, 603 F.2d 786, 788 n.1 (9th Cir. 1979) (fact that other employees could testify about husband's job responsibilities did not mean that wife was required to answer questions before a grand jury about her husband's job).

[16] *See* United States v. Neal, 532 F. Supp. 942 (D. Colo. 1982), *cert. denied,* 105 S. Ct. 1848 (1985).

[17] *Id.* at 949.

[18] *First Circuit:* United States v. Picciandra, 788 F.2d 39 (1st Cir.), *cert. denied,* 479 U.S. 847, 107 S. Ct. 166, 93 L. Ed. 2d 104 (1986); *Second Circuit:* United States v. Estes, 793 F.2d 465, 467 (2d Cir. 1986); *Third Circuit:* United States v. Ammar, 714 F.2d 238 (3d Cir.), *cert. denied,* 464 U.S. 936 (1983); *Fourth Circuit:* United States v. Broome, 732 F.2d 363, 365 (4th Cir.), *cert. denied,* 105 S. Ct. 181 (1984); *Fifth Circuit:* United States v. Mendoze, 574 F.2d 1372 (5th Cir.), *cert. denied,* 439 U.S. 988 (1978); *Sixth Circuit:* United States v. Sims, 755 F.2d 1239 (6th Cir.), *cert. denied,* 105 S. Ct. 3533 (1985); *Seventh Circuit:* United States v. Kahn, 471 F.2d 191, 194–95 (7th Cir. 1972), *rev'd on other grounds,* 415 U.S. 143 (1974).

reason that the benefits to be served by recognizing the privilege are outweighed by the public interest in ascertaining the truth and achieving justice in such circumstances. In this regard, the Third Circuit has drawn a distinction between the two marital privileges. It has refused to apply a joint participation exception to the testimonial privilege, because the privilege is concerned with the impact of judicially-compelled testimony on a marriage, but it has recognized that joint participation destroys the confidential communications privilege, because communications regarding ongoing or future crimes do not deserve protection.[19] The exception should be narrowly applied "to permit admission of only those conversations that pertain to patently illegal activities."[20]

As the discussion above indicates, the federal courts have recognized exceptions to the testimonial privilege when the testimony concerns injuries by one spouse to the other or to their children. Policy reasons would dictate the recognition of the same exceptions for the marital communications privilege.

¶ 18.04[03]   Summary of the Marital Privileges

As the foregoing discussion indicates, there are several differences between the testimonial and the communications privileges in terms of applicability and prerequisites for assertion. These differences reflect the different purposes of the privileges. Thus, the communications privilege applies only to communications between spouses made in confidence during a valid marriage; the testimonial privilege on the other hand, applies to all testimony against a spouse on any subject, including non-confidential matters. As indicated above, the courts are split on whether the testimonial privilege should apply to testimony about events predating the marriage. The testimonial privilege may not be asserted after the marriage has terminated, while the communications privilege, like other privileges intended to encourage confidences, survives the termination of the relationship. The communications privilege may be asserted by either spouse in both civil

---

[19] *See* United States v. Ammar, 714 F.2d 238 (3d Cir.), *cert. denied,* 464 U.S. 936 (1983).

[20] United States v. Sims, 755 F.2d 1239, 1243 (6th Cir.), *cert. denied,* 105 S. Ct. 3533 (1985).

and criminal proceedings, while the testimonial privilege may only be claimed by a testifying spouse, and is recognized only in criminal proceedings. More courts have been willing to recognize a joint participation exception to the confidential communications privilege than to the testimonial privilege.

¶ 18.05   Secrets of State and Other Official Information — Standard 509

¶ 18.05[01]   Scope of Rule

Standard 509 deals with two related, but separate privileges: an absolute privilege for diplomatic or military secrets, and a qualified privilege for official information. Although these privileges rest on constitutional grounds,[1] the courts have frequently used an evidentiary analysis and side-stepped the constitutional issues. Standard 509 therefore remains a useful guide for assessing privilege claims, since it substantially codified previous practice in the federal courts.[2] The Standard provides:

Supreme Court Standard 509

SECRETS OF STATE AND OTHER OFFICIAL INFORMATION

(a) Definitions.

(1) Secret of state. — A "secret of state" is a governmental secret relating to the national defense or the international relations of the United States.

(2) Official information. — "Official information" is information within the custody or control of a department or agency of the government the disclosure of which is shown to be contrary to the

---

[1] *See* United States v. Nixon, 418 U.S. 683, 94 S. Ct. 3090, 41 L. Ed. 2d 1039 (1974).

[2] Congressional and public reaction to proposed Rule 509 was extremely negative because the rule reached Congress just as the Watergate affair was unfolding and it was erroneously feared that the rule expanded executive prerogatives. See discussion in **Treatise** on Congressional Action on Standard 509, and at ¶ 509[02]. For a discussion of the views of the Department of Justice prior to the submission of the proposed rule to Congress *see* **Treatise** at ¶ 509[01].

public interest and which consists of: (A) intragovernmental opinions or recommendations submitted for consideration in the performance of decisional or policymaking functions, or (B) subject to the provisions of 18 U.S.C. § 3500, investigatory files compiled for law enforcement purposes and not otherwise available, or (C) information within the custody or control of a governmental department or agency whether initiated within the department or agency or acquired by it in its exercise of its official responsibilities and not otherwise available to the public pursuant to 5 U.S.C. § 552.

(b) General rule of privilege. — The government has a privilege to refuse to give evidence and to prevent any person from giving evidence upon a showing of reasonable likelihood of danger that the evidence will disclose a secret of state or official information as defined in this rule.

(c) Procedures. — The privilege for secrets of state may be claimed only by the chief officer of the government agency or department administering the subject matter which the secret information sought concerns, but the privilege for official information may be asserted by any attorney representing the government. The required showing may be made in whole or in part in the form of a written statement. The judge may hear the matter in chambers, but all counsel are entitled to inspect the claim and showing and to be heard thereon, except that, in the case of secrets of state, the judge upon motion of the government, may permit the government to make the required showing in the above form *in camera.* If the judge sustains the privilege upon a showing *in camera,* the entire text of the government's statements shall be sealed and preserved in the court's records in the event of appeal. In the case of privilege claimed for official information the court may require examination *in camera* of the information itself. The judge may take any protective measure which the interests of the government and the furtherance of justice may require.

(d) Notice to government. — If the circumstances of the case indicate a substantial possibility that a claim of privilege would be appropriate but has not been made because of oversight or lack of knowledge, the judge shall give or cause notice to be given to the officer entitled to claim the privilege and shall stay further proceedings a reasonable time to afford opportunity to assert a claim of privilege.

(e) Effect of sustaining claim. — If a claim of privilege is sustained in a proceeding to which the government is a party and it appears that another party is thereby deprived of material evidence, the judge shall make any further orders which the interests of justice require, including striking the testimony of a witness, declaring a mistrial, finding against the government upon an issue as to which the evidence is relevant, or dismissing the action.

¶ 18.05[02]   The Privilege for State Secrets[1]

Rule 509 defines a "secret of state" as a "governmental secret relating to the national defense or the international relations of the United States." The existence of a testimonial privilege against revealing military secrets has long been recognized.[2] While a privilege for secrets relating to international relations or diplomatic secrecy is generally acknowledged, litigation involving purely diplomatic secrets is unlikely to arise. Cases in which the claim is raised will undoubtedly involve issues of national defense as well.

The rationale for the privilege is obvious: the danger of harm to the nation outweighs any public or private interest in truthful and efficient fact-finding in an individual litigation. The privilege applies once the government makes "a showing of reasonable likelihood that the evidence will disclose a secret of state."

Rule 509 spells out some of the procedures for making the privilege claim. Consistently with the Supreme Court's decision in *United States v. Reynolds,*[3] it requires the claim to be asserted by the chief officer of the agency or department in charge of the matter to which the secret information relates.

The suggestion in Standard 509(c) that the required showing may be in writing, in whole or in part, conforms with the Supreme Court's approval of a "formal claim." It is hoped that in the

---

[1] *See* **Treatise** at ¶¶ 509[02]–[04].

[2] *See, e.g.,* United States v. Burr, 25 F.Cas. 30 (No. 14,692), 187 (No. 14,694) (C.C.D. Va. 1807); Totten v. United States, 92 U.S. 105, 23 L. Ed. 605 (1875); United States v. Reynolds, 345 U.S. 1, 73 S. Ct. 528, 97 L. Ed. 727 (1953). *Cf.* Guong v. United States, 860 F.2d 1063 (Fed. Cir. 1988) (complaint for breach of contract with CIA dismissed, since claimant could not prevail without revealing state secrets).

[3] 345 U.S. 1, 7–8, 73 S. Ct. 528, 97 L. Ed. 727 (1953) ("[T]he privilege belongs to the Government and must be asserted by it; it can neither be claimed nor waived by a private party. It is not to be lightly invoked. There must be a formal claim of privilege, lodged by the head of the department which has control over the matter, after actual personal consideration by that officer.").

course of committing its showing to paper, the executive will have to give careful consideration to the reasons underlying the claim. Standard 509(c) specifically provides that the judge, on motion by the government, may permit the showing to be made *in camera.*

Standard 509 is silent, however, about whether the judge can require the government to produce *in camera* the materials as to which the privilege claim is asserted, or whether the judge must honor the executive's claim of privilege once the government has shown that the information sought would contain state secrets. The silence of Rule 509 is attributable to the state of the law at the time it was drafted. The Supreme Court in its cases to date had equivocated on the power of a court to examine the materials sought to be protected, probably because of an unexpressed apprehension that it is unseemly for the judiciary to be privy to matters which are explicitly made the concern of the executive by the Constitution.[4] In its decision in *United States v. Nixon,*[5] however, which was handed down after Congress had deleted the subject matter of Standard 509 from inclusion in the Federal Rules of Evidence, the Court, in dictum, contemplated the possibility of *in camera* review even when state secrets are involved.[6]

Since *Nixon,* the federal courts have reviewed materials *in camera* to determine whether claims of state privilege should be upheld.[7] The *Reynolds* case suggests that a court should honor

---

[4] See discussion of United States v. Reynolds, 345 U.S. 1, 73 S. Ct. 528, 97 L. Ed. 727 (1953) in **Treatise** at ¶ 509[04].

[5] 418 U.S. 683, 94 S. Ct. 3090, 41 L. Ed. 2d 1039 (1974). See discussion in **Treatise** at ¶ 509[11].

[6] The last footnote of the opinion speaks of district judges examining material *in camera* in order to consider "the validity of particular excisions, whether the basis of excision is relevancy or admissibility under such cases as *United States v. Reynolds.*" *Id.,* 418 U.S. at 715, n.21. *Reynolds* is clearly a state secrets case, but the Court's comments in *Nixon* are dicta since the Court notes at three separate points that no claim of state or military secrets was made. *Id.,* 418 U.S. at 710–11.

[7] *See, e.g.,* Ellsberg v. Mitchell, 709 F.2d 51 (D.C. Cir. 1983), *cert. denied,* 465 U.S. 1038 (1984); Jabara v. Webster, 691 F.2d 272, 274 (6th Cir. 1982), *cert. denied,* 464 U.S. 863 (1983); National Lawyers Guild v. Attorney General, 96 F.R.D. 390, 399–401 (S.D.N.Y. 1982).

a privilege claim without further probing when the party that seeks the information as to which the privilege claim is asserted is unable to make a showing of necessity.[8] When a strong showing of necessity is made, the court may refuse to examine the materials *in camera* unless the government meets its burden of showing that the national security is endangered.[9] The Classified Information Procedures Act sets forth the procedures that a trial court must follow in ruling on questions of the admissibility of classified information in criminal cases.[10]

The consequences of a successful claim of state privilege are discussed below.

¶ 18.05[03]   The Privilege for Official Information[1]

Standard 509 accords a qualified privilege to nine categories of information defined as "official information" in subdivision (a)(2). Unfortunately, Standard 509 is of only limited use as a guide in determining what types of governmental information fall within this qualified privilege. That is because its drafters chose to define "official information" by reference to the Freedom of Information Act.[2] The Freedom of Information Act enables members of the public to obtain disclosure of governmental

----

[8] In *Reynolds,* 345 U.S. 1, 73 S. Ct. 528, 97 L. Ed. 727 (1953), widows of civilians killed in the crash of a military aircraft testing secret electronic equipment sued under the Federal Torts Claims Act. The Court stated, "[i]n each case, the showing of necessity which is made will determine how far the court should probe in satisfying itself that the occasion for invoking the privilege is appropriate." The Court found "a dubious showing of necessity" because "[t]here is nothing to suggest that the electronic equipment, in this case, had any causal connection with the accident." 345 U.S. at 11.

[9] *See* Ellsberg v. Mitchell, 709 F.2d 51 (D.C. Cir. 1983), *cert. denied,* 465 U.S. 1038 (1984).

[10] *See* **Treatise** at ¶ 509[11a] for provisions of the Act. The Act defines "classified information" as "information or material that has been determined by the United States Government pursuant to an Executive order, statute, or regulation, to require protection against unauthorized disclosure for reasons of national security and any restricted data, as defined in paragraph r. of section 11 of the Atomic Energy Act of 1954 (42 U.S.C. § 2014(y)) (18 U.S.C. App. ¶ 1).

[1] *See* **Treatise** at ¶¶ 509[05]–[11].

[2] 5 U.S.C. § 552.

information without making any showing of particularized need. The Act has, however, a number of exceptions which at the time Standard 509 was drafted were couched in terms of an evidentiary privilege. This convoluted draftsmanship in Standard 509 meant that the scope of the privilege had to be determined by reference to the Act, but the scope of disclosure then had to be measured by judicial opinions predating the Standard which had construed the common law privilege for governmental information.

Aside from the problems caused by the drafting of Standard 509, recent decisions of the Supreme Court strongly suggest that the authorization for barring disclosure in a litigated context will in each instance have its origin in a source outside the Freedom of Information Act since the Act is exclusively a disclosure statute.[3] Consequently, defining disclosure in terms of the categories of the Act as Standard 509 does is unhelpful. This is especially so since Exemptions 3 and 7 have been amended to make them function independently of standards of disclosure applicable to litigants. Nevertheless, counsel should be aware that the governmental evidentiary privilege is so intertwined with the Freedom of Information Act that requests for information brought under the Act may be resolved by case law construing the privilege, and litigants may rely on Freedom of Information Act cases when they dispute the applicability of an evidentiary governmental privilege.[4]

Standard 509 is of some use to litigants who face a claim of governmental privilege. The two main categories which give rise to privilege claims—intragovernmental communications and investigatory files—are singled out for special treatment, and the other FOIA exemptions incorporated into the Standard operate as a useful checklist when considering other possible governmental privilege claims. Furthermore, the Standard indicates the qualified nature of the privilege. The privilege applies only if the government can make a showing that disclosure would be "contrary to the public interest." A court is authorized to admit official

[3] Chrysler Corp. v. Brown, 441 U.S. 281, 99 S. Ct. 1705, 60 L. Ed. 2d 208 (1979) (Court relied on Trade Secrets Act rather than Freedom on Information Act to prohibit disclosure of information).

[4] See, e.g., United States v. Weber Aircraft Corp., 465 U.S. 792, 104 S. Ct. 1488, 79 L. Ed. 2d 814 (1984) (Exemption 5 of FOIA incorporates civil discovery privilege).

information if in the particular case the public's interest in the correct determination of the truth outweighs the public's interest in effective governmental operations. This balancing approach of Standard 509 is fully compatible with the Supreme Court's decision in *United States v. Nixon*.[5]

[a] Procedures for Claiming Privilege

Some of the procedures specified in Standard 509 for asserting the privilege must be viewed with caution. According to the Standard, the privilege may be asserted by any attorney representing the government. However, some courts have required that the claim of privilege be invoked by the head of the agency after personal consideration of the matter;[6] the head may delegate this responsibility to a subordinate, but only after issuing guidelines on the use of the privilege.[7]

Standard 509(d) gives the trial court the responsibility of notifying the government if there is "a substantial possibility that a claim of privilege would be appropriate but has not been made because of oversight or lack of knowledge." The court must then stay further proceedings a reasonable time so that the claim can be made.

Because the trial court must ascertain whether the public interest in non-disclosure is paramount before ruling on the applicability of the privilege, it necessarily has a good deal of discretion in how it requires the parties to develop the specific relevant factors which must be balanced in the particular case. The government may make its showing in whole or in part in a written statement, which all parties may inspect together with the statement of claim. The claim must describe with some specificity the information alleged to be privileged and state the

---

[5] 418 U.S. 683, 713, 94 S. Ct. 3090, 41 L. Ed. 2d 1039 (1974) (Supreme Court recognized that a privilege for presidential communications is constitutionally grounded but not absolute, and that it must yield upon a showing of "demonstrated, specific need for evidence in a pending criminal trial."). See discussion in **Treatise** at ¶ 509[11].

[6] *See, e.g.,* United States v. O'Neill, 619 F.2d 222 (3d Cir. 1980) (procedures should be the same as for state secret privilege).

[7] Exxon Corp. v. Dept of Energy, 91 F.R.D. 26, 43 (N.D. Tex. 1981); Mobil Oil Corp. v. Dept of Energy, 520 F. Supp. 414, 416 (N.D.N.Y. 1981).

reasons for preserving its confidentiality.[8] If the court finds that this provides insufficient information on which to rule, it may order the parties to produce additional information at a hearing. See subdivision (c) of Standard 509.

The hearing should be held in chambers so that in a jury case the jurors are not apprised of the claim, and to insure that sensitive government information is not made public. On the basis of this hearing the court may decide that it cannot determine the privilege claim without first examining in camera the materials as to which the claim was asserted.[9] The court must consider the particular facts of the case in deciding whether the government has made an adequate showing that it is entitled to the privilege. On the one hand, the court must examine such factors as the relevancy of the evidence,[10] the availability of other evidence,[11] the status of the litigant, and the nature of the case.[12] On the other hand, the court must determine to what extent disclosure of the information sought would undermine the policies protected by the privilege.[13]

After the in camera examination, the court may "take any protective measure which the interests of the government and the

---

[8] *See, e.g., In re* "Agent Orange" Product Liability Litigation, 97 F.R.D. 427 (E.D.N.Y. 1983).

[9] *See, e.g.,* Black v. Sheraton Corp. of America, 564 F.2d 531 (D.C. Cir. 1977) (court should have ordered in camera hearing where showing did not indicate which items were privileged but did justify in camera analysis); *In re* Franklin National Bank Securities Litigation, 478 F. Supp. 577 (E.D.N.Y. 1979) (handling of claim usually requires in camera inspection). *See also* Carl Zeiss Stiftung v. V.E.B. Carl Zeiss, Jena, 40 F.R.D. 318 (D.D.C. 1966), *aff'd on opinion below,* 384 F.2d 979 (D.C. Cir.), *cert. denied,* 389 U.S. 952 (1967).

[10] *See, e.g.,* United States v. American Telephone and Telegraph Co., 524 F. Supp. 1381, 1386–87 (D.D.C. 1981) (reasons individual members of FCC had for decisions were irrelevant to issue of whether defendant's compliance was reasonable).

[11] *Id.* (court balances interest in non-disclosure with defendants' need for evidence).

[12] Need may be greater in a criminal than in a civil case. *See* United States v. Nixon, 418 U.S. 683, 94 S. Ct. 3090, 41 L. Ed. 2d 1039 (1974).

[13] *See, e.g.,* Machin v. Zuckert, 316 F.2d 336, 337–38 (D.C. Cir.), *cert. denied,* 375 U.S. 896 (1963) (prohibiting disclosure of investigatory reports obtained under promise of confidentiality because efficiency of important government program might be hampered, but allowing disclosure of mechanics' factual reports which would be unaffected by promises of confidentiality).

furtherance of justice may require." It may, for instance, order the separation of internal opinions and recommendations which figured in the government's decision making process from purely factual findings and confine disclosure to the latter;[14] it may order the excision of the names of informants,[15] or that certain information only be made available to particular persons.[16] The court should make its protective orders "keeping in mind the issues of the case, the nature and importance of the interests supporting the claim of privilege, and the fundamental policy of free societies that justice is usually promoted by disclosure rather than secrecy."[17]

[b] Intragovernmental Opinions or Recommendations

Standard 509(a)(2)(A) restates a common law privilege[18] which will be accorded recognition pursuant to Rule 501.[19] The privilege recognizes that participants in governmental policy-making will not feel free to express their opinions fully and candidly when they fear that their views will be made public.[20] Purely factual material does not partake of the rationale for the privilege because its disclosure "would not hinder the flow of advice in any

---

[14] *See, e.g.,* Machin v. Zuckert, 316 F.2d 336, 340–41 (D.C. Cir.), *cert. denied,* 370 U.S. 896 (1963).

[15] *See, e.g.,* Olsen v. Camp, 328 F. Supp. 728, 732 (E.D. Mich. 1969).

[16] *Id.*

[17] Boeing Airplane Co. v. Coggeshall, 280 F.2d 654, 662 (D.C. Cir. 1960).

[18] Environment Protection Agency v. Mink, 410 U.S. 73, 86, 93 S. Ct. 827, 35 L. Ed. 2d 119 (1973), *superseded on other grounds by* Pub. L. 93-502, 88 Stat. 1561 (1974) ("the recognized rule that 'confidential intra-agency advisory opinions . . . are privileged from inspection' "); United States v. Weber Aircraft Corp., 465 U.S. 792, 104 S. Ct. 1488, 79 L. Ed. 2d 814 (1984).

[19] Whether intergovernmental communications are also qualifiedly privileged will also have to be decided pursuant to Rule 501. Standard 509 is silent about such communications but *cf.* Standard 510.

[20] Mobil Oil Corp. v. Department of Energy, 520 F. Supp. 414, 416 (N.D.N.Y. 1981) (purpose of privilege "is to encourage frank discussion of ideas and policies"; such discussions "would be inhibited were the participants to expect that their remarks would be disseminated publicly. . . . Thus, by protecting from disclosure the ebb and flow of the deliberative process, the pre-decisional privilege seeks to ensure the quality of governmental decision-making.").

decision-making process."[21] Standard 509 acknowledges this fact-opinion dichotomy by limiting this category of official information to "intragovernmental opinions or recommendations." A conclusion that does not go into the making of policy decisions and resolutions is not immune from discovery, because it is not "submitted for consideration in the performance of policy making functions."[22]

A memorandum embodying the final conclusion of the agency, and cited as the basis for the agency's action, does not require protection, so long as disclosure would not reveal the processes by which the decision was reached.[23] It is the decision-making process which requires shielding from public scrutiny, not the decision itself once it has been acted upon.

It must be remembered that this privilege is qualified. Disclosure of intragovernmental opinions or recommendations reflecting policy-making processes may be required in a given case because the scales tipped in favor of disclosure when the public

---

[21] Consumers Union of United States, Inc. v. Veterans Administration, 301 F. Supp. 796, 806 (1969), *dismissed as moot after full disclosure by government,* 436 F.2d 1363 (2d Cir. 1971); Environment Protection Agency v. Mink, 410 U.S. 73, 87–88, 89 n.16, 93 S. Ct. 827, 35 L. Ed. 2d 119 (1973), *superseded on other grounds by* Pub. L. 93-502, 88 Stat. 1561 (1974) ("memoranda consisting only of compiled factual material or purely factual material contained in deliberative memoranda and severable from its context would generally be available for discovery by private parties in litigation with the Government. . . . The proposed Federal Rules of Evidence appear to recognize this construction of Exception 5.").

[22] *Cf. In re* Grand Jury, 821 F.2d 946 (3d Cir. 1987), *cert. denied,* 108 S. Ct. 749 (1988) (although the court rejected a qualified speech or debate privilege for state legislators, it suggested a narrower deliberative privilege for confidential deliberative communications involving opinions, recommendations or advice about legislative decisions).

[23] *See* N.L.R.B. v. Sears Roebuck & Co., 421 U.S. 132, 151–52, 95 S. Ct. 1504, 44 L. Ed. 2d 29 (1975) ("it is difficult to see how the quality of a decision will be affected by communications with respect to the decision occurring after the decision is finally reached; and therefore equally difficult to see how the quality of the decision will be affected by forced disclosure of such communications, as long as prior communications and the ingredients of the decisionmaking process are not disclosed").

interest in effective governmental functioning was weighed against the public interest in accurate judicial determinations.[24]

[c] Investigatory Files Compiled for Law Enforcement Purposes

Standard 509(a)(2)(B) recognizes that there may be a qualified privilege for investigatory reports compiled for law enforcement purposes and not otherwise available. The premature disclosure of such reports could seriously hamper effective law enforcement.[25]

The rationale for non-disclosure does not apply if there is no prospect of law enforcement proceedings in which the investigative material will be germane,[26] or if the government's action has already been taken.[27] Some parts of the file may nevertheless

---

[24] *See* McClelland v. Andrus, 606 F.2d 1278, 1287, n.54 (D.C. Cir. 1979) (appropriate for the court to consider the litigant's need for the material); Bank of Dearborn v. Saxon, 244 F. Supp. 394, 402–03 (E.D. Mich. 1965), *aff'd,* 377 F.2d 496 (6th Cir. 1967) ("the real public interest under such circumstances is not the agency's interest in its administration but the citizen's interest in due process"); Timken Roller Bearing Co. v. United States, 38 F.R.D. 57 (N.D. Ohio 1964) (action for refund of alleged overpayment of taxes; court decided that in circumstances of case documents must be produced by government even though they would presumably reveal criteria by which commissioner assessed deficiency); Olsen Rug Company v. N.L.R.B., 291 F.2d 655, 661–62 (7th Cir. 1961) (even document containing policy recommendations is subject to disclosure when it bears on factual issue of defense to unfair labor charge).

[25] *See* Ferri v. Bell, 645 F.2d 1213 (3d Cir. 1981), *modified,* 671 F.2d 769 (3d Cir. 1982); Murphy v. FBI, 490 F. Supp. 1138 (D.D.C. 1980); Lamont v. Dep't of Justice, 475 F. Supp. 761 (S.D.N.Y. 1979). *Cf. In re* Department of Investigation, 856 F.2d 481, 486 (2d Cir. 1988) (material compiled in official investigation into city commissioner's fitness to continue in office was protected from disclosure, since materials were closely connected with simultaneous criminal investigation).

[26] *See, e.g.,* Frankenhauser v. Rizzo, 59 F.R.D. 339, 345 (E.D. Pa. 1973) (no need for privilege where over two years had elapsed since completion of the investigation, no criminal charges or interdepartmental disciplinary actions had resulted, and no party seeking discovery was a potential defendant in a criminal case).

[27] Wood v. Brier, 54 F.R.D. 7, 11–12 (E.D. Wis. 1972) ("once the investigation and prosecution have been completed discovery should be permitted").

remain privileged even if the investigation is closed or no enforcement proceedings are contemplated.[28] The file may, for instance, contain intragovernmental opinions or recommendations of the type barred by Standard 509(a)(2)(C), or the litigant may seek information which would be barred by the informer's privilege.

Even if the files relate to an investigation in which law enforcement is current or imminent, the privilege applies only when disclosure would be contrary to the public interest.[29]

[d] Other Governmental Information Exempted From Disclosure By the Freedom of Information Act[30]

Standard 509(a)(2)(C) is the catch-all provision that incorporated the remaining exemptions in the Freedom of Information Act,[31] not treated elsewhere, into the qualified privilege created for official information by Standard 509.

¶ 18.05[04] Effect of Sustaining Claim of Privilege for State Secrets or Official Information[1]

There are four categories of situations in which the consequences of a successful claim of privilege may be raised: (1) proceedings to which the government is not a party; (2) criminal proceedings instituted by the government; (3) civil proceedings instituted by the government, and (4) civil proceedings against the government.

Standard 509(e) is silent about the first category of case in which the government resists disclosure although it is not a party.

---

[28] Black v. Sheraton Corp. of America, 564 F.2d 531, 546 (D.C. Cir. 1977) (few would respond candidly to investigators if their remarks would become public after proceeding).

[29] See, e.g., Denver Policeman's Protective Association v. Lichtenstein, 660 F.2d 432, 437–38 (10th Cir. 1981) (police investigatory file sought by defendant for purpose of discovering exculpatory evidence not absolutely privileged where governmental interest in confidentiality outweighed by defendant's need).

[30] See Treatise at ¶ 509[08].

[31] The exemptions in the Freedom of Information Act, 5 U.S.C.A. § 552(b) have been amended a number of times since Standard 509 was drafted.

[1] See discussion in Treatise at ¶ 509[10].

The usual consequences are those that ordinarily occur when there is a loss of evidence, such as a dismissal if the plaintiff is unable to make out a prima facie case without the evidence. There may, however, be instances where the danger of revealing privileged information in the course of trying to establish a prima facie case may be sufficient to cause a dismissal.[2]

In the other three categories of cases, the drafters of Standard 509(e) recognized that the range of possibilities was too great to allow for a fixed rule because of the variety of ways in which privileged information may be relevant. In a criminal case, the documents suppressed may bear so directly upon a substantive element of the case that dismissal of the action is the only appropriate response if the government persists in non-disclosure.[3] On the other hand, if the material not produced is Jencks Act[4] material, the court is directed to strike the testimony of the witness and let the trial proceed unless "the interests of justice require that a mistrial be declared." Privileged materials may also bear on collateral matters such as the validity of an arrest or of a search and seizure. In all these instances, the trial court has discretion to tailor its order as justice requires.

Civil cases by or against the government also present a wide variety of situations. At one end of the spectrum are cases where the government is seeking to punish the defendant or regulate his activities and the claim of privilege prevents the defendant from obtaining facts essential to his defense. This situation may have to be handled on analogy to a criminal case. On the other hand, if the government is suing in a proprietary capacity, there may be less unfairness in allowing the successful claim of privilege to deprive the defendant of some useful information. Exactly how unfair—and what the trial court should consequently do—will depend on the particular facts of the case, such as the purposes

---

[2] Farnsworth Cannon, Inc. v. Grimes, 635 F.2d 268, 282 (4th Cir. 1980) (en banc court concluded that plaintiff's attempt to make out prima facie case would so threaten revelation of state secrets that in the overriding interest of the United States complaint should be dismissed).

[3] See, e.g., United States v. Andolschek, 142 F.2d 503 (2d Cir. 1944).

[4] 18 U.S.C. § 3500(d).

for which the information is sought, the consequences to the parties and the availability of other evidence.[5]

Generally, the plaintiff will be unable to make out a case because of the subsequent lack of evidence only if the privileged information is crucial to his cause of action and involves a state secret. If the information sought is classified as official information, the plaintiff's need will often result in the court ordering disclosure, although the plaintiff may have to wait until the active phase of an investigation is over when investigatory files are sought.

¶ 18.06 Identity of Informer—Standard 510

¶ 18.06[01] Scope of Privilege

Standard 510 recognizes that the government has a privilege not to disclose the identity[1] of a person who has furnished a law enforcement officer or member of a legislative committee or its staff with information relevant "to an investigation of a possible

[5] See, e.g., Attorney General of the United States v. Irish People, Inc., 684 F.2d 928, 949–55 (D.C. Cir. 1982), cert. denied, 459 U.S. 1172 (1983) (in action to compel defendant to register under Foreign Agents Registration Act defendant claimed selective prosecution and government claimed state secrets privilege as to certain documents defendant sought to support defense; district court dismissed action; appellate court reversed and remanded, holding that district court must balance the possibility of exculpation, the likelihood that privileged documents would exculpate defendant, the need for the documents, the government's interest in secrecy and in maintaining the action, what the defendant stands to lose, the availability of court orders other than dismissal or disclosure, and the parties' respective behavior; court suggested that dismissal was probably improper where likelihood of injustice to defendant was small and adverse consequences of disclosure would be great while alternatives were available such as requiring government stipulations as to some facts, or having district court look at files and marshal evidence on both sides). See discussion in In re United States, 872 F.2d 472 (D.C. Cir. 1989).

[1] The Advisory Committee's notes to Standard 510(a) state: "Only identity is privileged; communications are not included except to the extent that disclosure would operate also to disclose the informer's identity." Usually, of course, the informer expects the communication to be used, but at times, witnesses might be unwilling to cooperate in an investigation unless the confidentiality of their communications were assured. Cf. Standard 509(a)(2)(B).

violation of law."[2] The privilege is applicable in civil[3] as well as in criminal cases, and may be claimed not only by federal law enforcement officers[4] but also by state law enforcement agencies and their subdivisions.[5] The privilege is subject to two qualifications set forth in Standard 510(c). First, the privilege ceases once the identity of the informer is disclosed "to those who would have cause to resent the communication."[6] Second, the trial judge, on motion of the accused, must dismiss the charge if the government elects not to disclose the identity of an informer whom the judge has found reasonably likely to give testimony necessary to a fair determination of the issue of guilt or innocence. See discussion below.

Standard 510 provides:

Supreme Court Standard 510

IDENTITY OF INFORMER

(a) Rule of privilege. — The government or a state or subdivision thereof has a privilege to refuse to disclose the identity of a person who has furnished information relating to or assisting in an investigation of a possible violation of law to a law enforcement officer or member of a legislative committee or its staff conducting an investigation.

(b) Who may claim. — The privilege may be claimed by an appropriate representative of the government, regardless of whether the information was furnished to an officer of the government or of a state or subdivision thereof. The privilege may be claimed by an appropriate representative of a state or subdivision if the

---

[2] See **Treatise** at ¶¶ 510[01], [03] for discussion of why this formula was adopted by the Advisory Committee.

[3] See, e.g., Dole v. Local 1942, Int'l Bhd. of Elec. Workers, 870 F.2d 368 (7th Cir. 1989). See also discussion of civil cases in **Treatise** at ¶ 510[05].

[4] Ordinarily, government counsel will be the appropriate representative to claim the privilege, but in some situations the police officer who is being questioned may appropriately make the claim. See, e.g., Bocchicchio v. Curtis Publishing Co., 203 F. Supp. 403 (E.D. Pa. 1962).

[5] This provision furthers the rationale of the privilege because it is unrealistic to assume that informers distinguish between various governmental entities when furnishing information. In a criminal case, the federal government may, if it wishes, veto a local claim of privilege.

[6] See **Treatise** at ¶ 510[04].

information was furnished to an officer thereof, except that in criminal cases the privilege shall not be allowed if the government objects.

(c) Exceptions.

(1) Voluntary disclosure; informer a witness.—No privilege exists under this rule if the identify of the informer or his interest in the subject matter of his communication has been disclosed to those who would have cause to resent the communication by a holder of the privilege or by the informer's own action, or if the informer appears as a witness for the government.

(2) Testimony on merits.—If it appears from the evidence in the case or from other showing by a party that an informer may be able to give testimony necessary to a fair determination of the issue of guilt or innocence in a criminal case or of a material issue on the merits in a civil case to which the government is a party, and the government invokes the privilege, the judge shall give the government an opportunity to show in camera facts relevant to determining whether the informer can, in fact, supply that testimony. The showing will ordinarily be in the form of affidavits, but the judge may direct that testimony be taken if he finds that the matter cannot be resolved satisfactorily upon affidavit. If the judge finds that there is a reasonable probability that the informer can give the testimony, and the government elects not to disclose his identity, the judge on motion of the defendant in a criminal case shall dismiss the charges to which the testimony would relate, and the judge may do so on his own motion. In civil cases, he may make any order that justice requires. Evidence submitted to the judge shall be sealed and preserved to be made available to the appellate court in the event of an appeal, and the contents shall not otherwise be revealed without consent of the government. All counsel and parties shall be permitted to be present at every stage of proceedings under this subdivision except a showing in camera, at which no counsel or party shall be permitted to be present.

(3) Legality of obtaining evidence.—If information from an informer is relied upon to establish the legality of the means by which evidence was obtained and the judge is not satisfied that the information was received from an informer reasonably believed to be reliable or credible, he may require the identity of the informer to be disclosed. The judge shall, on request of the government, direct that the disclosure be made in camera. All counsel and parties concerned with the issue of legality shall be permitted to be present at every stage of proceedings under this subdivision except a disclosure in camera, at which no counsel or party shall be permitted to

be present. If disclosure of the identity of the informer is made in camera, the record thereof shall be sealed and preserved to be made available to the appellate court in the event of an appeal, and the contents shall not otherwise be revealed without consent of the government.

¶ 18.06[02]   Rationale [1]

Standard 510 is in accord with the views of commentators and courts—even those most reluctant to recognize any obstruction to the production of all relevant evidence—that a genuine privilege exists for the identity of persons supplying the government with information concerning possible violations of law.[2] Informers require a guarantee of anonymity.

> [I]t has been the experience of law enforcement officers that the prospective informer will usually condition his cooperation on an assurance of anonymity, fearing that if disclosure is made, physical harm or other undesirable consequences may be visited upon him or his family. By withholding the identity of the informer, the government profits in that the continued value of informants placed in strategic positions is protected, and other persons are encouraged to cooperate in the administration of justice.[3]

The government relies heavily on communications from informants in detecting criminal activity, particularly in cases involving narcotics offenses, liquor law violations and sexual crimes where an aggrieved victim rarely steps forward. Compared to the speculative benefits of, for instance, the privilege for communications between attorney and client, the importance of protecting an informer's identity can be statistically corroborated. An alarming number of government informers are murdered each year. While the consequences of disclosure may not be drastic in all criminal cases, or in civil cases, the likelihood of social ostracism, employer retaliation or malicious prosecution suits is

---

[1] *See* **Treatise** at ¶ 510[02].

[2] *See, e.g.,* McCray v. Illinois, 386 U.S. 300, 309, 87 S. Ct. 1056, 18 L. Ed. 2d 62 (1967) ("privilege . . . long . . . recognized in the federal judicial system").

[3] United States v. Tucker, 380 F.2d 206, 213 (2d Cir. 1967). *See also* McCray v. Illinois, 386 U.S. 300, 308, 87 S. Ct. 1056, 18 L. Ed. 2d 62 (1967).

reason enough to deter a potential informant from communicating with the authorities unless his anonymity is protected.[4]

But despite the values served by the privilege, the courts have recognized that the right to withhold the informer's identity is not absolute. Since, as Standard 510(a) acknowledges, the privilege belongs to the government and not to the informer, the interest of the public "in protecting the flow of information" must be balanced against the public interest in "a fair determination of the issues."[5] Society has an interest in fairness as well as efficiency, and in deterring lawless activities by law enforcement officers. Disclosure of the informant's identity may at times be decisive in determining whether the police are hiding their misbehavior behind the shield of privilege.

¶ 18.06[03]   Issue of Guilt or Innocence[1]

Standard 510(c)(2) rests squarely on the Supreme Court's decision in *Roviaro v. United States*[2] in requiring the trial judge, on motion of the accused, to dismiss the charge if the government elects not to disclose the identity of an informer whom the judge has found reasonably able to give testimony necessary to a fair determination of the issue of guilt or innocence. The Court in *Roviaro* stated:

> Whether a proper balance renders nondisclosure erroneous must depend on the particular circumstances of each case, taking into

---

[4] *In re* United States, 565 F.2d 19, 22–23 (2d Cir. 1977) ("[T]he likelihood of physical reprisal is not a prerequisite to the invocation of the privilege. Often, retaliation may be expected to take more subtle forms such as economic duress, blacklisting or social ostracism.").

[5] Roviaro v. United States, 353 U.S. 53, 62, 77 S. Ct. 623, 1 L. Ed. 2d 639 (1957) ("We believe that no fixed rule with respect to disclosure is justifiable. The problem is one that calls for balancing the public interest in protecting the flow of information against the individual's right to prepare his defense. Whether a proper balance renders nondisclosure erroneous must depend on the particular circumstances of each case, taking into consideration the crime charged, the possible defenses, the possible significance of the informer's testimony, and other relevant factors.").

[1] *See* **Treatise** at ¶ 510[06].

[2] 353 U.S. 53, 77 S. Ct. 623, 1 L. Ed. 2d 639 (1957).

consideration the crime charged, the possible defenses, the possible significance of the informer's testimony, and other relevant factors.[3]

The discussion which follows considers the factors the Court found to bear on the accused's need for the informer's testimony, and how these factors have been evaluated in subsequent decisions.[4]

[a] Informer a Material Witness

In *Roviaro,* the Supreme Court stressed that the informant was accused's "one material witness . . . who had been nearest to him and took part in the transaction."[5] Subsequent courts have likewise emphasized this factor. They have at times ordered disclosure when the informant was an active participant and eyewitness to the crime,[6] but have protected the identity of the informant who did not actively participate or was not a witness.[7]

[b] Informer's Testimony Must Be Material to Issue of Guilt

In *Roviaro,* the Supreme Court noted that defendant was not charged with mere possession of the heroin; he was charged with knowingly receiving it, knowing it to be imported contrary to law. The informer, said the Court, "was the only witness who might have testified to petitioner's possible lack of knowledge of the contents of the package."[8] Courts have interpreted this language

---

[3] *Id.,* at 62.

[4] *See* United States v. Fatico II, 458 F. Supp. 388 (E.D.N.Y. 1978), *aff'd,* 603 F.2d 1053 (2d Cir. 1979) for discussion of use of unidentified informers' statements at sentencing hearings.

[5] 353 U.S. at 64.

[6] *See, e.g.,* United States v. Ayaka, 643 F.2d 244 (5th Cir. 1981) (identity had to be disclosed where informer was more than merely passive observer and in camera transcript indicated that her testimony might be useful to defendant who was claiming alibi and had been identified only by DEA agent).

[7] *See, e.g.,* United States v. Gonzales, 606 F.2d 70, 75 (5th Cir. 1979) (even though informant is present during a critical transaction, fact that he does not actively participate favors nondisclosure); United States v. Turbide, 558 F.2d 1053 (2d Cir.), *cert. denied sub nom.* Perez v. United States, 434 U.S. 934 (1977) (informer could not have observed sale or final transfer of money).

[8] Roviaro v. United States, 353 U.S. 53, 64, 77 S. Ct. 623, 1 L. Ed. 2d 639 (1957).

in *Roviaro* as meaning that the informant's identity need not be disclosed if his testimony could not have any substantial probability of throwing doubt on element of the crime charged.[9]

[c] Law Enforcement Officer's Credibility Is Suspect

Although the *Roviaro* opinion does not discuss the point, the facts of the case indicate that the majority may have felt uncomfortable about the agents' credibility since the opinion notes some inconsistency about whether the informer and defendant had known each other before the events in question. Had the informer been produced, this conflict in testimony could perhaps have been resolved. The cases following *Roviaro* indicate that courts will not assume that law enforcement agents are prevaricating unless some tangible manifestation is brought to the court's attention. Mere speculation on the part of the defense is not enough.

[d] Entrapment

In *Roviaro,* the Supreme Court noted that the informant's testimony "might have disclosed an entrapment."[10] While numerous courts have in dictum suggested that they might order the informant's identity disclosed if essential to a defense of entrapment, in practice this factor rarely seems to account for disclosure.

[e] Other Relevant Factors

The other relevant factors to which the Supreme Court referred in formulating the balancing test in *Roviaro* are those which underlie the rationale for the privilege: the possibility of harm to the informer, the cessation of his usefulness to the government, the credibility of the informer, and the possible frustration of

---

[9] *See, e.g.,* United States v. Givens, 712 F.2d 1298 (8th Cir. 1983), *cert. denied,* 465 U.S. 1009 (1984) (trial court did not err in failing to require disclosure of confidential reliable informant's identity where he provided law enforcement officials only with information as to defendant's whereabouts and not about the substantive offense).

[10] 353 U.S. at 64.

other investigations. Since *in camera* disclosure prevents all of these consequences, there is less need for the court to be attentive to these factors when initially considering whether the informer may be able to give testimony needed for a fair determination. If the court decides to hold an *in camera* hearing and then decides that the informant can supply testimony necessary to a fair determination, the arguments for protecting the informant's identity must yield to the defendant's need for the evidence. The government must choose—between revealing the informant's name and thereby risking his safety and its investigative efficacy—or forfeiting its right to prosecute.

Standard 510(c) requires that it appear from the evidence in the case, or from a showing by a party, that the informer may have evidence necessary to a fair determination. Courts will not allow public disclosure solely on the basis of speculation by the defendant that the informer's testimony might be of help. The defendant must explain to the court as precisely as possible what testimony he thinks the informer could give and how his testimony would be relevant to a material issue of guilt or innocence.[11]

¶ 18.06[04]   Issue of Legality of Obtaining Evidence[1]

Standard 510(c)(3) states that a judge may require the identity of an informer to be disclosed if information provided by him was relied upon to establish probable cause for the issuance of an arrest or search warrant, or for an arrest without a warrant, on which the validity of a search depends. Upon the request of the government, this disclosure must be made *in camera*.

The restriction to *in camera* disclosure—except for the unlikely situation in which the government elects some other course—eliminates the possibility of the accused confronting the informant, except in those instances where the informant's testimony

---

[11] Rugendorf v. United States, 376 U.S. 528, 535, 84 S. Ct. 825, 11 L. Ed. 2d 887 (1964) ("Having failed to develop the criteria of *Roviaro* necessitating disclosure on the merits, we cannot say on this record that the name of the informant was necessary to his defense. . . . Never did petitioner's counsel indicate how the informants' testimony could help establish petitioner's innocence.").

[1] *See* **Treatise** at ¶ 510[07].

is also relevant to guilt, and disclosure is ordered pursuant to Standard 510(c)(2). This is in accord with the Supreme Court's decision in *McCray v. Illinois,* [2] which held that an accused does not have a constitutional right to confront an informer whose information is the sole basis for probable cause.

While holding that disclosure of an informant's identity is not a matter of constitutional right, the *McCray* opinion did indicate that disclosure may be called for because of evidentiary principles. The balancing test of *Roviaro v. United States* [3] must be applied to determine whether, in a particular case, the public interest in disclosure as a sanction against illegal police activity outweighs the public interest in protecting an informer's identity. [4]

According to Standard 510(c)(3), the judge "may require the identity of the informer to be disclosed," if "he is not satisfied that the information was received from an informer reasonably believed to be reliable or credible." This formulation sought to incorporate the test the Supreme Court was then using to determine the sufficiency of probable cause. [5] As the Supreme Court's test for probable cause changes, the need to have the informant's identity disclosed will also be affected. [6]

---

[2] 386 U.S. 300, 87 S. Ct. 1056, 18 L. Ed. 2d 62 (1967) (Court also found that inability to cross-examine arresting officers fully when identity of informant is not revealed does not deprive defendant of constitutional rights).

[3] 353 U.S. 53, 77 S. Ct. 623, 1 L. Ed. 2d 639 (1957).

[4] *See, e.g.,* United States v. Ordonez, 737 F.2d 793, 807–10 (9th Cir. 1984) (in a prosecution on drug-related charges, it was error of constitutional dimension to deny disclosure of identity of informant relied upon in police affidavit filed in support of search warrant where disclosure was highly relevant and might have been helpful to the defense and where record did not indicate that trial judge had applied *Roviaro* test; remand to conduct de novo *in camera Roviaro* hearing).

[5] *See, e.g.,* Aguilar v. Texas, 378 U.S. 108, 84 S. Ct. 1509, 12 L. Ed. 2d 723 (1964); Spinelli v. United States, 393 U.S. 410, 89 S. Ct. 584, 21 L. Ed. 2d 637 (1969).

[6] *See* Illinois v. Gates, 462 U.S. 213, 103 S. Ct. 2317, 76 L. Ed. 2d 527 (1983) (rejecting the test established in *Aguilar* and *Spinelli*).

¶ 18.07 Waiver of Privilege By Voluntary Disclosure — Standard 511 [1]

Standard 511 codifies standard practice in acknowledging that a privilege can be waived by disclosure or consent to disclosure. The Standard provides:

Supreme Court Standard 511

WAIVER OF PRIVILEGE BY VOLUNTARY DISCLOSURE

A person upon whom these rules confer a privilege against disclosure of the confidential matter or communication waives the privilege if he or his predecessor while holder of the privilege voluntarily discloses or consents to disclosure of any significant part of the matter or communication. This rule does not apply if the disclosure is itself a privileged communication.

Standard 511 must be read with reference to the particular privilege at issue. For instance, because the attorney-client privilege protects only the communication, the client does not waive the privilege when answering questions about the underlying information. Since only the witness spouse is the holder of the marital testimonial privilege after the Supreme Court's decision in *Trammel v. United States,* [2] only the witness spouse can waive the privilege by voluntary testimony. In the case of the informant's privilege, Standard 511 must be read in conjunction with Standard 510 which provides that, unlike the usual case in which waiver occurs through any voluntary disclosure, the informant's privilege ceases only if there has been disclosure to those who would have cause to resent the communication.

Some courts have declined to find that a waiver has occurred in cases of inadvertent disclosure. [3] However, Standard 511 does not limit the waiver of a confidential privilege to instances in

---

[1] *See* **Treatise** at ¶¶ 511[01]–[02].

[2] 445 U.S. 40, 100 S. Ct. 906, 63 L. Ed. 2d 186 (1980) (see discussion ¶ 18.04, *supra*).

[3] KL Group v. Case, Kay & Lynch, 829 F.2d 909, 918 (9th Cir. 1987) (no waiver of attorney-client privilege through inadvertent disclosure of a letter, one of 2,000 documents produced during discovery); Mendenhall v. Barber-Greene Corp., 531 F. Supp. 951, 954 (N.D. Ill. 1982) (no waiver when disclosure inadvertent).

which the holder of the privilege intentionally relinquishes a known right. Such a limitation, while it may be required in other contexts, does not conform with the realities of the confidential privilege situation. At some point after disclosure has occurred, it is no longer fair to honor the holder's claim of privilege; ascertaining at what point this occurs can be difficult.[4]

Courts frequently resort to the metaphor that the privilege may be used as a shield but not as a sword.[5] For example, when the question arises in the context of the attorney-client relationship, the client will be held to have waived the privilege by revealing the subject matter of the communication with the lawyer.[6] For

---

[4] See In re Sealed Case, 877 F.2d 976, 980–81 (D.C. Cir. 1989) ("The courts will grant no greater protection to those who assert the privilege than their own precautions warrant"; court discusses possible scope of an inadvertent waiver); In re Martin Marietta Corp., 856 F.2d 619 (4th Cir. 1988) (when corporation submitted otherwise privileged material to the United States Attorney and the Department of Defense in settling with the government, subject matter waiver was applied to the attorney-client privilege and to ordinary work product, but not to opinion work product); Permian Corp. v. United States, 665 F.2d 1214, 1221 (D.C. Cir. 1981) (where corporation permitted disclosure of communications to SEC staff it could not prevent disclosure by SEC; a "client cannot be permitted to pick and choose among his opponents, waiving the privilege for some and resurrecting the claim of confidentiality to obstruct others, or to invoke the privilege as to communications whose confidentiality he has already compromised for his own benefit"); Diversified Industries, Inc. v. Meredith, 572 F.2d 596 (8th Cir. 1978) (limited waiver when corporation elects to participate in voluntary disclosure program like the SEC's).

[5] See E.E.O.C. v. General Telephone Co. of Northwest, 885 F.2d 575, 578 (9th Cir. 1989) (even if there was a qualified privilege for self-critical portions of an employer's affirmative action plan, employer opened door and waived privilege by relying on the plan to show absence of discrimination).

[6] See United States v. Bernard, 877 F.2d 1463, 1464–65 (10th Cir. 1989) (witness testified that defendant had told him defendant had verified legality of loan with his attorney; government called the attorney, who denied ever having discussed the legality of the loan with the defendant; court held that defendant waived attorney-client privilege by disclosing his purported conversation with his attorney in an effort to induce witness to engage in loan). Cf. Joy v. North, 692 F.2d 880, 893–94 (2d Cir. 1982), cert. denied, 460 U.S. 1051 (1983) (motion for summary judgment precludes assertion of attorney-client or work product privilege with respect to documents on which motion is based). But cf. Greater Newburyport Clamshell Alliance v. Public Service Co. of New Hampshire, 838 F.2d 13, 20 (1st Cir. 1988) (in civil rights action, alleging that state police violated plaintiffs' Sixth Amendment rights by using

instance, the client cannot claim that counsel failed to advise him of the potential sentence he might receive upon pleading guilty, and then assert his privilege to keep the lawyer from testifying to the advice rendered.[7]

According to Standard 511 waiver occurs only if "any significant part of the matter or communication" is revealed. This formulation enables the court to exercise its discretion with reference to the objectives of the particular privilege involved.[8]

The last sentence of Standard 511 is intended to avert waiver when the revelation of the privileged matter occurs in another privileged communication. For instance, a spouse does not waive the privilege for confidential marital communications by telling a lawyer in confidence what had been said to the spouse.

¶ 18.08 Disclosure Under Compulsion or Without Opportunity to Claim Privilege—Standard 512[1]

Standard 512 is the converse of Standard 511. Standard 511 deals with waiver and its consequences; Standard 512 deals with the consequences of disclosure in the absence of waiver. The rule provides:

---

an informant to intercept privileged communications with attorneys, the court held that application of an automatic waiver rule would be too harsh).

[7] United States v. Miller, 600 F.2d 498 (5th Cir. 1979) (after defendant attempted to convince jury that he had relied on advice of counsel, cross-examination probing into actual advice received was proper); United States v. McCambridge, 551 F.2d 865, 873–74 (1st Cir. 1977) (defendant could not limit counsel's testimony to advice he had given with regard to defendant's prior convictions in advising defendant not to testify; defendant waived his privilege as to other reasons that were discussed concerning whether it was advisable for him to take the stand).

[8] In re Sealed Case, 877 F.2d 976, 980–81 (D.C. Cir. 1989) (discusses possible scope of an inadvertent waiver); In re Von Bulow, 828 F.2d 94, 102 (2d Cir.), cert. denied, 107 S. Ct. 1891 (1987) (after attorney wrote a book about a criminal trial at which his client had been acquitted, plaintiffs in a civil suit sought discovery regarding the attorney's conversations with the defendant, claiming that the privilege had been waived; court held that plaintiffs could not discover entire contents of all conversations, but only those portions that had been disclosed; there was no subject matter waiver because the disclosure was extra-judicial and without prejudice to plaintiffs).

[1] See **Treatise** at ¶¶ 512[01]–[02].

Supreme Court Standard 512

PRIVILEGED MATTER DISCLOSED UNDER COMPULSIONOR WITHOUT OPPORTUNITY TO CLAIM PRIVILEGE

Evidence of a statement or other disclosure of privileged matter is not admissible against the holder of the privilege if the disclosure was (a) compelled erroneously or (b) made without opportunity to claim the privilege.

The object of Standard 512 is to repair part of the damage which had already been done.

Subdivision (a) of Standard 512 recognizes that although a holder of a privilege could enforce the privilege by standing fast and risking a judgment of contempt, most witnesses are not capable of displaying such fortitude. To the extent that Standard 512(a) will apply in a given case, it has the effect of modifying the usual principles of res judicata.

Subdivision (b) of Standard 512 makes inadmissible evidence which was disclosed without the holder having an opportunity to claim his privilege. While it would cover situations where the nonholder party to a communication discloses without the holder's awareness, ethical considerations make such an eventuality unlikely in the case of a lawyer, psychotherapist or clergyman.

The main occasion for Standard 512(b) is that it is needed to implement those provisions in the Federal Rules which modify common law doctrine. For instance, because of ever more sophisticated techniques for intercepting confidential communications, new codifications, including the Federal Rules as submitted to Congress, contain provisions, in derogation of the common law, entitling the holder of a privilege to prevent eavesdroppers from disclosing confidential communications. Standard 512(b) implements this approach by mandating exclusion of the eavesdropper's testimony if he testifies before the holder has an opportunity to claim the privilege.

Standard 512(b) also protects the holder in instances where the standards have expanded the traditional scope of a privilege. For example, Standard 503(b)(3) extends the attorney-client privilege to the joint defense and pooled information situation; Standard 504(b) acknowledges that the psychotherapist-patient privilege continues in a group therapy setting. Standard 512(b) is needed to safeguard the holder's privilege from being destroyed by co-participants in these activities who may be laymen, unamenable to ethical restraints.

Standard 512(b) applies only if the criteria for the particular privilege have been met. The evidence of an eavesdropper or participant will be excluded only if the evidence would have been privileged had the holder had an opportunity to make a claim.[2]

The extent to which Standard 512 will bar the fruits of revealed matters is not clear. If the government was a party to the improper breach and a constitutional privilege was involved, the illegal fruits doctrine will apply. In other instances the court has some discretion. Generally it will admit, bearing in mind the general policy in favor of truth rather than exclusion.[3]

---

[2] *See, e.g.,* Young v. Taylor, 466 F.2d 1329, 1332 (10th Cir. 1972) (attorney's secretary testified to communication; not privileged because attorney was not acting as an attorney but as participant in transaction).

[3] S.E.C. v. OKC Corp., 474 F. Supp. 1031 (N.D. Tex. 1979) (even if report SEC obtained was privileged, it was not precluded from using privileged information to frame demands from unprivileged information; there is no prophylatic exclusionary rule to buttress the attorney-client privilege).

INDEX

[References are to paragraphs.]

A

ACCIDENT REPORT
Hearsay rule application, trustworthiness of report . . . 16.06[1][h]

ACCIDENTS
Character evidence, other accidents as . . . 7.01[12]
Rebuttal of claim of . . . 7.05[01]

ACCOMPLICES
Declaration against penal interest made in custody by accomplice . . . 2.04[02]

ACQUITTALS
Other crimes evidence . . . 7.01[08][b]

ACTS OF CONGRESS
Authentication of documents, presumption as to . . . 8.02[12]

ADJUDICATIVE FACTS
Judicial notice
    Facts subject to notice . . . 4.02
    Scope . . . 4.01

ADMISSION OF EVIDENCE
Coconspirators' declarations . . . 14.03[02]
Confession of nontestifying co-defendant . . . 2.04[02]
Confrontation clause . . . 14.03 *et seq.*
Extrinsic policy rules restricting . . 1.01[02]
Hearsay (See HEARSAY)
Limited admissibility (See LIMITED ADMISSIBILITY)
Misleading evidence . . . 2.05
Motion to strike (See MOTION TO STRIKE, subhead: Admission of evidence)
Objections (See OBJECTIONS, subhead: Admissions of evidence)
Preliminary questions . . . 15.02[06][b]
Preponderance of evidence standard . . . . 3.01[02]
Relevance, rules governing . . . 1.01
Similar acts, evidence of . . . 7.01[08][a]

AFFIRMATION (See OATH OR AFFIRMATION)

AGE DISCRIMINATION
Settlement offers . . . 7.05[01]

ALCOHOL
Juror's use of . . . 11.04[03]

ALFORD PLEAS
Impeachment of witnesses, grounds . . . . . 12.04[03]

ANCIENT DOCUMENTS
Authentication
    Age . . . 8.01[09][a]
    Appropriate custody . . . 8.01[09][c]
    Generally . . . 8.01[09]
    Hearsay exception rule, admissibility under . . . 16.06[03]
    Nonsuspicious condition . . . . 8.01[09][b]

APOSTILLE
Foreign public documents, certification . . . 8.02[05]

APPEALS
Impeachment of witness, pendency of appeal . . . 12.04[07]
In limine motions . . . 6.02[01]

ATTORNEY-CLIENT PRIVILEGE
Applicability of standard . . . 18.03[01]
Breach of duty by lawyer or client . . . . . . 18.03[07][c]
Claimants through same deceased claimant . . . 18.03[07][b]
Communications
    Eligibility . . . 18.03[04][a]
    Identifying facts about client, lawyer or representative . . . 18.03[04][c]
    Limitations . . . 18.03[04][b]
    Scope of privilege . . . 18.03[04]
Control group test . . . 18.03[05]
Corporate clients . . . 18.03[05]
Definitions
    Client . . . 18.03[03][a]
    Confidentiality . . . 18.03[03][d]
    Lawyer . . . 18.03[03][b]
    Representative of the lawyer . . . . . . 18.03[03][c]
Document attested by attorney . . . . 18.03[07][d]
Eligibility . . . 18.03[06]
Exceptions . . . 18.03[07] *et seq.*
Furtherance of crime or fraud . . . . 18.03[07][a]
Joint clients . . . 18.03[07][e]
Rationale . . . 18.03[02]
Waiver . . . 10.05[03][a]
Work product . . . 10.05[03][a]; 18.03[05]

[References are to paragraphs.]

ATTORNEYS

Competency as witnesses . . . 10.01[03]

Jurors, propriety of counsel interviewing . . . 11.04[04]

AUTHENTICATION AND IDENTIFICATION

Acknowledgment, certificate of . . 8.02[10]

Acts of Congress, presumptions under . . . 8.02[12]

Ancient documents . . . 8.01[09] *et seq.*

Ballistics comparison . . . 8.01[04][c]

Charts, summaries and calculations . . . . . 9.05[03]

Comparison with authenticated specimens . . . 8.01[04] *et seq.*

Contents of writing . . . 8.01[05][a]

Data compilations . . . 8.01[09] *et seq.*

Distinctive characteristics of writing . . . . 8.01[05] *et seq.*

Foreign public documents
"Apostille" . . . 8.02[05]
Certification . . . 8.02[04]
Convention abolishing legalization requirement . . . 8.02[05]

Generally . . . 8.01[01]

Government publications . . . 8.02[07]

Handwriting
Comparison . . . 8.01[04][a]
Nonexpert testimony . . . 8.01[02]

Internal patterns of writing . . . 8.01[05][c]

Newspapers . . . 8.02[08]

Originals . . . 9.02[03][a]

Periodicals . . . 8.02[08]

Physical attributes of writing . . 8.01[05][b]

Preliminary questions . . . 3.02

Presumptions under Acts of Congress as to documents . . . 8.02[12]

Process or system, accuracy of data . . . . . 8.01[10]

Psycholinguistics . . . 8.01[05][c]

Public records (See PUBLIC RECORDS)

Regulatory authentication . . . 8.01[11]

Relationship to other writings . . . . 8.01[05][d]

Reply letter technique . . . 8.01[05][e]

Self-authentication
Domestic public documents under seal . . . 8.02[02]
Generally . . . 8.02[01]

Statutory authentication . . . 8.01[11]

Subscribing witness' testimony . . 8.01[01]

Telephone calls (See TELEPHONE CALLS, subhead: Authentication)

Trade inscriptions . . . 8.02[09]

AUTHENTICATION AND IDENTIFICATION—Cont.

Typewriting comparison . . . . 8.01[04][b]; 8.01[04][c]

Uniform Commercial Code, effect on documents . . . 8.02[11]

Voice identification (See VOICE IDENTIFICATION)

AUXILIARY RULES

Probative value . . . 1.01[01]

AVAILABILITY

Hearsay exceptions (See HEARSAY, subhead: Availability of declarant immaterial)

B

BALLISTICS

Comparison with authenticated specimens . . . 8.01[04][c]

BEST EVIDENCE RULE

Application . . . 9.01[02]

Definitions . . . 9.01[03]

Drawings, form and content of . . 9.01[03]

Generally . . . 9.01[01]

Originals, applicability (See ORIGINALS)

Photographs defined . . . 9.01[03]

Public records exceptions . . . 9.04

Recordings defined . . . 9.01[03]

Writings defined . . . 9.01[03]

X-rays . . . 9.01[03]

BOOTSTRAPPING RULE

Preliminary determinations . . 15.02[06][b]

BRAIN-DAMAGED PERSONS

Competency as witnesses . . . 10.01[02]

BURDENS OF PROOF

Presumptions shifting burdens of proof in criminal cases . . . 5.04[05][a]; 5.04[05][b]

C

CALCULATIONS (See CHARTS, SUMMARIES AND CALCULATIONS)

CASH

Relevant evidence, sudden acquisition of . . . 6.01[06][d]

CERTIFICATE OF ACKNOWLEDGMENT

Authentication of documents . . . 8.02[10]

[References are to paragraphs.]

[References are to paragraphs.]

COMPROMISE—Cont.
Exceptions to exclusionary treatment . . . . 7.05[01][d]
Generally . . . 7.05[01]
Mistake or accident, rebuttal of claim of . . . 7.05[01]
Offers
    Disputes, to compromise . . . . 7.05[01][a]
    Other purposes, use for . . 7.05[01][d]
Settlement (See SETTLEMENT)

COMPULSION
Privileged matter disclosed under . . 18.08

COMPUTER PRINTOUTS
Originals, as . . . 9.02[02][c]
Summaries as . . . 9.05[04]

CONFESSION
Admissibility of nontestifying co-defendant's statement . . . 2.04[02]

CONFIDENTIAL COMMUNICATIONS
Attorney-client (See ATTORNEY-CLIENT PRIVILEGE)
Spouses (See MARITAL PRIVILEGES)

CONFRONTATION CLAUSE
Availability immaterial . . . 14.03[02]
Coconspirators' exception . . . 2.04[02]
Coconspirators' statements . . 15.02[06][e]
Cross-examination . . . 14.03[01]
Expert testimony . . . 13.03[03]
Hearsay exception . . . 14.03 *et seq.*
Identification statement . . . 15.01[04]
Indicia of reliability, examination for . . . . 15.02[06][e]
Jury instruction . . . 14.03
Testimony, declarant's . . . 14.03[01]
Unavailability of declarant . . . 14.03[03]

CONSISTENT STATEMENTS
Prior (See PRIOR STATEMENTS)

CONSPIRACIES
Coconspirators' statements (See COCON-SPIRATORS' STATEMENTS)
Confrontation clause . . 2.04[02]; 14.03[02]
Other crimes evidence . . . 7.01[07][c]
Preliminary questions . . . 15.02[06][b]
Preponderance of evidence standard . . . . 3.01[02]
RICO prosecution . . . 15.02[06][e]

CONSTITUTIONAL ERROR
Determination . . . 2.03[07]

CONSTITUTIONAL LAW
Confrontation clause . . . 14.03[01]
Objection to invalid conviction . . . . 12.04[03][e]
Penal interest, declaration against . . . . . . 2.04[02]
Sexually abused children, videotaped testimony of . . . 10.01[02]

CONSTRUCTION
Federal rules of evidence . . . 1.02

CONTROL
Court, generally . . . 2.02[2]
Ownership and . . . 7.08[02][a]
Trial judges, by . . . 2.01

CONTROL GROUP TEST
Attorney-client privilege . . . 18.03[05]

CONVICTION
Constitutionally invalid, objection to . . . . 12.04[03][e]
Hearsay exception for evidence of previous . . . 16.07[05]

CORPORATIONS
Attorney-client privilege . . . 18.03[05]

CORRESPONDENCE
Authentication by reply letter . . 8.01[05][e]

COUNSEL (See ATTORNEYS)

CREDIBILITY
Conviction, objection to constitutionally invalid . . . 12.04[03][e]
Evaluation of . . . 6.01[03]
Impeachment (See IMPEACHMENT OF WITNESSES)
Informer privilege, law enforcement officers' credibility as issue . . . 18.06[03][c]
Liability insurance . . . 7.08[02][b]
Pleas and plea discussions to attack defendant's . . . 7.07[04]
Rehabilitation (See REHABILITATION OF WITNESSES)

CRIME
Attorney-client privilege, furtherance as exception . . . 18.03[07][a]
Obscene matter, knowledge of importation of . . . 7.01[09][b]

CRIMINAL CASES
Advisory Committee on the Federal Rules of Criminal Procedure . . . 15.02[06][e]
Investigative reports of prior, hearsay exception applied . . . 16.06[01][i]

[References are to paragraphs.]

[References are to paragraphs.]

[References are to paragraphs.]

HEARSAY—Cont.

Exceptions—Cont.

Availability of declarant immaterial (See subhead: Availability of declarant immaterial)

Business records (See subhead: Business records exception)

Circumstantial guarantees of trustworthiness . . . 14.04[01]

Confrontation clause (See CONFRONTATION CLAUSE)

Reasonable person test . . . 17.04[2][c]

Residual hearsay . . . 14.04 et seq.

Unavailability of declarant (See subhead: Unavailability of declarant)

Excited utterances

Generally . . . 16.02

Perception . . . 16.02[03]

Rationale . . . 16.02[01]

Startling event or condition . . . . 16.02[02]

Stress of excitement . . . 16.02[04]

Time . . . 16.02[05]

Exclusions . . . 15.01 et seq.

Exculpatory statements . . . 17.04[03][a]

Federal rules, design . . . 14.01[02]

Former testimony

Direct or redirect examination . . . . . 17.02[03]

Generally . . . 17.02[01]

"Opportunity and similar motive" test . . . 17.02[02]

Party or predecessor in interest . . . . 17.02[04]

Generally . . . 14.01 et seq.

Identification statement . . . 15.01[04]

Impending death, statement under belief . . . 17.03

Inculpatory statements . . . 17.04[03][b]

Interests of justice . . . 14.04[04]

Judgment of previous convictions, admission of evidence . . . 16.07[05]

Marital privileges . . . 18.04[01][d]

Material fact, residual hearsay as evidence of . . . 14.04[02]

Medical diagnosis or treatment, statements relating to . . . 16.04; 16.06[01][g]

Mental or emotional condition

Generally . . . 16.03[02][a]

State of mind

In issue . . . 16.03[02][b]

Previous act, to show . . . . 16.03[02][d]

Subsequent act, to show . . . . . . 16.03[02][c]

HEARSAY—Cont.

Mental or emotional condition—Cont.

Then existing . . . 16.03

"More probative" requirement . . 14.04[03]

Notice of intention to offer . . . 14.04[05]

"Pedigree" exception . . . 17.05

Personal knowledge

Business records . . . 16.06[01][e]

Public records . . . 16.07[01][b]

Recorded recollection . . . 16.05[02]

Personal or family history statements, exception . . . 17.05

Physical condition . . . 16.03[01]

Preliminary questions . . . 15.02[06][b]

Private entities, records of . . . 16.06

Prior statements by witnesses (See PRIOR STATEMENTS)

Publications

Commercial publications, admissibility of . . . 16.08[02]

Market reports . . . 16.08[02]

Treatises learned, admissibility of . . . 16.08[01]

Public records

Absence of . . . 16.07[2]

Criminal cases . . . 16.07[01][d]

Generally . . . 16.07[01][a]

Investigative reports, criminal cases . . . 16.07[01][c]

Personal knowledge requirement . . . . 16.07[01][b]

Recorded recollection

Admissibility of memorandum . . . . . 16.05[05]

Freshness and accuracy of memorandum . . . 16.05[03]

Generally . . . 16.05

Insufficient recollection to testify accurately . . . 16.05[01]

Multiple participants . . . 16.05[04]

Personal knowledge requirement . . . . 16.05[02]

Regularly conducted activity, records of (See subhead: Business records exception)

Reputation evidence, use of . . . 16.09

Residual hearsay exceptions . . 14.04 et seq.

RICO prosecution . . . 15.02[06][e]

Statements

Ancient documents . . . 16.06[03]

Defined . . . 14.02[01]

Excluded categories . . . 14.02[02]

Personal or family history, exception . . . 17.05

Statements against interest

Contrary to interest . . . 17.04[02][e]

[References are to paragraphs.]

[References are to paragraphs.]

JURY TRIAL—Cont.
Relevancy, special rules of . . . 7.01[08][a]

JUVENILE ADJUDICATIONS
Impeachment of witnesses . . . 12.04[06]

K

KNOWLEDGE
Obscene matter, importation of . . . .
    7.01[09][b]
Other crimes evidence . . . 7.01[09][b]

L

LAW ENFORCEMENT
Informer privilege, officer's credibility as
    issue . . . 18.06[03][c]
Official information privilege for investiga-
    tory files . . . 18.05[03][c]

LAWYER-CLIENT PRIVILEGE (See AT-
TORNEY-CLIENT PRIVILEGE)

LAY OPINION (See OPINION TESTI-
MONY)

LIABILITY INSURANCE
Agency, issue of . . . 7.08[02][a]
Control . . . 7.08[02][a]
Credibility . . . 7.08[02][b]
Disclosure . . . 7.08[03]
Discovery . . . 7.08[03]
Exceptions to exclusionary treatment . . . .
    7.07[02] *et seq.*
Exclusionary treatment . . . 7.08[01]
Generally . . . 7.08[01]
Impeachment purposes . . . 7.08[02][b]
Jury instructions . . . 7.08[03]
Ownership . . . 7.08[02][a]

LIMITED ADMISSIBILITY
Application of rule . . . 2.04[02]
Civil cases . . . 2.04[02][a]
Criminal cases . . . 2.04[02][b]
Scope . . . 2.04[01]
Theory . . . 2.04[01]

M

MANN ACT
Marital privilege exception . . 18.04[01][b]

MARITAL PRIVILEGES
Adverse spousal testimony . . . 18.04[01]
Communications and testimonial privileges
    distinguished . . . 18.04[03]

MARITAL PRIVILEGES—Cont.
Confidential communications
    Exceptions . . . 18.04[02][a]
    Generally . . . 18.04[02]
Crime against other spouse . . 18.04[01][b]
Criminal participation exception applied to
    communication about intended crime . .
    18.04[02]
Exceptions . . . 18.04[01][a]; 18.04[01][b]
Generally . . . 18.04
Hearsay statements . . . 18.04[01][d]
Joint participation exceptions . . . .
    18.04[01][a]
Mann Act violations . . . 18.04[01][b]
Matters prior to marriage . . . 18.04[01][b]
Multi-party situations, applicability . . . . .
    18.04[01][c]
"Reason and experience" standard . . . . .
    18.04[01][a]
Sexual offenses with third person . . . . . .
    18.04[01][b]
Sham marriages . . . 18.04[01][b]
Testimonial and communications privileges
    distinguished . . . 18.04[03]
Trammel decision . . . 18.04[01]

MATERIAL FACT
Residual hearsay as evidence of . . . .
    14.04[02]

**MEDICAL AND SIMILAR EXPENSES,
PAYMENT OF**
Exclusionary treatment . . . 7.06

MEDICAL DIAGNOSIS OR TREATMENT
Hearsay exception for statements relating to
    . . . 16.04; 16.06[01][g]

MEMORY
Refreshing (See REFRESHING MEMORY)
Writings to refresh . . . 10.05 *et seq.*

MENTAL INCAPACITY
Impeachment of witnesses . . . 12.01[02]

MENTAL OR EMOTIONAL CONDITION
Hearsay exceptions (See HEARSAY)

MISLEADING EVIDENCE
Admissibility . . . 2.05

MISTAKE
Rebuttal of claim of . . . 7.05[01]

MOTION TO STRIKE
Admission of evidence
    Form . . . 2.03[02][c]
    Generally . . . 2.03[02]

MOTION TO STRIKE—Cont.
Admission of evidence—Cont.
   Specificity requirement . . . 2.03[02][c]
   Timing . . . 2.03[02][b]
   Waiver . . . 2.03[02][a]

MOTIVE
Other crimes evidence as proof . . . .
   7.01[09][c]

N

NEGLIGENCE
Character evidence, admissibility . . . . . .
   7.01[12]

NEWSPAPERS
Authentication . . . 8.02[08]

***NOLO CONTENDERE* PLEAS**
Exclusion . . . 7.07[02]
Impeachment of witnesses, plea as grounds
   . . . 12.04[03]

NOTICE
Hearsay, intention to offer . . . 14.04[05]

O

OATH OR AFFIRMATION
Identification statement . . . 15.01[04]
Prior inconsistent statements, requirement
   . . . 15.01[02][a]
Testimony . . . 10.04

OBJECTIONS
Admission of evidence
   Form . . . 2.03[02][c]
   Generally . . . 2.03[02]
   Procedures . . . 2.03[04]
   Specificity requirement . . . 2.03[02][c]
   Timing . . . 2.03[02][b]
   Waiver . . . 2.03[02][a]
Constitutionally invalid conviction . . . . .
   12.04[03][e]
Exclusion of evidence
   Generally . . . 2.03[03]
   Procedures . . . 2.03[04]
Pretrial motion, same issue raised in
   unsuccessful . . . 2.03[02][b]

OBSCENE MATTER
Knowledge of importation of . . 7.01[09][b]

OFFICIAL INFORMATION
Definition . . . 18.05[01]

OFFICIAL INFORMATION—Cont.
Privileges
   Freedom of Information Act . . . . . .
    18.05[03][d]
   Generally . . . 18.05[03]
   Intragovernmental opinions or recom-
    mendations . . . 18.05[03][b]
   Investigatory law enforcement files . .
    18.05[03][c]
   Procedures for claiming . . . .
    18.05[03][a]
Scope . . . 18.05[01]

OFFICIAL PUBLICATIONS
Authentication as governmental publications
   . . . 8.02[07]

OPINION TESTIMONY
Application . . . 10.02[02]
Generally . . . 10.02[01]
Helpfulness test . . . 10.02[02]
Personal knowledge requirement . . . .
   10.02[02]
Rational connection test . . . 10.02[02]

OPPORTUNITY AND SIMILAR MOTIVE
Hearsay exception, test of former testimony
   as . . . 17.02[02]

ORIGINALS
Authenticity . . . 9.02[03][a]
Best evidence rule, production of . . . . . .
   9.03[01]
Computer printouts as . . . 9.02[02][c]
Definition . . . 9.01[04]
Duplicates, admissibility . . . 9.02[01]
Production excused
   Collateral matters . . . 9.03[05]
   Generally . . . 9.03[01]
   Loss or destruction . . . 9.03[02]
   Opponent, in possession of . . . . . .
    9.03[04]
   Unobtainability . . . 9.03[03]
Recordings . . . 9.01[05]
Testimonial admissions of adverse parties,
   proof of contents through . . . 9.06
Written admissions of adverse parties, proof
   of contents through . . . 9.06

OTHER CRIMES EVIDENCE
Character evidence (See CHARACTER
   EVIDENCE)

OWNERSHIP AND CONTROL
Liability insurance . . . 7.08[02][a]

[References are to paragraphs.]

P

PEDAGOGICAL DEVICES
Charts, summaries and calculations as . . .
9.05[04][b]

PEDIGREE EXCEPTION
Hearsay . . . 17.05

PENAL INTEREST
Declaration against made in custody by
accomplice . . . 2.04[02]
Exculpatory statements against . . . .
17.04[03][a]
Hearsay exception for statements against
. . . 17.04[03]
Inculpatory statements . . . 17.04[03][b]

PERIODICALS
Authentication . . . 8.02[08]

PERSONAL HISTORY
Hearsay exception for statements of . . . . .
17.05

PERSONAL KNOWLEDGE
Expert testimony as basis . . . 13.03[02][a]
Hearsay exception (See HEARSAY)
Lack of . . . 10.03
Opinion testimony, requirement . . . .
10.02[02]

PHOTOGRAPHS
Definition . . . 9.01[03]
Preliminary questions concerning contents
Court determination . . . 3.03[01]
Jury determination . . . 3.03[02]

PHYSICAL CONDITION
Hearsay exception . . . 16.03[01]

PLAIN ERROR
Determination . . . 2.03[06]

PLEA BARGAINING (See PLEAS AND
PLEA DISCUSSIONS)

PLEAS AND PLEA DISCUSSIONS
Credibility, attacks on defendant's . . . . . .
7.07[04]
Criminal procedure rules . . . 15.02[06][e]
Exceptions to exclusionary treatment . . . .
7.07[05]
Impeachment, use for . . . 7.07[04]
Inadmissibility . . . 7.07[01]
Nolo contendere pleas, exclusion . . . . . . :
7.07[02]
Rejected pleas . . . 7.07[02]

PLEAS AND PLEA DISCUSSIONS—Cont.
Statements pursuant to plea bargaining . . .
7.07[03]
Withdrawn pleas . . . 7.07[02]

PREJUDICE
Other crimes evidence, balancing probative
value and prejudicial character of . . . . .
7.01[10]
Relevancy, special rules of . . . 7.01[08][a]
Relevant evidence, exclusion as . . 6.02[02]

PRELIMINARY HEARINGS
Jury presence . . . 3.01[04][b]
Testimony of accused . . . 3.01[04][c]

PRELIMINARY QUESTIONS
Admissibility . . . 15.02[06][b]
Allocation of responsibility
Court (See subhead: Court responsibil-
ity)
Jury . . . 3.01[03]
Authentication and identification require-
ments . . . 3.02
Coconspirators' statements, admissibility
. . . 15.02[06][b]
Court responsibility
Admissibility of evidence . . . .
3.01[02][d]
Coerced confessions . . . 3.01[02][d]
Generally . . . 3.01[02]
Hearsay rule, applicability . . . .
3.01[02][c]
Illegal searches . . . 3.01[02][d]
Improper trial procedures . . . .
3.01[02][d]
Privileges . . . 3.01[02][b]
Qualification of witnesses . . . .
3.01[02][a]
Evidentiary rules, applicability . . . .
3.01[04][a]
Jury responsibility . . . 3.01[03]
Photographs, contents of (See subhead: Writ-
ings, recordings and photographs, contents
of)
Preponderance of the evidence rule . . . . .
7.01[08][a]; 15.02[06][b]
Procedural aspects of preliminary fact deter-
minations . . . 3.01[04] *et seq.*
Recordings, contents of (See subhead: Writings, recordings and photographs, contents
of)
Scope . . . 3.01[01]
Self-incrimination, privilege against . . . . .
3.01[04][c]

[References are to paragraphs.]

[References are to paragraphs.]

PROBATIVE VALUE
Auxiliary rules . . . 1.01[1]
Other crimes evidence
    Prejudice v. probative value . . . . . .
    7.01[10]

PRODUCTS LIABILITY
Recall letters . . . 7.04[03]
Subsequent remedial measures . . 7.04[02]
Subsequent repairs, evidence of . . 7.04[02]

PROFILE EVIDENCE
Relevancy . . . 6.01[06][h]

PUBLICATIONS
Hearsay exception and (See HEARSAY, subhead: Publications)

PUBLIC DOCUMENTS (See PUBLIC RECORDS)

PUBLIC RECORDS
Authentication
    Domestic public documents
        Under seal . . . 8.02[02]
        Without seal . . . 8.02[03]
        Foreign public documents . . 8.02[04]
        Legal custodianship . . . 8.01[08]
Best evidence rule, exceptions . . . 9.04
Foreign (See FOREIGN RECORDS AND DOCUMENTS)
Hearsay rule and (See HEARSAY, subhead: Public records)

Q

QUESTIONS OF FACT
Preponderance of the evidence standard . . 3.01[02]

R

RACKETEER INFLUENCED AND CORRUPT ORGANIZATIONS ACT (RICO)
Character evidence in prosecutions under . . . 7.01[02]
Coconspirators' statements . . 15.02[06][e]

RAPE
Victim's past behavior, relevance . . . 7.09

RATIONAL CONNECTION TEST
Opinion testimony . . . 10.02[02]
Presumptions in criminal cases, applicability . . . 5.04[03]

REAL PROPERTY VALUE
Relevant evidence . . . 6.01[06][g]

(Matthew Bender & Co., Inc.)

REASONABLE PERSON TEST
Hearsay exception, statements against interest as . . . 17.04[02][c]

REASON AND EXPERIENCES STANDARD
Marital privileges . . . 18.04[01][a]

REBUTTAL
Confession of nontestifying co-defendant, reliability of . . . 2.04[02]
Mistake or accident, claim of . . . 7.05[01]

RECALL LETTERS
Products liability cases, admissibility in . . 7.04[03]
Subsequent remedial measures . . 7.04[03]

RECOLLECTION
Recorded (See HEARSAY, subhead: Recorded recollection)
Refreshment (See REFRESHING MEMORY)

RECORDED RECOLLECTION
Hearsay exception (See HEARSAY, subhead: Recorded recollection)

RECORDED STATEMENTS
Remainder of . . . 2.05

RECORDINGS
Definition . . . 9.01[03]
Duplicates . . . 9.02[02][b]
Originals . . . 9.01[05]
Preliminary questions concerning contents
    Court determination . . . 3.03[01]
    Jury determination . . . 3.03[02]

REFRESHING MEMORY
Attorney-client privilege, waiver . . . . . . 10.05[03][a]
Criminal cases . . . 10.05[02]
Depositions, work product use prior to . . . 10.05[03][d]
Generally . . . 10.05[01]
Jencks Act, applicability . . . 10.05[02]
Trial, use of work product at . . . . 10.05[03][c]
Work product issues . . . 10.05[03][b]
Writings . . . 10.05 *et seq.*

REHABILITATION OF WITNESSES
Character
    Opinion evidence . . . 12.03[05]
    Reputation . . . 12.03[05]
Generally . . . 12.01

[References are to paragraphs.]

[References are to paragraphs.]

[References are to paragraphs.]

TESTIMONY—Cont.

Opinion testimony by lay witnesses (See OPINION TESTIMONY)

Originals, proof of contents through adverse party's admissions . . . 9.06

Particularized guarantees of trustworthiness, examination for . . . 14.03[01]

Prior inconsistent statements . . . . 15.01[02][c]

Sexually abused children, videotaped testimony of . . . 10.01[02]

Truthfulness of . . . 12.01[06]

TRADE INSCRIPTIONS

Authentication . . . 8.02[09]

TRAMMEL DECISION

Marital privileges . . . 18.04[01]

TYPEWRITING IDENTIFICATION

Comparison with authenticated specimens . . . 8.01[04][b]; 8.01[04][c]

U

UNAVAILABILITY

Hearsay exception (See HEARSAY, subhead: Unavailability of declarant)

Statements against interest, admissibility . . . 17.04[02][a]

UNFAIRNESS

Duplicates, grounds for exclusion . . . . . . 9.02[03][b]

UNIFORM COMMERCIAL CODE

Authentication of documents under . . . . . 8.02[11]

V

VERDICT

Juror's use of alcohol or drugs, effect of . . 11.04[03]

VICTIMS

Character evidence . . . 7.01[05]

Rape victim's past behavior, relevance . . . 7.09

Sexually abused children, videotaped testimony . . . 10.01[02]

VIDEOTAPE

Sexually abused children, testimony of . . . 10.01[02]

VOICE IDENTIFICATION

Direct hearing . . . 8.01[06][a]

VOICE IDENTIFICATION—Cont.

Generally . . . 8.01[06]

Indirect hearing . . . 8.01[06][b]

Voicegram technique . . . 8.01[06][b]

W

WAIVERS

Privilege, waiver by voluntary disclosure . . . 18.07

WITNESSES

Calling . . . 2.06

Character of defendant exposed to attack by taking stand . . . 7.01[04]

Competency (See COMPETENCY OF WITNESS)

Exclusion (See EXCLUSION OF WITNESSES)

Expert (See EXPERT TESTIMONY)

Hypnotically refreshed testimony, exclusion of . . . 10.01[01]

Impeachment (See IMPEACHMENT OF WITNESSES)

Informer privilege for material . . . . 18.06[03][a]

Interrogation . . . 2.02[01]; 2.06

Non-party witnesses, testimony of . . . . . . 10.01[01]

Presentation . . . 2.02[01]

Prior inconsistent statements . . . . 15.01[02][c]

Rehabilitation (See REHABILITATION OF WITNESSES)

Special witness rules (See SPECIAL WITNESS RULES)

WORK PRODUCT

Attorney-client privilege . . . . . 10.05[03][a]; 18.03[05]

Claim . . . 10.05[03][b]

Depositions, to refresh recollections prior to . . . 10.05[03][d]

Refreshment of recollections . . 10.05[03] *et seq.*

Trial use to refresh recollections . . . . . . 10.05[03][c]

WRITINGS

Definition . . . 9.01[03]

Duplicates . . . 9.02[02][a]

Memory, use to refresh (See REFRESHING MEMORY)

Originals, proof of contents through adverse party's admissions . . . 9.06

[References are to paragraphs.]